BUILDING STRATEGIES
FOR COLLEGE READING

SECOND EDITION

BUILDING STRATEGIES FOR COLLEGE READING: A TEXT WITH THEMATIC READER

Jane L. McGrath

Maricopa Community Colleges

PRENTICE HALL, UPPER SADDLE RIVER, NEW JERSEY 07458

Library of Congress Cataloging-in-Publication Data

McGrath, Jane L.
  Building strategies for college reading: a text with thematic
reader/Jane L. McGrath.—2nd ed.
    p.   cm.
  Includes index.
  ISBN 0-13-262304-8
  1. College readers.   2. Reading (Higher education).   I. Title.
PE1122.M268   1997
808'.0427—dc21   97-14473
                                                   CIP

Editorial director: Charlyce Jones Owen
Acquisitions editor: Maggie Barbieri
Editorial assistant: Joan Polk
Director of production and manufacturing: Barbara Kittle
Managing editor: Bonnie Biller
Project liaison: Fran Russello
Project manager: Kari Callaghan Mazzola
Manufacturing manager: Nick Sklitsis
Prepress and manufacturing buyer: Mary Ann Gloriande
Marketing manager: Rob Mejia
Interior design and electronic page makeup: Kari Callaghan Mazzola
    and John P. Mazzola
Cover design: Bruce Kenselaar

*Grateful acknowledgment is made to the copyright holders on pages 457–465,
which are hereby a continuation of this copyright page.*

This book was set in 10/12 New Century Schoolbook by Big Sky Composition
and was printed and bound by Banta Company.
The cover was printed by Banta Company.

© 1998, 1995 by Prentice-Hall, Inc.
Simon & Schuster/A Viacom Company
Upper Saddle River, New Jersey 07458

Printed in the United States of America
10   9   8   7   6   5   4

ISBN 0-13-262304-8

PRENTICE-HALL INTERNATIONAL (UK) LIMITED, *London*
PRENTICE-HALL OF AUSTRALIA PTY. LIMITED, *Sydney*
PRENTICE-HALL CANADA INC., *Toronto*
PRENTICE-HALL HISPANOAMERICANA, S.A., *Mexico*
PRENTICE-HALL OF INDIA PRIVATE LIMITED, *New Delhi*
PRENTICE-HALL OF JAPAN, INC., *Tokyo*
SIMON & SCHUSTER ASIA PTE. LTD., *Singapore*
EDITORA PRENTICE-HALL DO BRASIL, LTDA., *Rio de Janeiro*

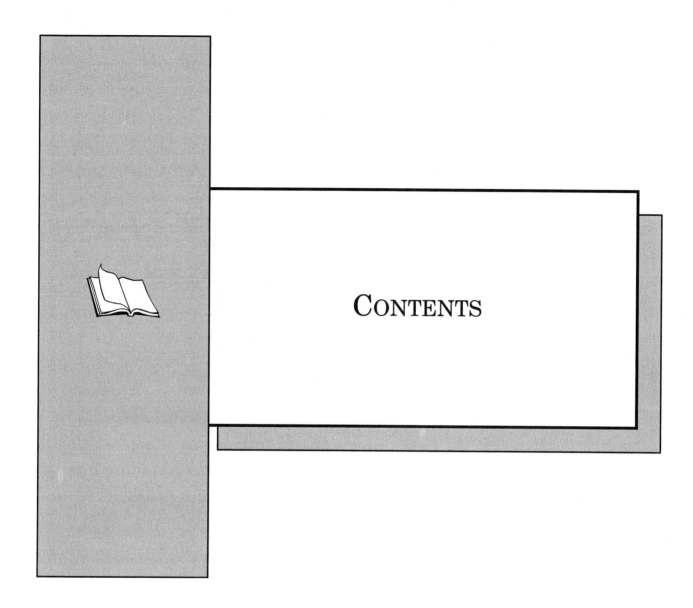

CONTENTS

CHAPTER 2
DETERMINE WHO THE AUTHOR IS AND WHY THE AUTHOR IS WRITING 21

CHAPTER 3
UNDERSTAND THE VOCABULARY THE AUTHOR USES 37

CHAPTER 4
IDENTIFY WHAT THE AUTHOR IS WRITING ABOUT   62

CHAPTER 5
ESTABLISH HOW THE AUTHOR DEVELOPS IDEAS 79

THEME 2
CONFRONTING VIOLENCE IN SOCIETY   243

THEME 3
"DOING PHILOSOPHY" IN EVERYDAY LIFE   306

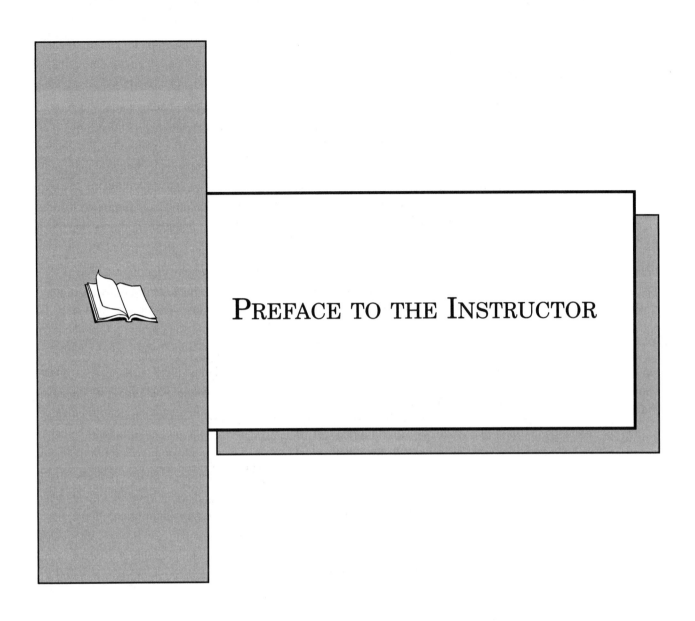

PREFACE TO THE INSTRUCTOR

Reading instructors share many common goals. For example, we want students to see themselves as active participants in the reading process. We also want students to become independent learners who are able to set and accomplish reading and study objectives.

To help students achieve these goals, this text encourages students to see the reading process as a dynamic, cognitive process that has variable demands depending on the task. It encourages them to build a large personal repertoire of reading and study strategies they can select from to meet the demands of any task. And, because students are able to transfer new strategies more easily to their own work when they have practiced on tasks they perceive to be real, the text provides authentic reading tasks using typical college prose.

Although there is still much discussion about the differences between a skill and a strategy, I consider a skill to be an accomplished technique and a strategy to be an action a reader consciously selects to achieve a particular goal. Strategies are therefore means to an end.

THE ORGANIZATION OF THE TEXT

The text emphasizes strategies for reading typical college-level expository prose and asks students to view reading for learning as a continuous process rather than as a one-shot activity.

I encourage students to (1) always develop a plan—clarify their purpose, activate their own knowledge, and set specific comprehension goals; (2) actively implement their plan—draw from their repertoire of learning and reading strategies; (3) regularly review what they've gathered—consolidate and integrate information, and decide what else they need to know; and (4) develop a new plan to further their comprehension goals.

CHAPTERS

The nine chapters investigate the skills of successful comprehension. Students examine and practice adapting and using a variety of strategies to help them fulfill their purpose. Each chapter contains instruction, examples, practice exercises (with suggested answers in the section titled "Suggested Answers for Practice Exercises," beginning on page 441) and at least four "Use Your Strategies" readings (many of which have been updated) with questions. Suggested answers for the "Use Your Strategies" exercises are in the Instructor's Manual.

Throughout the text, students work on identifying the author's purpose, understanding vocabulary in context, differentiating among different levels of information, and making valid inferences.

To facilitate a more systematic instructional progression, "Recognize the Author's Stance" is now Chapter 6, followed by "Integrate Text and Graphic Information," and "Organize the Information You Need." Chapter 9, "Decide What to Do with the Author's Information," serves as a summary.

THEMES

The four thematic units contain typical college reading material and comprehension tasks. Each contains a full textbook chapter along with six to eight pieces centered on a unifying topic. Each piece builds on previous readings to expand an understanding of the theme and students' relationship to it.

While some questions in the thematic units require the recall of specific information, others are more process-oriented—helping to dispel the black-and-white concept of the nature of comprehension. Using this combination of product- and process-oriented assessments encourages students to analyze their own strengths and needs in concert with the instructor. Various writing assignments provide another forum for students to interact with new concepts and ideas.

Theme 2, "Confronting Violence in Society," is entirely new. In addition, some of the readings in the other themes have been changed.

STUDY STRATEGIES

New to this edition is the section titled "Study Strategies," beginning on page 408. Every semester students ask me to give them strategies they can use to "remember more," or "take notes," or "do better on a test." These study strategies are ones that students can use in all their courses.

INSTRUCTOR'S MANUAL

The Instructor's Manual includes the following: course syllabus recommendations, presentation ideas and transparency masters, readability information on reading selections, suggested answers for exercises, and additional reading selections to use as quizzes for each of the nine chapters. It also contains a brief synopsis of Project Read-Aloud—the award-winning community service project for developmental reading students—and a complete *Project Read-Aloud Student Handbook*.

ACKNOWLEDGMENTS

The opportunity to create a second edition gave me the chance to incorporate ideas and requests from reading educators across the country. As I said in the first edition, although my name appears on the cover, countless women and men have contributed to its creation and publication. That assertion is even more accurate today.

I am exceedingly grateful to the thousands of students I have learned with during my years in the classroom. They have, directly and indirectly, shown me how critical it is to work on authentic tasks. Also, I thank numerous colleagues across the Maricopa Colleges. Over the years their knowledge, philosophies of teaching for learning, and experiences have provided meaningful insight into the realities of successful college reading.

I would like to thank the reviewers of this edition for their willingness to share their wisdom to make this a more useful tool for students: Mary L. Wolting, *Indiana University–Purdue University at Indianapolis*; Sylvia E. Roshkow, *Hunter College–CUNY*; Mary J. Holdway, *College of DuPage*; and Anita Podrid, *Queens College*.

In addition, my special thanks go to Ann Faulkner at Brookhaven College, Sally Rings at Paradise Valley Community College, and Ann C. Rogers at DeVry Institute of Technology in Irving Texas for their ongoing constructive recommendations.

The cadre of dedicated professionals at Prentice Hall is extraordinary and I'm indebted to everyone involved with this project. Sincere thanks to Kim Kitchen for first believing in my ability to deliver a relevant product, and to my anchor Joan Polk for her unfailing, efficient assistance. Also, a writer could never have a more understanding and knowledgeable editor than Maggie Barbieri; I'm most thankful she's mine.

And most importantly, my sincere gratitude goes to Larry McGrath, my partner in all of life's adventures. Without his continuing assistance, this book would not exist. His patience, wisdom, good humor, knowledge, and encouragement make all things possible.

A Final Note: I hope you will help me improve future editions of this book by taking a few minutes to send your comments to me at College Reading Development Group, Prentice Hall, One Lake Street, Upper Saddle River, New Jersey 07458, or E-mail me at Jellenjay@aol.com.

Jane L. McGrath

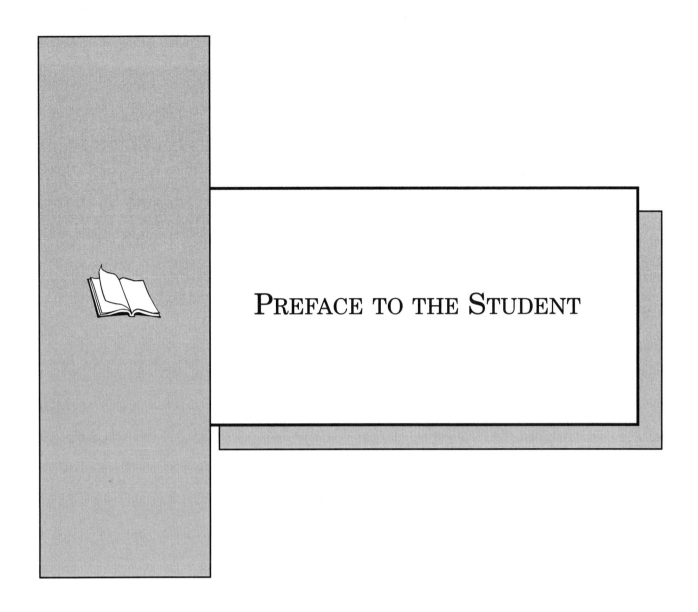

PREFACE TO THE STUDENT

Reading is the process of making meaning out of the 26 squiggles we call the alphabet. It is more than just knowing how to say words. Reading is the active thinking process of understanding an author's ideas, connecting those ideas to what you already know, and organizing all the ideas so you can remember and use them.

The demands of reading academic material are enormous—from studying a text assignment to prepare for class, to reading a magazine article for a discussion group, to reviewing for an exam. Research by Anderson and Armbruster (1984)* shows that a single text page can have as many as 50 separate but connected ideas. As a result, you are faced with sorting and understanding hundreds of ideas every time you study. But don't be discouraged. It is not an impossible task.

You can build a repertoire, or inventory, of reading and study strategies that helps you identify, understand, organize, and remember the information you need. Strategies are tools or techniques you consciously select to complete tasks accurately and efficiently.

*"Studying," by T. H. Anderson and B. B. Armbruster, in P. D. Pearson, ed., *Handbook of Reading Research* (New York: Longman, 1984), pp. 657–679.

Just learning about the strategies won't be enough, however. As an analogy, consider Jake. For the past month, Jake has been trying to shed a few pounds of extra weight and get in shape. He has learned some strategies for reaching his goals, including eating a low-fat diet and exercising regularly. He thinks about the strategies often and enjoys talking to his friends about his new fitness plan. He has just finished reading a book about planning healthy meals and he has made some sacrifices in his budget so he can buy a top-of-the-line exercise bike. Unfortunately, Jake hasn't lost any flab. Why? Because even though he has learned several strategies, he still spends his evenings eating chocolate cupcakes in front of the television. Until Jake starts actually using the strategies—eating right and riding the bike—he won't make much progress toward his goals.

Don't be like Jake. As you discover new reading and study strategies, apply them. Try them out in your classes and at work. Adapt them to fit your needs. Add them to your repertoire of strategies and use them *consistently*.

*A **Final Note:*** I hope you will help me improve future editions of this book by taking a few minutes to send your comments to me at College Reading Development Group, Prentice Hall, One Lake Street, Upper Saddle River, New Jersey 07458, or E-mail me at Jellenjay@aol.com.

Jane L. McGrath

ABOUT THE AUTHOR

Jane L. McGrath recently retired from 25 years of teaching reading, English, and computer applications courses in the Maricopa Community Colleges. She earned her undergraduate degrees in education and mass communications and her Ed.D. in reading education from Arizona State University. In 1991, McGrath was named *Innovator of the Year* by the Maricopa Colleges and the League of Innovation in Community Colleges for Project Read-Aloud, a college-community service program. She has also received *Outstanding Citizen* awards from the cities of Phoenix and Tempe for her community service work. In addition to teaching, McGrath is a freelance writer. She and her husband, Larry, an educator and professional photographer, combine talents on a wide range of projects from travel articles, to cookbooks, to technical pieces for the high-performance automotive industry. She is a member of the National Association of Developmental Educators and the College Reading and Learning Association.

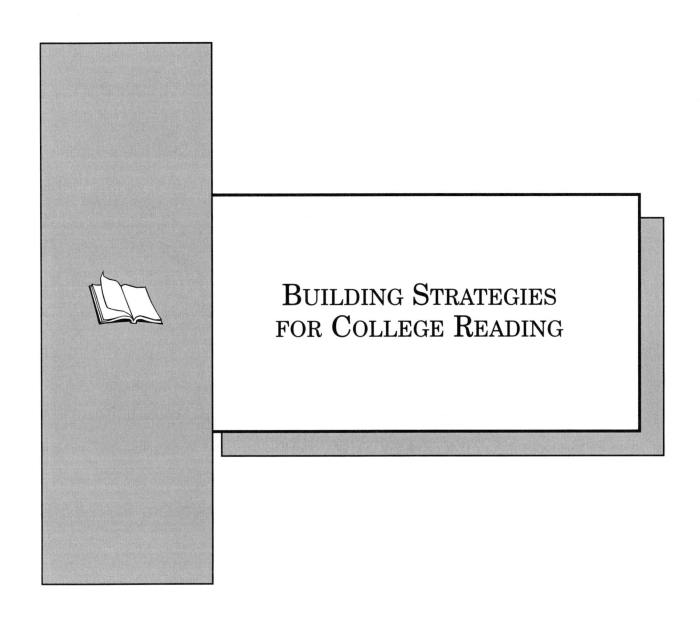

Building Strategies
for College Reading

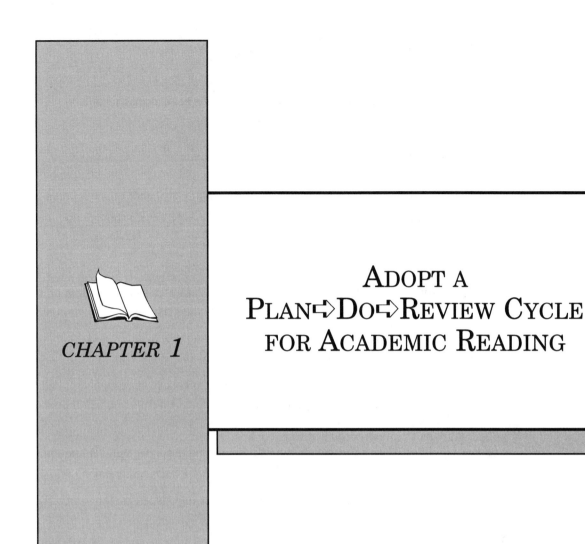

CHAPTER 1

ADOPT A PLAN⇨DO⇨REVIEW CYCLE FOR ACADEMIC READING

Reading is the active thinking process of understanding an author's ideas, connecting those ideas to what you already know, and then organizing all the ideas so you can remember and use them.

It is a complex process that involves your whole being. When you have trouble reading an assignment, no one can watch over your shoulder and "see" why you misunderstood the author's words or missed the author's main idea. Therefore, you must become an expert on your reading and study skills.

Just like the skilled carpenter who needs a toolbox full of specialized tools in order to select just the right ones to do each job, you need a toolbox full of reading and study strategies so you can select the ones appropriate to each of your tasks.

Start to fill your toolbox with the Plan⇨Do⇨Review cycle strategies. Add strategies as you work through the text. But remember that these strategies, like tools, are only means to an end—effective and efficient reading.

CHAPTER 1 OBJECTIVES

❏ Explain why you should develop a plan before beginning to read.

❏ List and explain pre-reading strategies.

❏ Explain why it's important to be an active reader.

❏ List and explain ways to monitor comprehension.

❏ List and explain fix-up strategies.

❏ Explain why review is necessary and list review strategies.

❏ Explain how you can use a Plan⇨Do⇨Review cycle to be a more successful reader.

WHAT IS A PLAN⇨DO⇨REVIEW CYCLE?

Everyone looks for ways to be successful. American executives strive to compete with aggressive competitors, teachers seek ways to enrich student learning, and students like you look for ways to improve academic performance.

So how can you, as a student, improve your chances for success? First, realize that whether your goal is to improve performance on a widget production line or a sociology final exam, the basic blueprint is the same: You plan what you need to do; you implement your plan; you review how well you did.

Since your goal of understanding more of what you read can't always be met the first time you complete your plan, you must view reading as a cycle instead of a one-shot activity. Using this cycle to become more successful at reading means that each time you have an assignment, you will *plan* before you begin, you will *do*, you will *review* what you have read, and you will continue to *plan*, *do*, and *review* until your comprehension goals are met. This chapter introduces a variety of reading and study strategies you can draw from to build your personal repertoire of strategies. Remember, a strategy is an action you consciously select to achieve a particular goal.

Plan⇨Do⇨Review Cycle

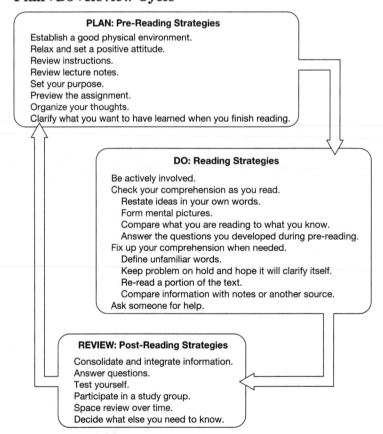

PLAN: Pre-Reading Strategies

Establish a good physical environment.
Relax and set a positive attitude.
Review instructions.
Review lecture notes.
Set your purpose.
Preview the assignment.
Organize your thoughts.
Clarify what you want to have learned when you finish reading.

DO: Reading Strategies

Be actively involved.
Check your comprehension as you read.
  Restate ideas in your own words.
  Form mental pictures.
  Compare what you are reading to what you know.
  Answer the questions you developed during pre-reading.
Fix up your comprehension when needed.
  Define unfamiliar words.
  Keep problem on hold and hope it will clarify itself.
  Re-read a portion of the text.
  Compare information with notes or another source.
Ask someone for help.

REVIEW: Post-Reading Strategies

Consolidate and integrate information.
Answer questions.
Test yourself.
Participate in a study group.
Space review over time.
Decide what else you need to know.

WHY DO I NEED TO DEVELOP A PLAN FOR EVERY ASSIGNMENT?

Task 1 Read this paragraph from a stockbroker's newsletter.

> Writing or selling Options against stock you already own is a strategy that is conservative and usually works well in a trading market. An Option is either a call (a right to buy 100 shares of stock at a specified price in the future) or a put (a right to sell 100 shares of stock at a specified price in the future). Thus an Option buyer or seller who owns no stock (called uncovered or naked) is a speculator who is looking at making large percentage returns on a small amount of invested capital in a short time. This individual would be paying the Option premium to us, the covered writer.

How successfully did you complete Task 1? How do you know if you were successful?

You may not be very confident of your success. Unless you have a working knowledge of the stock market, the content of the paragraph is hard to understand. In addition, since you didn't have a specific purpose for reading, it was probably difficult to know if you understood what was expected.

Task 2 Read this same paragraph from a stockbroker's newsletter to find out whether writing Options against your own stock is considered a risky or a conservative strategy.

> Writing or selling Options against stock you already own is a strategy that is conservative and usually works well in a trading market. An Option is either a call (a right to buy 100 shares of stock at a specified price in the future) or a put (a right to sell 100 shares of stock at a specified price in the future). Thus an Option buyer or seller who owns no stock (called uncovered or naked) is a speculator who is looking at making large percentage returns on a small amount of invested capital in a short time. This individual would be paying the Option premium to us, the covered writer.

How successfully did you complete Task 2? How do you know if you were successful?

I suspect you evaluated yourself "very successful" on Task 2. You found the information you were looking for—that writing Options against your own stock is a conservative strategy—in the first sentence. You clearly knew you had achieved your goal, and you stopped reading.

As you can see, even with the same paragraph, the reading requirements can be very different. So you begin every reading assignment by developing a plan.

The strategies you use to develop your plan will help you clarify two critical factors: (1) your specific purpose for reading the assignment, such as answering questions, preparing for a lecture, or reviewing for an exam; and (2) how difficult the material is for you, considering elements such as the vocabulary and your knowledge about the topic. You have a better chance of success when you plan.

WHAT PLANNING OR PRE-READING STRATEGIES CAN I USE?

Pre-reading strategies are tactics to give you a head start on good comprehension. They prime your brain. Pre-reading strategies include the following:

Establishing a Good Physical Environment Place yourself in surroundings that help your ability to concentrate on reading. Make certain that you have good lighting. Use a comfortable chair that encourages good posture and a ready-to-work attitude, and that allows you to hold or rest the book easily.

Relaxing and Setting a Positive Mental Attitude   Set yourself up to be successful. Arrange your schedule to do your study-reading when you are at your best mentally. Have confidence in yourself; know that you can read successfully and accomplish the goals you set.

Reviewing Instructions   Check any comprehension guidelines you have been given such as "Read this in preparation for tomorrow's lecture," or "Read to see how this author differs from what I've said today," or "Review all of the material we covered in preparation for the exam."

Reviewing Lecture Notes   Reread any notes you have taken on this topic, looking for topics or ideas you need to clarify, words you need to define, or names and dates you need to fill in. Once you have completed your reading, you will need to combine the information in your notes with the information from your reading.

Setting Your Purpose   Your purpose is your reason for reading and you will have slightly different reasons for reading different assignments. For instance, reading for enjoyment does not demand the attention or understanding that reading to prepare for a psychology lecture requires.

In addition, knowing your purpose is a clue to knowing how fast you should anticipate reading. For example, if you are reading a chapter called "How Do We Use Computers?" just to identify the ten general-usage categories, you will cover the material more quickly than if you are reading to understand all the facets of each of the categories. When you take time to set your purpose before you begin to read, you are more likely to understand what you need, and less likely to waste time.

Previewing the Assignment   Systematically surveying the material before you begin to read is like looking at a completed jigsaw puzzle before you start trying to put individual pieces together. Previewing should only take a few minutes because you read only specific elements:

    chapter objectives

    headings and subheadings

    introductory and concluding paragraphs

    boldface, underlined, and italic words and phrases

    graphics

    margin annotations

    end-of-chapter summaries and questions

In short, you read everything that will help give you a general understanding of the core ideas and their organization. Review the "Using Typography and Design Clues" strategies starting on page 414 for more ideas.

Organizing Your Thoughts   First, based on the chapter objectives and headings/subheadings, jot down the major topics. Then write a few words about what you know on each of the topics.

Clarifying What You Want to Have Learned When You Finish Reading   If you don't know what you are seeking as you read an assignment, how will you know when you are finished? If you don't read to identify and understand specific ideas and information, you probably won't understand the material you need to know.

Often your instructor will give you specific reading goals or there will be end-of-chapter questions. If not, one strategy is to rephrase the chapter's objectives or headings and subheadings as questions and then read to answer those questions. For example, you could rephrase this section's subhead as: "Why do I need to clarify what I want to have learned when I finish reading?" or "How can I clarify what I want to have learned when I finish reading?" Hopefully, you can answer those questions.

For example, if you were assigned the following selection, "Caring about Kids: When Parents Divorce," you could use some of the planning strategies this way:

Plan

1. Find an environment that allows for maximum concentration.
2. Allot time to complete assignment; then relax and adopt positive attitude.
3. Review professor's instructions (such as "Read this to prepare for tomorrow's lecture on Divorce in the United States").
4. Set your purpose: Read to identify main concepts and understand the vocabulary.
5. Preview assignment (read title, author, introduction, headings, and subheadings).

CARING ABOUT KIDS: WHEN PARENTS DIVORCE

*THE DIVISION OF SCIENTIFIC AND PUBLIC INFORMATION,
NATIONAL INSTITUTE OF MENTAL HEALTH*

Introduction

[1]Divorce: the breakup of a family. More than one-third—actually 40 percent—of all marriages in the United States now end in divorce. Although legally a separation of two people, divorce is, in reality, a family affair because more than half of all divorces involve children. Divorce ends the role of spouse; it doesn't end that of parent.

Working Out Issues

[2]Couples seeking a divorce will not always find it easy to reach agreement on issues that affect their children, but they should attempt to do so before telling their children about the impending separation. Children, even very young children, need to be prepared for the divorce. They need information about where they will live, who will take care of them, where they will go to school, and whatever other issues are of major concern to them.

Custody Issues

[3]When parents struggle over custody or are inconsistent in the arrangements agreed upon, problems are increased. When a child becomes the prize in a parental tug of war, the results can be emotionally damaging, causing the child to feel more insecure, angry, and guilty. The sooner parents face up to and work out custody details, the better the chances are that a child's anxiety about the divorce and his own future will begin to fade.

[4]Parents should carefully balance their own needs with those of the children. For example, the decision to keep the family home for the children's sake may cause a financial hardship. Or, if the family can't afford to buy a second car, it may be necessary for one parent to move closer to public transportation.

[5]Once the primary plans are made, many other issues need to be settled. How can the responsibility of child care and living expenses be fairly divided? Who will care for the children? Where? How? If both parents share expenses, how and when? Who will pay for medical care, insurance, transportation, food, and clothing? How will college costs be shared? Where will children spend holidays and vacations? And finally, will the visitations and responsibilities change as the children get older?

(CONTINUED)

CARING ABOUT KIDS: WHEN PARENTS DIVORCE (CONTINUED)

Types of Custody

[6]Custody is a responsibility as well as a right. It becomes obvious, when trying to consider the best interests of everyone involved, that there are no perfect answers. Custody does not have to be an all-or-nothing decision, however. There are a number of options available for sharing responsibility.

[7]*Single Parent Custody*   Neither parent relinquishes parenthood, but it is decided that one parent should be physically in charge.

[8]*Joint Custody*   Parents legally share responsibility for the children. The details of shared responsibility can be worked out in various ways.

[9]*Split Custody*   When there is more than one child in the family, children may be divided between parents. For example, the older children may live with the father and the younger with the mother, or the boys with the father and the girls with the mother.

[10]*Other Arrangements*   Single parents sometimes share responsibilities of parenting with other adults or grandparents so that a supervising adult is present at all times.

6. Organize your thoughts (use headings/subheadings to help organize what you know about the topics):

    Introduction

    Number of divorces—*I'm not surprised by the number of divorces quoted; at least one-third of my friends' parents and my parents' friends are divorced.*

    Divorced people are still parents—*I've seen movies where people getting divorced try to reassure the kids that the divorce won't affect them.*

    Working Out Issues

    I think it's important to work together—*I'll read to find out what the issues are.*

    Custody Issues

    I think parents can make life hard for children—*I'll read to see how to avoid problems!*

    Types of Custody

    There are several custody options—*The only type of custody I know about is where the mother has custody of the children. I'll read to find out what other types are allowed.*

7. Determine what you want to have learned when you finish reading (based on the headings):

    a. What is the current divorce rate in the United States?

    b. How/when should couples work out custody issues?

    c. What are major custody issues?

    d. What are the four types of custody?

Once you have developed your plan, you are ready to begin reading.

WHAT DO I DO ONCE I START TO READ?

Did you ever fall asleep while playing tennis or while you were watching your favorite television show? Probably not. How about while you were reading? Probably. What makes the difference? Your active involvement.

Active physical and mental involvement keeps you interested and committed. When you become passive, you rapidly lose interest and drift away. So, to read successfully you must be an active, thinking participant in the process.

HOW CAN I CHECK MY COMPREHENSION AS I READ?

As an active reader, you use comprehension monitoring, or checking, strategies to make certain that your understanding is satisfactory for your purpose. Comprehension monitoring strategies include the following:

Restating Ideas in Your Own Words   At the end of a sentence or paragraph, rephrase the idea in your own words.

Forming Mental Pictures   Build a mental picture of what the author is describing.

Comparing What You Are Reading to What You Know   Ask yourself how this new information fits with what you know. Does it reinforce your previous knowledge? Does it contradict what you previously thought? Does it add new information?

Answering Questions   Connect what you are reading to questions you need to answer.

IF I DON'T UNDERSTAND WHAT I'M READING, WHAT CAN I DO?

If you discover that you do not understand what you are reading, use one of these fix-up strategies to get yourself back on track. Fix-up strategies include the following:

Defining Unfamiliar Words   Make certain that you understand the words the author uses. If an unfamiliar word isn't defined in the context or the text's glossary, check your lecture notes, or a dictionary, or ask someone.

Using Chapter Objectives and Headings/Subheadings   Reread the objectives and headings/subheadings to see if there are ideas or concepts that help you to understand.

Reviewing Related Graphics   Review all associated graphics and their explanations to see if they clarify the text information.

Rereading a Portion   Try reading the sentence or paragraph a second time with the specific goal of clarifying your question.

Keeping the Problem on Hold and Hoping That It Will Clarify Itself   If the problem lies in only one sentence or paragraph, you may decide to mark it and continue reading. It is possible that the next sentence or paragraph will help your understanding.

Comparing Information with Notes or Another Source   Read about the topic or idea in your notes or in another book to see if a different approach helps your understanding.

Asking Someone   If after you have exhausted all other resources—clarified the vocabulary; reread the objectives, headings/subheadings, graphics, and unclear passages; and reviewed the other information you have on the topic—you still don't understand what you need to, ask someone for help. Potential resources could include your professor, a teaching assistant, a tutor, or a classmate.

For example, having developed a plan for the sample selection above, you could use some of the comprehension monitoring and fix-up strategies this way:

Do

8.   Begin reading.

9.   Monitor comprehension by answering the four questions in your plan:

a. What is the current divorce rate in the U.S.? (40 percent)

b. How/when should couples work out custody issues? (Couples should agree on issues that affect their children before telling them about the separation/divorce.)

c. What are major custody issues? (Major custody issues include: where child will live, responsibility of child care, living expenses, extra expenses, college costs, holidays and vacations, changes as children get older.)

d. What are the four types of custody? (1. single parent [problem: don't understand "neither parent relinquishes"].)

10.   Use the fix-up strategy: define relinquishes—gives up. Although neither parent gives up custody, one parent takes charge. Now, understandable.

11.   Continue reading for other types of custody arrangements (2. joint custody, 3. split custody, and 4. other arrangements.)

12.   Finish reading.

Even though you have finished reading (meaning you have understood what you set out to understand) your cycle is not complete. To successfully read for learning, you must review what you have read.

IF I UNDERSTAND WHAT I'VE READ, WHY DO I HAVE TO REVIEW?

Think about when you first learned to do something like drive a car, type, or play the guitar. If you practiced daily, you found yourself doing a little better each day. If, however, you didn't practice for two or three weeks, you had probably forgotten so much that you needed to start with some of the basics again.

It doesn't matter how old we are; without review, we forget information very quickly. In fact, without good review at regular intervals, you will probably forget as much as 80 percent of what you have read.

HOW CAN I REVIEW EFFECTIVELY?

Review strategies help you put information into perspective and help you remember it. To be most effective, your review sessions should be spaced out over time. Arrange your first review session within 24 hours of reading and continue to review the information on a regular schedule. Reviewing periodically helps you commit information to your long-term memory. Some review strategies include the following:

Rereading Thoughts You've Organized and Questions You've Answered during Reading   Make use of the work you did during your planning and reading.

Answering Questions   Write out or talk through the answers to the questions that you set out in your plan.

Consolidating and Integrating Information   Combine your knowledge with what you've gained from reading and your lecture notes to form one coherent picture.

Participating in a Study Group   Join a group of classmates to talk about what you have read. Try reviewing concepts, sharing notes, and taking practice tests with one another.

Testing Yourself   Make up a test on the material or have a classmate make one up and test yourself. Make a set of question-and-answer flash cards for a convenient carry-along review tool by writing the question on one side of a 3" x 5" card and the answer on the reverse side.

For example, using the sample, "Caring about Kids," and having developed a plan and read the selection to achieve your goals, you could use these review strategies:

Review

13.   Make up and take a test covering the necessary information.
14.   Correct the test.
15.   Review the information at least once before the next lecture.

WHY SHOULD I DO ANYTHING ELSE?

Occasionally, on small assignments or familiar material, you will achieve your reading comprehension goals at the end of one Plan⇨Do⇨Review cycle. On the other hand, when you're reviewing, don't be surprised to discover gaps in your knowledge. When you do, just develop a new plan that will help you fill in the gaps. Reread the portion of the assignment you need to get the information and then review, making sure to integrate the new information with what you already have.

As mentioned in the Preface, reading is thinking. Successful reading for learning requires you to understand what an author says and that doesn't happen without continuing effort.

CHAPTER 1 REVIEW QUESTIONS

1.   Explain why you should develop a plan before you begin reading.
2.   Identify the purpose of pre-reading activities and list three pre-reading activities.
3.   Explain why it's important to be an active reader.
4.   What are two ways to monitor your comprehension?
5.   What are two fix-up strategies for improving poor comprehension, and when should you use them?
6.   Explain why review is necessary, and list two review strategies.
7.   Explain how you can use a Plan⇨Do⇨Review cycle to be more successful.

CHAPTER 1 THINK AND CONNECT QUESTIONS

8.   Re-read the *Preface to the Student*. List two topics that were covered in both the *Preface* and this chapter. Why do you think these topics are in both places?

9. Where do you normally do your reading/studying? Do you think that environment helps or hurts your comprehension? How could you improve your environment?

CHAPTER 1 APPLICATION EXERCISES

10. Using one text section from one of your other textbooks, implement the Plan⇨Do⇨Review cycle: Develop a plan for reading, read, review, and continue the cycle until you have met your goal.

11. When you are having difficulty comprehending what you are reading, one of the fix-up strategies you can use is to ask someone for help. For each of your classes, identify at least two people you can call on. After you have checked with your sources, list when and where they are available, and how to contact them.

USE YOUR STRATEGIES: EXERCISE #1—"NUTRITION FOR THE '90S"

For this exercise, assume your instructor has asked you to read this selection—"Nutrition for the '90s"—as part of your preparation for tomorrow's introductory lecture on good nutrition: (1) Prepare a plan that includes what you will read during preview, how you will organize your thoughts, and four questions you will answer; (2) Explain how you will read to complete your plan (be sure to include answers to your planning questions); and (3) Describe the review strategies you will use to prepare for the lecture.

NUTRITION FOR THE '90S

AMY KEATING, M.S., R.D.

[1]You may know the merits of healthy eating. But often wanting to eat right and actually doing so are two separate things. For many, understanding how to eat right is the real challenge because the recommendations for good nutrition appear more complex than they actually are. Although several health organizations issue a variety of dietary recommendations, the basic message regarding diet and health are the same: Consume a diet low in fat, cholesterol and sodium and high in complex carbohydrates and dietary fiber to reduce the risk of chronic disease.

[2]To put these strategies into practice the focus should be on the big picture—the total diet over time. Here is a brief overview of major dietary concerns.

A Word on Variety

[3]Variety is not only the spice of life, it is also the secret to making sure you get the more than 40 nutrients you need each day. No one food supplies all the essential nutrients. That is why it is important to eat several types of food each day to get all the nutrients you need for good health. Choosing from the five food groups every day—Fruits, Vegetables, Grains, Meat and Dairy Products, with an assortment of foods within these groups, can help you get the variety you need.

Cut Back on Fat and Cholesterol

[4]Health authorities recommend that Americans reduce total dietary fat intake to no more than 30 percent of total daily calories. This guideline should apply to your total diet over time, not individual foods. One way to monitor your fat intake is to determine your Daily Fat Target. This is based on your calorie need which is influenced by your sex, age, weight and activity level. The following chart provides typical examples of how to calculate the daily fat gram target for men, women and dieters. Keep in mind that fat-containing foods can be balanced with lower fat foods over the course of the day.

(CONTINUED)

NUTRITION FOR THE '90s (CONTINUED)

[5]It is also recommended that we keep cholesterol intake below 300 mg per day. Remember that cholesterol is found only in foods of animal origin—meat, poultry, fish, eggs, milk and milk products.

	MEN	WOMEN	DIETERS
Calories/Day	2400	1800	1400
Drop last digit	240	180	140
Divide by 3 =			
FAT Grams/Day	80	60	47

Go Low on Sodium

[6]We get sodium from many sources, but mostly in the form of salt added to foods in processing, cooking and at the table. While we all need some sodium daily (about 500 mg) most Americans consume more than the 2400 mg per day recommended by the National Academy of Sciences. To put these numbers in perspective, just one teaspoon of salt contains about 2000 mg of sodium. Though it has not been proven that eating large amounts of sodium causes high blood pressure, many health professionals believe that reducing sodium intake is a good idea for everyone.

Eat Fiber Rich Foods

[7]Nutrition authorities recommend 20–30 grams of fiber per day, but many Americans consume much less. This is because we do not eat enough vegetables, fruits and grains in our current diets. Populations like ours with diets low in these types of foods and with higher than recommended amounts of fat tend to have a high incidence of heart disease, obesity and some types of cancers.

ONE POSSIBLE PLAN⇨DO⇨REVIEW APPROACH FOR "NUTRITION IN THE '90s"

Plan

1. Find an environment for maximum concentration.
2. Allot time to complete assignment, relax, and adopt positive attitude.
3. Review professor's instructions: "Read this for tomorrow's lecture."
4. Set your purpose: Read to identify main concepts and understand vocabulary.
5. Preview the assignment:

    Read (1) title and author, (2) two introductory paragraphs, (3) boldface headings, and (4) table.
6. Organize your thoughts (use headings/subheadings to organize):

    Introductory Paragraphs

    Basic message: Eat a diet low in fat, cholesterol, and sodium, and high in complex carbohydrates and dietary fiber to reduce risk of chronic disease

    Focus on "big picture"—total diet over time

Major Diet Concerns

Variety

Cut back on fat and cholesterol

Go easy on sodium

Eat fiber-rich foods

7. Determine specific reading outcomes: To prepare for lecture I will read to find out:

    a. How do you get good variety in your diet?

    b. How can you cut back on fat and cholesterol?

    c. Why should you cut back on sodium?

    d. What are fiber-rich foods?

Do

8. Begin reading.

9. Monitor comprehension by answering the four questions in the plan:

    a. How do you get good variety in your diet? Eat from the five food groups every day.

    b. How can you cut back on fat and cholesterol? Doesn't say how to cut back; advises that fat should be no more than 30 percent of total calories, how to calculate your own daily fat target, and to keep cholesterol below 300 mg per day.

    c. Why should you cut back on sodium? Too much sodium may cause high blood pressure; reducing sodium seems to just be a good idea.

    d. What are fiber-rich foods? Fiber-rich foods include vegetables, fruits, and grains.

10. Fix-up strategy: define "high incidence of heart disease," paragraph 7: high occurrence of—more people have heart disease.

11. Finish reading.

Review

12. Two to four hours before lecture, reread thoughts jotted down during planning (#6) and answers to four questions (#9).

USE YOUR STRATEGIES: EXERCISE #2—"FRACTIONS"

Allen Angel teaches at Monroe Community College. This selection—"Fractions"—is from his book *Elementary Algebra for College Students*, 3rd ed.

For this exercise, assume your instructor has asked you to read this portion of the section on "Fractions" to prepare for a quiz on basic algebraic terms. (1) Prepare a plan that includes what you will read during preview, how you will organize your thoughts, and four terms you will identify. (2) Explain how you will read to complete your plan (be sure to include answers to your planning questions). (3) Describe the review strategies you will use to prepare for your quiz.

FRACTIONS

ALLEN R. ANGEL

1. Learn multiplication symbols.
2. Recognize factors.
3. Reduce fractions to lowest terms.
4. Multiply fractions.
5. Divide fractions.
6. Add and subtract fractions.
7. Convert mixed numbers to fractions.

Students taking algebra for the first time often ask, "What is the difference between arithmetic and algebra?" When doing arithmetic, all of the quantities used in the calculations are known. In algebra, however, one or more of the quantities are often unknown and must be found.

Example 1

A recipe calls for 3 cups of flour. Mrs. Clark has 2 cups of flour. How many additional cups does she need?

Solution: The answer is 1 cup.

Although very elementary, this is an example of an algebraic problem. The unknown quantity is the number of additional cups of flour needed.

An understanding of decimal numbers and fractions is essential to success in algebra. The procedures to add, subtract, multiply, and divide numbers containing decimal points are reviewed in Appendix A. You may wish to review this material now.

You will need to know how to reduce a fraction to its lowest terms and how to add, subtract, multiply, and divide fractions. We will review these topics in this section. We will also explain the meaning of factors.

1. In algebra we often use letters called **variables** to represent numbers. A letter commonly used for a variable is the letter x. So that we do not confuse the variable x with the times sign, we use different notation to indicate multiplication.

- -

Multiplication Symbols

If a and b stand for (or represent) any two mathematical quantities, then each of the following may be used to indicate the product of a and b ("a times b").

$$ab \qquad a \bullet b \qquad a(b) \qquad (a)b \qquad (a)(b)$$

- -

Examples

3 times 4	3 times x	x times y
may be written	may be written	may be written
	$3x$	xy
$3(4)$	$3(x)$	$x(y)$
$(3)4$	$(3)x$	$(x)y$
$(3)(4)$	$(3)(x)$	$(x)(y)$
$3 \bullet 4$	$3 \bullet x$	$x \bullet y$

(CONTINUED)

FRACTIONS (CONTINUED)

2. The numbers or variables multiplied in a multiplication problem are called **factors**.

If $a \cdot b = c$, then a and b are **factors** of c.

For example, in $3 \cdot 5 = 15$, the numbers 3 and 5 are factors of the product 15. As a second example, consider $2 \cdot 15 = 30$. The numbers 2 and 15 are factors of the product 30. Note that 30 has many other factors. Since $5 \cdot 6 = 30$, the numbers 5 and 6 are also factors of 30. Since $3x$ means 3 times x, both the 3 and the x are factors of $3x$.

3. Now we have the necessary information to discuss fractions. The top number of a fraction is called the **numerator**, and the bottom number is called the **denominator**. In the fraction $\frac{3}{5}$ the 3 is the numerator and the 5 is the denominator.

A fraction is **reduced to its lowest terms** when the numerator and denominator have no common factors other than 1. To reduce a fraction to its lowest terms, follow these steps.

To Reduce a Fraction to Its Lowest Terms

1. Find the largest number that will divide (without remainder) both the numerator and the denominator. This number is called the **greatest common factor**.
2. Then divide both the numerator and the denominator by the greatest common factor.

If you do not remember how to find the greatest common factor (GCF) of two or more numbers, read Appendix B.

Example 2

Reduce $\frac{10}{25}$ to its lowest terms.

Solution: The largest number that divides both 10 and 25 is 5. Therefore, 5 is the greatest common factor. Divide both the numerator and the denominator by 5 to reduce the fraction to its lowest terms.

$$\frac{10}{25} = \frac{10 \div 5}{25 \div 5} = \frac{2}{5}$$

USE YOUR STRATEGIES: EXERCISE #3—"SOURCES OF GROUNDWATER POLLUTION"

Dr. Bernard J. Nebel is a biology professor at Catonsville Community College in Maryland, where he has taught environmental science for 21 years. He is a member of several professional associations and actively supports a number of environmental organizations. This selection—"Sources of Groundwater Pollution"—comes from his book *Environmental Science*, 3rd ed.

For this exercise, assume you have had one introductory lecture on sources of pollution and that your instructor has asked you to read this assignment before the next class. (1) Prepare a plan that includes what you will read during preview, how you will organize your thoughts, and four questions you will answer. (2) Explain how you will read to complete your plan (be sure to include answers to your planning questions). (3) Describe the review strategies you will use to prepare for lecture and a possible quiz.

SOURCES OF GROUNDWATER POLLUTION

BERNARD J. NEBEL

[1] As water infiltrates and percolates through the soil, it will tend to dissolve and carry any soluble chemicals into the groundwater. The soil will not filter out chemicals that are in solution. It is the old problem of leaching described in earlier chapters. Consequently, the general principle is: *Any chemical used on, disposed of, spilled, or leaked onto or into the ground can contaminate groundwater* (Figure 11–2).

[2] Major sources of groundwater pollution are currently recognized as the following:

[3] Inadequate landfills and other facilities where toxic chemicals have been dumped and from which they may leach into groundwater.

[4] Leaking underground storage tanks or pipelines. The leakage of gasoline from service station storage tanks is a particular problem.

[5] Pesticides and fertilizers used on croplands, lawns, and gardens.

[6] Deicing salt used on roads.

[7] Waste oils used on dirt roads to keep dust down.

[8] Over application of sewage sludges or wastewater.

[9] Transportation spills.

[10] Of all these, inadequate disposal and use of pesticides are considered to be the most widespread threat to groundwater.

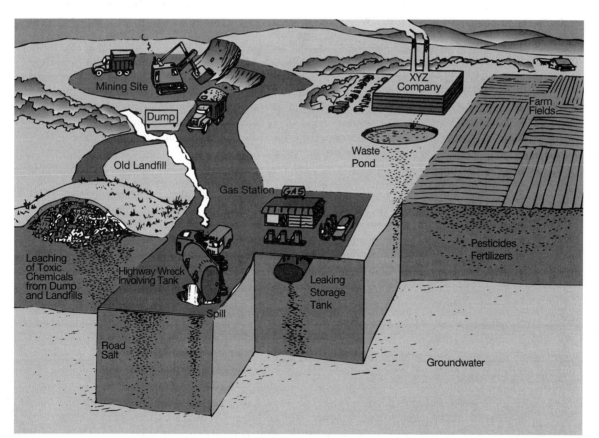

Figure 11–2 Any chemical used, stored, spilled, or disposed of on or near the surface may leach into the groundwater. This illustration depicts some of the most significant sources of groundwater contamination.

(*CONTINUED*)

SOURCES OF GROUNDWATER POLLUTION (CONTINUED)

Toxic Chemicals: Their Threat

[11]The most insidious of all groundwater pollution problems involves certain toxic chemicals that may go undetected because of being at very low concentrations, but which may gradually accumulate in the body to cause many adverse health effects including cancer.

What Are the Toxic Chemicals?

[12]Most toxic chemicals belong to one of two classes: heavy metals or synthetic organic chemicals.

Heavy Metals

[13]Heavy metals are metallic elements that in pure form are heavy. Lead, mercury, arsenic, cadmium, tin, chromium, zinc, and copper are examples. They are widely used throughout industry. Heavy metals are extremely toxic because, as ions or in certain compounds, they are soluble in water and may be ingested and absorbed into the body where they tend to combine with and inhibit the functioning of particular enzymes. Thus, very small amounts can have severe physiological or neurological consequences. The mental retardation caused by lead poisoning and the insanity and crippling birth defects caused by mercury are particularly well known.

Synthetic Organics

[14]Recall that all the complex molecules that make up plants and animals are natural organic chemicals. In contrast, chemists have learned to make hundreds of thousands of organic (carbon-based) compounds that are the basis for all plastics, synthetic fibers, synthetic rubber, paint-like coatings, solvents, pesticides, wood preservatives, and innumerable other chemicals. Such human-made organic compounds are referred to as synthetic organic chemicals.

[15]Many synthetic organic compounds are similar enough to natural organic compounds that they may be absorbed into the body and interact with particular enzymes or other systems, but here they cause problems. The body may not be able to break them down or metabolize them in any way; they are nonbiodegradable. The result is that they upset the system. With sufficient doses the effect may be acute poisoning and death. However, with low doses over extended periods, the effects are even more insidious, including mutagenic (mutation-causing), carcinogenic (cancer-causing), and tetratogenic (birth-defect-causing) effects. In addition, they may cause serious liver and kidney dysfunction, sterility, and numerous other physiological and neurological problems.

[16]A class of synthetic organics that is particularly troublesome is the halogenated hydrocarbons, organic compounds in which one or more of the hydrogen atoms have been replaced by an atom of chlorine, bromine, fluorine, or iodine. These four elements are classified as halogens; hence the name halogenated hydrocarbons.

[17]Among all the halogenated hydrocarbons, those containing chlorine and referred to as chlorinated hydrocarbons are by far the most common. Such compounds are widely used in plastics (e.g., polyvinyl chloride), pesticides (e.g., DDT, kepone, and mirex), solvents (e.g., carbon tetrachlophenol), electrical insulation (e.g., PCBs or polychlorinated biphenyls), flame retardants (e.g., TRIS), and many other products. PCBs and dioxin are examples of chlorinated hydrocarbons that are notorious for their pollution hazard....

USE YOUR STRATEGIES: EXERCISE #4—"COMPUTERS"

Dr. Larry Long and Dr. Nancy Long have written more than 30 books that have been used in over 600 colleges throughout the world. They both have many years of teaching and consultant experience. This selection—"Computers"—is from their book *Computers*, 4th ed.

For this exercise, assume your instructor has asked you to read this selection before the next class. The instructor often gives a quiz on terminology at the beginning of class. (1) List the planning strategies you will use, including what you will read during preview, how you will organize your thoughts, and four terms you will define as you read. (2) Describe your reading strategies. List definitions for the four terms you identified during preview and any additional terms you identified as you read. (3) List two review strategies you would use to prepare for lecture and a possible terminology quiz.

COMPUTERS: THE ESSENTIALS

LARRY LONG AND NANCY LONG

Anyone who lives in the information society has a basic understanding what a computer is and what it can do. This book is designed to add depth to this basic understanding. The best way to tackle computer concepts is incrementally, a little at a time. In the remaining sections of this chapter, we'll define the computer, identify its basic components, illustrate how it works, talk about its fundamental capabilities, list its strengths (as compared to the human computer), and talk briefly about the ways it is used. This section addresses the essentials.

Conversational Computerese: Basic Terms and Definitions

The **computer** is *an electronic device that can interpret and execute programmed commands for input, output, computation, and logic operations.* Computers may be technically complex, but they are conceptually simple. The computer, also called a **processor**, is the "intelligence" of a **computer system**. It performs all *computations* and *logic* operations. A computer system has four fundamental components: *input, processing, output,* and *storage.* Note that a computer system (not a computer) is made up of the four components. When the processor is combined with the other three components, it forms a *computer system* (see Figure 1–4).

Each of the components in a computer system can take on a variety of forms. For example, output (the results of processing) can be routed to a television-like monitor, audio speakers (like those on your stereo system), or a printer (see Figure 1–4). The output on a monitor is temporary and is called soft copy. Printers produce hard copy, or printed output. Data can be entered to a computer system for processing (input) via a keyboard (one character at a time), a microphone (for voice and sound input), or a point-and-draw device, such as a mouse (see Figure 1–4).

Storage of data and software in a computer system is either temporary or permanent. Random-access memory (RAM) provides temporary storage of data and programs during processing within solid state integrated circuits. Integrated circuits, or chips, are tiny (about .5 inch square) silicon chips into which thousands of electronic components are etched. The PC's processor is also a chip. Permanently installed and interchangeable disks provide permanent storage for data and programs (see Figure 1–4).

Computer Systems: Commuters to Wide-Bodies

The differences in the various categories of computers are very much a matter of scale. A good analogy can be made between airplanes and computers. Try thinking of a wide-body jet as a supercomputer, the most powerful computer, and a commuter plane as a personal computer. Both types of airplanes have the same fundamental capability: to carry passengers from one location to another. Wide-bodies, which fly at close to the speed of sound, can carry hundreds of passengers. In contrast, commuter planes travel much slower and carry about 30 passengers. Wide-bodies travel between large international airports, across countries, and between continents. Commuter planes travel short distances between regional airports. The commuter plane, with its small crew, can land, unload, load, and be on its way to another destination in 15 to 20 minutes. The wide-body may take 30 minutes just to unload. A PC is much like the commuter plane in that one person can get it up and running in just a few minutes. All aspects of the PC are controlled by one person. The supercomputer is like the wide-body in that a number of specialists are needed to keep it operational. No matter what their size, airplanes carry passengers and computers process data and produce information.

(CONTINUED)

COMPUTERS: THE ESSENTIALS (CONTINUED)

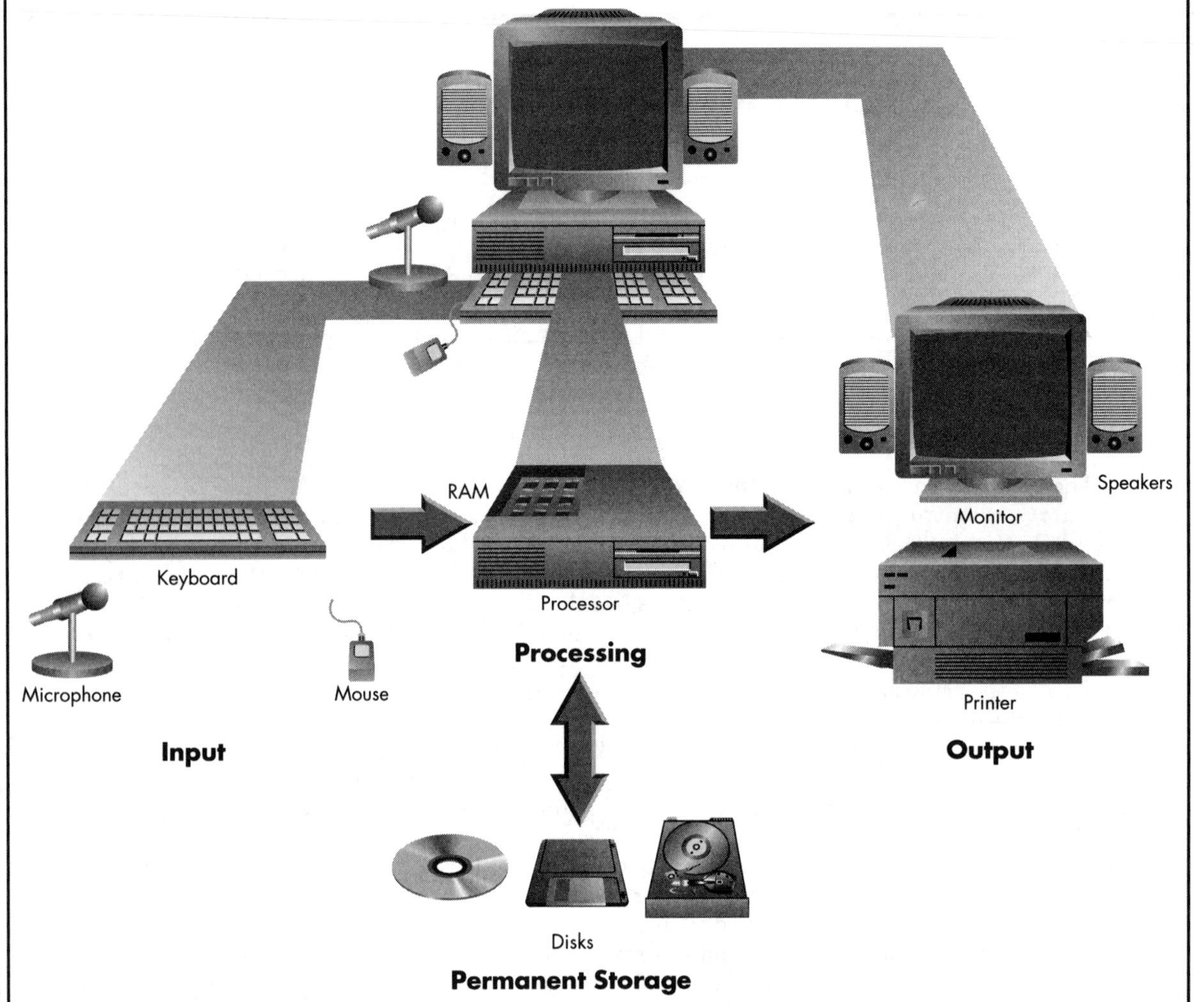

Figure 1–4   **The Four Fundamental Components of a Personal Computer System.** In a personal computer system, the storage and processing components are often contained in the same physical unit. In the illustration, the disk storage medium is inserted into the unit that contains the processor.

    Computers can be found in a variety of shapes, from cube-shaped to U-shaped to cylindrical to notebook-shaped. However, the most distinguishing characteristic of any computer system is its size—not its physical size, but its computing capacity. Loosely speaking, size, or computer capacity, is the amount of processing that can be accomplished by a computer system per unit of time. Mainframe computers have greater computing capacities than do personal computers, which are also called microcomputers (or micros). Mainframe computers vary greatly in size from midsized mainframes serving small companies to large mainframes serving thousands of people. And Supercomputers, the biggest of all, have greater computing capacities than do mainframe computers. Depending on its sophistication, a workstation's computing capacity falls somewhere between that of a micro and a mid-sized mainframe. Some vendors are not content with pigeonholing their products into one of these four major categories, so they have created new niches, such as desktop mainframes. In this book, we will limit our discussion to these four major categories (see Figure 1–5).

(CONTINUED)

COMPUTERS: THE ESSENTIALS (CONTINUED)

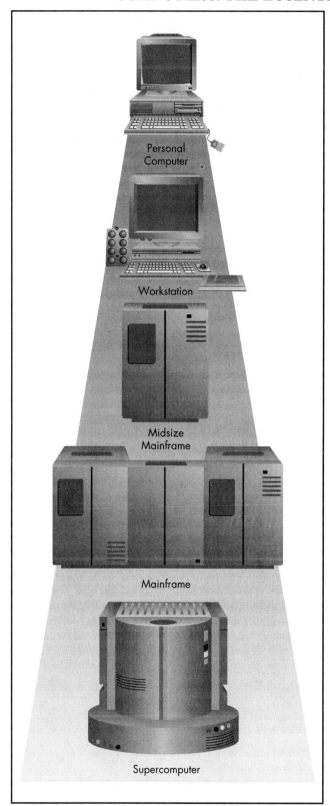

Figure 1–5

All computers, no matter how small or large, have the same fundamental capabilities—input, processing, output, and storage. Keep this in mind as you encounter the computer systems shown in Figure 1–5 in this book, at school, and at work. It should be emphasized that these categories are relative. What people call a personal computer system today may be called a workstation at some time in the future. In keeping with conversational computerese, we will drop the word system when discussing the categories of computer systems. Keep in mind, however, that a reference to any of these categories (for example, supercomputer) implies a reference to the entire computer system.

Micros, workstations, mainframes, and supercomputers are computer systems. Each offers many input/output or I/0 alternatives—ways to enter data to the system and to present information generated by the system. Besides obvious differences in size and capabilities, the various types of computers differ mostly in the manner in which they are used. Discussions in the following section should give you insight into when and where a particular system might be used.

CHAPTER 1 CONNECTIONS

A. Think about an area of your life in which you have been wanting to improve your performance—i.e., play better tennis, stick to a monthly budget, increase your productivity at work. What have you tried recently to help you improve? Do you think the Plan⇨Do⇨Review cycle could improve your chances for success? Why or why not? How would you start your plan to improve?

B. Using a Plan⇨Do⇨Review cycle to be a more successful reader asks you to approach reading differently than you have in the past. Which part(s) make the most sense to you? Why? Which part(s) are unclear or seem as if they will be the hardest to use? Do you think you will try using this approach? Why or why not?

CHAPTER 2

DETERMINE WHO THE AUTHOR IS AND WHY THE AUTHOR IS WRITING

As suggested in Chapter 1, before you start to read an assignment you should develop a plan of action. For this chapter you know that your general goal is to find, practice, and master strategies you can use to become more successful in reading for learning. But to get the most from this chapter you have to be more specific about your purpose and reading objectives.

Begin to develop your plan for this chapter by reviewing your instructor's directions and clarifying what you need to accomplish. For example, are you reading this chapter to prepare for listening to a lecture on the topic, as a follow-up to a class discussion, for information to use in completing the exercises, or a for a combination of reasons?

When you have decided why you are reading, and you are physically and mentally ready to work, you can activate additional pre-reading strategies. For example, your next step might be to read the content objectives, headings, subheadings, and chapter-ending questions to get your thoughts focused on the content.

Define this chapter's key vocabulary:

prose
infer and inference
purpose
exposition and expository
narration and narrative
description and descriptive
persuasion and persuasive

Next, think about and organize the information you've gathered. One way you could do this is to write down the chapter's major topics, a few words about what you already know on each of the topics, and what you need to find out as you are reading. Now you are ready to read this chapter.

CHAPTER 2 OBJECTIVES

❑ Determine why it's important to know the author.
❑ Identify and define four primary reasons authors have for writing.
❑ Identify strategies for inferring author's purpose.
❑ Understand why knowing the author's purpose helps comprehension.

WHAT IS MY BASIC STRATEGY FOR DETERMINING WHO AND WHY?

As You Plan:

1. Make certain you are ready to work.
2. Read about the author and the author's knowledge on this subject.
3. Determine the sources of the author's information.

As You Read:

4. Watch for references to information sources.
5. Follow the author's thoughts and clues.
6. Consider all the information.
7. Connect the author's information with your knowledge.
8. Infer the author's purpose.

As You Review:

9. Check validity of inferences with the information given.
10. Clarify the author's purpose.

WHY DOES IT MATTER WHO THE AUTHOR IS?

Think about the last time you had to talk with someone you didn't know. Remember how difficult that first conversation was? But do you also recall that as you learned about his or her background, job, hobbies, friends, and language, the talking and understanding became easier?

This also holds true for the silent conversation that takes place between you and the author during reading. Reading without knowing the writer, like talking with someone you don't know, makes communication difficult. Find out as much as you can about who the author is, his or her knowledge of the subject, and the source of the information.

There are strategies you can use to get to know an author and his or her qualification for writing. In books, look on the title page for basic data such as where the author teaches or what he or she does. Information about an author's background and professional activities is often included in the preface or a special "About The Author" section. Journals and magazines usually run a byline and short biography. Professors and librarians can also provide background data on authors. The more comprehensive picture of the author you construct, the more insight you will have for understanding what he or she is saying.

WHY DO WRITERS WRITE?

Once you know who is writing, read to find out why he or she is writing. Because an author doesn't often directly state his or her reason for writing, you must consider the information from all the sentences and infer, or put together, the reason for writing.

Inferring a writer's purpose is not just your opinion or a wild guess. An inference is your best reasoned conclusion based on the information you are given. Valid inferences follow logically from the information the author provides. As semanticist S. I. Hayakawa says in *Language in Thought and Action*, an inference is "a statement about the unknown made on the basis of the known."

Knowing an author's reason for writing will help you understand what the author writes. Four primary purposes for writing prose (writing other than poetry) are:

Exposition: The author wants to explain, set forth or make clear facts, events, and ideas.

Description: The author wants to paint a picture in words.

Narration: The author wants to tell a story.

Persuasion / Argumentation: The author wants to influence you—by engaging your emotions or by presenting logical arguments—to believe or feel a certain way or take a particular action.

But, just as in your own writing, authors often combine two or more purposes to clearly communicate their message. For example, an author may need to tell a story's sequence of events with vivid descriptions (but the primary purpose is still to tell you the story) or perhaps persuade you to take some action by giving you facts about the consequences of inaction (but the primary purpose is still to persuade you to act).

WHAT IS THE PURPOSE OF EXPOSITORY WRITING?

In your textbooks, you will most often find that an author's reason for writing is exposition—to give you information about ideas, events, people, or experiences without taking sides. Examples of exposition in textbooks include: physics—how gravity works, and art humanities—listing the major paintings by Rembrandt.

To establish writing as expository, look for definitions, facts and explanations that can be verified, rather than personal opinions. When reading exposition, have a clear purpose and concentrate on identifying main ideas first and then selecting the details that meet your purpose.

Expository Paragraph   John Macionis is a professor of sociology and author of numerous texts in the field. This excerpt comes from his text *Sociology*. The underlined phrases highlight how he defines his topic and give examples of its use. Taken together, you can infer his purpose is to give information about survey research.

<u>Survey Research</u>

<u>A survey is a research method in which</u> subjects respond to a series of items or questions in a questionnaire or an interview. Perhaps the most widely used of all research methods, <u>surveys are particularly suited to</u> studying what cannot be observed directly, such as political attitudes, religious beliefs, or the private lives of couples. Like experiments, <u>surveys can be used to</u> investigate the relationship among variables. <u>They are also useful for</u> descriptive research, in which subject responses help a sociologist to describe a social setting, such as a urban neighborhood or gambling casino.

WHAT IS THE PURPOSE OF DESCRIPTIVE WRITING?

When authors want you to visualize an object or a setting, they use sight, hearing, smell, taste, and touch words to create a picture that you can see in your mind. In your reading, description is often combined with exposition. Examples of description in textbooks include: political science—the detailed recounting of the sights and sounds of the exuberant celebration when the Berlin Wall came down, and American literature—Steinbeck allowing us to smell and feel the red dirt of the Oklahoma dust bowl in *Grapes of Wrath*.

To identify descriptive writing, look for details about the characteristics of people, places and things that engage your senses. When reading description, use the author's words to build pictures in your mind.

Descriptive Paragraph   From the title and the words that writer-naturalist Joseph Wood Krutch uses in *Desert Year*, we learn more than just that the desert is dry. Notice how, with phrases like those underlined, Krutch paints us a picture of the flower, sand, bird, and lizard. We can infer that his purpose is to sketch a picture of his beloved New Mexico desert.

<u>What It Looks Like</u>

What one finds, after one has come to take for granted the grand general simplicity, will be what one takes the trouble to <u>look for</u>—the <u>brilliant little flower springing</u> improbably out of the <u>bare, packed sand</u>, the <u>lizard scuttling with incredible speed</u> from cactus clump to spiny bush, the sudden <u>flash of a bright-colored bird</u>. This dry world, all of which seems so strange to you, is normal to them.

WHAT IS THE PURPOSE OF NARRATIVE WRITING?

In the narrative, the author tells a story. In academic reading, you will most likely read narration used with exposition; the author tells the story for a purpose or to make a point. Good expository narratives use many specific details. Examples of narration in textbooks include: American government—excerpts from a John Kennedy biography, and chemistry—what happens during combustion.

To identify narrative writing, watch for a retelling of events, situations and experiences told in the order in which they happen. When reading narration, determine if the author is telling the story just to entertain or if he or she is making a point, explaining a process, developing an idea, or providing information.

Narrative Paragraph Professor, scholar, and Pulitzer-Prize-winning author N. Scott Momaday tells of his life and the traditions of his Native American ancestors in his autobiography, *The Names*. The underlined phrases point out how he uses the sequence of events to pull us along. We can infer his purpose is to tell a story.

The End of My Childhood

The day before I was to leave I went walking across the river to the red mesa, where many times before I had gone to be alone with my thoughts. And I had climbed several times to the top of the mesa and looked among the old ruins there for pottery. This time I chose to climb the north end, perhaps because I had not gone that way before and wanted to see what it was. It was a difficult climb, and when I got to the top I was spent. I lingered among the ruins for more than an hour, I judge, waiting for my strength to return. From there I could see the whole valley below—the fields, the river, and the village. It was all very beautiful, and the sight of it filled me with longing.

WHAT IS THE PURPOSE OF PERSUASIVE WRITING?

In persuasive writing, authors present information, ideas, and opinions they hope will influence you to adopt a particular point of view, spend your money in a specific way, believe a concept, or do something. Authors can try to influence you by engaging your emotions or by presenting logical arguments to support their belief. For our purpose, whether an author wants to convince you through an appeal to emotions or an appeal to reason, we'll call their purpose *persuasion*. (As you continue with more advanced work, you will differentiate between an appeal to emotions—persuasion—and an appeal to reason—argumentation.) Examples of persuasion in textbooks include: computer programming—details on disk failure rates that make you want to keep back-up disks, and health—data from the American Cancer Society on cure rates and research costs that make you want to donate money.

To identify persuasive writing, look for information and opinions that support only one side of an issue or idea. Although skilled persuasive authors indicate they understand the other side of the issue by saying something about it, they spend their time discrediting ideas that go against their own. When reading persuasion, keep track of information without taking sides. All persuasive material is not bad and should not be discredited; you just need to recognize the author's attempt to influence you so you can decide whether to accept the information, reject the information, or find more information on the subject before you make up your mind.

Persuasive Paragraph In this preface to his book *Quality in America: How to Implement a Competitive Quality Program*, President of Technology Research Corporation V. Daniel Hunt discusses the importance of producing quality goods. Notice, in the underlined phrases, the words Hunt uses to appeal to patriotism and the desire for security to encourage readers to implement the Quality First™ program. We can infer his purpose is to persuade the reader to take action.

Preface

Producing quality goods and services is crucial not only to the continued economic growth of the United States, but also to our national security and the well-being and standard of living of each American family. America has been recognized for its leadership in producing quality products. However, in recent years, the position of America as quality leader has been challenged by foreign competition in domestic and overseas markets.

<u>Reasserting our leadership position will require a firm commitment to</u> <u>quality and the Quality First™ principle of continuous quality improve-</u> <u>ment.</u> America can, and must excel in this area, setting new standards for world-class quality and competing vigorously in international markets. (™ held by Technology Research Corporation)

CAN AN AUTHOR HAVE MULTIPLE REASONS FOR WRITING?

As mentioned earlier, an author often combines two or more purposes to communicate a message more clearly.

Harvard historian and Kennedy adviser Arthur M. Schlesinger, Jr. uses a combination of narration and exposition—using story form to tell what happened—in this excerpt from his book about Kennedy, *A Thousand Days.* What clues does Schlesinger give you?

A Thousand Days

When they arrived at Love Field, Congressman Henry Gonzalez said jokingly, "Well, I'm taking my risks. I haven't got my steel vest yet." The President, disembarking, walked immediately across the sunlit field to the crowd and shook hands. Then they entered the cars to drive from the airport to the center of the city. The people in the outskirts, Kenneth O'Donnell later said, were "not unfriendly nor terribly enthusiastic. They waved. But they were reserved, I thought." The crowds increased as they entered the city—"still very orderly, but cheerful." In downtown Dallas enthusiasm grew. Soon even O'Donnell was satisfied. The car turned off Main Street, the President was happy and waving, Jacqueline erect and proud by his side, and Mrs. Connally saying, "You certainly can't say that the people of Dallas haven't given you a nice welcome," and the automobile turning on to Elm Street and down the slope past the Texas School Book Depository, and the shots, faint and frightening, suddenly distinct over the roar of the motorcade, and the quizzical look on the President's face before he pitched over, and Jacqueline crying, "Oh, no, no... Oh, my God, they have shot my husband," and the horror, the vacancy.

The first narrative clues include *When they arrived,* and *The President, disembarking, walked immediately across the sunlit field to the crowd and shook hands.* What other narrative clues do you find?

Malcolm Rohrbough, a history professor and historian of the American West, tells the story of *Aspen: The History of A Silver Mining Town* using description and exposition—word picture and facts. What descriptive clues does Rohrbough use?

A Thrifty Mining Camp

The mining camp of Aspen lay at the end of a horseshoe, with the open end facing west down the valley of the Roaring Fork. Contact with the world of capital, supplies, technology, and people (in the form of immigrants) lay toward the east, however, across the axis of the horseshoe, by way of mountain ranges more than fourteen thousand feet high. The camp could be approached from only two directions: west from Leadville by way of Independence Pass; north from Buena Vista via the Taylor or Cottonwood Pass.

Rather than just tell where Aspen was located on a map, Rohrbough begins drawing a word picture of the location of Aspen in the first sentence: ... *Aspen lay at the end of a horseshoe, with the open end facing west down the valley of the Roaring Fork.*

PRACTICE: IDENTIFYING THE AUTHOR'S PURPOSE

Identify the author's purpose for writing in each paragraph.

1. Like traditional library research, there are a number of things you should do before you go on-line to do research in an electronic database. First, decide exactly what you want to know. Next, determine which database you will be using and how that database operates. Finally, write out your search strategy so that once you are on-line you can proceed through your search efficiently. (McGrath, *Magazine Article Writing Basics*)

2. Across the Great Plains, they erupt from the earth, tall and spindly with great round heads that spin and shine like galvanized bugs, twisting and clanking and spitting water. (Jim Carrier, "Windmill Creaks Echo in West's History," *The Denver Post*)

3. One of the strongest barriers to good thinking, then, is fear. Fear may show itself as anger, envy, selfishness, or hatred, but these are just expressions of our fear. And don't underrate the power of such emotions. History has shown what devastation fear and hatred among nations can wreak. Our personal fears can be just as damaging to our inner world, blinding our critical faculties with their dark energies. When we argue, then, we must be aware of what we feel as well as what we think. A good critical thinker may have to scrutinize not only the intellectual character of an argument, but its emotional temperature as well. (White, *Discovering Philosophy*)

4. The primary distinction between a bill, note and bond is the length of time, or term, the security will be outstanding from the date of issue. Treasury bills are short-term obligations issued for one year or less. Treasury notes are medium-term obligations issued with a term of at least one year, but not more than ten years. Treasury bonds are long-term obligations issued with a term greater than ten years. (Department of the Treasury)

5. By the early 1600s several religious minorities had abandoned hope of change in England and had begun to consider emigration. The first to depart was a small body of radical Puritan Separatists, the Pilgrims. In 1608 this group moved to Leiden in the Netherlands, then a refuge for religious minorities from all over Europe. For a while they prospered, but as time passed the little congregation began to fear for its survival and its orthodoxy in the face of the easygoing religious ways of the Dutch. In 1617 the Pilgrim leaders decided to move the congregation to "Virginia," where they could maintain their preferred mode of life and form of worship without distraction. (Unger, *These United States*)

CHAPTER 2 REVIEW QUESTIONS

1. Why is it important to know who the author is? Do you think this information is more critical for some types of material than others? Why?

2. What are strategies for identifying an author's expertise?

3. What is an inference?

4. List and define four primary purposes for writing.

5. List at least one strategy to use for identifying each of the purposes for writing.

6. Why is understanding who the author is and the author's purpose for writing helpful to accurate comprehension?

CHAPTER 2 THINK AND CONNECT QUESTIONS

7. Re-read the selections at the end of Chapter 1. Notice who the author is and determine the primary purpose for writing. Does knowing the author's background and purpose influence your willingness to accept the information? Why or why not?

8. Using one text section from one of your other textbooks and two magazine articles, identify the author and the primary purpose for writing.

CHAPTER 2 APPLICATION EXERCISES

9. Using the topic "cheating on a college exam," write an expository paragraph, a persuasive paragraph and a descriptive narrative paragraph.

10. From recent newspapers and magazines, identify articles that represent each of the primary purposes for writing, and an article where the author has multiple purposes for writing. Try to establish who the author is.

Note: If you have problems with any of the exercises, use one of the fix-up strategies described in Chapter 1, such as re-reading, to get the information you need to be successful.

USE YOUR STRATEGIES: EXERCISE #1

1. What can you infer best-selling author James Michener's purpose was in introducing readers of *Tales of the South Pacific* to character Luther Billis this way in this selection—"A Boar's Tooth"?

A BOAR'S TOOTH

The fat SeaBee was energetic and imaginative. He looked like something out of Treasure Island. He had a sagging belly that ran over his belt by three flabby inches. He rarely wore a shirt and was tanned a dark brown. His hair was long, and in his left ear he wore a thin golden ring. The custom was prevalent in the South Pacific and was a throwback to pirate days.

He was liberally tattooed. On each breast was a fine dove, flying toward his heart. His left arm contained a python curled around his muscles and biting savagely at his thumb. His right arm had two designs: Death Rather Than Dishonor and Thinking of Home and Mother. Like the natives, Luther wore a sprig of frangipani in his hair.

...On his left arm Billis wore an aluminum watch band, a heavy silver slave bracelet with his name engraved, and a superb wire circlet made of woven airplane wire welded and hammered flat. On his right wrist he had a shining copper bracelet on which his social security and service numbers were engraved. And he wore a fine boar's tusk.

2. What can you infer the National Resources Defense Council's purpose is in this excerpt—"A Brighter Idea"—from their booklet "What You Can Do to Save Energy and Our Environment"?

A BRIGHTER IDEA

For decades, Americans have used incandescent lightbulbs. We've grown used to their yellow light, their low price, even their shape. We've also gotten used to the fact that they burn out several times a year. And since we've never had an alternative, most of us haven't bothered to think about how much electricity they use. But it's time for a change.

Now there's a far more efficient alternative available—compact fluorescent lightbulbs. They're nothing like those long tubes with the harsh white light and annoying flicker. Compact flourescents are not much bigger than traditional household bulbs, and they give off a steady, soft light. Best of all, they use a fraction of the electricity. The compact fluorescent equivalent of a desk lamp bulb uses 15 to 18 watts instead of 60, and the equivalent of an overhead bulb uses 27 to 35 watts instead of 100. Compact flourescents are, however, heavier than the old bulbs and too bulky to fit under some lampshades. And they cost more. But every compact fluorescent you substitute for an incandescent bulb will save you $30 to $40 in electricity costs. And it will keep a half-ton of carbon dioxide out of the atmosphere. It's time to make the switch.

3. What can you infer professors Presley, Freitas, and Jones' purpose is in this excerpt—"Banks"—from their book *An Introduction to Business Using Works?*

BANKS

By the strictest definition, the word "bank" refers to commercial banks; however, in a broader application of the term, "bank" also includes other types of financial institutions, such as savings and loan associations and credit unions. Commercial banks are banking corporations which accept demand deposits and make loans to businesses. Savings and loan associations are financial corporations set up to sell shares to individuals, the proceeds of which are mostly invested in home mortgages. The investors are paid in the form of dividends rather than interest. Credit unions are cooperative financial societies organized by a group of people to accept deposits and make loans to its members.

4. What can you infer freelance writer Alexandra Greeley's purpose is in this article—"Getting the Lead Out ... of Just about Everything"— written for the *FDA Consumer?*

GETTING THE LEAD OUT ... OF JUST ABOUT EVERYTHING

A Puerto Rican family moved here from the Caribbean with high hopes for a better life. They set up housekeeping in low-income housing in eastern Massachusetts, and four of the six children developed lead poisoning, shattering family dreams.

When questioned, the 10-year-old son answers that he lives in the state of Boston and that George Washington is president of the United States. He cannot count to 30. His younger brother with severe lead poisoning is chronically restless. He is unable to sit still, and the doctor describes him as roaming around the doctor's office like a "caged animal."

(CONTINUED)

GETTING THE LEAD OUT ... OF JUST ABOUT EVERYTHING (CONTINUED)

In another case, the ninth of 10 children of a well-to-do Boston family had seizures and was in a coma as a child as a result of lead poisoning. She ultimately recovered and went to school and then to college. But her history shows she had tremendous emotional difficulties throughout her life and has managed to cope only because her family had the financial resources to help.

Not fictitious children, they represent but a few of the cases that John Graef, M.D., associate clinical professor at Harvard Medical School and chief of the lead and toxicology program at Children's Hospital in Boston, has encountered in his career. "I think we all get numbed by the numbers," he says. "These are real people. Statistics do not tell the whole story.... One of the things that worries us is that no matter where we look, there are ways for lead to enter our bodies."

Despite successful cleanup efforts—such as the reduction in the numbers of lead-soldered food cans, which the FDA has urged, and the removal of lead from gasoline—health problems caused by repeated exposure to lead continue to endanger Americans.

5. What can you infer Jane and Larry McGrath's purpose is in this *Performance Racing Industry* magazine excerpt—"Trends 2000"?

TRENDS 2000: POSITIONING FOR PROFIT

The future is bright for grassroots racing across the country—from Friday night drags and autocross to NHRA and NASCAR division racing. And all those racers are high-energy ingenious folks. They refuse to be satisfied with today's performance; they boldly search and research for the best of tomorrow.

That translates into a decade of unlimited business opportunities for high performance automotive retailers. With a proactive vitality, successful retailers are positioning themselves to increase profits well into the 21st century. "By the year 2000 we're going to look different and market our products differently," predicts Mike Oldham, Automotive Engineering, Clearwater, Florida. "We'll get rid of our old '60s look' and become more interesting and energetic," he said.

For many, however, building a long-range plan to achieve and profit from that competitive 'new look' is a mystery. To help unlock that mystery, here are the seven tactics that industry leaders forecast will propel retailers successfully into the future.

6. What can you infer the author's purpose is in this article excerpt on Bolivian silver mines—"Potosí"—from *Newsweek*'s Columbus issue?

POTOSÍ: A MOUNTAIN THAT EATS MEN

They say that Huayna Cápaj, king of the Incas, discovered the silver of Potosí, the Bolivian mines that lined the pockets of Spain and the rest of Europe for two centuries. ...The Spanish arrived 'from afar' in 1545 and by the turn of the century had extracted silver equal to three times the wealth in all of Europe's reserves. In 1592, the year of peak production, the mines yielded 220 tons of precious metal. Potosí itself became the jewel of the empire, a European-style metropolis with 36 gambling houses, ballrooms and theaters. When 16th-century Spaniards referred to something invaluable, they called it "worth a Potosí."

7. What can you infer the Alaskan Tourist Board's purpose is in this paragraph excerpted from the booklet they mail out to potential tourists?

ALASKA

This is a land of secrets, of ancient rainforests, of timeless rituals, with creatures of the land, the air, and the sea all taking part. When nature sings her ancient songs, birds wing their way north, and majestic whales begin their annual odyssey which may encompass thousands of miles. We, too, heed inner voices and turn north when the spirit calls. This is a land of mountain spires, of mighty rivers, and of whispering breezes. Some say if you listen carefully, you'll hear it calling your name.

---

8. What can you infer Janson and Janson's purpose is in this excerpt—"Form"—from the introduction to their text *A Basic History of Art?*

FORM

Every two-dimensional shape that we find in art is the counterpart to a three-dimensional form. There is nevertheless a vast difference between drawing or painting forms and sculpting them. The one transcribes, the other brings them to life, as it were. They require fundamentally different talents and attitudes toward material as well as subject matter. Although numerous artists have been competent in both painting and sculpture, only a handful have managed to bridge the gap between them with complete success.

Sculpture is categorized according to whether it is carved or modeled and whether it is relief or free-standing. Relief remains tied to the background, from which it only partially emerges, in contrast to free-standing sculpture, which is fully liberated from it. A further distinction is made between low (bas) relief and high (alto) relief, depending on how much the carving projects. However, since scale as well as depth must be taken into account, there is no single guideline, so that a third category, middle (mezzo) relief, is sometimes cited.

---

9. What can you infer professors McGrath and Rings' purpose is in this course syllabus statement—"Success"?

SUCCESS

Rarely can you get something for nothing. However, according to study skills expert David Ellis, students can get nothing for something—it happens when the only thing they invest in a course is their money.

We have no magic formulas, no new discoveries, no quick-fixes. The reading and studying strategies we will present have been around, in one form or another, for a long time. Some of the strategies will work for you and some will not but there is no way for you to know until you use them.

We can merely set the stage; you create learning through your own energy and action.

10. What can you infer Macionis's purpose is in this part of a "Sociology of Everyday Life" segment—"What's in a Name?"—in his *Sociology* text?

WHAT'S IN A NAME? SOCIAL FORCES AND PERSONAL CHOICE

On July 4, 1918, twins were born to Abe and Becky Friedman in Sioux City, Iowa. The first to be born was named Esther Pauline Friedman; her sister was named Pauline Esther Friedman. Today, these women are known to almost every American, but by new names adopted later: Ann Landers and Abigail ("Dear Abby") Van Buren.

These two women are not the only Americans to have changed their names to further their careers—it is a practice especially common among celebrities. At first glance, this may seem to be simply a matter of particular preference. However, examining the list below from a sociological perspective uncovers a general pattern. Historically, women and men of various national backgrounds have tended to adopt not just any name, but *English-sounding* names. Why? Because American society has long accorded high social prestige to those of Anglo-Saxon background.

USE YOUR STRATEGIES: EXERCISE #2—"CAN INTERPERSONAL SKILLS BE TAUGHT?"

Stephen Robbins teaches organizational behavior at San Diego State University and Southern Illinois University at Edwardsville. He is also the author of the best-selling *Organizational Behavior*, 4th ed. This selection—"Can Interpersonal Skills Be Taught?"—is from *Training in Interpersonal Skills*.

CAN INTERPERSONAL SKILLS BE TAUGHT?

STEPHEN P. ROBBINS

[1]Business and public-sector organizations spend tens of millions—maybe hundreds of millions—of dollars each year on development programs to improve their managers' interpersonal skills. You'd think, therefore, that there would be little debate over whether such skills can be effectively taught. But there are diverse opinions on this question.

[2]On one side are those who view interpersonal skills as essentially personality traits that are deeply entrenched and not amenable to change (Fiedler, 1965). Just as some people are naturally quiet, while others are outgoing, the antitraining side argues that some people can work well with others while many cannot. That is, it's a talent you either have or you don't. Their case is intuitively appealing when they single out individuals with highly abrasive interpersonal styles and propose that no amount of training is likely to convert them into "people-oriented" types. Most of their evidence, however, tends to be of this anecdotal variety.

[3]The skills advocates have an increasing body of empirical research to support their case. For instance, there is evidence that training programs focusing on the human relations problems of leadership, supervision, attitudes toward employees, communication, and self-awareness produce some improvement in managerial performance (Burke and Day, 1986).

[4]Nothing in the research suggests that skills training can magically transform the interpersonally incompetent into highly effective leaders. But that should not be the test of whether interpersonal skills can be taught. The evidence strongly demonstrates that these skills can be learned. Although people differ in their baseline abilities, the research shows that training can result in improved skills for most people.

EXERCISE #2 QUESTIONS—"CAN INTERPERSONAL SKILLS BE TAUGHT?"

1. Who is the author? What do you know about him?
2. Do you think that the author is knowledgeable about the subject? Why or why not?
3. What can you infer the author's purposes for writing are?
4. What does the author want to convince you of?

USE YOUR STRATEGIES: EXERCISE #3—"ADVICE TO BEGINNING WRITERS"

Robert McGrath is a freelance writer whose work appears in numerous national publications. This selection—"Advice to Beginning Writers"—is from *Byline*.

ADVICE TO BEGINNING WRITERS

ROBERT L. McGRATH

¹Countless successful writers—and some not so accomplished—have tried to unlock the secret of their triumphs to share it with others. Obviously, there is no patented method to achieve success. What works for one person may be a washout for others. But here's a method that works for me, and perhaps it will be helpful to you. I call it SWAP—a four-part approach to achievement in your writing efforts.

²**S**—Studying. Writing requires a lifetime of study. Your study may be concentrated at local colleges which offer writing courses at various levels, along with occasional seminars and local writers' groups. Or it may involve reading all the books about creative writing you can find. Constant review of magazines such as *Byline*, *Writer's Digest*, *The Writer*, and others will contribute immeasurably to your study program. Read the type of material you aspire to write. Saturate yourself with it. Have at hand several basic tools: A good dictionary, a thesaurus, a market list, books on technique covering the categories you hope to sell. Use them!

³**W**—Writing. This, of course, is the only way to succeed. A writer must write; otherwise, he is not a writer, and cannot lay claim to the appellation. Study courses, either in classroom situations or by correspondence, can be helpful, combining study with actual writing by requiring a certain amount of discipline—otherwise often elusive. I like an additional formula: SOP-2-SOC—seat of pants to seat of chair. So Hemingway stood at the mantel to write…do it your way, but do it. Pen, pencil, typewriter, word processor—they're all good tools. Use them! Form the habit of writing, every day if possible. Time or place do not matter. Just do it!

⁴**A**—Ambition. Set realistic goals for yourself. Be practical. Your first effort probably won't be The Great American Novel. But an expressive poem just might find print in an obscure journal and set you on your way. Or you might be a winner in one or more of the many *Byline* contests. You'll need a certain amount of self-confidence, for without it, you'll never reach those goals. Know that you have the native ability to put words on paper—words that will be worthwhile not only to you, but to others as well. Another formula comes to mind: SYI—scratch your itch. You have that urge to write. So write…write…write.

⁵**P**—Perseverance. Never give up on something you believe in. You can succeed, but only if you refuse to toss in the towel. My files contain irrefutable proof of the value of hanging in there. My short short story, "Payment Received," won tenth place in the 1955 *Writer's Digest* contest. I figured it had to be a worthy piece. But on thirty-nine trips to various editors, it failed to make the grade. The fortieth submission was to a magazine that previously had rejected it. I goofed; otherwise, I probably wouldn't have resubmitted it to Alfred *Hitchcock's Mystery Magazine*. It was later published in a hardcover collection of Hitchcock yarns, and reprinted in two separate paperback editions of the same anthology. It was read over a South African radio station (for which I was paid). It was the subject of a *Writer's Digest* experience report. Perseverance caused its sale. Other stories have parallel records. One sold to prestigious *Stories* magazine on its fifty-fifth trip out. The record for me is a sale on the eightieth trip to an editor's desk. Believe in yourself—persevere!

⁶Try the **SWAP** plan. Results aren't guaranteed, but it's worth a try.

EXERCISE #3 QUESTIONS—"ADVICE TO BEGINNING WRITERS"

1. Who is the author? What do you know about him?
2. Do you think the author is knowledgeable about the subject? Why or why not?
3. What can you infer the author's purposes for writing are?
4. What does the author want to convince you to do?

USE YOUR STRATEGIES: EXERCISE #4—"WILD THINGS"

Nick Taylor, who has written about fishing, family, the Mafia, and neo-Nazis in his diverse books, is an avid traveler in his spare time. This selection—"Wild Things"—is from *Travel Holiday*.

WILD THINGS

NICK TAYLOR

[1] I was snorkeling amid rainbow multitudes of fish, when something big hit the water. It plunged toward the bottom in a stream of bubbles, twisted, and headed toward me like a rocket. I felt just a moment of fascinated dread. Then it turned to look at me, and I confronted a pair of big brown eyes, cartoon whiskers, and naked curiosity, before the creature streaked away.

[2] You think you're prepared for the Galápagos. It's no news that these Ecuadorean islands, 600 miles off the mainland coast, are crawling with all but tame wildlife that will practically walk up and shake your hand and that you have to look sharp or you'll be stepping on a penguin nest. Their popularity has rendered the Galápagos familiar. You go expecting less a real wild-life experience than a sort of photographic petting zoo.

[3] Until you're nose to whiskers with a young sea lion.

[4] And that was only the beginning. During an eight-day cruise of the islands last December, my wife, Barbara, and I had more surprises as we hiked prehistoric landscapes thronged with birds, followed teeming shorelines, and swam in rock gardens. We watched marine iguanas butting heads over their harems and followed the slow march of giant tortoises across upland meadows. We were charmed by acrobatic seals and panhandled by mockingbirds. Far from being familiar, the islands constantly renewed our sense of wonder.

[5] A mockingbird greeted us as we waded ashore at Punta Suárez, on Isla Española, the most southerly of the Galápagos, on the first day of our excursion. It hopped from some bushes, cocked its head, and fixed us with sharp eyes. "Did anybody bring a water bottle?" asked our guide, Juan Carlos Naranio.

[6] Barbara handed him a water bottle from my backpack, and the bird leaped onto his arm. He handed the bottle back to Barbara, and the creature followed. It thrust its long, curved beak at the bottle top. "We're nearing the end of the dry season," said Juan Carlos. "You never see them when it rains." As our group of 10 set off along the rocky trail marked by the Galápagos National Park Service's low black-and-white posts, two more mockingbirds hopped along in hot pursuit. We—and they—stopped before a blue-footed booby in a nest on the ground beside the path. The brown-and-white bird fixed us with a wide-eyed, pixilated look, a look that seems to explain the booby's name. It comes from *bobo*, Spanish for foolish, but the sailors who named it did so because it was trusting and easy to kill. Its webbed feet, looking as if the bird had stepped into a can of sky blue paint, were equally absurd. As we watched, two downy, ungainly chicks clambered from the rocks.

[7] The trail continued along a rocky coastline watched over by a lone hawk. Soon we reached hundreds more birds—frigate birds, swallow-tailed gulls, and red-billed tropic birds with streamerlike tail feathers. Mating was in the air. We saw two albatrosses doing an elaborate courtship dance, flirting boobies lifting their blue feet and pointing their wingtips skyward, and a pair of copulating gulls.

[8] The thirsty mockingbirds gave up the chase. We emerged on the head of a sheer cliff high above a lava shelf glistening with sea spray. Sea lions sprawled on the rocks, among red spangles that were Sally Lightfoot crabs. As the surf rushed in, it found in the shelf's volcanic crevices a route to a spectacular release, roaring like a hurricane as it burst forth in a regular, geyserlike plume.

(CONTINUED)

WILD THINGS (CONTINUED)

[9]On another cliff, not far away, we entered the nesting grounds of the waved albatross. Most of the world's population of these seabirds nest on Española, but it was late in the year. The majority had left, the young on the extended pelagic journeys that make the albatross a bird of myth. One fledgling remained, among a few adults. Its head and neck were still covered with brown, curly down that made it look like a bearded old man. It could not yet fly, but it lifted its wings when we came too close, giving a hint of a wingspan that would grow to nearly eight feet.

[10]There seemed little left to see as we made our way back. Yet when we neared the beach where a dinghy would pick us up and return us to our cruise yacht, one of our group gave a cry of discovery. A sea lion had given birth while we were walking, leaving her placenta as evidence of this small miracle. Juan Carlos followed a path in the sand toward the water. He pointed to the weary mother, flopped behind a rock, and a mewing infant, still bloody, its eyes huge, its face wrinkled like any newborn's, crying to be nursed.

[11]It went like that throughout our seven-island cruise. At every turn, the Galápagos reinforced their famous claim as a unique and impressive outpost of the natural world.

EXERCISE #4 QUESTIONS—"WILD THINGS"

1. Who is the author? What do you know about him?
2. Do you think the author is knowledgeable about the subject? Why or why not?
3. What can you infer the author's purposes for writing are?

USE YOUR STRATEGIES: EXERCISE #5—"THE FIRST AMERICANS"

Pulitzer Prize winning historian Irwin Unger has been teaching American history for over twenty-five years on both coasts. He currently teaches at New York University, where he has been since 1966. This selection—"The First Americans"—is from *These United States*, 5th ed.

THE FIRST AMERICANS

IRWIN UNGER

[1]The first Americans were migrants from eastern Siberia on the Asian mainland. Physically, they belonged to the same human stock as the modern Chinese, Japanese, and Koreans—a relationship suggested by the straight black hair, broad face, and high cheekbones of most modern American Indians. The migrants were a hunting, fishing, and gathering people who depended on roots, berries, fish, and game for food. As decreasing rainfall reduced these resources in Siberia, scholars conjecture, the native peoples gradually moved eastward seeking sustenance. Today they would be stopped by the Bering Sea, but in that distant era we know that a land bridge joined Alaska in North America to Siberia. On the eastern side of this bridge the migrants probably found more abundant food supplies and a climate milder than in their homeland. Gradually they moved southward along various routes, and by the time Europeans arrived many thousands of years later, they had spread from just below the Arctic Ocean to Tierra del Fuego at the southern tip of South America and from the Atlantic to the Pacific. They had also grown enormously in numbers. From perhaps a few hundred or a few thousand migrants, by 1942 the Indian population of the Americas had swelled to 75 million, a figure equal to that of contemporary Europe.

(CONTINUED)

THE FIRST AMERICANS (CONTINUED)

[2]As their numbers grew over the centuries, the descendants of these Asian people diversified into many groups with distinct languages, cultures, and political and economic systems. By about 3000 B.C. some had begun to practice agriculture, with "maize" (corn), first developed from a grasslike native American plant, as their chief crop and the staple of their diet. They also grew tomatoes, squash, various kinds of beans, and, in South America, potatoes. Surpluses from agriculture transformed Indian life. Abundant food led to larger populations and also to more diverse societies. Not everyone was needed to produce food to sustain life, so classes of priests, warriors, artisans, and chiefs appeared. In the most fertile agricultural regions great civilizations arose with a command of technology, artistic sophistication, and political complexity comparable to the civilizations of Asia and Europe.

EXERCISE #5 QUESTIONS—"THE FIRST AMERICANS"

1. Who is the author? What do you know about him?
2. Do you think the author is knowledgeable about the subject? Why or why not?
3. What can you infer the author's purposes for writing are?

CHAPTER 2 CONNECTIONS

A. In what classes do you think you will have to do mostly expository reading? In what classes will you probably have a mixture of types of readings? Why the differences? What impact might these differences have on the way you study for particular classes?

B. Look again at the sample readings and exercises in this chapter. Who are your two favorite authors? Why are they your favorites? Do you tend to prefer a certain type of writer (for example, writers who use description more than straight exposition)? Do your preferences seem to affect your comprehension? If so, what strategies could you use to overcome potential problems?

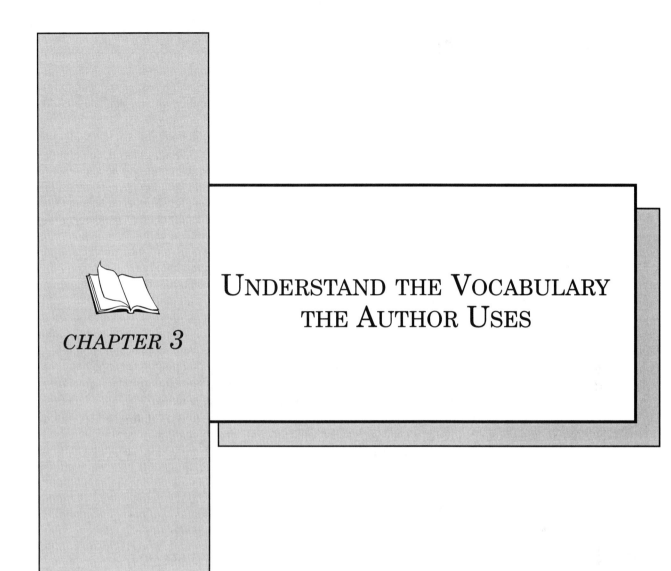

CHAPTER 3

UNDERSTAND THE VOCABULARY THE AUTHOR USES

English is the richest language with the largest vocabulary on Earth—over one million words. The average adult has a vocabulary of 40,000 to 50,000 words. So it's not surprising that in every reading assignment you encounter unfamiliar and confusing words.

As you develop your plan for reading this chapter, think about what you do when you run into a word you don't know. Perhaps you stop and look it up in the dictionary or find someone you can ask. What else have you tried? What strategies have you used when the definition you found in the dictionary didn't make sense in the context of the sentence or paragraph you were reading?

As you preview this chapter, jot down your answer to each of the main headings, which are in question form (e.g., "What Is My Basic Strategy for Understanding the Author's Vocabulary?"; "How Can I Use the Context to Help Define a Word?"; "How Can I Use the Word Itself as a Clue to Its Meaning?"; and so on). Then, as you read and gain new information, revise your answers.

Define this chapter's key vocabulary:

context
context clues
prefix
root
suffix
word analysis
literal meaning
denotation
connotation
figurative language
simile
metaphor

CHAPTER 3 OBJECTIVES

❏ Formulate an overall strategy for defining unfamiliar words.
❏ Understand how to use context to help define a word.
❏ Understand how to use the parts of the word to help define it.
❏ Identify other resources for defining unfamiliar words.
❏ Recognize the difference between the denotation and connotation of a word.
❏ Recognize when words are chosen by the author for a special purpose.
❏ Recognize and understand figurative language.

WHAT IS MY BASIC STRATEGY FOR UNDERSTANDING THE AUTHOR'S VOCABULARY?

As You Plan:

1. Review words that are highlighted—i.e., words in **boldface** or *italic* and words that are defined in footnotes or marginal notes.

As You Read:

2. Identify unfamiliar words.
3. Use context clues:

   Look at the surrounding words: Do they offer any clues?

   Look at the rest of the sentences or paragraphs: Do they offer any clues?

   Look for other clues, such as punctuation, the author's purpose, or setting.

4. Analyze word parts:

   Look at the word: Is it related to a known word?

5. Use your own experience.
6. Predict the possible meaning.
7. Try out the meaning in the sentence and see if it makes sense.
8. Decide if the definition makes sense, if you should try again, or if you should consult a dictionary or an expert.
9. Check for meanings beyond the literal definition.

As You Review:

10. Clarify any remaining definitions.
11. If it is important to your purpose, determine a way to review and remember the new words.

HOW CAN I USE THE CONTEXT TO HELP DEFINE A WORD?

Most of these words are familiar: *option, trading, call, put, uncovered, naked,* and *covered.* Yet in this paragraph from the stockbroker's newsletter you read in Chapter 1, your definitions for the words probably didn't help you understand the paragraph.

> Writing or selling *Options* against stock you already own is a strategy that is conservative and usually works well in a *trading* market. An Option is either a *call* (a right to buy 100 shares of stock at a specified price in the future) or a *put* (a right to sell 100 shares of stock at a specified price in the future). Thus an Option buyer or seller who owns no stock (called *uncovered* or *naked*) is a speculator who is looking at making large percentage returns on a small amount of invested capital in a short time. This individual would be paying the Option premium to us, the *covered* writer.

This is because words do not have just one isolated meaning. Words take on meaning from their context—how they are used in conjunction with other words.

When you read this paragraph, you could either skip over the words you didn't know or try to figure out their meanings. Fortunately, active readers—readers thinking about and looking for related information—can often use clues the author provides to help them understand unfamiliar words. In fact, I just used a context clue: I defined what I meant by "active reader" and set it off with a dash (—) as your clue.

For other examples of context clues, look in the stockbroker's paragraph. For the first two words—*Options* and *trading*—are there any words or information in the paragraph that help? Not really, so if you don't recognize them from your own experience, come back to them later. The next four of the words—*call, put, uncovered, naked*—are defined for you (parentheses are your clue). To define the final word—*covered*—the author gives the definition for its opposite—*uncovered*—as your clue.

USING CONTEXT CLUES

Assume you are reading your astronomy text and come to the unfamiliar words *perihelion* and *aphelion.* To comprehend the passage, you must understand the words. See how you can use the context clues the author provides.

> *Perihelion* is the point in the earth's orbit when the distance between the earth and the sun is at its minimum, as opposed to *aphelion.*

Here, the author defined *perihelion* directly (is the point in the earth's orbit when the distance between the earth and the sun is at its minimum) and has clued you to the definition of *aphelion* by stating it is the opposite (therefore, *aphelion* must be the point in the earth's orbit when the distance between the earth and the sun is at its maximum).

In addition to using punctuation, stating a definition or an opposite, an author can provide other clues such as giving an example or explanation, or restating the thought in more simple terms.

Making use of context clues to help define unfamiliar words is much like the work you did in Chapter 2 to infer the author's purpose. You combine all the information an author provides to determine the meaning the word has in this context. The meanings you construct through context clues are not reckless guesses; they are thoughtful suppositions supported by the author's information.

Unless the passage is extremely difficult and has too many unfamiliar words, using context clues can save you time and assure that you have the best definition for the context.

See how author John Macionis uses a variety of context clues in these passages from his text *Sociology*. As you read, look for words, phrases, and punctuation that relate to or seem to point to the unknown word.

Gives a Specific Definition of an Important Word (*sociology*):

A distinctive perspective is central to the discipline of *sociology*, which is defined as the scientific study of human social activity. As an academic discipline, sociology is continually learning more about how human beings as social creatures think and act.

Provides an Explanation of a New Word (*replication*):

One way to limit distortion caused by personal values is through the *replication* of research. When the same results are obtained by subsequent studies there is increased confidence that the original research was conducted objectively.

Uses Punctuation as a Clue to Meaning of Words (*experiment, hypothesis*):

The logic of science is clearly expressed in the *experiment*—a research method that investigates cause-and-effect relationships under highly controlled conditions. Experimental research tends to be explanatory, meaning that it is concerned not with just what happens but with why. Experiments are typically devised to test a specific *hypothesis*—an unverified statement of a relationship between any facts or variables. In everyday language, a hypothesis is simply a hunch or educated guess about what the research will show.

Gives Clue to Unknown Term (*ethnography*) by Comparison to Known Term (*case study*):

Cultural anthropologists describe an unfamiliar culture in an *ethnography*; a sociologist may study a particular category of people or a particular setting as a *case study*.

Gives Clue to New Term (*secondary analysis*) by Stating Its Opposite:

Each of the methods of conducting sociological investigation described so far involves researchers personally collecting their own data. Doing so is not always possible, however, and it is often not necessary. In many cases, sociologists engage in *secondary analysis*.

Gives Clue to New Word (*subculture*) with Examples:

When describing cultural diversity, sociologists often use the term *subculture*. Teenagers, Polish-Americans, homeless people, and "southerners" are all examples of subcultures within American societies. Occupations also foster subculture differences, including specialized ways of speaking, as anyone who has ever spent time with race-car drivers, jazz musicians, or even sociologists can attest.

PRACTICE: DEFINING WORDS USING CONTEXT CLUES

Use the author's context clues to unlock the meaning of the italicized words and phrases in these passages. Describe the context clues you used.

1. A magazine is custom-designed for its special audience. For example, *Redbook* and *Cosmopolitan* are both primarily women's magazines and may have articles on similar topics but their *slant*—their approach to the topic—is very different. Each must answer the questions and provide the information their readers expect. (McGrath, *Magazine Article Writing Basics Handbook*)

2. *Like terms* are terms that have the same variables with the same exponents. (Angel, *Elementary Algebra for College Students*, 3rd, ed.)

3. Typically, work outcomes are measured in *physical units* (i.e., quantity of production, number of errors), *time* (i.e., meeting deadlines, coming to work each day), or *money* (i.e., profits, sales costs). (Robbins, *Training in InterPersonal Skills*)

4. A composer often provides a marking for *tempo*, or overall speed, to help convey the character of a composition. (Politoske, *Music*)

5. Computerphobia, the fear of computers, is apparently affecting more and more people as microcomputers continue to be plugged into more and more homes, schools, and offices throughout the land. This relatively recent phenomenon, also known as *cyberphobia*, occurs in a large proportion of students and professionals. (Fuori and Gioia, *Computers and Information Processing*)

6. One problem in treating alcoholism is that it is hard to recognize. Although a person who is *chronically* drunk, as opposed to the occasional drinker, is more suspect. (*University of California at Berkeley Wellness Newsletter*, February 1993)

HOW CAN I USE THE WORD ITSELF AS A CLUE TO ITS MEANING?

You can't always rely on context clues; there may not be any or they may be confusing. Another strategy you can use to define an unfamiliar word is to analyze the parts of the word—its root and any prefixes and/or suffixes—as clues to the meaning of the entire word.

The root is the basic part of a word. Additional words are sometimes made by adding a prefix at the beginning of a root word and/or a suffix at the end of a root word. Prefixes and suffixes change the meaning of the root word. A suffix can also change the way a word can be used in a sentence and its part of speech. Combining the meanings of the word parts can help you understand the whole word.

When you learn the meaning of a few common word parts, you have a head start on defining other words that contain those parts. In fact, researchers estimate that for every word part you know, you have the key to unlock the meaning of about seven more words.

USING WORD PARTS

Let's assume you are reading a different astronomy text, this one with no context clues, and you come to the unfamiliar words *perihelion* and *aphelion*. If you know, or can look up the meanings of the basic word parts, you can define the words as easily as with context clues:

perihelion: peri from the Greek meaning *near,* + *helios* from the Greek meaning *the sun* = near the sun

aphelion: apo from the Greek meaning *away from,* + *helios* from the Greek meaning *the sun* = away from the sun

We arrive at similar meanings for *perihelion* and *aphelion* as when there were context clues to help. We just used a different strategy.

If you know that *apolune* means the point in the path of a body orbiting the moon that is farthest from the center of the moon, what does *perilune* mean? By combining what you already knew about *peri* (near) with the new information (*lune* means moon), you know that *perilune* means the point in the path of a body orbiting the moon that is nearest the center of the moon.

Use word parts to help define each of these words.

un = not	*able* = capable of
retro = backward	*spec* = see
trans = across	*anti* = against

a. un•read•able (not capable of being read)
b. retro•spec•tive (looking backward)
c. trans•atlantic (across the Atlantic ocean)
d. anti•inflammatory (against, or counteracting inflamation)

PRACTICE: DEFINING WORDS USING WORD PARTS

The following table lists some common word parts and their definitions. Use them to help you define the italicized words in the passages that follow.

ROOTS

aud, audit	hear	*demos*	people
graphy	writing, record	*mit, miss*	send
pathy	feeling	*port*	carry
divers	different	*phob*	fear
scribe, script	write	*spec*	see
literate, literatus	able to read and write	*geront, gerento*	old age
annus (ennal)	year	*mille*	1,000

PREFIXES

ec-, eco-	habitat	*chiz-* or *schizo-*	split
phren, phreno-	mind	*il-, im-, ir-*	in or into/or not
tele-	over a distance	*mega-, meg-*	large
trans-	across	*retro-*	backward
anti, contra, ob-	against	*quadri-, quadr-*	four
un-	not or opposite	*bi-, bio-*	living organisms
intra-	within, inside	*inter-*	among, between
semi-	half	*untra-*	super, excessive
micro-	small	*em-, en-*	within

SUFFIXES

-er, -or, -ist	one who	*-ly*	like
-ance, -ancy, -ency	act or fact of doing	*-able*	capable of
-ese	native to; originating in	*-ulent*	abounding in
-ine	having the nature of,	*-al*	characterized by
-ment	action	*-less*	without
-logy	oral/written expression	*-ism*	manner of action
-ity	condition, state	*-fy*	make, form into

1. It is the loss of this *biodiversity* and the loss of *irreplaceable* ancient forests that most concern environmentalists about the issue of logging in national forests. (Scott, "Hoots to Blame?")

2. In the industrialized countries, 3.3 percent of the adult population is *illiterate*. For the developing countries as a whole the figure is 35 percent, and rises as high as 60 percent in the 47 least developed countries. (Bequette, *UNESCO Courier*, January 1993)

3. In *telecommunications* we are moving to a single worldwide information network, just as economically we are becoming one global marketplace. (Naisbitt and Aburdene, *Megatrends 2000*)

4. Baca recalls her role in the beginning of the Chicano Mural Movement when she was searching for a way to express her own experience as a Hispanic American artist. Greatly influenced by the Mexican muralists, Baca discovered a means of community *empowerment*. (Estrada, "Judy Baca's Art for Peace")

5. Moving from our analysis of the term communication, we now examine the process of communication. We begin by studying a communication model and the three types of communication important to our study in this text: *intrapersonal*, *interpersonal*, and mass communication. (Bittner, *Each Other*)

6. The compost pile is really a teeming *microbial* farm. (Office of Environmental Affairs, *Backyard Composting*)

IF I STILL CAN'T FIGURE OUT THE MEANING, WHAT OTHER RESOURCES CAN I USE?

There will be times when you can't piece together any helpful information from the context or the structure of the word. When this happens, take the time to look the word up in the book's glossary or a dictionary, or ask one of your resource people (someone you identified in Chapter 1 as being a resource).

A glossary is a quick, easy-to-use resource because it only lists the specific meaning of the word as it's used in the book. Not all books provide a glossary (and even those that do sometimes won't provide enough information—such as how to pronounce the word), so sometimes you will need to consult a dictionary.

A dictionary is a reliable source of all the definitions for a word, plus correct spelling variations, pronunciations, parts of speech, and derivations. Since you will often find several definitions for a word, you must always fit the meaning you select back into the original context to be certain it makes sense.

USING A DICTIONARY

Assume that this time you come across *perihelion* and *aphelion* in your text and you don't have any context clues and you don't know the meaning of the word parts. Looking up the words in a dictionary gives you literal meanings similar to when you used context clues or word parts.

a|phe|li·on (ə fēʹlē ən, -fēlʹyən) *n.,* pl. **-li·ons** or **-li|a** (-ə) ⟦ModL, altered (as if Gr) by Johannes KEPLER < earlier *aphelium* < Gr *apo-,* from + *hēlios,* SUN[1]; modeled on L *apogaeum,* APOGEE ⟧ the point farthest from the sun in the orbit of a planet or comet, or of a man-made satellite in orbit around the sun: opposed to PERIHELI-ON

In this passage from the editors of *Syllabus*, you may have conflicting ideas about the meaning of rudimentary—does it mean low or high?

> The increasing power of the personal computer is making it possible to develop applications that are smarter and more responsive to the user.... Anyone who has used a spelling or grammar checker has experienced this type of application at a very *rudimentary* level. ("Advanced Technologies Lead the Way to the Future of Educational Computing," *Syllabus*)

If rudimentary is an unfamiliar word, you're best resource is the dictionary.

ru·di·men·ta|ry (ro͞o′də men′tər ē, -men′trē) **adj.** of, or having the nature of, a rudiment or rudiments; specif., *a)* elementary *b)* incompletely or imperfectly developed *c)* vestigial

Unfortunately, finding the correct meaning of a word in the dictionary is not always this clear-cut. Many words have more than one meaning and can be used as more than one part of speech. Each time you look up a word in the dictionary, your job is to sort through the definitions and select the one definition that best fits the context.

For example, if you look up the word *base* in a dictionary, you find a variety of definitions.

base¹ (bās) **n.**, *pl.* **bas′|es** (-iz) ⟦ME < OFr *bas* < L *basis*, BASIS⟧ **1** the thing or part on which something rests; lowest part or bottom; foundation **2** the fundamental or main part, as of a plan, organization, system, theory, etc. **3** the principal or essential ingredient, or the one serving as a vehicle /paint with an oil *base]* **4** anything from which a start is made; basis **5** *Baseball* any of the three sand-filled bags (*first base, second base,* or *third base*) that must be reached safely one after the other to score a run **6** the point of attachment of a part of the body /the *base* of the thumb] **7** a center of operations or source of supply; headquarters, as of a military operation or exploring expedition **8** *a)* the bottommost layer or coat, as of paint *b)* a makeup cream to give a desired color to the skin, esp. in the theater **9** *Archit.* the lower part, as of a column, pier, or wall, regarded as a separate unit **10** *Chem.* any compound that can react with an acid to form a salt, the hydroxyl of the base being replaced by a negative ion: in modern theory, any substance that produces a negative ion and donates electrons to an acid to form covalent bonds: in water solution a base tastes bitter, turns red litmus paper blue, and, in dissociation theory, produces free hydroxyl ions: see pH **11** *Dyeing* a substance used for fixing colors **12** *Geom.* the line or plane upon which a figure is thought of as resting /the *base* of a triangle] **13** *Heraldry* the lower portion of a shield **14** *Linguis.* any morpheme to which prefixes, suffixes, etc. are or can be added; stem or root **15** *Math. a)* a whole number, esp. 10 or 2, made the fundamental number, and raised to various powers to produce the major counting units, of a number system; radix *b)* any number raised to a power by an exponent (see LOGARITHM) *c)* in business, etc., a starting or reference figure or sum upon which certain calculations are made

Select the best definition of base for each of the following each sentences.

1. In the expression 42, the 4 is called the *base*, and the 2 is called the exponent.

2. The Ionic order's most striking feature is the column, which rests on an ornately profiled *base* of its own.

3. The closing of the military *base* in the region prompted a quick economic decline.

4. Today's experiment will show whether the compound is *base* or acid.

5. Both investigation teams were working from the same *base* information.

PRACTICE: SELECTING THE BEST DICTIONARY DEFINITION

Each of the italicized words or phrases has multiple meanings listed in the dictionary. Select the definition that best fits the context.

1. Your career depends not only on your efforts, but also on the efforts of many other people. You cannot be successful by yourself. You can only be successful as part of a joint effort by many different people, by acting in *harmony* with other people. All through your career, you will find yourself interdependent with other people. (Johnson, *Human Relations and Your Career*)

> **har·mo|ny** (här′mə nē) *n., pl.* **-nies** ⟦ME *armony* < OFr *harmonie* < L *harmonia* < Gr < *harmos*, a fitting < IE base **ar-* > ART, ARM[1]⟧ **1** a combination of parts into a pleasing or orderly whole; congruity **2** agreement in feeling, action, ideas, interests, etc.; peaceable or friendly relations **3** a state of agreement or orderly arrangement according to color, size, shape, etc. **4** an arrangement of parallel passages of different authors, esp. of the Scriptures, so as to bring out corresponding ideas, qualities, etc. **5** agreeable sounds; music **6** *Music a)* the simultaneous sounding of two or more tones, esp. when satisfying to the ear *b)* structure in terms of the arrangement, modulation, etc. of chords (distinguished from MELODY, RHYTHM) *c)* the study of this structure

2. Population increases, urban growth, and devastating poverty are three of the most *acute* problems facing the world in the twenty-first century.

> **a|cute** (ə kyōōt′) *adj.* ⟦L *acutus*, pp. of *acuere*, sharpen: see ACUMEN⟧ **1** having a sharp point **2** keen or quick of mind; shrewd **3** sensitive to impressions *[acute* hearing*]* **4** severe and sharp, as pain, jealousy, etc. **5** severe but of short duration; not chronic: said of some diseases **6** very serious; critical; crucial *[an acute* shortage of workers*]* **7** shrill; high in pitch **8** of less than 90 degrees *[an acute* angle*]*: see ANGLE[1], illus. **9** INTENSIVE (sense 3)

3. Science is an important foundation of all sociological research and, more broadly, helps us to *critically* evaluate information we encounter every day. (Macionis, *Sociology*, 3rd ed.)

> **crit|i·cal** (krit′i kəl) *adj.* **1** tending to find fault; censorious **2** characterized by careful analysis and judgment *[a* sound *critical* estimate of the problem*]* **3** of critics or criticism **4** of or forming a crisis or turning point; decisive **5** dangerous or risky; causing anxiety *[a critical* situation in international relations*]* **6** of the crisis of a disease **7** designating or of important products or raw materials subject to increased production and restricted distribution under strict control, as in wartime **8** *a)* designating or of a point at which a change in character, property, or condition is effected *b)* designating or of the point at which a nuclear chain reaction becomes self-sustaining —**crit′i·cal|ly** *adv.* —**crit′i·cal′i|ty** (-kal′ə tē) or **crit′i·cal·ness** *n.*

4. A *front* usually is in constant motion, shifting the position of the boundary between the air masses but maintaining its function as a barrier between them. Usually one air mass is actively displacing the other; thus the *front* advances in the direction dictated by the movement of the more active air mass. (Bergman and McKnight, *Introduction to Geography*)

front (frunt) *n.* ⟦ME < OFr < L *frons* (gen. *frontis*), forehead, front <
IE *bhren-*, to project > OE *brant*, steep, high⟧ **1** *a)* the forehead
b) the face; countenance **2** *a)* attitude or appearance, as of the face,
indicating state of mind; external behavior when facing a problem,
etc. *[to put on a bold* front*] b)* [Colloq.] an appearance, usually
pretended or assumed, of social standing, wealth, etc. **3** [Rare]
impudence; effrontery **4** the part of something that faces forward or
is regarded as facing forward; most important side; forepart **5** the
first part; beginning *[toward the* front *of the book]* **6** the place or
position directly before a person or thing **7** a forward or leading
position or situation ✰**8** the first available bellhop or page, as in a
hotel: generally used as a call **9** the land bordering a lake, ocean,
street, etc. **10** [Brit.] a promenade along a body of water **11** the
advanced line, or the whole area, of contact between opposing sides
in warfare; combat zone **12** a specified area of activity *[the home*
front, *the political* front*]* **13** a broad movement in which different
groups are united for the achievement of certain common political or
social aims ✰**14** a person who serves as a public representative of a
business, group, etc., usually because of his or her prestige ✰**15** a
person or group used to cover or obscure the activity or objectives of
another, controlling person or group **16** a stiff bosom, worn with
formal clothes **17** *Archit.* a face of a building; esp., the face with the
principal entrance **18** *Meteorol.* the boundary between two air
masses of different density and temperature —*adj.* **1** at, to, in, on,
or of the front **2** *Phonet.* articulated with the tongue toward the
front of the mouth: said of certain vowels, as (i) in *bid* —*vt.* **1** to
face; be opposite to **2** to be before in place **3** to meet; confront **4** to
defy; oppose **5** to supply or serve as a front, or facing, of —*vi.* **1** to
face in a certain direction *[a castle* fronting *on the sea]* ✰**2** to act as
a FRONT (senses 14 & 15): with *for*

5. The effects created by different intensities of sound, or dynamics, are
    basic to all musical expression. In traditional music, we often first
    become aware of the impact of dynamic effects upon hearing very
    sudden changes from soft to loud, or vice versa. For some of us, the
    first awareness of musical dynamics is very obvious, as in the so-called
    "Surprise" Symphony of Franz Joseph Haydn (1732–1809). Here, the
    surprise is a *radical* change in volume, a very loud chord coming on the
    heels of a gentle melody. (Politoske, *Music*)

rad‖i·cal (rad′i kəl) *adj.* ⟦ME < LL *radicalis* < L *radix* (gen. *radicis*),
ROOT[1] ⟧ **1** *a)* of or from the root or roots; going to the foundation or
source of something; fundamental; basic *[a* radical *principle] b)*
extreme; thorough *[a* radical *change in one's life]* **2** *a)* favoring
fundamental or extreme change; specif., favoring basic change in the
social or economic structure *b)* [R-] designating or of any of various
modern political parties, esp. in Europe, ranging from moderate to
conservative in program **3** *Bot.* of or coming from the root **4** *Math.*
having to do with the root or roots of a number or quantity —*n.* **1** *a)* a
basic or root part of something *b)* a fundamental **2** *a)* a person
holding radical views, esp. one favoring fundamental social or economic change *b)* [R-] a member or adherent of a Radical party **3**
Chem. a group of two or more atoms that acts as a single atom and
goes through a reaction unchanged, or is replaced by a single atom: it
is normally incapable of separate existence **4** *Math. a)* the indicated
root of a quantity or quantities, shown by an expression written
under the radical sign *b)* RADICAL SIGN

PRACTICE: *DEFINING WORDS USING OUTSIDE RESOURCES*

Define each of the italicized words or phrases and tell what resource you used
to find your definition.

1. America's love affair with the automobile was never any secret in Los
    Angeles. Built around the car, the Californian *megalopolis* is the
    biggest gas guzzler in the world. Its 13 million residents drive 9 million
    cars over 386 million kilometers (nearly 24 million miles) a day, using
    up 68 million liters (nearly 18 million gallons) of gasoline and diesel
    fuel, and producing 60 percent of the city's *notorious* smog. (*UNESCO
    Courier*, November 1992)

2. Since before the first *Gutenberg revolution*, paper has served as an indispensable all-purpose catalyst for much of one abstraction of what universities are all about: the creation, preservation, dissemination, and interpretation of data, information, and knowledge. (Lynn, "Publish Electronically or Perish," *Higher Education Product Companion*)

3. Few people could imagine that in a decade or so television would become a *preemptory force* in American culture, defining the news, reshaping politics, reorienting family life, and remaking the cultural expectations of several generations of Americans. (Gilder, *Life After Television*)

4. The automobile, one of the most *pervasive* symbols of modern culture, serves as an *apt metaphor* for the ways in which humans change the global environment. (Silver, *One Earth One Future*)

5. Our institutions of family, religion, education, business, labor, and community are attempting to keep afloat while wrestling with both internal and external combatants. Each group's *raison d'être* is challenged constantly while it seeks acceptable canons in which to function in modern society. (Rauch, "A Quality Life Should Be Full of Values," *USA Today*)

HOW CAN I USE THE STRATEGIES TOGETHER WHILE I'M READING?

Real reading tasks don't have the obvious look of these isolated samples. To successfully read (remember that reading and understanding are synonymous terms) the variety of material required in an academic setting requires that you use these strategies flexibly.

When you encounter a word that hinders your understanding, you may first check to see if there are any context clues you can use. On the other hand, if you recognize the parts of the word, perhaps that is all the clue you need. You work smarter, not harder. But you also realize that if context clues, word analysis, and your experience don't yield a probable meaning for the word, you must take time to consult an outside resource, like the dictionary.

For example, read this sentence from *Megatrends 2000*, by John Naisbitt and Patricia Aburdene. "Conceived under the influence of the next millennium, these new megatrends are the gateways to the 21st century." You probably read the passage by combining several strategies:

noting the context relationships between millennium and 21st century and between megatrends and gateways
using knowledge of word parts—mille = 1,000 and mega = big
remembering some prior knowledge—perhaps you've heard of megatrends.

Even if you used a slightly different set of strategies, when you fit the meanings together you understood that Naisbitt and Aburdene were saying "after thinking about the next thousand years—the 21st century—these are the big trends or ideas that will get us there successfully."

For a strategy to help remember new words, see the "Study Strategies" section entitled "Improving Vocabulary" on page 422.

PRACTICE: DEFINING WORDS USING CONTEXT CLUES, WORD PARTS, AND OTHER RESOURCES

Use your word sleuthing strategies to define the italicized words.

ENDANGERED SPECIES: ENDANGERED MEANS THERE'S STILL TIME

U.S. DEPARTMENT OF THE INTERIOR, U.S. FISH AND WILDLIFE SERVICE

[1]Since life began on this planet, countless creatures have come and gone—*rendered extinct* by naturally changing *ecological* conditions, and more recently by humans and their activities.

[2]If *extinction* is part of the natural order, and if so many species still remain, some people ask, "Why save *endangered species*? What makes a relatively few animals and plants so special that effort and money should be spent to preserve them?"

Why Save Endangered Species?

[3]Saving species is important to many people for a variety of reasons. People care about saving species for their beauty and the thrill of seeing them, for scientific and educational purposes, and for their ecological, historic, and cultural values.

[4]A *compelling reason* to preserve species is that each one plays an important role in an *ecosystem*—an intricate network of plant and animal communities and the associated environment. When a species becomes endangered, it indicates that something is wrong with the ecosystems we all depend on. Like the canaries used in coal mines whose deaths warned miners of bad air, the increasing numbers of endangered species warn us that the health of our environment has declined. The measures we take to save endangered species will help *ensure* that the planet we leave for our children is as healthy as the planet our parents left for us.

[5]Some species provide more immediate value to humans. For example, cancer fighting drugs have been *derived* from the bark of a *yew* that is native to the Pacific Northwest. Chemicals used to treat diseases of nerve tissue were found in an endangered plant in Hawaii. Valuable resources such as these could be lost forever if species go extinct.

Causes of Decline

[6]We can no longer attribute the *accelerating loss* of our wild animals and plants to "natural" processes. *Habitat destruction* is the single most serious worldwide threat to wildlife and plants, followed by *exploitation* for commercial or other purposes. Disease, *predation*, inadequate conservation laws, pollution, and introduction of non-native species, or a combination of these can contribute to a species' decline.

The Listing Process

[7]The U.S. Fish and Wildlife Service maintains the List of Endangered and Threatened Wildlife and Plants, which identifies species protected under the Endangered Species Act. The Act defines an "endangered" species as one that is in danger of extinction throughout all or a significant portion of its range. A "threatened" species is one likely to become endangered within the foreseeable future.

To understand the meaning of this passage you had to use several strategies together. For example,

> *rendered extinct* ([1]): Check surrounding words for clues. Prior phrase "have come and gone" clue to general meaning. I already know extinct means gone. Predict possible meaning: "made to disappear." Fit meaning into sentence. It makes sense.

ecological (¶1): Check surrounding words; no strong clues. Read ahead; no specific clues. Consider topic, and that *eco* means habitat. Predict possible meaning "environmental." Fit meaning into sentence. It makes sense, but since this appears to be an important word, I should also check for a dictionary definition.

extinction (¶2): Check surrounding words for clues. Following phrase "and if so many species still remain" seems to be opposite to meaning of extinction. Consider it has the same root as *extinct*. Predict possible meaning: "disappearing." Fit meaning into sentence. It makes sense.

endangered species (¶2): Check surrounding words; no strong clues. Read ahead; locate specific definition in last paragraph. Fit meaning into sentence. It makes sense.

compelling reason (¶4): Check surrounding words for clues. No direct restatement but phrase "each one plays an important role" makes me think it means "good reason." Fit meaning into sentence. It makes sense.

ecosystem (¶4): Check surrounding clues; punctuation indicates definition follows.

ensure (¶4): Check surrounding words for clues. No direct word clues but the sentence, taken as a whole, seems to suggest it's positive action. Consider the root *sure*. Predict possible meaning: "make sure." Fit meaning into sentence. It makes sense.

derived (¶5): Check surrounding words for clues. No direct clues but phrase "from the bark" makes me think it means "taken from or made out of." Fit meaning into sentence. It makes sense.

yew (¶5): Check surrounding words for clues. Prior phrase "from the bark of a" suggests it's a tree. Fit meaning into sentence. It makes sense.

Define these words from paragraph 6.

1. *accelerating loss*
2. *habitat destruction*
3. *exploitation*
4. *predation*

HOW CAN A WORD MEAN MORE THAN ITS DEFINITION?

In this chapter we've concentrated on finding an exact literal, or denotative, meaning of a word. But words often mean more than their explicit meaning or just what it says in the dictionary. Words can also suggest a variety of meanings that trigger an assortment of feelings and emotions. These associated meanings are called connotations—what the word implies to the reader. Because of these meanings beyond the literal, authors can subtly influence readers with the words they select. You should be especially wary of connotations when the author's primary purpose is to persuade. For example, which of these descriptions do you think I prefer?

> Dr. McGrath is petite, has reddish-brown hair, and a good sense of humor.
> Dr. McGrath is a runt, has reddish-brown hair, and a good sense of humor.

Yes, even though I have a good sense of humor, I do prefer being called petite.

Why? Because even though both petite and runt mean "short" in the dictionary, they make me feel differently because of their connotations. For me, the connotation of petite is positive: small and delicate. The connotation of runt, is negative: unnaturally short.

For example, consider the similarities and differences between the denotative and connotative meanings of the italicized words in each pair of passages.

> Jeff was very *confident* he would get the job because he scored well on the written exam.
>
> Jeff was very *cocky* he would get the job because he scored well on the written exam.
>
> Because they felt so strongly about the issue, Karen and Bill took part in a *rally* at the capital.
>
> Because they felt so strongly about the issue, Karen and Bill took part in a *demonstration* at the capital.

In everyday reading, however, you don't have two versions of the same passage to compare. Therefore, once you have determined the literal meaning, ask yourself if the word or phrase makes you feel or react—positively or negatively—beyond its meaning. Determine whether the word seems to soften the impact of the message (*anti-personnel weapon* instead of *bomb*) or intensify your reaction to the message (*guerrilla fighters* instead of *freedom fighters*). Authors choose words for their maximum impact—including their connotative meaning. You must understand both the denotative and connotative meaning of the words to fully understand the author's message. We'll take another look at how authors influence us by their choice of words in Chapter 6.

PRACTICE: CONSIDERING BOTH THE CONNOTATIVE AND DENOTATIVE MEANINGS

Read each pair of words. List their literal definitions and then describe their connotations.

1. a. jock   b. athlete
2. a. reserved   b. inhibited
3. a. collect   b. hoard
4. a. impertinent   b. bold

Read each passage with special attention to the italicized phrases. Why do you think the author selected those words? What message does the author want to convey? What other words or phrases could be used that would be more neutral?

1. After *unsuccessfully peddling his idea to every monarch of Western Europe*, Columbus finally interested the rulers of Spain. (Unger, *These United States*, 5th ed.)
2. By *crushing black leaders*, while *inflating the images of Uncle Toms* and celebrities from the world of sport and play, the mass media were *able to channel and control the aspirations and goals of the black masses*. (Cleaver, *Soul On Ice*)
3. To many minds, Hillary Clinton is the *quintessential yuppie mother* of the 1990s, juggling career and family with remarkable skill. (editorial, *The Arizona Republic*)

4. Exemptions from ESA (the Endangered Species Act) can be granted by the *so-called God Squad*, which is convened at the request of the U.S. Secretary of the Interior. (Berke, "The Audubon View," *Audubon*)

WHAT IS FIGURATIVE LANGUAGE?

From my drifting hot air balloon, the Hawaiian Islands looked like small bread crumbs floating in a full bowl of soup.

Enthusiasm bubbled out of petite 22-year old Chrissy Oliver with the effervescence of a just-opened split of champagne.

Homelessness is a rusty blade cutting through the soul of humanity.

Each of these statements is an example of figurative language: using words in an imaginative way to help the reader comprehend the message more clearly. Certainly, I could have written the statements literally: "The Hawaiian Islands look small," "Chrissy Oliver was happy to win the race," or "Homelessness causes untold problems," but I would have taken the risk that you would not be able to picture exactly what I wanted you to understand.

Although figurative language does not make sense literally, it does help you form a mental image, or picture, of what an author is talking about. Figurative expressions often compare something the author thinks you already know about to what he or she wants you to understand. The most basic of these comparisons are called similes (direct comparisons using the words "like" or "as") and metaphors (implied comparisons).

When a passage doesn't make sense to you at the literal level, check to see if the author is using figurative language. If so, use the author's words to draw a mental picture definition and fit that back into the context.

In this paragraph, to what does noted historian John Lukacs compare the problems of this country? What does he want you to picture and understand from the figurative expressions in this passage.

As the great French thinker Georges Beranos once wrote: "The worst, the most corrupting lies are problems wrongly stated." To put this in biological terms: without an honest diagnosis there can be no therapy, only further decay and perhaps even death. So I must sum up seven deadly sins of misdiagnosis: seven deadly problems that now face this country because of their intellectual misstatements. (Lukacs, *Our Seven Deadly Sins of Misdiagnosis*)

Lukacs wants you to picture the nation as a sick person to whom the doctor has given the wrong diagnosis. Before the person (the nation) can be cured, the illness (the problem) has to be correctly identified.

In this paragraph, training and development specialist Ron Zemke employs two comparisons. What does he want you to picture and understand from the figurative expressions?

The auditorium lights grow dim. A diffusion of sunrise hues washes languidly across a sweep of rear-projection screens. From beneath stage level, rising in single file like a septet of hunter's moons, come the seven letters of the sacred rite: Q-U-A-L-I-T-Y. (Zemke, "Faith, Hope and TQM" *Training*)

In the second sentence Zemke compares the slides coming on the screen to a slow, colorful sunrise. Then, he compares the appearance of the seven (septet) letters of the word QUALITY to the wondrous appearance of large and bright (hunter's) moons. (Note: When you have difficulty understanding a part of the figurative comparison, like "Hunter's moons," check with one of your resources to get the literal meaning of the expression. You must understand the literal before the figurative will make sense.)

PRACTICE: UNDERSTANDING FIGURATIVE LANGUAGE

Describe what the author is comparing, and what you should picture and understand from the figurative language in each of these passages.

1. This is our hope. This is the faith that I go back to the South with. With this faith we will be able to *hew out of the mountain of despair a stone of hope*. With this faith we will be able to *transform the jangling discords of our nation into a beautiful symphony of brotherhood*. (King, "I Have A Dream," speech delivered in Washington, D.C., August 28, 1963)

2. The *performance improvement efforts* of many companies *have as much impact on operational and financial results as a ceremonial rain dance has on the weather*. (Schaffer and Thompson, "Successful Change Begins with Program Results," *Harvard Business Review*, January–February 1992)

3. *The year 2000 is operating like a powerful magnet on humanity*, reaching down into the 1990s and intensifying the decade. It is amplifying emotions, accelerating change, heightening awareness, and compelling us to reexamine ourselves, our values, and our institutions. (Naisbitt and Aburdene, *Megatrends 2000*)

4. It wasn't long ago that school newspapers and campus newsletters were being churned out using slow processes that have now all but become extinct.... The print-oriented *classrooms of the '90s are now more or less jam-packed with computer terminals*, a *spaghetti feast of electronic wiring*, and students leaning toward computer terminals. (Morse, "Campus Publishing," *Higher Education Product Companion*)

5. *The flowering of Etruscan civilization* coincides with the Archaic age in Greece. During this period, especially near the end of the sixth and early in the fifth century B.C., Etruscan art showed its greatest vigor. (Janson and Janson, *A Basic History of Art*)

6. But time has proven that R.E. *"Ted" Turner*—Captain Outrageous to the press—is *crazy like a fox*. (Griffin and Ebert, *Business*, 2nd ed.)

CHAPTER 3 REVIEW QUESTIONS

1. Discuss your overall strategy for defining unfamiliar words.
2. Explain how to use context clues to help define a word and list two types of clues that authors use.
3. Explain what it means to use the parts of the word to help define it. Give one example.

4. List two other resources for defining unfamiliar words, and when you might use them.

5. State the difference between the denotation and connotation of a word. Give an example of how a word can have a connotative meaning beyond its dictionary meaning.

6. Explain why its important to understand both the denotative and connotative meanings of words and phrases.

7. Explain the purpose of figurative language and give an example.

CHAPTER 3 THINK AND CONNECT QUESTIONS

8. Re-read *Advice to Beginning Writers*, by Robert McGrath, Chapter 2, Exercise #3. Identify four of the unfamiliar words you came across when you first read it, and describe the strategies you used to figure them out. Now that you have some additional strategies, would you go about defining them any differently now? Why or why not?

9. Re-read *Wild Thing*, by Nick Taylor, Chapter 2, Exercise #4. Identify two figurative expressions and explain what the author wanted you to picture.

CHAPTER 3 APPLICATION EXERCISES

10. From recent newspapers or magazines, select an article you think uses a word or phrase for its connotative meaning. Explain why you think the author used the language. Rewrite the word or phrase keeping the literal meaning but changing the connotation.

USE YOUR STRATEGIES: EXERCISE #1—"OBSESSIVE-COMPULSIVE DISORDER"

Mary Lynn Hendrix is a science writer in the Office of Scientific Information, National Institute of Mental Health (NIMH). Scientific review was provided by NIMH staff members Thomas R. Insel, M.D.; Dennis L. Murphy, M.D.; Teresa A. Pigott, M.D.; Judith L. Rapoport, M.D.; Barry Wolfe, Ph.D.; and Joseph Zohar, M.D.

OBSESSIVE-COMPULSIVE DISORDER

MARY LYNN HENDRIX

What Is OCD?

[1]In the mental illness called *OCD* (obsessive-compulsive disorder), a person becomes trapped in a pattern of *repetitive* thoughts and behaviors that are senseless and distressing but extremely difficult to overcome. The following are typical examples of OCD:

(CONTINUED)

OBSESSIVE-COMPULSIVE DISORDER (CONTINUED)

[2]Troubled by repeated thoughts that she may have *contaminated* herself by touching door-knobs and other "dirty" objects, a teenage girl spends hours every day washing her hands. Her hands are red and raw, and she has little time for social activities.

[3]A middle-aged man is *tormented* by the notion that he may injure others through carelessness. He has difficulty leaving his home because he must first go through a lengthy *ritual* of checking and rechecking the gas jets and water faucets to make certain that they are turned off.

[4]If OCD becomes severe enough, it can destroy a person's *capacity to function* in the home, at work, or at school. That is why it is important to learn about the disorder and the treatments that are now available.

How Common Is OCD?

[5]For many years, mental health professionals thought of OCD as a very rare disease because only a small minority of their patients had the condition. But it is believed that many of those *afflicted* with OCD, in efforts to keep their repetitive thoughts and behaviors secret, fail to seek treatment. This has led to *underestimates* of the number of people with the illness. However, a recent survey by the National Institute of Mental Health (NIMH)—the Federal agency that supports research nationwide on the brain, mental illness, and mental health—has provided new understanding about the *prevalence* of OCD. The NIMH survey shows that this disorder may *affect* as much as 2 percent of the population, meaning that OCD is more common than *schizophrenia* and other severe mental illnesses.

EXERCISE #1 QUESTIONS—"OBSESSIVE-COMPULSIVE DISORDER"

1. What is Hendrix's purpose?
2. Do you think Hendrix is knowledgeable on this topic? Why or why not? What impact does the scientific review panel have on your view?
3. Write the meanings of these words and phrases and what strategies you used to get each one.
    a. OCD (¶1)
    b. repetitive (¶1)
    c. contaminated (¶2)
    d. tormented (¶3)
    e. ritual (¶3)
    f. capacity to function (¶4)
    g. afflicted (¶5)
    h. underestimates (¶5)
    i. prevalence (¶5)
    j. affect (¶5)
    k. schizophrenia (¶5)

USE YOUR STRATEGIES: EXERCISE #2—"HUMMINGBIRDS"

Robert McGrath is a freelance writer. His work appears in numerous national publications. This selection—"Hummingbirds"—is from *FEDCO Reporter*.

HUMMINGBIRDS: JEWELS ON WINGS

ROBERT L. McGRATH

[1]You've probably enjoyed watching those tiny rainbow-pinioned helicopters *hover* at the feeder in your backyard—or perhaps at your neighbor's. But how much do you really know about these jewels on wings?

[2]Hummingbirds come in a variety of colors, though mostly in the same *diminutive size* that makes them stand out as among nature's most remarkable creatures.

[3]There are more than 300 kinds, but amazingly, only the ruby-throated hummingbird is found east of the Mississippi River. Western states are home to as many as 18 different types, with the bulk of the others in the family inhabiting Central and South America. None are found outside the Western Hemisphere.

[4]Their kaleidoscopic plumage has no solid color. Instead, there are tiny barbs on each feather, placed so they break and refract light, just as a mirror or a diamond will do. While the male hummingbird is more colorful than his mate, underparts of both male and female are usually gray or a variety of other shades, while head and back are often a glowing green.

[5]The birds sport so many patches of different tints, they're often named after precious jewels—ruby, topaz, emerald, amethyst-throated.

[6]Those whirring wing-beats are made possible by special hinges within their bone-structure that permit helicopter-like rapid vibrating and feathering. Suspended or backward flight requires about 54 wing-beats per second, while normal dodging, darting flight reaching 50 miles per hour takes up to 75 beats of its narrow wings.

[7]Because it uses so much energy in flight, a hummingbird goes into a *state resembling hibernation* at night when it rests from a constant labor of gathering food. When awake, its normal temperature is over 100 degrees; it falls to as low as 64 degrees when it's asleep. The hummingbird's heartbeat, however, is super fast. While human beings average 72 beats a minute, the hummer's regular rate is 615 beats a minute when in flight.

[8]The *territorial-minded* male hummingbird vigorously defends his space against other birds, cats, or even snakes. Yet, once he has selected his mate and courtship is complete, the male leaves everything else to his partner. She alone builds the solid little nest—so small a quarter placed on top of it would stick out over the edges—using plant fibers, lichens, and bark, then cementing this miniature cup with saliva glue and spider webs.

[9]It takes 21 days for the female to hatch her two pea-sized pearly eggs. She then begins the endless duty of feeding the helpless, ever-hungry chicks by herself, a task lasting three weeks, when the *fledglings* are ready to fly.

[10]Anyone with a hummingbird feeder can enjoy a thrill a minute watching these winged wonders display their *aerial antics*—the most exciting in the world of birds.

EXERCISE #2 QUESTIONS—"HUMMINGBIRDS"

1.   What is McGrath's purpose?

2.   Do you think McGrath is knowledgeable on this topic? Why or why not?

3.   Write the meanings of these words and phrases:

      a. hover (¶1)

      b. diminutive size (¶2)

      c. state resembling hibernation (¶7)

      d. territorial-minded (¶8)

      e. fledglings (¶9)

      f. aerial antics (¶10)

4.   Identify and explain:

      a. 2 figurative phrases in paragraph 1

      b. 2 figurative phrases in paragraph 4

      c. 1 figurative phrase in paragraph 9

USE YOUR STRATEGIES: EXERCISE #3—"FOOD IRRADIATION"

Dale Blumenthal is a staff writer for *FDA Consumer*, the magazine of the U.S. Food and Drug Administration.

FOOD IRRADIATION: A SCARY WORD

DALE BLUMENTHAL

[1]*Irradiating* food to prevent illness from food-borne bacteria is not a new concept. Research on the technology began in earnest shortly after World War II, when the U.S. Army began a series of experiments irradiating fresh foods for troops in the field. Since 1963, FDA has passed rules permitting irradiation to *curb* insects in foods and microorganisms in spices, control *parasite contamination* of pork, and *retard spoilage* in fruits and vegetables.

[2]But to many people, the word irradiation means danger. It is associated with atomic bomb explosions and *nuclear reactor accidents* such as those at Chernobyl and Three Mile Island. The idea of irradiating food signals a kind of *"gamma alarm"* according to one British broadcaster. (Gamma rays are forms of energy emitted from some radioactive materials.)

[3]But when it comes to food irradiation, the only danger is to the bacteria that contaminate the food. The process damages their *genetic material*, so the organisms can no longer survive or multiply.

[4]Irradiation does not make food *radioactive* and, therefore, does not increase human exposure to radiation. The specified exposure times and energy levels of radiation sources approved for foods are *inadequate to induce radioactivity* in the products, according to FDA's Laura Tarantino, Ph.D., an expert on food irradiation. The process involves exposing food to a source of radiation, such as to the gamma rays from radioactive cobalt or *cesium* or to x-rays. However, no radioactive material is ever added to the product. Manufacturers use the same technique to sterilize many disposable medical devices.

[5]Tarantino notes that in testing the safety of the process, scientists used much higher levels of radiation than those approved for use in poultry. *But even at these elevated levels,* researchers found no toxic or cancer-causing effects in animals *consuming* irradiated poultry.

EXERCISE #3 QUESTIONS—"FOOD IRRADIATION"

1. What is Blumenthal's purpose?
2. Do you think Blumenthal is knowledgeable on this topic? Why or why not?
3. Write the meanings of these words and phrases:
   - a. irradiating (¶1)
   - b. curb (¶1)
   - c. parasite contamination (¶1)
   - d. retard spoilage (¶1)
   - e. nuclear reactor accidents (¶2)
   - f. gamma alarm (¶2)
   - g. genetic material (¶3)
   - h. radioactive (¶4)
   - i. inadequate to induce radioactivity (¶4)
   - j. cesium (¶4)
   - k. but even at these elevated levels (¶5)
   - l. consuming (¶5)

USE YOUR STRATEGIES: EXERCISE #4—"WHAT ECOSYSTEMS ARE AND HOW THEY WORK"

Dr. Bernard J. Nebel is a biology professor at Catonsville Community College in Maryland, where he has taught environmental science for 21 years. He is a member of several professional associations and actively supports a number of environmental organizations. This selection—"What Ecosystems Are and How They Work"—is from *Environmental Science*, 3rd ed.

WHAT ECOSYSTEMS ARE AND HOW THEY WORK

BERNARD J. NEBEL

[1]In 1968 astronauts returned with photographs of the earth taken from the moon. These photographs made it clear as never before that the earth is just a sphere suspended in the void of space. It is like a self-contained spaceship on an everlasting journey. There is no home base to which to return for repairs, more provisions, or disposal of wastes; there is just the *continuous radiation* from the sun. Indeed, the term "Spaceship Earth" was *coined* by futurist Buckminster Fuller as a result of this new perspective on our planet.

[2]Who is at the controls of Spaceship Earth? Unfortunately, no one! But Spaceship Earth is *equipped with an amazing array of self-providing mechanisms. Enormously diverse* plant and animal species *interact* in ways such that each obtains its needs from and provides for the support of others. Air and water are constantly *repurified and recycled*. Then there are self-regulating mechanisms as well, which tend to keep all the systems in balance with each other.

(CONTINUED)

WHAT ECOSYSTEMS ARE AND HOW THEY WORK (CONTINUED)

[3]But now problems are arising. In particular, the *human species is multiplying out of all proportion to others*. This is placing greater and greater demands on all systems and, at the same time, it is undercutting their productivity through pollution and over exploitation. The *natural regulatory mechanisms* are being upset. It is clear that such behavior aboard Spaceship Earth *cannot be sustained without catastrophic consequences*. Nor can we afford the happy-go-lucky luxury of trial-and-error learning when the fate of the whole world is at stake. We must gain an understanding of how Spaceship Earth works and then we must learn to conduct our activities within this context.

[4]Here in Part I our objective is to provide a general framework of understanding concerning the way our spaceship works. This understanding is gained through a study of natural ecosystems: what they are, how they function, how they are regulated, and how they develop and change. In keeping with the scientific method, we shall approach each area by describing the basic observations that have been made and showing how these observations have led to the formation of operating theories and principles. Finally, the understanding of these theories and principles will enable us to see more clearly where current trends are headed and *how certain human activities must be modified if modern society is to be sustained*.

EXERCISE #4 QUESTIONS—"WHAT ECOSYSTEMS ARE AND HOW THEY WORK"

1. What is Nebel's purpose for this section?
2. What does he compare the earth to and why?
3. Write the meaning of these words and phrases:

   a. continuous radiation (¶1)

   b. coined (¶1)

   c. equipped with an amazing array of self-providing mechanisms (¶2)

   d. enormously diverse (¶2)

   e. interact (¶2)

   f. repurified and recycled (¶2)

   g. human species is multiplying out of all proportion to others (¶3)

   h. natural regulatory mechanisms (¶3)

   i. cannot be sustained without catastrophic consequences (¶3)

   j. how certain human activities must be modified if modern society is to be sustained (¶4)

USE YOUR STRATEGIES: EXERCISE #5—"DROP THE BALL ON SPORTS METAPHORS IN POLITICAL COVERAGE"

Ellen Goodman is a syndicated columnist with the *Boston Globe*. Her articles appear in newspapers all around the world. This selection—"Drop the Ball on Sports Metaphors in Political Coverage"—appeared in the *Boston Globe*.

DROP THE BALL ON SPORTS METAPHORS IN POLITICAL COVERAGE

ELLEN GOODMAN

¹The crocuses are a-blooming, the Ides of March and the Ides of Super Tuesday are here. So, by all these *portents*, it must be time for my *quadrennial plea against the use of sports metaphors* in writing, speaking and thinking about politics.

²This has been a long, personal and so far entirely *futile* attempt on my part to have an impact on the *rhetoric of democracy*. By my calculations, politics has been described as the great American sport ever since the first election was called a race and the candidate became a winner.

Play-By-Play Analysis

³But sports reached a saturation point in the '80s when politicians began to sound like the Wide World of Sports, and the media turned from analysis to play-by-play. One favorite *mixed sports metaphor* came in 1984 from Lawton Chiles, now the governor of Florida, who described the "game plan" for the presidential debates this way: "It's like a football game…. Mondale can't get the ball back with one big play. But the American people love a horse race. I would advise him not to knock Reagan out."

⁴Well, as expected, the 1992 campaign began with the usual assortment of slam-dunks, knock-out punches, end runs and hard balls. But something happened after the campaign left New Hampshire and *relative civility*. While I was trying to get out of the locker room, we ended up in the trenches.

⁵The metaphors switched from sports to war. The *political coverage reads less like "Sports Illustrated" than "Soldier of Fortune."*

⁶We have campaign "assaults" and "attacks." The Super Tuesday states are "battlegrounds." The candidates "snipe" and "take aim" at each other. Jerry Brown is accused of using "slash-and-burn" tactics. Paul Tsongas is "under fire." And Pat Buchanan is a man who will "take no prisoners."

Playing Field to Killing Field

⁷How did this primary get off the playing field and onto the killing field? Kathleen Jamieson, political wordsmith and dean of the University of Pennsylvania's Annenberg School of Communication, says that war images creep in as a campaign gets, well, hostile.

⁸"When you are playing fairly within the rules of the game, the sports metaphors fit. The war metaphor is much more negative. It doesn't assume fair play or a referee."

⁹If words are the way we frame our ideas, *the war metaphor is more than rhetoric*. It forces us to talk and think about elections as if they were *lethally combative events* in which the object was to kill the enemy and declare victory. In the end, the war metaphor produces a victor or a commander-in-chief. But not necessarily a governor, or a leader, or a problem-solver.

¹⁰War talk doesn't allow the candidates to describe or stand on common ground. "It doesn't assume the goodwill and integrity of the other side," says Ms. Jamieson, "It doesn't talk about common good and collective ends. It assumes one person is right and the other's wrong."

(CONTINUED)

DROP THE BALL ON SPORTS METAPHORS IN POLITICAL COVERAGE (CONTINUED)

Search-and-Destroy Mission

[11]As for the media and the metaphor, fighting words frame the campaign as a search-and-destroy mission. It is not a coincidence that attack ads make the headlines. Nor is it a coincidence, says Ms. Jamieson, that men are much more likely to talk like warriors and write like war correspondents.

[12]Ms. Jamieson herself has been trying to elaborate a different political campaign language. She first played with a *courtship metaphor* since the candidates do woo the electorate and pledge forms of fidelity. That was, to put it mildly, fraught with sexual undertones.

[13]In New Hampshire, a focus group came up with the *metaphor of an orchestra*. The government is, after all, a collective entity that needs a leader to keep things in harmony. This had a nice ring, but it didn't hit all the right notes.

[14]Now Ms. Jamieson is toying with a metaphor that would picture the campaign as a quest. In the *vernacular* of the "quest" metaphor, the candidates would overcome "tests" that reveal their "character."

[15]The campaign would become a "search" for answers, not for the *soft underbelly of an opponent*.

[16]The point is to shift the verbal focus from strategy—"Is he doing what's necessary to win?"—to problems—"Does he understand them, can he solve them?" Her own quest for this "quest" metaphor has just begun. Any ideas are welcome in our metaphor mailbag.

[17]In the meantime, in the spirit of candidates and those who cover them, *block that war metaphor*. Tackle it if you must. There are already enough bodies on the combat field, careers blown to smithereens and land mines planted for the fall election. All we have learned so far this election year is that politics is hell.

EXERCISE #5 QUESTIONS—"DROP THE BALL ON SPORTS METAPHORS IN POLITICAL COVERAGE"

1. What is Goodman's purpose?
2. Explain these words and phrases:

   a. portents (¶1)

   b. quadrennial plea against the use of sports metaphors (¶1)

   c. futile (¶2)

   d. rhetoric of democracy (¶2)

   e. mixed sports metaphor (¶3)

   f. relative civility (¶4)

   g. political coverage reads less like "Sports Illustrated" than "Soldier of Fortune." (¶5)

   h. the war metaphor is more than rhetoric (¶9)

   i. lethally combative events (¶9)

   j. courtship metaphor (¶12)

   k. metaphor of an orchestra (¶13)

   l. vernacular (¶14)

   m. soft underbelly of an opponent (¶15)

   n. block that war metaphor (¶17)

CHAPTER 3 CONNECTIONS

A. Think about the reading demands you have this semester. Discuss how important you think your ability to understand the author's language is to successful comprehension. How important do you think understanding vocabulary is when you are listening to a lecture?

B. Describe a time when you used a particular word, in writing or speaking, because of its connotation. What was your purpose? Were you successful? Has anyone successfully convinced you to do or not do something by their choice of words?

CHAPTER 4

IDENTIFY WHAT THE AUTHOR IS WRITING ABOUT

A significant reason for developing a plan before you begin to read academic material is to make certain you set specific purposes for reading—to decide what you want to find out as you read. When you are reading for learning, your purpose will usually include understanding the author's main ideas. This is because a main idea is the framework that holds all the information together.

During your preview of this chapter, think back to a recent reading assignment for which your purpose was to understand the main ideas of the chapter. How did you begin your search? What did you look for? How did you know when you had found a main idea? When you found what you thought was a main idea, did you stop reading?

Define this chapter's key vocabulary:

paragraph
topic
controlling thought
main idea

thesis
directly stated main idea
implied main idea
multi-paragraph selection.

CHAPTER 4 OBJECTIVES

❏ Identify the main idea of a paragraph, whether it is directly stated or implied.
❏ Rephrase an author's main idea into a complete sentence using your own words.
❏ Identify the thesis of a multi-paragraph selection.
❏ Rephrase an author's thesis into a complete sentence using your own words.

WHAT IS MY BASIC STRATEGY FOR IDENTIFYING WHAT THE AUTHOR IS WRITING ABOUT?

As You Plan:

1. Understand the vocabulary.
2. Identify the topic—ask who or what the author is writing about.
3. Identify the controlling thought—ask what the author wants you to know about the topic.
4. Consider what you know about the topic and the controlling thought.
5. Combine the topic and controlling thought and predict the main idea.

As You Read:

6. Actively search for information that helps to clarify and refine your prediction about the main idea.
7. Do not allow your prior knowledge to distort what you read.

As You Review:

8. Revise and restate the main idea.

HOW CAN I IDENTIFY THE MAIN IDEA OF A PARAGRAPH?

Assume that 30 students in your English class are asked to write a paragraph on college grading systems. Would all 30 paragraphs tell your professor the same thing? Probably not. Although you would all write on the same topic, you would each focus on a specific thought. One of you might focus on the differences between high school and college grading systems, another on how college grading systems have changed over the years, another on the unfairness or worthwhileness of grades, while someone else might focus on the differences among college grading systems. The focus you selected—your controlling thought—is what would make your paragraph unique.

A paragraph is a group of related sentences that support and explain one main idea. Readers often mistake the topic—the who or what—for the main idea. But the topic is only a part of the author's idea. The main idea of a paragraph is the combination of the topic and the controlling thought—what the author wants you to know or understand about the topic.

To identify the main idea of a paragraph, find the topic by answering the question "Who or what is the author writing about?" and then clarify the controlling thought by answering "What does the author want me to know or understand about the topic?"

As stated earlier, the main idea is the frame that holds a paragraph together. Without understanding the main idea, you only have bits and pieces of details. It's very difficult to understand the relationships among the information without the main idea.

DIRECTLY STATED MAIN IDEAS

Often in expository and persuasive material, an author states his or her main idea in a sentence in the paragraph. This main idea sentence, or topic sentence, states the topic and controlling thought and clearly focuses the reader's attention on the author's message.

A topic sentence is often the first sentence in a paragraph, helping to prepare the reader for the rest of the paragraph. However, it can appear anywhere in a paragraph. It can be in the middle of the paragraph, tying the beginning and ending together; at the end of the paragraph, as a summary; or even split between two sentences in the paragraph.

No matter where the topic sentence is located, your strategy for finding and understanding the main idea is the same:

Identify the topic—ask who or what the author is writing about.

Identify the controlling thought—ask what the author wants you to know about the topic.

Consider what you know about the topic and controlling idea, being careful not to allow your prior knowledge to distort what you read.

Combine the topic and controlling thought and identify the topic sentence.

Rephrase the sentence in your own words.

For example, identify the topic, the controlling thought, and then the main idea in this excerpt from Barker and Barker's *Communication* text.

In a class where a professor used the sound "uh" some 20 times during the first five minutes of class, students could hardly help keeping count. The problem was that the professor didn't test the class on his "uhs," and many students didn't pass the test on the lecture. Of course it's easy to blame speakers for their sins. As effective listeners, however, we can't afford to let such mannerisms keep us from getting important points from the message. Focusing on the important elements in the communication setting rather than on the speaker's mannerisms is a much more profitable expenditure of listening energy. (Barker and Barker, *Communication*)

Who or what are Barker and Barker writing about? *Listening.*

What do they want you to understand about listening? *You should pay attention to what someone says, not how they say it.*

In this paragraph, the main idea is directly stated in the last sentence. However, to make sure you understand the author's main idea, you should rephrase the topic sentence using your words. For example, "To be an effective listener, you should pay attention to what a speaker says and not how he or she says it."

Read this paragraph to determine Grassian's main idea.

> Aristotle's sexist view is still shared by many people. For example, it is not uncommon to hear people say, "No woman should ever be President of the United States; women are too emotional for such responsibilities." Such a claim reflects the still common belief that the sex of an individual is highly correlated with psychological characteristics and, as such, may be used as an indicator of an individual's capacity to perform certain tasks. As a result of this belief, women are often treated unequally in our society. (Grassian, *Moral Reasoning*)

Who or what is Grassian writing about? *Many people still share Aristotle's sexist views.*

What does he want you to understand about the fact that many people still share Aristotle's sexist views? *It results in women often being treated unequally.*

In this paragraph, the main idea is split between the first and last sentence of this paragraph. Write one sentence that expresses the main idea.

The following is the opening paragraph from the "Weather and Climate" section in *Introduction to Geography* by Bergman and McKnight. Like many opening paragraphs, this one contains both the thesis for the entire section and a main idea for this paragraph. To find the main idea of this paragraph, identify the topic (who or what most of the paragraph is about) and the controlling thought. Combine them to form the main idea.

> The Earth is different from other known planets in a variety of ways. One of the most notable differences is the presence around our planet of a substantial atmosphere with components and characteristics that are distinctive from those of other planetary atmospheres. Our atmosphere makes life possible on this planet. It supplies most of the oxygen that animals must have to survive, as well as the carbon dioxide needed by plants. It helps maintain a water supply, which is essential to all living things. It serves as an insulating blanket to ameliorate temperature extremes and thus provide a livable environment over most of the Earth. It also shields the Earth from much of the sun's ultraviolet radiation, which otherwise would be fatal to most life forms. (Bergman and McKnight, *Introduction to Geography*)

Although the first sentence sounds like a possible main idea statement, it does not contain the answer to our two questions:

Who or what are Bergman and McKnight writing about? *The atmosphere.*

What do Bergman and McKnight want you to understand about the atmosphere? *Its (the atmosphere's) presence is one of the Earth's most notable differences among known planets.*

Thus, the first sentence, which is the most general, is actually the thesis for the entire section. (The remaining paragraphs in the text section cover other ways that the Earth is different from other planets.) The second sentence, which has the answers to our two questions, contains the main idea.

PRACTICE: IDENTIFYING DIRECTLY STATED MAIN IDEAS

Identify the main idea in each paragraph.

1. To be successful in school, students must be able to understand and remember information presented in classroom lectures. This is not an easy task. In order to learn from a lecture, students need to engage in a number of different cognitive tasks. They must focus their attention on the lecture while it is being delivered, understand the ideas presented, organize the content in some manner, accurately store the new material in their memory, and be able to recall it at a later time, such as on an exam. (King, "Reciprocal Peer-Questioning," *The Clearinghouse*)

2. We created our twenty-four-hour society, in part, as a way to cut costs, a way to squeeze more output from our scarce resources. Even the most rudimentary cost-benefit analysis shows that it is far cheaper to build one facility or one assembly line and operate it twenty-four hours a day, seven days a week, than to build four facilities or assembly lines and operate them only forty hours a week. More product can be manufactured in that single continuous operation, because daily start-ups and shutdowns are eliminated, and the savings on the capital costs of the equipment are enormous, particularly if by turning your facility or assembly line into a continuous facility you increase the opportunity for automation and thus reduce the need for personnel. (Moore-Ede, *The Twenty Four Hour Society*)

3. The economic status of the aged has been a topic of great interest to researchers and policymakers for many years. The conventional wisdom formerly was that the economic status of the aged was low. In recent years that view has been replaced by the conventional wisdom that the aged are well off. The former view led to sentiment for increases in government assistance, while the latter view has led to cutbacks. Both views, however, are too simplistic. The assessment of the economic status of the aged is far more complex than most popular articles and analyses suggest. (Radner, "The Economic Status of the Aged," *Social Security Bulletin*, Fall, 1992)

4. In spite of the good intentions of many writers, fictional characters are predominantly white and do not accurately portray reality. The population of the United States consists of about 12 percent blacks, 8.2 percent Hispanics, 2.1 percent Asians, and 2 percent Native Americans, and 20 percent of all people have a disabling condition—but most fiction portrays quite a different reality. (Seger, *Creating Unforgettable Characters*)

5. Carbon monoxide is a by-product of combustion, present whenever fuel is burned. It is produced by common home appliances, such as gas or oil furnaces, gas refrigerators, gas clothes dryers, gas ranges, gas water heaters or space heaters, fireplaces, charcoal grills and wood burning stoves. Fumes from automobiles and gas powered lawn mowers also contain carbon monoxide and can enter a home through walls or doorways if an engine is left running in an attached garage. (BRK Brands, *What You Need to Know about the Leading Cause of Poisoning*)

WHAT CAN I DO IF THE MAIN IDEA ISN'T DIRECTLY STATED?

Sometimes, especially in descriptive and narrative pieces, an author doesn't directly state the main idea. The author leaves it up to the reader to add together the information from all the sentences and infer, or put together, the main idea. The author implies; you infer.

Like determining the author's purpose or defining a word through context, to infer an unstated main idea you combine what the author says directly, the author's clues, and your own knowledge. Inferring a main idea requires your best reasoned conclusion based on the information you are given.

IMPLIED MAIN IDEAS

Even when there isn't a topic sentence, your basic strategy for finding the main idea is the same: you identify the topic and controlling thought. Then, however, instead of locating a topic sentence, you combine the topic and controlling thought into your own main idea statement.

For example, in this paragraph from *Who Are the Investment Swindlers?* by the National Futures Association (NFA), there isn't one sentence that directly states the main idea. But when you add together the title and what is directly stated, you can infer the main idea.

> They are a faceless voice on the telephone. Or a friend of a friend. They may perform surgery on their victims' savings from a dingy back office or boiler-room or from an opulent suite in the new bank building. They may wear three-piece suits or they may wear hard hats. They may have no apparent connection to the investment business or they may have an alphabet-soup of impressive letters following their names. They may be glib and fast-talking or so seemingly shy and soft-spoken that you feel almost compelled to force your money on them. (National Futures Association, *Who Are the Investment Swindlers?*)

Who or what is the NFA writing about? *Who are investment swindlers.*

What do they want you to understand about investment swindlers? *There is no single description of them; they can be anybody.*

Thus we can infer that the main idea is: *There is no single description for investment swindlers; anyone could be one.*

Identify the main idea of this paragraph by the President's Committee on Employment of the Handicapped. Again, there isn't one sentence that directly states the main idea, but when you add together what is directly stated, you can infer the main idea.

> In 1943 Public Law 16 significantly advanced vocational rehabilitation services for veterans. A year later, the G.I. Bill of Rights provided veterans with allowances for educational training, loans for the purchase and construction of homes, farms, and business property, and compensation for periods of unemployment. Benefits were continued and enlarged in subsequent years in response to the Korean and Vietnam wars. (The President's Committee on Employment of the Handicapped, *Performance*)

Who or what is the Committee writing about? *Government services for veterans.*

What do they want you to understand about government services for veterans? *An increasing array of benefits have been offered since 1943.*

Thus we can infer that the main idea is: *Since 1943 the government has provided an increasing array of benefits for veterans.*

PRACTICE: IDENTIFYING IMPLIED MAIN IDEAS

Write the main idea of each paragraph.

1. In the Dick and Jane readers some of us remember from our childhoods, a family consisted of a married couple, two or three well-behaved children, and a dog and a cat. Father wore suits and went out to work; mother wore aprons and baked cupcakes. Little girls sat demurely watching little boys climb trees. Home meant a single-family house in a middle-class suburban neighborhood. Color the lawn green. Color the people white. Family life in the textbook world was idyllic; parents did not quarrel, children did not disobey, and babies did not throw up on the dog. (Delfattore, *What Johnny Shouldn't Read— Textbook Censorship in America*)

2. On the job you will periodically face challenges not directly related to the work you do. Prejudice and discrimination based on factors such as age, sex, race, ethnicity, and disability are common problems. Sexual harassment—any uninvited verbal or physical behavior related to sexuality—is of concern in today's work environment. Knowing what to do if you are confronted and then making wise choices can lessen the trauma. Being sensitive to others in the work environment so that you don't unwittingly create problems is most advisable. Refraining from sexist or racist comments and language may require effort, but it is the fair and decent way to behave. Challenging your own stereotypes and eliminating personal prejudice will make this easier. Acceptance and equal treatment of others are keystones of positive human relations. (Hanna, *Person to Person: Positive Relationships Don't Just Happen*)

3. A famous figure in sixteenth-century English history, Thomas More lived from 1478 to 1535. He was the son of judge John More and was an unusually talented individual. Legend has it that More was marked for greatness even as a youth. Educated at Oxford University and London's Lincoln Inn, More began his career as a lawyer after giving up the idea of being a monk. More developed an active law practice, he was visible in London politics, and he established a reputation as a Renaissance humanist through his writings in literature, history, and philosophy. He is best know to most people, however, for being a member of the court of King Henry VII. More held a series of posts and ultimately rose to the important position of Lord Chancellor. (White, *Discovering Philosophy*)

4. The day before I was to leave I went walking across the river to the red mesa, where many times before I had gone to be alone with my thoughts. And I had climbed several times to the top of the mesa and looked among the old ruins there for pottery. This time I chose to climb the north end, perhaps because I had not gone that way before and wanted to see what it was. It was a difficult climb, and when I got to the top I was spent. I lingered among the ruins for more than an hour, I judge, waiting for my strength to return. From there I could see the whole valley below, the fields, the river, and the village. It was all very beautiful, and the sight of it filled me with longing. (Momaday, *The Names*)

5. The Federal Clean Air Act mandates that employers with more than 100 employees who are located in selected metropolitan areas reduce car commuting by 25 percent by 1996. Consequently, many U.S. corporations, nonprofit organizations and government agencies are

taking a new look at the option of telecommuting—having some of their employees regularly work from home a few days a week, connected to the office via computer and modem. (Conroy, "Away From Their Desks," *Compuserve Magazine*)

HOW CAN I BE SURE I HAVE IDENTIFIED THE MAIN IDEA OF A PARAGRAPH?

If you aren't certain you have selected the main idea of the paragraph, try this strategy: After each sentence of the paragraph, read your main idea sentence. If you have identified the main idea, your sentence will unify all of the other sentences of the paragraph into a coherent unit. Your sentence will be more general than all the other sentences. It will sum-up the other sentences.

PRACTICE: IDENTIFYING MAIN IDEAS IN PARAGRAPHS

Use your strategy for finding the main idea:

Do I understand the vocabulary the author is using?

Who or what is this paragraph about?

What does the author wants me to know about this topic?

What do I know about this topic and controlling thought?

When I combine the topic and controlling thought, what do I think the main idea is?

What information can I find that helps me clarify and refine my prediction about the main idea?

Can I state the main idea in my own words?

1. Business education has undergone more change in the last ten years than it has in the last century. The education reform movement, recent technological innovations, increasing cultural diversity in the workforce, and the emergence of the global marketplace have all had a dramatic impact on the office support curriculum. Businesspersons and educators alike are trying to cope with what Tom Peters calls "a world turned upside down." What was appropriate just a few years ago must be continually evaluated and updated to keep pace with the rapidly changing workplace. (Jaderstrom, White, and Ellison, "The Changing Office Support Curriculum: Preparing Students for the Future," *The Balance Sheet*)

2. Since all of my recommendations call upon you to prepare for speaking by writing out, in some form, what you wish to say, it is, first of all, of great importance to recognize that what is written to be read has a radically different character from what is written to be heard. The remarkable difference between listening and reading—the one requiring you to keep moving forward irreversibly with the flow of speech, the other allowing you to proceed at your own pace and to go forward or backward at will by simply turning the pages—demands that you accommodate what you write for listening, as contrasted with what you must do for readers. (Adler "Preparing and Delivering a Speech," *How to Speak, How to Listen*)

3. "Manners makyth man," wrote the poet William of Wykeham. Ah—but what makyth the manners? We might, perhaps, venture "Mother makyth manners"—along, of course, with a dash of early experience

and more than a little spicing of genetic inheritance. The relative roles of "nature" versus "nurture" caused much bitter argument in scientific circles in recent years. But the flames of the controversy have now died down, and it is generally accepted that, even in the lower animals, adult behavior is acquired through a mix of genetic make-up and experience gained as the individual goes through life. The more complex an animal's brain the greater the role that learning is likely to play in shaping its behaviour, and the more variation we shall find between one individual and another. Information acquired and lessons learned during infancy and childhood, when behaviour is at its most flexible, are likely to have particular significance. (Goodall, "Mothers and Daughters," *Through a Window*)

4. Ozone-destroying chemicals are extremely stable, so they last in the atmosphere for many decades. That means even if production of all chlorofluorocarbons (CFSs) and halons stopped today, the chemicals already in the atmosphere would go on destroying ozone well into the 21st century. And because large quantities of these chemicals are contained in existing air conditioners and refrigerators, from which they continue to escape through malfunction or intentional venting, it may be a century before the ozone layer has built itself back up. (Cooper, "Ozone Depletion," *CQ Researcher*)

5. Of all the traditional presentation media, 35mm slides promise to make the best impression on an audience. There is something attention-grabbing and impressive about seeing well-executed color slides on a big screen. At the same time, slides are the greatest challenge to produce from the desktop (computer). Creating 35mm slides is not a solo activity like running the company newsletter off a laser printer. Making slides requires either additional hardware in the form of a slide recorder, and maybe even another computer. (Thompson, "Sliding Home," *PC Publishing and Presentations*)

HOW CAN I IDENTIFY THE THESIS OF A MULTI-PARAGRAPH SELECTION?

A multi-paragraph selection, like an essay or text chapter, is a group of related paragraphs—each with a main idea—that support and explain one thesis, or over-all main idea. The thesis of a multi-paragraph selection is the umbrella idea that unifies the main ideas of all the paragraphs.

Just as the main idea is the frame that holds a paragraph together, the thesis is the frame that holds the many paragraphs of the essay or chapter together. If you don't identify the thesis, you have a series of ideas with nothing to connect them.

The thesis sentence is often stated in the first paragraph to prepare the reader for the rest of the chapter. However it can appear anywhere in the chapter or, like the main idea of a paragraph, it may not be directly stated at all. It may be up to you to put all of the author's ideas together and infer the thesis.

No matter where the thesis is located, your strategy for finding it is the same:

Identify the topic—ask who or what the entire selection is about.

Identify the controlling thought—ask what the author wants you to know about the topic.

Consider what you know about the topic and controlling idea.

Combine the topic and controlling thought to form the thesis.

PRACTICE: IDENTIFYING THE THESIS OF A MULTI-PARAGRAPH SELECTION—"SPECIAL NUTRITIONAL NEEDS OF ATHLETES AND ACTIVE INDIVIDUALS"

Jerrold Greenberg teaches at the University of Maryland. George Dintiman teaches at Virginia Commonwealth University. This selection—"Special Nutritional Needs of Athletes and Active Individuals"—is from *Exploring Health: Expanding the Boundaries of Wellness.*

SPECIAL NUTRITIONAL NEEDS OF ATHLETES AND ACTIVE INDIVIDUALS

JERROLD S. GREENBERG AND GEORGE B. DINTIMAN

[1]Athletes and active individuals have a few special nutritional needs to meet the demands of *vigorous* activity, to prevent heat exhaustion and heat stroke and to maximize and store energy from food.

More Calories

[2]If you are neither losing nor gaining weight and have sufficient energy, you are probably taking in the correct number of calories daily. Weigh yourself at the same time and under the same conditions daily, preferably upon rising. If no weight gain or loss is occurring, there is no need to keep complicated records in *caloric intake and expenditure*. In general, very active male college-age athletes need approximately 25 to 27 calories per pound compared to 20 to 21 per pound for female athletes. Moderately active individuals need approximately 20 to 23 (males) and 16 to 18 (females) calories per pound. *Sedentary* individuals, on the other hand, need approximately 15 to 18 (males) and 11 to 12 (females) calories per pound.

More Water

[3]To avoid dehydration, electrolyte imbalance, and heat-related disorders, as well as early fatigue, it is necessary to *hydrate* approximately fifteen minutes before exercising by drinking 12–48 ounces of cold water (one to four glasses), then drinking water freely during and after exercise. Since thirst will underestimate your needs, you must form the habit of drinking *when no thirst sensations exist*.

Proper Nutrition

[4]*Electrolytes*—water, sodium, potassium, and chloride—lost through sweat and water vapor from the lungs should be replaced as rapidly as possible. It is the proper balance of each electrolyte that prevents dehydration, cramping, heat exhaustion, and heat stroke. Too much salt without adequate water, for example, actually draws fluid from the cells, *precipitates nausea*, and increases potassium loss. Although water alone will not restore electrolyte balance, it is the single most important element in preventing heat-related disorders. Eating extra portions of potassium-rich foods several days before a contest and using extra table salt is all most individuals need. If commercial electrolyte drinks are used, they should be diluted with twice the normal amount of water to reduce the sugar content. Lower sugar content will speed absorption time and prevent the body's release of insulin and possible reduction of quick energy.

Iron Supplements

[5]Iron deficiency can lead to a loss of strength and endurance, early fatigue during exercise, loss of visual perception, and impaired learning. Needs vary according to age, activity level, and sex. Iron is the only nutrient that adolescent female and male athletes need in greater quantity.

PRACTICE QUESTIONS—"SPECIAL NUTRITIONAL NEEDS OF ATHLETES AND ACTIVE INDIVIDUALS"

1. What is Greenberg and Dintiman's purpose?
2. Define these words or phrases:
    a. vigorous (¶1)
    b. caloric intake and expenditure (¶2)
    c. sedentary (¶2)
    d. hydrate (¶3)
    e. when no thirst sensations exist (¶3)
    f. electrolytes (¶4)
    g. precipitates nausea (¶4)
3. Write the main idea of each paragraph.
4. What is the thesis of the selection?

CHAPTER 4 REVIEW QUESTIONS

1. What is your strategy for identifying the main idea of a paragraph?
2. Why is it important to restate the main idea in your own words?
3. What is your strategy for identifying the thesis of a multi-paragraph selection?

CHAPTER 4 THINK AND CONNECT QUESTIONS

4. Re-read "Sources of Groundwater Pollution," Chapter 1, Exercise #3. What is the author's purpose? State the thesis in your own words.
5   Re-read "Endangered Species," in Chapter 3. What is the author's purpose? Write the main ideas of paragraphs 3, 4, and 5. State the thesis in your own words.

CHAPTER 4 APPLICATION EXERCISES

6. Select three paragraphs in a current reading assignment from another class. Identify the main idea of each paragraph.
7. Assume that you need to write a paragraph on the topic of health care costs. Decide what your controlling thought will be and write a topic sentence (main idea) for your paragraph.

USE YOUR STRATEGIES: EXERCISE #1

Define the italicized words. Write the main idea of each paragraph in your own words.

1. If stating an idea were enough, there would be no books or essays. Each piece of writing would consist of only a topic sentence. Of course more is needed. Writers must explain, expand, and support their ideas. Sometimes facts or logic are called for, sometimes narration of events, and sometimes examples, illustrations, and reasons. A mathematics

textbook calls for clear, step-by-step reasoning, with many examples and exercises to *reinforce* each lesson. New interpretations of historical events call for background information, direct evidence, and support from *authoritative* sources. The way that an author chooses to develop a main idea depends on the work's purpose and its intended audience. (Veit, Gould, and Clifford, *On Writing*)

2. At times we half-heartedly make efforts to remember facts that stand out, and completely miss the speaker's main points. This habit has also been referred to as "majoring in minors." Unless we listen with an intent to understand the *essence* of the message, we may fall into the habit of picking and choosing only selected tidbits to process and remember. When we put these bits together at the end of the presentation or conversation, we may find that we have a totally incorrect perception of what the speaker was trying to get across. (Barker and Barker, *Communication*)

3. Couples seeking a divorce will not always find it easy to reach agreement on issues that affect their children, but they should attempt to do so before telling their children about the *impending* separation. Children, even very young children, need to be prepared for the divorce. They need information about where they will live, who will take care of them, where they will go to school, and whatever other issues are of major concern to them. (NIMH, *Caring About Kids: When Parents Divorce*)

4. A *compelling reason* to preserve species is that each one plays an important role in an ecosystem—an intricate network of plant and animal communities and the associated environment. When a species becomes endangered, it indicates that something is wrong with the ecosystems we all depend on. Like the canaries used in coal mines whose deaths warned miners of bad air, the increasing numbers of endangered species warn us that the health of our environment has declined. The measures we take to save endangered species will help ensure that the planet we leave for our children is as healthy as the planet our parents left for us. (U.S. Department of the Interior, U.S. Fish and Wildlife Service, *Endangered Species*)

5. Overweight is a hefty problem in the United States. It's estimated that 24 percent of men and 27 percent of women in this country—about 34 million Americans—are obese. And sometimes it seems that there are 34 million different diets or diet products promoted to combat the problem. The latest to win the nation's *fervent* attention is a revival of a sort—a return to very low calorie diets, generally 400 to 800 calories per day. (*FDA Consumer*)

6. In countries where two or more languages *coexist*, confusion often arises. In Belgium, many towns have two quite separate names, one recognized by French speakers, one by Dutch speakers, so that the French Tournai is the Dutch Doornik, while the Dutch Luik is the French Liège. The French Mons is the Dutch Bergen, the Dutch Kortrijk is the French Courtrai, and the city that to all French-speaking people (and indeed most English-speaking people) is known as Bruges (and pronounced "broozsh") is to the locals called Brugge and pronounced "broo-guh." Although Brussels is officially bilingual, it is in fact a French-speaking island in a Flemish Lake. (Bryson, *Mother Tongue*)

7. You may know the merits of healthy eating. But often wanting to eat right and actually doing so are two separate things. For many, understanding how to eat right is the real challenge because the

recommendations for good nutrition appear more *complex* than they actually are. Although several health organizations issue a variety of dietary recommendations, the basic message regarding diet and health are the same: Consume a diet low in fat, cholesterol and sodium and high in complex carbohydrates and dietary fiber to reduce the risk of chronic disease. (Keating, "Nutrition for the '90s")

8. Despite the rich variety of *indigenous* local cultures around the globe, the world is increasingly coming to look like one place. In consumer goods, architecture, industrial technology, education, and housing, the European model is pervasive. (Bergman and McKnight, *Introduction to Geography*)

9. Breathing. It may be something you never think about or it may be your major focus when you're meditating, swimming laps, *trekking* at high altitudes, or having an asthma attack. In any case, it is a remarkable physical process that provides our bodies with the oxygen we need for metabolism and eliminates metabolism's waste product, carbon dioxide. (Vernick, "Every Breath You Take," *Good Housekeeping*)

10. As water infiltrates and percolates through the soil, it will tend to dissolve and carry any soluble chemicals that are in solution. It is the old problem of leaching described in earlier chapters. Consequently, the general principle is: Any chemical used on, disposed of, spilled, or leaked onto or into the ground can *contaminate* groundwater. (Nebel, *Environmental Science*)

USE YOUR STRATEGIES: EXERCISE #2—"WHO AM I?"

David Johnson teaches at the University of Minnesota. This selection—"Who Am I?"—is from *Human Relations and Your Career*, 3rd ed.

WHO AM I?

DAVID W. JOHNSON

[1]How you describe yourself as a person is your identity. Your Identity is a consistent set of attitudes that defines who you are. These attitudes contain both a view of how you are similar to other people and a view of how you are *unique* as a person. The world can change. Other people can change. Your career can change, but there is something about yourself that stays the same. And that something is your identity.

[2]There are three ways you build your identity. The first is by comparing yourself with other people. The second is by trying to be like people you admire. And the third is by taking on social roles.

[3]Being part of a cooperative effort allows you to compare yourself with others. It is within cooperative relationships that you increase your self-awareness (by finding out how other people see you). Through cooperating with people, you become aware of how you are similar to and different from others. The better you know other people, the clearer you will be about your identity. The more feedback you receive from other people, the better you will know yourself as a person. It is from your cooperative relationships that you find out whether you are an emotional or unemotional person, whether you are *diplomatic* or blunt, or whether you are sensitive or nonsensitive as a person. From hearing about other people's attitudes, you become more aware of your own attitudes. By sharing experiences and feelings, you become more self-aware. Cooperation promotes the type of relationships in which you can get to know other people and yourself.

(CONTINUED)

WHO AM I? (CONTINUED)

[4]A second way you build your identity is by deciding who you want to be like. Everyone has people they like, admire, and see as unusually competent or powerful. You will want to be like such people. So you will adopt their attitudes and actions. One of the interesting things about wanting to be like other people whom you admire is that the people do not have to be real. The can be *fictional* or fantasy persons! You may decide that you want to be like a character in a movie. You may decide that you want to be like a person in a book. Most of the people you will want to be like, however, will be people you cooperate with. Your parents, older brothers and sisters, older friends, and even teachers are all people you may wish to be like in certain ways. You can strengthen your identity by choosing people with positive qualities and trying to develop the same qualities in yourself.

[5]A third way you build your identity is by taking on a *stable set* of social roles. A social role is a set of actions that other people expect of you. Examples of social roles are the roles of student, friend, spouse, sibling, child, parent, and citizen. Every social role has a set of expected actions. The social roles you take on help tell you who you are as a person. The more stable your social roles, the more stable your identity will be.

EXERCISE #2 QUESTIONS—"WHO AM I?"

1. What is Johnson's purpose?
2. Define these words:
   a. unique (¶1)
   b. diplomatic (¶3)
   c. fictional (¶4)
   d. stable set (¶5)
3. Write the main idea of paragraphs 3, 4, and 5.
4. Write the thesis of the selection.

USE YOUR STRATEGIES: EXERCISE #3—"THE HYDROLOGIC CYCLE"

Frederick Lutgens and Edward Tarbuck teach at Illinois Central College. This selection—"The Hydrologic Cycle"—is from *The Atmosphere—An Introduction to Meteorology*, 6th ed.

THE HYDROLOGIC CYCLE

FREDERICK K. LUTGENS AND EDWARD J. TARBUCK

[1]An adequate supply of water is vital to life on earth. In all, the total water content of the earth's hydrosphere is about 1.36 billion cubic kilometers (326 million cubic miles). The vast bulk, about 97.2 percent, is stored in the global oceans. In addition, about 2.15 percent of the earth's moisture is tied up as ice (glaciers, snow, and ice fields). Less than 1 percent is found in freshwater lakes, streams, and as groundwater. Furthermore, a tiny fraction of 1 percent exists as water vapor within the earth's atmosphere.

(CONTINUED)

THE HYDROLOGIC CYCLE (CONTINUED)

[2]The increasing demands on this *finite* resource have led scientists to pay a great deal of attention to the *continuous* exchanges of water among the oceans, the atmosphere, and the continents. This unending circulation of the earth's water supply has come to be called the *hydrologic cycle*.It is a gigantic system powered by energy from the sun in which the atmosphere provides the vital link between the oceans and continents. Water from the oceans, and to a much lesser extent from the continents, is constantly evaporating into the atmosphere. Winds transport the moisture-laden air, often great distances, until the complex processes of cloud formation are set in motion that eventually result in precipitation. The *precipitation* that falls into the ocean has ended its cycle and is ready to begin another. The water that falls on the continents, however, must still make its way back to the oceans.

[3]Once precipitation has fallen on land, a portion of the water soaks into the ground, some of it moving downward, then *laterally*, and finally seeping into lakes and streams or directly into the ocean. When the rate of rainfall is greater than the earth's ability to absorb it, the additional water flows over the surface into streams and lakes. Much of the water that soaks in or runs off eventually finds its way back to the atmosphere. In addition to evaporation from the soil, lakes, and streams, some water that infiltrates the ground surface is absorbed by plants, which then release it into the atmosphere, a process called *transpiration*.

[4]Although the amount of water vapor in the air at any one time is but a *minute* fraction of the earth's total water supply, the absolute quantities that are cycled through the atmosphere in 1 year are immense, some 380,000 cubic kilometers—enough to cover the earth's surface to a depth of about 100 centimeters. Estimates show that over North America, almost six times more water is carried within the moving currents of air than is transported by all the continent's rivers. Because the total amount of water vapor in the atmosphere remains about the same, the average annual precipitation over the earth must be equal to the quantity of water evaporated. However, for all the continents taken together, precipitation exceeds evaporation. Conversely, over the oceans, evaporation exceeds precipitation. Because the level of the world ocean is not dropping, runoff from land areas must balance the deficit of precipitation over the oceans.

[5]In summary, the hydrologic cycle represents the continuous movement of water from the oceans to the atmosphere, from the atmosphere to the land, and from the land back to the sea. The movement of water through the cycle holds the key to the distribution of moisture over the surface of our planet and is *intricately* related to all atmospheric *phenomena*.

EXERCISE #3 QUESTIONS—"THE HYDROLOGIC CYCLE"

1. What is Lutgens and Tarbuck's purpose?
2. Define these words or phrases:
   a. finite (¶2)
   b. continuous (¶2)
   c. hydrologic cycle (¶2)
   d. precipitation (¶2)
   e. laterally (¶3)
   f. transpiration (¶3)
   g. minute (¶4)
   h. intricately (¶5)
   i. phenomena (¶5)
3. Write the thesis of this selection.

USE YOUR STRATEGIES: EXERCISE #4—"THEORIES OF HUMAN BEHAVIOR"

Jerrold Greenberg teaches at the University of Maryland. George Dintiman teaches at Virginia Commonwealth University. This selection—"Theories of Human Behavior"—is from *Exploring Health*.

THEORIES OF HUMAN BEHAVIOR

JERROLD S. GREENBERG AND GEORGE B. DINTIMAN

[1]Why do people adopt certain health-related behaviors and not others? Although many *theories* have been proposed to explain why people behave as they do, no one knows for sure. The theories described below, however, are often cited as the most adequate explanations of why some people smoke cigarettes and others do not, and generally why some people behave in a healthy way and others do not. This is no magic list, though. Your instructor or other sources can provide you with additional theories of human behavior.

Hierarchy of Needs

[2]Abraham Maslow proposed that human beings behave in ways that are designed to satisfy certain needs. Further, there exist levels of needs, and the high-level needs do not *emerge* until the low-level needs are satisfied.

[3]Until hunger and thirst (physiological needs) are satisfied, you will not be concerned with safety. In fact, if you need food badly, you might even chase a lion away from a *felled prey*. Until you feel safe and secure (safety needs), you will not be concerned with others loving you. Until you are loved (love needs), you will not be concerned about whether others respect you (esteem needs). And until you are respected by others, you will not care whether you can achieve your potential (self-actualization needs).

[4]In our society, most of these needs are met to some degree. However, the degree to which they are met varies and consequently our behavior varies. Some of us might display sexual behavior that is *contrary to our nature* because of our need for love. Others might conform to friends' drug behavior because of the need for esteem.

Force Field Theory

[5]According to Kurt Lewin, human behavior is characterized by a *constant tension* between *driving and restraining forces*. When one set of forces becomes stronger than another, you behave one way. When the other set of forces becomes stronger, you behave another way.

[6]For example, you might want to lose weight but you live with someone who eats high-calorie foods. If the attraction of these foods is stronger than your desire to lose weight, your diet goes down the drain.

Adjustment Theory

[7]Others believe that human beings are constantly striving to adjust to their environments. The adjustment is needed to maintain an *equilibrium* necessary for a healthy existence. When the environment places us in *disequilibrium* we behave in ways designed to right ourselves. Thus, when a student enters college and leaves home for the first time, he or she seeks to replace the family with close friends. To acquire these friends might mean joining college organizations, taking drugs, or acquiring other behaviors designed to restore equilibrium.

EXERCISE #4 QUESTIONS—"THEORIES OF HUMAN BEHAVIOR"

1. What is the Greenberg and Dintiman's purpose?
2. Define these words or phrases:
    a. theories (¶1)
    b. emerge (¶2)
    c. felled prey (¶3)
    d. contrary to our nature (¶4)
    e. constant tension (¶5)
    f. driving and restraining forces (¶5)
    g. equilibrium (¶7)
    h. disequilibrium (¶7)
3. Write the main idea of paragraphs 2, 5, and 7.
4. What is the thesis of the selection?

CHAPTER 4 CONNECTIONS

A. In the first four chapters of this text you have read paragraphs and multi-paragraph selections about many subjects—i.e., ecology, nutrition, sociology, and business. In your other classes, at work, and at home, you read about many other subjects. In which subjects is the reading easiest for you? In which subjects is it most difficult? By that I mean, when is it easiest or hardest for you to identify the main idea? Why do you think that is true? What do you think you can do to make the hardest reading easier?

B. Based on the reading assignments you have done for your classes during the last few weeks, how important is it to understand the vocabulary the author uses? What do you do when you encounter an unfamiliar word? Is what you do different in any way than what you did six months ago? Why or why not?

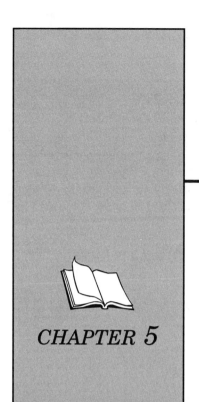

CHAPTER 5

ESTABLISH HOW THE AUTHOR DEVELOPS IDEAS

Understanding main ideas is crucial to good comprehension. For some purposes, such as preparing to listen to a lecture, knowing the main ideas may be all you need. But many times, just understanding the main ideas will not provide enough information. When your purpose for reading requires a more detailed understanding, such as answering questions, writing a paper, or learning the steps in a procedure, you must go beyond the thesis and main ideas and be able to identify the details you need.

Think about how you decide what is important to remember. Do you try to remember everything you read? Do you try to remember more details in some subjects than in others? Do you vary the amount of detail you try to remember depending on what you are going to do with the information?

Define this chapter's key vocabulary:

major supporting detail

minor supporting detail

signal words

methods of development

CHAPTER 5 OBJECTIVES

❑ Identify and understand different kinds of details.

❑ Determine the relationships among details and/or sentences.

❑ Identify and understand the use of signal words.

❑ Understand how the way that an author develops and supports the thesis and/or main idea can help comprehension.

❑ Use signal words, punctuation, and the methods authors use to develop and support the thesis and/or main ideas as clues to understanding.

WHAT IS MY BASIC STRATEGY FOR ESTABLISHING HOW THE AUTHOR DEVELOPS IDEAS?

As You Plan:

1. Understand the vocabulary.
2. Predict the thesis and/or main idea.
3. Determine how much detail you need to know.

As You Read:

4. Actively search for information that helps to clarify and refine your prediction about the thesis and/or main idea.
5. Identify useful signal words.
6. Determine the relationships among details and/or sentences.
7. Determine if the way the author develops the thesis and/or main idea helps you to understand the details.
8. Use the author's signal words, punctuation, and development as clues to help you identify information and ideas you need.

As You Review:

9. Revise and restate the thesis and/or main idea.
10. Restate the supporting details you need to fulfill your purpose.

HOW CAN I IDENTIFY AND UNDERSTAND DIFFERENT KINDS OF DETAILS?

Remember what Veit, Gould, and Clifford said about writing in one of the practice paragraphs in Chapter 4:

> If stating an idea were enough, there would be no books or essays. Each piece of writing would consist of only a topic sentence. Of course more is needed. Writers must explain, expand, and support their ideas. Sometimes facts or logic are called for, sometimes the narration of events, and sometimes examples, illustrations, and reasons. A mathematics textbook calls for clear, step-by-step reasoning, with many examples and exercises to reinforce each lesson. New interpretations of historical events call for background information, direct evidence, and support from authoritative sources. The way that an author chooses to develop a main idea depends on the work's purpose and its intended audience.

The work you did in Chapter 4 reinforced the concepts that: (1) a multi-paragraph selection has only one thesis, (2) there may be any number of paragraphs in the selection but each paragraph has only one main idea, (3) a para-

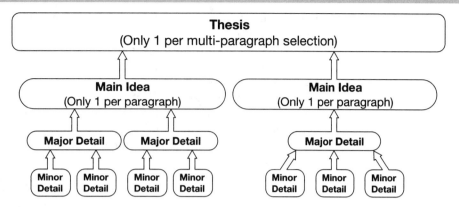

graph may contain any number of sentences and thus any number of major and minor details.

A major supporting detail is a specific piece of information that directly supports and explains a main idea. A minor supporting detail is a very specific piece of information that supports and explains a major detail.

Being able to distinguish among the thesis, main idea, major supporting detail(s), and minor supporting detail(s), and determine how they relate to one another, is critical for the reader who is to reading to fulfill a specific purpose and be able to remember what he or she has read. Identifying the relationships among the ideas and/or sentences helps you make connections among ideas and improve comprehension.

For example, take another look at the opening paragraph from Bergman and McKnight's "Weather and Climate" chapter. We established in Chapter 4 that sentence 1 is the thesis for the entire section and sentence 2 is the main idea for this paragraph. Now, read to see what additional information the authors provide.

[1]The Earth is different from other known planets in a variety of ways. [2]One of the most notable differences is the presence around our planet of a substantial atmosphere with components and characteristics that are distinctive from those of other planetary atmospheres. [3]Our atmosphere makes life possible on this planet. [4]It supplies most of the oxygen that animals must have to survive, as well as the carbon dioxide needed by plants. [5]It helps maintain a water supply, which is essential to all living things. [6]It serves as an insulating blanket to ameliorate temperature extremes and thus provide a livable environment over most of the Earth. [7]It also shields the Earth from much of the sun's ultraviolet radiation, which otherwise would be fatal to most life forms.

How do the details they provide support and explain the main idea?

Sentence 3 directly supports main idea; therefore it is a major detail.
Sentences 4–7 give examples of the major detail; therefore they are minor details.

      Sentence 4—supplies oxygen and carbon dioxide
      Sentence 5—helps maintain water supply
      Sentence 6—insulation from temperature extremes
      Sentence 7—shield from ultraviolet radiation

Now that you have identified several different levels of information, how much of it should you remember? Just the thesis? The thesis and main idea?

The thesis, main idea, and the major detail? The thesis, main idea, major detail, and the four examples?

How much you need to remember about what you read depends on your purpose for reading. If this had been an actual geography assignment, you would have decided as part of your plan specifically what you needed to find out as you read. For example, if you were reading this chapter as preparation for a lecture, you might have decided to concentrate only on the thesis and main idea. On the other hand, if you were preparing for an extensive exam on the chapter, you might have decided you needed to memorize several levels of detail, including the examples.

Reread this paragraph from Macionis's *Sociology*. Like many authors, Macionis often combines major and minor details in one sentence. Identify his main idea and distinguish between major and minor supporting details.

> [1]A survey is a research method in which subjects respond to a series of items or questions in a questionnaire or an interview. [2]Perhaps the most widely used of all research methods, surveys are particularly suited to studying what cannot be observed directly, such as political attitudes, religious beliefs, or the private lives of couples. [3]Like experiments, surveys can be used to investigate the relationship among variables. [4]They are also useful for descriptive research, in which subject responses help a sociologist to describe a social setting, such as an urban neighborhood or gambling casino.

Main idea: A survey is a research method in which subjects respond to a series of items or questions in a questionnaire or an interview.

Sentence 2:
Major—widely used, suited to studying what can't be observed
Minor—such as political attitudes, religious beliefs, private lives

Sentence 3:
Major—like experiments, used to investigate relationships among variables

Sentence 4:
Major—useful for descriptive research where subject helps describe social setting
Minor—such as urban neighborhood or gambling casino

To help you understand the relationships among the details and/or sentences, an author uses a variety of clues including signal words, punctuation, and paragraph structure.

WHAT ARE SIGNAL WORDS AND PHRASES?

Signal words, sometimes called transition words, are words and phrases an author uses to point you in a specific direction of thought or to alert you to particular types of information. These words can be clues for identifying different kinds of details.

In the preceding Macionis paragraph, you used several signal words and phrases to point you to different types of information.

is a—to alert you to a definition
are particularly suited to—to point out a use of surveys

such as—to alert you to examples

Like—to point out a similarity

also—to point out an additional use of surveys

such as—to alert you to examples

Signal words that can point to major details include words such as: *central, principal, chief, major, main, key, primary,* and *significant.*

Signal words that suggest a continuation of the same type of thought include: *and, too, in addition, moreover, or, also, furthermore, as well as, besides, furthermore, in other words,* and *another.*

Words that signal a recap of the author's ideas include phrases like: *in summary, in conclusion,* and *to sum up.*

Other signal words and phrases are used to guide you through a paragraph or multi-paragraph selection. These additional signal words are listed later in this chapter with each of the methods of development.

PRACTICE: USING THE AUTHOR'S CLUES

1. [1]Divorce: the breakup of a family. [2]More than one-third—actually 40 percent—of all marriages in the United States now end in divorce. [3]Although legally a separation of two people, divorce is, in reality, a family affair because more than half of all divorces involve children. [4]Divorce ends the role of spouse; it doesn't end that of parent. (NIMH, *Caring about Kids: When Parents Divorce*)

    a. How does the author define divorce?

    b. What punctuation clue did the author use?

2. [1]Today about 10 percent of the Earth's land surface, amounting to some 6 million square miles (15 million km^2) is covered with ice. [2]More than 96 percent of that area comprises the Antarctic and Greenland ice caps. [3]In addition, many of the high mountains of the world contain glaciers, which are large natural accumulations of land ice that flow downslope or outward from their centers of accumulation. (Bergman, *Human Geography*)

    a. Besides the Antarctic and Greenland ice caps, what other areas are covered with ice?

    b. What signal phrases does the author use as a clue?

3. [1]The 1990s have been designated the "decade of the brain," so it is not surprising that one of the emerging specialties in psychology is concerned with brain functioning. [2]Neuropsychologists are trained to diagnose disorders of the brain. [3]Using various tests, they try to identify specific brain areas that may be malfunctioning. [4]They also conduct research to identify early symptoms that predict the development of disorders such as Huntington's disease (Diamond, White, Myers, and Mastromauro, 1992). (Davis and Palladino, *Psychology*)

    a. What do Neuropsychologists do in addition to diagnosing disorders of the brain?

    b. What signal word does the author use as a clue?

4. [1]Fats (or lipids), another group of basic nutrients, are perhaps the most misunderstood of the body's required energy sources. [2]Most of us do not realize that fats play a vital role in the maintenance of healthy skin and hair, insulation of the body organs against shock, maintenance of

body temperature, and the proper functioning of the cells themselves. (Donatelle and Davis, *Access to Health*)

      a. What is the common name for lipids?

      b. What punctuation clue does the author use?

5. [1]Donald Cressey's book *Other People's Money* (1953) is a classic study of embezzlers. [2]On the basis of interviews with convicted embezzlers, Cressey concluded that three basic conditions are necessary before people will turn to embezzlement. [3]First, they must have a financial problem that they do not want other people to know about. [4]Second, they must have an opportunity to steal. [5]Third, they must be able to find a formula to rationalize the fact that they are committing a criminal act—such as "I'm just borrowing it to tide me over." (Kornblum and Julian, *Social Problems*)

      a. According to Cressey's research, what primary conditions are necessary for people to embezzle?

      b. What signal phrase do the authors use as a clue in sentence 2?

      c. What signal words do the authors use in sentences 3, 4, and 5 to alert you to the primary conditions?

HOW DOES THE AUTHOR DEVELOP THE MAIN IDEA?

How the author develops and supports the thesis or main idea refers to the structure he or she gives the information. Six common ways authors develop and support main ideas are example, comparison and/or contrast, division or classification, cause and effect, process, and definition.

It is useful to determine the structure, or method of development, because it provides a clue to locating and sorting out the relationships among details you need. By that I mean, when you spot one of the common methods of development such as comparison/contrast, you think and read actively because you know to look for the similarities and differences the author is providing to support and explain the main idea.

Please remember, however, that discovering the author's method of development is not your reason for reading; you are just using what you can discover about the development as a clue to understanding the ideas and details you need.

HOW DOES THE AUTHOR USE EXAMPLES?

One of the most common and easily recognized methods of development in academic material is the use of examples to support and develop the thesis or main idea.

Using this method of development, authors support and develop their general statement—the thesis or main idea—with specific, relevant examples, instances, or illustrations.

Topic sentences such as these often lead to the use of examples:

The best strategy for staying warm is to rely on an old mountaineering technique known as layering, a method that helps the body maintain a comfortable balance between heat generated and heat lost. For example, the first layer... (*The reader should watch for details that give examples of layering.*)

A magazine is custom-designed for its special audience. For example, Redbook and Cosmopolitan... (*The reader should watch for details that give examples of magazines that are custom-designed for an audience.*)

Words that signal examples or illustrations include: *for example, to illustrate, for instance, such as, specifically, namely,* and the abbreviations *i.e.,* and *e.g.*

Determine the main idea of this paragraph on cardiovascular diseases. What kind of details do Donatelle and Davis use to develop and support their main idea?

> We can prevent or reduce the risks for cardiovascular diseases by taking steps to change certain behaviors. For example, controlling high blood pressure and reducing our intake of saturated fats and cholesterol are two things we can do to reduce the risk for heart attacks. By maintaining our weight, lowering our intake of sodium, and changing our lifestyles to reduce stress, we can lower blood pressure. We can also monitor the levels of fat and cholesterol in our blood and adjust our diets to prevent clogging of arteries. (Donatelle and Davis, *Access to Health*)

In this paragraph, Donatelle and Davis support their main idea (*we can prevent or reduce the risk of heart diseases by changing some of our behaviors*) through a series of specific examples (*control high blood pressure and reduce intake of saturated fats and cholesterol to reduce risk of heart attacks; maintain weight, lower intake of sodium and reduce stress to lower blood pressure; monitor fat, cholesterol and adjust diet*).

HOW DOES THE AUTHOR USE COMPARISON AND/OR CONTRAST?

To compare means to tell how two things or ideas or people are alike. Contrast means to tell how two things or ideas or people are different.

Authors can choose to develop and support their main idea by giving the likenesses, the differences, or both the likenesses and differences between or among things or ideas or people.

Topic sentences such as the following alert you to watch for likenesses and/or differences:

> Running for the local school board is similar to running for a major political office in many ways, but there are also important differences. (*The reader should watch for details that tell how running for the school board and a major office are alike and how they are different.*)

> Despite the diversity of ecosystems, they are alike in some ways. (*The reader should watch for details that tell how various ecosystems are alike.*)

> Although there may be some similarities between the lighting techniques of studio and outdoor photographers, their differences are critical. (*The reader should watch for details that tell how the lighting techniques are different.*)

Signal words to watch for that may indicate comparison include: *similarly, like, the same as, compared to, in the same way, likewise, parallels, resembles, equally,* and *just as.*

Signal words that may indicate contrast include: *but, yet, on the other hand, however, instead, nevertheless, on the contrary, unlike, in contrast to, whereas, in spite of, although, conversely, different from, rather than,* and *just the opposite.*

Read the following paragraph to determine Long's main idea. How does he develop the details he uses to support that idea?

> A computer system can also be likened to the biological system of the human body. Your brain is the processing component. Your eyes and ears are input components that send signals to the brain. If you see someone

approaching, your brain matches the visual image of this person with others in your memory (storage component). If the visual image matches that of a friend, your brain sends signals to your vocal cords and right arm (output components) to greet your friend with a hello and a handshake. Computer system components interact in a similar way. (Long, *Introduction to Computers and Information Processing*)

In this paragraph, Long supports his main idea (*a computer system is like a human biological system*) by describing how the two systems are alike (*brain is like processing component*; *eyes and ears like input components*; *memory is like storage component*; *vocal cords and arm are like output components*).

Read the following paragraph to determine the author's main idea about Canyonlands National Park and the Grand Canyon. How are the details developed?

For diversity, Canyonlands National Park gives even the Grand Canyon a run for its money. Its 337,570 acres range in elevation from 3,700 feet at the head of Lake Powell to more than 7,000 feet at the highest point on the south boundary above Salt Creek. Like the Grand Canyon, Canyonlands protects a great inner gorge carved by the Colorado River, with a rim high above that offers awesome views. But here, too, are flats studded with slickrock needles and spires, an intricate system of side canyons decorated with massive stone arches, and rich archeological resources famous for fine rock art. (*The Sierra Club Guides to the National Parks*)

The authors of this paragraph develop their main idea (*Canyonlands National Park is at least as diverse as the Grand Canyon*) by giving information on how they are alike (*they both have an inner gorge carved by the Colorado River and a high rim with an awesome view*) and how they are different (*Canyonlands has flats studded with slickrock needles and spires, an intricate system of side canyons decorated with massive stone arches, and rich archeological resources famous for fine rock art*).

HOW DOES THE AUTHOR USE DIVISION OR CLASSIFICATION?

Division or classification is commonly used when the author wants to break a larger subject into parts to examine how each part contributes to the whole. Additionally, when an author needs to bring order to a group of ideas, activities, or things, he or she will often divide or classify them according to their characteristics. In classification, an author uses categories or groups, not individual items.

The main idea usually identifies what will be divided or classified and often tell how many divisions will be considered. Topic sentences such as these point to division or classification of information:

We can divide the color input/output process into five areas: planning, scanning, color correction, proofing, and printing. (*The author is breaking a large topic—color input/output process—into parts; the reader should watch for details that examine each part.*)

There are four basic ways to accomplish the purchase of mutual fund shares at that day's net asset value. These ways are to transfer from a money fund, with a wire transfer from your bank, through a telephone purchase, or by opening a new account by wire. (*The author is dividing ways to buy mutual funds at a specific value; the reader should watch for details that tell how each way works.*)

Signal words you should watch for include: *categories*, *classifications*, *groups*, *classes*, *ways*, *elements*, *features*, *methods*, *kinds*, *types*, *parts*, *factors*, *issues*, *reasons*, and *sorts*.

Read the following paragraph to determine Bittner's main idea. How does it appear he will develop the details of Eric Berne's approach to understanding human interaction?

> The psychiatrist and proponent of transactional analysis, Eric Berne, developed an interesting approach to understanding human interaction. At the core of his approach is what he called the ego state. In the simplest terms, there are three types of ego states which are, according to Berne, present in every individual (adult state, parent state, child state). To better understand these three types in relation to what we have already been discussing about self-concept, think of them as different self-concepts which we possess and relate to at any given time. (Bittner, *Understanding Self-Concept*)

Bittner develops his main idea (*the concept of the ego state is at the center of Berne's theory of human interaction*) by dividing it into three types (*adult state, parent state, child state*). He follows this paragraph with an in-depth look at each of the three states.

HOW DOES THE AUTHOR USE CAUSE AND EFFECT?

An author uses cause and effect—reasons and results—to explain why or how something happened and the result of the action. Using a cause-and-effect pattern of development, an author can examine the reasons for events or situations and their consequences, look at the known benefits or outcomes of a set of conditions, or predict the possible consequences of a given situation.

An author can begin with the cause(s) and give the result(s), or can begin with the result(s) and give the cause(s). There can be a single cause with multiple effects, multiple causes and a single effect, or a causal chain—where, like falling dominoes, an action results in an effect, which causes something else, which causes something else, and so on.

Topic sentences such as the following alert you to look for a cause-and-effect relationship:

> Many factors contributed to the increase in college enrollments in the 1980s. (*The author gives the effect—increased college enrollment; the reader should watch for details that give the causes.*)

> Although it is difficult to predict all of the long-term effects of air pollution, a few are already known. (*The author gives the cause—air pollution; the reader should watch for details that give the effects.*)

Words that signal cause include: *because*; *for this reason*; *due to*; *cause*; *on account of*; and the phrase, *if this, then this*.

Words that signal a result include: *as a result, since, consequently, therefore, thus, in effect, resulting*, and *the outcome is*.

Read the following paragraph to determine Strongman's main idea. How does he develop the main idea?

> Within psychology, there has been a long-standing link between personality and abnormal behavior, an understanding of the former often being regarded as important to the study of the latter. Perhaps one reason for this is the impact of the early psychoanalysts on both fields. A very brief

comment therefore might be useful on some of the links between emotion and personality. (Strongman, *The Psychology of Emotion*)

Strongman develops his main idea—the effect (*that there has been a long-standing link between personality and abnormal behavior*) by looking at one cause (*the impact of the early psychoanalysts on both fields*).

HOW DOES THE AUTHOR USE PROCESS?

When an author wants you to understand how to do something yourself or how something is or was done, he or she must give or describe the sequence of steps or behaviors needed to complete the process.

Topic sentences such as the following alert you to look for a sequence of activities:

> The interview, like any research, is a time-consuming process that involves a number of steps. (*The reader should watch for details that give the steps.*)

> The imaging technique known as ISI (Idealized Self-Image), developed by Dr. Dorothy Susskind, asks the subject to perform the following behaviors. (*The reader should watch for details that give the behaviors.*)

Signal words that may indicate process include: *first, second, third, ...; next*; *then*; *finally*; *eventually*; *following this*; *steps*; *at the start*; *to begin*; *initially*; *during the next minute, hour, day, year*; and specific times or dates.

Read the following paragraph to determine Tocquet's main idea. How does he develop and support his main idea?

> For the extraction of a square root the mental calculation broadly follows the normal method: first, you divide the number into groups of two figures, you look for the largest square contained in the first group, you carry the root as the first result and subtract this square from the first group. Next, you mentally add on to the remainder the first figure of the second group and divide the number thus obtained by twice the first figure carried; you retain this quotient as the second figure of the root required. As can be seen, the process is rather complicated and lengthy. (Robert Tocquet, *The Magic of Numbers*)

Tocquet supports his main idea (*to mentally calculate a square root you use about the same procedure as when you calculate with pencil and paper*) by giving the sequence of steps needed to complete the process. He uses two signal words—first and next—and a series of punctuation marks to help you follow the process.

HOW DOES THE AUTHOR USE DEFINITION?

In academic material, authors often need to restrict and clarify a definition or explain their personal interpretation of the meaning of a term or concept.

This is done in a variety of ways. Common methods of providing definitions include: giving one or more dictionary definitions or one or more connotative meanings, by tracing the etymology, by comparing and/or contrasting the word with other terms, providing examples, and by negation—telling what it doesn't mean.

Topic sentences such as the following alert you to watch for definitions:

> The word "politician" has many meanings. (*The reader should watch for details that give various meanings.*)

Psychologists are wary when asked to write about aggression; it is a definitional minefield. (*The reader should watch for details that give various definitions.*)

Words that signal definition include: *define as, is, known, the term means, is stated as,* and *is used to mean.*

Read the following paragraph by Grassian to determine the main idea. How does he develop the details to support his idea?

> The concept of euthanasia is used today with varying meanings. In its original Greek meaning, "euthanasia" meant no more than an easy and painless death (*eu* = well; *thanatos* = death) and was later extended to refer to the work of a physician in alleviating as far as possible the suffering of dying. Today, however, "euthanasia" is often used synonymously with that of "mercy killing" and as such entails the bringing about of death. *The American Heritage Dictionary* (1975) defines "euthanasia" as "the action of inducing the painless death of a person for reasons assumed to be merciful." As this definition demonstrates, central to our current concept of euthanasia is the idea that such an action be motivated by a desire to be merciful to or to do good to the recipient. As such, when most people are asked to think of a case of euthanasia they imagine a person who is dying of a painful terminal illness, such as cancer, and is given some lethal drug or injection that is meant to "put him out of his misery." (Grassian, *Moral Reasoning*)

Grassian develops and supports his main idea (*"euthanasia" has different meanings*) by giving five definitions of the word. He begins with the original meaning from Greek and traces the meaning through to today's usage.

HOW DOES THE AUTHOR USE A COMBINATION OF METHODS?

Up to this point, you have been working with sample paragraphs that I have selected because they showed one primary method of development. But don't be misled. Much of the material you read is not this clear-cut; it does not adhere to only one method of development. Most authors use a combination of methods to develop their paragraphs, chapters, and articles.

For example, what do Donatelle and Davis want you to understand about manic depressives? What details do they provide to help you understand their idea? How do they develop the details?

> Endogenous and exogenous depression are sometimes called unipolar depression because their victims suffer depression only. Conversely, victims of manic-depressive mood disorder suffer from violent mood swings. Manic depressives may be energetic, creative, vivacious, and "happy" for a time and then become severely depressed. Thus the characteristic mania of happiness followed by the melancholy of depression classifies the disorder as a bipolar affliction. Between 10 and 15 percent of the total American population is afflicted with manic-depressive mood disorders. (Donatelle and Davis, *Access to Health*)

Donatelle and Davis mainly want you to understand that manic depression is a bipolar affliction because it causes significant highs and lows. They first contrast victims of manic depression with victims of endogenous and exogenous depression (termed unipolar depression) by telling how their moods are different from each other—unipolar depressives suffer only depression; manic depressives suffer great mood swings. Then they give an effect of this mood swing—it's classified as bipolar.

PRACTICE A: DETERMINING HOW THE AUTHOR DEVELOPS IDEAS

1. [1]The origin of the term "Baroque" is uncertain. [2]Possibly it derives from the Portuguese word *barroco*, an irregularly shaped pearl. [3]Or it may have come from the Italian word *baroco*, a far-fetched syllogistic argument. [4]Or perhaps it came from the name of a sixteenth-century Italian painter, Frederigo Barocci. (Politoske, *Music*)

   a. What is the main idea?

   b. What is the relationship of sentences 2–4 to sentence 1? Do they summarize, introduce a contrast, or provide an illustration/example? Explain.

   c. What is the relationship of sentence 4 to sentences 2 and 3? Does it define, summarize, introduce a contrast, or continue the thought? Explain.

2. [1]Couples seeking a divorce will not always find it easy to reach agreement on issues that affect their children, but they should attempt to do so before telling their children about the impending separation. [2]Children, even very young children, need to be prepared for the divorce. [3]They need information about where they will live, who will take care of them, where they will go to school, and whatever other issues are of major concern to them. (NIMH, *Caring about Kids: When Parents Divorce*)

   a. What is the main idea?

   b. What is the relationship of sentence 3 to sentences 1 and 2? Does it define a term, introduce a contrast, or provide an illustration/example? Explain.

   c. Does sentence 3 contain major or minor details? Explain.

3. [1]Various behavioral theories have been studied as they relate to health. [2]Ideas and concepts such as self-efficacy, locus of control, and health locus of control are becoming more widely understood. [3]Self-efficacy refers to a person's appraisal of his or her own ability to change or to accomplish a particular task or behavior. [4]Locus of control refers to a person's perceptions of forces or factors that control his or her destiny. [5]Health locus of control focuses specifically on those factors that influence health. [6]These constructs influence how we view ourselves and also how we behave or seek to change behaviors. (Donatelle and Davis, *Access to Health*)

   a. What is the main idea?

   b. What is the relationship of sentence 2 to sentence 1? Does it define, summarize, introduce a contrast, or provide an illustration/example? Explain.

   c. What is the relationship of sentences 3–5 to sentence 2? Do they define, continue the same thought, or provide an illustration/example? Explain.

4. [1]Many (of the North American Indian) tribes were skilled in handicrafts, making beautiful pottery, light and swift birchbark canoes, and implements of copper. [2]Some wove a kind of cloth from the inner bark of trees. [3]Others, however, lived very simply, with few artifacts. [4]The numerous peoples of California, for example, blessed with a mild climate and abundant food, made do with simple clothing and crude houses. [5]Only their beautiful basketwork revealed their skills with materials. (Unger, *These United States*)

   a. What is the main idea?

b. What is the relationship of sentence 3 to sentences 1 and 2? Does it define, summarize, introduce a contrast, or continue the same thought? Explain.

c. What word does Unger use in sentence 3 to signal its purpose?

5. ¹It is estimated that advertisers in the United States now spend more than $57 billion each year, compared with $1.69 billion spent in 1935, according to census reports. ²As the nation's gross national product (GNP) has risen beyond $2.6 trillion, advertising expenditures have kept pace, ranging close to 2 percent of the GNP each year. ³Advertising, with its marketing aids of sales promotions, product design, point-of-purchase displays, product publicity, and public relations, thus plays an obvious role in the growth of the nation's economy. (Agee, Ault, and Emery, *Introduction to Mass Communications*)

    a. What is the main idea?

    b. What is the relationship of sentence 3 to the sentences 1 and 2? Does it define, summarize, introduce a contrast, or provide an illustration/example? Explain.

6. ¹Mechanical industries that processed tobacco, grain, soap, and canned foodstuffs dramatically increased their output through the use of continuous-process machinery. ²A cigarette-making machine developed in 1881 was so productive that just fifteen of them satisfied America's entire annual demand for cigarettes. ³Procter & Gamble developed a new machine for mass-producing Ivory soap. ⁴Diamond Match began using a machine that produced and boxed matches by the billions. ⁵Industries that distilled and refined petroleum, sugar, animal or vegetable fats, alcohol, and chemicals reaped enormous savings from new heat and chemical technologies, giant furnaces, whirling centrifuges, converters, and rolling and finishing equipment. ⁶Standard Oil, American Sugar Refining, and Carnegie Steel, among others, gained unprecedented efficiencies. ⁷Metalworking industries benefited from larger and more efficient machine tools and a wider variety of semifinished materials. ⁸International Harvester and Singer Sewing Machine expanded their production far beyond the imaginings of past generations. (Reich, *The Work of Nations*)

    a. What is the main idea?

    b. What is the relationship of sentences 2–4 to sentence 1? Do they provide a contrast, or an illustration/example? Explain.

    c. What is the relationship of sentence 6 to sentence 5? Does it provide a contrast, or an illustration/example? Explain.

    d. What is the relationship of sentence 8 to sentence 7? Does it provide a contrast, or an illustration/example? Explain.

PRACTICE B: DETERMINING HOW THE AUTHOR DEVELOPS IDEAS

1. The age of the average worker has gradually increased over the past few decades…. This trend has affected businesses in two ways. First, older workers tend to put greater demand on a company's health insurance, life insurance, and retirement benefit programs. And second, younger workers taking the places of retirees tend to want different things from employers—things like more opportunities for self-expression or more leisure time. (Griffin and Ebert, *Business*)

      a. What is the main idea?

      b. How do Griffin and Ebert develop and support the main idea?

      c. What signal words were helpful?

      d. In what two ways has the aging of the workforce affected businesses?

2. The most serious disciplinary problems facing managers undoubtedly involve attendance. For instance, in a study of two hundred organizations, 60 percent of which employed over one thousand workers, absenteeism, tardiness, abuse of sick leave, and other aspects of attendance were rated as the foremost problems by 79 percent of the respondents (Bureau of National Affairs, 1973). Importantly, attendance problems appear to be even more widespread than those related to productivity—such as carelessness in doing work, neglect of duty, and not following established procedures. (Robbins, *Training in Interpersonal Skills*)

      a. What is the main idea?

      b. What kind of details does Robbins use to support the main idea?

      c. If you were reading this paragraph to prepare for listening to a lecture, what would you concentrate on remembering?

      d. If you were reading this paragraph to prepare for taking a test, would you concentrate as much, more, or less?

3. ¹Being shy can cause many problems for adults. ²They are often hesitant to seek out others and are excluded from social relationships. ³Shy or withdrawn individuals are less likely to be promoted at work. ⁴In addition, adults who are hesitant to talk with others are often taken advantage of by aggressive salespeople. (McGrath, *Self-Defeating Behaviors*)

      a. What is the main idea?

      b. What kind of details does McGrath use to develop the main idea?

      c. What is the cause? What are the results?

      d. What is the relationship of sentence 4 to sentences 2 and 3? Does it define, summarize, introduce a contrast, continue the same thought, or provide an illustration/example?

4. To be convincing, presentation graphics must be fitted to the message and to the audience.... Begin with a plan. The most important part of your presentation preparation is deciding on just one primary idea with which to leave your audience. State it in a dozen words or less. Next, develop a complete outline of what you want to say.

    When you've clearly identified your theme, the time, and the relative emphasis of each portion of your presentation, you can begin to create individual elements. Decide on the best way to illustrate your message for this audience. Then, draw small sketches of each overhead, slide, or handout you want to use. (Adapted from Hengesbaugh, *Typography for Desktop Publishers*)

      a. What is the main idea?

      b. List the steps in the process described by Hengesbaugh

5. Perhaps these (communication) difficulties arise because public speaking differs from other forms of communication in two ways. First, a public speaking situation includes two distinct and separate roles: speaker and audience. Second, in this speaker-audience relationship,

the speaker carries more responsibility than does the audience. In other communication situations, speakers and listeners exchange roles and share this responsibility. (Barker and Barker, *Communication*)

   a. What is the main idea?

   b. How do Barker and Barker develop their main idea?

   c. How does public speaking differ from other forms of communication?

6. We all want to have positive influence with certain people in our personal and professional lives. But how do we do it? How do we powerfully and ethically influence the lives of other people? There are three basic categories of influence: (1) model by example (others see); (2) build caring relationships (others feel); (3) mentor by instruction (others hear). (Covey, *Seven Habits of Highly Effective People*)

   a. What is the main idea?

   b. How does Covey develop his main idea?

   c. What do you predict the paragraphs that follow this one contain?

CHAPTER 5 REVIEW QUESTIONS

1. What is the difference between a thesis, a main idea, a major detail, and a minor detail? Why do you need to know the difference?

2. What is the purpose of signal words? Give two examples of signal words and tell how you would use them.

3. List and explain six methods authors use to develop and support their main ideas.

4. Explain how you can use author clues such as signal words, punctuation, and methods of development to help your comprehension.

CHAPTER 5 THINK AND CONNECT QUESTIONS

5. Re-read "Endangered Species" in Chapter 3, page 48. In paragraphs 3–5, look beyond the main ideas you identified to the details the authors provide to support them. For each of the three paragraphs, list the major supporting details and the development clues you used, such as signal words or method of development.

6. Re-read "Theories of Human Behavior" in Chapter 4, Exercise #4, page 77. Identify the major details Greenberg and Dintiman use to develop and support the main ideas of paragraphs 2/3/4 and 5/6.

CHAPTER 5 APPLICATION EXERCISES

7. Review the topic sentence about health care costs you wrote for the Chapter 4 Application Exercise on page 72. Using the method of paragraph development that you think will best support and explain your main idea, write one paragraph. Your paragraph should include at least two major supporting details and one minor supporting detail.

8. Using your texts or other expository material, identify one paragraph in which the author develops the main idea using example, one in

which the author uses comparison/contrast, one in which the author uses process, and one in which the author uses either division/classification or cause/effect.

USE YOUR STRATEGIES: EXERCISE #1

1. [1]Exercise has several beneficial effects. [2]It burns calories, enhances weight loss, and increases the likelihood that weight loss will be maintained. [3]It also increases metabolism, which counteracts the opposing effects of dieting, suppresses appetite, and minimizes the loss of lean tissue. [4]Aerobic exercise in particular strengthens the heart; enhances general muscle tone, strength, and elasticity; and has a positive effect on serum lipids, coronary efficiency, and blood pressure (Brownell, 1980). [5]At the same time, aerobic exercise decreases the risk of coronary artery disease, diabetes, and high blood pressure. [6]It is also associated with decreased anxiety and depression and an enhanced sense of well-being. [7]However, exercise also carries some risks. [8]If initiated by someone who is unfit or if carried to extremes, it may result in orthopedic discomfort and injury and, more rarely, may precipitate a heart attack (Haskell, 1984). (Snyder, *Health Psychology and Behavioral Medicine*)

    a. What is the main idea?

    b. How does Snyder develop and support the main idea?

    c. What is the relationship of sentence 7 to sentence 1? Does it define, restate, introduce a contrast, continue the same thought, or provide an illustration/example?

2. [1]Computers are designed to be either special-purpose or general-purpose computing devices. [2]Special-purpose computers, also known as dedicated computers, are designed around a specific application or type of application.... [3]For example, the Lunar Excursion Module (LEM), which landed the first man on the moon, had a special-purpose computer on board intended to do only one thing: control the altitude or relative position of the vehicle during descent and ascent to and from the moon.... [4]General-purpose computers are designed to handle a variety of tasks.... [5]Thus the same combination of hardware can be used to execute many different programs. [6]General purpose computers have the advantage of versatility over special-purpose computers but typically are less efficient and slower than special-purpose computers when applied to the same task. (Fuori and Gioia, *Computers and Information Processing*)

    a. What is the main idea?

    b. How do Fuori and Gioia develop and support their main idea?

    c. What is the purpose of sentence 3?

3. Animals, known technically as fauna, occur in much greater variety than do plants. As objects of geographical study, however, they are less important than plants, for at least two reasons. First, animals are much less prominent in the landscape. Apart from extremely localized situations, animals tend to be secretive and inconspicuous, whereas the vegetation is not only fixed in position, it also serves as a relatively complete ground cover wherever it has not been removed by human interference. In addition, animals do not provide the clear evidence of

environmental interrelationships that plants do. (Bergman and McKnight, *Introduction to Geography*)

    a. What is the main idea?

    b. How do Bergman and McKnight develop and support their main idea?

    c. List the two reasons animals are less important than plants to geographical study.

4.   A clause is a group of words containing both a subject and a predicate. A clause functions as an element of a compound or a complex sentence. There are two general types of clauses: the main or independent clause and the subordinate or dependent clause. The main clause (such as "it is hot") is an independent grammatical unit and can stand alone. The subordinate clause (such as "because it is hot") cannot stand alone. A subordinate clause is either preceded or followed by a main clause. (*Webster's Guide to Business Correspondence*)

    a. What is the main idea?

    b. How does the author develop and support the main idea?

    c. If you were preparing to take a test where you had to explain clauses and give examples, which details would you remember? Which ones would you ignore? Why?

5.   The sociological perspective was sparked by three basic and interrelated changes. First, rapid technological innovation in eighteenth-century Europe soon led to the spread of factories and an industrial economy. Second, these factories drew millions of people from the countryside, causing an explosive growth of cities. Third, people in these expanding industrial cities soon began to entertain new ideas about the world, leading to important political developments. (Macionis, *Sociology*)

    a. What is the main idea?

    b. How does Macionis develop and support his main idea?

    c. What signal words does Macionis use?

6.   About 300 million years ago the conditions for the subsequent formation of petroleum (mineral oil) were established in shallow coastal waters by the teeming tiny creatures and plants that lived and died in vast numbers. The ooze formed on the bottom by the remains of these organisms was unable to decompose because of a lack of oxygen. As a result of climatic changes, these coastal areas became buried under layers of earth, and the organic remains were subjected to high pressures and temperatures over periods of millions of years. The fats, carbohydrates and proteins were thereby subjected to conditions in which they were decomposed and underwent extensive chemical changes. As a result of these changes, a large number of compounds were formed which all enter into the composition of petroleum. (*The Way Things Work*)

    a. What is the main idea?

    b. How does the author develop and support the main idea?

7.   A number of factors contribute to overweight and obesity in the United States population. Inactivity and overeating, in that order, are the two leading causes among both children and adults. Early eating patterns, the number of fat cells acquired early in life, metabolism, age, and environmental and genetic factors also play a significant role. (Greenberg and Dintiman, *Exploring Health*)

    a. What is the main idea?

b. How do Greenberg and Dintiman develop and support their main idea?

c. List eight factors that contribute to obesity.

8. [1]Studying philosophy helps you to develop insight into some of life's great puzzles and to fashion your own vision of what life is all about. [2]As you go through life, you will be challenged all along the way to make decisions about who you are and what's important to you. [3]What will you do with your life? [4]What career will you pursue? [5]Will you marry? [6]And if so, what kind of person? [7]Will you have children? [8]How will you rear them? [9]What will you tell them is important? [10]What are you willing to do for money and success? [11]How will you cope with the crises you will encounter in your own life or in the lives of those you love—illnesses, accidents, problems on the job or at home, death? [12]Philosophy helps you develop a sense of what life is all about and where you're going. (White, *Discovering Philosophy*)

a. What is the main idea?

b. How does White develop and support the main idea?

c. What is the relationship of sentence 12 to sentence 1. Does it define, restate, introduce a contrast, continue the same thought, or provide an illustration/example?

9. The Colorado Avalanche Information Center (CAIC) in Denver advises skiers to stay alert for avalanche conditions. The threat of avalanches is greatest in the late winter because of higher snow accumulations, warmer temperatures that make snow wet and heavy, and the presence of more unstable snow layers. Avalanche conditions are more likely to occur in terrain sloping 30° or more, and during and immediately after bad weather involving snow and high winds.

If it is not possible to stay out of such conditions, the CAIC advises skiers to stay near the end or flanks of narrow valleys and away from the middle or lower reaches, cliffs, tree stands, and gullies, where there is limited room to maneuver in an emergency. (adapted from information from the Colorado Avalanche Information Center)

a. What is the main idea of paragraph 1? What is the main idea of paragraph 2?

b. How does the author develop and support the main ideas?

c. What are three conditions that increase the threat of avalanches?

10. In the early years of the new nation, two types of newspapers were developing. One was the mercantile paper, published in the seaboard towns primarily for the trading and shipping classes interested in commercial and political news. Its well-filled advertising columns reflected the essentially business interest of its limited clientele of subscribers—2000 was a good number. The other type was the political paper, partisan in its appeal and relying for reader support on acceptance of its views, rather than upon the quality and completeness of its news. Most editors of the period put views first and news second; the political paper deliberately shaped the news to fit its views. (Agee, Ault, and Emery *Introduction to Mass Communications*)

a. What is the main idea?

b. How do Agee, Ault, and Emery develop and support their main idea?

c. List the major differences between the two types of newspapers.

USE YOUR STRATEGIES: EXERCISE #2—"WHEN X-COLD STRIKES"

Robert McGrath is a successful freelance writer. His work appears in numerous national publications. This selection—"When X-Cold Strikes"—is from *Young Americans*.

WHEN X-COLD STRIKES

ROBERT L. MCGRATH

[1]X-cold is hypothermia—body temperature lowered too rapidly by chilling from wet, wind and cold. It brings quick collapse of mental and physical functions, affecting anyone, young or old.

[2]It's exception-cold, extensive-cold. X-cold happens when unexpected winter wind, rain or snow arrives. Your clothes get wet and lose up to 90 percent of their insulating value. Water is held against your body with a chilling effect, even though outside temperatures can be as high as 50 degrees Fahrenheit.

[3]Your body temperature, normally 98.6°F, drops to 94°F or below. If it cools further, it's a danger point—X-cold—because cooling to 80°F can produce death.

[4]If you know how to prevent it, X-cold won't spoil your outdoor fun. Watch for these signals:

Chattering teeth and shivering.

Slow, hard-to-understand speech.

Forgetfulness, confusion.

Fumbling hands.

Stumbling, difficulty in walking.

Sleepiness—The person going to sleep may never wake up.

Exhaustion—If the person can't get up after a brief rest, X-cold has taken over.

[5]X-cold reduces reasoning power and judgment because of lack of oxygen to the brain. The affected person usually denies that anything is wrong.

[6]What can you do? Find shelter. Build a fire. Get the victim out of wind, rain, snow. Strip off wet clothing and put on dry clothes or wrap up in a sleeping bag. Give warm drinks. Avoid medicines—they may slow down body processes even more.

[7]Body heat trapped by insulating clothing is the best protection against cold. Wear loose-fitting, lightweight clothing in several layers. Put on a knit cap—more than half the body's heat can be lost through the head. That extra warmth will send added blood to your feet, making them feel more comfortable.

[8]Remember, weather may pull surprises. Unexpected changes can bring sharp wind, driving rain, snow—conditions producing X-cold.

[9]Use your head. Wear seasonal clothing. Don't let X-cold—hypothermia—keep you from enjoying our great outdoors the year around.

EXERCISE #2 QUESTIONS—"WHEN X-COLD STRIKES"

1. What is McGrath's purpose?
2. Write a sentence that expresses McGrath's thesis.
3. What is X-cold? What is hypothermia?
4. In paragraph 1, what is the relationship between sentence 2 and sentence 1?

5. What is the main idea of paragraph 4?
6. What is the main idea of paragraph 7?
7. What are four warning signs of hypothermia?
8. Why does hypothermia reduce a person's reasoning power?
9. What are four positive actions you can take to counteract hypothermia?
10. What is the primary action McGrath urges you to take to avoid hypothermia?

USE YOUR STRATEGIES: EXERCISE #3—"RUNNING THE SMALL BUSINESS"

Ricky Griffin teaches business at Texas A&M University. Ronald Ebert teaches business at the University of Missouri-Columbia. This selection—"Running the Small Business"—is from *Business*, 2nd ed.

RUNNING THE SMALL BUSINESS: REASONS FOR SUCCESSES AND FAILURES

RICKY W. GRIFFIN AND RONALD J. EBERT

[1a]Why do many small businesses succeed and others fail? [b]While there is no set pattern, there are some common causes of both success and failure.

Reasons for Failure

[2a]Four common factors contribute to small business failure. [b]One major problem is managerial incompetence or inexperience. [c]If managers do not know how to make basic decisions, they are unlikely to make them effectively. [d]A second contributor to failure is neglect. [e]That is, after the glamour and excitement of the big grand opening, some *entrepreneurs* get discouraged and don't concentrate as much on their business as they should.... [f]Third, weak control systems can also be a cause of failure. [g]If control systems fail to alert managers to *impending problems*, they are likely to be caught unprepared to deal with them. [h]Finally, many small businesses fail because the owner does not have enough capital to keep it going. [i]New business owners are almost certain to fail if they expect to pay the second month's rent from the first month's profits.

Reasons for Success

[3a]Likewise, four basic factors contribute to small business success. [b]One factor is hard work, drive, and dedication. [c]Owners must be committed to succeeding and willing to put in the time and effort necessary to make it happen. [d]Another factor is *market demand* for the products or services being provided. [e]If a large college town has only a single pizza parlor, a new one is more likely to succeed than if there are already thirty in operation. [f]Managerial competence is also important. [g]Successful small business-people have at least a *modicum of ability and understanding* of what they should do. [h]And finally, luck is often a key variable in determining whether the business succeeds or fails. [i]For example, when Debbi Fields first opened Mrs. Fields' Cookies, she literally had to give cookies away in order to tempt people to buy them. [j]Had she not found eager customers that first day she might well have given up and quit.

EXERCISE #3 QUESTIONS—"RUNNING THE SMALL BUSINESS"

1. What is Griffin and Ebert's purpose?
2. Define each of these words or phrases from the selection:
    - a. entrepreneurs (¶2)
    - b. impending problems (¶2)
    - c. market demand (¶3)
    - d. modicum of ability and understanding (¶3)
3. What type of context clue do Griffin and Ebert use to help define market demand?
4. Write a sentence that expresses Griffin and Ebert's thesis.
5. In each sentence in paragraphs 2 and 3, identify whether the sentence is the main idea, a major detail, or a minor detail.
6. In paragraph 2, what is the relationship of sentence b to sentence a?
7. In paragraph 2, what is the relationship of sentence c to sentence b?
8. What are four common causes of failure for small businesses?
9. What are four common causes of success for small businesses?
10. What four words do Griffin and Ebert use in paragraph 2 to signal the four causes?

USE YOUR STRATEGIES: EXERCISE #4—"THE BENEFITS OF THE SOCIOLOGICAL PERSPECTIVE"

Dr. Macionis is an associate professor of sociology at Kenyon College in Gambier, Ohio. He teaches a wide range of upper-level courses, but his favorite course is Introduction to Sociology. His doctorate is in sociology and he is the author of several articles and papers on topics such as community life in the United States, interpersonal relationships in families, effective teaching, and humor. This selection—"The Benefits of the Sociological Perspective"—is from *Sociology*, 3rd ed.

THE BENEFITS OF THE SOCIOLOGICAL PERSPECTIVE

JOHN J. MACIONIS

[1]The knowledge that has been amassed within sociology is immense and can be readily applied to our lives in countless ways. There are, however, four general ways in which the sociological perspective can enrich our lives.

[2a]The first benefit of using the sociological perspective is learning that our world contains a remarkable variety of human social patterns. [b]North Americans represent only about 5 percent of the world's population, and, as the remaining chapters of this book explain, the rest of humanity lives in ways that often differ dramatically from our own. [c]As members of any society, people define their ways of life as proper and often "natural." [d]But looking over the course of human history, and examining the world today, we find countless competing versions of correct behavior. [e]*The sociological perspective helps us to recognize human diversity and to begin to understand the challenges of living within a diverse world.*

(CONTINUED)

THE BENEFITS OF THE SOCIOLOGICAL
PERSPECTIVE (CONTINUED)

[3]The second benefit comes from realizing that, within particular societies, people come to accept as "true" certain ideas that may or may not be factual. *The sociological perspective challenges our familiar understandings of ourselves and of others, so that we can critically reconsider what has been assumed to be "true."*

[4]As we have already seen, a good example of a widespread but misleading "truth" is that Americans are "autonomous individuals," independent of others and personally responsible for their lives. By thinking this way, we are sometimes too quick to praise particularly successful people as being personally superior to those who have not fared as well. On the other side of the coin, people who do not measure up may be unfairly condemned as personally deficient. A sociological approach encourages us to ask whether these beliefs are actually true and, to the extent that they are not, why they are so widely held.

[5]As we consider American society in global context, we might also wonder if the American conception of "success," with its emphasis on materialism rather than, for instance, spiritual well-being, is the best way by which to judge others, as well as to evaluate our own lives.

[6]The third benefit provided by the sociological perspective involves understanding that, for better or worse, American society operates in a particular and deliberate way. No one is able to live with complete disregard for society's "rules of the game." In the game of life, we may decide how to play our cards, but it is society that deals us the hand. The more effective player is generally one who better understands how the game works. Here again, sociology is valuable. *The sociological perspective allows us to recognize both the opportunities and the constraints that affect our lives.* Knowledge of this kind is power. Through it, we come to understand what we are likely and unlikely to accomplish for ourselves, and we are able to see how the goals we adopt can be realized more effectively.

[7a]Of course, the more we understand about the operation of society, the more we can take an active part in shaping social life. [b]On the other hand, with little awareness of how society operates, we are likely passively to accept the status quo. *The sociological perspective, therefore, empowers us as active members of our world.* For some, this may mean embracing society as it is; others, however, may attempt nothing less than trying to change the entire world in some way. The discipline of sociology advocates no one particular political orientation. Indeed, sociologists are widely spread across the political spectrum. But evaluating any aspect of social life—whatever one's eventual goal—depends on the ability to identify social forces and to assess their consequences....

EXERCISE #4 QUESTIONS—"THE BENEFITS OF THE SOCIOLOGICAL PERSPECTIVE"

1. What is Macionis's purpose?
2. Write a sentence that expresses Macionis's thesis.
3. How does Macionis develop and support his thesis?
4. In paragraph 2, what is the relationship of sentence e to sentence a?
5. How do paragraphs 4 and 5 relate to paragraph 3?
6. What words does Macionis use in paragraphs 2, 3, and 6 to signal the key points?
7. What other clues—in addition to, or in place of signal words—does he use to signal key points?
8. In paragraph 7, what is the relationship of sentence b to sentence a?
9. List the benefits of the sociological perspective.
10. What percentage of the world's population do North Americans represent? Are you surprised by this percentage? Did you think it would be higher or lower? Why?

11. What does Macionis think is "a widespread but misleading 'truth' about Americans"?

12. How does Macionis think we judge success in America? Does he think it is the best criteria? Do you?

13. What political viewpoint do most sociologists hold?

14. What is necessary, according to Macionis, for us to become active members of society?

15. Assume you are going to have a short quiz tomorrow on the benefits of the sociological perspective. What details would you remember?

USE YOUR STRATEGIES: EXERCISE #5—"GLITTERING ALICE; SAD ELEANOR"

Richard Cohen is an American writer on national affairs for the *Washington Post*.

GLITTERING ALICE; SAD ELEANOR

RICHARD COHEN

[*Note: Eleanor Roosevelt was the wife of President Franklin D. Roosevelt. She was an active and effective First Lady during his 13 years as President. Even after his death she continued her work as a distinguished diplomat, writer, and speaker. Alice Roosevelt Longworth was the oldest daughter of President Theodore Roosevelt. She was married in the White House to Speaker of the House Nicholas Longworth and enjoyed a long and glamorous social life.*]

[1]It is one of those coincidences of history that Alice Roosevelt Longworth, daughter of the grand and unforgettable Teddy and wife of the totally forgettable Nicholas, died the very same week two more books were published about her cousin, Eleanor. The two hated each other—at least Alice hated Eleanor—thinking probably that they had little in common but a family name. They had something else: They were prisoners of their looks.

[2]Alice, of course, was radiant and pretty—daughter of a president, a Washington *debutante*, a standard of style and grace, the one who gave the color Alice Blue to the nation as surely as her father gave his name to a certain kind of stuffed toy bear.

[3]She married in the White House, took the speaker of the House of Representatives for her husband, and stayed pretty much at the center of things Washingtonian for something like 70 years. She was, as they say, *formidable*.

[4]Eleanor, on the other hand, was homely. She had a voice pitched at the level of chalk on a blackboard, and the teeth of a beaver. She was awkward in both speech and manner and when she talked—when she rose to speak—the experience was both painful to her and her audience. She had a husband, but there is reason to believe that she was unloved by him. There is about Eleanor Roosevelt an aura of aching sadness, yet in her own way she, too, was formidable. She certainly *endures*.

[5]It is interesting to consider how their looks—the way they looked to the world—shaped these two women. It is interesting because in some ways they were so similar. They were both Roosevelts—one of the Oyster Bay branch, the other of the Hyde Park—both well-off, both of the *aristocracy*, and both *manifestly bright*.

[6]Eleanor's intelligence proclaimed itself. She threw herself into causes. She spoke for people who had no spokesperson and she spoke well. She championed the poor, the black, women and other minorities. She campaigned and lectured and gave speeches and she did this with such intensity and such effect that it is not too much to say that before her death she was either a goddess or a witch to most Americans.

(CONTINUED)

GLITTERING ALICE; SAD ELEANOR (CONTINUED)

[7]I am partial to the goddess side, thinking that the worst you can call a person is not "do-gooder" but rather "do-nothinger." That is something you could never call Eleanor Roosevelt.

[8]As for Alice, she showed her intelligence in her wit. It was she who said, "The secret of eternal youth is arrested development," and who commented on Wendell Willkie after he received the presidential nomination: "He sprang from the grass roots of the country clubs of America."

[9]Her most admired remark, the one about Thomas Dewey looking like the "bridegroom on a wedding cake," was not hers at all. The reason we know is that she admitted it. She borrowed it, popularized it, but did not invent it.

[10]No matter. She invented enough so that Washington adored her and presidents more or less routinely elbowed themselves to her side so that they could hear what she had to say.

[11]Yet with Alice, there it stopped. She was what she was, and what she was was beautiful. She did more or less what was expected of pretty girls. She was perfect just being—just being Alice and being pretty—and in the America of both her youth and her maturity there was nothing better than to be rich and pretty and well-married.

[12]That she was also intelligent was almost besides the point, like the *gilding on a lily*. And while she later became cherished for her wit, it was not because she could use it for any purpose, but because it was like her beauty itself: something of a jewel. She was the perfect *appurtenance*, the one men wanted seated next to them.

[13]With Eleanor, the story is different. Her looks were not her strong suit and so she had to declare herself in another way—by intellect, character, *indomitability*. She did this well, found causes, gave purpose to her life and left this earth with the certainty that she had mattered.

[14]The conventional view is to see Eleanor as sad and Alice as glittering. To an extent, I'm sure, that's true. But in reading the obituaries, in reading how Alice cruelly imitated Eleanor and *mocked* her good causes, you get the sense that Alice herself realized that *something ironic had happened*, that she had somehow become trapped by her own good looks, by her perfection, by her wit—that she had become the eternal debutante, frozen in time. Eleanor was actually doing something.

[15]So now Eleanor and Alice are dead. One led a sad life, the other a glittering one. But one suspects that as the books came out on Eleanor, Alice realized the tables had turned. There is something sad about being an ugly duckling, but there is something sadder yet about being the belle of the ball after the music has stopped, the guests have gone home and the rest of the world has gone to work.

EXERCISE #5 QUESTIONS—"GLITTERING ALICE; SAD ELEANOR"

1. What is Cohen's purpose?
2. Have you ever heard of Alice Roosevelt or Eleanor Roosevelt? What did you already know about either of them?
3. Define each of these words and phrases from the selection:
    a. debutante (¶2)
    b. formidable (¶3)
    c. endures (¶4)
    d. aristocracy (¶5)
    e. manifestly bright (¶5)
    f. gilding on a lily (¶12)
    g. appurtenance (¶12)
    h. indomitability (¶13)
    i. mocked (¶14)
    j. something ironic had happened (¶14)

4. Write a sentence that expresses Cohen's thesis.

5. How does Cohen develop and support his thesis?

6. What is the relationship of paragraph 4 to paragraphs 2 and 3?

7. List three descriptors of each woman's physical appearance.

8. List three descriptors of each woman's intelligence and life's work.

9. In paragraph 15, Cohen says "But one suspects that as the books came out on Eleanor, Alice realized the tables had turned." What do you think he meant?

10. Based on Cohen's article and your previous knowledge, do you agree with his statement in paragraph 1, "They were prisoners of their looks"? Why or why not?

CHAPTER 5 CONNECTIONS

A. When you are reading an assignment, how do you decide what to remember? Do you vary the amount of detail you try to remember depending on what you are going to do with the information? Do some of your classes require you to remember more details than others? If so, why?

B. Are you pleased with the results of your reading and study strategies this semester? If you are pleased, what attitudes do you have and what things are you doing that help you the most? If you are not pleased with your success, what are two changes you could make this week that might help? Have you been using any of the Plan⇨Do⇨Review cycle? How successful is it for you?

CHAPTER 6

RECOGNIZE THE AUTHOR'S STANCE

An important reason to plan before you read is to prime your brain. Planning helps you to start thinking, not just about the tasks you have to do, but about ideas. It gives you the chance to make connections between what you already know and what you are going to learn.

As you prepare to read this chapter, think about your stance, or position, on an issue—for example, "getting older." Consider what kind of words and actions you use when you want to let others know how you feel about your upcoming birthday. How do you communicate that you're delighted about finally getting older or, on the other hand, that you're feeling ancient and need some quiet understanding?

Could you write an essay that equally presents the positive and negative aspects of getting older even if you have strong feelings about the issue? What precautions would you take if you wanted to make sure you were presenting both sides of the issue? Do you think it would be wrong if you wrote only your feelings? Do you think it would be important for someone reading your essay to know if you had personal feelings about aging that influenced what you wrote?

Define this chapter's key vocabulary:

stance

reliable

bias

point of view

fact

opinion

tone

irony and ironic

satire

sarcasm

CHAPTER 6 OBJECTIVES

❑ Identify and understand the components of an author's stance.
❑ Identify strategies to determine if an author is reliable.
❑ Identify and understand an author's point of view.
❑ Distinguish between fact and opinion.
❑ Define tone and identify strategies for recognizing tone.

WHAT IS MY BASIC STRATEGY FOR RECOGNIZING THE AUTHOR'S STANCE?

As You Plan:

1. Understand the vocabulary.
2. Predict the thesis and/or main idea.
3. Determine how much detail you need to know.
4. Review the sources of the author's information.
5. Try to determine if the author is reliable as well as knowledgeable.

As You Read:

6. Actively search for information that helps to clarify and refine your prediction about the thesis and/or main idea.
7. Identify words with connotative meanings.
8. Identify the author's point of view.
9 Determine which information is fact and which is opinion.
10. Determine the author's tone.

As You Review:

11. Revise and restate the thesis/main idea.
12. Confirm the author's reliability and the source of the information.
13. Compare the author's point of view with your own.
14. Review the facts and the opinions given to support the thesis/main idea.
15. Based on your purpose, and considering the author's stance, organize the thesis, main ideas, and supporting details.

WHAT IS THE AUTHOR'S STANCE?

You discovered early on that all writing is purposeful; an author wants to communicate information and ideas to you for a reason. In addition, you found that it is important to look at the author's knowledge of the subject and the sources of information. Now, you must go beyond the author's expertise and basic reason for writing. This will enable you to go beyond what the author says to what the author means. You need to determine the author's stance, or position, on the subject—in short, where the author is "coming from."

Much of the time an author does not directly state his or her stance. As you have done when you have made other inferences, you must carefully combine what the author says directly with the author's clues and your own knowledge to infer the author's stance. Uncovering the author's motivation and point of view gives you additional perspective on the author's message.

IS THE AUTHOR RELIABLE?

It is difficult to find out an author's motivation for writing, so it is often hard to know whether he or she is reliable. By reliable, I mean you can trust the author to give you a fair analysis of the topic without undue influence from others.

For example, a professional athlete and a sports medicine doctor could both write knowledgeably on the topic of athletic footwear—from different perspectives—but with knowledge about the topic. It would be difficult, however, to know whether their writing would be reliable—giving a fair analysis of the footwear without undue influence from a sponsor or manufacturer.

To investigate an author's reliability, read other pieces the author has written, read what others have to say about him or her, and ask teachers and librarians for information.

WHAT IS POINT OF VIEW?

Another element of the author's stance is point of view—his or her position or opinion. Two broad categories of writing are: objective, meaning without the author's point of view, or neutral and impartial; and biased, reflecting the author's point of view about the topic.

Typically, you expect expository pieces such as encyclopedia entries and scientific reports to be objective, and persuasive works like political brochures and editorials to be biased. What you, as a careful, critical reader must watch for is a biased point of view, even when the primary purpose is exposition.

Writers of academic material strive to write objectively—without displaying their point of view. But all writers are human so even texts and journal articles can reflect the author's personal bias.

Writing that reflects the author's point of view is not necessarily bad. Although the connotations of the word "objective" make it seem positive and those of the word "biased" make it seem negative, do not assume that only objective writing is good writing or biased writing is bad writing. Writing is not good or bad as long as you identify the author's bias and factor that into your comprehension of the information.

HOW CAN I IDENTIFY POINT OF VIEW?

To identify point of view in writing, you must use all available clues, including background information about the author, the title of the selection, and the sources of quotations, references, and illustrations. In addition, watch for words and phrases that have special connotations and emotional effects and a preponderance, or majority, of one-sided information.

The following is the first three paragraphs from "Computers Can't Teach Awareness" by political and environmental columnist Liz Caile. She wrote this column for *The Mountain-Ear*, a small Colorado mountain town weekly newspaper. Read to discover her point of view about computers and humans.

In a recent discussion of careers, young people were told to master computer skills and math if they wanted to "work for the environment." That stuck in my mind the way the limited concept of outdoor education sometimes sticks. It's OK as far as it goes, but are we going to solve global warming or ozone holes with computers, or just diagnose them that way? Are we going to reverse population growth through mathematical models, or just extrapolate the possibilities?

The key to solutions is awareness of what constitutes a healthy environment. You can't get that awareness staring into a glass tube lit by electricity generated someplace out of sight, out of mind (in our neighborhood by burning coal). You can't feel the complex relationships of air, water, plants and animals. No matter how sophisticated our technology gets, it will never be as intricate as the real thing. Would you like to make love to your computer? They're making great strides in "virtual reality," but....

Holly Near has a line in one of her songs, a song both political and environmental, "love disarms." Being disarmed is part of being aware. Disarmed, we become observers. We enlarge our receptiveness to the planet's needs to balance out our active manipulations of it. Awareness requires that we love wild ecosystems as much as ourselves—that we give them life and soul. That kind of awareness can't be taught by a computer.

Based on the questions Caile asks and the words and phrases she uses, we can infer Caile's point of view is that it's up to people, not computers, to help the environment. She appears to view the computer's role as very limited. Do you think Caile is reliable? Why or why not?

Professors Fuori and Gioia in their text *Computers and Information Processing*, 3rd ed., conclude their final chapter, "Computers Down the Road," with the following paragraphs. Read to find their point of view about computers and humans.

Whereas some computer experts believe that computers hold the key to great progress for the human race, others feel that computers will eventually lead to depersonalization, unemployment, an invasion of our privacy, and the nuclear destruction of our planet. While some are moving with the flow and striving to acquire computer knowledge and skills, others are laying back and hoping computer technology will not disrupt their lives too much.

As with any powerful scientific advancement, the computer can be a curse or a blessing. Historically, human beings have never reached a new level of technological advancement and deemed it too dangerous to use. Despite its destructive capabilities, there is little chance that we will ever ban the use of nuclear energy; similarly, it looks as though computers are here to stay. But is it the computer we should fear? Or is it the nature of those who would harness its power for good or evil? As always, it is not the *tool* but the *tool user* that must be monitored.

One of the goals of artificial intelligence research is to help us determine how we think, why we interpret as we do, and ultimately, who we are. We humans have been perplexed by our existence since earliest history. By providing us with a clearer understanding of the human mental process, perhaps AI research may eventually lead us to a better understanding of self. As was once said many years ago, "The answer lies within."

Fuori and Gioia present two sides of the controversial technology issue: computers provide the key to success for humanity, versus computers provide the key to destruction of humanity. But because of the questions they ask in paragraph 2 and the words and phrases they use—it's not the tool (computer) but the tool user (human) that needs watching, and that possibly computer research will provide insight to a better humanity—we can infer their point of view is that computers do have a vital role. Do you think Fuori and Gioia are reliable? Why or why not?

PRACTICE: IDENTIFYING POINT OF VIEW

1. Cigarette smoking accelerates artery clogging and greatly increases the risk of death from coronary artery disease, heart attack, and stroke in the adult years. The incidence of cancer, chronic bronchitis, and emphysema also increases. (Greenberg and Dintiman, *Exploring Health*)

     a. What is Greenberg and Dintiman's point of view on smoking?

     b. What point of view might a representative of the tobacco industry have?

     c. Assume that you have to write a research paper on the effects of smoking. Why would it be necessary to read more than one source for your research? List three types of sources you would consult.

2. As long as Americans spend more time watching [TV] than reading, educators must address the need for critical viewing as well as critical reading. If readers are trained to read interpretively, so too must viewers be taught to look critically at TV. And if we succeed with this teaching, we'll have changed the present pattern in which 70 percent of what Americans hear in a political campaign consists of thirty- and sixty-second commercials consisting of half-truths and innuendo....

     As E. B. White noted a half century ago, television is "the test of the modern world." Used correctly, it can inform, entertain and inspire. Used incorrectly, television will control families and communities, limiting our language, dreams, and achievements. It is our "test" to pass or fail. (Trelease, "Television")

     a. What is Trelease's point of view on current television viewing habits?

     b. Who might have a different point of view about the effects of television?

     c. What is your point of view about the effects of television?

3. New scientific advances promise to multiply future food yields. Biotechnology offers genetically altered crops that can be custom designed to fit the environment, produce bountiful harvests, and resist plant diseases. One bacterial gene eliminates the need for chemicals to

kill worms by producing a natural protein that disintegrates the worms' digestive system. Genetically engineered viruses can be used as pesticides. In 1988 scientists mapped the genome of rice—the set of 12 chromosomes that carries all the genetic characteristics of rice. This development could enable geneticists to produce improved strains of rice. Biotechnology can replace chemical pesticides and fertilizers, whose biological or even genetic impact on our own bodies is not fully understood. (Bergman and McKnight, *Introduction to Geography*)

> a. What is Bergman and McKnight's point of view about the impact of biotechnology?
>
> b. What point of view might a person who prefers health foods or natural foods have?
>
> c. What point of view might a representative of a pesticide company have?

WHICH INFORMATION IS FACT AND WHICH IS OPINION?

An author can use facts, opinions, or a combination of facts and opinions to support his or her point of view. A fact is an objective statement that can be proved true or false. A fact can be verified—no matter where you look or whom you ask, the information is the same. Examples of facts include:

> In the mid-1800s the work of Louis Pasteur and others revealed that epidemic diseases were caused by microorganisms.
>
> A lobbyist is a person hired by an individual, interest group, company, or industry to represent its interests with government officials.

An opinion is a subjective statement that cannot be proved true or false. An opinion cannot be verified; the information can change depending on where you look or whom you ask. An opinion is not true or false, right or wrong, or good or bad. But depending on the amount and type of evidence the author considered before forming the opinion, his or her opinion can be valid or invalid. Sometimes an author will evaluate a significant amount of information and offer an opinion that helps your understanding of the topic. Just remember it is an opinion. Examples of opinions include:

> Louis Pasteur made the most significant contributions to the world of medicine of any scientist in history.
>
> Lobbyists are the primary cause of problems in the government today.

As a reader, you can have confidence in facts and valid opinions. You need to be skeptical of invalid opinions.

PRACTICE: DISTINGUISHING BETWEEN FACT AND OPINION

Indicate whether a sentence is fact, opinion, or contains both facts and opinions.

1. [1]In managing the planning process, more and more firms have adopted a management by objectives (MBO) approach. [2]MBO is a system of collaborative goal setting that extends from the top of the organization to the bottom. [3]Under this system, managers meet with

each of their subordinates individually to discuss goals. [4]This meeting usually occurs annually and focuses on the coming year. [5]The manager and the subordinate agree on a set of goals for the subordinate. [6]The goals are stated in quantitative terms (for example, "I will decrease turnover in my division by 3 percent") and written down. [7]A year later, the subordinate's performance is evaluated in terms of the extent to which the goals were met. [8]MBO has been shown to be quite effective when applied at all levels of the company. [9]Tenneco, Black & Decker, General Motors, General Foods, and Alcoa have all reported success using MBO. [10]However, MBO involves quite a bit of paperwork and is sometimes used too rigidly. (Griffin and Ebert, *Business*, 2nd ed.)

2. [1]A major federal program aimed at identifying and cleaning up existing waste sites was initiated by the Comprehensive Environmental Response, Compensation, and Liability Act of 1980, popularly known as Superfund. [2]Through a tax on chemical raw materials, this legislation provided a fund of 1.6 billion over the period 1980–1985 to identify and clean up sites that posed a threat to groundwater. [3]However, the Environmental Protection Agency's (EPA's) record in administering this program over the first five years was disgraceful. (Nebel, *Environmental Science*, 3rd ed.)

WHAT IS TONE?

As noted in Chapter 3, words by themselves don't have much meaning. The words "I don't care" can be a simple phrase meaning "I just don't have a preference," or a complex of emotions translated from "you've made me so angry it doesn't matter." If you misunderstand the meaning, you can be in big trouble. But how do you know which meaning to select?

You know the intended meaning when you put the words into a context. Part of that context is the tone—the emotional feeling or attitude we create with our words. Tone is one indication of an author's point of view. When you're talking with someone you identify tone by listening to the pitch and volume of his or her voice, and watching gestures and facial expressions. Using these clues, you determine if someone is being serious or humorous, straightforward, or ironic. And knowing that helps you understand their meaning.

WHAT KINDS OF TONE DO AUTHORS USE?

Like a speaker, a writer can create any emotion. In some of your reading assignments you may need to narrowly define the author's tone—e.g., decide whether the tone is funny, witty, whimsical, or comical. However, most of the time you can place the tone of the writing into one of eight general groupings.

GENERAL TYPES OF TONE

	GENERAL DESCRIPTION OF TONE	*SIMILAR TYPES OF TONE*
straightforward	objective; without bias	honest, objective, fair
ironic	means opposite of what it says	contradictory, paradoxical
serious	very thoughtful and sincere	solemn, dignified
humorous	intended to be enjoyable	funny, joking, amusing, comical
emotional	subjective: with strong feeling	passionate, sympathetic, fervent
positive	confident and up-beat attitude	optimistic, enthusiastic, hopeful
negative	skeptical and gloomy attitude	cynical, angry, grim, pessimistic
sarcastic	witty, biting humor	satire, mockery, acerbic

HOW DO WORDS AND DETAILS CHANGE TONE?

Although you don't have a speaker's verbal or visual clues available when you are reading, you can understand the author's tone by paying attention to the words and details the author chooses to use or chooses to leave out. Using these clues, along with what the author says directly and your own knowledge, will help you correctly infer the author's tone.

Read to determine the author's tone in these paragraphs. How does the author want you to feel about the person being described? What elements contribute to the differences?

Description A: He had apparently not shaved for several days and his face and hands were covered with dirt. His shoes were torn and his coat, which was several sizes too small for him, was spotted with dried mud.

Description B: Although his face was bearded and neglected, his eyes were clear and he looked straight ahead as he walked rapidly down the road. He looked very tall; perhaps the fact that his coat was too small for him emphasized that impression. He was carrying two books snugly under his left arm and a small terrier puppy ran at his heels.

Both paragraphs could be describing the same man but the words and details the author has chosen present two very different impressions of the man. Notice how the negatives in Description A (unshaven, coat too small) have been reworded and turned into assets in Description B. Also, leaving out details (like torn shoes) and adding details like the books and the puppy in Description B contributes to the different tone.

WHAT IS AN IRONIC TONE?

Recognizing tone is especially important when an author doesn't intend for the reader to take his or her words literally. If you don't realize that the author is being ironic—saying the opposite of what he or she means—you misinterpret the message.

For example, consider this portion of a scientist's presentation to his colleagues. If they take his words literally and follow his principles of good writing, will they be good writers? What clues does he provide to let you know that he is deliberately saying the opposite of his real message?

The Principles of Good Writing

Write hurriedly, preferably when tired. Have no plans; write down items as they occur to you. The article will thus be spontaneous and poor. Hand in your manuscript the moment it is finished. Rereading a few days later might lead to revision—which seldom, if ever, makes the writing worse. If you submit your manuscript to colleagues (a bad practice), pay no attention to their criticisms or comments. Later, resist any editorial suggestions. Be strong and infallible; don't let anyone break down your personality. The critic may be trying to help you or he may have an ulterior motive, but the chance of his causing improvement in your writing is so great that you must be on guard.

The scientist's title tells us that his purpose is to give information on techniques for good writing. But, when his first details—e.g., writing hurriedly, when tired, and without plans—seem to contradict what you know about good writing practices, you begin to question his real meaning. Then, in his third sentence when he actually says his advice will lead to a poor article—the opposite of his stated purpose—you know that he's being ironic. Rather than just listing the practices of good writing, he used a bit of ironic humor to make his point.

WHAT KIND OF TONE ARE SATIRE AND SARCASM?

Satire and the more caustic sarcasm often use ironic statements to poke fun at people and deride foolish or dishonest human behaviors. Satire and sarcasm make use of ridicule, mockery, exaggeration, and understatement. This type of biting humor is used by cartoonists like Doonesbury's Gary Trudeau and comedians on shows like *Saturday Night Live*. When you're reading a cartoon or watching one of these comedy shows and you understand the words but don't understand that they are making fun of the politician or the movie star, you miss the point and the humor. You also miss the point when you don't understand that an author is using satire or sarcasm. Analyze the words and details an author uses as clues to tone.

Veteran Chicago columnist Mike Royko is known for his acerbic style. He begins his jab at trendy public television viewing habits this way in a 1985 column. Look for words and details Royko uses as clues to his sarcasm in the following selection—"Work the Bugs Out, Channel 11."

WORK THE BUGS OUT, CHANNEL 11

MIKE ROYKO

A friend of mine asked if I had seen some wonderful television show recently presented on the public channel. When I told him that I hardly ever watch that channel, he looked amazed.

"You don't watch public TV?" he said, "But that's the only station that shows anything of *quality*."

That's what everybody always says. If you want to see thoughtful drama or fine music shows with deep social significance, you are supposed to watch public TV.

Well, maybe they have such shows, but they're never on there when I turn my set on. No matter when I turn my set on, all I ever see is one of four shows:

1. Insects making love. Or maybe they are murdering each other. With insects it's hard to tell the difference. But after a day's work, my idea of fun isn't watching a couple of bugs with six furry legs and one eye trying to give each other hickies.

2. A lion walking along with a dead antelope in its jaws. I don't know how many times I've seen that same mangy lion dragging that poor antelope into a bush. The tourist bureau in Africa must bring him out every time a TV crew shows up. But the question is, why do they keep showing it? Does somebody at the channel think that we must be taught that lions don't eat pizza?

3. Some spiffily dressed, elderly Englishman sitting in a tall-backed chair in a room that is paneled in dark wood. He is speaking to a younger Englishman who wears a WWI uniform and stands before a crackling fire. The older bloke says things like: "Well Ralph, see you're back from the front. Jolly good you weren't killed. Sorry to hear about your brother. Bloody bad luck, that. Shell took his head clean off. Oh, well, we must go on. Will you be joining us for dinner?" And the younger man says: "Thank you, Father."

(CONTINUED)

WORK THE BUGS OUT, CHANNEL 11 (CONTINUED)

4. The station announcer, talking about what great shows they have on Channel 11. The last time I tuned in, he talked about it for so long that I dozed off. When I awoke, he was talking about how great the show had been. Before I could get to the dial, two insects started making love again.

That's it. That's all I ever see on public TV.
Wait, I forgot. There are a couple of others. Some skinny, bearded, squeaky-voiced, wimpy guy from Seattle does a cooking show....

If you read only the words written by Royko, you miss the message; you must infer—read between the lines—to determine what he means by what he says. For any form of wit or humor like irony, satire, or sarcasm to be effective, the reader must clearly understand the author's intended message, not just the words he or she uses.

PRACTICE: IDENTIFYING TONE

1. There are those who believe that a rapidly advancing computer technology exhibits little regard for the future of the human race. They contend that computers are overused, misused, and generally detrimental to society. This group argues that the computer is dehumanizing and is slowly forcing society into a pattern of mass conformity. To be sure, the computer revolution is presenting society with complex problems, but they can be overcome. (Long, *Introduction to Computers and Information Systems*)

    a. What is Dr. Long's point of view about computers?

    b. Would you describe Dr. Long's tone as optimistic or cynical? Why?

2. Donald Trump had not granted an interview or smirked into a camera in nearly a month. It was his longest media dry spell since 1986— when he started taking reporters on grand tours aboard his black Puma helicopter, laying claim to the Manhattan-to-Atlantic City landscape with a lordly wave of his hand. At forty-four, despite almost daily, banner-headlined catastrophes since the beginning of 1990, he was still willing to play posterboy, and a birthday was a great photo opportunity. So, after weeks of hiding from a suddenly carnivorous press, he decided to surface at a birthday blast organized by his casino dependents. With his golden hair backing up beneath his starched collar, a wounded half smile on his silent lips, and perfectly protected by his ever-present blue pinstriped suit, the icon of the eighties— slowed in the first six months of the new decade to an uncertain pace—worked his way out onto a Boardwalk blanketed by a mid-June haze. (Barrett, *Trump: The Deals and the Downfall*)

    a. What is Barrett's point of view about Trump?

    b. How would you describe Barrett's tone? Why?

3. One of the strongest barriers to good thinking, then, is fear. Fear may show itself as anger, envy, selfishness, or hatred, but these are just

expressions of our fear. And don't underrate the power of such emotions. History has shown what devastation fear and hatred among nations can wreak. Our personal fears can be just as damaging to our inner world, blinding our critical faculties with their dark energies. When we argue, then, we must be aware of what we feel as well as what we think. A good critical thinker may have to scrutinize not only the intellectual character of an argument, but its emotional temperature as well. (White, *Discovering Philosophy*)

    a. What is White's point of view about the impact of fear?

    b. How would you describe White's tone? Why?

CHAPTER 6 REVIEW QUESTIONS

1. What is the author's stance?

2. What does the word *reliable* mean? Why is it difficult to determine if an author is reliable?

3. What is point of view? How can you recognize an author's point of view?

4. What is a fact? What is an opinion?

5. What is tone?

6. What are strategies for recognizing tone?

CHAPTER 6 THINK AND CONNECT QUESTIONS

7. Reread "Nutrition for the '90s," Chapter 1, Exercise #1, pages 10–11.

    a. Do you consider the author to be knowledgeable and reliable? Why or why not?

    b. What is the author's point of view and tone?

    c. Does the author use primarily facts or opinions? Give examples to support your answer.

    d. Does this analysis change your view of the author's message? Why or why not?

8. Make a list of the following:

    things you have bought recently (like shoes, jeans, cereal, a car)

    things you have done recently (such as gone to a movie, drunk a soft drink, voted)

    views you have adopted (such as for or against abortion, for or against nuclear energy, for or against affirmative action)

Can you identify what you saw or read that influenced you to buy, do, or believe? Did you realize you were being influenced? What types of thing will you watch for in the future?

CHAPTER 6 APPLICATION EXERCISES

9. Using the topic "getting older," write a humorous paragraph and then a serious paragraph. Notice how you can make the change easily by the type of words, details, and punctuation you use.

10. Using the primary reading materials (texts, journals, etc.) in each of

your classes, determine the authors' general tone and point of view. Also, investigate their backgrounds and evaluate their expertise and reliability.

USE YOUR STRATEGIES: EXERCISE #1—"EXECUTION HAS BENEFITS—DOESN'T IT?"

E. J. Montini's column appears daily in the *Arizona Republic*. He writes on social and political issues and their effect on people. This selection— "Execution Has Benefits—Doesn't It?"—is from the *Arizona Republic*.

EXECUTION HAS BENEFITS—DOESN'T IT?

E. J. MONTINI

[1]Now that Don Harding is dead, now that we've killed him, it's time to *reap* the rewards, to count up the ways we're benefiting from his death. There must be plenty.

[2]Two days ago, the convicted murderer was alive and in prison. Today, he's dead. He was killed at our expense. In our name. By us. Which means we must have thought it was important to kill him. We must have believed there were benefits in it for us.

[3]Like, for instance, safety.

[4]Maybe we're safer today than we were Sunday, when Harding was still alive.

[5]No, that's not it.

[6]Harding was in a maximum-security prison cell Sunday, as he had been every day for the past 10 years. We were as safe from him then, while he was alive, as we are from him now.

[7]It must be something else. There must be some other benefit to having strapped Harding into a chair in a tiny room and filled the space with poison gas. It took him about 10 minutes to die.

$16,000 to Keep Him Alive

[8]How about money?

[9]Some people say that killing Harding saved us a lot of money. It was costing us $16,000 a year to keep him alive, and we no longer have to spend the cash. That's the benefit, right?

[10]Wrong.

[11]Our efforts to kill Harding (and anyone else on death row) probably cost us more than it would have cost to keep him in prison for life. In fact, several states have *abolished* the death penalty partly because it costs so much.

[12]It must be something else.

[13]There must be some other *extremely beneficial* reason for standing by calmly as the tiny capillaries in Harding's lungs were exploded by the cyanide gas, filling his chest with blood. Drowning him from the inside.

[14]Maybe we figured that, if we execute Harding, others will think twice before killing. That would be nice.

[15]Too bad it's not true. Not even those who foam at the mouth at the thought of executing people, like *high-profile proponent* Arizona Attorney General Grant Woods, believe the death penalty is a *deterrent*. Studies in states that execute people—as we now do—show that it's not, that murder rates don't go down.

[16]It must be something else.

We Don't Kill All Murderers

[17]I know. Everyone says there's a benefit to the families of the victims. We kill people like Harding for them. So the families can get revenge.

(CONTINUED)

EXECUTION HAS BENEFITS—DOESN'T IT? (CONTINUED)

[18]What about other cases, though?

[19]There are hundreds of inmates in Arizona prisons who have killed people. Yet there are only 99 on death row. We don't kill all murderers, even though the families of all victims suffer the same loss.

[20]We're willing to kill 100 but not 1,000. Killing 1,000 would be considered *too barbaric*, wouldn't it? A little death goes a long way.

[21]Still, the fact that we don't kill all murderers proves we're really not interested in satisfying the revenge of all victims' families.

[22]If there's a benefit to having killed Harding, it must be something else.

[23]Like the fact that it freed up a prison cell. That's something. We might say there's now room for one more criminal in Arizona prisons.

[24]Except, unfortunately, there isn't. The prisons already contain about 1,000 more inmates than they're designed to handle. Killing one or two people won't help. We'd have to kill a thousand or so, and, like I said, we don't have the stomach for that.

[25]So, it must be something else.

[26]Maybe the benefit we got from killing Harding is *less tangible*. Maybe we killed him only to prove, as Attorney General Woods likes to say, that "justice is being served."

[27]In other words, to send a message. To teach a lesson.

[28]That must be it. The execution was a lesson. Our children, I figure, will learn something by it. They'll find out we're willing to strap a man down, poison him, then stand around and watch him slowly and painfully die.

[29]That's the benefit.

[30]The boys and girls we sent to bed Sunday night, before the killing, eventually will learn something very important from what we did. They'll learn what type of people their parents really are.

EXERCISE #1 QUESTIONS—"EXECUTION HAS BENEFITS—DOESN'T IT?"

1. What is Montini's purpose?
2. What is his thesis?
3. What is Montini's point of view on the death penalty?
4. What is his tone?
5. How does his tone relate to his point of view and/or bias?
6. Do you think he has the knowledge to write this article? Why or why not?
7. Do you think he is reliable? Why or why not?
8. Do you think anything could cause him to change his point of view?
9. Define these words or phrases as used by Montini:

   reap (¶1)

   abolished (¶11)

   extremely beneficial (¶13)

   high-profile proponent (¶15)

   deterrent (¶15)

   too barbaric (¶20)

   less tangible (¶26)

10. What event happened to make Montini write this column?
11. How and where was Harding killed?

12. Montini lists and discounts five "benefits" of Harding's execution. Name them.
13. What is the "benefit" that Montini decides "must be it"? Does he really think it is a benefit?
14 Montini says that children will "learn what type of people their parents really are." What does he mean?
15. Do you agree or disagree with Montini? Why or why not?
16. If you wanted to get more information on the death penalty, list three places you would likely find more information.

USE YOUR STRATEGIES: EXERCISE #2—"U.S. KIDS NEED MORE SCHOOL TIME"

Ellen Goodman is a nationally syndicated columnist known for her writings on American social and political issues. This column—"U.S. Kids Need More School Time"—was written in the summer of 1990. This selection is from *The Boston Globe*.

U.S. KIDS NEED MORE SCHOOL TIME

ELLEN GOODMAN

[1] The kids are hanging out. I pass small bands of once-and-future students on my way to work these mornings. They have become a familiar part of the summer landscape

[2] These kids are not old enough for jobs. Nor are they rich enough for camp. They are school children without school. The calendar called the school year ran out on them a few weeks ago. Once supervised by teachers and principals, they now appear to be in "*self care*." Like others who fall through the cracks of their parents' makeshift plans—a week with relatives, a day at the playground—they hang out.

[3] Passing them is like passing through a time zone. For much of our history, after all, Americans framed the school year around the needs of work and family. In 19th-century cities, schools were open seven or eight hours a day, 11 months a year. In *rural America*, the year was arranged around the growing season. Now, only 3 percent of families follow the agricultural model, but nearly all schools are scheduled as if our children went home early to milk the cows and took months off to work the crops. Now, three-quarters of the mothers of school-age children work, but the calendar is written as if they were home waiting for the school bus.

[4] The six-hour day, the 180-day school year is regarded as somehow *sacrosanct*. But when parents work an eight-hour day and a 240-day year, it means something different. It means that many kids go home to empty houses. It means that, in the summer, they hang out.

[5] "We have a huge *mismatch* between the school calendar and the realities of family life," says Dr. Ernest Boyer, head of the Carnegie Foundation for the Advancement of Teaching.

[6] Dr. Boyer is one of many who believe that a *radical revision* of the school calendar is *inevitable*. "School, whether we like it or not, is *custodial* and educational. It always has been."

[7] His is not a popular idea. Schools are routinely burdened with the job of solving all our social problems. Can they be asked now to *synchronize* our work and family lives?

(CONTINUED)

U.S. KIDS NEED MORE SCHOOL TIME (CONTINUED)

⁸It may be easier to promote a longer school year on its educational merits and, indeed, the educational case is *compelling*. Despite the complaints and studies about our kids' lack of learning, the United States still has a shorter school year than any industrial nation. In most of Europe, the school year is 220 days. In Japan, it is 240 days long. While classroom time alone doesn't produce a well-educated child, learning takes time and more learning takes more time. The long summers of forgetting take a toll.

⁹The opposition to a longer school year comes from families that want to and can provide other experiences for their children. It comes from teachers. It comes from tradition. And surely from kids. But the *crux of the conflict* has been over money.

¹⁰But we can, as Boyer suggests, begin to turn the hands of the school clock forward. The first step is to extend an optional after-school program of education and recreation to every district. The second step is a summer program with its own staff, paid for by fees for those who can pay and *vouchers* for those who can't.

¹¹The third step will be the hardest: a true overhaul of the school year. Once, school was carefully *calibrated* to arrange children's schedules around the edges of family needs. Now, working parents, especially mothers, even teachers, try and blend their work lives around the edges of the school day.

¹²So it's back to the future. Today there are too many school doors locked and too many kids hanging out. It's time to get our calendars updated.

EXERCISE #2 QUESTIONS—"U.S. KIDS NEED MORE SCHOOL TIME"

1. Who is the author?
2. What is the author's purpose?
3. What is the author's thesis?
4. What major reasons does the author use to support her thesis?
5. What is the author's tone?
6. What is the author's point of view?
7. Do you feel the author has the knowledge to write this article? Why or why not?
8. Do you feel the author is reliable? Why or why not?
9. Define these words or phrases as used by the author:
    - a. self care (¶2)
    - b. rural America (¶3)
    - c. sacrosanct (¶4)
    - d. mismatch (¶5)
    - e. radical revision (¶6)
    - f. inevitable (¶6)
    - g. custodial (¶6)
    - h. synchronize (¶7)
    - i. compelling (¶8)
    - j. crux of the conflict (¶9)
    - k. vouchers (¶10)
    - l. calibrated (¶11)

10. Around what has the school year been built for much of our history?

11. How long was the typical school year of nineteenth-century cities?

12. Why is there a mismatch between the school calendar and the realities of twentieth-century family life?

13. Which industrialized nation has the shortest school year?

14. What three groups or things, according to Goodman, are against a longer school year?

15. What does she say is the biggest obstacle to a longer school year?

16. Who is Dr. Ernest Boyer? What is his point of view?

17. What are Boyer's three steps to changing the school calendar?

18. What do you think is one major advantage of a longer school year? What do you think is one major disadvantage of a longer school year?

19. Do you agree or disagree with Goodman? Why?

20. If you wanted to get more information on changing the school calendar, list three places you would likely find more information.

USE YOUR STRATEGIES: EXERCISE #3—"WHAT DO YOU MEAN YOU DON'T LIKE MY STYLE?"

Mr. Fielden is a professor of management communication at the University of Alabama. He has been an associate editor at Harvard Business Review and dean of the business schools at Boston University and the University of Alabama. As managing partner of Fielden Associates, he has consulted on management communication with many of the nation's leading corporations. This selection—"What Do You Mean You Don't Like My Style?"—is the seventh article he has written for *Harvard Business Review*.

WHAT DO YOU MEAN YOU DON'T LIKE MY STYLE?

JOHN S. FIELDEN

Introduction

What you say in a letter or a memorandum is partly how you say it. Your message—your real intentions—can get lost in your words. Seeing the whole message a communication can convey is more than understanding the dictionary definitions of the words you choose. It is also discerning the intentions and emphases and relationships reflected in the connotations of those words and the sentence structures you use. Writing an effective letter is far more than stating the basic message you wish to give to someone. It is also conveying how you wish to relate to the recipient and what you want him or her to feel in response. And that's important because it may determine what the reader does about the message.

You convey these additional meanings through the style you choose to write with. There is no single style for all occasions. Sometimes it's tactful to be personal, and sometimes it's best to be fairly impersonal. At times it feels right to be simple and direct, and at other times roundabout and colorful. Sometimes you just need to be forceful. One thing is sure: strategy is part of style. The message you want to send is partly in your tone. Any message varies according to the way you phrase it.

The [following material] describes six styles that you will find appropriate for various writing situations in business.

(CONTINUED)

WHAT DO YOU MEAN YOU DON'T LIKE MY STYLE? (CONTINUED)

In large corporations all over the country, people are playing a game of paddleball—with drafts of letters instead of balls. Volley after volley goes back and forth between those who sign the letters and those who actually write them. It's a game nobody likes, but it continues, and we pay for it. The workday has no extra time for such unproductiveness. What causes this round robin of revision?

Typos? Factual misstatements? Poor format? No. *Style* does. Ask yourself how often you hear statements like these:

> "It takes new assistants about a year to learn my style. Until they do, I have no choice but to bounce letters back for revision. I won't sign a letter if it doesn't sound like me."

> "I find it difficult, almost impossible, to write letters for my boss's signature. The boss's style is different from mine."

In companies where managers primarily write their own letters, confusion about style also reigns. Someone sends out a letter and hears later that the reaction was not at all the one desired. It is reported that the reader doesn't like the writer's "tone." A colleague looks over a copy of the letter and says, "No wonder the reader doesn't like this letter. You shouldn't have said things the way you did. You used the wrong style for a letter like this." "Style?" the writer says. "What's wrong with my style?" "I don't know" is the response. "I just don't like the way you said things."

Everybody talks about style, but almost nobody understands the meaning of the word in the business environment. And this lack of understanding hurts both those who write letters for another's signature and those who write for themselves. Neither knows where to turn for help. Strunk and White's marvelous book *The Elements of Style* devotes only a few pages to a discussion of style, and that concerns only literary style. Books like the *Chicago Manual of Style* seem to define style as all the technical points they cover, from abbreviations and capitalizations to footnotes and bibliographies. And dictionary definitions are usually too vague to be helpful.

Even such a general definition as this offers scant help, although perhaps it comes closest to how business people use the word:

> Style is "the way something is said or done, as distinguished from its substance." (*The American Heritage Dictionary of the English Language*)

Managers signing drafts written by subordinates, and the subordinates themselves, already know that they have trouble agreeing on "the way things should be said." What, for instance, is meant by "way"? In trying to find that way, both managers and subordinates are chasing a will-o'-the-wisp. There *is* no magical way, no perfect, universal way of writing things that will fend off criticism of style. There is no one style of writing in business that is appropriate in all situations and for all readers, even though managers and subordinates usually talk and behave as if there were.

But why all the confusion? Isn't style really the way we say things? Certainly it is. Then writing style must be made up of the particular words we select to express our ideas and the types of sentences and paragraphs we put together to convey those ideas. What else could it be? Writing has no tone of voice or body gesture to impart additional meanings. In written communication, tone comes from what a reader reads into the words and sentences used.

Words express more than *denotations*, the definitions found in dictionaries. They also carry *connotations*. In the feelings and images associated with each word lies the capacity a writing style has for producing an emotional reaction in a reader. And in that capacity lies the tone of a piece of writing. Style is largely a matter of tone. The writer uses a style; the reader infers a communication's tone. Tone comes from what a reader reads into the words and sentences a writer uses.

In the business environment, tone is especially important. Business writing is not literary writing. Literary artists use unique styles to "express" themselves to a general audience. Business people write to particular persons in particular situations, not so much to express themselves as to accomplish particular purposes, "to get a job done." If a reader doesn't like a novelist's tone, nothing much can happen to the writer short of failing to sell some books. In the business situation, however, an offensive style may not only prevent a sale but may also turn away a customer, work against a promotion, or even cost you a job.

(CONTINUED)

WHAT DO YOU MEAN YOU DON'T LIKE MY STYLE? (CONTINUED)

While style can be distinguished from substance, it cannot be divorced from substance. In business writing, style cannot be divorced from the circumstances under which something is written or from the likes, dislikes, position, and power of the reader.

A workable definition of style in business writing would be something like this:

Style is that choice of words, sentences, and paragraph format which by virtue of being appropriate to the situation and to the power positions of both writer and reader produces the desired reaction and result.

Which Style Is Yours?

Let's take a case and see what we can learn from it. Assume that you are an executive in a very large information-processing company. You receive the following letter:

Mr. (Ms.) Leslie J. Cash
XYZ Corporation
Main Street
Anytown, U.S.A.

Dear Leslie:

As you know, I respect your professional opinion highly. The advice your people have given us at ABC Corporation as we have moved into a comprehensive information system over the past three years has been very helpful. I'm writing to you now, however, in my role as chairman of the executive committee of the trustees of our hospital. We at Community General Hospital have decided to establish a skilled volunteer data processing evaluation team to assess proposals to automate our hospital's information flow.

I have suggested your name to my committee. I know you could get real satisfaction from helping your community as a member of this evaluation team. Please say yes. I look forward to being able to count on your advice. Let me hear from you soon.

Frank J. Scalpel
Chairman
Executive Committee
Community General Hospital
Anytown, U.S.A.

If you accepted the appointment mentioned in this letter, you would have a conflict of interest. You are an executive at XYZ, Inc. You know that XYZ will submit a proposal to install a comprehensive information system for the hospital. Mr. Scalpel is the vice president of finance at ABC Corp., a very good customer of yours. You know him well since you have worked with him on community programs as well as in the business world.

I can think of four typical responses to Scalpel's letter. Each says essentially the same thing, but each is written in a different business style:

(CONTINUED)

WHAT DO YOU MEAN YOU DON'T
LIKE MY STYLE? (CONTINUED)

Response 1

Mr. Frank J. Scalpel
Chairman, Executive Committee
Community General Hospital
Anytown, U.S.A.

Dear Frank,

As you realize, this litigious age often makes it necessary for large companies to take stringent measures not only to avoid conflicts of interest on the part of their employees but also to preclude even the very suggestion of conflict. And, since my company intends to submit a proposal with reference to automating the hospital's information flow, it would not appear seemly for me to be part of an evaluation team assessing competitors' proposals. Even if I were to excuse myself from consideration of the XYZ proposal, I would still be vulnerable to charges that I gave short shrift to competitors' offerings.

If there is any other way that I can serve the committee that will not raise this conflict-of-interest specter, you know that I would find it pleasurable to be of service, as always.

Sincerely,

Response 2

Dear Frank,

Your comments relative to your respect for my professional opinion are most appreciated. Moreover, your invitation to serve on the hospital's data processing evaluation team is received with gratitude, albeit with some concern.

The evaluation team must be composed of persons free of alliance with any of the vendors submitting proposals. For that reason, it is felt that my services on the team could be construed as a conflict of interest.

Perhaps help can be given in some other way. Again, please be assured that your invitation has been appreciated.

Sincerely,

Response 3

Dear Frank,

Thank you for suggesting my name as a possible member of your data processing evaluation team. I wish I could serve, but I cannot.

XYZ intends, naturally, to submit a proposal to automate the hospital's information flow. You can see the position of conflict I would be in if I were on the evaluation team.

Just let me know of any other way I can be of help. You know I would be more than willing. Thanks again for the invitation.

Cordially,

(CONTINUED)

WHAT DO YOU MEAN YOU DON'T LIKE MY STYLE? (CONTINUED)

Response 4

Dear Frank,

Thanks for the kind words and the invitation. Sure wish I could say yes. Can't, though.

XYZ intends to submit a sure-fire proposal on automating the hospital's information. Shouldn't be judge and advocate at the same time!

Any other way I can help, Frank—just ask. Thanks again.

Cordially,

What Do You Think of These Letters?

Which letter has the style you like best? Check off the response you prefer.

Response   __ 1   __ 2   __ 3   __ 4

Which letter has the style resembling the one you customarily use? Again, check off your choice.

Response   __ 1   __ 2   __ 3   __ 4

Which terms best describe the style of each letter? Check the appropriate boxes.

Response 1	__ Colorful __ Passive __ Personal __ Dull __ Forceful __ Impersonal
Response 2	__ Colorful __ Passive __ Personal __ Dull __ Forceful __ Impersonal
Response 3	__ Colorful __ Passive __ Personal __ Dull __ Forceful __ Impersonal
Response 4	__ Colorful __ Passive __ Personal __ Dull __ Forceful __ Impersonal

Let's Compare Reactions

Now that you've given your reactions, let's compare them with some of mine.

Response 1 seems cold, impersonal, complex. Most business people would, I think, react somewhat negatively to this style because it seems to push the reader away from the writer. Its word choice has a cerebral quality that, while flattering to the reader's intelligence, also parades the writer's.

Response 2 is fairly cool, quite impersonal, and somewhat complex. Readers' reactions will probably be neither strongly positive nor strongly negative. This style of writing is "blah" because it is heavily passive. Instead of saying "I appreciate your comments," it says "Your comments are most appreciated"; instead of "I think that my services could be construed as a conflict of interest," it says "It is felt that my services could be construed…." The use of the passive voice subordinates writers modestly to the back of sentences or causes them to disappear.

This is the impersonal, passive style of writing that many with engineering, mathematics, or scientific backgrounds feel most comfortable using. It is harmless, but it is certainly not colorful; nor is it forceful or interesting.

(CONTINUED)

WHAT DO YOU MEAN YOU DON'T LIKE MY STYLE? (CONTINUED)

Response 3 illustrates the style of writing that most high-level executives use. It is simple; it is personal; it is warm without being syrupy; it is forceful, like a firm handshake. Almost everybody in business likes this style, although lower-level managers often find themselves afraid to write so forthrightly (and, as a result, often find themselves retreating into the styles of responses 1 and 2—the style of 1 to make themselves look "smart" to superiors and the style of 2 to appear unbossy and fairly impersonal). Persons who find response 2 congenial may feel a bit dubious about the appropriateness of response 3. (Although I have no way of proving this judgment, I would guess that more readers in high positions—perhaps more owner-managers—would like response 3 than would readers who are still in lower positions.)

Response 4 goes beyond being forceful; it is annoyingly self-confident and breezy. It is colorful and conversational to an extreme, and it is so intensely personal and warm that many business people would be offended, even if they were very close acquaintances of Frank Scalpel's. "It sounds like an advertising person's chitchat," some would probably say.

Strategy Is Part of Style

As you compared your responses with mine, did you say, "What difference does it make which style *I* like or which most resembles *my* customary style? What matters is which style will go over best with Mr. Scalpel in this situation"? If you did, we're getting somewhere.

Earlier, when we defined business writing style, some may have wanted to add, "And that style should sound like me." This was left out for a good reason. Circumstances not only alter cases; they alter the "you" that it is wise for your style to project. Sometimes it's wise to be forceful; at other times it's suicidal. Sometime being sprightly and colorful is appropriate; at other times it's ludicrous. There are times to be personal and times to be impersonal.

Not understanding this matter of style and tone is why the big corporate game of paddleball between managers and subordinates goes on and on. The subordinate tries to imitate the boss's style, but in actuality—unless the boss is extremely insensitive—he or she has no single style for all circumstances and for all readers. What usually happens is that after several tries, the subordinate writes a letter that the boss signs. "Aha!" the subordinate says. "So that's what the boss wants!" And then the subordinate tries to use that style for all situations and readers. Later, the superior begins rejecting drafts written in the very style he or she professed liking before. Both parties throw up their hands.

This volleying is foolish and wasteful. Both superior and subordinate have to recognize that in business writing, style cannot be considered apart from the given situation or from the person to whom the writing is directed. Expert writers select the style that fits a particular reader and the type of writing situation with which they are faced. In business, people often face the following writing situations:

Positive situations:
Saving yes or conveying good news

Situations where some action is asked of the reader:
Giving orders or persuading someone to do as requested

Information-conveying situations:
Giving the price of ten widgets, for example

Negative situations:
Saying no or relaying bad news

In each of these situations, the choice of style is of strategic importance.

(CONTINUED)

WHAT DO YOU MEAN YOU DON'T LIKE MY STYLE? (CONTINUED)

In positive situations a writer can relax on all fronts. Readers are usually so pleased to hear the good news that they pay little attention to anything else. Yet it is possible for someone to communicate good news in such a cold, impersonal, roundabout, and almost begrudging way that the reader becomes upset.

Action-request situations involve a form of bargaining. In a situation where the writer holds all the power, he or she can use a forceful commanding style. When the writer holds no power over the reader, though, actions have to be asked for and the reader persuaded, not ordered. In such cases, a forceful style will not be suitable at all.

Information-conveying situations, getting the message across forcefully and straightforwardly is best. Such situations are not usually charged emotionally.

In negative situations, diplomacy becomes very important. The right style depends on the relative positions of the person saying no and the person being told no.

For instance, if you were Leslie Cash, the person in the example at the beginning of the article whom Frank Scalpel was inviting to serve on a hospital's evaluation team, you would be in a situation of having to say no to a very important customer of your company. You would also be in a doubly sensitive situation because it is unlikely that Mr. Scalpel would fail to recognize that he is asking you to enter a conflict-of-interest situation. He is probably asking you *anyway*. Therefore, you would not only have to tell him no, but you would have to avoid telling him that he has asked you to do something that is highly unethical. In this instance, you would be faced with communicating two negative messages at once or else not giving Scalpel any sensible reason for refusing to serve.

Suit Your Style to the Situation

Now that we've thought about the strategic implications of style, let's go back to look at each of the responses to Scalpel's request and ask ourselves which is best.

Do we *want* to be personal and warm? Usually yes. But in this situation? Do we want to communicate clearly and directly and forcefully? Usually yes. But here? Do we want to appear as if we're brushing aside the conflict, as the third response does? Or do we want to approach that issue long-windedly, as in the first response, or passively, as in the second? What is the strategically appropriate style?

In the abstract, we have no way of knowing which of these responses will go over best with Mr. Scalpel. The choice is a matter of judgment in a concrete situation. Judging the situation accurately is what separates successful from unsuccessful executive communicators.

Looking at the situation with strategy in mind, we note that in the first response, the writer draws back from being close, knowing that it is necessary to reject not only one but two of the reader's requests. By using legalistic phraseology and Latinate vocabulary, the writer lowers the personal nature of the communication and transforms it into a formal statement. It gives an abstract, textbooklike response that removes the tone of personal rejection.

The very fact that response 1 is difficult to read and dull in impact may be a strategic asset in this type of negative situation. But if in this situation a subordinate presented response 1 to you for your signature, would it be appropriate for you to reject it because it is not written in the style *you* happen to *like* best in the abstract—say, the style of response 3?

Now let's look at response 2. Again, we see that a lack of personal warmth may be quite appropriate to the situation at hand. Almost immediately, the letter draws back into impersonality. And by using the passive constantly, the writer avoids the need to say "I must say no." Furthermore, the term *construed* reinforces the passive in the second paragraph. This term is a very weak but possibly a strategically wise way of implying that *some* persons (*other* people, not the writer) could interpret Scalpel's request as an invitation to participate in an improper action. Now we can see that, instead of seeming dull and lacking in personal warmth as it did in the abstract, response 2 may be the type of letter we would be wise to send out, that is, when we have taken the whole situation into careful consideration and not just our personal likes and dislikes.

(CONTINUED)

WHAT DO YOU MEAN YOU DON'T LIKE MY STYLE? (CONTINUED)

The third response, and to even greater extent the fourth, have styles that are strategically inappropriate for this situation. In fact, Scalpel might well regard the colorful style of the fourth response as highly offensive. Both responses directly and forcefully point out the obvious conflict, but by being so direct each runs the risk of subtly offending him. (The third response is "you can see the position of conflict I'd be in if I were on the evaluation team," and the fourth is "Shouldn't be judge and advocate at the same time!") We could make a pretty strong argument that the direct, forceful, candid style of the third response and the breezy, warm, colorful, intensely personal "advertising" style of the fourth response may both prove ineffectual in a delicate, negative situation such as this.

What Effect Do You Want?

At this point, readers may say, "All right. I'm convinced. I need to adjust my style to what is appropriate in each situation. And I also need to give directions to others to let them know how to adjust their styles. But I haven't the foggiest notion of how to do either!" Some suggestions for varying your writing style follow. I am not implying that a communication must be written in one style only. A letter to be read aloud at a colleague's retirement party, for instance, may call not only for a warm, personal style but for colorfulness as well. A long analytic report may require a passive, impersonal style, but the persuasive cover letter may call for recommendations being presented in a very forceful style.

Forceful Style   This style is usually appropriate only in situations where the writer has the power, such as in action requests in the form of orders or when you are saying no firmly but politely to a subordinate.

Passive Style   This style is often appropriate in negative situations and in situations where the writer is in a lower position than the reader.

Personal Style   This style is usually appropriate in good-news and persuasive action-request situations.

Impersonal Style   This style is usually appropriate in negative and information-conveying situations. It's always appropriate in technical and scientific writing and usually when you are writing to technical readers.

Colorful Style   Sometimes a lively style is appropriate in good-news situations. It is most commonly found in the highly persuasive writing of advertisements and sales letters.

Less Colorful Style   By avoiding adjectives, adverbs, metaphors, and figures of speech, you can make your style less colorful. Such a style is appropriate for ordinary business writing.

Please bear in mind that these six styles are not mutually exclusive. There is some overlap. A passive style is usually far more impersonal than personal and also not very colorful. A forceful style is likely to be more personal than impersonal, and a colorful style is likely to be fairly forceful. Nevertheless, these styles are distinct enough to justify talking about them. If we fail to make such distinctions, style becomes a catchall term that means nothing specific. Even if not precise, these distinctions enable us to talk about style and its elements and to learn to write appropriately for each situation.

Discuss Needs First

What conclusions can we draw from this discussion? Simply that, whether you write your own letters or have to manage the writing of subordinates, to be an effective communicator, you must realize that:

(CONTINUED)

WHAT DO YOU MEAN YOU DON'T LIKE MY STYLE? (CONTINUED)

1. Each style has an impact on the reader.
2. Style communicates to readers almost as much as the content of a message.
3. Style cannot be isolated from a situation.
4. Generalizing about which style is the best in all situations is impossible.
5. Style must be altered to suit the circumstances.
6. Style must be discussed sensibly in the work situation.

These conclusions will be of obvious help to managers who write their own letters. But what help will these conclusions be to managers who direct assistants in the writing of letters? In many instances, writing assignments go directly to subordinates for handling. Often, manager and assistant have no chance to discuss style strategy together. In such cases, rather than merely submitting a response for a signature, the subordinate would be wise to append a note: e.g., "This is a very sensitive situation, I think. Therefore, I deliberately drew back into a largely impersonal and passive style." At least, the boss will not jump to the conclusion that the assistant has written a letter of low impact by accident.

When they do route writing assignments to assistants, superiors could save much valuable time and prevent mutual distress if they told the subordinates what style seemed strategically wise in each situation. Playing guessing games also wastes money.

And if, as is often the case, neither superior nor subordinate has a clear sense of what style is best, the two can agree to draft a response in one style first, and if that doesn't sound right, to adjust the style appropriately.

Those who write their own letters can try drafting several responses to tough but important situations, each in a different style. It's wise to sleep on them and then decide which sounds best.

Whether you write for yourself or for someone else, it is extremely unlikely that in difficult situations a first draft will be signed by you or anyone else. Only the amateur expects writing perfection on the first try. By learning to control your style and to engineer the tone of your communications, you can make your writing effective.

EXERCISE #3 QUESTIONS—"WHAT DO YOU MEAN YOU DON'T LIKE MY STYLE?"

1. What is Fielden's purpose?
2. What is Fielden's thesis?
3. How does Fielden develop and support his thesis?
4. What is Fielden's point of view on writing style?
5. What is Fielden's tone?
6. Do you think Fielden has the knowledge to write this article? Why or why not?
7. In the Introduction, Fielden says getting the whole message from a letter "...is also discerning the intentions and emphases and relationships reflected in the connotations of those words...." What does he mean?
8. What is Fielden's workable definition of style in business writing? Do you agree with it? Would you change it in any way?
9. What are the six conclusions Fielden says we can draw from his discussion of style?
10. In the last paragraph, Fielden says "Only the amateur expects writing perfection on the first try." What does he mean? Do you agree with him? Why or why not?

USE YOUR STRATEGIES: EXERCISE #4—"ENDORSEMENTS JUST A SHELL GAME"

The funny, acerbic syndicated columnist Mike Royko takes on any and all social and political issues in his daily column that appears in hundreds of newspapers daily. This selection—"Endorsements Just a Shell Game"—is from *Dr. Kookie You're Right*.

ENDORSEMENTS JUST A SHELL GAME

MIKE ROYKO

[1]The man from an advertising agency had an unusual proposition.

[2]His agency does the TV commercials for a well-known chain of Mexican restaurants in Chicago.

[3]"You may have seen our commercials," he said. "They include a *cameo appearance* by Lee Smith and Leon Durham of the Cubs. It shows them crunching into a tortilla."

[4]No, I somehow missed seeing that.

[5]"Well, anyway, we'd like to have you in a commercial."

[6]Doing what?

[7]"Crunching into a tortilla."

[8]I thought tortillas were soft. I may be wrong, but I don't think you can crunch into a tortilla. Maybe you mean a taco.

[9]"Well, you'd be biting into some kind of Mexican food."

[10]What else would I have to do?

[11]"That's it. It would be a cameo appearance. You'd be seen for about four seconds. You wouldn't have to say anything."

[12]I'd just bite into a piece of Mexican food?

[13]"Right. For a fee, of course."

[14]How big a fee?

[15]He named a figure. It was not a *king's ransom*, but it was more than *walking-around money*.

[16]"It would take about forty-five minutes to film," he said.

[17]Amazing. In my first newspaper job almost thirty years ago, I had to work twelve weeks to earn the figure he had mentioned.

[18]It was a small, twice-a-week paper, and I was the only police reporter, the only sports reporter, the only investigative reporter and the assistant political writer, and on Saturday I would edit the stories going into the entertainment page. The publisher believed in a day's work for an hour's pay.

[19]Now I could make the same amount just for spending forty-five minutes biting into a taco in front of a TV camera.

[20]And when I was in the military, it would have taken eight monthly paychecks to equal this one taco-crunching fee. Of course, I also got a bunk and meals and could attend free VD lectures.

[21]"Well, what do you think?" he asked.

[22]I told him I would think about it and get back to him.

[23]So I asked Slats Grobnik, who has sound judgment, what he thought of the deal.

[24]"That's a lot of money just to bite a taco on TV. For *that kind of scratch*, I'd bite a dog. Grab the deal."

[25]But there is a question of ethics.

[26]"Ethics? What's the ethics in biting a taco? Millions of people bite tacos every day. Mexicans have been biting them for hundreds of years. Are you saying that Mexicans are unethical? Careful, some of my best friends are Mexicans."

[27]No, I'm not saying that at all. I like Mexicans, though I'm opposed to bullfighting.

[28]"Then what's unethical?"

[29]The truth is, I can't stand tacos.

(CONTINUED)

ENDORSEMENTS JUST A SHELL GAME (CONTINUED)

[30]"What has that got to do with it? I can't stand work, but I do it for the money."

[31]It has everything to do with it. If I go on TV and bite into a taco, won't I be endorsing that taco?

[32]"So what? You've endorsed politicians and I've never met a politician that I liked better than a taco."

[33]But endorsing a taco I didn't like would be dishonest.

[34]"Hey, that's the American way. Turn on your TV and look at all the people who endorse junk. Do you think they really believe what they're saying?"

[35]Then it's wrong. Nobody should endorse a taco if they don't like a taco.

[36]"Then tell them you'll bite something else. A tortilla or an enchilada."

[37]But I don't like them either. The truth is, I can't stand most Mexican food. The only thing I really like is the salt on the edge of a margarita glass. Oh, and I do like tamales.

[38]"Good, then bite a tamale."

[39]No, because the only tamales I like are the kind that used to be sold by the little Greeks who had hot dog pushcarts on the streets. They were factory-produced tamales about the size and weight of a lead pipe. But I don't think anybody would want me to do a TV commercial for hot dog stand tamales.

[40]"Can't you just bite the taco and spit it out when the camera is turned off?"

[41]That would be *a sham*. Besides, even if I liked tacos or tortillas, what does it matter? Why should somebody eat in a restaurant because they see me biting into that restaurant's taco? Am I a taco expert? What are my credentials to tell millions of people what taco they should eat? I'm not even Mexican.

[42]"Well, you're a sucker to turn it down. Why, it's almost un-American. Do you think that in Russia any newsman would ever have an opportunity to make that much money by biting into a pirogi?"

[43]That may be so. But maybe someday a food product will come along that I can lend my name to, something I can truly believe in.

[44]"I doubt it. Not unless they start letting taverns advertise shots and beers on TV."

EXERCISE #4 QUESTIONS—"ENDORSEMENTS JUST A SHELL GAME"

1. What is Royko's purpose?
2. What is his thesis?
3. What is Royko's point of view on endorsements?
4. What is his tone?
5. How does his tone relate to his point of view and/or bias?
6. Do you think he has the knowledge to write this article? Why or why not?
7. Do you think he is reliable? Why or why not?
8. Do you think anything could cause him to change his point of view?
9. Explain these phrases or figures of speech used by Royko:
   - a. cameo appearance (¶3)
   - b. king's ransom (¶15)
   - c. walking-around money (¶15)
   - d. that kind of scratch (¶24)
   - e. a sham (¶41)
10. What did the advertising agency want Royko to do?
11. Do you think Royko made the commercial? Why or why not?

12. How much of a factor do you think money was in Royko's decision?

13. How does Royko's thesis match or contradict your concept of reliability? Explain.

14. If you were in Royko's position, what would you have decided to do? Why?

15. This type of situation is often referred to as a moral dilemma. Have you ever had a moral dilemma? How did you resolve the dilemma?

USE YOUR STRATEGIES: EXERCISE #5—"THE FUTURE"

Edward F. Bergman is chairman of the geography department at Lehman College of the City University of New York. He has taught widely in Europe, and he has written about New York City, U.S. history, political geography, and international affairs.

Tom L. McKnight teaches geography at the University of California, Los Angeles. Most of his professional life has been based at UCLA, but he has also taught temporarily at other schools in the United States, Canada, and Australia.

This selection—"The Future"—is from *Introduction to Geography*.

THE FUTURE

EDWARD F. BERGMAN AND TOM L. MCKNIGHT

[1]Until now all the factors just discussed have held off the *specter of worldwide starvation*. Is it possible that humankind is now, at last, at the end of its ability to increase food supplies?

[2]The answer to this question is no. There is no reason to fear that humankind is, technologically, in danger. If demographers are correct in their projections of the Earth's future population, the population can be fed. Although farmers now utilize almost all potential cropland, and the amount of cropland per capita is declining, humankind has scarcely begun to maximize productivity even with present-day technology. The leading contemporary technology has been applied to only a small portion of the Earth, and *newly emerging technology* offers still greater possibilities.

[3]A 1983 study by the Food and Agriculture Organization (FAO, a UN agency) of the world's soil and climate determined that with basic fertilizers and pesticides, all cultivable land under food crops, and the most productive crops grown on at least half the land, the world in the year 2000 could feed four times its projected 2000 population. (That study discounted any possible technological breakthroughs between 1983 and 2000.) If average farm yields rose just from the present 2 tons of grain equivalent *per hectare* (2.47 acres) to 5 tons, the world could support about 11.5 billion people. Each person could enjoy "Plant energy"—food, seed, and animal feed—of 6,000 calories per day, the current global average. (North America currently uses about 15,000 calories per person per day, but most of that is consumed by animals, which are then eaten by people.)

[4]In addition, humankind could improve its diet by concentrating on raising those domesticated animals that most efficiently transform grain into meat. Chickens are the most efficient. They yield 1 pound (0.46 kg) of edible meat for every 4 pounds (1.8 kg) of grain they consume. Pigs produce 1 pound for every 7 pounds of grain, and beef cattle 1 pound for every 15 pounds (6.8 kg) of grain. In addition, chickens reach maturity—and therefore can be consumed—much faster than do pigs and cattle. Therefore, a greater emphasis placed on raising chickens could immensely improve the human diet. China is widely replacing swine with chicken farming, and several other countries have established programs to multiply their chicken populations. In many societies, however, cattle are viewed as a status symbol, and this preference delays the switch into more productive livestock.

(CONTINUED)

THE FUTURE (CONTINUED)

Biotechnology in Agriculture

[5]New scientific advances promise to multiply future food yields. Biotechnology offers *genetically altered crops* that can be custom designed to fit the environment, produce bountiful harvests, and resist plant diseases. One bacterial gene eliminates the need for chemicals to kill worms by producing a natural protein that disintegrates the worms' digestive system. Genetically engineered viruses can be used as pesticides. In 1988 scientists mapped the genome of rice—the set of 12 chromosomes that carries all the genetic characteristics of rice. This development could enable geneticists to produce improved strains of rice. Biotechnology can replace chemical pesticides and fertilizers, whose biological or even genetic impact on our own bodies is not fully understood.

[6]Scientists have also conducted research on *halophytes*, plants that thrive in salt water. Interbreeding halophytes with conventional crops has made these crops more salt-resistant, which means that they can grow in more diverse environments. Farmers are today harvesting lands in Egypt, Israel, India, and Pakistan once thought too salt-soaked to support crops. Conventional crops may someday be grown in salt water.

[7]Mechanized fishing on technologically advanced ships has already multiplied yields from the sea, but humankind has scarcely begun the shift from hunting and gathering seafood (fishing and gathering a few aquatic plants) to aquaculture, which involves herding or domesticating aquatic animals and farming aquatic plants. Humankind took this step with agriculture and livestock herding on land thousands of years ago. Presumably this food frontier will be expanded.

[8]All these possibilities justify optimism. The economist Henry George (1839–1897) succinctly contrasted the rules of nature with the multiplication of resources through the application of human ingenuity. He said, "Both the jayhawk and the man eat chickens, but the more jayhawks, the fewer chickens, while the more men, the more chickens."

[9]This principle is key to understanding and counting all resources, but technological solutions to problems can still trigger unexpected new problems. Over reliance on insecticides, for example, can lead to the poisoning of farm workers or the contamination of water supplies. The debate between the optimists and the pessimists continues.

EXERCISE #5 QUESTIONS—"THE FUTURE"

1. What is Bergman and McKnight's purpose?
2. What is their thesis?
3. What is their point of view on the ability of the world to provide food for its population in the future?
4. What is their point of view on the promise of genetically altered crops?
5. What is their general tone?
6. How does their tone relate to their point of view and/or bias?
7. Do you think Bergman and McKnight have the knowledge to write this article? Why or why not?
8. Do you think they are reliable? Why or why not?
9. What, if anything, do you think could cause them to change their point of view?
10. Explain these words or phrases:
    a. specter of worldwide starvation (¶1)
    b. newly emerging technology (¶2)
    c. per hectare (¶3)
    d. genetically altered crops (¶5)
    e. halophytes (¶6)

11. If farmers are currently using almost all available cropland and the amount of available cropland is diminishing, how do Bergman and McKnight suggest food yields can be increased to meet future demands?

12. Why do the authors suggest that raising a greater percentage of chickens could improve the human diet?

13. Name the three advantages of genetically altered crops.

14. Why do Bergman and McKnight compare aquaculture to agriculture and livestock herding? Do you think it is a useful comparison? Explain.

15. Explain, in your own words, the meaning of economist Henry George's quote in paragraph 8 "Both the jayhawk and the man eat chickens, but the more jayhawks, the fewer chickens, while the more men, the more chickens." Do you agree or disagree with George? Why?

CHAPTER 6 CONNECTIONS

A. Reread the paragraphs on pages 107–108 by Caile and those by Fuori and Gioia about computers. Which piece most closely matches your point of view about the use and impact of computers? Why? Did either Caile or Fuori and Gioia spark an idea you hadn't thought about? Did either author change your mind?

B. In paragraphs 1 and 2 of the excerpt from Bergman and McKnight's *Introduction to Geography* text "The Future" (page 130), they ask the question: "Is it possible that humankind is now, at last, at the end of its ability to increase food supplies?" They then answer the question: "no." Do you think it is acceptable for textbook authors to include their point of view in the text? Why or why not?

CHAPTER 7

INTEGRATE TEXT AND GRAPHIC INFORMATION

Because of computer technology, expository authors are using an increasing number of graphics—such as graphs, tables, charts, diagrams, and photographs—to complement and supplement their words. Rarely in academic reading do graphics stand alone. Authors use graphics to condense, clarify, illustrate, highlight, or add details that aren't covered in the text. You must be skillful in understanding the information provided by the graphic, and integrating that information with the words.

As you preview this chapter, recall what types of graphics you have seen recently in your text assignments, in newspapers and magazines, and on television. Did you read the graphic? If so, did you understand the main idea? If you read the graphic, did you skip over the words? Did you read both the words and the graphic? Did you compare the information between the words and the graphic?

Define this chapter's key vocabulary:

graphic

graph

table
pie chart
diagram
flow chart
caption
row
column
map
legend
key
scale

CHAPTER 7 OBJECTIVES

❑ Recognize that graphics contain valuable information.
❑ Understand how to read different types of graphics.
❑ Identify and consider the source of the information used in graphics.
❑ Integrate words and graphics.

WHAT IS MY BASIC STRATEGY FOR INTEGRATING TEXT AND GRAPHIC INFORMATION?

As You Plan:

1. Read the graphic's title and subtitles.
2. Read the graphic's labels, captions, legend, key, and/or scale.
3. Determine how the information is organized.
4. Answer the question, who or what is this graphic is about?
5. Identify the relationships, changes, or trends represented.
6. Answer the question, what does the author want me to understand about this subject?
7. Consider the quality of the information.
8. Predict the relationship of the information in the graphic to the written information.

As You Read:

9. Integrate the information in the graphic with the written information.

As You Review:

10. Revise and restate the thesis and/or main idea.
11. Restate the supporting details you need to fulfill your purpose.

HOW CAN I UNDERSTAND GRAPHIC INFORMATION?

For our purpose, a graphic is any visual representation that authors use to highlight, clarify, illustrate, summarize, or complement their text.

When you read a graphic, you must first understand the graphic's information. Just as you do with written material, consider the source or quality of the graphic's data. Information about who collected and prepared the data should be included in the graphic's caption or footnote.

Then, like reading a paragraph, identify the author's main idea and the relationships among the details.

Next, compare the information from the graphic with what is presented in the text—is it the same or are there some differences? Does the graphic highlight a portion of what is written, give an example of a concept or idea, summarize the written material, or add details not covered in the text? Finally, based on your overall purpose for reading, decide how much of the graphic's information you need to know.

HOW DO I READ A GRAPH?

A graph uses bars or lines to show the relationships between or among quantities. Graphs can be used in almost every subject. For example, a graph can be used in a mass communications text to show the change in the number of newspapers published in the United States over the last 50 years, in a psychology text to show the divorce rates by sex and age, or in your reading class to show the distribution of grades on the last exam.

When reading a graph, you are concerned with at least two variables—one indicated, or labeled, on the vertical axis (up and down the side), and the other labeled on the horizontal axis (across the bottom). The main idea of the graph will often be summarized in its title or by the text's discussion of the graph. Source lines or captions under the graph often give the source of the information. A key, or reference center, defines any other codes being used. Two common types of graphs are bar graphs and line graphs.

BAR GRAPH

An author can use a simple bar graph to show the comparison of quantities within a category. See how the bar graph in Example 1.1 uses data from the U.S. Census Bureau (caption), to show the number of gallons (vertical axis) of three kinds of milk (key) consumed in the United States during four different years (horizontal axis).

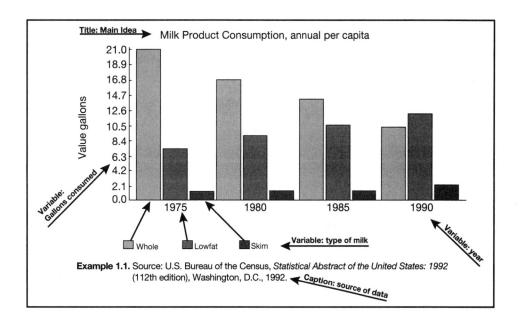

Example 1.1. Source: U.S. Bureau of the Census, *Statistical Abstract of the United States: 1992* (112th edition), Washington, D.C., 1992.

Stacked Bar Graph   A stacked bar graph is effective when an author wants you to concentrate on component parts of a total. See how Example 1.2 uses the same U.S. Census data and variables as Example 1.1, but focuses your attention on the changes in the proportion of each kind of milk consumed to the total consumption.

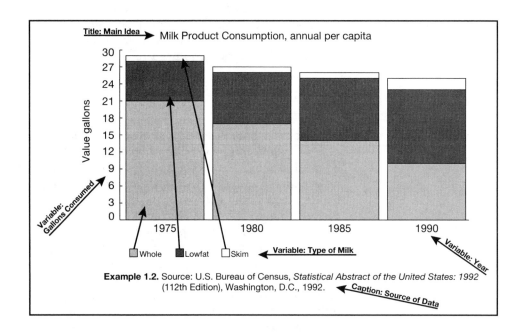

Example 1.2. Source: U.S. Bureau of Census, *Statistical Abstract of the United States: 1992* (112th Edition), Washington, D.C., 1992.

LINE GRAPH

An author uses a line graph to focus your attention on a pattern or an upward or downward trend. See how the line graph in Example 1.3, using the same U.S. Census Bureau data as above, directs your attention to the downward trend in whole milk consumption and the upward trends in lowfat and skim milk consumption.

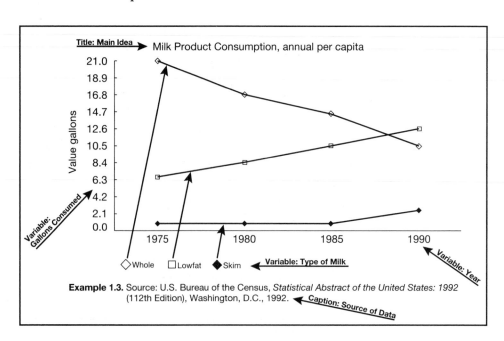

Example 1.3. Source: U.S. Bureau of the Census, *Statistical Abstract of the United States: 1992* (112th Edition), Washington, D.C., 1992.

PRACTICE: READING AND INTEGRATING TEXT AND A GRAPH

In each of the following, read the paragraph, read the graph, integrate the information, and then answer the questions.

1. Oceans respond very differently than do continents to the arrival of solar radiation. In general, land heats and cools faster and to a greater degree than does water. Therefore, both the hottest and coldest areas of the Earth are found in the interiors of continents, distant from the moderating influence of oceans. In the study of the atmosphere, probably no single geographical relationship is more important than the distinction between continental and maritime climates. A continental climate experiences greater seasonal extremes of temperature—hotter in summer, colder in winter—than does a maritime climate (see Figure 2–1). (Bergman and McKnight, *Introduction to Geography*)

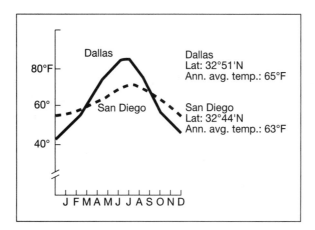

Figure 2–1   Temperature Curves for San Diego and Dallas   San Diego, situated on the coast, experiences milder temperatures in both summer and winter than inland Dallas.

a. What is the topic of Figure 2–1?

b. Is the purpose of this line graph to highlight one portion of the paragraph, give an example of the concept, or summarize the paragraph?

c. If your purpose for reading this selection was to understand why there is a difference between continental and maritime climates, would you need to memorize the details from the graph? Explain.

2. *Financing the Small Business*   Although determining whether to start from scratch or buy an existing firm is an important decision, it is meaningless unless a small businessperson can obtain the money to set up shop or purchase a business. As Figure 6.5 [on page 138] shows, a bewildering variety of monetary resources—ranging from private to governmental—await the small businessperson. (Griffin and Ebert, *Business*)

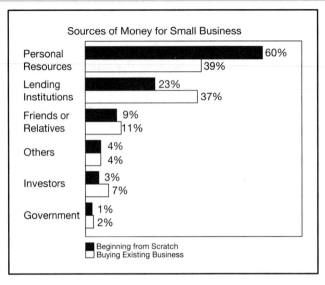

Figure 6.5

a. What is the topic of Figure 6.5?

b. The paragraph refers to "a bewildering variety of monetary resources." How is the graph more specific?

c. What is the largest source of money for a small businessperson starting a new business from scratch?

d. What is the second largest source of money for a small businessperson buying an existing business?

HOW DO I READ A TABLE?

Authors use a table when they want you to have several pieces of specific data rather than a summary. The data, often numbers or statistics, are arranged systematically in rows (horizontal) and columns (vertical). The information in a table often compares qualities or quantities or shows how things change over time (the trend). Tables can be used to display data in almost any subject, from the growth of government spending in an economics text, to the number of calories found in alcoholic beverages in a health text.

When reading a table, use the title or written reference to the table to help predict the main idea. Next, identify the variables by reading the column labels (across the top of the table) and the row labels (down the left side of the table). Clarify the type of data presented for each variable—e.g., raw numbers, percentages. And, as always, check the source line and/or caption for source information and clarification.

See how the table in Example 1.4 (on page 139) displays data from the U.S. Department of Agriculture to show the specific number of calories and grams of fat in average servings of common foods.

Title: Main Idea

Column Labels: Variables

Low Fat Foods§

	Serving	Calories	Grams of Fat*
Dairy Products			
Cheese:			
Low-fat cottage (2%)	1/2 cup	100	2
Mozzarella, part skim	1 oz.	80	5
Parmesan	1 Tbs	25	2
Milk:			
Low-fat (2%)	1 cup	125	5
Nonfat, skim	1 cup	85	trace
Ice Milk	1 cup	185	6
Yogurt, low-fat, fruit	1 cup	230	2
Poultry Products			
Chicken, roasted:			
Dark meat, no skin	3 oz.	175	8
Light meat, no skin	3 oz.	145	4
Turkey, roasted:			
Dark meat, no skin	3 oz.	160	6
Light meat, no skin	3 oz.	135	3
Egg, hard cooked	1 large	80	6

Row Labels: Variables

Example 1.4. *From Nutritive Value of Foods*, U.S. Department of Agriculture, Home and Garden Bulletin No. 72, 1985.

Source of Fat Data

§From *Diet, Nutrition & Cancer Prevention: The Good News*, U.S. Department of Health and Human Services, NIH Publication No. 87-2878, December 1987.

Source of Low Fat Data

PRACTICE: READING AND INTEGRATING TEXT AND A TABLE

Read the paragraph below, read Table 3–1 (on page 140), integrate the information, and then answer questions a, b, and c.

3. Table 3–1 indicates some changes in attitudes among first-year college students over a single generation: those entering college in 1968 and those entering in 1987. The figures in the table indicate that some things have not changed very much: about the same proportion of students come to college in order to "gain a general education" and to "learn more about things." But students of the late 1980s certainly appear more interested in gaining skills, especially those that will lead to a high-paying job. Moreover, the political activism of the 1960s seems to have declined significantly in favor of pursuing personal success. Note that changes have generally been greater among women than among men. This, no doubt, reflects the fact that the women's movement, concerned with social equality for the two sexes, intensified after 1968. (Macionis, *Sociology*)

    a. What is the topic of Table 3–1?

    b. Is the purpose of Table 3–1 to highlight one portion of the paragraph, summarize the paragraph, or add details not covered in the paragraph?

    c. The paragraph says "students of the late 1980s certainly appear more interested in gaining skills, especially those that will lead to a high-paying job." What specific data from the table supports this statement?

TABLE 3–1   ATTITUDES AMONG STUDENTS ENTERING AMERICAN COLLEGES, 1968 AND 1987

		1968	*1987*	*CHANGE*
Reasons to Go to College (Very Important)				
Gain a general education	male	60	61	+1
	female	67	67	0
Learn more about things	male	69	72	+3
	female	74	76	+2
Improve reading and writing skills	male	22	36	+14
	female	23	43	+20
Get a better job	male	74	83	+9
	female	70	83	+13
Prepare for graduate or professional school	male	39	44	+5
	female	29	50	+21
Make more money	male	57	75	+18
	female	42	68	+26
Life Objectives (Essential or Very Important)				
Develop a philosophy of life	male	79	40	−39
	female	87	39	−48
Keep up with political affairs	male	52	43	−9
	female	52	33	−19
Raise a family	male	64	56	−8
	female	72	60	−12
Help others in difficulty	male	50	50	0
	female	71	67	−4
Be successful in my own business	male	55	55	0
	female	32	46	+14
Be well off financially	male	51	80	+29
	female	27	72	+45

Note: To allow comparisons, data from early 1970s rather than 1968 are used for some items.
Source: Richard G. Braungart and Margaret M. Braungart. "From Yippies to Yuppies: Twenty Years of Freshman Attitudes."
Public Opinion, Vol. 11, No. 3 (September–October 1988):53–56.

HOW DO I READ A PIE CHART OR CIRCLE GRAPH?

Authors use pie charts (also called circle graphs) to illustrate the ratio of the values of a category to the total. The whole pie, or circle, represents 100% and various segments, or pieces of the pie, show relative magnitude or frequencies. The larger the pie wedge, the larger fraction of the total it represents. Pie charts can be used to illustrate a variety of data. For example, a study skills author might use one to illustrate the percentage of time a student spends in various activities—e.g., studying, working, sleeping; or an accounting text author could use a pie chart to show the relative amounts to budget for household expenses—e.g., rent, food, clothing.

As with other graphics, use the title or the written reference to help predict the main idea. The main idea will tell you what 100% of the pie graph represents. Next, check the key to see how many segments of the whole are included, what they are, and what fill pattern is used to identify each. Check the caption or footnote for the source of the information.

Look at the pie chart in Example 1.5 (on page 141) that displays Social Security benefits data from the U.S. Census Bureau. The whole pie represents all people (100 percent) who received monthly Social Security benefits in 1990. The pieces of the pie represent the proportion of the total received by each eligible category.

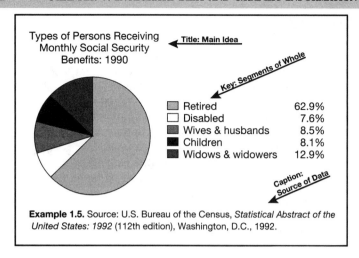

Types of Persons Receiving
Monthly Social Security
Benefits: 1990

Title: Main Idea

Key: Segments of Whole

Retired	62.9%
Disabled	7.6%
Wives & husbands	8.5%
Children	8.1%
Widows & widowers	12.9%

Caption:
Source of Data

Example 1.5. Source: U.S. Bureau of the Census, *Statistical Abstract of the United States: 1992* (112th edition), Washington, D.C., 1992.

PRACTICE: READING AND INTEGRATING TEXT AND A PIE CHART

Read the paragraph, read Figure 19.2, integrate the information, and then answer the questions.

4. Non-direct distribution channels do mean higher prices to the ultimate consumer. The more members involved in the channel, the higher the final price to the purchaser. After all, each link in the distribution chain must charge a markup or commission in order to make a profit. Figure 19.2 shows typical markup growth through the distribution channel. (Griffin and Ebert, *Business*)

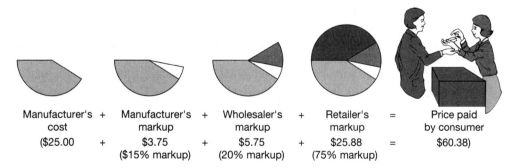

Manufacturer's cost	+	Manufacturer's markup	+	Wholesaler's markup	+	Retailer's markup	=	Price paid by consumer
($25.00	+	$3.75	+	$5.75	+	$25.88	=	$60.38)
		($15% markup)		(20% markup)		(75% markup)		

Figure 19.2   Typical Price Markup: Manufacturer to Consumer

a. What is the topic of Figure 19.2?

b. Is the purpose of Figure 19.2 to highlight one portion of the paragraph, give a specific example of the concept, or summarize the paragraph?

c. What is the manufacturer's cost for the item? What does the consumer pay for the item?

d. Why does each member of the distribution chain mark up the item? Where did you find that information?

HOW DO I READ A DIAGRAM?

Diagram is a general term that refers to any type of drawing an author uses to help you understand ideas, objects, plans, processes, or sequences. Diagrams include everything from a simple labeled line drawing of the parts of a flower in a biology text, to an organizational chart in a management text, to a complex correlation-and-cause diagram in a sociology text.

Begin by identifying the topic and main idea of the diagram. Next, try to establish the purpose of the diagram—what it shows and why the author is using it. In addition, clarify what each portion of the diagram represents.

Look at the diagram in Example 1.6 that I developed for the chapter on "researching information" in my *Magazine Article Writing Basics* text. It shows (with the filled circles) and tells (in words) the differences in the information you will find when you use the three key terms of Boolean Logic.

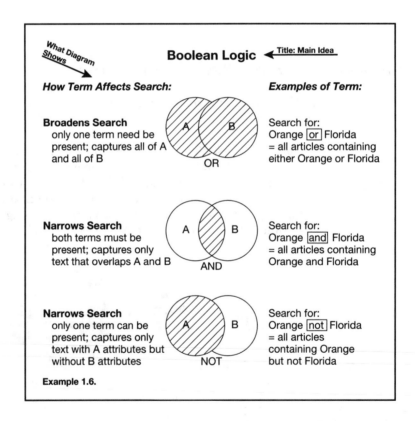

Example 1.6.

FLOW CHART

A Flow Chart is a type of diagram that uses boxes, rectangles, diamonds, or circles, with connecting lines or arrows, to show the step-by-step procedure of a complicated process. These sequential diagrams are designed to be read from top to bottom or left to right. Flow charts can be constructed to show many different kinds of processes—from how a computer program operates in a data processing text, to the procedure for analyzing the elements in a laboratory sample in a chemistry lab manual, to how to write an essay (see Example 1.7—on page 143—that I developed for students in writing classes).

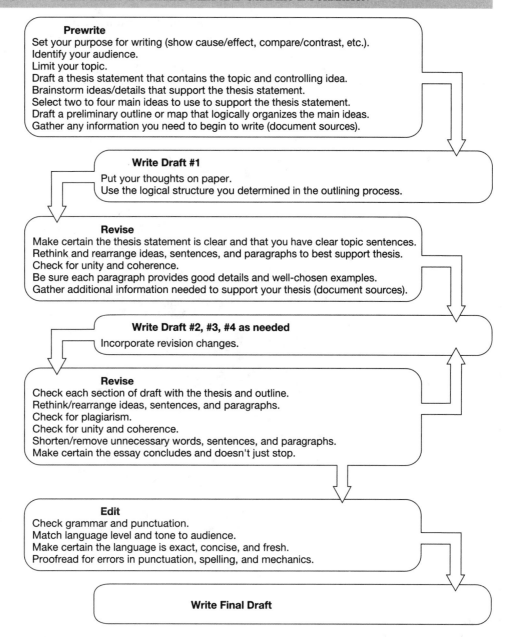

Prewrite
Set your purpose for writing (show cause/effect, compare/contrast, etc.).
Identify your audience.
Limit your topic.
Draft a thesis statement that contains the topic and controlling idea.
Brainstorm ideas/details that support the thesis statement.
Select two to four main ideas to use to support the thesis statement.
Draft a preliminary outline or map that logically organizes the main ideas.
Gather any information you need to begin to write (document sources).

Write Draft #1
Put your thoughts on paper.
Use the logical structure you determined in the outlining process.

Revise
Make certain the thesis statement is clear and that you have clear topic sentences.
Rethink and rearrange ideas, sentences, and paragraphs to best support thesis.
Check for unity and coherence.
Be sure each paragraph provides good details and well-chosen examples.
Gather additional information needed to support your thesis (document sources).

Write Draft #2, #3, #4 as needed
Incorporate revision changes.

Revise
Check each section of draft with the thesis and outline.
Rethink/rearrange ideas, sentences, and paragraphs.
Check for plagiarism.
Check for unity and coherence.
Shorten/remove unnecessary words, sentences, and paragraphs.
Make certain the essay concludes and doesn't just stop.

Edit
Check grammar and punctuation.
Match language level and tone to audience.
Make certain the language is exact, concise, and fresh.
Proofread for errors in punctuation, spelling, and mechanics.

Write Final Draft

Example 1.7.

MAP

A map is a diagram that depicts on a two-dimensional flat surface all or part of the earth's three-dimensional surface. Maps translate data into spatial patterns by using distance, direction, size, and shape. Maps are used in geography and history to show the locations of places and events, but they can also be used to show everything from distributions of various religious populations in a philosophy text, to acid rain affected areas in a book on environmental biology.

When reading a map, begin by identifying the topic and main idea. Use the words, scale, legend, or other reference points to establish how the information is represented on the map. A scale is a map element that shows the relationship between a length measured on a map and the corresponding distance on the ground. A legend, like a key on a chart, is a reference center that defines codes being used. As always, consider the source of the data.

Look at the map of Colorado's Indian Peaks Wilderness Area in Example 1.8. The map shows the portion of Indian Peaks where a backcountry permit is required. It's scale is in miles and the legend includes an explanation for the nine symbols used on the map.

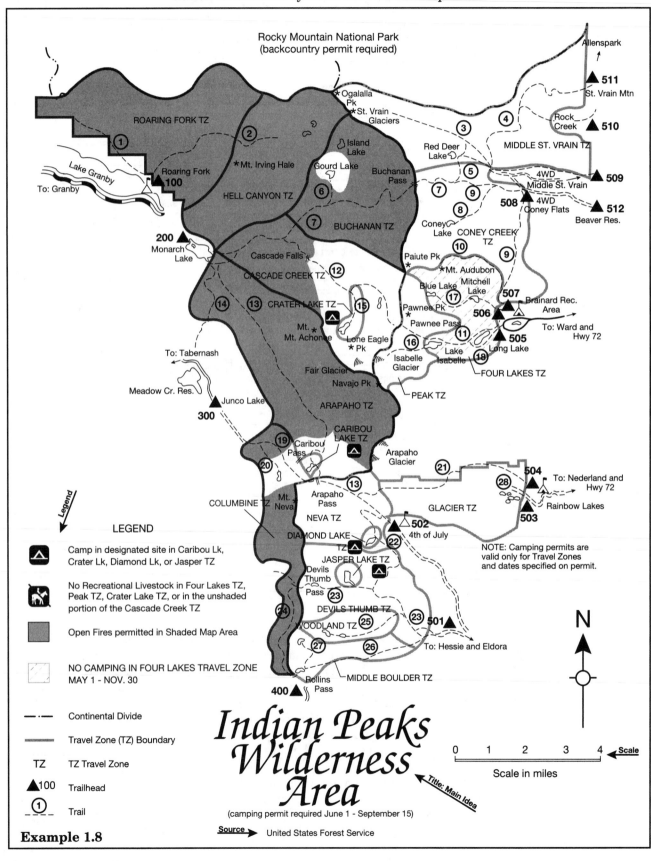

Example 1.8

PRACTICE: READING AND INTEGRATING TEXT AND A DIAGRAM

Read the paragraphs, read the map, integrate the information, and then answer the questions.

5. The Federal Reserve System (the Fed) also serves commercial banks by clearing checks. Imagine you are a photographer living in New Orleans, who wants to participate in a photography workshop in Detroit, Michigan. In order to do so you must send a check for $50 to the Detroit studio. Figure 20.3 traces your check through the clearing process.

    After the studio deposits your check in a Detroit bank (step 1), the bank deposits the check in its own account at the Federal Reserve Bank of Chicago (step 2). The check is sent from Chicago to the Atlanta Federal Reserve bank for collection (step 3) because you, the check writer, are in the Atlanta Federal Reserve Bank district. Your New Orleans bank receives the check from Atlanta and deducts the $50 from your account (step 4). Your bank then has $50 deducted from its deposit account at the Atlanta Federal Reserve Bank (step 5). Finally, the $50 is shifted from Atlanta to the Chicago Federal Reserve Bank (step 6). The studio's Detroit bank gets credited, and the studio's account then gets credited $50, normally within two weeks. Your bank then returns the canceled check to you by mail. (Griffin and Ebert, *Business*)

Figure 20.3

a. Is the purpose of Figure 20.3 to highlight one portion of the paragraph, illustrate what the paragraph says, or add details not covered in the paragraph?

b. What does the map illustrate?

c. Do you think the author wants you to concentrate on remembering the names of the cities? Why or why not?

d. What is the main idea you think the author wants you to remember from the paragraph and graphic?

HOW DO I READ A PHOTOGRAPH OR ILLUSTRATION?

Photographs and drawings are also common in expository material. They could be used to show examples of nonverbal communication in a speech communications text, the results of a chemical reaction in a physics text, or caste marks of Indian society in a sociology text.

They often lack a title or labels common to other graphics but usually include a caption—a brief description of the contents of the illustration. Like other types of graphics, authors use photographs and drawings to help you visualize information. Use the caption and words to direct your attention to specific elements.

Look at the photographs in Example 1.9 from Larry McGrath's *Travel Photography Handbook*. Note how the caption points out the main idea of Photo A and Photo B.

Photo A   **Photo B**

Example 1.9   In many cases, selecting a slightly different vantage point and/or using a different lens permits the photographer to exclude distracting elements in a picture. Notice how the distracting wires and light post in Photo A have been eliminated in Photo B by moving closer to the chapel and changing from a normal to a wide angle lens.

PRACTICE: READING AND INTEGRATING TEXT AND A PHOTOGRAPH OR ILLUSTRATION

Read the paragraphs and the illustration, integrate the information, and then answer the questions.

6. To see how the mind can shape what we perceive, look at the two pictures on page 147:

What do you see? Each would present you with two distinctly different images. When you look at the first one in one way, you see a vase. Look at it differently and you see two faces. The second picture presents either a beautiful young woman facing away from you or an ugly old crone in profile.

How is this possible? The sense data that your eyes take in—the arrangement of lines and shading—remain the same. But you can "shift" the pictures you see. What you "see," then, is the meaning your mind imposes on the data, and your mind can reprocess that data so that they represent something different. (White, *Discovering Philosophy*)

> a. What is the purpose of the illustration in this example?
>
> b. What do you think White wants you to remember from the illustration?

CHAPTER 7 REVIEW QUESTIONS

1. Why do authors use graphics?
2. List and describe four common types of graphics used with expository writing.
3. How can you identify the source and reliability of the information?
4. Why do you need to integrate the words and graphics?

CHAPTER 7 THINK AND CONNECT QUESTIONS

5. Re-read the first portion of Chapter 1. What does the Plan⇨Do⇨Review flowchart on page 2 show? What is the purpose of the flowchart? Does it fulfill its purpose? Why or why not?
6. Re-read "Sources of Groundwater Pollution," Chapter 1, Exercise #3, page 15. What is the purpose of Figure 11–2?

CHAPTER 7 APPLICATION EXERCISES

7. Select a text assignment from another class that includes at least one graphic. What is the purpose of the graphic? How do the words help you to understand the graphic? How does the graphic help you understand the words?

8. From a current newspaper or magazine, select an article that includes at least one graphic. What is the purpose of the graphic? How do the words help you to understand the graphic? How does the graphic help you understand the words?

USE YOUR STRATEGIES: EXERCISE #1

1. Although America does not have large numbers of people dying from starvation, a condition that characterizes other regions of the world, nutritionists believe that our "diets of affluence" are responsible for many diseases and disabilities, including heart disease, certain types of cancer, hypertension (high blood pressure), cirrhosis of the liver, tooth decay, and chronic obesity. The food choices that Americans make have changed over the past three decades. Some of the changes are outlined in Table 6.1. (Donatelle and Davis, *Access to Health*)

TABLE 6.1   CHANGES IN ANNUAL FOOD CONSUMPTION OF AMERICANS, 1960–1987

The following table illustrates changes in annual food consumption per person during the past three decades. Unless otherwise indicated, the amounts are presented in pounds. Are these trends generally healthy or unhealthy?

FOOD PRODUCT	*1960*	*1970*	*1984*	*1987*
Red meat	173.7	162.8	151.9	144.0
Fish and shellfish	10.3	11.8	13.7	15.4
Poultry	34.0	48.2	66.5	77.8
Eggs (number)	334.0	309.0	259.0	249.0
Whole milk	263.9	219.1	126.6	109.9
Lower-fat milk (1% and 2%)	—	50.0	99.1	113.6
Nonfat milk	10.7	11.6	11.5	14.0
Fats and oils	—	52.6	58.6	62.7
Flour (white, whole-wheat)	—	110.8	118.1	128.0
Pasta	—	7.7	11.3	17.1
Breakfast cereals	—	10.8	14.0	15.2
Sugar and corn sweeteners	111.5	121.0	125.1	130.0
Saccharin	—	5.8	10.0	5.5
Aspartame	—	—	5.8	13.5
Fruit (fresh)	—	76.9	87.8	98.6
Fruit (canned)	—	14.4	8.9	8.7
Vegetables (fresh)	—	64.0	78.8	78.6
Coffee (gallons)	—	33.4	26.5	26.5
Soft drinks (gallons)	—	20.8	27.2	30.3
Beer (gallons)	—	30.6	35.0	34.4
Wine (gallons)	—	2.2	3.4	3.4
Distilled spirits (gallons)	—	3.0	2.6	2.3

— = data not available

Source: U.S. Department of Commerce, Bureau of the Census, *Statistical Abstracts of the United States*, 1989.

a. What is the topic of Table 6.1?

b. Is the purpose of Table 6.1 to highlight one portion of the paragraph, summarize the paragraph, or add details not covered in the paragraph?

c. What quantity do the numbers for red meat, flour, and pasta represent?

d. Would you say these trends are generally healthy or unhealthy? List three specific food product trends to support your answer.

2. Several programs have been proposed to provide job opportunities for America's inner-city unskilled. One is to rebuild the blue-collar economies of the central cities by encouraging industry to locate there in urban enterprise zones, where manufacturers receive government subsidies. The federal government has been slow to act, but several states and cities have designated such zones in their poorest communities (see Figure 9–27). (Bergman and McKnight, *Introduction to Geography*)

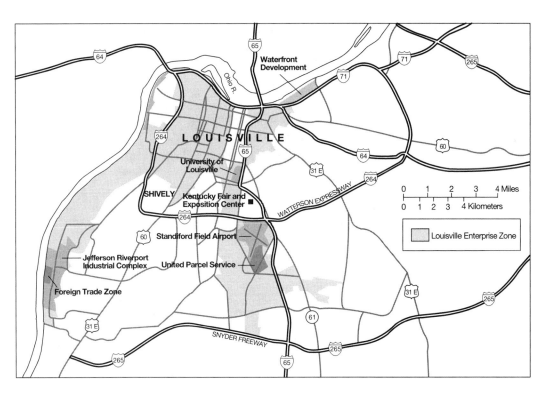

Figure 9–27

a. Is the purpose of Figure 9–27 to highlight one portion of the paragraph, give an example of a concept, or summarize the paragraph?

b. Which portion of which city is represented on this map?

c. What type of businessperson might be interested in looking at this map? Why?

d. What does urban mean?

3. From 1965 to 1987, health-care expenses increased 1000 percent: from an average of approximately $176 to $1758 annually for every person in the United States, as shown in Figure 20.2. As of 1989, Americans spent $1.3 billion dollars daily for health care. (Greenberg and Dintiman, *Exploring Health*)

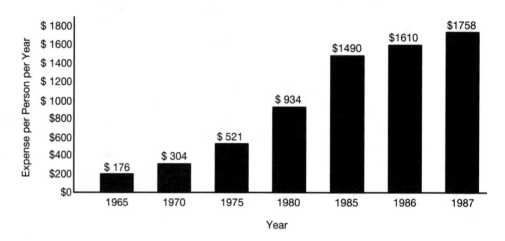

Figure 20.2   Health Care Expenses per Person, 1965 to 1987
Source: Health Insurance Association, *1989 Source Book of Health Insurance Data* (Washington, DC: Health Insurance Association of America, 1989).

a. What is the topic of Figure 20.2?

b. What does Figure 20.2 show?

c. What is the source of the data? Do you think this is a reliable source? Why or why not?

d. In this example, would you use the words or the graphic to determine the percent of increase from 1965 to 1987? Which would you use to determine the dollar amount spent in 1980?

4. For the purpose of this discussion, we will classify the uses of computers into six general categories: information systems/data processing, personal computing, science and research, process control, education, and artificial intelligence. Figure 1–4 [on page 151] shows how the sum total of existing computer capacity is apportioned to each of these general categories. In the years ahead, look for personal computing, process control, education, and artificial intelligence to grow rapidly and become larger shares of the computer "pie." (Long, *Introduction to Computers and Information Systems*)

a. What does this pie chart show?

b. What information is in the pie chart and in the paragraph?

c. What information is in the pie chart but not in the paragraph?

d. What information is in the paragraph but not in the pie chart?

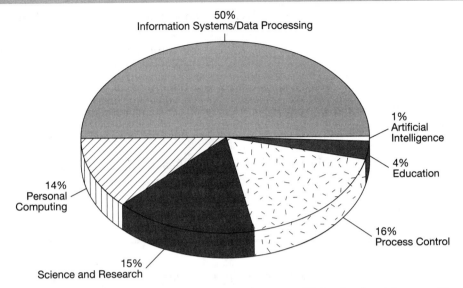

Figure 1–4   The Way We Use Computers. This pie chart is an estimate of how existing computer capacity is distributed among the general categories of computer usage.

5.   Management is the process of planning, organizing, leading, and controlling an enterprise's financial, physical, human, and information resources in order to achieve the organization's goals of supplying various products and services.... The planning, organizing, leading, and controlling aspects of a manager's job are interrelated, as shown in Figure 5.1. But note that while these activities generally follow one another in a logical sequence, sometimes they are performed simultaneously or in a different sequence altogether. In fact, any given manager is likely to be engaged in all these activities during the course of any given business day. (Griffin and Ebert, *Business*)

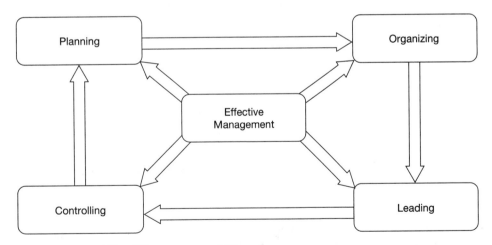

Figure 5.1   The Management Process

a. What is the topic of Figure 5.1?

b. Is the purpose of Figure 5.1 to illustrate the concept, or add details not covered in the paragraph?

c. Why do you think Griffin and Ebert chose a flowchart to illustrate the management process?

d. Assume you are preparing for a test on the management process. List the information you would need to remember.

USE YOUR STRATEGIES: EXERCISE #2—"THE HEALTH-ILLNESS CONTINUUM"

Jerrold Greenberg teaches at the University of Maryland. George Dintiman teaches at Virginia Commonwealth University. This selection—"The Health-Illness Continuum"—is from *Exploring Health*.

THE HEALTH-ILLNESS CONTINUUM

JERROLD S. GREENBERG AND GEORGE B. DINTIMAN

It is important to consider health as being separate from illness. You may wonder why, for many people define illness as lack of health, and health as lack of illness. These people might depict health and illness as a straight line and call that line a "health continuum," with ill health at one end and perfect health at the other (see Figure 1.1).

Figure 1.1   The Health Continuum

However, when we consider illness and health as separate entities, the continuum will not show them overlapping. That is, at some point one must stop and the other must begin. Figure 1.2 shows the model for this conceptualization. Illness occupies the right half of the continuum and ends at the midpoint; health begins there and occupies the left half of the continuum.

Figure 1.2   The Health-Illness Continuum

Of course, one may argue that even if someone is ill, that person may have some degree of health. For example, a physically handicapped person who exercises regularly and participates in the Wheelchair Olympics may be healthier than a person who is not ill, but who is not physically fit. For now, though, let's withhold objection until we can explain how we intend to use the health-illness continuum.

(CONTINUED)

THE HEALTH-ILLNESS CONTINUUM (*CONTINUED*)

Wellness

We'd now like you to look at the health-illness continuum under a microscope. Notice that the line isn't a line at all, but a series of dots. The continuum would then look like Figure 1.3.

| Perfect health | Health | Illness | Death |

Figure 1.3   The Magnified Health-Illness Continuum

If we could get an even more powerful microscope and focus it on just one of the dots on the continuum, you might see something like Figure 1.4. Each dot on the continuum, then, is composed of the five components of health. When we integrate social, mental, emotional, spiritual, and physical health at any level of health or illness, we achieve what we will call wellness. Put another way, you can be well regardless of whether you are ill or healthy. Paraplegics, for example, may not be defined as healthy; but they could have achieved high-level wellness by maximizing and integrating the five components of health so that, within their physical limitations, they are living a quality life. They may interact well with family and friends (social health); they may succeed at school, on the job, or with a hobby (mental health); they may be able to express their feelings when appropriate (emotional health); they may have a sense of how they fit into the "grand scheme of things" through a set of beliefs (spiritual health); and they may exercise within the boundaries of their capabilities, for example, by finishing a marathon on crutches or in a wheelchair (physical health).

Figure 1.4   A Single Health-Illness Continuum Dot

EXERCISE #2 QUESTIONS—"THE HEALTH-ILLNESS CONTINUUM"

1. Define *continuum*. How do Greenberg and Dintiman use a graphic to represent a continuum?
2. What is the difference between "The Health Continuum" (Figure 1.1) and the "The Health-Illness Continuum" (Figure 1.2)? Did you find the written or the graphic explanation easier to understand? Why?
3. Where is "health" located on the continuum in Figure 1.2? Do you get the same explanation from the written text and the graphic?

4. How is the continuum graphic in Figure 1.3 different than Figure 1.2?

5. What is the relationship of Figure 1.4 to "The Health-Illness Continuum"?

6. What are the five components of health? Where is this information stated?

7. According to Greenberg and Dintiman, you can be well regardless of whether you are ill or healthy. How is this possible?

8. How do Greenberg and Dintiman define wellness?

9. What example does Greenberg and Dintiman use to support and develop their definition of wellness?

10. Describe one other topic or subject you could graphically represent on a continuum.

USE YOUR STRATEGIES: EXERCISE #3—"HIGHER EDUCATION MANIFESTS THOSE GREATER EXPECTATIONS"

This selection—"Higher Education Manifests Those Greater Expectations"—comes from Rachel L. Jones of *Knight-Ridder Newspapers*, February 29, 1996.

HIGHER EDUCATION MANIFESTS THOSE GREATER EXPECTATIONS

RACHEL L. JONES

[1] When Cyrus Khorrami was deciding on his future profession, his doctor father offered some advice about economic security.

[2] "He said, 'You'll always be well off, because no matter what else happens in the world, people will always get sick,'" recalls Khorrami, a 20-year-old premed student at George Washington University here.

[3] That logic about the rewards of a professional degree is vividly highlighted by the results of a Census Bureau report released Wednesday detailing the value of education.

[4] The study shows enormous differences in income among Americans, based on how much education and what kinds of education they have received. And census data show that the relative rewards of education have grown over time.

[5] A person with a bachelor's degree could expect to earn about $2,339 a month in 1993—an amount 4 1/2 times the $508 a high-school dropout would make, the study shows. And an advanced degree paid even more: an average of $3,331 a month.

[6] And the extra earning power of a degree clearly increased from 1984 to 1993, census data show. The average earnings of high school graduates went up about 22 percent in that period, while college grads saw their earnings jump 47 percent.

[7] Career choices such as medicine, the law and engineering are, on average, far more lucrative than liberal arts, education or the social sciences. A person with a bachelor's degree in education earned an average of $1,699 a month in 1993. just over half the $3,189 that an engineering major could expect to pull down.

[8] But in an economy overshadowed by the threat of downsizing, many young Americans receive some ominous mixed messages about advanced education. More and more, college-bound teenagers who may see their degreed parents laid off believe that higher education is no shield against unemployment.

(CONTINUED)

HIGHER EDUCATION MANIFESTS
THOSE GREATER EXPECTATIONS (CONTINUED)

[9]"Our students see a completely different world than students of 10 years ago," said Marva Gumb, director of career services at the George Washington University Career Center.

[10]While Khorrami expects to earn $300,000 a year after taking over his father's medical practice in about 12 years, psychology major Karen Lipp thinks she'll be lucky to make $30,000 with a bachelor of arts degree.

[11]"I might be able to double it with a Ph.D.," said 19-year-old Lipp, who's minoring in art and hopes to combine the two fields by practicing art therapy. "The only way I'll be able to live like my parents is if I marry someone successful and we combine our incomes."

[12]But despite worries about economic uncertainties, the Census Bureau study confirms everything that parents, teachers and career counselors have admonished through the years: advanced education and training, as much as you can get, can pay very large dividends compared with life without them.

[13]"What we found was that with increased education, overall income is usually better and more stable in the long run." said Rosalind Bruno, the Census Bureau demographer who wrote the report. "There's no disputing the relationship between advanced training and larger economic rewards."

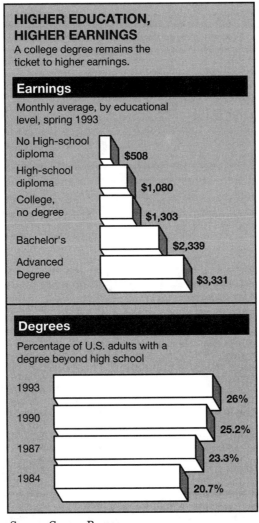

HIGHER EDUCATION, HIGHER EARNINGS
A college degree remains the ticket to higher earnings.

Earnings
Monthly average, by educational level, spring 1993

No High-school diploma	$508
High-school diploma	$1,080
College, no degree	$1,303
Bachelor's	$2,339
Advanced Degree	$3,331

Degrees
Percentage of U.S. adults with a degree beyond high school

1993	26%
1990	25.2%
1987	23.3%
1984	20.7%

Source: Census Bureau

(CONTINUED)

HIGHER EDUCATION MANIFESTS THOSE GREATER EXPECTATIONS (CONTINUED)

[14]And the study shows that by and large, more Americans are finishing high school, and have heeded the societal prod toward advanced education.

[15]By 1993, more than one of four adults had a degree beyond high-school level, an increase from the 21 percent in 1984. The proportion of adults without a high-school diploma decreased to 19 percent from 26 percent in 1984.

[16]Also, in that year, 28 percent of men and 26 percent of women held degrees above the high-school level, compared with 23 percent of men and 19 percent of women in 1984. Women were less likely to have an advanced degree, or more likely to have an associate or vocational degree, compared to men.

[17]Not surprisingly for those worried about gender inequities, men far outnumber women among high-paid engineers while women dominate among low-paid educators. The report also highlights gaps between the educational and economic attainment of minorities versus whites.

[18]The percentage of blacks earning Ph.D.s was lower in 1994 than in 1978, falling from nearly four percent to just over two, he says. While blacks were most likely to have earned business-management degrees, the report found 46 percent of those were at the associate/vocational level, compared to over 28 percent for whites.

EXERCISE #3 QUESTIONS—"HIGHER EDUCATION MANIFESTS THOSE GREATER EXPECTATIONS"

1. What is Jones's thesis?
2. What year was this article written? What year is the "earnings" data from? Why do you think there is a difference?
3. Who is the source of the "earnings" data? Do you think they are a reliable source? Why or why not?
4. The number/percentage of Americans with a degree beyond high school in 1993 is given in both the words and the graphic. How is it listed in the words? In the graphic?
5. How did the percentage of U.S. adults with a college degree change between 1984 and 1993? Where did you locate the information?
6. Between 1984 and 1993, how much did the earnings of high school graduates increase? During this same time period, how much did the earnings of college graduates increase? Where did you find the information?
7. In 1993, how much more would a person with a bachelor's degree earn than a person without a high school diploma? Where did you find the information?
8. In 1993, how much more would a person with a bachelor's degree in engineering earn than a person with a bachelor's degree in education? Where did you find the information?
9. In today's economy, does a college degree guarantee a high income? Why or why not? If not, is it still worthwhile? Why or why not?
10. In paragraph 17, Jones states, "The report also highlights gaps between the educational and economic attainment of minorities versus whites." What example does she use to support her statement?

USE YOUR STRATEGIES: EXERCISE #4—"THE GREYING OF THE PLANET"

Jean-Claude Chasteland is a French demographer who was head of the United Nations Population Division in New York until 1990, and is now a consultant with the French National Institute of Demographic Studies in Paris. He has published many articles on the demographic problems of the Third World and on questions of population and development in general. This selection—"The Greying of the Planet"—is from *UNESCO Courier*.

THE GREYING OF THE PLANET

JEAN-CLAUDE CHASTELAND

The world has just experienced three decades of rapid demographic change. In the past thirty years, world population has grown from 2.7 billion to a little over 5 billion. During this period of unprecedented expansion, something occurred, at first unremarked, that, nevertheless, was of great importance for the future—for the first time since the eighteenth century, during the early 1970s, the growth rate of the world population began to decline.

This new trend was an indication that, following the industrialized countries, Third World countries were in their turn entering the phase of demographic transition (see Chart). In other words their fertility was dropping. The speed with which this demographic transition is completed is likely to be the factor which determines not only the future size of the populations concerned but also their age structure. The faster the transition phase is completed the more quickly their populations will age; for, as the French demographer Alfred Sauvy used to say, populations have no other choice than to grow or to grow old.

When all is said and done, the aging of a population, defined here as an increase in the proportion of old people in relation to total population, is striking evidence of the successes achieved in gaining technological mastery over certain aspects of life and death. The sometimes excessive fears expressed about population aging seem, therefore, somewhat paradoxical. Perhaps this rather pessimistic attitude finds its roots in the negative idea that the individual has of his or her own aging—an ineluctable process that ends in death. No one can halt the passage of time and, for the individual, rejuvenation is merely a metaphor. Populations, however, do not stand in the same relationship with time; through the interplay of fertility and mortality rates, they can indeed grow younger or older or maintain a stable age structure. Of course, there are thresholds above which the aging of a population becomes virtually irreversible, but it is possible to achieve a stable state in which the process of aging is, as it were, suspended in time.

WORLD POPULATION TRENDS BY AGE GROUP BETWEEN 1950 AND 2025 (PERCENT)

	WORLD POPULATION				*INDUSTRIALIZED COUNTRIES*				*DEVELOPING COUNTRIES*			
	0–14	15–59	60 AND OVER	TOTAL	0–14	15–59	60 AND OVER	TOTAL	0–14	15–59	60 AND OVER	TOTAL
1950	35	57	8	100	28	61	11	100	38	56	6	100
1990	32	59	9	100	21	62	17	100	36	57	7	100
2000	31	59	10	100	20	61	19	100	34	58	8	100
2025	24	61	15	100	18	57	25	100	26	62	12	100

Source: United Nations data, New York 1988.

EXERCISE #4 QUESTIONS—"THE GREYING OF THE PLANET"

1. What does the title, "The greying of the planet," mean?
2. How much has the world population grown in the past three decades? Is this an unusual amount?
3. What is the "demographic transition" referred to in paragraph 2?
4. How does Chasteland define an "aging population"?
5. To what does Chasteland attribute the aging of the population? Do you agree? Why or why not?
6. What does the chart contain? Which of the entries are actual percentages and which are projected percentages?
7. Describe the membership of the three categories in the chart: World Population, Industrialized Countries, and Developing Countries.
8. What is the population expected to look like in the world's industrialized countries in the year 2000?
9. How will that population (described in #8) be like and/or different than the population in the world's developing countries in the year 2000?
10. What does Chasteland mean by the phrase "an ineluctable process" in paragraph 3?

CHAPTER 7 CONNECTIONS

A. Do you usually read graphics or skip over them? Do you often read graphics and skip over the words? Are there some types of graphics you find easy to understand? Are there some types of graphics you often have difficulty reading? What makes a graphic difficult for you to understand? What is one thing you will try to make reading graphics easier?

B. For the next two days, keep track of the graphics you read in your textbooks, during classes, at work, in newspaper and magazines—everywhere. Then answer these questions. Were you surprised at the number of graphics you had to read—either more or less than expected? Where did you encounter the largest number of graphics? Describe the graphic that was the hardest for you to read. What did you do to help your understanding? Describe the graphic that was the easiest for you to read. Why do you think it was easy for you?

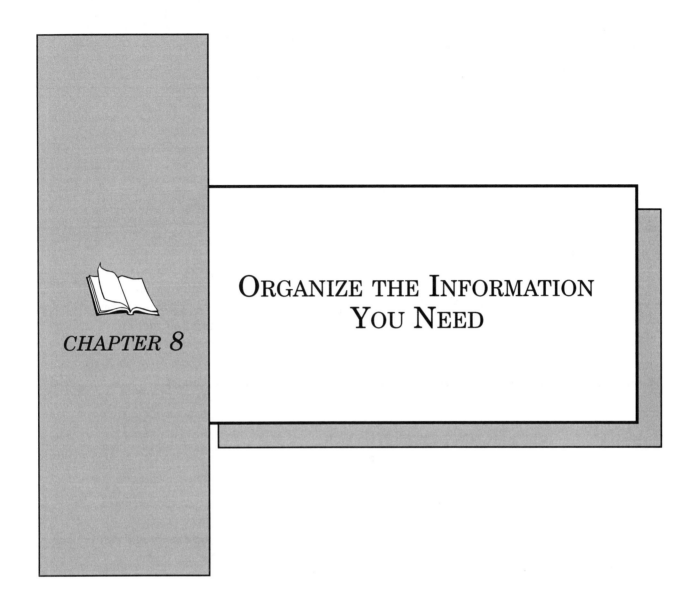

ORGANIZE THE INFORMATION YOU NEED

CHAPTER 8

So often we hear the phrase, "I've got to get organized!" But what do people want to accomplish by getting organized, and how do they go about getting organized? The dictionary says you organize something by systematically arranging a collection of interdependent parts with relation to the whole. In other words, you introduce an overall order to things. For example, you prioritize a list of tasks you have to get done at work or you arrange the errands you have to run according to your route of travel. You organize, or bring order to things, because it makes your work and life more efficient.

As you develop your plan for this chapter, consider how you organize various tasks and activities in your life. Do you consciously spend part of each day "getting organized" or do you unconsciously order things? Do you have different organization strategies for different kinds of tasks? Does anyone ever say they wish you were better organized? What do you think they mean?

Define this chapter's key vocabulary:

annotate
graphic organizers
outline
information map
paraphrase
summary and summarize

CHAPTER 8 OBJECTIVES

❏ Use annotating as a strategy for organizing information.
❏ Use outlining and mapping as a strategy for organizing information.
❏ Use summarizing as a strategy for organizing information.

WHAT IS MY BASIC STRATEGY FOR ORGANIZING THE INFORMATION I NEED?

As You Plan:

1. Understand the vocabulary.
2. Predict the thesis and/or main idea.
3. Determine how much detail you need to know.

As You Read:

4. Actively search for information that helps you clarify and refine your prediction about the thesis and/or main idea.
5. Identify useful signal words.
6. Determine if the way the author develops the thesis or main idea helps you to understand the details.
7. Use the author's signal words, punctuation, and development as clues to help you identify information and ideas that you need.
8. Identify the author's stance.
9. Integrate graphic and text information.

As You Review:

10. Revise and restate the thesis and/or main idea.
11. Restate the supporting details you need to fulfill your purpose.
12. Organize thesis, main ideas, and supporting details.

WHY DO I NEED TO ORGANIZE INFORMATION?

In everyday life you have to keep track of a variety of information—tax records, baseball cards, recipes, holiday card mailing list, appointments, and outings. For each type of information, you analyze which parts are most useful and figure out a way to sort, organize, and store the information so you can easily find and use it when you want it.

Since there isn't just one way to organize and store all information, based on your purpose and the type of information, you design an appropriate organizational strategy. For example, you might keep tax records in envelopes by deduction category, baseball cards in binders by player or team, recipes in a box divided by meal course, mailing lists in a notebook in alphabetical order, and appointments and outings on a calendar.

In academic life you also have to keep track of a variety of information—text information, supplemental readings, lecture notes, study group explanations, and research data. And, just like you do with everyday information, you must analyze your purpose and the type of information and then design a way to sort, organize, and store it so you can easily find, review, and use it.

In sociology for example, you might annotate your text, outline the supplemental readings and study group explanations in your notebook on pages opposite your lecture notes, and summarize the research data. On the other hand, in biology you might integrate information from all sources into a series of information maps, or in a personal development class you might summarize information in a journal.

The most difficult part of designing an effective organizational strategy is knowing and identifying what you need to know: thesis, main ideas, major details, and minor details. Once you identify the information you need, organizing it so you can efficiently and effectively access it is relatively easy. Common strategies include annotating, creating graphic notes, and summarizing.

HOW CAN I EFFECTIVELY ANNOTATE TEXT?

By annotate I mean write brief, useful information in the margins of your text in your own words. Annotation is an effective strategy whether you need to organize only main ideas or all the information the author gives, down through the minor examples.

For most students, any discussion of marking texts includes how they use their arsenal of highlighting markers. Unfortunately, using highlighters to mark a text is not always a good idea. First, it encourages you to passively mark the author's words rather than restating ideas in your own words. Second, highlighters seem to encourage you to mark too much text without regard to the type or level of information. And finally, page after page of rainbowed lines make it difficult for you to review only the important information.

Annotating, on the other hand, makes you an active participant—you must translate the author's words and ideas into your own. In addition, since you must fit your notes legibly into the text's margins, annotating encourages you to carefully sift and sort ideas. And finally, when it comes time to review, you have already brought order to the information you need.

As with all strategies for organizing information, do not try to annotate, or mark, material the first time you read it. Only after you have read and thought about the material and have a clear understanding of what you need to know, can you begin to annotate.

The better your annotations are, the more organized and effective your review will be. You will have clarified the ideas and concepts that are important to your purpose. Although your annotations will vary depending on your purpose for reading and the content, typically you will do the following when making annotations:

Restate the thesis and/or main ideas.

Mark key words and major details or concepts.

Note examples you need to know.

Restate information from graphics.

Tag confusing ideas you want to clarify.

Jot down possible test questions.

Cite a useful method of development—e.g., cause/effect, comparison/contrast.

In addition to your marginal summaries, common symbols you might use include: T for *thesis*, MI for *main idea*, EX for *example*, S for *summary*, DEF for *definition*; 1, 2, 3, for major points; ? for items to be clarified, and * for important concepts. Underline judiciously. As you practice annotating various texts, you will develop additional shorthand, or codes, that make the strategy more effective for you.

I've used some of the common notations on this paragraph from Bergman and McKnight's *Introduction to Geography* "Weather and Climate" section.

T: Earth different from other planets in many ways
MI: major diff.—our atmosphere

T The Earth is different from other known planets in a variety of ways. MI One of the most notable differences is the presence around our planet of a substantial atmosphere with components and characteristics that are distinctive from those of other planetary atmospheres. *Our atmosphere makes life possible on this planet. It ① supplies most of the oxygen that animals must have to survive, as well as the carbon dioxide needed by plants. It ② helps maintain a water supply, which is essential to all living things. It serves as an ③ insulating blanket to ameliorate temperature extremes and thus provide a livable environment over most of the Earth. It also ④ shields the Earth from much of the sun's ultraviolet radiation, which otherwise would be fatal to most life forms.

*atmosphere makes life possible
4 ways:

The annotations reinforce what you established in Chapters 4 and 5: sentence 1 is the thesis for the section, sentence 2 is the main idea for this paragraph, sentence 3 is a major detail, and sentences 4–7 are minor details.

Consider the annotations on Macionis's paragraph on surveys from *Sociology*.

MI: survey research: people respond to QS.

MI A survey is a research method in which subjects respond to a series of items or questions in a questionnaire or an interview. Perhaps the ①most widely used of all research methods, surveys are particularly ②suited to studying what cannot be observed directly, such as political attitudes, religious beliefs, or the private lives of couples. Like experiments, surveys can be used to ③investigate the ④relationship among variables. They are also useful for descriptive research, in which subject responses help a sociologist to describe a social setting, such as an urban neighborhood or gambling casino.

Annotations are your notes to yourself about what's important to remember.

PRACTICE: ANNOTATING TEXT—"WRITING ABOUT HISTORY"

The excerpt from "Writing about History" by Dr. Robert Weiss in Unger's *These United States*, 5th ed., provides some fundamental principles for reading historical reports and essays. Assume you are preparing to answer an essay question about how to read history effectively. Annotate it only after you have read and thought about the material and have a clear understanding of what you need to know.

WRITING ABOUT HISTORY

DR. ROBERT WEISS

Reading History

An understanding of the fundamentals of historical writing will make the student of history a more discerning and selective reader. Although no two historical works are identical, most contain the same basic elements and can be approached in a similar manner by the reader. When reading a historical monograph, concentrate on the two basic issues discussed in the preceding section: facts and interpretation.

(CONTINUED)

WRITING ABOUT HISTORY (CONTINUED)

Interpretation

The first question the reader should ask is: What is the author's argument? What is his theme, his interpretation, his thesis? A theme is not the same as a topic. An author may select the Civil War as a topic, but he then must propose a particular theme or argument regarding some aspect of the war. (The most common, not surprisingly, is why the war occurred.)

Discovering the author's theme is usually easy enough because most writers state their arguments clearly in the preface to their book. Students often make the crucial error of skimming over the preface—if they read it at all—and then moving on to the "meat" of the book. Since the preface indicates the manner in which the author has used his data to develop his arguments, students who ignore it often find themselves overwhelmed with details without understanding what the author is attempting to say. This error should be avoided always.

The more history you read, the more you will appreciate the diversity of opinions and approaches among historians. While each author offers a unique perspective, historical works fall into general categories, or "schools," depending on their thesis and when they were published. The study of the manner in which different historians approach their subjects is referred to as *historiography*. Every historical subject has a historiography, sometimes limited, sometimes extensive. As in the other sciences, new schools of thought supplant existing ones, offering new insights and challenging accepted theories. Below are excerpts from two monographs dealing with the American Revolution. As you read them, note the contrast in the underlying arguments.

1. "Despite its precedent-setting character, however, the American revolt is noteworthy because it made no serious interruption in the smooth flow of American development. Both in intention and in fact, the American Revolution conserved the past rather than repudiated it. And in preserving the colonial experience, the men of the first quarter century of the Republic's history set the scenery and wrote the script for the drama of American politics for years to come."*

2. "The stream of revolution, once started, could not be confined within narrow banks, but spread abroad upon the land. Many economic desires, many social aspirations were set free by the political struggle, many aspects of colonial society profoundly altered by the forces thus set loose. The relations of social classes to each other, the institution of slavery, the system of landholding, of business, the forms and spirit of the intellectual and religious life, all felt the transforming hand of revolution, all emerged from under it in shapes advanced many degrees nearer to those we know."†

What you have just read is nothing less than two conflicting theories of the fundamental nature of the American Revolution. Professor Jameson portrays the Revolution as a catalyst for major social, economic, and political change, while Professor Degler views it primarily as a war for independence that conserved, rather than transformed, colonial institutions. The existence of such divergent opinions makes it imperative that the reader be aware of the argument of every book and read a variety of books and articles to get different perspectives on a subject.

All historical works contain biases of some sort, but a historical bias is not in itself bad or negative. As long as history books are composed by human beings, they will reflect the perspectives of their authors. This need not diminish the quality of historical writing if historians remain faithful to the facts. Some historians, however, have such strong biases that they distort the evidence to make it fit their preconceived notions. This type of history writing (which is the exception rather than the rule) is of limited value, but when properly treated can contribute to the accumulation of knowledge by providing new insights and challenging the values—and creative abilities—of other historians.

*Carl N. Degler, *Out of Our Past*, rev. ed. (New York: Harper and Row, Harper Colophon Books, 1970), p. 73.
†J. Franklin Jameson, *The American Revolution Considered as a Social Movement* (Boston: Beacon Press, 1956), p. 9.

(CONTINUED)

WRITING ABOUT HISTORY (CONTINUED)

Evidence

Once you are aware of the author's central argument, you can concentrate on his use of evidence—the "facts"—that buttress that argument. There are several types of questions that you should keep in mind as you progress through a book. What types of evidence does the author use? Is his evidence convincing? Which sources does he rely on, and what additional sources might he have consulted? One strategy you might adopt is to imagine that you are writing the monograph. Where would you go for information? What would you look at? Then ask yourself: Did the author consult these sources? Obviously no writer can examine everything. A good historical work, however, offers convincing data extracted from a comprehensive collection of materials.

As you begin to ask these questions, you will develop the skill of critical reading. Used in this sense the word critical does not mean reading to discern what is wrong with the narrative. Rather, it refers to analytic reading, assessing the strengths and weaknesses of the monograph, and determining whether the argument ultimately works. All historical works should be approached with a critical—but open—mind.

One important point to remember is that you need not accept or reject every aspect of a historical monograph. In fact, you most likely will accord a "mixed review" to most of the books you read. You may accept the author's argument but find his evidence inadequate, or you may be impressed by his data but draw different conclusions from it. You may find some chapters tightly argued, but others unconvincing. Even if you like a particular book, almost inevitably you will have some comments, criticisms, or suggestions.

HOW CAN I CREATE AN OUTLINE OR MAP TO ORGANIZE INFORMATION I NEED?

Another way to organize information is to put your notes on separate paper in a graphic, or picture, format. Graphic organizers are especially effective when you need to order several pieces of information of different levels of importance.

Let's look at two types of graphic organizers—an informal outline and an information map—using Bergman and McKnight's "Weather and Climate" and Macionis's "survey" paragraphs.

WHAT IS AN INFORMAL OUTLINE?

An informal outline is a type of graphic organizer for information that uses differing amounts of indentation to create a picture of the relationships among ideas. When you create a formal outline, you follow several rules and you designate different levels of information in two primary ways: (1) different letters and numbers at the start of each line and (2) different amounts of indentation, or space, at the start of each line. When you create an informal outline, however, you are not bound by the rules of formal outlining. You are only interested in using different amounts of indentation to draw a picture of the relationships among ideas.

To create an informal outline, identify the thesis, main idea(s), major supporting details, and minor supporting details you need to know. Then, on notebook paper, write down each piece of information indented under the information it supports and explains.

For example, if you were creating an informal outline of a multi-paragraph selection it might look like this:

Thesis (of the whole selection)
    Main Idea (of first paragraph)
       Major Detail
          Minor Detail
    Main Idea (of second paragraph)
       Major Detail
       Major Detail
          Minor Detail
          Minor Detail
       Major Detail

If you were creating an informal outline of a paragraph it might look like this:

Main Idea (of whole paragraph)
    Major Detail
    Major Detail
       Minor Detail
    Major Detail

If you needed to know all the information, including the examples, in Bergman and McKnight's "Weather and Climate" section, your outline might look like this:

The Earth is different from other known planets in a variety of ways.
    A major difference is the presence around our planet of an atmosphere very different from other planets.
       Our atmosphere makes life possible on this planet.
          It supplies most of the oxygen and carbon dioxide.
          It helps maintain a water supply.
          It serves as an insulating blanket to lessen temperature extremes.
          It shields the Earth from much of the sun's ultraviolet radiation.

Now, assume you need to know all the information presented in the following Macionis paragraph.

A survey is a research method in which subjects respond to a series of items or questions in a questionnaire or an interview. Perhaps the most widely used of all research methods, surveys are particularly suited to studying what cannot be observed directly, such as political attitudes, religious beliefs, or the private lives of couples. Like experiments, surveys can be used to investigate the relationship among variables. They are also useful for descriptive research, in which subject responses help a sociologist to describe a social setting, such as an urban neighborhood or gambling casino.

Complete this informal outline.

A survey is a research method in which subjects respond to a series of items or questions in a questionnaire or an interview.

_____

_____

_____

_____

_____

_____

WHAT IS AN INFORMATION MAP?

Another graphic, or visual, way you can organize information is to map it. Just like a road map that shows the relationships of small towns, cities, and metropolitan areas with different size dots and different sizes and styles of type, an information map shows the relationships among information with different size boxes or circles and different size type.

Like the process of creating an outline, the first step in creating an information map is to identify the thesis, main idea(s), major supporting details, and minor supporting details you need to know. Then you can begin to construct your map to show the relationships of the different levels of information. Begin by writing the thesis or main idea in a large box or circle. Add the major supporting information as branches off the central idea. Continue adding branches for each level of detail you need to know.

For example, a map of the Macionis paragraph could look like this:

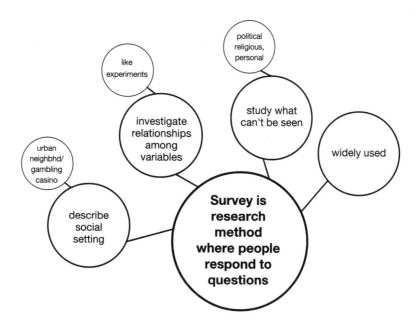

Complete a map of the information from Bergman and McKnight's "Weather and Climate" paragraph. Again, assume you need to know all the information.

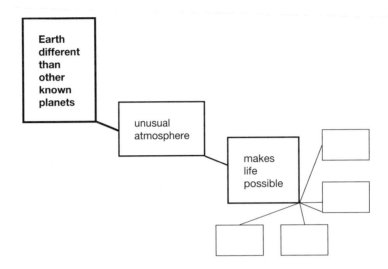

You can also create different types of maps to reinforce the development or organizational clues the author has used.

For example, a map of Long's comparison paragraph from Chapter 5 might look like this.

A computer system can also be likened to the biological system of the human body. Your brain is the processing component. Your eyes and ears are input components that send signals to the brain. If you see someone approaching, your brain matches the visual image of this person with others in your memory (storage component). If the visual image matches that of a friend, your brain sends signals to your vocal cords and right arm (output components) to greet your friend with a hello and a handshake. Computer system components interact in a similar way. (Long, *Introduction to Computers and Information Processing*)

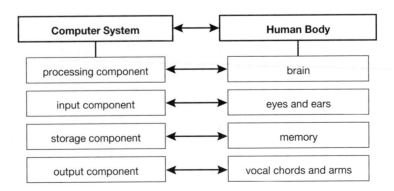

Or, if an author wanted you to understand the steps of a process, like Tocquet does in this paragraph, you might make a simple map like the one that follows the paragraph.

For the extraction of a square root, the mental calculation broadly follows the normal method: first, you divide the number into groups of two figures, you look for the largest square contained in the first group, you carry the root as the first result and subtract this square from the first group. Next, you mentally add on to the remainder the first figure of the second group and divide the number thus obtained by twice the first figure carried; you retain this quotient as the second figure of the root required. As can be seen, the process is rather complicated and lengthy. (Tocquet, *The Magic of Numbers*)

To calculate square root mentally:

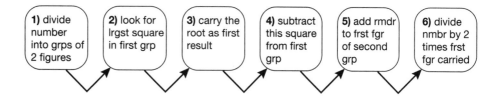

PRACTICE: CREATING AN INFORMAL OUTLINE OR INFORMATION MAP

Create an informal outline or information map using the excerpt from pages 163–165, "Writing about History" by Dr. Robert Weiss from Unger's *These United States*, 5th ed. Again, assume you are preparing to answer an essay question about how to read history effectively. Create your outline or map only after you have read and thought about the material and have a clear understanding of what you need to know.

HOW CAN I CREATE A SUMMARY TO ORGANIZE THE INFORMATION I NEED TO KNOW?

A summary is a condensed version of the original in your own words. Begin your summary with a restatement of the thesis or main idea. Include the main ideas or major supporting details in the same order and with the same emphasis as the original. Paraphrase—put all information in your own words. For tips on when to paraphrase, see the study strategy entitled "Avoiding Plagiarism" on page 434.

When you need to concentrate on just the thesis and main ideas or on the main ideas and major details, writing a summary is a good strategy. A summary does not include examples and minor details that may be included in annotations or graphic organizers.

Your summary must be:

In your own words: Do not copy from the original.

In standard paragraph form: Use good writing techniques (i.e., complete sentences with capital letters, transitions, and punctuation.)

Brief: Include only the thesis and main ideas or main idea and major details.

Complete: Do not leave out any main ideas or major details.

Objective: Include only the author's information; do not include your opinion of the information.

To write an effective summary:

1. Reread the portion you need to summarize.
2. Write the thesis or main idea in your own words. As with all thesis or main idea statements, do not include your opinion.
3. Identify each main idea and/or major detail in the selection.
4. Paraphrase each idea or detail into a sentence.
5. Revise and edit your paragraph.
6. Make certain your summary is an accurate capsule version of the original.

This is a sample summary of Bergman and McKnight's "Weather and Climate" paragraph. Because you must use your own words in a summary, yours probably wouldn't read exactly like this one. The basic content, however, would be the same.

The Earth differs from other planets in several ways. The biggest difference is the Earth's unique atmosphere. It is the makeup of our atmosphere that makes life possible.

This is a sample summary of Macionis's survey paragraph.

A survey is a method used in research where people are asked to answer written or oral questions. Surveys are the most common research method and are very useful when studying things that can't be seen. Surveys can also be used to examine the connection among variables and for descriptive research.

PRACTICE: WRITING A SUMMARY

Write a summary of the excerpt "Writing about History" by Dr. Robert Weiss (on pages 163–165) from Unger's *These United States*, 5th ed., to help you prepare to answer an essay question about how to read history effectively.

CHAPTER 8 REVIEW QUESTIONS

1. What is annotating? When would you use annotating as a strategy for organizing information?
2. What are graphic organizers? When would you use a graphic organizers as a strategy for organizing information?
3. What does *paraphrase* mean?
4. What is a summary? When would you use summarizing as a strategy for organizing information?

CHAPTER 8 THINK AND CONNECT QUESTIONS

5. Create an information map for "Theories of Human Behavior," Chapter 4, Exercise #4, page 77.

6. Write a summary of "The Health-Illness Continuum," Chapter 7, Exercise #2, pages 152–153.

CHAPTER 8 APPLICATION EXERCISES

7. Select a one-page reading assignment from another text. Assume your purpose is to prepare for a quiz on the information. Annotate the text selection.

8. Select a five paragraph reading assignment from another class. Based on your purpose and the content, use one of these strategies: Annotate it, create an informal outline or map, or write a summary of the selection.

USE YOUR STRATEGIES: EXERCISE #1—"FEEDBACK"

Kittie Watson is an associate professor at Tulane University. The chapter on listening and feedback, from which this selection—"Feedback"—is excerpted, was written specifically for the sixth edition of Barker and Barker's text, *Communication*.

FEEDBACK

KITTIE W. WATSON

[1]Communication is a circular process. As a message is transmitted from sender to receiver, a return message, known as feedback, is transmitted in the opposite direction. Feedback is a message that indicates the level of understanding or agreement between two or more people in communication in response to an original message. Feedback represents a listener's verbal or nonverbal commentary on the message being communicated.

[2]Feedback is an ongoing process that usually begins as a reaction to various aspects of the initial message. For example, a definite response is being fed back to the speaker when we shake our heads affirmatively or look quizzically at the speaker. Feedback plays an essential role in helping us to determine whether or not our message has been understood; whether it is being received positively or negatively; and whether our audience is open or defensive, self-controlled or bored. Feedback can warn us that we must alter our communication to achieve the desired effect. If we are not aware of feedback or don't pay any attention to it, there is a strong possibility that our efforts at communicating will be completely ineffective.

[3]To emphasize the importance of the feedback mechanism in communication, you need only imagine yourself growing up for the last 18 years or so, never having received any feedback. No one has praised you as you learned to walk or ride a bike. No one has warned you not to chase a ball into the street or to put your hand on a hot stove. No one has shared your tears or laughter. You probably would not function well at all. How would you appraise your self-concept? What values or morals would you possess? While such an existence is impossible, since a certain amount of feedback comes from you yourself as well as from others in the environment, this example does suggest the various functions and effects of feedback in the communication process.

(CONTINUED)

FEEDBACK (CONTINUED)

Types of Feedback

[4]There are two types of feedback: self-feedback and listener feedback. See Figure 3.5.

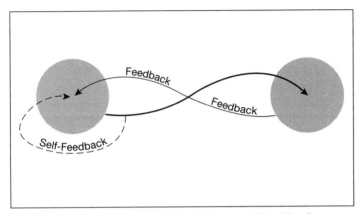

Figure 3.5   Self-Feedback and Listener Feedback

[5]Self-feedback applies to the words and actions that are fed back into your central nervous system as you perceive your own muscular movements and hear yourself speak. Feeling your tongue twist as you mispronounce a word or, in a library, suddenly realizing that you are speaking too loudly are examples of self-feedback. Another example would be hearing yourself use a word incorrectly, or reversing sounds—for example, asking, "Were you sappy or had?" instead of "happy or sad."

[6]Research indicates that self-feedback plays an important role in the nature and form of our judgmental processes, especially when listener feedback is absent. For example, Hagafors and Brehmer have found that our judgments become more consistent when we are required to justify them to others and when no other form of listener feedback is present. In addition, under these conditions our judgments seem to become more analytical and less intuitive. It seems that self-feedback in the form of justification alters the nature and form of our overall judgmental process.

[7]The other major type of feedback, listener feedback, involves verbal and nonverbal responses. Verbal feedback may take the form of questions or comments. A listener may, for instance, ask a speaker to explain the last point or give praise for making the story so interesting. Nonverbal feedback may be transmitted by applause or laughter, to indicate approval, or by a blank stare, which might indicate disinterest or confusion. Even silence can act as feedback. If a teacher asks a question and no one answers, the silence may indicate understanding, or perhaps dislike of the teacher. If a father asks his son if he has finished his homework and the son doesn't reply, that silence is meaningful.

Functions of Feedback

[8]Feedback serves various functions in the communication process. The first of these functions is to evaluate what is right or wrong about a particular communication. If you give a speech to the class, your teacher will offer criticism and suggestions for improving your delivery. If someone is watching you hang a painting, he or she will give you feedback as you try various positions, to help you find the right place for it. As will be discussed in Chapter 4, nonverbal feedback, in the form of nods and hand movements helps to regulate turn taking in conversation.

(CONTINUED)

FEEDBACK (CONTINUED)

[9]Secondly, feedback can serve to stimulate change. For example, a popular soft-drink company, after changing its century-old formula, received so much mixed feedback in the form of letters and phone calls that the company not only retained the new formula but brought back the original formula and placed both on grocery-store shelves.

[10]A third function of feedback is to reinforce, to give reward or punishment. A father says, "I'm proud of you, son," or "Jim, can't you ever keep quiet!" When used in this way, rewarding feedback encourages certain behaviors, while punishing feedback is intended to discourage certain behaviors. Comedians rely on positive reinforcement from their audience in the form of laughter; their performance may improve if they sense that the audience feedback is positive.

EXERCISE #1 QUESTIONS—"FEEDBACK"

Assume you are going to have a quiz on what feedback is, the types of feedback, and the functions of feedback.

1. Annotate this text selection.
2. Write a sentence that expresses the author's thesis.
3. What is feedback?
4. True or False: If we don't pay attention to feedback, we may not communicate effectively.
5. What are the two types of feedback?
6. Identify three major functions of feedback.
7. What is the purpose of Figure 3.5?

USE YOUR STRATEGIES: EXERCISE #2—"ALCOHOL IN PERSPECTIVE"

This selection—"Alcohol in Perspective"—appeared in the *University of California at Berkeley Wellness Letter*, which is published in association with the School of Public Health.

ALCOHOL IN PERSPECTIVE

UNIVERSITY OF CALIFORNIA AT BERKELEY WELLNESS LETTER

Double Messages

[1]Alcohol, a natural product of fermentation, is probably the most widely used of all drugs. It has been a part of human culture since history began and part of American life since Europeans settled on this continent. "The good creature of God," colonial Americans called it—as well as "demon rum." At one time, beer or whiskey may have been safer to drink than well water, but there have always been many other reasons for drinking: the sociability of drinking, the brief but vivid sense of relaxation alcohol can bring, and the wish to celebrate or participate in religious and family rituals where alcohol is served. In some cultures, abstention is the rule. In others, the occasional use of alcohol is regarded as pleasurable and necessary—but such use is carefully controlled and intoxication frowned upon. Tradition and attitude play a powerful role in the use of this drug.

(CONTINUED)

ALCOHOL IN PERSPECTIVE (CONTINUED)

²Some people, unfortunately, drink because of depression and/or addiction to alcohol. Apart from such needs, powerful social and economic forces encourage people to drink. For starters, alcoholic beverages are everywhere—from planes and trains to restaurants and county fairs. Also, drink is cheap. The relative cost of alcohol has declined in the last decades. Since 1967 the cost of soft drinks and milk has quadrupled, and the cost of all consumer goods has tripled, but the cost of alcohol has not even doubled. This is because the excise tax on alcohol is not indexed to inflation. Congress has raised the federal tax on beer and wine only once in 40 years (in 1990). The tax on hard liquor has been increased only twice—small raises in 1985 and 1990. Opinion polls have shown that the public is in favor of raising federal excise taxes on alcohol, but the alcohol industry successfully fights increases. Furthermore, about 20 percent of all alcohol is sold for business entertainment and is thus tax deductible, making it that much less costly to whoever pays the bar bill.

³Finally, the alcohol, advertising, and entertainment industries tirelessly promote the idea that it's normal, desirable, smart, sophisticated, and sexy to drink. In print, on television, and at the movies, we see beautiful, healthy people drinking. Beer ads associate the product with sports events, fast cars, camaraderie, and sex. Hollywood's stars have always imbibed plentifully, on and off camera: "Here's looking at you, kid," echoes down the ages. Among modern American male writers, alcoholism has been a badge of the trade: Hemingway, Fitzgerald, and Faulkner were all alcoholics. In *The Thirsty Muse*, literary historian Tom Dardis cites the deadly effect of alcohol on male American writers, many of whom made a credo of heavy drinking.

⁴Considering all these pro-drinking forces, it is amazing that 35 percent of us over 18 never drink, and another 35 percent drink lightly and only occasionally. It's equally amazing that our drinking levels have been declining for the past 10 years. But it's estimated that only 8 percent of us consume more than half of all the alcohol. Still, out-and-out alcoholism is only one factor in the grief caused by drinking, and alcohol problems are not a simple matter of the drunk versus the rest of us.

Alcohol's Toll

⁵It's a rare person in our society whose life goes untouched by alcohol. Alcohol causes, or is associated with, over 100,000 deaths every year, often among the young. In 1990, alcohol-related traffic crashes killed more than 22,000 people—almost the same number as homicides. Half the pedestrians killed by cars have elevated blood alcohol levels. At some time in their lives, 40 percent of all Americans will be involved in an alcohol-related traffic crash. Alcoholism creates unhealthy family dynamics, contributing to domestic violence and child abuse. Fetal alcohol syndrome, caused by drinking during pregnancy, is the leading known cause of mental retardation. After tobacco, alcohol is the leading cause of premature death in America. The total cost of alcohol use in America has been estimated at $86 billion annually, a figure so huge as to lose its meaning. But money is a feeble method for measuring the human suffering.

⁶In a free society, banning alcohol is neither desirable nor acceptable. But government, schools, and other institutions could do more than they do to protect the public health, teach the young about the dangers of alcohol, and treat alcoholics. As individuals and as citizens, we could all contribute to reducing the toll alcohol exacts on American life.

EXERCISE #2 QUESTIONS—"ALCOHOL IN PERSPECTIVE"

Assume you are preparing to answer two essay questions on this selection—one about society's double messages and another on alcohol's toll.

1. Based on your need to prepare to answer two essay questions on this selection, what method would you use to organize the information? Explain.

2. Use the organization strategy of your choice on this selection.

3. What does the subheading "double messages" mean? How does the author develop and support the idea that society sends double messages?

4. Do you agree that society sends double messages about alcohol? Give an example to support your answer.

5. What are four reasons people drink?

6. True or False: The relative cost of alcohol to the consumer has dropped over the last several years.

7. True or False: The percentage of people who drink has declined over the last ten years.

8. True or False: Only 8 percent of the people consume 50 percent of all the alcohol.

9. True or False: Opinion polls show that Americans do not want an increase in liquor taxes.

10. Who promotes the idea that it's alright to drink? Why do you think these industries promote drinking?

11. What is the main idea of paragraph 5?

12. How does the author develop and support the main idea of paragraph 5?

13. What does the author mean by the phrase "money is a feeble method for measuring the human suffering" in paragraph 5?

14. What is the author's purpose for writing this selection?

USE YOUR STRATEGIES: EXERCISE #3—"THE UNITED STATES AND THE METRIC SYSTEM"

THE UNITED STATES AND THE METRIC SYSTEM: A CAPSULE HISTORY

NATIONAL INSTITUTE OF STANDARDS AND TECHNOLOGY

[1]The United States is the only *industrialized country* in the world not officially using the metric system. Because of its many advantages (e.g., easy conversion between units of the same quantity), the metric system has become the internationally accepted system of measurement units.

[2]Most Americans think that our involvement with metric measurement is relatively new. In fact, the United States' increasing use of metric units has been underway for many years, and the *pace has accelerated* in the past two decades. In the early 1800s the U.S. Coast and Geodetic Survey (the government's surveying and map-making agency) used meter and kilogram standards brought from France. In 1866 Congress authorized the use of the metric system in this country and supplied each state with a set of standard metric weights and measures.

[3]In 1875, the United States *reinforced its participation* in the development of the internationally recognized metric system by becoming one of the original seventeen signatory nations to the Treaty of the Meter. This agreement established the International Bureau of Weights and Measures (BIPM) in Sèvres, France, to provide standards of measurement for worldwide use.

(CONTINUED)

THE UNITED STATES AND THE METRIC SYSTEM:
A CAPSULE HISTORY (CONTINUED)

[4]In 1893, the metric measurement standards, resulting from international cooperation *under the auspices* of BIPM, were adopted as the fundamental standards for length and mass in the United States. Our "customary" measurements—the foot, pound, quart, etc.—have been defined in relation to the meter and the kilogram ever since.

[5]In 1960, the General Conference of Weights and Measures, the governing body that has overall responsibility for the metric system, and which is made-up of *signatory nations* to the Treaty of the Meter, approved a modernized version of the metric system. The "modernized" system is called Le Système International d'Unités or the International System of Units, abbreviated SI.

[6]In 1965, Great Britain, as a condition for becoming a member of the European Common Market, began a transition to the metric system in its trade and commerce. The conversion of England and the Commonwealth Nations to SI created a new sense of urgency regarding the use of metric units in the United States. Congress authorized a three-year study of this Nation's systems of measurement, *with particular emphasis on the feasibility of adopting SI.* Known as the "Metric Study Act of 1968," the study was conducted by the Department of Commerce. As part of the study, an advisory panel of 45 representatives consulted with and took testimony from hundreds of consumers, business organizations, labor groups, manufacturers, and state and local officials. The panel's report, "A Metric America, A Decision Whose Time Has Come," concluded that measurement in the United States was already based on metric units in many areas and that it was becoming more so every day. The majority of participants in the study believed that conversion to the metric system was in the best interests of the Nation, particularly in view of the increasing importance and influence of technology in American life and our foreign trade.

[7]The study recommended that the United States change to predominant use of the metric system over a ten-year period. Congress passed the Metric Conversion Act in 1975. The stated purpose of the Act was "to coordinate and plan the increasing use of the metric system in the United States." A process of voluntary conversion was initiated with the establishment of the U.S. Metric Board. The Board was charged with "devising and carrying out a broad program of planning, coordination, and public education, consistent with other national policy and interests, with the aim of implementing the policy set forth in this Act." However, the Act did not specify the ten-year conversion period recommended by the study. Further, much of the American public ignored the efforts of the Metric Board. In 1981, the Board reported to Congress that it *lacked the necessary clear Congressional mandate to bring about National conversion to predominant use of metric measurements.*

[8]Because of the Board's apparent ineffectiveness and efforts to reduce Federal spending, *it was disestablished* in the fall of 1982.

[9]The Board's demise increased doubts about the United States' commitment to metrication. *Public and private sector* metric transition slowed at the same time that the very reasons for the United States to adopt the metric system—the increasing competitiveness of other nations and the demands of global marketplaces—made completing United States metric conversion even more important.

[10]Congress, *recognizing the criticality of the United States' conformance* with international standards for trade, included new strong incentives for United States industrial metrication in the Omnibus Trade and Competitiveness Act of 1988. That legislation designated the metric system as the "preferred system of weights and measures for United States trade and commerce." It also required that all federal agencies use the metric system in their procurement, grants and other business-related activities by a "date certain and to the extent economically feasible, by the end of fiscal year 1992."

[11]The Act's mandates are based on the conclusion that industrial and commercial productivity, effectiveness in mathematics and science education, and competitiveness of American products in world markets, will be enhanced by completing the change to the metric system of units. Failure to do so will increasingly handicap the Nation's industry and economy. The Federal Government's mandate is intended to encourage United States producers to develop their ability to provide goods and services expressed in metric units.

EXERCISE #3 QUESTIONS—"THE UNITED STATES AND THE METRIC SYSTEM"

Assume you are preparing for a quiz on the history of the metric system.

1. Define each of these words or phrases from the selection:
   - a. industrialized country (¶1)
   - b. pace has accelerated (¶2)
   - c. reinforced its participation (¶3)
   - d. under the auspices of (¶4)
   - e. signatory nations (¶5)
   - f. with particular emphasis on the feasibility of adopting SI (¶6)
   - g. lacked the necessary clear Congressional mandate to bring about National conversion to predominant use of metric measurements (¶7)
   - h. it was disestablished (¶8)
   - i. public and private sector (¶9)
   - j. recognizing the criticality of the United States' conformance (¶10)

2. Write a sentence that expresses the author's thesis.

3. Consider the way the author developed the details to support the thesis. What would best organize the major details—a comparison/contrast chart, a cause/effect diagram, or a timeline? Why?

4. Using the method you think is best, map the major details.

5. True or False: The United States is the only industrialized country in the world that doesn't officially use the metric system.

6. True or False: The United States began using the metric system in the early 1800s.

7. True or False: The United States refused to sign the Treaty of the Meter in 1875.

8. True or False: Great Britain began its transition to the metric system in 1965.

9. True or False: The Omnibus Trade and Competitiveness Act of 1988 is intended to discourage U.S. businesses from using the metric system.

10. Why is the metric system the internationally accepted system of measurement units?

11. When and why was the U.S. Metric Board established?

12. When and why was the U.S. Metric Board disestablished?

13. By what date did the Omnibus Trade and Competitiveness Act of 1988 require federal agencies to use the metric system?

14. The mandates of the Omnibus Trade and Competitiveness Act of 1988 are based on three conclusions. What are they?

15. Do you use the metric system of units at home, at school, or at work? Do you think its use has increased since the end of 1992? Do you think the United States will make a complete transition to the metric system in the next ten years? Why or why not?

USE YOUR STRATEGIES: EXERCISE #4—"AREAS OF COMPUTER APPLICATIONS"

William Fuori and Louis Gioia teach in the Mathematics and Computer Processing Department at Nassau Community College in Garden City, New York. This selection—"Areas of Computer Applications"—is from *Computers and Information Processing*, 3rd ed.

AREAS OF COMPUTER APPLICATIONS

WILLIAM M. FUORI AND LOUIS V. GIOIA

[1]A computer is a very useful tool, but it is certainly not the answer to all of our problems. There are certain types of problems that a computer is equipped to handle more economically and efficiently than other devices or people.

Computers Do It Better

[2]Computers are superfast. Because they can perform tasks a lot more quickly than we can, we spend less time waiting. This frees us up to do other things. Computers are capable of performing boring or dangerous tasks (and without complaining). Computers, believe it or not, are extremely dependable. When something goes wrong and service is disrupted or there is an error in your paycheck, statistics reveal that usually it is not the computer's fault; the problem generally lies elsewhere. "Sorry, the computer is down" usually translates into a human error, not a mechanical malfunction.

[3]It should be apparent that computers are ideally suited to handle such primary business functions as payroll, personnel, accounting, and inventory, as each of these functions is justifiable, definable, repetitive, and deals with a large volume of data. New applications of computers are continually being discovered. If we were to attempt to produce a list of all the application areas to which computers are presently being applied, it would be obsolete before it could be completed. Some general areas that extensively employ computers are the following:

[4]1. General business: accounts receivable, accounts payable, inventory, personnel accounting, payroll
[5]2. Banking: account reconciliation, installment loan accounting, interest calculations, demand deposit accounting, trust services
[6]3. Education: attendance and grade-card reports, computer-assisted instruction, research analysis, registration
[7]4. Government: income tax return verification, motor vehicle registration, budget analysis, tax billing, property rolls.

[8]Other areas of application include law enforcement, military affairs, sports, transportation, real estate, business forecasting, medicine, broadcasting, commercial arcade games, publishing, and personal use in the home, to mention but a few. The uses of computers are indeed boundless, and present applications are only a sample of things to come.

EXERCISE #4 QUESTIONS—"AREAS OF COMPUTER APPLICATIONS"

Assume you are preparing to answer an essay question about the effective applications of computers.

1. Write a sentence that expresses the author's thesis.

2. Based on your need to prepare to answer an essay question about the effective applications of computers, what method would you use to organize the information? Explain.

3. Use the organization strategy of your choice on this selection.

4. Assume that instead of preparing to answer an essay question about the effective uses of computers, you are preparing to take a multiple choice test on the selection. What, if anything, would you do differently? Explain.

CHAPTER 8 CONNECTIONS

A. When you read a text assignment, what is usually the most difficult part for you—e.g., identifying the main idea, separating levels of details, organizing information? How do you think you can use one or more new strategies to make your reading more successful?

B. Do you consciously spend part of each day "getting organized" or do you unconsciously order things? Do you have different organization strategies for different kinds of tasks? Does anyone ever say they wish you were better organized? What do you think they mean? Do you ever wish other people were more organized? What advice would you give them?

CHAPTER 9

DECIDE WHAT TO DO WITH THE AUTHOR'S INFORMATION

As you've worked through the first eight chapters you discovered that reading for learning requires more than just reporting what an author says. To be successful, you must become involved with the author's thoughts and ideas. Now you must decide what to do with those thoughts and ideas. As Edgar Dale says,

Reading, we must remember, is a process of getting meaning from the printed page by putting meaning into the printed page. Reading taste and ability are always tethered to past experience. But reading itself is one way of increasing this capital fund of past experience. Reading, therefore, must be seen as more than saying the word, more than seeing the sentences and paragraphs. Good reading is the way a person brings his whole life to bear on the new ideas which he finds on the printed page. It is reading the lines, reading between the lines, and reading beyond the lines. It is an active, not a passive process. The good reader becomes involved with the writing and the writer. He agrees, he argues back. He asks: Is it true? Is it pertinent? What, if anything, should I or could I do about it?

How did you decide whom to vote for during the last election? If you had to vote on "English Only" legislation, what sources would you read? Among all the organizations that ask for contributions, how do you decide whom to give your time and money? As you plan for reading this chapter, think about how you reach decisions such as these and the impact reading has on your life.

Define this chapter's key vocabulary:

critical reader
objectively analyze
argument
evidence

CHAPTER 9 OBJECTIVES

❏ Identify the strategies of a responsible reader.
❏ Understand what it means to be a critical reader.
❏ Understand the need to make a conscious decision to accept, reject, or suspend judgment on the author's information.

WHAT IS MY BASIC STRATEGY FOR DECIDING WHAT TO DO WITH THE AUTHOR'S INFORMATION?

As You Plan:

1. Think about how you form opinions and how you decide what to do.
2. Think about what makes you believe or disbelieve an author.
3. Understand the vocabulary.
4. Predict the thesis/argument and main ideas.
5. Determine how much detail you need to know.

As You Read:

6. Actively search for information that helps to clarify and refine your prediction about the thesis/argument and main ideas.
7. Consider what you know about the topic; how does the new information agree and/or disagree with what you know?
8. Keep an open mind; do not unquestioningly accept or reject what you read.

As You Review:

9. Revise and restate the thesis/argument and main ideas.
10. Organize the thesis/argument, main ideas, and supporting details.
11. Make a conscious decision to accept, reject, or suspend judgment on the author's ideas and information. If you have suspended judgment, plan where you will gather more information on the topic.

WHAT ARE MY STRATEGIES AS A RESPONSIBLE READER?

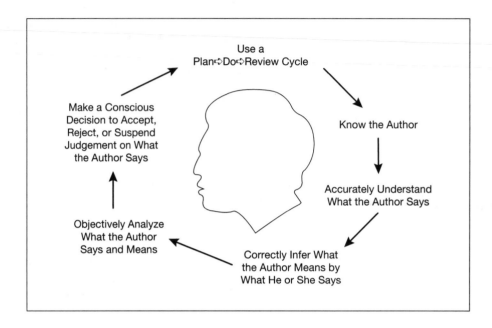

INITIAL STRATEGIES

Use a Plan⇨Do⇨Review Cycle (Review Chapter 1)   You begin with a systematic approach to reading because it promotes objectivity and decreases opportunities for impulsive or emotional reactions to an author's ideas and information.

When you develop and implement a plan based on an assignment's two critical factors—your purpose for reading the assignment and the difficulty of the material—you are more likely to be an active, thinking participant in the process. And, as you have discovered, reading requires thinking.

By viewing reading as a continuing, or cyclic, activity you have time to integrate new information with what you know, and are able to link ideas into the larger perspective.

Know the Author (Review Chapters 2 and 6)   Reading without knowing the writer, like talking with someone you don't know, makes communication difficult.

First, recognizing why an author wants to communicate information and ideas to you—to explain or make clear facts, events, and ideas; paint a picture in words; tell a story; or influence you to believe or feel a certain way or take a particular action—helps you understand what the author writes.

Then, staying aware of the author's knowledge, reliability, and stance provides additional insight into what the author means by what she or he says.

Accurately Understand What the Author Says (Review Chapters 1–8)   Your purpose when you are reading for learning always requires you to accurately understand the author's thesis—or argument as it is called when the author's purpose is to persuade—and main ideas. This is because the thesis or argument and main ideas are the framework that holds the author's information together. As Weiss said in his "Reading History" excerpt in Chapter 8, "The first question the reader should ask is: What is the author's argument? What is his theme, his interpretation, his thesis?"

Next, you turn your attention to how the author supports and develops the thesis or argument and main ideas. Investigate the kinds of details or evidence provided. Remember what Veit, Gould, and Clifford said about writing: "If stating an idea were enough, there would be no books or essays. Each piece of writing would consist of only a topic sentence. Of course more is needed. Writers must explain, expand and support their ideas. Sometimes facts or logic are called for, sometimes the narration of events, and sometimes examples, illustrations, and reasons.... The way that an author chooses to develop a main idea depends on the work's purpose and its intended audience."

In addition, it is useful to determine the structure, or method of development, because it provides a clue to locating and sorting out the relationships among details you need for good comprehension.

Correctly Infer What the Author Means by What He or She Says (Review Chapters 2, 3, 4, 5, 6)   In your reading assignments you have discovered instances in which an author doesn't directly state what she or he wants you to know. In these situations you have had to infer what the author meant. You have logically developed your best reasoned conclusion based on the information the author provided.

Because inferences are perceptive thoughts about the author's information, not just reckless guesses or opinions, your knowledge of the author and an accurate understanding of what he or she does say is critical.

Revisit the inferences you've made in previous chapters: in Chapter 2 you connected information from all the sentences and inferred the author's reason for writing, in Chapter 3 you carefully combined the author's information to identify the denotative and connotative meanings of a word from context, in Chapter 4 you added together information from all the sentences to determine an unstated main idea, in Chapter 5 you used all of the author's clues to establish how ideas were developed, and in Chapter 6 you linked together a variety of clues and information to determine the author's stance.

ANALYZE AND ACCEPT, REJECT, OR SUSPEND JUDGMENT

Objectively Analyze What the Author Says and Means   Contrary to the common connotation, a critical reader's goal is *not* to find fault or criticize. Quite the opposite, a critical reader comprehends, questions, clarifies, and analyzes to reach objective, responsible judgments.

The most difficult aspect of analysis for most readers is trying to separate their personal opinions and biases from the author's ideas and information. Our first inclination is to agree with authors who provide information that supports our views, and discount authors who provide information that contradicts our views. One of the best defenses against opinionated or impulsive reactions to an author's ideas and information is to maintain an honest awareness of your own ideas and views.

You should not unquestioningly accept what an author says just because it is in print. Likewise, you should not automatically reject what an author says just because it differs from your point of view.

Once you have an accurate understanding of what the author says and means, you examine it objectively. By objectively, I mean without being influenced by your own biases. You thoughtfully and impartially analyze the soundness and significance of the author's information. These strategies for analyzing the support, or evidence, the author provides for the thesis or argument and main ideas will provide a solid base for the more sophisticated analysis techniques you will encounter in advanced course work.

First, determine if the author is using facts, opinions, or a combination of facts and opinions to develop and support his or her thesis or argument. In your analysis you can have confidence in facts and valid opinions but you should be skeptical of unsubstantiated opinions. Also review the sources the author used—are they sufficient and reputable?

Other criteria to consider in evaluating the author's information and ideas include the relevance, logic, and clarity of the support or evidence. Relevant evidence directly supports the author's thesis or argument. The relationship between relevant evidence and the thesis or argument is obvious. It includes pertinent and specific details that advance the author's position. Logical evidence provides reasonable and rational support for the author's thesis or argument. Logical evidence makes sense to you. Evidence clarifies; it seeks to simplify and make clear the author's thesis or argument.

Try to locate other information, ideas, or points of view and compare them with the author's.

Make a Conscious Decision to Accept, Reject, or Suspend Judgment on What the Author Says   The most important point to remember is that you need not accept or reject every aspect of what an author says. In fact, you will likely give a "mixed review" to most of what you read. You may accept an author's argument but find the evidence inadequate, or you may be impressed by the data but draw different conclusions from it. Even if you like a particular author or book, you will probably have some comments, criticisms, or suggestions. I have liberally paraphrased Dr. Weiss' comments about reading history to focus attention on your complex and difficult task as a critical reader.

Also remember that your decision to accept, reject, or suspend judgment on an author's thesis or argument is not irreversible. As a critical reader, you are open-minded; new information, changing facts, and fresh material give you the opportunity to review, rethink, and grow.

PRACTICE: USING YOUR CRITICAL READING STRATEGIES

Consider again these two paragraphs from "Writing about History" by Dr. Robert Weiss in Unger's *These United States*, 5th ed.

1. Despite its precedent-setting character, however, the American revolt is noteworthy because it made no serious interruption in the smooth flow of American development. Both in intention and in fact, the American Revolution conserved the past rather than repudiated it. And in preserving the colonial experience, the men of the first quarter century of the Republic's history set the scenery and wrote the script for the drama of American politics for years to come. (Carl N. Degler, *Out of Our Past*, rev. ed. [New York: Harper & Row, Harper Colophon Books, 1970], P. 73.)

2. The stream of revolution, once started, could not be confined within narrow banks, but spread abroad upon the land. Many economic

desires, many social aspirations were set free by the political struggle, many aspects of colonial society profoundly altered by the forces thus set loose. The relations of social classes to each other, the institution of slavery, the system of landholding, of business, the forms and spirit of the intellectual and religious life, all felt the transforming hand of revolution, all emerged from under it in shapes advanced many degrees nearer to those we know. (J. Franklin Jameson, *The American Revolution Considered as a Social Movement* [Boston: Beacon Press, 1956], p. 9.)

Because these authors present two conflicting theories of the fundamental nature of the American Revolution, you cannot accept both of them. Using your strategies as a responsible, critical reader, what do you do?

a. Do you accept one thesis or argument and reject the other? Explain why you accepted or rejected each author's thesis or argument.

b. Do you reject them both? Explain why you rejected each author's thesis or argument.

c. Do you suspend judgment on both? If you suspend judgment, indicate where you would look for additional clarifying information.

CHAPTER 9 REVIEW QUESTIONS

1. What are the strategies of a responsible reader?
2. What does it mean to be a critical reader?
3. What are your personal guidelines for accepting or rejecting an author's information, and seeking additional information?

CHAPTER 9 THINK AND CONNECT QUESTIONS

4. Reread "Food Irradiation: A Scary Word" by Blumenthal, Chapter 3, Exercise #3, pages 56–57. Also, read "Irradiated Food: Some Facts to Consider" by Greene, Exercise #1, pages 186–187. In what ways do the two authors agree and/or disagree? Based on the information provided by Blumenthal and Greene, what is your point of view on irradiated food? Will you buy irradiated food? Why or why not? Where could you look for more information?

5. Reread the selection "Can Interpersonal Skills Be Taught?" by Robbins, Chapter 2, Exercise #2, page 32. Do you accept or reject that interpersonal skills can be taught or do you suspend judgment until you have more information? What is the basis for your decision? Where could you look for information with a different point of view?

CHAPTER 9 APPLICATION EXERCISES

6. From recent newspapers and magazines, identify one article in which you accept the author's thesis or argument, one article in which you reject the author's thesis or argument, and one article in which you

are suspending judgment until you gather more information. In each case, explain why you reached the conclusion you did.

7. From any of your textbooks, identify a section in which you accept the author's thesis or argument, a section in which you reject the author's thesis or argument, and a section in which you are suspending judgment until you gather more information. In each case, explain why you reached the conclusion you did.

USE YOUR STRATEGIES: EXERCISE #1—"IRRADIATED FOOD"

Linda Greene is a feature writer for *Vitality*, from which this selection—"Irradiated Food"—is taken.

IRRADIATED FOOD: SOME FACTS TO CONSIDER

LINDA GREENE

[1]The idea of irradiated food may conjure up images of glowing vegetables that would send a Geiger counter reading through the ceiling. But does irradiation make food radioactive?

[2]When food is irradiated, it is sent on a conveyor belt into a room containing cobalt 60 rods (a radioactive isotope). The room is then flooded with gamma rays. After treatment, the food looks and tastes the same as before.

[3]According to Edward Josephson, professor of food science and nutrition at the University of Rhode Island in West Kingston, irradiated food is no more radioactive than luggage is after it passes through an airport X-ray machine. The gamma rays used to irradiate food pass right through without leaving waste products behind.

[4]However, Michael F. Jacobson, Ph.D., executive director of the Center for Science in the Public Interest in Washington, D.C., explains that just because the food isn't radioactive doesn't mean it is safe to eat. Research indicates that irradiated food contains tiny amounts of a few unsavory chemicals. And the amount of nutrients in the food are reduced by the process.

Irradiated Food—The Pros

[5]The reasons to treat foods with radiation sound reasonable in theory. Radiation can kill bacteria (such as salmonella) that cause food poisoning and parasites that cause disease. It can destroy insects in produce, lengthen the shelf life of fruits and vegetables and offer an alternative to the use of certain fumigants and chemicals that have been linked to cancer. Irradiation holds the promise of dramatically reducing food-related disease and expanding the world food supply.

[6]Currently, the FDA has approved the use of radiation to treat fruit, vegetables, grains, pork, poultry, wheat and wheat flour, white potatoes, spices and dry or dehydrated enzyme preparations used in many processed foods.

Irradiated Food—The Cons

[7]Irradiation eliminates some problems with food but has the potential to create others. The process causes molecules to break down, and a few stray parts called free radicals may recombine into new derivatives called radiolytic products (such as benzene and formaldehyde), some of which have been linked to cancer.

(CONTINUED)

IRRADIATED FOOD: SOME FACTS TO CONSIDER (CONTINUED)

[8]With low doses of radiation, the number of radiolytic products produced is minimal. Moreover, some radiolytic products also occur naturally in foods and are sometimes created during cooking or processing. But no tests exist that can detect food that has received abnormally high doses of radiation and that could contain many radiolytic products. Also, some scientific research indicates irradiated foods have a degree of toxicity.

[9]An additional concern is irradiation's effect on food nutrients. Studies have shown that irradiation reduces levels of vitamin C, thiamin, vitamin E and polyunsaturated fats. This may prove to be a critical problem because the FDA estimates that, eventually, as much as 40 percent of the food we eat could be irradiated.

The Bottom Line

[10]Much of the food we eat will never undergo irradiation. Some foods, such as dairy products and water-based vegetables, aren't suitable for the process. And because U.S. food distribution and hygiene systems are good, irradiation is not cost-effective for most products. If you don't want to eat irradiated food until more research has been completed, pay attention to packaging in the grocery store: All radiation-treated foods must bear a special green symbol. Avoiding them when eating out is more of a challenge because restaurants aren't required to identify dishes made with irradiated ingredients. Each of us, weighing the pros and cons, will have to make our own decision about eating irradiated food. Irradiated food can lower our risk of food poisoning, but its long-range cancer-causing potential is still largely unknown.

EXERCISE #1 QUESTIONS—"IRRADIATED FOOD"

1. What is Greene's purpose?
2. What is Greene's thesis or argument?
3. What is Greene's point of view on irradiated foods?
4. Would you characterize Greene's article as biased or objective? Give a specific example to support your answer.
5. Do you accept, reject, or suspend judgment on Greene's thesis or argument?
6. Explain your decision and what, if any, next steps you would take.

USE YOUR STRATEGIES: EXERCISE #2—"IN PERSPECTIVE"

Dr. Nebel is a biology professor at Catonsville Community College in Maryland where he has taught environmental science for 21 years. He is a member of several professional associations and actively supports a number of environmental organizations.

Dr. Richard T. Wright is chairman of the Division of Natural Sciences, Mathematics, and Computer Science at Gordon College in Massachusetts, where he has taught environmental science for 22 years. He has received research grants from the National Science Foundation for his work in aquatic microbiology, and works on many professional and environmental endeavors. This selection—"In Perspective"—is from *Environmental Science*, 3rd ed.

IN PERSPECTIVE: NATURE'S CORPORATIONS

BERNARD J. NEBEL AND RICHARD T. WRIGHT

[1]The Spotted Owl controversy pits jobs against the preservation of the old-growth forests of the West. Timber interests maintain that preservation will result in 20,000 lost jobs. In their view, the controversy comes down to this: We should continue to cut the old-growth forests for the sake of keeping loggers employed.

[2]General Motors and other major businesses facing hard times lay off thousands of workers, and no one questions their need or right to do so. Clearly, the survival of General Motors is more important than keeping all their workers employed. It is assumed that those laid off will find other employment. According to conventional wisdom, corporate America must survive if the economy is to have a chance of recovering from economic bad times.

[3]In a real sense, ecosystems are the corporations that sustain the economy of the biosphere. If we want those ecosystems to survive and recover, we may have to tighten our belt and withdraw some of the work force engaged in exploiting them. The maintenance of these systems is obviously more important than some jobs. Why can't laid-off loggers seek other employment the way laid-off autoworkers, steelworkers, or computer engineers do? Why should a natural ecosystem be "bankrupted" just to maintain the temporary employment of a few (temporary because the loggers will be out of a job in a few years when the old-growth forests are finally all cut)?

[4]Clearly, it is short-sighted to assume that ecosystems are there just to provide jobs and that the jobs are more important than the ecosystems. When the old-growth forests are gone, we shall have lost more than just loggers' jobs—we shall have lost a priceless heritage and a major part of the natural world that provides us with vital services.

EXERCISE #2 QUESTIONS—"IN PERSPECTIVE"

1. What is Nebel and Wright's purpose?
2. What is Nebel and Wright's thesis or argument?
3. What do Nebel and Wright compare ecosystems to? Do you think this is a valid comparison? Why or why not?
4. Do Nebel and Wright use mostly facts or opinions to support their thesis or argument? Give two examples.
5. Do you accept, reject, or suspend judgment on Nebel and Wright's thesis or argument?
6. Explain your decision and what, if any, next steps you would take.

USE YOUR STRATEGIES: EXERCISE #3—"PROBLEMS IN AMERICAN EDUCATION"

Dr. Macionis is an associate professor of sociology at Kenyon College in Gambier, Ohio. He teaches a wide range of upper-level courses, but his favorite course is Introduction to Sociology. His doctorate is in sociology and he is the author of several articles and papers on topics such as community life in the United States, interpersonal relationships in families, effective teaching, and humor. This selection—"Problems in American Education"—is from *Sociology*, 3rd ed.

PROBLEMS IN AMERICAN EDUCATION—BUREAUCRACY AND STUDENT PASSIVITY

JOHN J. MACIONIS

[1]A problem more specific to schools themselves is pervasive *student passivity*—a lack of active participation in learning. This problem is not confined to any particular type of school: It is commonly found in both public and private schools and at all grade levels (Coleman, Hotter, and Kilgore, 1981).

[2]Schooling would seem a wonderful opportunity. In medieval Europe, children assumed many adult responsibilities before they were teenagers; a century ago, American children worked long hours in factories, on farms, and in coal mines—for little pay. Today, however, the major responsibility faced by youths is to study their human heritage, learn the effective use of language, master the manipulation of numbers, and acquire knowledge and skills that will *empower* them *and enhance* their comprehension, enjoyment, and mastery of the surrounding world.

[3]Yet the startling fact is that many students do not perceive the opportunities provided by schooling as a privilege, but rather as a *series of hurdles that are mechanically cleared* in pursuit of credentials that may open doors later in life. Students are, in short, bored. Some of the blame must be placed on students themselves, and on other factors such as television, which now takes up more of young people's time than school does. Even so, much of the *pervasive* passivity of American students is caused by the educational system.

[4]In the nineteenth century, American children were typically taught in one-room schoolhouses: small and highly personal settings in their local communities. During this century, with rising costs, many local schools were dissolved; at the same time, expanding state and federal governments favored large regional schools as a more efficient means of supervising educational curricula and *ensuring uniformity*. Schools today, therefore, reflect the *high level of bureaucratic organization* found throughout American society. As Chapter 7 ("Groups and Organizations") explained, such rigid and impersonal organization can negatively affect administrators, teachers, and students.

[5]After studying high schools across the United States, Theodore Sizer (1984) acknowledged that the bureaucratic structure of American schools is necessary to meet the massive educational demands of our vast and complex society. Yet he found that a bureaucratic educational system *fosters* five serious problems (1984:207–209).

[6]First, bureaucratic uniformity ignores the *cultural variation* within countless local communities. It takes schools out of the local community and places them under the control of outside "specialists" who may have little understanding of the everyday lives of students.

[7]Second, bureaucratic schools define success by numerical ratings of performance. School officials focus on attendance rates, dropout rates, and achievement test scores. In doing so, they overlook dimensions of schooling that are *difficult to quantify*, such as the creativity of students and the energy and enthusiasm of teachers. Such bureaucratic school systems tend to define an adequate education in terms of the number of days (or even minutes) per year that students are inside a school building rather than the school's contribution to students' personal development.

[8]Third, bureaucratic schools have rigid expectations of all students. For example, fifteen-year-olds are expected to be in the tenth grade, and eleventh-grade students are expected to score at a certain level on a standardized verbal achievement test. The high-school diploma thus rewards a student for going through the proper sequence of educational activities in the proper amount of time. Rarely are exceptionally bright and motivated students allowed to graduate early. Likewise, the system demands that students who have learned little in school graduate with their class.

[9]Fourth, the school's bureaucratic division of labor requires specialized personnel. High-school students learn English from one teacher, receive guidance from another, and are coached in sports by others. No school official comes to know the "full" student as a complex human being. Students experience this division of labor as a continual shuffling among rigidly divided fifty-minute periods throughout the school day.

(CONTINUED)

PROBLEMS IN AMERICAN EDUCATION—BUREAUCRACY AND STUDENT PASSIVITY (CONTINUED)

[10]Fifth, the highly bureaucratic school system gives students little responsibility for their own learning. Similarly, *teachers have little latitude* in what and how they teach their classes; they dare not accelerate learning for fear of disrupting "the system." Standardized policies dictating what is to be taught and how long the teaching should take render many teachers as passive and unimaginative as their students.

[11]*Several factors have enhanced bureaucracy* in American schools. Bureaucratic schools, Sizer claims, were needed to effectively process the rapid influx of immigrant children during the last century; since then, the student population of New York City alone has grown larger than that of all of America in 1900. Cultural values are also at work: Americans tend to believe that the most effective way to accomplish any task is to formulate a system, and for better or worse, that is precisely what formal education in the United States has become.

[12]Since bureaucracy discourages initiative and creativity, students become passive. The solution, drawing on the discussion in Chapter 7 ("Groups and Organizations"), is to "humanize" bureaucracy, or in this instance, Sizer claims, to humanize schools. He recommends eliminating rigid class schedules, reducing class size, and training teachers more broadly to enable them to become more fully involved in the lives of their students. Perhaps his most radical suggestion is that graduation from high school should depend on what a student has learned rather than simply on the length of time spent in school.

EXERCISE #3 QUESTIONS—"PROBLEMS IN AMERICAN EDUCATION"

1. What is Macionis's purpose?
2. What is Macionis's thesis or argument?
3. Define these words or phrases:
   a. student passivity (¶1)
   b. empower and enhance (¶2)
   c. series of hurdles that are mechanically cleared (¶3)
   d. pervasive (¶3)
   e. ensuring uniformity (¶4)
   f. high level of bureaucratic organization (¶4)
   g. fosters (¶5)
   h. cultural variation (¶6)
   i. difficult to quantify (¶7)
   j. teachers have little latitude (¶10)
   k. several factors have enhanced bureaucracy (¶11)
4. What is the primary cause of student passivity according to Macionis?
5. What are the five ways bureaucracy encourages student passivity?
6. What does Macionis say is Sizer's "most radical" suggestion? Do you think that it is a radical suggestion?
7. Give one reason why you think Sizer's "radical suggestion" would work and one reason why it would not work.
8. What is Macionis's point of view on bureaucracy? Explain your answer.

USE YOUR STRATEGIES: EXERCISE #4—"THE ROAD TO SUCCESS IS PAVED WITH DETERMINATION, FOCUS"

Harvey Mackay is the author of *Swim with the Sharks without Being Eaten Alive* and *Sharkproof*. This selection—"The Road to Success Is Paved with Determination, Focus"—is from his *United Features Syndicate* column.

THE ROAD TO SUCCESS IS PAVED WITH DETERMINATION, FOCUS

HARVEY MACKAY

There were only two times in my life when I wanted to be older. When I was 15 and the minimum age for a driver's license was 16. And when I was 59, and a marathoner, I knew the next year I'd be ranked against 60- to 64-year-olds instead of 55- to 59-year-olds.

I ran in the Boston Marathon this year. By Mile 10, I didn't think I was going to get even a minute older. It was my 10th marathon and the toughest. With one mile to go, I hooked up with an old friend, Hal Higdon, editor of the fabulous magazine *Runners' World*. He was just about to complete his 100th (and this is not a typo, folks) marathon—100th Boston and his own 100th. He was grimacing and not looking too good, so I hollered out, "What's wrong?... You should be on Cloud 9 ... They can't take this away from us!"

He said he had fallen apart at Mile 10, a point at which, for the running elite, the real race hasn't even started. For the past 15 miles, he was just gutting it out.

Twenty-five yards from the finish line, I had to slow down and take in the whole scene. My running partner, Bill Wenmark, had taken out his camera so he could take a picture as I crossed the finish line.

At that moment, Higdon, who by now was five to 10 runners ahead of me, turned back, cupped his hands and said, "Harvey, that will teach you to stop for a picture."

Hal Higdon, my hero, a gutsy performer, his competitive juices still flowing down to the last nanosecond. The truth is, except for the elite, marathoners do not compete against each other.

When you are running with 38,000 other people, how can it really matter whether you finish 8,651st, 18,651st or 28,651st?

What matters is, you finish ... period.

There is only one thing runners really compete against: It is the little voice that grows louder at every split that says: "Stop."

It is, unfortunately, a familiar sound. We hear it all our lives, at work, at school, in our personal relations.

It tells us we cannot succeed.

We cannot finish.

The boss expects too much.

The company is too demanding.

The homework assignment takes too long.

Our family is too unappreciative.

The truth is that many successful people are no more talented than unsuccessful people.

The difference between them lies in the old axiom that successful people do those things that unsuccessful people don't like to do.

Successful people have the determination, the will, the focus, the drive to complete the tough jobs.

Why run 26 miles, 385 yards?

(CONTINUED)

THE ROAD TO SUCCESS IS PAVED
WITH DETERMINATION, FOCUS (CONTINUED)

Why torture yourself to achieve a goal with no tangible reward or significance other than what you yourself assign to it?

The answer lies in the question.

Because only you can know what it means, only you are able to make yourself do it.

When you do, then you know there isn't anything you can't do.

No amount of hype, no cheering section, no personal glory, no place in the annals of history can carry you all those miles.

You have to do it yourself.

Your chances of success in life are probably just as good as anyone else's.

Don't shortchange yourself through fear or a preconceived notion that the cards are stacked against you.

At the Boston Marathon, Heartbreak Hill is at Mile 18. There are Mile 18s in everyone's life. Some come earlier in the race. Some later.

But wherever you find them, you can overcome them.

Running a marathon is not about winning the race against 38,000 other runners. It's about winning the race against yourself.

Mackay's Moral:

"Nothing in the world can take the place of persistence. Talent will not.... Genius will not.... Education will not.... Persistence and determination alone are omnipotent. Press on."

—Ray Kroc, McDonald's founder

EXERCISE #4 QUESTIONS—"THE ROAD TO SUCCESS IS PAVED WITH DETERMINATION, FOCUS"

1. What is Mackay's purpose?
2. What is Mackay's thesis or argument? What does he want you to do?
3. What analogy does Mackay use to develop and support his thesis?
4. What does Mackay say are the main differences between successful people and unsuccessful people? Do you agree or disagree? Why?
5. In what ways do you agree with Ray Kroc? In what ways do you disagree?

CHAPTER 9 CONNECTIONS

A. What tasks or situations at school, work, and home require you to make inferences? What kinds of clues do you use to help you make valid inferences? What tasks or situations are easiest for you to make inferences? What are the most difficult? What strategies do you use to check the validity of your inferences?

B. During most of your prior school experience you have probably been taught to accept the information in textbooks without question. What are the advantages of accepting text information without question? What are the disadvantages? What changes in this approach, if any, would you suggest to elementary and high school teachers?

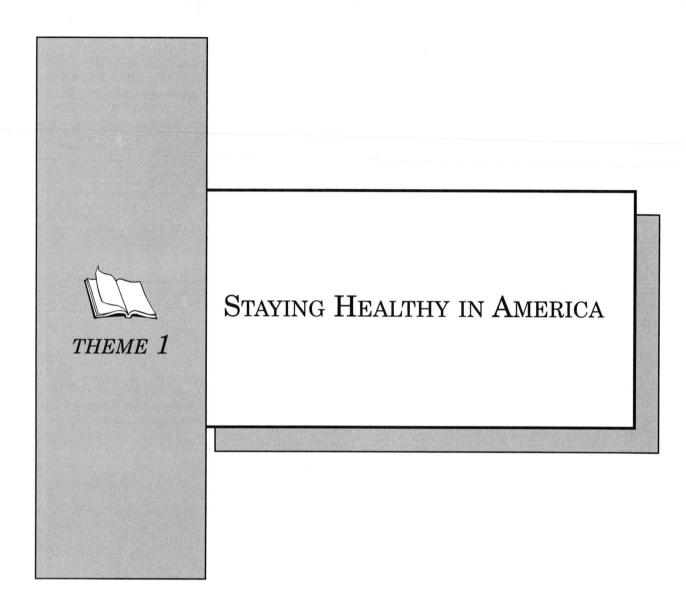

THEME 1

STAYING HEALTHY IN AMERICA

The first wealth is health.—Emerson, *The Conduct of Life*

How do you define "health"? Being able to play in sports? Not missing a day of work? Feeling good about yourself? Leading a balanced life? Good health may be difficult for us to define in just a few words but I suspect we all agree that being healthy means more than just being free of a disease. Being healthy involves a combination of physical, psychological, social, environmental, and spiritual elements.

This unit looks at health and the activities, behaviors, and attitudes that affect health and the quality of life.

The textbook chapter that opens this theme, "Promoting Your Health," from *Access to Health* by Dr. Rebecca Donatelle and Dr. Lorraine Davis, defines both health and wellness. It describes the benefits of achieving optimal health and presents a framework for developing behaviors that promote health and wellness.

Next, in "Fitness for Every Body," Mary-Lane Kamberg says you don't have to be a world-class athlete to enjoy the benefits of fitness. She analyzes three major components of fitness—strength, endurance, and flexibility—as they apply to "regular" people.

"Fruits and Vegetables" from the *Mayo Clinic Health Letter* reports on the research surrounding the current focus on increasing fruits, vegetables and grains in the diet and reviews the USDA's food guide pyramid. Then, Deborah Jones tells us how to feel better and perhaps even live longer with "Seven Keys to Good Health."

"Growing older isn't what it used to be," says Carl Sherman. So, in "The New Aging," he looks at what you can do to "head off the effects of time." Next, "Good Friends Are Good Medicine" by the *Prevention* magazine staff provides a sampling of research findings on the relationship between personal friendships and good health. "Jest for the Health of It" is Susan Goodman's prescription for a good giggle.

And finally, Peggy Noonan asks us to consider if we are thinking too much about prolonging life and not enough about living it in her column "Looking Forward."

Each of the readings is by a different author(s), of a different length, and requires different tasks.

STRATEGIES FOR SUCCESS

Develop a plan for each of the readings.

Determine who the author is and why he or she is writing.

Know the vocabulary the author uses.

Identify what the author is writing about.

Establish how the author develops and supports the thesis.

Recognize the author's stance.

Integrate graphic and text information.

Organize the information you need.

Decide what you can do with the author's information.

"PROMOTING YOUR HEALTH"

Rebecca J. Donatelle, Ph.D., CHES, is an associate professor and Coordinator of Graduate Studies in the Department of Public Health at Oregon State University. A nationally recognized health educator, Dr. Donatelle has taught thousands of students over the years in a wide range of health promotion and disease prevention areas that are directly related to, or serve as the basis for, chapters in this text. In addition to her teaching experience, her research areas have focused on health behaviors and those factors that serve to reduce risk and promote health in social and political environments.

Lorraine Davis, Ph.D., CHES, is a professor of health education and Vice Provost for Academic Personnel at the University of Oregon. Dr. Davis has taught a variety of classes to scores of undergraduate and graduate students focusing on the multifaceted areas of health promotion and education, disease prevention, and analysis of health data. She has been awarded the Ersted Award for excellence in teaching and inducted into the Hall of Excellence at the University of Wisconsin for professional excellence in health education.

This selection—"Promoting Your Health"—is from *Access to Health*, 3rd ed.

Promoting Your Health

THE KEYS TO

CHAP

CHAPTER OBJECTIVES

- Provide a definition of health, including the physical, social, mental, emotional, environmental, and spiritual components.
- Define wellness and characterize the continuum from illness to wellness.
- Provide examples of primary, secondary, and tertiary prevention.
- Discuss the health status of Americans in terms of life expectancy, chronic disease, risk factors, the environment, violence and abusive behaviors, mental health, and access to health care.
- Contrast quantity of life and quality of life.
- Identify factors that influence health status and provide examples of each.
- List the benefits of achieving optimal health.
- Discuss the role of beliefs, values, self-efficacy, and locus of control in making decisions about health.

PERSONAL WELLNESS

WHAT DO YOU THINK?

• Jennifer is an active college sophomore who watches her weight, tries to eat healthful foods and limits her alcohol consumption. She also claims to be an adult child of an alcoholic, dysfunctional family and has seen a counselor twice a week for the last four years. She goes to numerous support groups and likes to associate with people who have had similar experiences. Whenever she talks with someone, she always refers to her therapist or what her therapist or support group has said. She prefaces many of her conversations with new people with: "I'm an adult codependent child of an alcoholic and am recovering from a dysfunctional family." Whenever she has a problem, she blames her abusive father and codependent mother.

• John is 100 pounds overweight and does not like to work up a sweat exercising. He is a sensitive, caring young man with many close friends and a volunteer for many health-related agencies, helping people in need. He likes to be out enjoying nature and likes the inner peace he derives from a walk on the beach or a quiet night by the campfire in the wilderness. Recently he was arrested for spiking trees in the Pacific Northwest, which promotes the preservation of old growth forests, but endangers the lives of loggers.

• Martha is a college freshman who has been a paraplegic since she was in a car accident at the age of 10. She is bright and extremely funny, and she gets along well with people around her. Martha spends her free time at the local homeless shelter, talking to people who she feels are much worse off than she is. She eats a diet extremely high in fat and cholesterol and says that if she's going to die, she might as well exit after eating what she wants.

Which of these people is the healthiest? Which is the most unhealthy? Based on your own definition of health, in what areas are they most "unhealthy"? What factors may have contributed to these problems? Among the people you know, who would you consider to be the most "healthy"? Why?

I f someone were to ask you and your close friends to list the most important things in your lives, you might be surprised at the differences in the responses. Some of you would probably list family, love, financial security, significant others, and happiness. Others, including yourself, also might view health as one of the most important factors. Raised on a steady diet of clichés—"If you have your health, you have everything," "Be all that you can be," "Use it or lose it," "Just do it"—many people readily acknowledge that health is a desirable goal. But what does it really mean to be healthy? How healthy are *you?* What can you do to influence your own health? Why bother trying to change or improve your health status? Why all this fuss over health, anyway?

In this book, we attempt to answer these questions and many more in ways that are relevant for you. We will also help you to attain the basic knowledge and skills necessary to make the best health-related decisions in an area laden with conflicting research reports, deliberate attempts by some to mislead you into purchasing worthless products and services for their own financial gain, and an ever-changing, often overwhelming, mass of new information.

Attaining good health is no easy task. Each of us is a unique product of our genetic history, our family interactions, our experiences with friends and significant others, our sex, culture, race, socioeconomic status, and a host of other subtle and not-so-subtle influences. We are also influenced by the environment we navigate through and live in and by all the external political, economic, and social forces that help or hinder us along the way. Some of us may discover very few obstacles in our quest for optimum health and wellness. Others may come upon significant barriers, many of which may be difficult to overcome. There is no one recipe for obtaining health. As a unique individual with a unique blend of attitudes, beliefs, values, knowledge, and experiences, you must find your own best way to achieve health goals within your own special set of environmental conditions.

This text is designed to offer fundamental information that will provide an *Access to Health* that is consistent with who you are and what you want to become. Health is not an all-or-none proposition that is always totally within your control. But, there are many major and minor changes and adaptations that you can make in your behavior that may significantly impact on your risk factors. For those risk factors beyond your control, you must learn to react, adapt, and make optimum use of your existing resources to create the

Your health status is the result of many influences, some of which are immediate, such as what you ate during the last week and how much you exercised. But other influences extend back to your family environment when you were a child. Warm and loving families contribute positively to the mental and emotional health of members not only when they are children but throughout their lives.

best situation for yourself. By making informed, rational decisions, you will be able to improve both the quality and the quantity of your life.

FINDING THE RIGHT HEALTH VOCABULARY

Defining Health

Definitions of the term **health** have changed dramatically over the years, evolving from its earliest definitions as synonymous with hygiene and sanitation, to the widely accepted definition by the World Health Organization (WHO) in the 1940s: "Health is the state of complete physical, mental and social well-being, not merely the absence of disease or infirmity."[1]

René Dubos later clarified the WHO definition of health by stating, "Health is a quality of life, involving social, emotional, mental, spiritual and biological fitness on the part of the individual, which results from adaptations to the environment."[2] Each of these definitions describes health as being multidimensional, including many different components and encompassing many different aspects of life. These components typically include the following:

Health is neither static nor single dimensional. Healthy people understand that their health is not based merely on the absence of illness, but on an optimal level of physical, emotional, social, spiritual, and environmental responsiveness.

- *Physical Health*—Includes such characteristics as body size and shape, sensory acuity, susceptibility to disease and disorders, body functioning, recuperative ability, and ability to perform certain tasks.

- *Social Health*—Refers to our interactions with others, our ability to adapt to various social situations, and our daily behaviors—the ability to have satisfying interpersonal relationships.

- *Mental Health*—Includes the ability to learn—our rational thinking component and intellectual capabilities.

- *Emotional Health*—Includes the ability to control emotions so that we feel comfortable expressing them when appropriate as well as expressing them appropriately—our feeling component; the ability to *not* express emotions either when it is inappropriate to do so or in an inappropriate manner.

- *Environmental Health*—An appreciation of our external environment and the role we play in preserving, protecting, and improving environmental conditions.

- *Spiritual Health*—May involve a belief in a higher form of being or a specified way of living prescribed by a particular religion, but it also extends to the feeling of being part of some wider form of existence—a sense of unity with the larger environment or a guiding sense of meaning or value. It includes a feeling of oneness with others, with nature, and with the larger environment. It also may include our ability to understand and express our own basic purpose in life, to feel that we are part of the greater spectrum of existence, to experience love, joy, pain, sorrow, peace, contentment, and wonder over life's experiences, and to care about and respect all living things.

The current definition of health proposes a positive view that focuses on individual attempts to achieve optimum well-being within a realistic framework of individual potential. In Figure 1.1, health is described as a continuum from illness to optimum well-being. Where you are on this continuum may vary from day to day as you are buffeted by life's ups and downs. But if you persist in your attempts to change behaviors and reduce risk, the likelihood of remaining on the positive end of the continuum will be greatly improved. "Keeping Track of Yourself" will help you locate your own health status within the continuum.

Health relates to who we are as individuals, how we respond to others and the environment, what we value and perceive as important in our lives, and how we respond to the daily challenges of life. Health is an ever-changing dimension of our lives, in which we strive to be the best possible physical, emotional, social, spiritual, and environmentally sensitive beings we can. The current definition of health acknowledges that each of us must attempt to achieve this optimum level of being in a "sometimes hostile environment." Each of us must come to terms with the adversity and obstacles obstructing the way to optimal health in our own special way, focusing on our positive attributes whenever possible, changing those things about ourselves that we can change, and learning to recognize and deal with those that we cannot change.

---

health A quality of life, involving social, emotional, mental, and spiritual, biological fitness on the part of the individual, which results from adaptations to the environment.

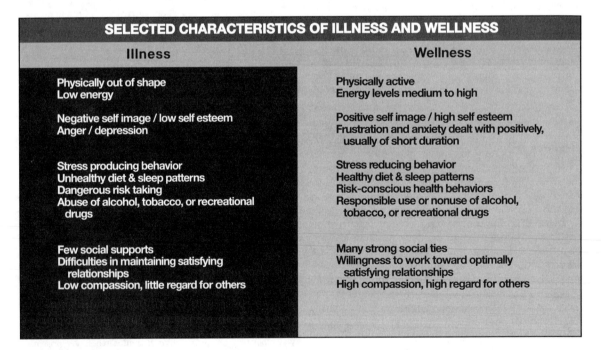

Optimum Wellness

High Level of Wellness

Good Health

Average Health

Signs of Illness

Symptoms of Illness

Disability (reversible)

Disability (irreversible)

Death

Lifespan

SELECTED CHARACTERISTICS OF ILLNESS AND WELLNESS

Illness	Wellness
Physically out of shape Low energy	Physically active Energy levels medium to high
Negative self image / low self esteem Anger / depression	Positive self image / high self esteem Frustration and anxiety dealt with positively, usually of short duration
Stress producing behavior Unhealthy diet & sleep patterns Dangerous risk taking Abuse of alcohol, tobacco, or recreational drugs	Stress reducing behavior Healthy diet & sleep patterns Risk-conscious health behaviors Responsible use or nonuse of alcohol, tobacco, or recreational drugs
Few social supports Difficulties in maintaining satisfying relationships Low compassion, little regard for others	Many strong social ties Willingness to work toward optimally satisfying relationships High compassion, high regard for others

Figure 1.1   *The continuum from illness to wellness.*

Defining Wellness

Wellness is a term that has been popularized in the last decade. Like the modern definitions of health, *wellness* refers to an ever-changing movement toward optimum well-being. The two terms are not mutually exclusive. In fact,

most health professionals agree that the term *health* no longer implies the mere absence of disease, but is instead a dynamic, lifelong process in which the physical, psychological, social, environmental, and spiritual dimensions are all considered essential. The closer we get to achieving the ideal level of functioning in and balance between each of the

Promoting Your Health

KEEPING TRACK OF YOURSELF

1. How would you define being healthy? Whom do you know who you think is very healthy? What criteria have you used to make this assessment?

2. How do you rate yourself on the wellness continuum shown in Figure 1.1? How many characteristics do you have that are listed on the "Illness" side of the continuum? The "Wellness" side of the continuum?

3. What areas are your major weaknesses in terms of achieving optimal health? What things could you change now that might improve your health? Are there any barriers that might stop you from changing?

above dimensions, the closer we are to achieving **high-level wellness.**

The wellness continuum described in Figure 1.1 also illustrates the various dimensions of wellness. "Well" individuals take an honest look at their personal capabilities and limitations and make an effort to change those factors that are within their control. They try to achieve a *balance* in each of the wellness dimensions while trying to achieve a *positive wellness position* on an imaginary continuum. Many people believe that, like health, wellness can best be achieved by adopting a *holistic* approach in which the interaction and positive balance between mind, body, and spirit are emphasized. Persons on the illness and disability end of the continuum have failed to achieve this integration and balance and may be seriously deficient in one or more of the wellness dimensions. But the disability component of the wellness continuum does not imply that a physically handicapped person cannot achieve wellness. A handicapped person may in fact be very "healthy" in terms of relationships with others, level of self-confidence, environmental sensitivity, and overall attitude toward life. In contrast, a person who spends hours in front of a mirror lifting weights to perfect the size and shape of each muscle may be "unhealthy" in interactions with others, level of self-esteem, and attitude toward life. Although we often place a premium on physical attractiveness and external trappings, appearance is actually only one indicator of a person's overall health. Typically, the closer you get to your potential in the five components of health, the more "well" you will be. Both health and wellness are ongoing *active* processes, including those positive attitudes and behaviors that continually improve the quality of your life.

Health Promotion: A New Focus

In discussions of health and wellness, terms such as **health promotion** are often used. Health promotion has been de-fined as "any combination of educational, organizational, economic, and environmental supports for behaviors that are conducive to health." More recently, health promotion has also been viewed as the "science and art of helping people change their lifestyles to move toward a state of optimal health." Regardless of how it is defined, health promotion identifies healthy people who are at a certain risk for disease and attempts to motivate them to improve their health status. It encourages those whose health and wellness behaviors are already sound to maintain and improve them. But health promotion goes one step further by attempting to modify behaviors, attitudes, and values and introduce health-enhancing activities.

Whether we use the term *health* or *wellness,* it is commonly understood that we are talking about a person's overall reactions or responses to the nuances of living. Occasional dips into the ice cream bucket and other dietary slips, failure to exercise every day, flare-ups of anger, and other deviations from optimal behavior should not be viewed as major failures. Actually, our ability to recognize that we are imperfect beings, attempting to adapt in an imperfect world, is considered an indicator of individual well-being.

We must also remember to be tolerant of others who are attempting to improve their health. Rather than being "warriors against pleasure" in our zeal to reform or transform the health behaviors of others, we need to be supportive, under-

---

wellness An ever-changing movement toward optimum well-being, involving multiple dimensions of health.

high-level wellness The ideal level of functioning in and balance between each of the health and wellness dimensions.

health promotion Any combination of educational, organizational, economic, and environmental supports for behaviors that are conducive to health. Includes the science and art of helping people change their lifestyles to move to a state of optimal health.

standing, nonjudgmental, and positive in our interactions with others. **Health bashing**—intolerance or negative feelings, words, or actions toward people who fail to meet our own expectations of health—may indicate our own deficiencies in the psychological, social, and/or spiritual dimensions of the health continuum.

Prevention: The Key to Future Health

Although a great deal can be done to promote healthy behaviors, a key goal of Americans today is the **prevention** of premature death and disability. Instead of relying on medical professionals to fix you when you're broken, the focus of prevention is on taking positive actions now, making the best health decisions to avoid even becoming sick. Getting immunized against diseases such as polio, never starting to smoke cigarettes, using condoms during sexual intercourse, and similar measures constitute **primary prevention**: taking actions to stop a health problem *before* it starts. Another form of prevention focuses on **secondary prevention**, or recog-

Since the connection between a healthy lifestyle and the prevention of disease is clear, choosing an exercise or sports activity you enjoy is not only fun, but is also a positive step toward good health.

nizing a health problem early in its development and intervening (also referred to as *intervention*) in the process to eliminate the underlying causes before serious illness develops. Attending health education seminars to help you cut down or stop cigarette intake is an example of secondary prevention.

Because so many deaths and illnesses are directly related to aspects of lifestyle such as tobacco use, obesity, alcohol abuse, sedentary activities, overeating (particularly fats), and so forth, primary and secondary prevention are essential to reducing the **incidence** (numbers of new cases) and **prevalence** (number of existing cases) of a disease or disability. (For a comparison of health indicators between blacks and whites, see "Disparities in Health: Real or Imagined?")

Unfortunately, health education and health promotion activities have historically been seriously underfunded by governmental officials, with less than 5 percent of the total health care expenditures in the United States focusing on these areas. Instead, governmental monies have been primarily allocated for research and **tertiary prevention**, treatment and/or rehabilitation efforts after a person has gotten sick. This form of prevention is not only the most costly; it is also less effective in promoting health than is any other prevention method.

If the government and the health care system are primarily interested in taking care of you only *after* you are sick, who is responsible for helping you remain well? Although many health agencies, programs, and public health prevention specialists are available to assist you, much of the responsibility for your health rests with you. As costs for treatment rise in the years ahead, people will have increasing difficulty in paying for them. What are your options? Clearly, the best option is for you to take action now that will help you to achieve your optimal health level and to make responsible and informed decisions so that you stay well in the future.

---

health bashing Intolerance, negative feelings, and a general placing of total blame on the victim that is expressed in terms of feelings, words, or actions toward people who fail to meet our own expectations of health.

prevention Taking positive actions now to avoid even becoming sick.

primary prevention Taking prevention steps that stop a health problem before it starts. Getting vaccinations, using condoms during intercourse, and so forth are common examples.

secondary prevention Form of prevention that recognizes a health problem early in its development and intervenes early to address the underlying cause before serious illness develops.

incidence Numbers of new cases of a disease or disability.

prevalence Number of existing cases of a disease or disability.

tertiary prevention Prevention efforts that occur after a person has become sick or disabled. Efforts aimed at treatment (medical model) and/or rehabilitation.

Multicultural Perspectives

DISPARITIES IN HEALTH: REAL OR IMAGINED?

While current arguments rage over the best system of health care in the United States, it is useful to remember the vast differences between the haves and the have-nots when it comes to certain health indicators. Achieving a healthier America depends on significant improvements in the health of population groups now at higher risk of premature death, disease, and disability. For example:

INDICATOR OF HEALTH	WHITE MALE	BLACK MALE	WHITE FEMALE	BLACK FEMALE
1. Death rates for suicide*	19.6	12.5	4.8	2.4
2. Death rate for homicide and legal intervention*	8.1	61.5	2.8	12.5
3. Maternal mortality rates for complications during pregnancy and childbirth*	NA	NA	5.4	18.6
4. Death rates for breast cancer*	NA	NA	22.9	26.0
5. Life expectancy at birth	72.6	66.0	79.3	74.5
6. Infant mortality rates**	8.2	17.7	8.2	17.7
7. Years of potential life lost*** (Before age 65—all causes)	6,525.1	14,186.5	3,403.8	7,431.5
8. Persons under 65 years of age without health care	14%	22%	14%	22%
9. Death rates for human immunodeficiency* virus	13.1	40.3	0.9	8.1
10. Death rates for heart disease*	205.9	272.6	106.6	172.9
11. Death rates for cancer*	157.2	230.6	110.7	130.9
12. Death rates for stroke*	28.0	54.1	24.1	44.9
13. Self-reported poor/fair health status	8.1%	15.1%	8.1%	15.1%
14. Age-adjusted percentage who are regular cigarette smokers	27.6%	32.2%	23.9%	20.4%

*Age-adjusted rates per 100,000.

**Per 1,000 live births.

***Years of potential life lost are calculated by multiplying the number of deaths for each age group by the years of life lost (the difference between age 65, which is used as the standard, and the midpoint of the age group). For example, the death of a person aged 15–24 years counts as 45 years of potential life lost.

WHAT DO YOU THINK?

1. Of all the factors listed, where do there appear to be the greatest disparities between whites and blacks? Which factors are worse for whites than for blacks? For females than for males? Why do you think these differences occur?

2. What factors do you believe have contributed to these disparities?

3. What actions might be taken to improve each of the above health indicators? Which ones may be modified through individual actions? Which ones must be modified through community (legislative, economic, environmental, health care system) measures? By both individual and community actions?

SOURCES: C. Hogue and M. Hargraves (1993), "Class, Race, and Infant Mortality in the United States," *American Journal of Public Health, 83*(1): 9–13. U.S. Department of Health and Human Services (1992), *Health: United States 1991 and Prevention Profile*, DHHS Publication No. (PHS) 92: 1232.

HEALTH STATUS INDICATORS

How Healthy Are We?

The health status of a group of people, a community, a state, a nation, or the world is often reduced to statistical data for descriptive and comparative purposes. In 1979, the surgeon-general of the United States observed that "the health of the people has never been better." In his assessment, he looked at statistical data on death rates from disease (particularly the childhood diseases), injuries, life expectancy, and other criteria. This information helped lay the foundation for *Healthy People 2000: The National Health Promotion and Disease Prevention Objectives for the United States.* (See Table 1.1.)

Although this and other documents provide an important source of information for health planners, they typically do not offer a complete assessment of our current health status. Data used in developing documents such as these typically do not assess levels of human suffering, emotional health, spiritual health, and other *quality-of-life* measures. Instead they often focus on *quantity-of-life* variables.

Life Expectancy By 1993, the average life expectancy (number of years a person is expected to live) was over 79.3 years for white females, 72.6 for white males, 74.5 for black females, and 66.0 for black males. Life expectancy for a white female born in 1990 exceeds 83.4 years, and a white male born in 1990 can expect to live to over 76 years.[3]

Chronic Disease During the 1980s, death rates for three of the leading causes of death among Americans declined: heart disease, stroke, and unintentional injuries. Infant mortality also decreased, and some childhood infectious diseases were nearly eliminated. These gains provide hope that the 1990s will see progress against other diseases. Heart disease continues to kill more people than all other diseases combined. Lung cancer deaths have increased steadily since the 1960s, and breast cancer deaths remain stubbornly high.

Risk Factors Since the 1970s we made dramatic improvements in high blood pressure detection and control, experienced declines in cigarette consumption, increased our awareness of cholesterol and dietary fats as risk factors, and reduced alcohol consumption and use of alcohol when driving.

TABLE 1.1 HEALTHY PEOPLE 2000: SELECTED OBJECTIVES OF THE NATION FOR CHILDREN AND YOUNG ADULTS

1. Reduce overweight to a prevalence of no more than 20 percent among people aged 20 and older.
2. Reduce dietary-fat intake to an average of 30 percent of calories or less and average saturated-fat intake to less than 10 percent of calories. (Now nearly 40 percent for both.)
3. Increase complex carbohydrate and fiber-containing foods in the diets of adults to 5 or more daily servings for vegetables (including legumes) and fruits, and to 6 or more daily servings for grain products. (Now slightly over 2 1/2 servings of vegetables and fruits and 3 of grains.)
4. Reduce alcohol consumption by people aged 14 and older to an annual average of no more than 2 gallons of ethanol per person. (Was 2.50 gallons in 1989.)
5. Reduce to no more than 30 percent the proportion of all pregnancies that are unintended. (During past 5 years, 56 percent of pregnancies were unintended, unwanted, or earlier than desired.)
6. Reduce coronary heart disease deaths to no more than 100 per 100,000. (Now over 135 per 100,000.)
7. Reduce the prevalence of mental disorders (exclusive of substance abuse) among adults to less than 10.7 percent. (Now over 12 percent.)
8. Reduce homicides to no more than 7.2 per 100,000. (Now over 8.5 per 100,000.)
9. Reduce deaths from work-related injuries to no more than 4 per 100,000. (Now more than 6 per 100,000.)
10. Reduce destructive periodontal disease to a prevalence of no more than 15 percent among people aged 35–44. (Now 24 percent or more.)
11. Reverse the rise in cancer deaths to achieve a rate of no more than 130 per 100,000. (Now over 133 per 100,000.)
12. Reduce rape and attempted rape of women aged 12–34 to no more than 225 per 100,000. (Now in excess of 400 per 100,000.)
13. Increase to at least 30 percent the proportion of people aged 6 and older who engage regularly, preferably daily, in light-to-moderate physical activity for at least 30 minutes per day. (Only 22 percent of people aged 18 and older are active 30 minutes or more 5 times per week; only 12 percent are active 7 days per week.)
14. Increase to at least 20 percent the proportion of people aged 18 and older who engage in vigorous physical activity that promotes the development and maintenance of cardiorespiratory fitness. (Now only about 12 percent.)
15. Reduce the proportion of college students engaging in recent occasions of heavy drinking of alcoholic beverages to no more than 32 percent. (Now over 42 percent.)
16. Increase to at least 50 percent the proportion of people with high blood pressure whose blood pressure is under control. (Now an estimated 26 percent for persons 18 and older.)
17. Reduce the mean serum cholesterol among adults to no more than 200 mg/dL. (Now over 215 mg/dL.)
18. Increase to at least 20 percent the proportion of people aged 18 and older who seek professional help in coping with personal and emotional problems. (Now slightly over 13 percent.)
19. Increase to at least 60 percent the proportion of sexually active, unmarried women aged 15–19 whose partners used a condom at last sexual intercourse. (Now approximately 30 percent.)

SOURCE: *Healthy People 2000: The National Health Promotion and Disease Prevention Objectives for the United States* (Boston: Jones and Bartlett, 1992).

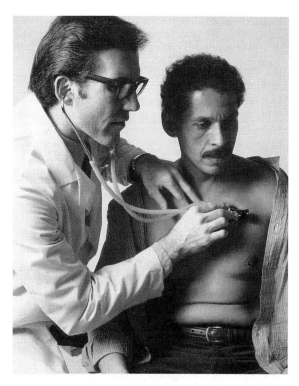

Healthy people in our society feel committed to increasing access to good health care for themselves and also for all Americans.

The Environment During the last decade, there has been increasing concern about toxic substances, solid waste, acid rain, the ozone level, dying oceans, global warming, polluted water supplies, food supplies, and many other life-threatening conditions.

Violence and Abusive Behaviors Child abuse, spouse abuse, and other forms of intrafamilial violence threaten millions of Americans each year. The United States ranks first among industrialized nations in violent deaths. Taken together, suicides and homicides constitute the fourth leading cause of potential years of life lost. Suicide is the third leading cause of death among people aged 15–24, and homicide is the leading cause of death for African Americans aged 15–34.

Mental Health Depression has been described as the "common cold of mental illness," affecting at least 5 percent of the population at any given time.

- Between 10 and 12 percent of children and adolescents suffer from mental disorders, including autism, attention-deficit disorder, hyperactivity, and depression.

- Over 23 million adults are severely incapacitated by mental disorders, not including substance abuse, and more than twice that number have experienced at least one diagnosable mental problem.

Access to Health Care Nearly 25 percent of the American public is uninsured or underinsured, and these numbers are increasing daily. Millions of Americans need medical care or will need it in the near future and will be shut out of the system. The number of homeless, undernourished, and mentally ill persons continues to grow in direct proportion to economic and social service problems. Some critics argue that we are moving toward a society of haves and have-nots when it comes to health and well-being. While one group focuses on whether to join a health club, another group wonders if they will be safe sleeping under the bushes in the park. While one group fastidiously reads labels on food products to ensure that they don't consume too much saturated fat, another group wonders where their next meal may come from. The dichotomy between a middle-class perspective on health and the "survival" health status of many other Americans and people throughout the world is reason for growing concern.

By definition, a truly healthy person possesses a sense of both individual and social responsibility. Rather than focusing on their own personal health, genuinely healthy people are concerned about others and the greater environment. This concern translates into taking actions designed to help them live a high-quantity and high-quality life, as well as to help others who are less fortunate.

IMPROVING YOUR HEALTH STYLE

Benefits of Achieving Optimal Health

Table 1.2 provides an overview of the leading causes of death in the United States today. Risks for each of these leading killers have been reduced significantly by practicing specific lifestyle patterns—for example, consuming a diet low in saturated fat and cholesterol, exercising regularly, reducing sodium, managing stress, and other practices. Lifestyle and individual behavior are believed to account for over 58 percent of good health (see Figure 1.2). Heredity, access to health care, and the environment are other factors that influence health status. While you can't change your genetic history, and improving your environment and the health care system is difficult, you can influence your future health status by the behaviors you choose today.

Reduction in risk for major diseases is just one of the benefits that you can hope to achieve. Among the others are:

- Improved quality of life, in addition to increased longevity
- Increased capacity for pleasure
- Greater zest for living
- Greater energy levels, improved productivity, more interest in having fun
- Improved self-image

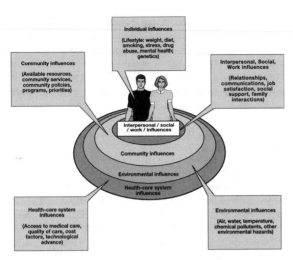

Figure 1.2 *Factors that influence your health status.*

- Improved immunological functioning with enhanced ability to fight off infections
- Enhanced relationships with others due to better communication and "quality" time spent with others
- Improved ability to control and manage stress
- Enhanced levels of self-efficacy, more personal control of your life

- Reduced reliance on the health-care system, increased ability to engage in self-care, health-enhancing behaviors, lower health-care costs
- Adding life to years, as well as adding years to life
- Improved cardiovascular functioning
- Increased muscle tone, strength, flexibility, and endurance, resulting in improved physical appearance, performance, and self-esteem
- More positive outlook on life, fewer negative thoughts, ability to view life as challenging and negative events as a potential for growth
- Improved self-confidence and ability to understand and reach out to others
- Improved environmental sensitivity, responsibility, and behaviors
- Greater appreciation for nature and our place in the larger frame of existence.
- Enhanced levels of spiritual health, awareness, and feelings of oneness with self, others, and the greater environment

Although mounting evidence indicates that there are significant benefits to being healthy, many people find it difficult to become and stay healthy. Rather than realistically assessing their lifestyles, they tend to make excuses for their behavior.

TABLE 1.2 LEADING CAUSES OF DEATH IN THE UNITED STATES FOR ALL RACES BY AGE			
All Ages and Races Combined	**1–4 Years**	**5–14 Years**	**15–24 Years**
1. Diseases of the heart	1. Accidents and adverse effects	1. Accidents and adverse effects	1. Accidents and adverse effects
2. Malignant neoplasms	2. Congenital anomalies	2. Malignant neoplasms	2. Homicide & legal intervention
3. Cerebrovascular diseases	3. Malignant neoplasms	3. Homicide and legal intervention	3. Suicide
4. Accidents and adverse effects (includes motor vehicle and other accidents and adverse effects)	4. Homicide and legal intervention	4. Congenital anomalies	4. Malignant neoplasms
5. Chronic obstructive pulmonary diseases and allied conditions (COPD)	5. Diseases of the heart	5. Diseases of the heart	5. Diseases of the heart
6. Pneumonia and influenza	6. Pneumonia and influenza	6. Suicide	6. Human immunodeficiency virus
7. Diabetes mellitus	7. Certain conditions originating in the perinatal period	7. Pneumonia and influenza	7. Congenital anomalies
8. Suicide	8. Human immunodeficiency syndrome	8. Chronic obstructive pulmonary disease	8. Pneumonia and influenza
9. Chronic liver disease and cirrhosis	9. Meningitis	9. Benign neoplasms, carcinoma in situ, and neoplasms of uncertain nature	9. Cerebrovascular disease
10. Homicide and legal intervention	10. Septicemia	10. Cerebrovascular disease	10. Chronic obstructive pulmonary disease
11. Human immunodeficiency virus infection			
12. Nephritis, nephrotic syndrome, and nephrosis			
13. Atherosclerosis			
14. Septicemia			
15. Certain conditions originating in the perinatal period.			

SOURCE: National Center for Health Statistics (January 7, 1992), *Monthly Vital Statistics Report: Final Mortality, 40,* (8), 1–51.

By the simple act of choosing to eat nutritious and attractively served foods in a relaxing environment, people increase their chances for a long and healthy life.

well we are doing in several of these key areas. This information indicates many areas in which people can make changes to improve the quality of their lives.

Change is not easy. In our culture, it is normal to eat when we're not hungry, to be overweight, to take the elevator instead of the stairs, and to drive around the parking lot for five minutes to avoid a one-minute walk. We don't relax because we don't know how. We eat high-fat foods because they were a part of our upbringing. We don't exercise because exercise is often equated with work. Health behaviors are learned behaviors that are encouraged by both peers and family. Decisions to change old, negative thinking patterns or behaviors take conscious effort, planning, and an awareness of individual barriers to success.

Typically, sleeping seven to eight hours a day, eating a nutritious breakfast, not eating between meals, maintaining proper weight, not smoking cigarettes, limiting intake of alcohol, and exercising regularly are recognized as essential components of a long and healthy life. These commonsense recommendations have withstood the test of time, remaining unsurpassed as sound health advice. How close do we come to meeting these goals? Table 1.3 offers an overview of how

Factors Influencing Health Changes

Mark Twain once said that "habit is habit, and not to be flung out the window by anyone, but coaxed downstairs a step at a time." Changing negative behavior patterns into healthy ones is often a time-consuming and difficult process. The chances of success are better when people make gradual changes that give them time to unlearn negative patterns and substitute positive ones. We have not yet developed a foolproof method for effectively changing people's behavior, but we do know that certain behaviors can benefit both individu-

TABLE 1.2 LEADING CAUSES OF DEATH IN THE UNITED STATES FOR ALL RACES BY AGE		
25–44 Years	**45–64 Years**	**65 Years +**
1. Accidents and adverse effects	1. Malignant neoplasms	1. Diseases of the heart
2. Malignant neoplasms	2. Diseases of the heart	2. Malignant neoplasms
3. Human immunodeficiency virus	3. Cerebrovascular diseases	3. Cerebrovascular accidents
4. Diseases of the heart	4. Accidents and adverse effects	4. Chronic obstructive pulmonary disease
5. Suicide	5. Chronic obstructive pulmonary disease	5. Pneumonia and influenza
6. Homicide and legal intervention	6. Chronic liver disease and cirrhosis	6. Diabetes melioidosis
7. Chronic liver disease and cirrhosis	7. Diabetes mellitus	7. Accidents and adverse effects
8. Cerebrovascular diseases	8. Suicide	8. Atherosclerosis
9. Pneumonia and influenza	9. Pneumonia and influenza	9. Nephritis, nephrotic syndrome, and nephrosis
	10. Human immunodeficiency virus	10. Septicemia

TABLE 1.3
SELECTED PERSONAL HEALTH BEHAVIORS IN THE UNITED STATES, 1989 (BY PERCENTAGE)

Health Behavior	Sleeps 6 Hours or Less	Never Eats Breakfast	Snacks Every Day	Less Physically Active	5 or More Alcoholic Drinks a Day	Current Smoker	30% or More Above Ideal Weight
All persons	22.0	24.3	39.0	16.4	37.5	30.1	13.1
Age							
18–29	19.8	30.4	42.2	17.1	54.4	31.9	7.5
30–44	24.3	30.1	41.4	18.3	39.0	34.5	13.6
45–64	22.7	21.4	37.9	15.3	24.6	31.6	18.1
65 +	20.4	7.5	30.7	13.5	12.2	16.0	13.2
Gender							
Male	22.7	25.2	40.7	16.5	49.3	32.6	12.1
Female	21.4	23.6	37.5	16.3	23.3	27.8	13.7
Race							
White	21.3	24.5	39.4	16.7	38.3	29.6	12.4
Black	27.8	23.6	37.2	13.9	29.3	34.9	18.7
Other	21.4	21.5	32.6	16.5	33.3	24.8	6.7

SOURCE: *Statistical Abstract of the United States 1989,* 109th ed. (Washington, DC: U.S. Government Printing Office, 1989).

als and society as a whole. To understand how the process of behavior change works, we must first identify specific behavior patterns and attempt to understand the reasons for them.

Unfortunately, the development or maintenance of health behaviors is not necessarily a linear model in which we can assume that if we have knowledge, our attitudes and behaviors will automatically change. Knowledgeable people would not then behave in ways detrimental to their health. The reasons people behave in unhealthy ways, despite known risks, are complex and not easily understood. Health researchers have studied health behaviors for decades and continue to analyze the reasons that one person chooses to act responsibly while another ignores obvious health risks.

Figure 1.3 identifies the major factors that influence behavior and behavior-change decisions. These factors can be divided into three general categories: predisposing, enabling, and reinforcing factors.

• **Predisposing factors** are those things we bring to the situation, such as our life experiences, knowledge, cultural and ethnic inheritance, and current beliefs and values.

• **Enabling factors** are factors such as skills or abilities, physical, emotional, and mental capabilities, resources and accessible facilities that make our health decisions more convenient or more difficult. For example, if you like to

swim for exercise but the only available pool is inaccessible, you might be less likely to go swimming than if the pool were located nearby. Although it is easy to use negative enabling factors as excuses for not behaving in a positive manner, it is often possible to devise strategies for dealing with difficult circumstances.

• **Reinforcing factors** relate to the presence or absence of support, encouragement, or discouragement that significant people in your life bring to a situation. For example, if you decide to stop smoking and members of your family smoke in your presence, you might be tempted to start smoking again. Internal reinforcement that comes from the *self-talk* you give yourself is another key reinforcing factor.

The manner in which you reward or punish yourself for your own successes and failures may affect your chances of adopting healthy behaviors. Learning to accept small failures and to concentrate on your successes may foster further successes. Berating yourself because you binged on ice cream, argued with a friend, or didn't jog because it was raining might create an internal environment in which failure becomes almost inevitable. Telling yourself that you're worth the extra time and effort and giving yourself a pat on the back for small accomplishments is an often overlooked aspect in positive behavioral change.

Although a variety of factors influence our decisions, each of us decides either consciously or unconsciously to behave in a particular manner. Our decision-making process is motivated by a complex interaction between our values, beliefs, and selected factors in our social environment, as discussed earlier.

When we make decisions about our health, our underlying beliefs play a role. Proponents of the *Health Belief Model* note that people are more likely to alter a given behavior if several conditions are met (see Chapter 2).

An example of the Health Belief Model would be a college student who is extremely overweight but, although he has suffered several episodes of chest pain, does not believe that he is old enough to be at risk. After a brief jog he passes out, only to wake up in the emergency room. The doctor tells him that he has had a mild heart attack and that some blockage has been detected in his coronary arteries. He is warned that unless he loses 80 pounds, lowers his intake of saturated fat, and begins to exercise regularly, he faces major coronary by-pass surgery or death in the months ahead. The student goes on a medically supervised diet, loses weight, and starts an aerobic exercise program. Clearly, he responded to the risk, realized the consequences, and saw the benefits of changing his behavior.

Mentally stimulating activities like collecting stamps or watching baseball or going to the movies can contribute to mental and emotional health at any age.

Figure 1.3
Influences on your health decisions and behaviors.

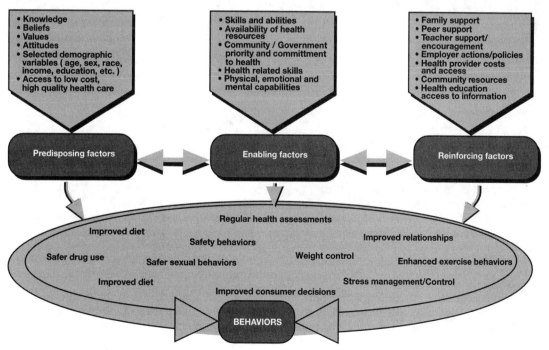

Promoting Your Health

FACT OR FALLACY? MAKING SENSE OF HEALTH REPORTS

One of the most difficult problems you may have when trying to *inform* yourself about health issues is in determining what to believe and what not to believe out of all the conflicting claims about various health risks. Is oat bran really of any help in warding off cardiovascular disease? Is sodium as bad as we once thought it was? Does a glass of wine a day keep the doctor away? If you're puzzled by it all, you are not alone. Although no 100 percent foolproof methods exist for determining the merits of all health claims, there are some basic questions you can ask when reading reports of new findings about foods, products, services, or behaviors. Acquiring the analytical skills necessary to critique such claims and make prudent behavioral changes will help ensure that the actions you take are the best ones for you.

1. *What is the source of the information?* **Finding out where the study was done and who paid for the research will often uncover possible unreliable or biased research objectives. Data supplied by independent investigators working for agencies that do not have a vested interest in the outcome may reduce the potential threat of error.**

2. *Who are the authors of the study? Who conducted the research?* **If possible, try to discover who the researchers themselves were. What were their credentials for doing the research? Are they working at a reputable institution or agency? Have they done similar research in these areas previously?**

3. *What research methods were used in the study?* **Familiarity with basic research terms and principles of sound research methods may help you determine the merit of a study. You should consider the following:**
Sample size: **Always look at the numbers of people involved in the study that supposedly proved a health effect. Studying 100 people in one geographical area may provide some interesting preliminary data on a particular subject, but it would not be enough to**

generalize the findings to everyone. Obviously, the more people participating in the study, the better, particularly if the researchers are generalizing their findings to the population. While some studies using small numbers of subjects may be valid, certain research protocols must be followed before this is true.
Subjects: **How were the subjects selected? From volunteers, by random selection into groups, and so forth? Were both men and women in the group? What were the ages of participants? Were persons from different races, regions, and so forth, represented in the study group?**
Study design: **Does the study have a *control group* (a group of people with similar characteristics but who did not receive the treatment being used to study a given effect)? Were adequate controls for inherent differences in race, age, gender, socioeconomic factors, and so forth, taken into consideration? Were subjects from different groups *matched* to try to equalize potential confounding effects? Did all subjects think that they were receiving a scientifically tested treatment? (The *placebo effect* is the subject's tendency to experience a desired effect because he or she thinks that a certain medical or other treatment will help.)**
Source of information: **Although you may not have access to all of the preceding information, try to note where the article or report was published. Consider the following sources:**
Tabloids. **These news headlines are usually found at the checkout lines in grocery stores. Typical headlines might include: "Man mates with alien woman and produces new race," "Baby raised by dinosaur found in the jungles of Africa." Suffice to say, you should be skeptical of health "facts" found in these formats.**
News Magazines/Newspapers. **Weekly or daily news magazines or newspapers may have a "sensational" twist in their news reporting. Often, they have interesting articles written by health writers who are not necessarily**

FACT OR FALLACY? MAKING SENSE OF HEALTH REPORTS *(cont.)*

knowledgeable about the subject. They may have a one-sided approach to an issue, or provide inaccurate or incomplete information. Although you may find out some very good information in these formats, it is best to dig deeper before coming to any health conclusions.

Self-Help Books. Reader beware. In the effort to "make a buck" in the health arena, many self-made authorities have been successful in getting people to buy their books. Keep in mind that the key factor here is "selling" and that publishers often do not verify facts in these books. Just because something is published in a book doesn't make it accurate or reliable! Stick to reputable authors with degrees or academic training in the area and be critical of what is said. Check their statements against textbooks in the field, or call health professionals in your area to verify particular points.

Professional Journals. Although sometimes more difficult to read, *refereed journals (peer-reviewed)* are perhaps the most reliable sources of information. A refereed article is reviewed very carefully by at least three experts in the field before it is accepted for publication. Peer reviewing helps to ensure reliability and credibility. Do not confuse an *edited* journal with a peer-reviewed journal. Edited journals have paid editors who review the work for style, and so forth, but they may have no background to deal with content. Most peer-reviewed journals publish guidelines for submitting manuscripts to their journal. These guidelines typically give information about the peer review process. Most college and university journals are probably peer-reviewed.

Values are also significant factors in determining behavior change. People may be more likely to engage in a weight-training or fitness program if they believe that these activities will improve other aspects of their social lives or interpersonal relationships. Selected *cues to action* may provide those underlying stimuli that motivate people to take aggressive, firm action to change a given behavior. Finding out that her total cholesterol level is over 300 may be a cue that influences one person to reduce her saturated-fat intake. Another person may read an article about the harmful effects of high cholesterol levels and reduce cholesterol intake. Remember that each person's cue to action may be different. Determining which ones work for you is a key aspect of any behavior change strategy.

If you believe health to be a result of factors beyond your control, you will not take personal responsibility for your health. A certain sense of internal control over your health coupled with a high degree of confidence in your ability is the ideal situation for positive health-behavior change. If you believe that you can change negative health behavior (self-efficacy) and that your actions will make a difference in your health (health locus of control), positive change becomes much more likely.

Readiness is the state of being that precedes behavioral change. People who are ready to change (see Figure 1.4) possess the attitudes, skills, and internal and external resources that make change a likely reality. To be ready for change, certain basic steps and adjustments in thinking must occur.

CHOICES FOR CHANGE

Various behavioral theories have been studied as they relate to health. Ideas and concepts such as self-efficacy, locus of control, and health locus of control are becoming more widely understood. **Self-efficacy** refers to a person's appraisal of his or her own ability to change or to accomplish a particular task or behavior. **Locus of control** refers to a person's perceptions of forces or factors that control individual destiny. **Health locus of control** focuses specifically on those factors that relate to health actions and activities. These constructs influence how we view ourselves and also how we behave or seek to change behaviors.

self-efficacy Refers to a person's appraisal of his or her own ability to change or accomplish a particular task or behavior.

locus of control Personal perceptions of forces or factors that control individual destiny. Some people are more internally controlled and believe that they are powerful instruments for change in their situation. Others are more externally controlled and believe that external forces beyond their control dictate their behaviors.

health locus of control Locus-of-control factors relating specifically to health-related actions/activities.

readiness State of being that precedes a behavioral change.

Being able to express feelings and talk through problems with friends is part of good health.

What Do You Need to Know to Change?

- *Facts and information about topics and issues in health.* You may have many questions about various issues regarding your health status. How much and what types of fat are O.K. in your diet? What are the best body-toning exercises you can do to achieve a given result? How can you improve your weak interpersonal communication skills? How can you have an intimate sexual relationship and avoid STDs? Knowing where to go for accurate information and how to make good decisions based on sometimes conflicting reports are important first steps in being ready to change. The box "Fact or Fallacy" will help you become a more cautious, skilled reader of health materials. Although there is a tremendous amount of information available, using the best resources and thinking critically will permit you to make the best choices.

- *Important information about your own health.* People seldom change their behaviors until they believe that they are really at risk or that the perceived benefits are worth their efforts. Self-awareness is usually created by the process of *self-assessment* or *self-appraisal*. One method used extensively by individuals, organizations, health-care professionals, and educational institutions is the *Health Risk Appraisal (HRA)*. The U.S. Department of Health and Human Services questionnaire gives you a basic indicator of your overall health status and the areas in which you may need improvement (see box on pages 17 to 19). Some HRAs are much more complex and use actual physical tests of blood chemistry, cholesterol counts, urinalysis, and other measures of health status combined with pencil-and-paper-questions to determine health. Regardless of the type of instrument used, such analyses provide a starting point. If you have high cholesterol or high blood pressure, or if you have a family risk for breast cancer, these may be key

areas to focus on. Once you understand the health facts and they become personally relevant, you may value change more. Valuing change and seeing it as beneficial may encourage you to believe that change is good, right, and important. In addition, such information may strengthen your own beliefs in your ability to change (self-efficacy).

- *Knowing how to choose from options.* Understanding the facts, valuing the facts, and believing in the importance and likelihood of change are essential elements of basic change. But, unless you know *how* to go about change, your efforts may be futile. Knowing what your resources are, practicing certain optional health-related skills and behaviors, and developing the ability to continue a behavior are the next steps in initiating and continuing change. If you start jogging and you don't like it or can't stick to it, try swimming or another activity rather than giving up.

- *Making the commitment to change.* Because behaviors are learned responses that often develop into subconscious rituals and procedures, they become a significant part of a person's identity. Changing these behaviors is difficult. In general, the younger you are, the less likely that these behavioral patterns will have become deeply ingrained and the better your chances for change.

Figure 1.4
The steps and stages in becoming ready for behavioral change.

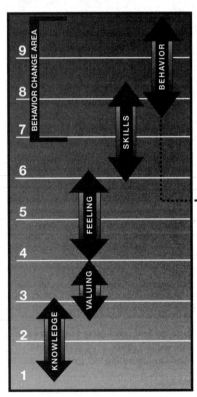

Promoting Your Health

U.S. DEPARTMENT OF HEALTH AND HUMAN SERVICES HEALTH BEHAVIOR QUESTIONNAIRE

This is not a pass-fail test. Its purpose is simply to tell you how likely your behavior is to keep you healthy. The behaviors covered in the test are recommended for most Americans. Some of them may not apply to persons with certain chronic diseases or handicaps. Such persons may require special instructions from their physicians or other health professionals.

You will find that the test has six sections: smoking, alcohol and drugs, eating habits, exercise and fitness, stress control, and safety. Complete one section at a time by circling the number corresponding to the answer that best describes your behavior (2, 3, or 4 for "Almost Always," 1 for "Sometimes," and 0 for "Almost Never"). Then add the numbers you have circled to determine your score for that section. Write the score on the line provided at the end of each section. The highest score you can get for each section is 10.

CIGARETTE SMOKING

If you never smoke, enter a score of 10 for this section and go to the next section, "Alcohol and Drugs."

	Almost Always	Sometimes	Almost Never
1. I avoid smoking cigarettes.	2	1	0
2. I smoke only low-tar and low-nicotine cigarettes, *or* I smoke a pipe or cigars only.	2	1	0

Cigarette Smoking Score: _____

ALCOHOL AND DRUGS

	Almost Always	Sometimes	Almost Never
1. I avoid drinking alcoholic beverages, *or* I drink no more than one or two drinks a day.	4	1	0
2. I avoid using alcohol or other drugs (especially illegal drugs) as a way of handling stressful situations or the problems in my life.	2	1	0
3. I am careful not to drink alcohol when taking certain medicines (for example, medicine for sleeping, pain, colds, and allergies).	2	1	0
4. I read and follow the label directions when using prescribed and over-the-counter drugs.	2	1	0

Alcohol and Drugs Score: _____

EATING HABITS

	Almost Always	Sometimes	Almost Never
1. I eat a variety of foods each day, such as fruits and vegetables, whole grain breads and cereals, lean meats, dairy products, dry peas and beans, and nuts and seeds.	4	1	0
2. I limit the amount of fat, saturated fat, and cholesterol I eat (including fat on meats, eggs, butter, cream, shortenings, and organ meats such as liver).	2	1	0
3. I limit the amount of salt I eat by cooking with only small amounts, not adding salt at the table, and avoiding salty snacks.	2	1	0
4. I avoid eating too much sugar (especially frequent snacks of sticky candy or soft drinks).	2	1	0

Eating Habits Score: _____

HEALTH BEHAVIOR QUESTIONNAIRE

EXERCISE AND FITNESS	Almost Always	Sometimes	Almost Never
1. I maintain a desired weight, avoiding overweight and underweight.	3	1	0
2. I do vigorous exercises for fifteen to thirty minutes at least three times a week (examples include running, swimming, brisk walking).	3	1	0
3. I do exercises that enhance my muscle tone for fifteen to thirty minutes at least three times a week (examples include yoga and calisthenics).	2	1	0
4. I use part of my leisure time participating in individual, family, or team activities that increase my level of fitness (such as gardening, bowling, golf, and baseball).	2	1	0

Exercise and Fitness Score: _____

STRESS CONTROL			
1. I have a job or do other work that I enjoy.	2	1	0
2. I find it easy to relax and express my feelings freely.	2	1	0
3. I recognize early, and prepare for, events or situations likely to be stressful for me.	2	1	0
4. I have close friends, relatives, or others whom I can talk to about personal matters and call on for help when needed.	2	1	0
5. I participate in group activities (such as church and community organizations) or hobbies that I enjoy.	2	1	0

Stress Control Score: _____

SAFETY			
1. I wear a seat belt while riding in a car.	2	1	0
2. I avoid driving while under the influence of alcohol and other drugs.	2	1	0
3. I obey traffic rules and the speed limit when driving.	2	1	0
4. I am careful when using potentially harmful products or substances (such as household cleaners, poisons, and electrical devices).	2	1	0
5. I avoid smoking in bed.	2	1	0

Safety Score: _____

HEALTH BEHAVIOR QUESTIONNAIRE

YOUR HEALTH STYLE SCORES

After you have figured your score for each of the six sections, circle the number in each column that matches your score for that section of the test.

Cigarette Smoking	Alcohol and Drugs	Eating Habits	Exercise and Fitness	Stress Control	Safety
10	10	10	10	10	10
9	9	9	9	9	9
8	8	8	8	8	8
7	7	7	7	7	7
6	6	6	6	6	6
5	5	5	5	5	5
4	4	4	4	4	4
3	3	3	3	3	3
2	2	2	2	2	2
1	1	1	1	1	1
0	0	0	0	0	0

Remember, there is no total score for this test. Consider each section separately. You are trying to identify aspects of your lifestyle that you can improve in order to be healthier and to reduce the risk of illness. So let's see what your scores reveal.

WHAT YOUR SCORES MEAN TO YOU

Scores of 9 and 10 Excellent! Your answers show that you are aware of the importance of this area to your health. More important, you are putting your knowledge to work for you by practicing good health habits. As long as you continue to do so, this area should not pose a serious health risk. It's likely that you are setting an example for your family and friends to follow. Although you received a very high score on this part of the test, you may want to consider other areas where your scores could be improved.

Scores of 6 to 8 Your health practices in this area are good, but there is room for improvement. Look again at the items you answered with a "Sometimes" or an "Almost Never." What changes can you make to improve your score? Even a small change can often help you achieve better health.

Scores of 3 to 5 Your health risks are showing! Would you like more information about the risks you are facing and about why it is important for you to change these behaviors? Perhaps you need help in deciding how to make the changes you desire. In either case, help is available in this book.

Scores of 0 to 2 You may be taking serious and unnecessary risks with your health. Perhaps you are not aware of the risks and what to do about them. In this book you will find the information and help you need to improve your scores and, thereby, your health.

SOURCE: U.S. Department of Health and Human Services, *Health Style: A Self Test* (Washington, D.C.: Public Health Service, 1981).

T A K I N G   C H A R G E
P E R S O N A L   A N D   C O M M U N I T Y   A C T I O N

Although people are more concerned today about health issues than at any time in our nation's history, many of us feel that we can do little to reduce our own risk. We find it even more difficult to bring about change at the community level. Following are suggestions that may improve your own health status and that of those around you.

MANAGING YOUR PERSONAL HEALTH BEHAVIORS

- *Are you really ready to do whatever it takes to change?* Assess your readiness by analyzing where you are in terms of a readiness scale.

- Complete a personal health history, including individual risks from your genetics, inheritance, lifestyle, environment, and health care system. Prioritize those that *your behavior* can have an impact on, either short- or long-term.

- Develop a short-term plan of action to reduce your immediate risks, and begin to control your long-term risks. Improve your diet, increase your fitness levels, avoid harmful substances, improve your social skills, help others, consider spiritual issues more often, take time to control stress, get adequate amounts of sleep, practice self-care activities, use the health care system wisely, practice responsible sexual behaviors, etc.

- *Decide how things will improve or be different in your life as a result of the change.* What will really be different if you succeed? How much will the ultimate change matter to your relationships? Your health? Your self-concept? How important are these things to you?

- *Listen to the things that you are telling yourself (self-talk) that are affecting your emotional response to change.* Are your past experiences, values, and attitudes causing you to make unrealistic excuses or to defend your past behaviors? Are you making this change because you really want to, or are you being pressured by others?

- *Assess your resources.* What things will help you achieve your goals? Will friends, community support groups, or other networks help you in your efforts to change?

- *Determine what things have previously stood in the way of reaching your goals.* What are the barriers or blocking agents? Which of these can you avoid?

- *Establish priorities for change.* Determine what things are most important for you to change now. Which is *the* most important factor? The *next* most important?

- *Develop a plan of action.* Break the parts of your action into small components or objectives. Tackle each component one at a time, being careful not to try too many changes at a time.

- *Determine how you will know when you have satisfactorily met your goal.* How will you evaluate success? Will you evaluate success by a series of small objectives to be met or only in terms of the ultimate goal? For example, people who begin an exercise program often find it helpful to start with a graduated program that will enable them to reach their goal after a specified period of time (say, one month). This is often easier than saying "By this time next year, I will be running the Boston Marathon."

- *Determine what things will keep you going.* What will help you maintain the behavior change? The most difficult part of any behavior change strategy is to be able to continue for prolonged periods of time.

- If you have already tried several of the items on this list and failed, don't be discouraged. The problems you have encountered may be due to influences you've never really thought about, or to a lack of support or encouragement. Sometimes people will even help you fail—by sabotaging your diet, for example, or encouraging you to take another drink. Positive reinforcement is essential.

MANAGING YOUR COMMUNITY HEALTH BEHAVIORS

- Act responsibly to preserve the environment. Consume fewer resources, use fewer prepackaged products, *reuse, recycle, and reduce consumption* whenever possible. Water, air, natural resources, and animals are important legacies, and each of us can play a significant role in protecting them.

- Analyze what is going on in your school, your community, your state, and the nation. *Read, discuss, and develop opinions* about the critical health issues likely to have an impact on you, your parents, your friends, and society in general.

- Listen to the opinions of your school administrators, your state elected officials, and your national elected representatives. If an important health issue is being considered, *write or call* these officials and let them know how you feel about the issues. *Become involved* in city government and in social services, particularly when the health of others is likely to be affected.

- *Vote* for elected officials whose policies, rhetoric, and past histories have indicated that they support improvements in health care, environmental issues, education, minority health, and other critical issues facing the nation.

- *Purchase* products and services from companies that have proven records of protecting the environment, providing safe foods and products, and supporting the health and well-being of others through their organizational practices.

SUMMARY

- There are no simple definitions of what it means to be healthy.

- Health can be defined as the ability of an organism to achieve optimal well-being within a realistic framework of individual potential and in a sometimes hostile environment.

- Total health or wellness involves physical, mental, emotional, environmental, spiritual, and social components in addition to the absence of physical infirmity.

- Overemphasizing one component of the wellness continuum and ignoring other components can lead to serious health deficiencies.

- Health promotion can be defined as any combination of educational, organizational, economic, and environmental supports for behaviors conducive to health.

- The benefits of good health include improved self-image, life satisfaction, enhanced creativity, increased energy levels, and reduced medical costs.

- Lifestyle, environment, biology and heredity, health care, and other factors are major influences in individual health and longevity.

- Disease prevention refers to a variety of techniques used to prevent worsening of health conditions. In general, there are three types of prevention: primary, secondary, and tertiary.

- Health status can be measured by analysis of such factors as incidence, prevalence, morbidity, mortality, and infant mortality rates. However, many nonstatistical factors must be considered as well. Disparities in health are important future considerations.

- Behavior change is a complex task, and a deliberate plan is required. Logical steps include identifying a behavior change, listening to yourself, determining why it's important that you change, developing a plan of action, evaluating your progress, and maintaining the behavior change.

- Predisposing, enabling, and reinforcing factors affect our ability to change our behaviors.

- Our beliefs, values, and readiness for change may significantly affect our ability to change.

- We must each accept personal responsibility for keeping current, evaluating priorities, and choosing viable options regarding health.

FURTHER READINGS

U.S. Department of Health and Human Services. *Health United States: 1991.* Washington, DC: Government Printing Office.

Contains the 1991 *Prevention Profile,* submitted by the secretary of the Department of Health and Human Services to the president and the congress of the United States. This is the sixteenth report on the health status of the nation and provides vital health statistics.

U.S. Department of Health and Human Services. (1993) *Monthly Vital Statistics Report,* vol. 41 no. 7. Washington, DC: Centers for Disease Control and Prevention, National Center for Health Statistics.

This publication includes the final data from the CDC/National Center for Health Statistics. Includes statistics on deaths and death rates, causes of death, infant mortality, and other important data.

U.S. Department of Health and Human Services. (1992) *Healthy People 2000: National Health Promotion and Disease Objectives.* Boston, MA: Jones and Bartlett.

This document contains a national strategy for significantly improving the health of the nation over the coming decade. It addresses the prevention of major chronic illnesses, injuries, and infectious diseases.

Mary-Lane Kamberg is a frequent contributor to *Current Health 2*, from which this selection—"Fitness for Every Body"—is taken.

FITNESS FOR EVERY BODY

MARY-LANE KAMBERG

[1]The starting gun fires. The track star *propels* himself from the starting block. He sprints around the track. He breaks the tape with his chest as he crosses the finish line.

[2]No argument here: Everyone agrees that sports celebrities are physically fit. What you may not know is that you don't have to be a world-class athlete to enjoy the benefits of fitness.

[3]Forty years ago, fitness tests measured only athletic skills. Participants were scored in such events as the 50-yard dash and the standing long jump. If you weren't a star athlete, you wouldn't rate well—but you might have been fit by today's more accurate standards.

The Big Three

[4]Today, experts test fitness levels by looking at three major *components* that contribute to good health: strength, endurance, and flexibility.

[5]*Strength* is the amount of force the muscles can exert. Strength is what lets you lift a barbell or do a pull-up. However, you don't have to do weight training to build strength. Any weight-bearing activity—walking, gymnastics, or exercises such as push-ups, for example—will make you stronger.

[6]*Endurance* is the ability to exercise over a period of time. Endurance keeps you going in a cross-country run; it lets you swim another lap after you've already done 10. *Aerobic exercise*—exercise that increases the body's consumption of oxygen and improves both the respiratory and circulatory systems' functioning—develops endurance. Swimming, walking, and bicycling are examples of aerobic activities. So are dancing, jumping rope, and running. Aerobic exercise makes the heart and lungs work harder, which, in turn, improves the capacity to work longer and harder. Experts say that you need about 20 minutes of aerobic exercise three times per week to be physically fit.

[7]*Flexibility* is the ability to stretch. People with good flexibility have full use of the muscles and joints through what experts call the range of motion. A baseball pitcher, for example, must be able to use the entire range of motion of his shoulder to be able to throw well. Stretching before and after exercise improves flexibility, but be careful not to stretch cold muscles. Warm up first with some easy running, rope jumping, or a similar activity. Activities such as dance and gymnastics require lots of stretching, so they are good ways to improve flexibility.

Testing, One, Two, Three!

[8]Fitness tests measure a person's strength, endurance, and flexibility. They can also measure a person's percentage of body fat compared with his or her lean muscle tissue. Body-fat measurement tells more about a person's fitness level than weight, because muscle weighs three times more than fat. Someone who weighs more than another person might be more physically fit if the weight is muscle tissue. Excess fat is associated with risk factors for disease.

[9]Just how is body fat measured? A doctor or other health professional measures body fat percentage with an instrument called a skin-fold *caliper*. The caliper takes a "pinch" of flesh and measures its thickness.

(CONTINUED)

FITNESS FOR EVERY BODY (CONTINUED)

[10]The person being tested is usually checked in the abdomen, the front of the thigh, the back of the arm, and the angle of the shoulder blade. Boys between the ages of 5 and 17 should have between 10 percent and 20 percent body fat. Girls in that age group should have body fat between 20 percent and 25 percent.

[11]Other tests that tell how fit someone is include blood pressure and heart rate screenings and tests that measure how well the heart is pumping blood past your lungs. Another test measures how much air you can hold in your lungs and breathe out in one second. Healthy habits—eating nutritious food, exercising, and not smoking—improve scores on these tests.

Fitness and Fatness

[12]Most athletes, to be sure, qualify as being fit using these criteria. So do many people who aren't interested in competitive sports, but who do care about their well-being. Unfortunately, even by today's standards, many adults and children are not fit.

[13]A 1989 study by the Amateur Athletic Union found that 68 percent of 9 million Americans between the ages of 6 and 17 couldn't pass tests of strength, endurance, and flexibility. The research also documented a steady decline in fitness in this age group between 1980 and 1989. The number of students who scored satisfactory on the tests declined from 43 percent in 1980 to 32 percent in 1989.

[14]In another study, the U.S. Department of Health and Human Services compared school-age children of today with those of 20 years ago. Researchers found that today's children have a higher percentage of body fat than children had 20 years ago. Obesity is a growing problem for Americans between the ages of 6 and 17. (Obesity is defined as weighing 20 percent or more over ideal weight, which is based on a combination of individual and statistical factors.) A study reported in the *American Journal of Diseases of Children* found that during the last 15 years, obesity in 6- to 11-year-old children went up 54 percent, and increased 39 percent in children aged 12 to 17. This information, however, must also be seen in the light of the increasing incidence of eating disorders in young people. Fear of fatness has its own set of serious problems.

Fit Families

[15]Generally, fit children have fit parents. In many families, fitness is a way of life, with parents and their children frequently participating together in sports and other physical activities. On the other hand, children who are obese usually have obese parents. Research has shown that a *tendency* to be overweight may be inherited.

[16]Heredity is only part of the story, however. Too much fast food, as well as more television viewing and avid interest in home video games have all been blamed for playing a part in the decline in fitness among children and adolescents. It's obvious: The more time you sit in front of the tube, the less time you spend riding your bike, walking, or playing sports.

Fitness Facts

[17]Why do we care about fitness? The fact is, people who are physically fit stay healthy longer.

[18]Five years ago, a study of 17,000 Harvard University graduates that was reported in the *New England Journal of Medicine* found that people who stayed active lived longer than their classmates who didn't exercise.

[19]But good health is only one benefit of regular exercise. Here's another fact: Being physically fit improves self-esteem, helps relieve stress, and can improve appearance. And some educators think fitness is linked to better grades!

(CONTINUED)

FITNESS FOR EVERY BODY (CONTINUED)

[20]A fifth-grade teacher in California had his students run 20 minutes to 40 minutes every morning. The teacher found that the students were more ready to learn after they ran. He also compared his runners to other students who didn't run. The runners not only scored better than nonrunners on academic tests, the runners also missed fewer days of school because of illness. Runners missed about two days per year; nonrunners missed an average of 17 days per year. Another study that linked exercise with academic achievement kept track of more than 500 Canadian children for more than six years. Researchers found a connection between fitness and how well students learned math and writing skills.

[21]A third benefit of physical fitness is social adjustment. Young children relate to other children through movement. As people grow up, movement plays an important part in social development. During physical activity, children learn to get along with each other. Sports and physical play activities offer opportunities to learn to share, negotiate, and work together to solve problems. It worked that way when you were young; it works today now that you're in your teens.

[22]If you want to improve your fitness level, consider asking your school physical education instructor for advice. Explain your plans and ask about a fitness screening. A screening helps identify areas in which you need improvement. Your instructor may tell you to *modify* your program, avoid certain exercises, or increase others to strengthen weak muscles or *stabilize* joints to prevent injury. For instance, the instructor may say you have good strength and endurance, but need to work for more flexibility.

Fitness Fun-damentals

[23]Teens with certain medical conditions may need to discuss their fitness plans with their parents and physician. Your fitness plan will include some form of exercise, but how can you tell which exercise or sport is best for you? One fitness expert says that the best exercise is the one you actually do. Try different activities until you find something you like. If exercise isn't fun, you probably won't do it for long.

[24]Organized sports teams are good because they offer social contact as well as exercise. But what if you're not a great athlete? Try recreational sports classes or leagues. Many community youth groups sponsor co-ed volleyball games, for example. Your local parks and recreation department may offer tennis lessons or basketball clinics.

[25]You also can exercise on your own or with just a couple of friends. Meet a few times a week for a group walk. Or use an exercise videotape to work out together. Walking, running, bicycling, and other aerobic activities offer fitness benefits and don't require athletic *prowess*.

[26]While you're trying new activities, don't forget that exercise is not always sports-related. Ballet lessons or a square dance club can give you plenty of exercise. You might want to try bench stepping or water walking. Because water increases resistance and reduces the effect of gravity, 15 minutes of walking in water equals an hour on land. (Get in the water about chest deep, and walk as if you were on land. Swing your arms for better results.)

[27]Some high schools are setting up on-site fitness centers that students and teachers alike may use. If you can afford it, look for a fitness center nearby. Many health clubs allow only adults, but some have programs designed especially for children and teens. And don't forget that cleanliness is an important *finale* to a fitness program. Shower and put on clean clothes (including socks) after you're finished.

Stumbling Blocks

[28]If getting exercise is as simple as taking a brisk walk, why don't more people get fit? Fears and *misconceptions* get in the way.

(CONTINUED)

FITNESS FOR EVERY BODY (CONTINUED)

[29]Some people think they can't become physically fit. Or they don't want to exercise. Teens who are overweight, for instance, might be uncomfortable with the way they look in a leotard or sports uniform, so they'd rather not participate. Those who are small for their age may feel the same way. Also, teens who have never been good at competitive sports sometimes don't want to try anything that involves exercise. The battle is even tougher for teens whose family is inactive.

[30]Misconceptions also keep some people from exercising. Many girls mistakenly believe that they will build bulky, unattractive muscles if they do too much exercise. The truth is, even the most muscular women body-builders don't look like Arnold Schwarzenegger. That's because female hormones don't allow the same muscle development as male hormones do.

[31]Boys who build muscles through weight lifting may look good, but if that's their only exercise, they may be neglecting the endurance and flexibility components of true fitness. Big biceps have little or no effect on the efficiency of the heart. Girls who care about the way they look most often think in terms of eating for an attractive body shape instead of exercising. If they are underweight, they may fear exercise will make them lose weight. The truth is exercise will tone their muscles and make a skinny body more attractive.

Food for Fitness

[32]A last component in the fitness equation is food. Food gives your body the energy it needs to perform the physical activities that lead to fitness. The important thing to remember is that the right kinds food really do make a difference in how fit you are. A healthy diet includes the correct proportions of carbohydrates, proteins, and fats. And within those categories some food choices are better than others.

[33]Limit fat intake to 30 percent of your daily calories. You can limit fat by choosing protein sources with less fat. Choose lean meats. Trim the *visible* fat. Remove the skin from chicken before cooking. Eat more fish. Some beans are good protein sources without fat. When you cook use polyunsaturated oils. Substitute salads (beware of the dressing!) and frozen yogurt for french fries and ice cream.

[34]Remember that complex carbohydrates—apples, broccoli, and carrot sticks, for example—are better for you than simple sugars because they provide more nutritional value. Have fruit for dessert. Try whole grain bread. These foods also provide more fiber and more fiber is more healthful.

Solving the Diet Dilemma

[35]Changing your attitudes about food choices will make a better contribution to your overall fitness than dieting to lose weight. Some experts believe that dieting doesn't work without exercise. Their theory is that when someone diets, his or her body thinks it is starving. It reacts by slowing the *metabolism*, the chemical and physical processes involved in living. The body then tries to store fat—just when the dieter is hoping to lose that fat.

[36]Still, health experts are concerned about the 40 percent of high school students who say they have been on diets. Life-threatening eating disorders often follow periods of extended and/or fad dieting. If you want to lose weight, change your food choices and increase your activity level. That will prove to be the best route to physical fitness.

What's in It for You

[37]The most important steps you ever take may well turn out to be those you take to become physically fit. You'll be healthier and feel better if you watch what you eat and set aside time each week for physical activity—even if you never reach the ranks of the superstars.

CONTENT QUESTIONS—"FITNESS FOR EVERY BODY"

TRUE OR FALSE

If the statement is false, rewrite it to make it true.

1. Today's fitness tests are much the same as they were 40–50 years ago.
2. Strength is the amount of force the muscles can exert.
3. Exercise means playing an organized sport.
4. Today's children have a higher percentage of body fat than children 20 years ago.
5. You should limit fat intake to 30 percent of your daily calories.

COMPLETION

6. Experts test fitness levels by looking at three major components. Name them.
7. Why does a body-fat measurement tell more about a person's fitness level than their weight?
8. Why do some people resist participating in a fitness program?
9. A healthy diet includes the correct proportions of what three elements?
10. If you want to lose weight, what two major things should you do?

VOCABULARY—"FITNESS FOR EVERY BODY"

1. propels (¶1)
2. components (¶4)
3. aerobic exercise (¶6)
4. caliper (¶9)
5. tendency (¶15)
6. modify (¶22)
7. stabilize (¶22)
8. prowess (¶25)
9. finale (¶27)
10. misconceptions (¶28)
11. visible (¶33)
12. metabolism (¶35)

CONTENT ANALYSIS QUESTIONS—"FITNESS FOR EVERY BODY"

1. State Kamberg's thesis.
2. Compare and contrast strength, endurance, and flexibility.
3. What reasons does Kamberg give for the growing problem of obesity for Americans between the ages of 6–17?
4. What age was this article's primary target audience? What specific clues did you use?
5. What are the major benefits of regular exercise? Do you see any disadvantages?

APPLICATION QUESTION—"FITNESS FOR EVERY BODY"

1. How do you define being physically fit? Do you feel you are physically fit? Why or why not? Do you think most of your family and friends are physically fit? Why or why not? What do you think are the major factors that keep you, your family, and your friends physically fit? What do you think would improve your fitness level and the fitness level of others?

2. Assume that you have been assigned to a college committee charged with recommending general fitness guidelines for students, faculty, and staff. What would you recommend as the major components of such a program? Why?

"FRUITS AND VEGETABLES"

The *Mayo Clinic Health Letter*, from which this selection—"Fruits and Vegetables"—is taken, is written and published by the Mayo Foundation for Medical Education and Research, a subsidiary of Mayo Foundation.

FRUITS AND VEGETABLES

MAYO CLINIC HEALTH LETTER EDITORIAL STAFF

Eat Five a Day Every Day

[1]How many fruits and vegetables did you eat today? One? Two? Even if you can say three, there's room for improvement.

[2]The Food and Nutrition Board of the National Academy of Sciences recommends that you eat five servings of fruits and vegetables daily. The reason: Fruits and vegetables can help you control your weight and reduce your risk of coronary heart disease and cancer.

Why More Is Better

[3]At the forefront of research into the relationship between diet and disease is a new focus on fruits and vegetables. These foods are a natural fit for diets aimed at reducing the risk of obesity and heart disease.

[4]Fruits and vegetables contain *virtually* no fat and most have fiber. They also are rich in a variety of vitamins, minerals and other chemicals that scientists suspect may be related to disease prevention, particularly cancer protection.

[5]Although research has given no clear-cut answers, health and government agencies are calling for Americans to eat five servings from a variety of fruits and vegetables every day. One serving equals one-half cup of cooked vegetables, canned fruit or juice. Count one cup of chopped vegetables or fruit, or a medium whole fruit, as one serving.

[6]Here's a closer look into how eating fruits and vegetables may protect your health:

[7]**Beta Carotene**   Deep-yellow and dark-green vegetables are rich sources of beta carotene—a substance that your body uses to make vitamin A.

(*CONTINUED*)

FRUITS AND VEGETABLES (CONTINUED)

[8]Low blood levels of beta carotene are linked with the development of lung cancer.

[9]Good sources of beta carotene are carrots, spinach, tomatoes, winter squash, sweet potatoes, pumpkin, papaya, cantaloupe, mango, apricots, and watermelon.

[10]In addition to beta carotene, fruits and vegetables contain other carotenoids that may be involved in cancer prevention.

[11]***Vitamins C and E*** These nutrients act as antioxidants. They fight free radicals—molecules that may cause disease by injuring cells or harming your body's natural healing ability. (See *Mayo Clinic Health Letter*, January 1992.)

[12]Look for vitamin C in broccoli, broccoflower, oranges, brussels sprouts, grapefruit, strawberries, cantaloupe, cauliflower and baked potatoes. Vegetable oils, nuts, leafy greens, and whole grains contain vitamin E.

[13]***Phytochemicals*** These chemicals are contained naturally in fruits, vegetables, and grains.

[14]Scientists used to believe phytochemicals were not essential to human nutrition. Yet new studies suggest substances in *cruciferous* vegetables may be related to cancer protection.

[15]Cruciferous vegetables include brussels sprouts, cauliflower, broccoli, broccoflower, kale, mustard greens, cabbage (bok choy, green, red and savoy), turnips, rutabaga, and kohlrabi. Many of these vegetables also contain vitamin C.

[16]The National Cancer Institute (NCI) began a five-year project in 1990 to study how foods rich in phytochemicals may prevent cancer or slow its progress. The first year of the Designer Foods program focused on garlic, licorice root, flax-seed, citrus fruits, and a group of vegetables that includes parsley, carrots, and celery.

[17]***Fiber*** The NCI recommends that you eat 20 to 30 grams of fiber daily. The recommendation stems from evidence suggesting that a high-fiber, low-fat diet lowers your risk of colon and rectal cancer. (See *Mayo Clinic Health Letter*, May 1992.)

[18]Fruits and vegetables, especially *legumes*, are good sources of fiber. One-half cup of cooked legumes provides an average of 5 grams of fiber and less than 1 gram of fat. Legumes include split peas, blackeyed peas, and lentils, as well as kidney, pinto, black, navy, and garbanzo beans.

[19]Data from a national food consumption survey show that diets with five servings of fruits and vegetables contained about 17 grams of fiber. Adding just two slices of whole-wheat bread brings the total to at least 20 grams of fiber—and meets the NCI daily goal for fiber.

[20]***Low Fat*** The same food consumption survey found that eating fruits and vegetables can help you control fat.

[21]In diets with no fruits and vegetables, fat contributed about 38 percent of daily calories. Eating two servings of vegetables and at least three servings of fruits lowered daily calories from fat to around 34 percent.

[22]Limiting fat to no more than 30 percent of daily calories may reduce your risk of obesity, coronary heart disease, and cancer.

Limit Fat and Boost Fiber

[23]Eating more fruits and vegetables is not a *panacea*. The relationship of diet to disease is overwhelmingly complex, influenced by many lifestyle and environmental factors. No one food is perfect. It's your overall diet that counts.

(CONTINUED)

FRUITS AND VEGETABLES (CONTINUED)

[24]Yet, at a minimum, eating five servings of fruits and vegetables every day can improve your diet by helping control fat and boosting fiber.

Here Are Ways to Eat Five a Day

[25]Does eating five servings of fruits and vegetables a day sound like a lot? If so, try these ideas:

[26]*Serve soup*: Use vegetables and legumes as a base for soups or as added ingredients.

[27]*Moisturize lean ground meats*: Add raw, grated carrot, potato, or apple to lean ground beef or turkey to make meat loaf or meatballs.

[28]*Thicken sauces without fat*: Substitute cooked and pureed vegetables for cream or whole milk.

[29]*Be creative*: Pasta and stir-fry dishes are ideal ways to serve lots of different vegetables and small portions of meat.

[30]*Enhance old standbys*: Add fruit to your breakfast cereal and raw, grated vegetables or fruit to muffins and cookies.

[31]*Try new and unusual vegetables*: The *genetically engineered* broccoflower is a good example. A cross between broccoli and cauliflower, this vegetable looks like a light green head of cauliflower with a milder, sweeter taste.

[32]*Don't let lettuce limit salads*: Choose a wider variety of greens, including arugula, chicory, collards, dandelion greens, kale, mustard greens, spinach, and watercress.

New Guide to Healthy Eating: Focus Is on Fruits, Vegetables, and Grains

[33]On April 28, 1992, the U.S. Department of Agriculture (USDA) gave a fresh, new look to its guide for healthy eating. The federal agency unveiled its new "food guide pyramid"—a change in geometry that offers updated advice on nutrition.

[34]The pyramid conveys three essential elements of a healthy diet:

[35]*Proportion*: Eat different amounts every day from the basic food groups.

[36]The shape of the pyramid tells you at a glance that grains, vegetables, and fruits should make up the bulk of your diet.

[37]*Moderation*: Use fats and sugars sparingly. Although this point is reflected in the 1990 Dietary Guidelines for Americans, the food guide pyramid adds visual impact to the message.

[38]*Variety*: Choose different foods from each major food group every day. The pyramid doesn't claim that any food is better or worse than another.

[39]As you look at the pyramid, keep this important point in mind:

[40]The USDA groups foods according to the most important nutrients they contain and how they're used. That's why you see legumes grouped with meat, poultry, fish, eggs, and nuts.

[41]Legumes contain protein in amounts comparable to these other protein-rich foods. But they also provide fiber with virtually no fat—healthful qualities none of the other foods in this group have.

[42]Don't worry about where legumes are grouped—with meats or with fruits and vegetables. Just remember to eat them.

(CONTINUED)

FRUITS AND VEGETABLES (CONTINUED)

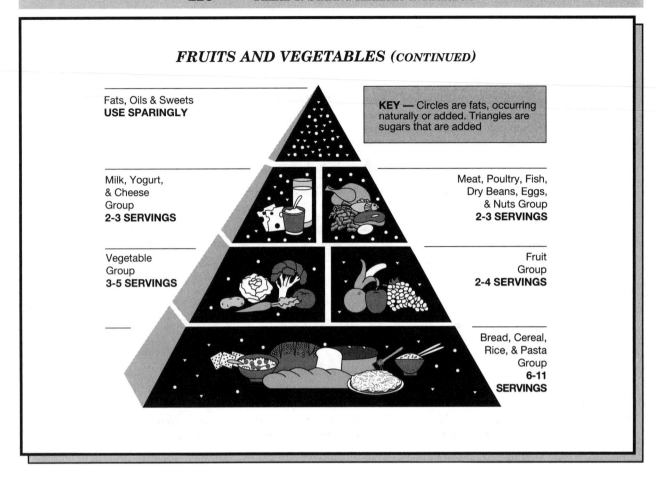

CONTENT QUESTIONS—"FRUITS AND VEGETABLES"

TRUE OR FALSE

If the statement is false, rewrite it to make it true.

1. It is recommended that you eat five servings of fruits and vegetables daily.
2. Fruits and vegetables contain very little fat.
3. It is thought that beta carotene causes lung cancer.
4. A high-fiber, low-fat diet may lower your risk of colon cancer.
5. Eating more fruits and vegetables is all you need to do for a perfect diet.

COMPLETION

6. List two reasons you should eat five servings of fruits and vegetables daily.
7. List three essential elements of a healthy diet according to the USDA.
8. Name three health risks that can be reduced by limiting your fat intake to no more than 30 percent of daily calories.

9. Name two ways in which eating five servings of fruits and vegetables every day can improve your diet.
10. What is the advantage of legumes over other protein-rich foods?

VOCABULARY—"FRUITS AND VEGETABLES"

1. virtually (¶4)
2. beta carotene (¶7)
3. cruciferous (¶14)
4. legumes (¶18)
5. panacea (¶23)
6. enhance (¶30)
7. genetically engineered (¶31)

CONTENT ANALYSIS QUESTIONS—"FRUITS AND VEGETABLES"

1. What is the source of the food guide pyramid? Do you think this is a reliable source? Why or why not?
2. Why are legumes grouped with meat, poultry, fish, eggs, and nuts? Explain your answer.
3. What do the writers mean by "no one food is perfect"?
4. Why do you think scientists are engineering food genetically? What do you see as the positive aspects of such food experiments? What do you see as negative aspects? *Note:* If you are not familiar enough with the concept of genetically engineered food to state any positive or negative aspects, where could you find more information?

APPLICATION QUESTIONS—"FRUITS AND VEGETABLES"

1. Make a list of what you have eaten during the last three days (or keep a record for the next three days). How closely does your diet match the USDA Food Guide Pyramid? Is one of the food groups consistently under- or over-represented in your diet? How could you change your diet to include more fruits and vegetables?

2. Assume you belong to a community service group on campus that has been asked to develop a "healthy eating" campaign for a local primary school. What would you stress in your campaign? Why? How would you present the information to the youngsters?

"SEVEN KEYS TO GOOD HEALTH"

Deborah Jones is a writer whose work often appears in national magazines. This selection—"Seven Keys to Good Health"—is from *Chatelaine*.

SEVEN KEYS TO GOOD HEALTH: HOW TO FEEL BETTER—MAYBE LIVE LONGER

DEBORAH JONES

[1]A recent medical study links seven common lifestyle practices with disabilities and *premature death*. Besides well-known health hazards—excessive drinking, smoking, social inactivity—the list includes snacking, skipping breakfast and sleeping less than seven or more than eight hours a night. These last practices aren't as risky as the others but point to an unhealthy *chaotic lifestyle*, according to Dr. Lester Breslow of the University of California's School of Public Health in Los Angeles and Dr. Norman Breslow of the University of Washington in Seattle.

[2]Studying nearly 7,000 people for more than 25 years, the Breslows found that the more bad habits a person had, the higher the risk. Those with all seven habits were twice as likely to die prematurely or to develop disabilities serious enough to interfere with routine activities, such as getting dressed and climbing stairs or to prevent them from working for six months or more.

[3]What steps can you take to lead a healthier, and perhaps longer, life? Dr. Patricia Beresford, director of the Preventive Medicine Centre at the Halifax YMCA, offers these suggestions:

Sufficient Sleep

[4]Dr. Beresford, who feels best with four hours of sleep a night says everyone's requirements are different and that the need for sleep generally declines with age. Still, research shows that most people require seven to eight hours of sleep on a daily basis, and that North Americans tend to deprive themselves of sleep, contributing to stress and physical and emotional problems. As a general rule, you should sleep enough hours each night to feel rested and alert throughout the day.

Cardiovascular Exercise

[5]Do *cardiovascular exercise*, such as brisk walking, jogging, or cycling for a minimum of 15 minutes at least three times a week to make your heart and lungs more efficient. The pace should be *vigorous*, but you should be able to walk without being breathless. Regular exercise, particularly walking and other weight-bearing activities, also helps reduce the risk of *osteoporosis*.

Nutritious Snacks

[6]The unhealthy snack-eaters in the Breslows' study were probably indulging in chocolate bars, potato chips, buttered popcorn and other fare high in fat, sugar or salt. Instead, have popcorn without butter and salt, fresh fruit, raw vegetables, whole grains, or unsalted nuts and seeds.

Wholesome Breakfasts

[7]Eat a complete breakfast daily, including a protein, a fruit or vegetable and a whole grain. It can be as fast and simple as a cheese sandwich with juice; cheese and crackers with juice; toast with peanut butter and a piece of fruit or just a piece of cold pizza topped with vegetables.

Limited Drinking

[8]While some research suggests that one drink a day may reduce the risk of heart disease, other studies link even moderate drinking with increased risk of breast cancer and liver disease. Here's what Dr. Beresford advises: "If you drink alcohol it should only be an occasional social occurrence. I would never suggest that anybody have one drink a day."

(*CONTINUED*)

SEVEN KEYS TO GOOD HEALTH:
HOW TO FEEL BETTER—MAYBE LIVE LONGER (CONTINUED)

No Smoking

[9]Smoking is linked with increased risk of lung and cervical cancer, heart disease, respiratory diseases (such as bronchitis and emphysema), osteoporosis, strokes among oral contraceptive users, and even with wrinkles. When smokers kick the habit, their risks start to decrease; their chances of getting lung cancer and heart disease may eventually become similar to those of people who have never smoked.

A Sensible Weight

[10]Obesity increases the risk of such diseases as heart disease and diabetes; weight lost through quick diets is always regained. Being underweight impairs energy levels; in severe cases, underweight causes menstrual disorders and may increase the risk of osteoporosis. Dr. Patricia Beresford's prescription for a healthy weight includes good eating habits, stress management and regular exercise.

CONTENT QUESTIONS—"SEVEN KEYS TO GOOD HEALTH"

TRUE OR FALSE

If the statement is false, rewrite it to make it true.

1. Everyone needs at least eight hours of sleep each night to stay healthy.
2. The Breslows found that people with all seven of the bad habits were twice as likely to die early or develop serious problems.
3. Quitting smoking does not reduce a person's health risks.
4. Regular exercise can help reduce the risk of osteoporosis.
5. Weight lost through quick diets is always regained.

COMPLETION

6. List Dr. Beresford's seven keys to good health.
7. List three unhealthy snacks. List three healthier snacks.
8. What is the recommended amount of exercise?
9. According to Jones, what are the three well-known health hazards?
10. What is Dr. Beresford's prescription for maintaining a healthy weight?

VOCABULARY—"SEVEN KEYS TO GOOD HEALTH"

1. premature death (¶1)
2. chaotic lifestyle (¶1)
3. cardiovascular exercise (¶5)
4. vigorous (¶5)
5. osteoporosis (¶5)

CONTENT ANALYSIS QUESTIONS—"SEVEN KEYS TO GOOD HEALTH"

1. How many people were included in the Breslows' research study? How long did the study follow the participants? Do you think this was enough people over a long enough time period to provide useful information? Why or why not?
2. Research shows that North Americans tend to deprive themselves of sleep. What do you think are some of the causes? What are some of the results?
3. Why do you think breakfast is the one meal that is listed as important to good health?
4. Some research suggests than one drink a day may reduce the risk of some illnesses. Other research suggests even moderate drinking may increase the risk of some illnesses. What do you think? What would you read to find out more information?

APPLICATION QUESTIONS—"SEVEN KEYS TO GOOD HEALTH"

1. Assume that you are a part of a group developing a ten-minute presentation for the adults at the downtown homeless shelter. Which of these seven keys to good health would you concentrate on in your presentation? Why? What other keys would you add?
2. How do you fare on the seven keys to good health? What steps can you take to lead a healthier, and perhaps longer, life?

"THE NEW AGING"

Carl Sherman is a freelance health and psychology writer trying to survive in Brooklyn. This selection—"The New Aging"—is taken from *Working Woman*.

THE NEW AGING

THE RESEARCH IS IN: HOW WE GROW OLDER IS BEING REDEFINED

CARL SHERMAN

[1]Growing older isn't what it used to be. Today's 40-year-old looks, acts and feels like yesterday's 30-year-old, says trend-spotter Faith Popcorn, and 50 now is like 40 was a generation ago. Popcorn calls it *"down-aging,"* a culturewide revision of life's timetable.

[2]Has an obsession with youth turned into a national inability to act our age? Not quite. Science is in fact *validating* our new youthful lifestyle and outlook. As Americans live longer—about 30 million are over 65, compared with 17 million 25 years ago—research on aging has boomed. For example, the Baltimore *Longitudinal Study* of Aging, conducted by the National Institute on Aging (NIA), has tracked over 2,000 men and women, ranging from their 20s through their 90s, with thorough physiological and psychological tests every two years. One major finding: Much of the slowing and breakdown that a decade ago was considered the *inevitable* result of time is actually due to disease, lifestyle, and environmental wear and tear. Most symptoms of age can be postponed, and in some cases prevented.

[3]"To an extent, you can take control of your own aging," says James Fozard, who directs the Baltimore study. If you eat right, stay active and avoid health-sapping habits, you're likely to be younger—physically, mentally and in spirit—than your 40-, 50-, or 60-year-old counterpart was a generation ago. Here's what you can do to head off the effects of time.

The Senses

[4]Vision generally remains unchanged through the 30s, but as the lens of the eye loses flexibility, it becomes harder for it to bend to bring close objects into focus. Farsightedness will almost certainly force you to hold the newspaper at arm's length sometime in your 40s and to keep trading up to ever-stronger glasses.

[5]But beneath the surface, *a far graver threat* to vision may be slowly progressing, beginning in your teens. Cataracts, the clouding of the lens that often dims vision in the 60s, are the result of lifelong oxidation damage, a by-product of normal body chemistry, says Paul Jacques, research associate at the USDA Human Nutrition Research Center on Aging at Tufts University. Jacques's study found that people without cataracts had higher levels of antioxidant nutrients—vitamins E and C and beta carotene—in their blood and got them more from natural sources (fruits and vegetables) than from supplements. Studies done at Johns Hopkins University have linked cataracts to smoking and sun exposure, both avoidable.

[6]By your 20s, you also begin to lose your ability to hear high tones, according to James Jerger, a professor of audiology at Baylor College of Medicine in Houston. Most people don't notice the slow, progressive muffling until their 60s, when they start to find speech hard to follow, although women are less likely to go deaf than men. Jerger also points out that some people still have perfectly good hearing into their 90s.

[7]Maybe it's not just luck. A high-fat diet can clog the blood vessels that nourish the delicate hearing organs, and years of rock concerts can cause *cumulative trauma*. Tribes in the deserts of the Sudan, who *subsist* largely on fruit and berries, keep acute hearing all their life, while Scandinavians ("They put a little coffee in their cream," says Jerger) suffer hearing loss early.

[8]Our sense of smell remains practically unchanged as we age, but our voice box tissue becomes less elastic, leading to a slightly deeper voice for women (men's voices actually get higher).

(CONTINUED)

THE NEW AGING (CONTINUED)

The Body

[9]A gradual decline in organ efficiency occurs throughout adulthood. The kidneys filter waste a little more slowly each decade. By your 40s, kidney stones will have appeared if you're *predisposed* to them. Women who've had children may find by their 40s that they leak a few drop of urine when they cough or sneeze, but simple exercises are very effective in strengthening stretched pelvic muscles. It won't be until your 60s that your liver will metabolize toxin more slowly, but barring heavy drinking and/or chronic hepatitis, it will function perfectly well for a lifetime. Between your early 20s and age 80, it's natural to lose 40 percent of your pulmonary function. Yet nature gave us lung power to spare: If you're healthy, you won't notice the difference.

[10]Blood pressure goes up every decade after 40 among Americans; overall, fewer women suffer from hypertension than men, but it still strikes 32 percent of women between 25 and 74. Coronary heart disease is uncommon in premenopausal women; estrogen seems to work as a kind of special protector, possibly by affecting the level of HDLs, the "good" cholesterol that keeps the bad cholesterol in check. The benefits of estrogen seem to last for 10 years after menopause, but by age 65 women's death rate from heart disease is almost as high as men's. According to statistics from the NIA, one out of every four women over 65 suffers from some form of cardiovascular disease. Yet despite these statistics, abundant research shows that a lifelong low-fat diet and an ongoing exercise program can help protect against heart disease, even during the most *vulnerable* later years.

[11]As for the more visible shape we're in, the decades do leave their mark. At 20, the average woman's body is 26.5 percent fat; by her 40s, it's 33 percent; and by her 50s, 42 percent. By 70, she'll have lost 30 percent of the muscle she had at 20. Flabbiness in the thighs, tummy and upper arms can show up as early as the 30s. But in fact, changes in muscle tone and body composition— the ratio of fat to muscle—can be minimal until close to 50 for women who keep up a good fitness program, says Everett Smith, director of the *biogerontology laboratory* at the University of Wisconsin. "I have a lot of staffers in their mid-30s who have better muscle tone now than in their 20s." (Breasts have no muscle tissue, and with age the ligaments above them stretch, especially after nursing.)

[12]Your functional capacity—the ability to generate energy for work and play—will drop 7.5 percent per decade, after a peak in the early 30s. At 40, many women find that stairs seem steeper and that they run out of steam earlier in the day. Much of this outgo may be accounted for by the fact that most women in their 40s are under more pressure than they were at 20, and they devote less time to exercise, says Smith. Those who exercise regularly cope better with business and family stresses, and exercise can dramatically slow or even reverse the energy drop. In one study, *sedentary* women from 35 to 65 were enrolled in a program of aerobic exercise. "After 10 years their functional capacity was 6 percent higher than when they started," says Smith.

[13]Training can build muscle at any age. In one program, a group of men and women with an average age of 90 worked with weights, increasing muscle size by 10 percent and nearly tripling their strength. Since lean tissue burns more calories than fat, muscle maintenance also makes it easier to stay slim.

[14]Creaky knees and stiff shoulders may creep into your life between 35 and 50. The health of your joints depends on the strength of the muscles supporting them, so again, regular exercise, especially weight lifting, running or walking, is important. Stress and physical changes make lower-back pain more common in the 30s, 40s and 50s (the disks that cushion the vertebrae in your spine gradually degenerate), but pain can often be prevented by strengthening lower-body and abdominal muscles.

(CONTINUED)

THE NEW AGING (CONTINUED)

[15]Healthy bones are crucial for heading off osteoporosis, one of the major health problems suffered by older women. This disease, which causes bones to become thin and porous enough to fracture easily, accelerates at menopause and strikes one out of four white women past age 65 (black women tend to have denser bones and so are less susceptible). The stronger your bones are before menopause, the less affected you'll be, so it's important to "bank bone" when you're young, says Sheryl Sherman, project director for osteoporosis at the NIA. Adequate calcium in your diet, about 1,000 milligrams a day (8 ounces of skim milk has 302 milligrams), and regular weight-bearing exercise (walking or running) will help build strong bones while you're young, then slow the drain.

The Mind

[16]Brain tissue begins to deteriorate in your 20s, but it will take 50 years or more before there's a noticeable change in your mental functions. Although some people feel they've already lost some of their edge by their 30s—they forget names and don't concentrate as well—there's no evidence at all to tie this to aging, according to Dr. Gene Cohen, acting director of the NIA.

[17]If you do tend to forget more, it may be that remembering some facts just isn't as important to you as it was when you were a student, and you have more years of information and names to sort through. The stress of business and family life can also lead to lapses. Still, scientific tests show that, for most people, true memory doesn't change until the 70s.

[18]From the 30s onward there is a slight mental slowdown, such as in reaction time, which determines how quickly you step on the brake and how fast you come up with the answers in "Jeopardy." But other functions, like vocabulary, get better through your 50s and 60s.

[19]Biologically, the brain actually continues to develop throughout your adult life. Although a number of brain cells die each year, the connecting branches between them—pathways for the nerve impulses that create thought, feeling and memory—keep on sprouting and spreading, *compensating* for the loss of cells, says Cohen. Studies show that intellectual challenge can enhance this growth. Mice that were put in a complex maze (the rodent equivalent of an adult-education class) sprouted extra intercell bridges.

[20]Physical exercise can help brain function, too. Robert Dustman, chief of the neuropsychology laboratory at the Salt Lake City, Utah, V.A. Hospital, found that aerobically fit individuals in their 50s, as well as those in their 20s, had more mental flexibility, adjusting more quickly to changing tasks, than same-age couch potatoes. "Fitness seems to slow mental decline, perhaps by bringing more oxygen to the brain," Dustman says. In fact, says Fozard of the Baltimore study, "a physically fit 60-year-old may have the same reaction time as a sedentary 20-year-old."

[21]The bottom line is that the passing years should leave mental powers pretty much *unscathed*. The deterioration we used to blame on age, it seems, can often be due to illnesses such as thyroid disease, lung disease and depression, which are more common in middle age and later. Alzheimer's disease strikes more women than men, primarily because more women live to be old enough to suffer from it. The disease occurs most commonly in people over age 85 who, it is suspected, have a genetic predisposition to it, coupled with some environmental trigger. More controllable is a condition called multi-infarct dementia, caused by ministrokes that block blood flow to the brain, killing tissue. Improving your circulation through a low-fat, low-cholesterol diet and exercise can help prevent strokes. "In healthy people," says Cohen, "intellectual performance remains robust throughout life." When the Social Security Administration surveyed centenarians some years age, it found no lack of creativity and intellectual activity; one still wrote a daily newspaper column.

(*CONTINUED*)

THE NEW AGING (CONTINUED)

Sexuality

[22]If you're already enjoying a satisfying sex life in your 30s and 40s, you have even more to look forward to. "Woman tend to report that sex is better as they get older—much better," says Patricia Schreiner-Engel, director of psychological services at the obstetrics-and-gynecology department at Mount Sinai Medical Center in New York. "They become more sexually responsive and comfortable with sex." The longer a woman has been orgasmic, the more easily she will achieve orgasm.

[23]For most women, the hormone shifts of menopause have little impact on desire or responsiveness. Although it's true that the drying and thinning of vaginal tissues at menopause can make intercourse painful, a topical estrogen cream can usually help. Regular sex is actually the best treatment for the problem.

[24]There's no age limit on the joy of sex. Schreiner-Engel describes a conference in which a group of doctors, all women, were discussing this issue: "At what point does sexual desire really start to go down?" they asked one doctor, who was 75 years old. "I'll let you know," she said.

[25]At any age, a drop in desire or sexual interest is probably due to depression, physical illness, relationship difficulties or the lack of a partner. All treatable.

Illness

[26]The risk of heart disease, the biggest killer of women as well as men, accelerates with menopause because of the loss of estrogen. The risk of cancer, the number two killer, rises sharply each decade after 30. Lung cancer has become the leading cause of cancer death for women as the number of female smokers has risen. Of course, it is highly preventable. The incidence of breast cancer has risen dramatically, although survival rates have also increased. Meanwhile, researchers are accumulating more information about possible causes of this disease (a high-fat diet is clearly one culprit), and thus potential preventive measures.

[27]Adult-onset diabetes is 10 times more likely at 60, when it strikes 20 out of 1,000 women, than it is at 30. Immune function starts to drop off in your 40s, but the change isn't significant until your 60s, when infections become more frequent.

[28]How well we can fight off illnesses, from cancer to colds, is one of the biggest health issues of the last 20 years. It's now known that a low-fat diet can lower the risk of heart disease, as well as a range of cancers. Recent research suggests that antioxidant nutrients help, too. Exercise seems to protect against heart disease, cancer and diabetes.

[29]Even the decline in immune defense may be negotiable. Dr. Ranjit Chandra, a research professor at Memorial University of Newfoundland, recently found that nearly one third of people over 65 have deficiencies of nutrients like iron, zinc, vitamin C and beta carotene, probably due to a poor diet. When a group of older men and women were given multivitamin supplements, they had 40 percent fewer colds, flus and other illnesses than a control group who had not taken vitamin supplements.

Longevity

[30]Life expectancy has risen dramatically, from 47 at the turn of the century to nearly 80 today. But *optimum life span* is still about 116 years, says Huber Warner, deputy associate director of the biology of aging program at the NIA. Some scientists believe that sooner or later we must run into a brick-wall genetic program for death.

[31]The future may revise this, too. Studies of animals have shown that drastically limiting food intake can vastly extend the maximum life span. Rats given a very low calorie diet live to 50 months, compared with their normal 32. Whether the same thing can he done with humans, creating a race of 170-year-old Methuselahs, is far from certain. "It's not a goal of modern research," says Warner. "Extending the healthy life span is."

CONTENT QUESTIONS—"THE NEW AGING"

TRUE OR FALSE

If the statement is false, rewrite it to make it true.

1. Americans have a longer life span than they did in past centuries.
2. Men are less likely to go deaf than women.
3. A high-fat diet can contribute to hearing problems.
4. We have no control over the aging process.
5. Biologically, the brain continues to develop throughout adult life.

COMPLETION

6. What are three possible contributors to the formation of cataracts?
7. List three general things you can do to take control of your own aging.
8. What is the biggest killer of women and men? What is the number two killer?
9. We used to think that growing older meant an inevitable physical and mental slowing and breakdown. What is the current thinking?
10. What is the goal of modern health research?

VOCABULARY—"THE NEW AGING"

1. down-aging (¶1)
2. validating (¶2)
3. longitudinal study (¶2)
4. inevitable (¶2)
5. a far graver threat (¶5)
6. cumulative trauma (¶7)
7. subsist (¶7)
8. predisposed (¶9)
9. vulnerable (¶10)
10. biogerontology laboratory (¶11)
11. sedentary (¶12)
12. compensating (¶19)
13. unscathed (¶21)
14. optimum life span (¶30)

CONTENT ANALYSIS QUESTIONS—"THE NEW AGING"

1. What is Sherman's thesis?
2. How does Sherman develop and support his thesis? Give examples to support your answer.

3. In paragraph 29 Sherman writes, "Even the decline in immune defense may be negotiable." What does he mean?

4. Based on Sherman's information, what are four positive steps you can take to keep your mind alert?

5. Do you believe we are "down-aging?" To explain and support your answer, compare and contrast your attitudes and behavior today with the attitudes and behavior of someone older when he or she was your age; and compare and contrast the attitudes and behaviors you had when you were younger with the attitudes and behaviors of today's young teens.

APPLICATION QUESTIONS—"THE NEW AGING"

1. Assume that members of your campus community service group are going to be working with a group of folks in their 70s at a neighborhood senior adult center for five hours a week. Design two activities or projects you think would be enjoyable and beneficial for the seniors.

2. Assume that you've decided to "head off the effects of time." Outline the changes you are going to make in your life.

"GOOD FRIENDS ARE GOOD MEDICINE"

GOOD FRIENDS ARE GOOD MEDICINE

PREVENTION STAFF

[1]Exercise is great for health. And so are vitamins, steam baths, SmokeEnders and the "Richard Simmons Show." But something else is great for health, and it doesn't take running shoes. It's called friendship.

[2]"More and more, research is teaching us that healthy, long lives depend on deepening our bonds with other human beings."

[3]That's Richard Grossman talking, who's director of the Center for Health in Medicine at the Montefiore Hospital and Medical Center in the Bronx, New York. What he's talking about is something that should come as especially good news: Good friends can be good medicine.

[4]Grossman isn't saying party till you drop, but he is saying get out and "make meaningful contacts with people. An active social life can nourish the mind, the feelings, and the spirit, and it's clear that good physical health depends as much on these parts of ourselves as it does on a strong and well-functioning body."

[5]Grossman isn't saying that regular exercise and a healthy diet aren't important. But he is saying that the fitness buff who does all the right things—but does them alone—might be missing out on what new research suggests could be the greatest health protector of all. He's missing out on the peace of mind in knowing he's got people he can turn to in times of need.

[6]It may, in short, be as important to talk heart to heart with a good friend each week as to go to the spa.

[7]Sound like your kind or fitness program?

(CONTINUED)

GOOD FRIENDS ARE GOOD MEDICINE (CONTINUED)

[8]Good, because the evidence looks quite convincing. Here's just a sampling of what research has come up with.

[9]A study of 7,000 residents of Alameda County, California, by researchers from Yale University found that people with good social-support systems were two to five times more likely to outlive people with fewer social involvements.

[10]An investigation by researchers reporting in the *Journal of Health and Social Behavior* found that a strong social support system was a powerful protector of both physical and mental health in 100 men who had been laid off from their jobs.

[11]A study of 170 pregnant women reported in the *American Journal of Epidemiology* recalled that pregnancy complications were three times more likely in women with weak social-support systems as compared with women with strong ones.

[12]No surprise, kids need meaningful companionship, too. A report in the *Journal of Youth and Adolescence* showed significantly greater rates of illnesses of all kinds in children lacking close contact with their folks. Like the saying goes, people need people. And not just for emotional health, but for physical health, too.

CONTENT ANALYSIS QUESTIONS—"GOOD FRIENDS ARE GOOD MEDICINE"

1. What are the writers' purposes?
2. What is the writers' thesis?
3. What type of details do the writers use to support and develop the thesis?
4. Is the information presented in paragraphs 9–12 primarily fact or opinion? Explain your answer.
5. Did the writers achieve their purpose? Why or why not?

"JEST FOR THE HEALTH OF IT"

Susan Goodman is a staff writer for *Current Health 2* magazine, from which this selection—"Jest for the Health of It"—is taken.

JEST FOR THE HEALTH OF IT

SUSAN GOODMAN

[1]Your friend comes up to you and asks if you've heard what Tom replied to the English teacher when she asked him the meaning of "derange." You haven't, but you want to. He delivers his funny line, and you groan—but then together you have a big laugh.

(CONTINUED)

JEST FOR THE HEALTH OF IT (CONTINUED)

[2]It isn't just your mouth or vocal cords that are getting a humorous workout. When you laugh, your chest, thorax, and abdominal muscles contract along with your diaphragm, heart, and lungs. When you really let go and howl, your blood pressure soars from an average of 120 to about 200. Your pulse rate doubles from 60 to 120 beats per minute. Laughter pumps more adrenaline into your bloodstream. It may also cause endorphins, the body's natural painkillers, to flood through your body.

Good Exercise

[3]People always knew that a good giggle could brighten any day, but now science tells us it can do much more than that. For one thing, laughter is good exercise. When you just read about what happens when you laugh, you might have thought it resembled your body's efforts when playing tennis or going up for a jump shot. If so, you were not far from wrong.

[4]Even mild laughter is good exercise, explains William F. Fry Jr., M.D., a professor of psychiatry at Stanford University. A hearty laugh stimulates almost every system in your body. It helps you breathe more deeply, bringing oxygen to the blood and expelling carbon dioxide. Laughing has even been called a form of internal jogging.

[5]All these benefits seem reason enough to run to the circus or to a Pee Wee Herman movie. Yet laughter improves health in additional ways that can't easily be measured by a blood pressure cuff. The amazing story of Norman Cousins is an example.

Mind over Matter

[6]In 1964, Cousins, an editor of *Saturday Review*, was told he had a crippling spinal disease and a one-in-500 chance for survival. Cousins rejected the traditional medical approach in favor of his own laugh-yourself-to-health cure. He checked into a hotel with lots of funny books, tapes of Marx Brothers' movies, and reruns of the old television show "Candid Camera." Regular laughter not only gave him some pain-free time to sleep, it also helped him beat the odds and make a full recovery.

[7]At first medical science put cases like Cousins' in the same category as faith healing and wearing copper bracelets to cure arthritis. Now, they are putting humor where it belongs—in places that help sick people get well. St. Joseph's Hospital in Houston, for instance, created a "Living Room" complete with funny books and magazines and live performances by comics and magicians. Patients are welcome to come to the room for a little comic relief. Other hospitals wheel carts of funny stuff—from video tapes to comic books—around to patients.

Stress Reducing

[8]Just like jogging and other forms of exercise, laughing helps reduce stress. You see, once laughing stops, your muscles are much more relaxed than they were before you started. Your heartbeat and blood pressure also fall to lower levels. With all these bodily functions running at a low and easy pace, you can feel a little slower and easier yourself. Researchers now know that laughter can relieve certain types of headaches, even help lessen hypertension. Psychologist Jeffrey Goldstein of Temple University even believes laughter, with its reduction of stress and hypertension, helps people with a good sense of humor live longer.

(CONTINUED)

JEST FOR THE HEALTH OF IT (CONTINUED)

Laughter and Learning

[9]Before you get set to snicker, wait! Let us stretch laughter's list of good points even further. Does the idea of chortling your way to better grades tickle your fancy? A study conducted by Dr. Dolf Zillmann at Indiana University found that children learn better and remember more when lessons are mixed with laughter. For one thing, humor keeps their attention focused upon the material. Also, everybody is more willing to enter into an activity wholeheartedly if they think they are going to have a good time.

[10]People with a full-blown funnybone reap its rewards long after they graduate from school. Studies have shown that a sense of humor is the most consistent characteristic among executives promoted in major companies. Scientists have found that if you smile, you are more likely to be hired for a job. You are also more likely to be trusted once in that job.

Prescription for Mirth

[11]Sounds like it's time to put a little more humor in your life, doesn't it? *Mad Magazine*, funny movies, and the daily newspaper comics will help, but it's also important to develop your own internal resources. Here are a few suggestions:

[12]1. *Adopt a playful attitude*: Keep your mind open to silly thoughts. If you're too worried about being cool to appear silly, remember that the word silly itself comes from the Old English word "saelig" meaning "happy, prosperous, and blessed."

[13]2. *Think funny*: Try to see the amusing side of every situation, especially ones that could otherwise be difficult. So when you discover you left your homework at home after you're already late for school because you stained your brand new white shirt which you only put on because you ripped your favorite sweater, make a joke out of the whole thing. It sure beats crying.

[14]3. *Laugh at yourself and take yourself lightly, but don't make jokes that put yourself or others down*: And make sure to take important responsibilities seriously. After that, a dose of humor makes all of life's worries and burdens a little lighter.

[15]4. *Make others laugh*: Laughter is contagious; making others happy often makes you feel happy. So pass on a good joke when you hear one. Some people say that health and happiness aren't laughing matters—but maybe they should be.

[16]Oh, yes, how did Tom define that word? "A place where de cowboys ride."

CONTENT QUESTIONS—"JEST FOR THE HEALTH OF IT"

TRUE OR FALSE

If the statement is false, rewrite it to make it true.

1. Laughter is good exercise.
2. A good laugh primarily benefits your lungs.
3. During a hearty laugh, your blood pressure drops.

4. Norman Cousins used traditional medicine in addition to his laugh-cure.
5. Traditional medical science does not believe there are any real benefits to humor and laughter.

COMPLETION

6. List four benefits of laughing.
7. Goodman talks about big laughs, mild laughs, and hearty laughs but also uses four synonyms for laugh. List them.
8. What is the most consistent characteristic among executives promoted in major companies?
9. What are endorphins?
10. List two reasons children learn better and remember more when their studies are mixed with laughter.

CONTENT ANALYSIS QUESTIONS—"JEST FOR THE HEALTH OF IT"

1. Explain the title "Jest for the Health of it."
2. Why is laughing called a form of internal jogging?
3. State Goodman's thesis.
4. What does the phrase "mind over matter" mean?
5. Write yourself a prescription for mirth.

APPLICATION QUESTIONS—"JEST FOR THE HEALTH OF IT"

1. List four adjectives that describe a person you know who has as good sense of humor and smiles often. List four adjectives that describe a person you know who doesn't laugh or smile very often. Which list has more words with positive than negative connotations? If someone were describing you, what kind of words would they use?
2. Design a plan that one of your instructors could use to appropriately mix humor into his/her course. Your plan should include a minimum of three specific suggestions.

"LOOKING FORWARD"

Peggy Noonan was a special assistant and speechwriter for President Reagan. She now writes on current issues and is a frequent guest on PBS. Her latest book is *Life, Liberty and the Pursuit of Happiness*. This selection—"Looking Forward"—is from her regular column in *Good Housekeeping*.

LOOKING FORWARD

ARE WE THINKING TOO MUCH ABOUT PROLONGING LIFE, AND NOT ENOUGH ABOUT HOW TO LIVE IT?

PEGGY NOONAN

[1]I was on a plane the other day, looked out the window, and started thinking about pictures of clouds. Do you remember them? Back in the fifties, sixties, and early seventies, when it was still unusual to fly, people got excited about being up in the sky on a plane. They'd get out their cameras and click away. Later, back home, they'd bring out the pictures: "This is the stewardess. This is the wing outside my window. And look, these are the clouds." There was a particular bright clarity to the pictures, the sky so blue and endless, the clouds thick, white-silver, and majestic.

[2]They stopped taking those pictures somewhere in the mid-seventies, when the 747 had become a common fact and everyone had flown. Everyone had seen clouds from the top, looking down.

[3]We look back at past decades and think of phrases like "a more innocent age." But we were never innocent. In fact, in terms of a greater easiness and excitement about life, I wonder if people weren't in a way more knowing then than we are now.

[4]I was the first in my family to travel by airplane, when in 1967 my aunt and uncle took me, at age 16, to San Juan for a vacation. We buckled in, took off, and soon we were soaring over the Atlantic going east and south in a big stomach-churning arc … and then immediately everybody lit up Marlboros and began drinking to calm their nerves and alert their bodies that vacation had begun.

[5]Pretty soon the plane was full of chatter and laughter, and vacationers were aisle hopping. It was gay and noisy and heightened somehow. People worked hard. Now they were going to play hard.

[6]The plane I was on the other day was quiet. The only sound around me, aside from the engines, was the dry rustling of big newspapers and the dry tap-tap of computers. A flight attendant came by with the cart, and I asked for orange juice, and we got talking. She'd worked for the airline for almost 25 years.

[7]"When I first started, the passengers all drank," she said. "Minute they'd ask for a drink, I'd give 'em a double." Then the whole country changed in the eighties, she said, and it was all bottled water and juices. She wasn't complaining, but there was a little *nostalgia* in her tone as if she were also saying, That was fun back then.

[8]We're a more sober nation now, and not only on planes. Americans are more earnest and purposeful, less willing to endanger their health or *imperil* their attractiveness by smoking, drinking, or eating the wrong things.

[9]I belong to a gym. I even enjoy it. But I have to admit I respect those who don't worry too much about fitness and health, who know that you actually have to die someday. I certainly am more moved by them than by the friend who recently at lunch flexed her muscles, and told me she works out every day, and to watch out for the pasta, the problem is what you put on it, and if you even *think* about that meat sauce it will take you three days to get rid of it. She was disciplined and, in this context, virtuous. She was also a little *sanctimonious*. The way people are when they don't understand anything about life and so find A Truth and lecture you about it to show you, and themselves, that they're not confused and lost.

[10]When I'm with them, I miss these: the Sinatra-listening, Johnny Walker-drinking, steak-eating, overweight Americans of my youth who were by and large less educated, *less affluent* than we are, but a little more human.

[11]There was a kind of *dashing quality* to their unhealthfulness. There was something to their sense that life is a gift and it's ungrateful not to enjoy it. They knew how to be merry, to be silly, to happily waste time, to be loud and foolish. And I suspect that we, their sons and daughters, think too much about prolonging life and not enough about how to live it.

(CONTINUED)

LOOKING FORWARD (CONTINUED)

[12]Which is not to say that we should drink more or smoke. But we might remember this: Take care of yourself but don't make it your main mission in life, be disciplined but not rigid. And don't stress perfection. If you're perfect, only the perfect will be comfortable with you, and you'll wind up lonely.

[13]While we're all making our New Year's resolutions—"I'm going to walk a mile each day," or whatever—maybe we should add this: I'm going to relax. Be imperfect. Be nice. Have fun. Get a little looser around the edges—and *enjoy* life.

VOCABULARY—"LOOKING FORWARD"

1. nostalgia (¶7)
2. imperil (¶8)
3. sanctimonious (¶9)
4. less affluent (¶10)
5. dashing quality (¶11)

CONTENT ANALYSIS QUESTIONS—"LOOKING FORWARD"

1. What is Noonan's purpose?
2. What is Noonan's thesis? How does she develop and support her thesis?
3. In paragraph 3, what do you think Noonan is referring to and asking when she says "...I wonder if people weren't in a way more knowing then than we are now"?
4. How does Noonan characterize people of her parents' generation? How does she characterize people of her generation? What has changed?
5. How do you think Noonan would define health? Explain your answer.

APPLICATION QUESTION—"LOOKING FORWARD"

1. Write a realistic resolution for yourself for living healthier and happier, even if it isn't the start of a new year.

CONFRONTING VIOLENCE IN SOCIETY

Although there are many theories and much blame and finger-pointing, no consensus exists on the reasons for the violence or its solutions. Consider the following:

The rate of violent crime rose more than 370 percent from 1960 to 1991.

The number of juveniles arrested for homicide increased 85 percent between 1987 and 1991.

More than 2 million children are abused or neglected each year.

Every fifteen seconds a woman is battered; more than 2 million women are victims of domestic violence each year.

Someone is murdered in the United States every twenty-two minutes.

One in 25 elderly persons is victimized each year, and that number is growing.

Every day more than 100,000 children take a gun to school.

There are 600 cases every year of mothers killing their children.

One in five homicides occurs in families.

More than 1 million Americans are in jail or prison.

If firearm violence continues to increase at its current rate, by the year 2003 it will likely be the leading cause of injury-related deaths.

The level of deadly violence in the United States is about seventeen times higher than that in England, France, or Japan.

The authors in this theme discuss violence in our homes, our schools, our television, our sports, and our society to give insight into what Delaware Senator Joseph R. Biden has called "the most dangerous country in the world."

Professors Kornblum and Julian's chapter on "Violence," from *Social Problems* opens the theme. They discuss violence as a concept, including the distinction between institutional and noninstitutional violence. Next, they give various explanations of violence, including the biological viewpoint, frustration-aggression and control theories, violence as a subculture, violence as a rational choice, and the influence of the mass media. They evaluate criminal violence, family violence, and juvenile violence. The text chapter ends with current issues and their implications for future policy-making in the United States.

In "Why Rocky III?" from *Sex, Violence, and Power in Sports: Rethinking Masculinity*, Sociologist Mike Messner looks at a type of violence that we reward with celebrity status and money.

Newton Minow and Craig Lamay, in "Strangers in the House," from *Abandoned in the Wasteland: Children, Television, and the First Amendment*, examine the impact of the violence we bring into our homes via television.

Using real-people stories to illustrate the point that family violence is not a new phenomenon, Sandra Arbetter, in "Family Violence: When We Hurt the Ones We Love," covers spousal, child, elder, and sibling abuse.

The U.S. Department of Education's *Gangs and Victimization at School* studies gangs in schools and student victimization and fear, dispelling the myth that only minority students in inner cities are plagued by gangs.

In "Guns and Drugs," from *Teen Violence*, Susan Lang shows that the mix of youth with guns and drugs is killing thousands of young men and women and thousands of bystanders.

In *The Bookmobile*, college student Arleen Knowles remembers the bookmobile that brought happiness, self-respect, and hope to a south Chicago ghetto.

Each of the readings is by a different author(s), of a different length, and required different tasks.

STRATEGIES FOR SUCCESS

Develop a plan for each of the readings.

Determine who the author is and why he or she is writing.

Know the vocabulary the author uses.

Identify what the author is writing about.

Establish how the author develops and supports the thesis.

Recognize the author's stance.

Integrate graphic and text information.

Organize the information you need.

Decide what you can do with the author's information.

"VIOLENCE"

William Kornblum is a professor of sociology in the Graduate School and University Center at the City University of New York. Joseph Julian is a professor of sociology at San Francisco State University. This selection is from their text *Social Problems*, 8th ed.

CHAPTER

7

Violence

Chapter Outline

FACTS ABOUT VIOLENCE

- Between 1820 and 1945, human beings killed 59 million other human beings—one every 68 seconds—in wars, murders, quarrels, and skirmishes.
- At least 1 million children are physically abused each year, and many die as a result.
- It is estimated that more than 2 million women are victims of domestic violence each year.
- The rate of death by homicide among white men aged 15–24 is 21.9 per 100,000 population; among black men the rate is 85.6 per 100,000.
- Over 68 percent of the homicides reported in 1992 were committed by people using firearms; over 80 percent of those homicides involved handguns.

Within the space of a week two European tourists are murdered in cold blood in Florida. In North Carolina the father of the nation's most famous basketball player, Michael Jordan, is murdered by two young men with histories of violent crime. A student is shot outside a high school in New York City. In Houston, Los Angeles, and Washington, D.C., there are numerous incidents of random shootings and innocent victims killed by errant bullets. On Long Island a serial killer who preyed on prostitutes is apprehended, but not before he has ended the lives of almost a score of young women. All this lethal violence is only a fraction of that which occurred during a single year, 1993.

The level of deadly violence in the United States is about seventeen times higher than that in England or France or Japan. No other major industrialized nation has homicide rates that come close to those in the United States, and for black men in the United States the chances of living beyond age 40 are worse than in the poorest nations in the world, mainly because of the toll taken by violence. The overall rate of homicide among men aged 15–24 in the United States is about 22 per 100,000; for black men it is about 86 per 100,000. The widespread availability of guns and the

Scenes of extreme violence and its consequences—here, the random shooting of passengers on a Long Island Rail Road commuter train in 1993—have brought the problem of violence in the United States to greater public prominence.

Although we think of ourselves as a peace-loving people, we continually resort to violence in defense of what we consider our vital interests. The American Civil War was among the bloodiest in world history.

contribution of drugs to violence are important factors in this situation, but those who study the problem of violence in America also point to the pervasiveness of violence in our culture. The stability of American institutions may depend on efforts to reduce the level of violence in this nation.

Much violent action is not recognized as such. This is particularly true of violence associated with the rise or expansion of a political party or social movement; most groups try to forget, justify, or disguise their use of violence for these purposes. While extralegal violent acts such as murder, rape, or gang wars elicit public condemnation, other forms of violence are accepted or even praised; this is the case, for example, in most wars. Likewise, in troubled times and in frontier areas, vigilante activities are often approved by the local community as the only available means of maintaining order. In general, violence by or on behalf of the state is less likely to be condemned than violence by private citizens or violent acts in defiance of authority.

Despite the relative stability of its institutions, the United States has witnessed more violent behavior than other Western industrial nations. According to official statistics, approximately 22,540 murders were committed in 1992, as well as 109,062 rapes, 1,126,974 aggravated assaults, and 672,478 robberies (*UCR,* 1993). (See Figure 7–1.) The significance of the problem of violence and the need to find means to control and prevent it are apparent.

THE CONCEPT OF VIOLENCE

The word *violence* has a generally negative connotation; it has been defined as "behavior designed to inflict injury to people or damage to property" (Graham & Gurr, 1969, p. xiv). It may be considered legitimate or illegitimate, depending on who uses it and why and how it is used. Some special uses of violence, particularly in athletic activities like football and hockey, are so socially accepted that they are usually perceived not as violence but as healthy and even character-building behaviors.

Also not generally thought of as violence is *structural violence*, that is, "the

VIOLENCE   **199**

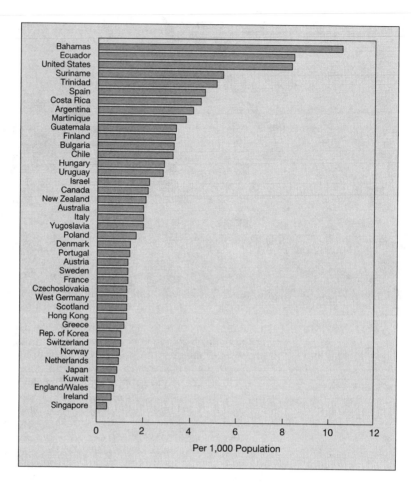

FIGURE 7–1   Homicide Rates, Selected Countries

dominance of one group over the other, with subsequent exploitative practices" (Galtung, 1971, p. 124). In such a situation the threat or potential of violence is usually sufficient to keep the dominated group "in its place," but the effect on social relations is very much like that of overt violence. This aspect of violence will not be discussed at length in this chapter, but it should be noted that a dominated group's recognition that it has experienced structural violence may engender overt group violence such as civil disorder and rebellion.

Jerome Skolnick (1969) pointed out that violence "is an ambiguous term whose meaning is established through political processes" (p. 3). What a society classifies as violent is likely to depend largely on who provides the definitions of violence and has the resources to publicize and enforce those definitions. War is a classic example: The actions of one's own side are generally viewed as honorable, while the other side is described as the aggressor and its violent acts are viewed as atrocities. Similarly, within a nation accusations of violent behavior are exchanged by those in power and their relatively powerless adversaries:

Within a given society, political regimes often exaggerate the violence of those challenging established institutions. The term violence *is frequently employed to discredit forms of be-*

bavior considered improper, reprehensible, or threatening by specific groups which, in turn, may mask their own violent response with the rhetoric of order or progress. (Skolnick, 1969, p. 4)

Several writers have attempted to justify the use of violence by a colonized people against the colonial regime or by the "have-nots" against the "haves." Frantz Fanon (1968), the Caribbean French psychiatrist whose experiences in the Algerian war made him a revolutionary, spoke of violence as a "cleansing force" that frees the spirit and restores self-esteem; it unifies the people and teaches them to assert themselves against any attempt at tyranny, even by their own leaders. Herbert Marcuse (1964) wrote about the revolutionary potential of people who have been denied full participation in the social life of advanced industrial nations—"the substratum of the outcasts and outsiders, the exploited and persecuted of other races and other colors, the unemployed and the unemployable" (p. 256).

There are, thus, many dimensions to the concept of violence. A useful distinction can be made between *institutional violence*, or violence exercised on behalf of or under the protection of the state, and the *noninstitutional violence* of those who are opposed to established authority. Violence in both of these categories may be either constructive or destructive; but institutional violence is usually presumed to be legitimate until proven otherwise, whereas people who engage in noninstitutional violence are punished. Thus, wars or violent police actions are usually considered legitimate because they are conducted under the aegis of the state; violent protests and demonstrations, revolutionary activity, civil disorders, and violent criminal activity are not. Although this difference is partly a matter of the difference in power between the "ins" and the "outs," it is also based on the traditional idea that the state may do some things that an individual citizen may not do in order to meet its responsibility for protecting the general welfare. It is when the state is seen as using force for purposes contrary to the general welfare that noninstitutional violence—sabotage, terrorism, rebellion, or revolution—is likely to occur.

EXPLANATIONS OF VIOLENCE

The Biological Viewpoint

"No person living today can question the statement that man, *Homo sapiens,* self-proclaimed to represent the pinnacle of evolution, is the most dangerous living species" (Boelkins & Heiser, 1970, p. 15). Between 1820 and 1945, human beings killed 59 million other human beings—one every 68 seconds—in wars, murders, quarrels, and skirmishes (Boelkins & Heiser, 1970). Violence is also commonplace in many American homes. As Steinmetz and Straus (1973) put it, "It would be hard to find a group or institution in American society in which violence is more of an everyday occurrence than it is within the American family" (p. 50).

Is it simply human nature to engage in violence? Since violence among humans is such a common occurrence, some social scientists have argued that human aggressive tendencies are inherent or instinctual. According to this view, only social organization keeps violent tendencies under control. Other experts argue that aggression is natural but violence is not. In an exhaustive review of research on the causes of interpersonal violence, a panel of experts convened by the National Academy of Sciences concluded that there is no solid evidence to support neurological or biological explanations of violent behavior. The panel did note, however, that findings from studies of animals and humans point to several features of the nervous system as possible sources of such explanations and recommended continued research on the subject (Reiss & Roth, 1993). Given the weight of evidence in favor of social and psychological explanations of violent behavior, this recommendation drew considerable criticism from social scientists (Kornblum, 1993).

Frustration–Aggression and Control Theories

Some theorists have argued that violence is a form of aggression that results from frustration. An unfulfilled need produces the frustration, and the frustration is vented in aggression. The strength of the impulses, needs, or wishes that are blocked determines the amount of frustration experienced, which in turn determines the degree of aggression. Failure, lack of affection, and poverty are suggested as possible causes of frustration. The *frustration–aggression theory* has been described as the easiest and most popular explanation of social violence of all kinds, including riots, political turmoil, robberies, and juvenile delinquency (Berkowitz, 1993). The main problems with this theory are that it fails to explain why frustration leads to aggression in some instances and not in others, and that frustration–aggression can be defined so broadly that it can cover almost any conceivable situation.

Related to the frustration–aggression theory is the *control theory,* which states that a person's ability to restrain or control impulsive behavior is correlated with the existence of close relationships with significant others. In this view, people may resort to violence when their attempts to relate to others in their own fashion are frustrated. The fact that violence is significantly more prevalent among ex-convicts, alcoholics, and others who are out of the mainstream of society and estranged from family and friends is also cited as evidence for the control theory. Thus, from the standpoint of control theory, murderers are likely to be "egocentric, impulsive, rebellious, or sadistic persons who cannot control their emotions" (Lunde, 1975, p. 39).

Of course, not all people who fit this description become murderers, nor do all murderers fit this description. One study suggested that there are actually two common personality types among murderers. One is *under*controlled: The person is unable to restrain aggressive impulses, has "never developed internal taboos against lashing out when provoked, and [has] few inhibitions about satisfying . . . acquisitive or sexual desires aggressively." The second is the exact opposite: an *over*controlled person who inhibits aggressive impulses almost completely and for whom "even socially acceptable outlets for aggression, such as swearing or pounding on a table, [are] off-limits" (Lunde, 1975, p. 39). Such people are said to repress their anger or hostility to the breaking point, until they suddenly and unpredictably explode.

It is difficult to demonstrate the validity of the control theory, since most murders and many other violent crimes are spontaneous, and their causes are not always clear. The lack of close relationships could simply be one factor among many that lead to violent behavior. The control theory does, however, suggest one clue to why violent crimes are increasing in frequency. In the past, various social factors—generally accepted moral standards; church membership; smaller, more intimate communities—aided in the development of controlled personalities. As a result of the erosion of these traditional social controls, people feel isolated and are more likely to resort to violence.

Violence as a Subculture

Many sociologists believe that violence is a learned behavior, one that is acquired through the process of socialization. Accordingly, aggressive or violent actions are most likely to occur in a culture or subculture in which violence is accepted or encouraged. Originally devised to explain juvenile gang behavior, the subculture theory has also been seen as the key to violence in general. In this model, members of violent subgroups have a low threshold for provocation, perceiving threats to their integrity in situations that would not be perceived as such by members of the dominant society. The norms of such groups require a combative response to provocation (Felson & Tedeschi, 1993).

In North America hockey is notoriously violent, but most other professional sports also have difficulty controlling the violent behavior of both players and fans.

It has also been suggested that all American males participate to some extent in a subculture of violence; the relatively low rate of violent acts by women is cited as evidence. Eugene C. Bianchi (1974), for example, sees professional football as a metaphor for America's "physical brutality, profit-maximizing commercialism . . . authoritarian-military mentality, and sexism" (p. 842). He notes that school and family join in forming "male children into competitors and achievers" (p. 843).

If violence is a consequence of social learning, frustration is not a prerequisite for violent behavior. Rather, violent habits are acquired through imitation or as a result of reinforcement of aggressive behavior. Along these lines, it has been shown that physically aggressive parents tend to have physically aggressive offspring. In addition, laboratory studies indicate that children who observe adults displaying physical aggression will be more aggressive in their later play activities than children who are not similarly exposed (Bandura, 1986). On the basis of this and other research, Frederick Ilfeld (1970) concluded that

> *physical punishment by parents does not inhibit violence and most likely encourages it. It both frustrates the child and gives him a model to imitate and learn from. The learning of violence through modeling applies to more than just parental behavior. It is also relevant to examples set by the mass media, one's peer or other reference groups, and local and national leaders. (p. 81)*

The subculture theory asserts that aggression is a by-product of a culture that idealizes a tough, "macho" image. This theory developed from analyses of official statistics, which suggest that certain subcultures have higher rates of violent crime than other segments of society. But as we suggested in Chapter 6, the stereotype that most acts of aggression are committed by young, minority males is erroneous because official statistics do not register the actual incidence of crime. Moreover, since the statistics do not reflect the attitudes or ideologies of individual offenders, it is difficult to discover the motives for their crimes. Data collected for the National Commission on the Causes and Prevention of Violence indicated that interpersonal violence received a low rate of approval in all socioeconomic groups (Reiss & Roth, 1993). A study of British men who had been convicted of acts of hostile aggression found that none of the men had committed their crimes in order to protect their reputation or win peer approval. The highest percentage of the crimes sprang from the aggressor's desire to inflict harm on the victim (Berkowitz, 1993).

In sum, people who commit acts of hostile aggression seem to share not an adherence to external subcultural norms but, rather, a similar set of psychological traits that can be found in any social, economic, or ethnic group.

Violence as Rational Choice

Although the implications of violence for human life and society seem wholly irrational, in many instances violent behavior can be interpreted as a rational means of attaining otherwise impossible ends. *Rational-choice theory* looks at all forms of human behavior for evidence of the actor's conscious or unconscious weighing of costs versus benefits (Hechter, 1987). Thus, rational-choice theorists would ask how criminals weight the chance of punishment against the likelihood of gain from breaking the law. Although it would seem that crimes involving terror and bloodshed are highly irrational acts committed by crazed individuals, in fact in many of these situations a rational strategy is at work.

Crimes such as extortion, kidnapping, and blackmail are often accompanied by the threat of violence. They are referred to as *strategic* crimes, however, because the violent act is one move in a complex "game" played by the criminal, the victim, and law enforcement agencies (Laver, 1982). In these "games," the criminals often wish to achieve their goals without resorting to maximum violence, but they must be prepared to use maximum force to convince the authorities that they are serious. To take just one example, "The successful kidnapper is the one who is perfectly prepared to kill the hostage and who can get this point across to his victim" in such a way that the law enforcement agencies involved will agree to meet the kidnapper's demands (Laver, 1982, p. 91).

The rational-choice approach is limited as an explanation of violence, but it is useful in situations in which it is important to understand what the violent actor hopes to gain in a situation. It stresses the importance of communication in cases of kidnapping, siege, and the like. Without communication, the strategic criminal and the authorities cannot reach an agreement that would prevent further violence. An example of such a situation is the standoff between the FBI and David Koresh, the leader of the Branch Davidian cult, which eventually led to the tragic deaths of many cult members in a fire that engulfed their fortified compound near Waco, Texas, in 1993. It is for this reason that the media often play such a crucial role in situations like hijackings, in which hostages are held until the terrorist's demands are met. In fact, the role of the media in violence of all kinds is significant and controversial, as will become clear in the next section.

The Influence of the Mass Media

A major issue in the study of violence is the role of the mass media in communicating or fostering violent attitudes. A survey of television programming conducted by the *Christian Science Monitor* six weeks after the assassination of Senator Robert Kennedy in 1968 found portrayals of 84 killings in 85.5 hours of prime-time evening and Saturday morning programming. The bloodiest evening hours were between 7:30 and 9:00, when the networks estimated that 26.7 million children between the ages of 2 and 17 were watching television (cited in Siegel, 1970). Since the 1970s there have been some changes in programming, and a portion of prime time has been devoted to family viewing. Despite these efforts to address the problem, levels of violence on television remain very high. So-called "action-adventure" programs are standard fare during prime time because they are relatively inexpensive to produce (and therefore more profitable) and because violence is an effective plot device. In addition, there is a great deal of violence in children's programming, especially cartoons.

Since the 1950s, when television viewing became widespread, its impact on young audiences has been the subject of a great deal of research. By the early 1970s it was generally agreed that there is some evidence linking television viewing to short-term aggression, but the debate over its long-term effects continued. In 1982 the National Institute of Mental Health released a report stating that "there is now 'overwhelming' scientific evidence that 'excessive' violence on television leads directly to aggression and violent behavior among teen-agers" (Reinhold, 1982).

Some researchers believe that the effects of television are more subtle. Hartnagel, Teevan, and McIntyre (1975) found that the effect of televised violence on behavior is indirect: "Values and attitudes or perceptions of the world may be substantially affected by television programming which may, in turn, influence behavior" (p. 348). This suggests that young viewers may become calloused by overexposure to violent programming and that, although they may not become violent themselves, they may more readily tolerate violent behavior in others.

Eli Rubinstein (1981) suggests that the problem of media violence may be especially acute for troubled children who already suffer from psychological disturbances that distort their perceptions of reality. He examined the television-viewing habits of ninety-four emotionally disturbed children in a state-operated inpatient facility for children in New York. He found that the behaviors of the children seemed to be related to what they watched on television: They imitated aggressive behavior and pretended to be characters in their favorite TV programs. Although much remains to be learned about the effects of televised violence on troubled children, Rubinstein believes that research must also focus on television's potential for helping this population.

The influence of the mass media, particularly television, in the reporting of protests, demonstrations, civil disorders, and other forms of potentially violent activity is another important issue. There are two questions here: Do the media distort the facts by stressing the violent aspects of news events, and does the presence of media reporters at such events tend to increase the possibility that violence will occur? The answer to both questions may be yes, in some instances. Distortion and provocation are difficult concepts to measure, however, and the matter is far from settled. Gladys Engle Lang and Kurt Lang (1972) have suggested that although the media "both contribute to the appearance of increased frequency and accelerate the cycle of protest," the presence of television and other news media in specific potentially violent situations "probably acts more as a *deterrent of violence* at such events than as an instigator" (pp. 108–109). On the other hand, there is some reason to fear that the extensive publicity given to such events as bomb scares, airplane hijackings, prison riots, and political assassinations may be "contagious," inspiring other attempts to engage in similar behavior. The rash of kidnappings, hijackings, and assassination attempts in recent years has been attributed in part to such media "contagion."

It is an oversimplification, of course, to assume that any portrayal of violence will tempt spectators to act out what they have seen. Both the context of the stimulus and the attitude of the viewer must also be considered. The desire to imitate what is seen on the television or movie screen is likely to depend largely on how it is presented, although we still lack hard evidence on what the relevant variables are. Similarly, the emotional condition of individual viewers will predispose them to react to what they see in different ways. Scenes of a prison riot are likely to evoke quite different reactions from a high school dropout who feels oppressed by "the system" than they would from an ambitious young executive.

CRIMINAL VIOLENCE

Statistically, violent crimes are the least prevalent types of crime. According to the FBI's *Uniform Crime Reports (UCR)* , the violent crimes of murder, robbery, aggravated assault, and forcible rape account for 13.5 percent of all reported crimes; the remainder are property crimes and status offenses. But while violent crime is not the most common type of crime, it is the most frightening. People who return to a burglarized home often report a feeling of revulsion at the thought of strangers handling their personal possessions; the intrusion itself is felt as a defilement. But the defilement of one's body in a violent attack is a far more terrifying prospect. More than any other crime, it threatens one's integrity and sometimes one's life.

In this section we will examine three types of violent crime: homicide, assault, and rape. Later in the chapter we will discuss the violence that occurs in families and the possible links between gangs and violence.

Criminal Homicide

Criminal homicide takes two forms. *Murder* is defined as the unlawful killing of a human being with malice aforethought. *Manslaughter* is unlawful homicide without malice aforethought. In practice, it is often difficult to distinguish between manslaughter and murder. Someone may attack another person without intending to kill, but the attack may result in death. Depending on the circumstances, one case might be judged to be murder and another to be manslaughter. Often the deciding factor is the extent to which the victim is believed to have provoked the assailant.

Paradoxically, most murderers do not have a criminal record. Of course, there are those who use actual or threatened violence as tools in a criminal career, but these are exceptions; as a rule, professional criminals try to keep violence—especially killing—to a "necessary" minimum because of the "heat" it would bring upon them from the law. Most murderers do not see themselves as real criminals, and until the murder occurs, neither does society. Murderers do not conform to any criminal stereotype, and murder does not usually form part of a career of criminal behavior.

Murder does, however, follow certain social and geographic patterns. Reported murders occur most often in large cities. The murder rate for large metropolitan areas is 10 per 100,000 population, compared to 5 per 100,000 in rural counties and cities outside metropolitan areas (*UCR,* 1993). The incidence of murder is unevenly distributed within cities; as Donald T. Lunde (1975) has pointed out, "most city neighborhoods are just as safe as the suburbs" (p. 38). There are also regional differences; for example, murder is more likely to occur in the South, even though it is one of the more rural parts of the country. This seems to be a result of the culture of the region, which tends to legitimize personal violence and the use of weapons.

Most murderers are men, who generally are socialized to be more violent than women and to use guns for recreation or for military purposes; guns are the most common murder weapon. Most murderers are young: In 1992, 55 percent of those arrested for murder were under age 25. The victims are young, too; in 1992, 33.8 percent were between the ages of 20 and 30 (*UCR,* 1993). More than half of all murder victims are members of minority groups. About 90 percent of the time, the killer and the victim are of the same race (*UCR,* 1990).

More significant than the demographic characteristics of murderers and their victims is the relationship between them. Several studies have indicated that this relationship is generally close; often the murderer is a member of the victim's family or an intimate friend. A high proportion of murderers are relatives of their victim, often the husband or wife. Victim studies suggest that there is a great deal of unreported domestic violence and that the majority of violent crimes are committed by family members, friends, or acquaintances (Reid, 1991). One study found that *more than 40 percent of murder victims are killed in residences. . . . More women die in their own bedrooms than anywhere else. One in every five murder victims is a woman who has been killed there by her spouse or lover. Husbands are most vulnerable in the kitchen; that's where wives are apt to pick up knives to finish family arguments.*

The other half of murders involving close relatives include parents killing children, children killing parents, or other close relatives killing each other. These victims usually die in the living room from gunshot wounds. Another 6 percent of murders [are] between more distant relatives. (Lunde, 1975, pp. 35–36)

Most murders occur during a quarrel between two people who know each other well. Both the murderer and the victim may have been drinking, perhaps together, before the event; as noted in Chapter 5, many homicides are alcohol related. Even though many homicides occur during the commission of other crimes, these killings, too, are usually unpremeditated—a thief surprised by a security officer, a bank robber confronted by an armed guard, and so on. In addition, many homicides involve police officers, many of whom are killed in the line of duty. In 1960, 48 law enforcement officials were killed in the states and territories of the United States. This number reached a peak of 134 in 1975 and stood at 61 in 1992 (*UCR, 1993*).

The mentally ill commit murder at the same rate as the general population, but serial killers are almost always psychotic—either paranoid or sexual sadists (Lunde, 1975). These murderers may hear voices commanding them to kill, think they are superhuman or chosen for a special mission, or kill to avert imagined persecution. Sadists may torture before killing and/or mutilate their victims afterward. Unlike most murderers, psychotic killers are seldom acquainted with their victims, who are often representatives of a type or class—rich businessmen, for example, or young middle-class women.

Mass Murders There is some evidence that mass murders (in which four or more people are killed by the same person in a short time) are becoming more frequent. Although the number of such murders fluctuates from year to year, some of the worst cases of the century have occurred since 1980.

On July 18, 1984, James Oliver Huberty, a recently fired security guard, opened fire in a McDonald's restaurant, killing twenty-one people and injuring twenty others. This was the worst massacre by a single person in a single day in U.S. history. In 1989, Theodore (Ted) Bundy, an articulate and rather charming drifter, was executed for the murder of numerous children and teenagers throughout the United States. These two cases, one a psychotic who murders in a fit of rage, the other a cool but also psychotic individual who organizes a series of killings (and therefore is known as a serial killer), illustrate quite well the types of people who commit mass murders. Generally, a mass murderer like Huberty kills in a fit of spontaneous rage; a serial killer often is highly organized and seeks to perfect a murder technique that will also prevent detection and apprehension. Most serial killers also have deep emotional problems concerning sexuality and describe the act of violence itself as thrilling and compelling (Holmes & DeBurger, 1987; Levin & Fox, 1985; Reid, 1991).

Assault and Robbery

Murder and assault are similar. *Assault* is a threat or attempt to injure. Murder therefore is a form of aggravated assault in which the victim dies. Often an extreme case of assault becomes murder accidentally; it may depend on the weapon used or the speed with which the injured person receives medical attention.

Since murder and assault are similar kinds of crime, most observations concerning murder also apply to assault. However, a person who commits assault is somewhat more likely to have a criminal record than one who commits murder.

Robbery may be defined as taking another person's property by intimidation. It accounts for 37 percent of all reported crimes of violence (*Statistical Abstract,* 1993). (A robbery in which violence was actually used is recorded as an assault.) Unlike murder or assault, robbery usually occurs between strangers; it is also the only major violent crime that is likely to occur between members of different races or classes.

Rape

Forcible rape is the act of forcing sexual intercourse on another person against his or her will. *Statutory rape,* for which the penalties are less severe, is the act of having sexual relations with a man or woman who is below a particular age established by state law. Although most arrests are for statutory rape, forcible rape attracts the most attention.

In the past, forcible rape was an extremely difficult crime to prove. Evidence requirements—the presence of bruises or torn clothing, eyewitnesses, or medical proof of intercourse—were unrealistic. Relatively few rapes occur in front of witnesses, and recent findings indicate that many rapists experience sexual dysfunction—which makes it less likely that rape can be verified by the presence of semen in the victim. Such difficulties discouraged victims from reporting the crime, and those who did press charges often encountered further problems. Defending attorneys sought to discredit the plaintiff's testimony by suggesting that she had provoked or cooperated with her assailant. In some cases the victim's previous sexual behavior was used to imply that she was promiscuous and, hence, not a reliable witness. Women who had suffered from the trauma of rape often found themselves the further victims of unresponsive and even hostile court proceedings. Many victims also feared revenge by the rapist.

These conditions persisted as long as rape was viewed as an exclusively sexual crime. The perpetrator of the "crime of passion" was thought to be driven by overwhelming and uncontrollable desire. Rapists were believed to be different from other people who commit violent crimes. This is only partially true; unlike murderers and those who commit assault, rapists often have a long history of criminal offenses. These offenses, however, tend to be for crimes other than rape (Reiss &

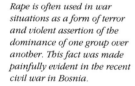

Rape is often used in war situations as a form of terror and violent assertion of the dominance of one group over another. This fact was made painfully evident in the recent civil war in Bosnia.

Roth, 1993). This relatively high rate of criminal involvement suggests that the rapist's motivation may be violent rather than sexual. A team of Massachusetts researchers found that rapists' feelings of anger, need for power, and desire to control the victim are significant factors; sex itself does not seem to motivate them. Rather, sex becomes the means through which the assailant expresses hostility (*Human Behavior,* June 1978).

Defining forcible rape as a crime of violence rather than one of passion helps place it in the proper perspective and invalidates the idea that the victim can initiate the crime by arousing desire in the rapist. It also suggests that women are not the only victims of this crime—men also can be raped, either by other men or by women. The old stereotypes of men as masters and women as objects of desire and domination worked to the disadvantage of both male and female rape victims. The women's movement and changing attitudes have led to a new understanding of this crime. Although rape laws still vary from one state to another, the nationwide trend is to revise existing statutes in favor of the victim. Corroboration by a witness is no longer necessary, and the plaintiff's sexual history is admissible only if it involves previous contact with the accused; moreover, although women are still the most likely victims of rape, men are now entitled to press charges against their attackers.

Rape victims are generally treated with more consideration and sensitivity today than they were in the past. Round-the-clock medical and counseling services are available, and police units staffed with specially trained personnel help victims overcome the trauma of the experience. As a result of these measures, more victims are willing to seek justice. Despite these changes, however, rape remains one of the most underreported of all crimes. According to the FBI, many women are too embarrassed or afraid to report a rape. They feel shamed by the attack and do not want others to know about it. Many also fear that the assailant will attack them again if they report the incident to the police.

Victim studies show that the vast majority of forcible rapes are not reported to the police. A recent study financed by the National Institute on Drug Abuse found that 683,000 adult women were raped in 1990, a figure more than five times higher than the number of rape cases recorded in official reports (Johnston, 1992). The study found that 61 percent of the victims were under 18 and that 22 percent had been raped by strangers. (The latter statistic suggests that family sexual abuse and acquaintance rape account for the majority of rapes.) On the basis of these findings, the researchers estimated that 6.8 million women would say that they had been raped once and 4.7 million that they had been raped more than once. More than 70 percent of the victims said that they were concerned about family members discovering that they had been raped, and about 60 percent said that they worried about being blamed for being raped (Koss & Harvey, 1991).

Date Rape   Date rape, or *acquaintance rape,* is forcible sex in which the victim is known to the offender. Although the victim has agreed to engage in some form of social interaction with the offender, she has not agreed to have sexual intercourse with him. When a woman is raped on a date, she is much less likely to report the incident than if she were raped by a stranger. Moreover, some people do not consider such incidents to be actual rapes. For example, a survey of junior high school students found that 51 percent of the boys and 41 percent of the girls believed a man has a right to force a woman to kiss him if he has spent a "lot of money" on her (*Dallas Morning News,* May 3, 1988).

Studies have found that between 11 and 25 percent of college women have been in situations in which their boyfriends forced them to have sexual intercourse. As many as 35 percent of male college students report that they have become so sexually aroused on a date that they have forced themselves upon the woman or felt that they were capable of doing so (Malamuth, 1981; Shotland & Goldstein, 1983). Often date rape on college campuses takes the form of gang rapes, usually at parties following heavy drinking or use of other drugs.

The frequency of *reported* date rape began to increase in the late 1980s. Officials at the Santa Monica Rape Treatment Center note that the women involved came from all parts of the nation and that the incidents occurred on all types of college campuses and included "fraternity-party gang rapes, dormitory rape, date rape, stranger rape" (Hendrix, 1988). Until recently, colleges and universities were totally unprepared to respond to such cases, but as the idea of date rape gains acceptance and incidents of such rape are given greater publicity, college administrations are adopting measures designed to prevent such incidents and providing counseling and other resources to victims. In 1993, for example, Antioch College added to a lively debate over issues of consent and coercion in sexual relations by publishing guidelines that require verbal consent at every stage of sexual behavior.

FAMILY VIOLENCE

Child Abuse

Child abuse is a serious problem in the United States. At least 1 million children are physically abused each year, and many die as a result. Because it is such a taboo subject and so often is not reported to the authorities, statistics on child abuse are even more unreliable than data on other crimes. However, a random survey of parents in Boston found that one person in six claimed that his or her child had been a victim of sexual or other abuse, and nearly half of those interviewed claimed to know a child who had been victimized sexually. Fifteen percent of mothers and 6 percent of fathers said that they had been abused as children (Finkelhor & Meyer, 1988). An earlier survey reported significant increases in the incidence of

TABLE 7–1   VIOLENCE AGAINST CHILDREN IN INTACT FAMILIES

Percentage of households where each type of violence occurred at least once in the past year. Nationwide poll was of two-caretaker households with at least one child 3 to 17 years old at home; 1,146 families were polled in the first survey and 1,428 were polled in the second.

	1975	1985
Slapped or spanked	58.2%	54.9%
Pushed, grabbed, or shoved	31.8	30.7
Threw something	5.4	2.7
Hit or tried to hit with something	13.4	9.7
Kicked, bit, or hit with fist	3.2	1.3
Beat up	1.3	0.6
Threatened with a gun or knife	0.1	0.2
Used gun or knife	0.1	0.2
All violence	63.0	62.0
Severe violence (Last five items)	14.0	10.7
Very severe violence (Last four items)	3.6	1.9

Source: New York Times, November 11, 1985. Copyright © 1985 by the New York Times Company. Reprinted by permission.

child abuse in communities throughout the United States and in other nations as well (Russell, 1984). Only in the last few years has a serious attempt been made to deal with the problem on a national scale—with limited success, as illustrated in Table 7–1.

Child abuse may be defined as a deliberate attack on a child by a parent or other caregiver that results in physical injury. A major obstacle to research on child abuse is concern for the traditional rights of parents; a parent has the right to inflict physical violence on his or her child (Justice & Justice, 1990). According to Suzanne Steinmetz and Murray Straus (1973), "The most universal type of physical violence is corporal punishment by parents. Studies in England and the United States show that between 84 and 97 percent of all parents use physical punishment at some point in their child's life" (p. 50).

If parents are to be responsible for raising and training children, they need to exercise a certain degree of authority, including the right to punish. Our culture strongly defends the right of parents to govern their children as they see fit, and it has traditionally approved of the use of corporal punishment for this purpose ("Spare the rod and spoil the child"). Thus, one of the first court cases in which an outside agency successfully intervened to protect an abused child was the 1866 Mary Ellen case, in which the plaintiff was the Society for the Prevention of Cruelty to Animals.

Increased concern with "children's rights" has changed this picture somewhat. Child labor laws, actions of the Society for the Prevention of Cruelty to Children, and changes in the handling of juvenile delinquents have helped reinforce these rights. However, the rights of parents and the preservation of the family unit are still regarded as primary concerns, even when in any other situation the nature of the injury would warrant criminal investigation and possible prosecution. Indeed, even in some of the worst cases the traditional autonomy of the family unit prevents the authorities from intervening or even learning about the problem. Some researchers estimate that only one case in three is ever discovered (Reiss & Roth, 1993).

According to a study by David Gil (1966), the victims of child abuse appear to be fairly evenly distributed over all age groups and between the sexes, although there are some changes in sex distribution during different stages of childhood and adolescence. At least half the victims in the study had been abused prior to the reported incident. A significant proportion of children seem to invite abuse through provocative behavior, although this plays a much smaller role in explaining attacks on children than the cultural norms discussed earlier. Of all cases of abuse, almost 90 percent were committed by the children's parents, and 14 percent of the mothers who abused their own children had themselves been victims of abuse as children.

A family in which there is child abuse typically has one or more of the following characteristics:

1. There is only one parent.
2. The parent's level of education and socioeconomic status are low.
3. The parent is highly authoritarian.
4. The family includes four or more children and has received some kind of public assistance within a year of the abuse incident.
5. The family changes its place of residence frequently.

Although these characteristics are found in many poor families, it is important to note that any correlation between abuse and poverty is biased by the fact that the behavior of the poor is more likely to be reported in official records than that of members of other classes, who are better equipped to conceal their activities. However, there are some specific problems, such as stress and anxiety, that are particularly prevalent in poor families.

Because studies based on official statistics have an inherent bias against the poor, the findings of a study by Brandt Steele and Carl Pollock (1974) are of interest. For five and a half years the researchers, both psychiatrists, studied sixty families in which significant child abuse had occurred. These families were not chosen by any valid sampling technique and therefore cannot be regarded as statistically representative; they were merely families that happened to come to the attention of the investigators. They did, however, span a wide range of socioeconomic and educational levels, and they included urban, rural, and suburban residents. The information obtained from them led the researchers to conclude that poverty, alcoholism, unemployment, broken marriages, and similar social and demographic factors are less significant than previous studies seemed to indicate. Instead, they found a typical personality pattern among abusive parents: The parent demands a high level of performance from the child at an age when the child is unable to understand what is wanted and unable to comply; and the parent expects to receive from the child a degree of comfort, reassurance, and love that a child would ordinarily receive from a parent. When the expected performance and nurturance are not forthcoming, the parent retaliates the way a small child might, with violence; but in this case the violence is not by the weak against the strong but by the strong parent against the weak, defenseless child.

It is important to note that *in every case studied*, Steele and Pollock found that the abusive parents had themselves been subject to similar unreasonable demands in childhood, and in a few cases they found evidence of the same experience among the grandparents. It seems, therefore, that child abuse could be part of a behavior pattern that is transmitted through the generations in some families and that it might be found to correlate with other aspects of family organization (Wisdom, 1989; Wyatt & Powell, 1988).

Spouse Abuse

On a rainy day in March 1992, Shirley Lowery, a Milwaukee bus driver, was stabbed to death by the man from whom she had fled a few days before. She was attacked as she hurried into the county courthouse to seek an injunction against her former companion, whom she accused of beating and raping her and threatening her life. Like many abusive husbands and boyfriends, her companion could not tolerate the idea of her leaving him. Lying in wait for her in the courthouse hallway, he stabbed her nineteen times with an eight-inch butcher knife.

Instances of violence between spouses have long been acknowledged and even tolerated as part of domestic life. Wives are the most frequent victims of such violence, although cases of battered husbands are sometimes reported. Very often the victims are seriously injured, yet, as with violence directed against children, the traditional autonomy of the family, together with the traditional subordination of women within the family, have made the authorities reluctant to intervene. Only recently has spouse abuse become an issue of social concern, and it is still difficult to assess its frequency and its impact on American family life.

Many researchers believe that spouse abuse is directly related to the high incidence of violence in American families. According to Straus (1977), "There seems to be an implicit, taken-for-granted cultural norm which makes it legitimate for family members to hit each other. In respect to husbands and wives, in effect, this means that the marriage license is also a hitting license (p. 444)." A study of more than 2,100 couples found that 3.8 percent of the husbands had physically assaulted their wives within the previous twelve months (Straus, 1977). The Justice Department estimates that more than 2 million women are victims of domestic violence each year. The vast majority of these women fail to notify the police of the incident, either because they consider it a private matter or because they fear further violence. Each year between 2,000 and 4,000 women are beaten to death by their spouses, and 25 percent of all female suicides are preceded by a history of battering (Reid, 1991).

Even when faced with constant violence, a surprising number of women make no attempt to leave the men who abuse them. Lenore Walker (1977) has suggested that this passivity is a form of fatalism. A pattern of dependency, of "learned helplessness," is established early in many women's lives:

> *It seems highly probable that girls, through their socialization in learning the traditional woman's role, also learn that they have little direct control over their lives no matter what they do. . . . They learn that their voluntary responses really don't make that much difference in what happens to them. Thus, it becomes extremely difficult for such women to believe their cognitive actions can change their life situation. (pp. 528–529)*

Other experts have described wife abuse as "a complicated and cumulative cycle of tension, belittlement, violence, remorse, and reconciliation that can lead to a paralysis of will and extinction of self-respect" (Erlanger, 1987, p. 1). This "battered women's syndrome," they claim, is a result of the deliberate undermining of a woman's sense of independence and self-worth by a possessive, overly critical man. "There is a sense of being trapped," one victim reports. "You live in terror and your thinking is altered" (quoted in Erlanger, 1987, p. 44).

Recent research has uncovered a high correlation between child abuse and spouse abuse: Between 30 and 40 percent of the time, a man who abuses his wife also abuses his children (Erlanger, 1987). In such situations a battered wife may remain with her husband in an attempt to protect the children. Conversely, the children may try to intervene and defend their mother, thereby causing the father to turn on them.

Elder Abuse

A form of violence that has recently come to public attention is abuse of the elderly by members of their own families, sometimes referred to as "granny bashing." (Abuse of the elderly may take other forms besides outright violence, such as withholding of food, stealing of savings and social security checks, and verbal abuse and threats.) Accurate data on elder abuse are not available, and it is difficult to prove that such violence has occurred. Elderly people bruise easily and fall often, and physicians are not trained to detect abuse in elderly patients. Moreover, because social scientists have only recently begun to study this type of violence, little is known about its causes. It is possible that family members are simply unable to cope with the problems of an aging parent or grandparent yet are unwilling, because of feelings of guilt, to place the parent in a nursing home. As the proportion of elderly people in the population increases, it can be expected that the frequency of elder abuse will also increase.

GANGS, GUNS, AND VIOLENT DEATH

Why is the homicide rate in the United States as much as twenty times the rate in other industrialized nations? (See Figure 7–1.) There is no one answer, but important explanations may be found in an analysis of changing patterns of juvenile violence, the increased firepower available to violent persons, and the inability of American society to agree on appropriate controls over lethal weapons.

In many sensational headlines one reads of brutal violence by juvenile gangs in large cities. In an especially infamous case in New York City, a gang of youths described as a "wolf pack" raped and nearly murdered a female jogger in Central Park. In Los Angeles, the "Crips" and "Bloods" are said to be especially violent gangs engaged in the distribution of crack cocaine. In Chicago and elsewhere, violence is attributed to the activities of armed gangs of various kinds. But in recent years there has been a sudden upsurge of gang activity and gang-related violence in smaller cities and suburban areas. In some instances gangs of skinheads and other groups of teenagers and young adults have perpetrated what are known as hate crimes, often involving violent attacks on homosexuals, Jews, or Asian immigrants. Even more dangerous, however, is the increase in the lethal gang violence associated with the sale and use of crack cocaine in some smaller cities and towns (Eckholm, 1993).

Figure 7–2 shows that homicide arrests among juveniles aged 14 to 17 have risen precipitously since 1983. The teenagers accused of killing an English tourist in northern Florida, for example, had accumulated long histories of arrests for violent criminal acts before age 14. This pattern of early involvement in crime among children from poverty-stricken and socially isolated neighborhoods is a strong signal to society that creative programs to combat poverty and neglect are urgently needed in large and small communities throughout the nation.

Gangs range from the peer groups that hang out on street corners to the well-organized, hierarchical gangs of crime syndicates. Perhaps the most violent gangs are those of organized crime. Their killings are often done by contract killers, professional murderers who kill for a payment. But organized-crime–sponsored murders account for only a small percentage of all murders. Do deaths caused by other types of gangs account for the remainder? This does not seem to be the case.

Juvenile and young-adult gangs often begin as street corner cliques and become incorporated into a larger gang confederation. Such gang organizations are often located in poor, segregated communities, where much of their activity is dedicated to the defense of local territory or turf. But experts on the sociology of gangs are quick to point out that there are many types of juvenile gang structures and many different types of gang activity, not all of which are violent or criminal.

In a thorough study of gang confederations in Milwaukee, John M. Hagedorn (1988) found that while gangs in large cities like Los Angeles, Chicago, and New York have been present more or less continuously for generations, in smaller cities and suburban areas gangs may be a new phenomenon. And simply because a community does not have recognizable gangs does not mean that gangs may not form in the near future. Much depends on relations between teenagers and the police, on the drug trade and its control, and on how young people perceive the need (or lack of it) to defend their turf from other teenagers. Thus, in Milwaukee, although there

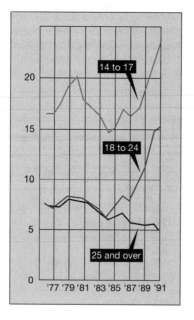

FIGURE 7–2   Homicide Arrests Nationwide per 100,000 People, by Age of Suspect

Source: Eckholm, 1993.

Young members of ethnic groups seeking to adapt to life in American cities often band together in gangs that may engage in violent conflicts with other gangs.

is some fighting, especially as young men strive to gain prestige within the gangs, there is relatively little "gang warfare" or homicide attributable to gang warfare. In Chicago, in contrast, there seems to be far more gang-related homicide, especially among Hispanic gangs.

A large majority of the gang members whom Hagedorn interviewed admitted owning at least one handgun. Hagedorn concludes that the problem of violence and homicide is related more to the increasing availability of guns and the involvement of some gangs in the illegal drug industry than to inherent features of the gangs themselves; this conclusion is shared by most students of gang behavior. Martin Sanchez Jankowsky, one of the nation's foremost authorities on violent gangs, notes that contrary to what some members of the public—and some sociologists—think, gang members typically do not like violence and the risks to personal safety that it entails. But most gang members believe that "if you do not attack, you will be attacked." This worldview implies that much gang violence is premeditated in order to take the opponent by surprise. In addition, Sanchez Jankowski notes, "the injuries incurred as a result of organizational violence [in the gang] become the social cement that creates group bonds in a deviant individualist setting." Overall, he concludes, gang violence "is understood to be the instrument used to achieve objectives that are not achievable in other ways" (1991, p. 177).

Another study of gang activity and involvement in drug dealing supports Hagedorn's conclusions and reinforces the idea that high rates of lethal violence are attributable more to the widespread use of guns than to the presence of gangs themselves. Terry Williams (1989) spent three years following the activities of a mobile drug "crew" in New York. This small and highly entrepreneurial gang was in the retail crack business. Its success depended on discipline: on ensuring that members did not become too high to function in their jobs or so careless that they became victims of violent robberies. Williams, like Hagedorn, documents the widespread and routine possession of handguns, but he also notes the increasing availability of more powerful automatic weapons and submachine guns.

While the crack epidemic is clearly responsible for an increasing number of homicides in poor communities since 1985, the United States had extremely high homicide rates even before the advent of crack; drugs alone therefore do not provide a sufficient explanation. But the availability of easily concealed handguns, together with the traditions of interpersonal violence that date at least from the period of the American frontier, probably accounts for much of the higher levels of deadly violence found in the United States.

Franklin E. Zimring, one of the nation's foremost experts on guns and gun control, reports that the "proportion of all households reporting handgun ownership has increased substantially over a twenty-year period" (1985, p. 138). On the basis of survey research, Zimring estimates that between one-fifth and one-fourth of all American households have one or more handguns. This represents an enormous increase since the late 1950s, when the proportion was probably well below one in ten households. Studies of the relationship between handgun possession and homicide find that when people arm themselves out of fear and a desire for protection there is also an increased risk of fatalities due to accidents involving guns, as well as homicides caused by mistaken recourse to fatal force—as in the tragic case of a Japanese exchange student in New Orleans who was killed when he tried to enter the wrong house in search of a party to which he had been invited (Reiss & Roth, 1993).

SOCIAL POLICY

Researchers at the National Center for Health Statistics report that 4,223 American men between the ages of 15 and 24 were killed in 1987, or 21.9 per 100,000. The rate for black men in the same age group was 85.6 per 100,000. Michigan was the most dangerous state for young black men, with a homicide rate of 232 per 100,000 compared to 155 in California, 139 in the District of Columbia, and 137 in New York. Among young white men the highest rate occurred in California (22 per 100,000), followed by Texas (21), New York (18), and Arizona (17). The safest state for whites was Minnesota (1.9 per 100,000); for blacks it was North Carolina (34.2 per 100,000).

These are alarming statistics, and the American public is clearly justified in its demand that society "do something" about violent crime. However, exactly what should be done is much less clear, as can be seen in the controversies over gun control, media violence, and ways of dealing with family violence.

Gun Control

In recent decades there has been increasing demand for stricter federal supervision of the purchase and sale of firearms, particularly the cheap handguns that are readily available in many areas. However, opponents of gun control legislation, represented primarily by the National Rifle Association (NRA), constitute one of the most powerful interest groups in the nation. The NRA draws much of its strength from areas of the nation where hunting is popular and there is a strong feeling that people need to be able to protect themselves and their families. NRA members claim that gun control measures would violate the "right to bear arms" that is contained in the United States Constitution. This is a strong position and one that most political leaders are unwilling to challenge directly.

The statistics on violence by means of guns—especially handguns—are alarming. Over 68 percent of the homicides reported in 1992 were committed by people using firearms; more than 80 percent of those homicides involved handguns. (See Figure 7–3.) In addition, over 40 percent of robberies and almost 25 percent of aggravated assaults involved the use of a firearm (*UCR*, 1993). The United States leads all other Western nations not only in number of homicides by guns but also in rates of suicide and accident by guns. And about 300 children die in accidental shootings each year.

Opponents of gun control claim that the decision to commit murder has nothing to do with possession of a gun; a killer can stab, strangle, poison, or batter a victim to death. Gun control therefore would make little difference. Although this argument sounds logical, it ignores the lethal potential of guns, which are about five times more likely to kill than knives, the next most commonly used murder weapon. One study found that for every 100 reported knife attacks, an average of 2.4 victims die, whereas for every 100 gun attacks, an average of 12.2 victims die (Gillin & Ochberg, 1970). And since most murders are spontaneous results of passion rather than carefully planned acts, it follows that the easy availability of guns is likely to increase the death rate in criminal assaults. In most cases murders are a result of three factors: impulse, the lethal capacity of the weapon, and the availability of the weapon. Strict gun control would eliminate or at least reduce the latter two factors.

In response to what has come to be perceived as a national epidemic of gunshot injuries and deaths, a majority of Americans now appear to favor strict controls on the sale of handguns. A 1993 Louis Harris survey of 1,250 adults found that for the first time since polling on this issue began, 52 percent of all respondents (61 percent of women) favored a ban on the possession of handguns unless a court has granted an exception. The survey also estimated that nine out of ten Americans support the Brady Bill, which calls for a five-day waiting period before purchase of a handgun and allows local authorities to check the background of the buyer (Barringer, 1993); the bill was passed by Congress and signed by President Clinton in 1993. Proponents of gun control argue that a stronger federal law is needed; they cite countries that have such regulations, such as Japan and England, in which rates of murder by means of guns are very low (Reiss & Roth, 1993).

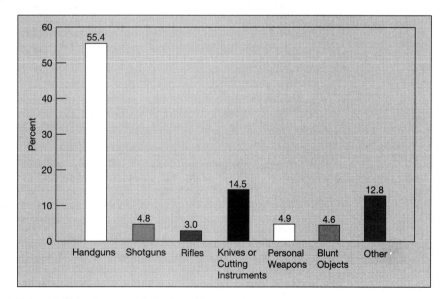

FIGURE 7–3   Percent of Murders Committed with Various Weapons, 1989

Source: UCR, 1990.

James Brady looks on as President Clinton signs the Brady Bill, which requires a five-day waiting period and a background check on individuals who wish to buy handguns.

Not all anti-gun, anti-violence policy is made at the federal level. Throughout the United States communities and voluntary associations are devising ways to reduce the number of guns "on the street." A popular approach that has had surprising results is the "gun buy-back," in which community residents are paid or given gift certificates for local stores if they turn in their guns. Such programs, which are highly publicized, at least give people the feeling that they can do something to help reduce the level of handgun violence.

After some states and cities passed gun control legislation in 1968, studies began to show some evidence that fewer crimes were committed with guns, but such evaluations are hampered by a number of problems in the research: First, it is impossible to know how effective a city's gun control legislation is when guns are so widely available in illegal markets. Second, social scientists can study the effects of policies only when they are significant. In many cases the gun control legislation was rather weak, making it difficult to compare conditions before and after enforcement. Third, assessments of the effects of legislation require longer-term study than is possible in cases in which gun control legislation has been passed only recently. Studies based on statistics covering only a few years have trouble distinguishing effects from mere fluctuations in crime rates that could be due to other causes (Zimring, 1985).

Today the NRA's power seems to be waning as Americans become more alarmed about the level of lethal violence and police departments increasingly side with gun control advocates. Despite NRA opposition, Congress passed legislation banning certain types of automatic weapons, "cop-killer" bullets that can penetrate police vests, and plastic guns that can evade electronic detection. The NRA is also finding it much more difficult to enlist the support of police professional associations and unions.

An important issue related to gun control is the extent to which women who are heads of households will choose to arm themselves with handguns for protection. Since the number of female-headed households is rising rapidly, any increase in the propensity of women to arm themselves could raise the overall level of handgun ownership to 50 million in the next decade. But research shows that women are still far more reluctant than men to purchase handguns; female-headed households are half as likely to have handguns as male-headed households (Zimring, 1985). This suggests that the outcome of the political battle over handguns may eventually depend on how both sides manage to appeal to female voters.

Media Violence

Another way of reducing violence in society might be to deemphasize violence in the media. In 1972 the United States Surgeon General's Study of Television and Social Behavior concluded that

> *the causal relationship between televised violence and antisocial behavior is sufficient to warrant appropriate and immediate remedial action. The data on social phenomena such as television and violence and aggressive behavior will never be clear enough for all social scientists to agree on the formulation of a succinct statement of causality. But there comes a time when the data are sufficient to justify action. That time has come. (quoted in Bogart, 1972–1973, p. 521)*

It should be possible, through either legislation or voluntary regulation, to reduce the incidence of killings and the reliance on shoot-and-slug formulas, especially in movies and television programming. The media have agreed to devote the first hour of prime-time television—from 8 P.M. to 9 P.M., called the "family hour"—to programming that is considered suitable for family viewing, with the more violent programs being shown at later hours. However, no serious effort has been made to reduce the overall level of televised violence.

Since the early 1970s a team of researchers at the University of Pennsylvania has provided counts of media violence. These counts show that despite the family hour, rates of televised violence have not fallen and in fact have increased steadily. Children's television is even more violent than adult programming (Donnerstain & Linz, 1987; Hirsh, 1987). In addition, changes in the technology of television—particularly the advent of video cassette recorders and cable television—have made it difficult to regulate the amount of televised violence available to the public.

The ready availability of videotapes has become a matter of widespread concern in recent years. Children and teenagers routinely obtain videotapes of movies that feature extreme violence, including dismemberment and sexual mutilation, and watch them without their parents' knowledge. Some organizations have taken a stand against easy access to violent films; they have called for legislation requiring prominent display of Motion Picture Association of America ratings of videotapes and, in some cases, for bans on the sale or rental of certain types of cassettes. To date, however, few states have enacted such requirements. At this writing it is fair to

Although the results of research on the effects of televised violence on viewers are ambiguous, large segments of the American public are increasingly convinced that there is a connection between high levels of televised violence programming and aggressive behavior by viewers of such programs.

say that most attacks on media content are directed against sexuality and against depictions that are thought to legitimate homosexuality and pre- and extramarital sex, rather than against violence.

Dealing with Family Violence

Child abuse is widely recognized as a serious national problem. In recent decades there have been numerous efforts, both by government and by private agencies, to increase public awareness of the problem and to prevent it where possible. The Child Abuse Prevention and Treatment Act was passed by Congress in 1974 to help states and communities organize programs for parents who abuse their children. Also in 1974, the National Institute of Mental Health established a national center in Denver to study the problem more thoroughly and set up a national commission to resolve the complicated legal problems and recommend changes in federal and state laws involving child abuse. Grant programs have also been funded to identify the causes of child abuse and provide treatment through self-help programs and lay therapy. Increasingly, states are requiring social workers and psychologists to report all cases of known or suspected child abuse to child protection authorities in their communities.

In order to break the cycle of abuse, some therapy groups have attempted to teach parenting techniques to mothers and fathers who were abused children themselves. The clinic workers try to supply these parents with alternative outlets for their frustration and anger and encourage them to call for help whenever they feel tempted to strike their children. Parents are also encouraged to seek meaningful relationships with other adults and not to invest their children's behavior with so much significance. C. Henry Kempe, who initiated the first treatment programs for parents at the Denver Child Abuse Center, found that 80 percent of the children could be returned to their parents "without risk of further injury, if their parents received intensive help [while the child lived in a foster home] and if there was a follow-up program after the child went home" (MacLeod, 1974, p. 719). For parents who resist this approach because of previous unfavorable experiences with the mental health system, there is Parents Anonymous. Established in 1970, this organization is similar in many ways to Alcoholics Anonymous. Regular meetings are held during which parents help each other stop mistreating their children.

Like child abuse, spouse abuse has received increased public attention in recent years. This problem is usually dealt with at the local rather than the national level. For example, in the 1970s many municipalities created shelters for battered wives, and others formed crisis intervention teams that attempt to negotiate with or "cool out" couples who are engaging in physical conflict. The need for both shelters and active intervention has not been met on a large scale, however, owing to lack of public funds.

More recently there has been a trend toward efforts to prevent spouse and child abuse by encouraging neighbors, friends, or family members themselves to notify the authorities when they have reason to believe that abuse is likely or is occurring. However, even when the authorities know that abuse is occurring in a particular household, they often are unable to act, especially in cases of child abuse. One problem, as noted earlier, is that there is little agreement on where child protection ends and rights to family privacy begin. Another is the lack of coordination between agencies dealing with spouse and child abuse—the former is treated as a routine police matter and the latter as a concern of child welfare agencies. Increasing cooperation among police investigators, medical professionals, and social workers has therefore become a high priority in many communities.

Race, Poverty, and Violence: The Unfinished Agenda

The links between socioeconomic inequalities and the level of violence in society have been demonstrated in numerous studies. At the end of the 1960s the National Commission on Civil Disorders (the Kerner Commission), after studying rioting in more than 150 cities, warned that the United States was moving toward "two separate societies, one black, one white—separate and unequal." Another commission, the National Commission on the Causes and Prevention of Violence (the Violence Commission), was appointed in 1968 following the assassinations of Dr. Martin Luther King, Jr., and Senator Robert Kennedy. It concluded that violence occurs when groups in a society are denied access to opportunities to obtain a decent living and to participate in the decisions that affect their lives. A third presidential commission, the Commission on Law Enforcement and Administration of Justice (the Katzenbach Commission), also concluded that "the roots of violence and disorder lie deep in the social fabric of American society, in its traditions, inequalities, and conflicts and ineffective governance" (Ball-Rokeach & Short, 1985).

These three major federal studies marked a shift from an emphasis on the psychological disorders underlying violence to a more sociological understanding of the origins of violence. The redress of legitimate grievances and the equitable sharing of the American pie became more important considerations in formulating policy than the search for personality profiles or biological predispositions that would explain violent behavior. The conservative climate of the 1980s did not alter this fundamental shift. Instead, conservative critics of liberal social policies called for increased severity of sentencing and higher rates of incarceration and punishment in lieu of a focus on more equal distribution of wealth and greater integration of the disadvantaged into the nation's economic institutions. While these were far from liberal policies, they did not constitute a challenge to the basic social (rather than psychological) orientation of the 1970s.

BOX 7–1   CURRENT CONTROVERSIES: THE MYTH OF BLACK VIOLENCE

It is widely believed, not only by the public but also by the media and the government, that blacks—especially young black males—are more prone to violence than whites. Official statistics seem to confirm this view: Although blacks make up 13 percent of the population, they account for more than half of those arrested for murder, rape, and nonnegligent manslaughter; this is five times the arrest rate of whites for these crimes. In addition, the victims of violent crime are far more likely to be black. Homicide is the primary cause of death for younger black men as well as for black women under age 40 (FBI, 1990).

Official statistics may be misleading, however. They reflect official attitudes and behavior—particularly the greater likelihood that black offenders will be arrested. Victim surveys provide more accurate information than arrest reports about crimes committed. Thus, while the FBI reported that the proportion of blacks arrested for aggravated assault in 1987 was more than three times greater than the proportion of whites, the National Crime Survey found that the actual proportions were very similar: 32 per 1,000 for blacks and 31 per 1,000 for whites.

If rates of violence are comparable among blacks and whites, why are the consequences of violence, in terms of both imprisonment and death by violence, so much more severe for blacks than for whites? One explanation is the "double standard" of police protection. Police are seven times more likely to charge black teenagers than white teenagers with felonies than to charge white teenagers with similar offenses, and the courts are more likely to imprison black teenagers. More telling, perhaps, is the belief that violent behavior is normal in inner-city black neighborhoods; arrest and imprisonment occur only if violence reaches extreme levels. In cases of domestic violence, for example, law enforcement officials do not intervene until a serious injury or fatality occurs. A similar pattern can be seen in police response to assault and homicide among black males, including gang members (Stark, 1990). One outcome, ironically, is that the life expectancy of males is greater in Bangladesh than in inner-city neighborhoods in the United States (McCord & Freeman, 1990).

The myth of black violence, with its consequences in actual experience, flies in the face of two of the nation's most cherished ideals: equal protection of the laws and social equality. It is further evidence of the need for policies that address the correlation between social inequality and violence rather than stereotyping any particular group as more prone to violence than others.

In the 1990s policy makers with various ideological perspectives once again began debating the issues of crime control that had been raised in the 1960s and 1970s. The primary question was how to diminish rates of crime and violence by increasing the share of the pie available to those at the bottom of the social order. (See Box 7–1, on page 221.) But social scientists are also discovering that they need to develop more varied policy recommendations that also address serious problems of media violence, the targeting of enforcement and rehabilitation programs to communities in greatest need, and the role of educators in combating the epidemic of juvenile violence now claiming so many American lives.

SUMMARY

1. Violence may be considered legitimate or illegitimate, depending on who uses it and why and how it is used. One distinction that is sometimes made is between institutional violence, which is exercised on behalf of or under the protection of the state, and noninstitutional violence, which is exercised by those who are opposed to established authority.

2. Biological explanations of violence are based on the idea that there are instinctive violent or destructive urges in all humans. The frustration–aggression theory holds that an unfulfilled need produces frustration, which is then vented in aggression. A related view is the control theory, in which the ability to control impulsive behavior is correlated with the existence of close relationships with other people.

3. Many sociologists believe that violence is a learned behavior and that violent actions are most likely to occur in a culture or subculture in which violence is accepted. In this theory violent behavior is learned by imitation and is a by-product of a culture that values toughness.

4. Rational-choice theorists have explored the role of violence in so-called strategic crimes such as extortion, kidnapping, and blackmail. In such instances, violent behavior can be interpreted as a rational means of attaining otherwise impossible ends.

5. The role of the mass media in fostering violent attitudes has been a subject of considerable research. The evidence shows that excessive violence on television leads directly to violent behavior among teenagers. It is also thought that the reporting of civil disorders and other forms of violence by the mass media may increase the possibility that further violence will occur.

6. Murder is the unlawful killing of a human being with malice aforethought. Most murderers are young men; more murders occur in cities than in rural areas; and in a large proportion of the cases the relationship between murderer and victim is a close one. Mass murderers are either psychotics who murder in a fit of rage or serial killers who are also psychotic but are cool and well organized.

7. Robbery may be defined as the taking of another person's property by intimidation. It usually occurs between strangers.

8. Forcible rape is the act of forcing sexual intercourse on another person against his or her will. In recent years rapes by offenders who are known to the victim—date or acquaintance rape—have become a matter of concern, especially on college and university campuses.

9. Child abuse, sometimes leading to death, is a serious problem in the United States. Many abusive parents were themselves subjected to abuse in childhood. Spouse abuse is also common and appears to be highly correlated with child abuse.

10. The high rate of homicide in the United States compared to other industrialized nations is sometimes attributed to violence by juvenile gang members, but the available evidence indicates that it is not the presence of gangs per se but the ready availability of guns that accounts for the prevalence of lethal violence in American cities.

11. Policy makers do not agree on what should be done to reduce or eliminate violent crime. Although most Americans favor gun control (i.e., supervision of the purchase and sale of firearms), opponents of such measures are powerful and well organized and until recently have succeeded in preventing the passage of meaningful legislation in this area. There are some signs that the dominance of the gun lobby is weakening, but legislators and the public are still divided on this issue. Efforts to reduce the level of media violence have also met with little success.

12. Family violence is widely recognized as a serious national problem, and there have been numerous efforts to increase public awareness of the problem and to prevent it where possible. There is a need for greater cooperation among police investigators, medical professionals, and social workers who deal with families in which abuse occurs.

13. The relationship between socioeconomic inequality and violence has recently become the focus of analyses of violence and debates over policies directed toward its abatement. Numerous important studies have demonstrated the need for the redress of legitimate grievances and a more equitable sharing of values and resources if the overall level of violence in American society is to be reduced.

SUGGESTED READINGS

ALLEN, JOHN. *Assault with a Deadly Weapon: The Autobiography of a Street Criminal,* eds. Dianne Hall Kelly and Philip Heymann. New York: McGraw-Hill, 1978. A frank account of the life of a street criminal; argues that the criminal-justice system must attempt to rehabilitate communities rather than criminals.

BROWNMILLER, SUSAN. *Against Our Will: Men, Women and Rape.* New York: Simon & Schuster, 1975. A provocative description of the violent aspects of sexual norms and of rape as a form of aggression against women.

COMSTOCK, GEORGE, ET AL. *Television and Human Behavior.* New York: Columbia University Press, 1978. An examination of television's impact on the daily lives of Americans, particularly children.

FANON, FRANTZ. *The Wretched of the Earth.* New York: Grove Press, 1968. A classic analysis by a psychoanalyst of the relationships between colonizers and colonized that sees extreme violence as a common condition of colonialism.

HAGEDORN, JOHN M. *People and Folks: Gangs, Crime, and the Underclass in a Rustbelt City.* Chicago: Lake View Press, 1988. An excellent firsthand account of gangs and gang violence in a medium-sized city.

KRAMER, RITA. *At a Tender Age: Violent Youth and Juvenile Justice.* Fort Worth, TX: Holt, Rinehart and Winston, 1987. A searing account of failures in the criminal-justice system's treatment of violent young people by an author who has marshalled many important facts and brings a decidedly critical and conservative perspective to her observations.

LAVER, MICHAEL. *The Crime Game.* Oxford, England: Martin Robertson, 1982. A readable and useful introduction to the theory of games as applied to crime, with special treatment of bargaining in hostage and other terrorist situations.

PRICE, BARBARA RAFFEL, and NATALIE J. SOKOLOFF. *The Criminal Justice System and Women.* New York: Clark Boardman, 1982. An excellent anthology of research papers and essays about women and crime; includes some fine studies of violence against women and its effects.

REISS, ALBERT J., JR., and JEFFREY A. ROTH (EDS.). *Understanding and Preventing Violence.* Washington, DC: National Academy Press, 1993. A thorough review of recent social-scientific research on the causes of violence, with special emphasis on the possible biological basis of violence; also describes measures that have achieved relative success in controlling or preventing some patterns of interpersonal violence.

"WHY ROCKY III?"

Mike Messner has a Ph.D. in sociology from the University of California at Berkeley. He is currently an associate professor in the Department of Sociology and the Program for the Study of Women and Men in Society at the University of Southern California in Los Angeles. He is a former athlete and the author of *Power at Play*.

This selection—"Why Rocky III?"—is from *Sex, Violence, and Power in Sports: Rethinking Masculinity*, which Mike Messner wrote with Don Sabo.

WHY ROCKY III?

MIKE MESSNER

[1] I faithfully watched the first two. But I can't go see the third one. Not *Rocky III*. The Italian Stallion will have to go this final round without me.

[2] Lately, I've been thinking more about boxing and enjoying it less. While watching the sports news on TV recently I saw a "promising young boxer" by the name of Dave Moore finishing off an opponent. I have never enjoyed watching a man being beaten into unconsciousness, but this particular instance was especially chilling. I felt as though I were seeing a ghost, for the fight brought back to me a song written by Bob Dylan in 1963 about a boxer of the same name, who was killed in the ring.* Dylan angrily asks several times through the song,

Who killed Davey Moore?
Why did he die
And what's the reason for?

[3] This *question has plagued me* for some time. Just who *is* responsible when a man is seriously injured or loses his life in the boxing ring? This issue was raised following last year's highly promoted championship bout between Sugar Ray Leonard and Thomas Hearns. Nearing the end of the fight, when Hearns was ahead on points, Leonard stung him with what was described as a "vicious combination of lefts and rights to the head" that left Hearns "dazed and staggering." The referee, who concluded that Hearns was "out on his feet," called the fight and awarded Leonard a technical knockout. Although the fight was applauded as a great one, some people were not so happy with its finish. For instance, the next day a young man commented to me that "the ref shouldn't have called the fight— you've gotta go down in a championship fight."

[4] Indeed, boxing referees are caught in an extremely difficult bind. On the one hand, they are responsible for seeing that the fight ends before someone gets seriously injured. On the other hand, they face tremendous pressure from fans, promoters, television networks, and sometimes the fighters themselves to let the fight go on until there is a clear-cut victory—until someone "goes down."

*In *Blood and Guts: Violence in Sports* (New York and London: Paddington Press, 1979; page 173), Don Atyeo tells the story of Davey Moore's last fight. In 1963, when Moore was featherweight champion, he was pounded in the ring by his opponent, Sugar Ramos. He died seventy-five hours later. A week after his death, three more boxers were killed in the ring, leading the Pope (among others) to call for the abolition of boxing.

(CONTINUED)

WHY ROCKY III? (CONTINUED)

Not I, said the referee,
Don't point your little finger at me.
Sure, I coulda stopped it in the eighth
And saved him from his terrible fate.
But the crowd would have booed, I'm sure,
At not getting their money's worth.
Too bad that he had to go,
But there was pressure on me, too, you know.
No, it wasn't me that made him fall,
You can't blame me at all.

[5]The *need for a "clear decision"* to end every boxing contest seems to be a growing problem. An earlier title fight between Leonard and Roberto Duran (the Animal, the Destroyer who had previously dethroned Leonard) was yet another example. After several hard-fought rounds, Duran was clearly being beaten. He was hurt, and was losing the ability to defend himself. Between rounds, he decided to quit, claiming that he had stomach cramps. He was soundly booed. The fans, who had paid large sums of money to witness what was promised to be a "monumental battle," were disappointed and angry. The criticism of Duran has not died down to this day. Some say he threw the fight. Most boxing fans agree that when the chips were down, he was a "gutless quitter."

[6]At about the same time that the Leonard-Duran fight was making news, I was following another story about the Welsh boxer Johnny Owen, who had been critically injured in a boxing match. "Owen Still in Coma" read the small blurbs—and, later, "Owen Dies." Like the *mythological* Rocky Balboa, Owen was a hard-working, ambitious young man from a poor, working-class background. He had said that his goal was to "fight a few more times and then get out of it before I get hurt." Certainly he was not a "gutless" man. He stayed in the fight to the end, undoubtedly pleasing the fans.

Not I, said the angry crowd,
Whose screams filled the arena loud
Too bad that he died that night,
But we just like to see a good fight
You can't blame us for his death,
We just like to see some sweat
There ain't nothing wrong in that
No, it wasn't us that made him fall,
You can't blame us at all.

[7]Why do we fans push boxers to their limits, always demanding a clear-cut victory? This *phenomenon can be seen as a result of a social-psychological malaise* in modern life. Increasing instability and uncertainty in daily life, brought on by high unemployment, rising living costs, and increasingly shaky international relations (the United States, no longer the undisputed heavyweight champ, has been pushed around by relative lightweights like Iran), as well as insecure family relations and challenges to the traditional bases of masculinity, all bring about a need for *some* arena where there are obvious "good guys and bad guys"—clear winners and losers. For many people, sports has provided that arena. The National Football League has in recent years instituted a "fifth quarter" to decide games that end in a tie during regulation time. For players and for fans, it seems that "a tie is as good as a loss—it's like kissing your sister," as one fan told me.

(CONTINUED)

WHY ROCKY III? *(CONTINUED)*

[8]Added to the fans' emotional investment is financial investment in boxing. Millions of dollars are bet on big matches. Fans pay hefty sums to watch the matches on cable television at home or on closed-circuit television in theaters. Like any other multimillion-dollar product on the market, boxing is heavily hyped by promoters and by the media. After all the hype and heavy betting preceding a match, a man can't just quit because he has stomach cramps. He's *gotta* go down.

> *Not I, says the boxing writer,*
> *Pounding the print on his old typewriter.*
> *Who says, boxing ain't to blame,*
> *There's just as much danger in a football game.*
> *Boxing is here to stay,*
> *It's just the old American way.*
> *No, you can't blame me at all,*
> *It wasn't me that made him fall.*

[9]But what about the boxers themselves? What is it that made Sugar Ray Leonard return to the ring and risk losing the sight in an injured eye? As many would argue, the fighters know what they're getting into—they know the dangers. Of course, they also want the glory and the money that go with being on top. But those of us who watch boxing matches should ask some other questions. For instance, who are these men who risk life and limb for our entertainment? Most boxers are from poor, working-class backgrounds. Many are members of minority groups for whom boxing may seem to be one of the few ways out of the misery they were born into. According to Chris Dundee, a Miami boxing promoter, "Any man with a good trade isn't about to get knocked on his butt to make a dollar" (Atyeo 1979, 176–77). But an *impoverished society* (such as in many Latin American nations) or an economically depressed city (such as Detroit) is fertile ground for a flourishing boxing industry.

[10]So even though nobody forces young boxers to enter the ring, it would be foolish to suggest that most of them freely choose boxing from a number of attractive alternatives. (Although many of the elite may romanticize the strength, stamina, courage, and masculinity of a John Wayne, we don't see many of the Rockefellers or the Kennedys taking up careers as pugilists, duking it out in the ring.) In any society which restricts the opportunities of certain groups of people, one will be able to find a significant number of those people who will be willing to pursue very dangerous careers for the slim chance of "making it big." Boxers are modern-day equivalents of Roman gladiators—they are both our victims and our heroes—and we are increasingly giving them the "thumbs down."

[11]For every millionaire Ali and for every smiling Sugar Ray we see on our TV, there are hundreds of fighters who have never made enough money boxing even to live on. All they have received for their efforts are a few scattered cheers, some boos, and some permanent injuries. But to the fans they are mostly invisible—unless one of them has the *impertinence* to die in the ring. We just don't see the long-term damage a boxer takes from years of severe jolts to the internal organs and to the brain. According to J. A. N. Corsellis, a neurologist who has studied boxers and their injuries, "By the time a fighter has had even as few as 150 bouts, he is really, I think, very likely to have suffered brain damage" (Atyeo 1979, 182).

[12]Does it make us wonder when we hear Muhammad Ali's once poetic and lightning-quick tongue, which used to "float like a butterfly," now often sticking to the roof of his mouth, as though it had been stung by a bee? And do we think about what boxing does to the people who watch the spectacle of boxing? Do we wonder to what extent boxing may serve to legitimate violence in everyday life?

(CONTINUED)

WHY ROCKY III? (CONTINUED)

Who killed Davey Moore?
Why did he die
And what's the reason for?

[13]Dylan's question still troubles me. I think we can begin to find the answer by examining *our own complicity* in turning a brutal tradition into a profitable sport. The boxing business both meets the needs of an alienated and frustrated populace and at the same time generates millions of dollars for promoters, the media, and big-time bettors. And part of the problem is in our society's conception of manhood. When the traditional bastions of masculinity are crumbling or being undermined by historical forces, few things are so affirming to the threatened male ego as a good boxing match. Boxing lets us feel our solidarity with other men as we *vicariously express our repressed anger and violence.*

[14]When I was in junior high school, my friend Ron asked me to meet him after school because he was going to fight another boy and wanted some moral support. I watched as they fought. Ron's opponent was bigger, quicker, and a better fighter. Before long, Ron was bleeding from the mouth. In a last-ditch effort, he let out a terrible scream and came at his opponent with a desperate and reckless windmill-like flailing of the arms. His pitiful attempt to take the offensive was answered with a stiff right to the nose that put him down on the ground, sobbing and humiliated. Two young men then showed up and broke up the fight. To my surprise, they did not say a thing to the two fighters, but, rather, they *chastised* those of us who had been watching and cheering the fighters on. "You're worse than those two," they told us. "Their fight would have ended before someone got hurt if you hadn't been here *egging them on* like you did. You should be ashamed of yourselves."

[15]*...and what's the reason for?*

Reference

Atyeo, Don. 1979. *Blood and Guts: Violence in Sports* New York and London: Paddington Press.

CONTENT QUESTIONS—"WHY ROCKY III?"

COMPLETION

1. Why weren't people happy with the finish of the Leonard-Hearns fight or the Leonard-Duran fight? In both fights, what outcome did people want?

2. Why are boxing referees in a "difficult bind"?

3. List four of the reasons Messner gives for why Americans need an arena where there are obvious "good guys and bad guys." What other reasons would you add?

4. According to Messner, who typically becomes a boxer? Do you agree with his analysis? Why or why not?

5. In the story Messner recalls from junior high school, why did the young men who broke up the fight yell at the spectators? Do you think it was appropriate? Why or why not?

VOCABULARY—"WHY ROCKY III?"

1. question has plagued me (¶3)
2. need for a "clear decision" (¶5)
3. mythological (¶6)
4. phenomenon … result of a social-psychological malaise (¶7)
5. impoverished society (¶9)
6. impertinence (¶11)
7. our own complicity (¶13)
8. vicariously express our repressed anger and violence (¶13)
9. chastised (¶14)
10. egging them on (¶14)

CONTENT ANALYSIS QUESTIONS—"WHY ROCKY III?"

1. What is Messner's thesis?
2. Why does Messner use the lyrics from the Bob Dylan song throughout his essay? Do you think it is an effective device? Why or why not? How do the lyrics help to develop and support his thesis?
3. In paragraph 14, Messner recalls a personal experience of watching a fight. How does the story help to develop and support his thesis?
4. In paragraph 13, Messner says that "part of the problem is in our society's conception of manhood." Do you agree? Why or why not?
5. How do you answer Messner's question "to what extent does boxing serve to legitimize violence in everyday life?" How do you think Messner would answer this question?
6. How do you answer Messner's question "Just who is responsible when a man is seriously injured or loses his life in the boxing ring?" How do you think Messner would answer this question?

APPLICATION QUESTIONS—"WHY ROCKY III?"

1. Assume that a much talked about championship fight is going to be broadcast on pay-per-view in your area. The local cable company offers your college's student organization the opportunity to show the event on the large screen television in the student center as a profitable fund-raising activity. Do you vote to show it? Why or why not?
2. Assume that your young next-door neighbor, who looks up to you, asks what you think about him taking boxing lessons at the local boys' club. What do you tell him? Why?

"STRANGERS IN THE HOUSE"

Newton Minow is chairman of the board of the Carnegie Corporation and the Walter H. Annenberg Professor of Communications Law and Policy at Northwestern University. In 1961, as President Kennedy's chairman of the Federal Communications Commission, he astonished the American public when he characterized television broadcasting as a "vast wasteland." He is a past chairman of PBS.

Craig Lamay is associate director of the Public-Service Television Project and former editor of the *Media Studies Journal*.

This selection—"Strangers in the House"—is from their book *Abandoned in the Wasteland: Children, Television, and the First Amendment*.

STRANGERS IN THE HOUSE

NEWTON N. MINOW AND CRAIG L. LAMAY

Shall we just carelessly allow children to hear any casual tales which may be devised by casual persons, and to receive into their minds ideas for the most part the very opposite of those which we should wish them to have when they are grown up?

—Plato

[1]Every day, millions of Americans leave their children in the care of total strangers. Many do so reluctantly. Child care is hard to come by and they take what they can get. Fortunately, many of the strangers are good company. They know something about the needs of children, and are caring, even loving, in trying to meet them. But because the financial rewards for child care are few, these people rarely stay. Those who do stay usually neglect the children altogether. When they do pay attention, they hustle the children for money, bribing them with toys and candy. They bring guns to the house, and drugs, and they invite their friends over; sometimes they use the house for sexual liaisons. Often things get out of hand. Fights break out, and frequently someone gets hurt or killed.

[2]Many parents eventually catch on. Some are horrified; some don't care. Amazingly, however, most accept the situation, believing it beyond their power to change. They may be right. Better care is expensive and hard to find, and the strangers, once there, refuse to leave. Like drug dealers on the corner, they control the life of the neighborhood, the home, and, increasingly, the lives of the children in their custody. Unlike drug dealers, they cannot be chased away or deterred; they claim a constitutional right to stay.

[3]This is not a horror story from the tabloids. Nor, upon meeting the parents of these children, would most of us think them criminal, unfit, or even irresponsible. The fact is, if you own a television set, there is a good chance that this is *your* family, and these are *your* children. Every day, all across the United States, a parade of louts, losers, and con men whom most people would never allow in their homes enter anyway, through television. And every day the strangers spend more time with America's children than teachers do, or even in many cases the parents themselves. "If you came home and you found a strange man...teaching your kids to punch each other, or trying to sell them all kinds of products, you'd kick him right out of the house," says Yale psychology professor Jerome Singer. "But here you are; you come in and the TV is on, and you don't think twice about it."[1]

(CONTINUED)

STRANGERS IN THE HOUSE (CONTINUED)

[4]We should. Those strangers are raising and educating our children. They occupy a special place in our children's lives, as important for what they teach them as the family, the school, or the church is. By the time most American children reach first grade, they will have already spent the equivalent of three school years *in the tutelage of* the family television set. Between the ages of six and eighteen they will spend more time each week in front of that set than they will engaged in any other activity, whether schoolwork, playing, or talking with friends and family. For millions of them, television is not only the first but also the most enduring educational and social institution they will know. For those in unstable or abusive families, a television set may be the nearest thing to a parent they can hope for, providing whatever *intellectual nourishment* they are likely to get during the critical development period between birth and their sixth birthday. For millions of other children in loving families, whose lives are more stable, television still occupies more of their waking time than their parents do. Nearly 70 percent of the day-care facilities at which their parents leave them have a television on for several hours each day.[2]

...

[5]Television is the most violent part of a nation that is itself the most violent country in the developed world. Every year in the United States there are more than 1.9 million violent crimes and more than 20,000 homicides. Someone is murdered in the United States every twenty-two minutes. These are the numbers that television executives like to quote when they say that the violence on the screen mirrors the violence in real life. But it doesn't. The simple arithmetic is this: in a country of more than 250 million people, an American's chance of being a victim of violent crime is statistically very small; by comparison, a random walk through prime-time television reveals a world in which almost half the characters are either victims or perpetrators of violent crimes (the percentage comes from research by George Gerbner at the University of Pennsylvania); in children's programs, the percentage rises to 79 percent. Critics complain that these percentages are grossly inflated by narrow definitions of violence that include everything from pie-in-the-face jokes to news programming. But even a generous allowance for such narrowness still leaves the world of television an exaggeratedly brutal place. In one eighteen-hour period in April 1992, for example, the Center for Media and Public Affairs monitored ten broadcast and cable channels in Washington, D.C., and counted 1,846 violent scenes, 175 of which resulted in a fatality.[15] If only half of the latter group—87 or 88 scenes—were homicides, that would give television a murder rate of one every twelve minutes, almost twice the rate of real murder. Most important of all is that this statistical comparison greatly understates the point: television homicides, unlike those on the street, are witnessed by hundreds of millions of people, among them, every weekday night, about 13 million children.[16] Even in a nation where a gun can be found in every other home, television's portrayal of violence is so *skewed* as to have made a norm out of the extreme, the sensational, and the improbable. Through television, Americans have *created a cosmology of terror* that overshadows reality itself.

[6]So routinely do Americans accept television's version of their lives that on January 18, 1993, when seventeen-year-old Gary Scott Pennington walked into his high-school English class in Grayson, Kentucky, and fired a .38-caliber bullet into his teacher's forehead, killing her, one of the students who witnessed the murder remembered thinking, "This isn't supposed to happen. This must be MTV."[17] Must be. The average student in Gary's senior class had already seen 18,000 murders on television. The average student in the class had spent between 15,000 and 20,000 hours watching television, compared with 11,000 in school; every year the average American child watches more than a thousand stylized and explicit rapes, murders, armed robberies, and assaults on television.[18]

(CONTINUED)

STRANGERS IN THE HOUSE (CONTINUED)

[7]Small wonder that countless studies and reviews over the past decades have argued that there *is* a link between aggressive behavior and exposure to television violence. Small wonder that the Surgeon General in 1972, the National Institute of Mental Health in 1982, and the American Psychological Association in 1992 have all said such a link exists. Broadcasters like to say that these studies don't prove anything, and in one respect they're right. Social science is not in the proof business, but in the business of identifying relationships and measuring their significance, strength, and direction. Where television violence is concerned, social science relies on several methods of testing the relationships, ranging from simple laboratory experiments to thirty-year studies of people's lives that take into account all the factors—family income, education, family cohesion—that contribute to social violence. Virtually all this research has been done in the studies of television, and all of them consistently show that television violence contributes to real violence, and to a *pervasive sense of fear*.

[8]The most famous of these studies is the 1972 Surgeon General's report *Television and Growing Up: The Impact of Televised Violence*.[19] The report had its roots in earlier congressional inquiries into social violence, in 1961 and again in 1964, and in the Kerner Commission, convened by President Lyndon B. Johnson to examine the root causes of unrest in a nation that had borne witness to three major political assassinations and disastrous urban riots. As part of its work, the commission established a task force to study media violence. The task force drew the attention of Rhode Island senator John Pastore, then chairman of the Senate Subcommittee on Communications, who wanted *a definitive answer* to the question of whether violence on television affected behavior. In 1969 Pastore directed the Surgeon General to look into the matter and to report the following year.

[9]Broadcasters immediately saw the project as a threat and moved to cripple whatever results it might present. They did so by challenging the credentials of seven of the distinguished social scientists who were selected to the project's advisory committee, and by eventually installing on the board five additional members to their own liking, some of whom were, or had once been, employed by the networks. The move angered many social scientists, who thought it damaged the project's credibility, but the work went forward anyway. The research included twenty-three different studies based on laboratory experiments, field research, and organizational and institutional studies and surveys; and the final report, completed on December 31, 1971, greatly increased what we then knew about children and television. Despite fears that special interests would compromise the findings, the report stated unequivocally that there was a causal relationship between aggressive behavior and watching violence on television.

[10]That was not, however, what the public learned. In one of his few errors in a distinguished reporting career, *New York Times* television writer Jack Gould, who had obtained a copy of the report's final chapter (which almost certainly came from a source friendly to the networks), overlooked its central conclusion and misinterpreted the rest. Gould reported, in a front-page story, that the "Surgeon General has found that violence in television programming does not have an adverse effect on the majority of the nation's youth, but may influence small groups of youngsters predisposed by many factors to aggressive behavior."[20] Compounding the error, the headline read: "TV Violence Held Unharmful to Youth."

[11]Gould's report caused a furor among many members of the Surgeon General's Advisory Committee, as well as among members of Congress and academia who labeled the report a "whitewash." Despite subsequent news conferences in which Surgeon General Jesse Steinfeld declared that the study showed "for the first time a causal connection between violence shown on television and subsequent behavior by children,"[21] the damage was done. Gould's report set the tone for the majority of media reports around the country, not the least one which appeared in the industry trade magazine *Broadcasting*. "A blue ribbon committee of social scientists has concluded that there is no causal relationship between television programs that depict violence and aggressive behavior by the majority of children," the magazine reported.[22]

(CONTINUED)

STRANGERS IN THE HOUSE (CONTINUED)

[12]So distorted was the coverage of the Surgeon General's report, and *so acrimonious the ensuing debate* about it, that Senator Pastore convened hearings to review the research and the findings. Pastore called to testify virtually all the researchers whose work comprised the report, and eventually established that, indeed, they had found television violence a cause for serious public concern. Ithiel de Sola Pool, a political scientist, summarized the report for Senator Pastore in one sentence: "Twelve scientists of widely different views unanimously agreed that scientific evidence indicates that the viewing of television violence by young people causes them to behave more aggressively."[23] The networks' own researchers concurred, and, pressed by Senator Pastore, the television executives who testified did also.

[13]Nothing happened. In 1974, the communications scholar Douglass Cater reviewed the background of the Surgeon General's report, its findings, and the controversy that swirled around them:

> That was the high-water mark. At the time of this writing—two years since those initial hearings—there has been less than persuasive evidence that the commitments given to Pastore have been met with alacrity. Violence on the television screen...has continued at a high level. Violent incidents on prime time and Saturday morning programs maintain a rate of more than twice the British rate, which is itself padded with American imports...The FCC has not yet dealt with the issue of violence in children's programming. Thus promise *still* lies ahead.[24]

It *still* does. The greatest legacy of the Surgeon General's report has probably been the doubt sown by Jack Gould's report in *The New York Times*. Their admissions before Congress notwithstanding, television executives have challenged every subsequent report with the refrain that the connections between viewing television violence and behavior are tenuous at best and, in any case, prove nothing. Their denials, and even many of their counterarguments, are similar to those made by cigarette-industry executives who refuse to acknowledge the connection between smoking and heart and respiratory diseases.

[14]Where television and entertainment people do admit connections, *they simultaneously debunk them*. Society's ills cannot be laid at television's door, they say, certainly not in a country where guns are emblematic of freedom, where vast disparities of income exist, as well as of educational and economic opportunity, where divisions of race and ethnicity have caused violence for two hundred years, where more families fall apart than stay together. "TV is not the sole culprit," says Jack Valenti. "You cannot press a button and make your child immune to watching his school kid friends pack a .357 Magnum to school. You can't press a button and keep your child from knowing that there is drug dealing and drugs around the neighborhood. You can't press a button and repair broken homes...and you can't press a button and tell your child not to succumb to peer pressure."[25]

[15]All this is patently true, but arguing that any one action is the key to ending violence makes a mockery of moral responsibility. Here is the communications professor George Gerbner, who has been monitoring television violence for two decades:

> We're dealing with a syndrome to which there are many contributing factors. We happen to be talking about just one of them, but let us not assume it's the only one, or, under all circumstances, the primary one. To make it the only one is, I agree, an evasion of our responsibility for the condition of our cities. Equally harmful is to say that it makes no contribution...But the notion that, sure, there is violence in fairy tales, there is violence in Shakespeare, and therefore we shouldn't be concerned about it, is a powerfully misleading notion.[26]

(CONTINUED)

STRANGERS IN THE HOUSE (CONTINUED)

Misleading indeed. Brandon Tartikoff, former president of NBC, says, "I definitely think moving images influence behavior. In television, I had different views than the social scientists my network was hiring from places like Yale to provide data that violence on TV does not lead to acts of violence. TV is basically funded by commercials, and most commercials work through imitative behavior. They show somebody drinking a cup of hot coffee, saying, 'Mmmm.' They expect you to go out and buy Yuban."[27]

[16]The movie producer Lawrence Gordon, whose credits include *Die Hard*, *48 Hours*, and *Field of Dreams*, discovered the connection between entertainment and behavior when teenage viewers of his 1979 film about street gangs, *The Warriors*, left theaters and tore into each other; nationwide, three killings were attributed to the film. "I'd be lying if I said that people don't imitate what they see on the screen," Gordon says. "I would be a moron to say they don't, because look how dress styles change. We have people who want to look like Julia Roberts and Michelle Pfeiffer and Madonna. Of course we imitate. It would be impossible for me to think they would imitate our dress, our music, our look, but not imitate any of our violence or our other actions."[28]

[17]Like all media, television is a teacher. But television is a more powerful teacher than most, and its principal pupils are very young children. Today, in most American homes, children aged two to eleven watch television for twenty-two hours a week; teenagers watch about the same, about twenty-three hours a week.[29] This means that most children spend more time each week watching television than doing anything else except sleeping. For black and Hispanic children, regardless of their families' income levels, these numbers are even higher; and for poor children, who typically have few alternative activities, the numbers go higher still.[30]

[18]Over the last two decades the level of violence on broadcast television has been fairly steady, with twenty to twenty-five violent acts per hour in children's programs compared to about five to six violent acts per hour in prime time.[31] What *has* changed, as anyone who watches television knows, is that television violence is far more graphic now, and far more likely to be sexual. A lot of the violence children see occurs in adult programs, but, amazingly, most of it is in material created specifically for them, in cartoons and animated features. The National Institute of Mental Health reported a decade ago that more than 80 percent of children's programs contain some sort of violent act.[32] Researchers typically define an "act of violence" as, for example, "an overt physical action that hurts or kills, or threatens to do so."[33]

[19]Yet television executives go on ridiculing these definitions and their implications that *Road Runner* or the *Teenage Mutant Ninja Turtles* teaches violence. At a 1994 conference, USA Network president Kay Koplovitz said flatly, "I don't believe it." Why not? Anyone who has seen a young child enthralled by *Barney and Friends* or *Mr. Rogers' Neighborhood* should know that children perceive television quite differently than adults do. Why is it so hard to believe that children who learn well from simplified, exaggerated presentations can also learn from graphic depictions of violence?* Indeed, it may be that the violent messages which television sends to the very young, however, *innocuous* they may appear to adults, are the most damaging in the long run. As the researcher Brandon Centerwall writes:

> The average American preschooler watches more than 27 hours of television per week. This might not be bad if these young children understood what they were watching, but they don't. Up through ages three and four, most children are unable to distinguish fact from fantasy on TV, and remain unable to do so despite adult coaching. In the minds of young children, television is a source of entirely factual information regarding how the world works. There are *no limits to their credulity*. To cite one example, an Indiana school board had to issue an advisory to young children that, no, there is no such thing as Teenage Mutant Ninja Turtles. Children had been crawling down storm drains looking for them.

*Sadly, many adults cannot bring themselves to tolerate, much less appreciate, the one or two quality children's programs on television that are made *only* for children, without adults in mind at all. In the last two years, "Barney," friend to millions of preschoolers, has been the target of hate columns in the national press, including at least one, on the *Wall Street Journal* editorial page, that pictured the purple dinosaur in the crosshairs of a rifle scope. That same day, on the same page, the *Journal* featured an unsigned column on the breakdown of "simple decency" and "civility" in public life.

(CONTINUED)

STRANGERS IN THE HOUSE (CONTINUED)

Naturally, as children get older, they come to know better, but their earliest and deepest impressions are laid down at an age when they still see television as a factual source of information about the outside world. In that world, it seems, violence is common, and the commission of violence is generally powerful, exciting, charismatic and effective. In later life, serious violence is most likely to erupt at moments of severe stress—and it is precisely at such moments that adolescents and adults are most likely to revert to their earliest, most visceral sense of the role of violence in society and in personal behavior. Much of this sense will have come from television.[34]

[20]Centerwall's comments added spark to the congressional inquiries held during the summer of 1993, for they received enormous press attention, mostly because of the data he had gathered in remote towns in the United States and Canada that, for technical reasons, did not receive television signals until the mid-1970s, long after everyone else. In each of these towns, Centerwall discovered, the introduction of television was followed by an increase in aggressiveness among boys. Was there, he wondered, a connection? He tested the hypothesis by comparing the homicide rates of the United States and Canada with those of South Africa, which did not get television until 1975. After controlling for factors such as economic growth, alcohol consumption, and firearm availability, Centerwall found that the homicide rates in the United States and Canada rose by more than 90 percent between 1945 (about the time television was introduced in those countries) and 1974, while over the same period homicide rates among white South Africans declined by 7 percent.

[21]But even many who admired Centerwall's argument often missed his most compelling point. Responding to research done by NBC that showed screen violence to be only "modestly" related to violent behavior, affecting only about 5 percent of 2,400 children in a three-year study, Centerwall observed that such a seemingly small effect is actually quite significant:

It is an *intrinsic property* of such "bell curve" distributions that small changes in the average imply major changes at the extremes. Thus if exposure to television causes 8 percent of the population to shift from below-average aggression to above-average aggression, it follows that the homicide rate will double. The findings of the NBC study and the doubling of the homicide rate are two sides of the same coin.[35]

In other words, the effects of violence can have *exponential consequences*. The issue is not, as Sam Donaldson once asked, whether people "watch movies, then grab their guns and go out to do mayhem"—the proverbial straw man raised by the industry—but whether the totality of depictions creates a climate that fosters violence in general. It's like dropping a stone into the calm surface of a large pond: suddenly the water is not so still anymore.

Notes

1. Dr. Jerome Singer, quoted in *On Television: Teach the Children*, produced by Mary Megee, On Television Ltd., New York.
2. "Television Usage in Child-Care Centers," Statistical Research, Inc., May 1994.

...

(CONTINUED)

STRANGERS IN THE HOUSE (CONTINUED)

15. Neil Hickey, "How Much Violence Is There?" *TV Guide*, June 1992.

16. Child viewing data from *Neilsen Total Viewing Sources Report*, February 1993.

17. See "Reading, Writing, and Murder," *People*, June 14, 1993.

18. See David A. Hamburg, *Today's Children: Creating a Future for a Generation in Crisis* (New York: Random House, 1992), and William Dietz and Victor Strasburger, "Children, Adolescents and Television," *Current Problems in Pediatrics*, Vol. 21, No. 1, 1991, pp. 8–14.

19. Surgeon General's Scientific Advisory Committee on Television and Social Behavior, *Television and Growing Up: The Impact of Televised Violence* (Washington, D.C.: U.S. Government Printing Office, 1972).

20. "TV Violence Held Unharmful to Youth," *The New York Times*, January 11, 1972.

21. Quoted in Douglass Cater and Stephen Strickland, *TV Violence and the Child: The Evolution and Fate of the Surgeon General's Report* (New York: Russell Sage Foundation, 1975), p. 80.

22. "Violence on Air and in Life: No Clear Link," *Broadcasting*, January 17, 1972.

23. Quoted in Cater and Strickland, op. cit., p. 88.

24. Ibid., p. 3.

25. "TV Violence Labels Not Expected to Affect Kids," *The Hollywood Reporter*, July 1, 1993.

26. *Violence on Television: A Symposium and Study Sponsored by the Editors of TV Guide*, June 1992, pp. 9–10.

27. Quoted in Peter Biskind, "Drawing the Line," *Premiere*, November 1992.

28. Quoted in Ken Auletta, "What Won't They Do?" *The New Yorker*, May 17, 1993.

29. These figures are from Nielsen Data Research for the period from September 14, 1992, to September 13, 1993. See Larry McGill, "By the Numbers—What Kids Watch," *Media Studies Journal*, Fall 1994, pp. 95–96. Some researchers believe that smaller children, aged two to eleven, watch as much as twenty-eight hours of television each week. See Aletha Huston et al., *Big World, Small Screen: The Role of Television in American Society* (Lincoln: University of Nebraska Press, 1992).

30. See J. P. Tangney and S. Feshbach, "Children's Television-Viewing Frequency: Individual Differences and Demographic Correlates," *Personality and Social Psychology Bulletin*, Vol. 14, 1988, pp. 145–58; and Ronald Kuby and Mikael Csikszentmihalyi, *Television and the Quality of Life: How Viewing Shapes Everyday Experience* (Hillsdale, N.J.: Earlbaum, 1990).

31. Huston et al., op. cit., p. 53. These per-hour figures are also cited by Edward Donnerstein, Ron Slaby, and Leonard Eron in *Violence and Youth: Psychology's Response* (Washington, D.C.: American Psychological Association, 1994).

32. National Institute for Mental Health, *Journal*, Vol. I, 1982.

33. See "Number of Violent Scenes on TV Drops by Half," *Los Angeles Times*, July 29, 1993. The definition is the one used by George Gerbner and his colleagues; other researchers use similar definitions. The 1992 study done for *TV Guide* by the Center for Media and Public Affairs defined an act of violence as "any deliberate act involving physical force or the use of a weapon in an attempt to achieve a goal, further a cause, stop the action of another, act out an angry impulse, defend oneself from attack, secure a material reward, or intimidate others."

34. Brandon Centerwall, "Television and Violent Crime," *The Public Interest*, Spring 1993, pp. 56–58.

35. Ibid., pp. 65–66.

CONTENT QUESTIONS—"STRANGERS IN THE HOUSE"

TRUE OR FALSE

If the statement is false, rewrite it to make it true.

1. By the time most American children start first grade, they have spent the equivalent of three school years in front of the television.
2. Most American children spend more time each week watching television than doing anything else except sleeping.
3. The violence on television simply mirrors the violence in real life.
4. Television violence has become less graphic and less sexual over the years.
5. Countless studies have demonstrated a causal link between aggressive behavior and exposure to television violence.

COMPLETION

6. In the first few paragraphs, Minow and Lamay talk about the "total strangers" Americans are letting take care of their children. Who are they really talking about?
7. Why do Minow and Lamay think we should be concerned about these strangers?
8. In paragraph 4, Minow and Lamay say that for millions of children "television is not only the first but also the most enduring educational and social institution they will know." What do they mean? Do you agree? Why or why not?
9. In paragraph 5, Minow and Lamay say that "... television's portrayal of violence is so skewed as to have made a norm out of the extreme, the sensational, and the improbable." What do they mean? Do you agree? Why or why not?
10. Does movie producer Lawrence Gordon think there is a connection between entertainment and behavior? What evidence does he use to support his view?

VOCABULARY—"STRANGERS IN THE HOUSE"

1. in the tutelage of (¶4)
2. intellectual nourishment (¶4)
3. skewed (¶5)
4. created a cosmology of terror (¶5)
5. pervasive sense of fear (¶7)
6. a definitive answer (¶8)
7. so acrimonious the ensuing debate (¶12)
8. they simultaneously debunk them (¶14)
9. innocuous (¶19)
10. no limits to their credulity (¶19)
11. intrinsic property (¶21)
12. exponential consequences (¶21)

Content Analysis Questions—"Strangers in the House"

1. What is Minow and Lamay's purpose? What do you think they would like to see happen?
2. What is Minow and Lamay's thesis?
3. How do they develop and support their thesis?
4. In paragraph 15, what do you think Minow and Lamay and Professor Gerbner are saying?
5. Minow and Lamay assert that "the effects of violence can have exponential consequences"—like the ripples in the water from a stone tossed in a pond. What do you think they mean? Do you agree? Why or why not?

Application Questions—"Strangers in the House"

1. Assume that a local child care center asks the members of your child development class to work with them to draft a set of "suggested viewing guidelines" for parents. What three ideas or concepts would you want to make sure were included in such guidelines? Explain.
2. If you went home today and asked that the television set be turned off for two full weeks—with no exceptions—what type of reactions do you think you would get? Why? What would be your own reaction? Why? What negative and/or positive results do you think might result from such an experiment?

"Family Violence"

Sandra Arbetter has a master's degree in social work and writes on mental health issues for a variety of audiences. This selection—"Family Violence"—is from *Current Health 2.*

FAMILY VIOLENCE: WHEN WE HURT THE ONES WE LOVE

Sandra Arbetter

[1]When the lake waters swirled over the car holding Susan Smith's two little boys, the ripple was felt around the nation. How could the sweet-looking mother from the peaceful town of Union, South Carolina, drown her own children?

[2]Wake up, America. There are 600 cases every year of mothers killing their children, according to the U.S. Department of Justice. The Smith case jolted folks out of the numbness created by daily headlines of beatings, rapes, shootings, stabbings, and torture—all in the family. Maybe it was the news photos of the two handsome little faces. Maybe it was the murders coming so soon after O. J. Simpson was charged with stabbing to death his ex-wife, Nicole, and her friend Ron Goldman. How could a national sports hero be associated with such messy business as spousal abuse and murder?

(CONTINUED)

FAMILY VIOLENCE:
WHEN WE HURT THE ONES WE LOVE (CONTINUED)

[3]The facts about family violence are coming out of the closet, and they reveal that children and wives are not the only family members mistreated. The web of family violence entangles husbands abused by wives, parents abused by their children, and brothers and sisters abused by each other.

[4]The statistics on family violence are staggering:

[5]Every 15 seconds a woman in this country is battered. Almost 2 million women are severely assaulted every year. One-third of female homicide victims are killed by a husband or partner.

[6]Spousal abuse occurs in families of every racial, ethnic, and economic group. In a recent study at the University of Rhode Island, for example, nearly 20 of every 1000 women with family incomes over $40,000 reported being victims of severe violence.

[7]Last year more than 1 million teens ran away from home. Most left, not for the excitement of the streets or to be grown-up, but to escape beatings and sexual abuse and worse at home.

[8]One in 25 elderly persons is victimized. Almost one-third of this maltreatment is by adult children of the elderly, according to the U.S. Department of Health and Human Services.

[9]Three million cases of child abuse or neglect were reported in 1994. About half involve neglect, which means that adults are not providing a safe environment with adequate shelter, clothing, food, and sanitation. Abuse includes physical or emotional injury or sexual abuse.

Effects on Victims

[10]But the numbers don't tell the whole story. It's the suffering of each victim that matters most.

[11]"I can't trust anyone," says 21-year-old Dan. "I feel lonely all the time." When the people who are supposed to take care of you are hurting you instead, then nothing is safe. It can be hard to get along with friends and co-workers, or to have a long-term intimate relationship.

[12]Children who witness (or are victims of) abuse are at risk for school problems, drug abuse, sexual acting out, running away, suicide, and becoming abused themselves. Their self-esteem is shattered by feelings of powerlessness to protect themselves or the parent who is being abused. Girls from abusive homes tend to become victims. Boys tend to see violence as the way to deal with frustration.

[13]Children from abusive families learn a false lesson: love and violence go together. The person who loves you hits you, so you hit the person you love.

An Old Story

[14]The violence is nothing new, but until recently there was an *unwritten conspiracy* to ignore it. Americans wanted to hang onto the image of the family as all sweetness and light. When there was abuse, often a husband beating a wife, it was dismissed with a knowing smile as part of being in love.

[15]Sweetness and light? Tell that to the 3.3 million children between the ages of 3 and 17 who are at risk from parental violence, according to Peter Jaffe, author of *Children of Abused Women*. Tell that to the thousands of children who have been wrenched from their abusive home to live in shelters or foster care.

[16]Tell that to Patricia, who wears long-sleeved shirts and more makeup than her pretty features need, to cover up bruises from beatings by her father.

(CONTINUED)

FAMILY VIOLENCE:
WHEN WE HURT THE ONES WE LOVE (CONTINUED)

[17]"When I heard my father coming home at night, my stomach curled into a tight knot. He's got a terrible temper, and once he got upset he couldn't stop until he'd beat me and my mom.

[18]"One night he hit my mother with a wrench, and then he choked her until I thought she was dead. I made the mistake of running over to see if she was OK. He picked me up and threw me against the stove. A burner was on and I burned my arm.

[19]"But the worst time was when he made my mom sit under the kitchen table and beg for food like a dog. If I had a gun, I think I would have killed him. I hated myself for not sticking up for my mom, but I was too scared."

[20]It was right after that incident that Patricia's mother got in touch with a shelter for abused women, one of almost 1,300 in the United States. She and Patricia lived there for three weeks while she looked for a job and a place to live. After many tears and second thoughts and counseling sessions, Patricia's mother *resolved* never to go back to being abused.

[21]Patricia said that gave a tremendous boost to her own feelings about being female—that someone can be strong and brave and demand respect.

[22]"It was pretty tough," says Patricia. "We had no money, and I was cut off from my friends. And all the time I was afraid my dad would find us."

[23]Patricia's fear was real. Many men can't tolerate their wife or partner leaving. Some men beg to come back, swearing never to hurt again. Some men threaten at home and at work. Many states now have *anti-stalking laws* to protect women from men who pursue them against their will. Even with the new laws, officials admit that it's difficult to protect a woman from a man who is *obsessed* with regaining control over her. The terrifying truth is that women who leave are at greater risk of being killed than those who stay.

[24]On the subject of murder, of 35 women on death row in 1993, almost half had murdered an abusive partner. Recently, there has been strong feeling that abuse victims act in self-defense and should not be imprisoned. Some governors have pardoned them. It's a sensitive subject, with people on the other side saying that pardoning those women *condones* murder.

Why Men Abuse

[25]More than 90 percent of reported battering is done by the male partner, although the whole story of abuse by women is yet to be told. The shame of it keeps many men from reporting it, according to experts.

[26]Men abuse women by:

[27]physical abuse

[28]emotional abuse

[29]economic abuse (taking her money; making her ask for money)

[30]sexual abuse (making her do things against her will. Until recently, few states even
recognized that rape could occur within a marriage.)

[31]isolation (controlling what she does, who she sees and talks to)

[32]What causes men to abuse women they say they love? Experts say it has a lot to do with feelings of powerlessness. A man who abuses may look tough on the outside, but he often has low self-esteem and is very dependent on the woman. He expects her to meet all his needs, solve his loneliness, make him feel good about himself. If she wants to go out with friends or make some decisions of her own, he feels abandoned. Violence steps in to keep the woman fearful of going against his wishes. The man often puts down his partner, calling her dumb or ugly or useless. Heard often enough, that wears down the woman's self-esteem so that she questions her ability to leave and make it on her own.

(CONTINUED)

FAMILY VIOLENCE:
WHEN WE HURT THE ONES WE LOVE (CONTINUED)

[33]There are other factors that influence men to use abuse to control their partner: a previous head injury; low levels of a brain chemical called seratonin, which affects mood; a gene that promotes violence; stress, such as financial problems; substance abuse; lack of training to be a parent; and coming from an abusive family.

Child Abuse

[34]Every day in this country, children are killed by parents and caretakers. Men more than women tend to shake babies to stop them from crying, according to a report from the U.S. Advisory Board on Child Abuse and Neglect. This can cause death: Neck muscles are not fully developed; the baby's head moves violently; the brain is pulled different directions, and brain cells tear. The problem is how to get untrained parents to understand that babies do not cry to irritate their mothers and fathers. Their crying communicates some need, and they can't stop just because someone is angry at the noise.

[35]Women kill most often through severe neglect—like the mother in Memphis who left two toddlers in the car last June in 90-degree heat while she partied with friends. Temperatures in the car soared, and the children died.

[36]New statistics show an increase in the rate of abuse of adolescents. Teen abuse has been underreported, possibly because adults see teens as able to protect themselves.

[37]In young children, boys are abused more often than girls; but over age 12, girls bear the brunt. A partial explanation is that adolescents are abused when they disobey their parents. Since parents are less likely to grant autonomy to girls, there are more instances of parent-daughter dispute. Girls are also sexually abused more frequently. Some experts say boys often don't report sexual abuse because the abusers usually are male, and boys—at a vulnerable time in their sexual development—worry about being labeled homosexual or wimpy.

Elder Abuse

[38]Grandparents are for hugs and I-Love-You drawings and visits on holidays. But did you know that some are abused? The elderly who are abused are often too frail to defend themselves and too ashamed to report mistreatment.

[39]Dr. David Finkelhor of the University of New Hampshire has identified three kinds of elder abuse:

[40]psychological abuse: name-calling, insulting, ignoring, threatening

[41]financial abuse: illegal or unethical use of the elderly person's funds or property

[42]physical abuse: hitting, pushing, confining someone against his or her will; sexual abuse

[43]Most elderly are abused by those they live with, partly the result of the stress of caring for a person who is ill or disabled, who needs to be fed and toileted, and who provides little satisfying companionship. Abusers usually have a history of substance or mental illness. Two-thirds of them are financially dependent on the victim. There can even be an element of the adult child "getting even" for past abuse by the parent.

[44]Some states have passed laws for mandatory reporting of elder abuse, which means that doctors and social workers must report suspected abuse. Mandatory reporting of suspected child abuse has been the law for many years.

[45]Communities are encouraging neighbors to keep an eye on seniors. Some are considering shelters like the ones organized for battered women, and they are expanding senior day care services and support services for caregivers.

(CONTINUED)

FAMILY VIOLENCE:
WHEN WE HURT THE ONES WE LOVE (CONTINUED)

Between Brothers and Sisters

[46]If we have ignored spousal and elder abuse, we have all but denied the existence of sibling abuse, which often is chalked up to "normal sibling rivalry."

[47]"I begged my parents not to go out and let my sister, Lila, baby-sit," says Sam, now 17. "She'd sit on me and put a pillow over my face and punch my head. She'd tickle me until I wet my pants, and then threaten to tell everyone at school about it. Once she pointed my father's gun at me and said she'd kill me if I didn't do what she asked."

[48]Sam's mother and father thought his complaints were just childish squabbles between brother and sister. It turned out that Lila's behavior was a call for help. When Sam got a concussion after Lila tripped him, the whole family went for counseling. As they all learned to communicate their feelings verbally and to express praise and appreciation for one another, Lila's abusive behavior lessened.

[49]Sibling sexual abuse is an *underreported phenomenon*, partly because parents resist recognizing it and partly because there is confusion about where normal sex play ends and incest begins. Sex play usually occurs between children who are close in age, and before puberty. If there is an age difference of even a few years, there is an imbalance of power and the younger child is being coerced.

[50]Most sibling sexual abuse involves a boy between 8 and 16 years old molesting a younger sister. He, himself, may be the victim of sexual abuse.

[51]"The good news is that children who abuse siblings can recover," says Michael O'Brien, director of PHASE, a family treatment program for sexually abusive adolescents in St. Paul, Minnesota. He says that with intensive therapy with all family members, 95 percent of offenders do not repeat their abuse.

Getting Help

[52]If you're being abused, tell someone. Some people are afraid to tell for fear they'll be sent away, the family will be torn apart, or that other family members will be angry. But what is the alternative: to continue to live with an abuser, to have your self-esteem plunge to zero, to risk getting into trouble, to be badly injured?

[53]When 14-year-old Sue told her school social worker that her father was coming into her room at night and touching her in a sexual way, the worker called the state child welfare agency. A woman from the agency came to school that same day to talk with Sue, and then went to the house to talk with Sue's parents. Sue's father was asked to leave the house until Sue's safety could be assured. Her father went before a judge, and was ordered to undergo counseling before he would be allowed to rejoin his family.

[54]In counseling, abusers learn that anger is not the only emotion. Underneath, there may be hurt, worry, sadness, or fear. They learn to recognize these feelings and put them into words. They hear that they do not own the woman, that it is OK for her to have an opinion that differs from his, and that there are ways to control the impulse to hit.

[55]Of course, many children from abusive homes go on to have successful lives with loving relationships. While some studies say 80 percent of abusers were abused as children, other research puts the figure closer to 30 percent. While that is still higher than the base rate of 5 percent for abuse in the general population, it means that up to 70 percent of children who were abused do not grow up to be abusive to their family members.

[56]In many ways, family violence remains a terrible puzzle. But now that personal histories are being made public and problems are being recognized as such, we have a chance to put some of the pieces together.

CONTENT QUESTIONS—"FAMILY VIOLENCE"

TRUE OR FALSE

If the statement is false, rewrite it to make it true.

1. Children and wives are the only victims of family abuse.
2. Every 15 seconds a woman in America is battered.
3. Women who leave abusive partners are at greater risk of being killed than those who stay.
4. Most elderly are abused by attackers who break into their homes.
5. Sibling abuse is underreported.

COMPLETION

6. Arbetter says that "children from abusive families learn a false lesson." What is the lesson? Why is it false?
7. List six factors that contribute to men's abuse of women.
8. List three kinds of elder abuse. Why is elder abuse so rarely reported?
9. What are the chances that children who abuse their siblings can stop the abusive behavior and recover? What type of intervention is needed?
10. What do abusers learn in counseling? Why is this helpful?

VOCABULARY—"FAMILY VIOLENCE"

1. unwritten conspiracy (¶14)
2. resolved (¶20)
3. anti-stalking laws (¶23)
4. obsessed (¶23)
5. condones (¶24)
6. underreported phenomenon (¶41)

CONTENT ANALYSIS QUESTIONS—"FAMILY VIOLENCE"

1. Arbetter describes the "web of family violence." Do you think the analogy to a "web" is appropriate? Why or why not? If not, what analogy would you use?
2. Arbetter says, "But the numbers [statistics on family violence] don't tell the whole story. It's the suffering of each victim that matters most." What do you think she means? Do you agree?
3. Arbetter says, "The violence is nothing new, but until recently there was an unwritten conspiracy to ignore it." What does she mean? Why do you think society was like that? What do you think is happening to change things?
4. Do you think we will see an increase or a decrease in elder abuse in the next ten years? Explain your answer.
5. Why do you think Arbetter says, "In many ways, family violence remains a terrible puzzle"? Explain your answer.

APPLICATION QUESTIONS—"FAMILY VIOLENCE"

1. Assume that after class you often join a group of students for coffee in the cafeteria. Over the last couple of weeks, someone in the group, a woman in her late twenties, has tried to hide a variety of bruises on her face and arms. Today she has a broken arm. She talks with you and describes an abusive relationship. She asks for your advice. What do you tell her?

2. Assume that three months ago your next-door neighbor's father moved in with him. During the first few weeks you saw the elderly father walking or sitting outside. However, for the last three weeks you haven't seen him and have heard your neighbor's loud voice issuing threats and insults. What, if anything, do you do?

"GANGS AND VICTIMIZATION AT SCHOOL"

This brief was prepared by John H. Ralph, National Center for Education Statistics (NCES); Kelly W. Colopy and Christine McRae, Policy Studies Associates; and Bruce Daniel, Pinkerton Computer Consultants, Inc. This selection—"Gangs and Victimization at School"—is from the *Education Policy Issues" Statistical Perspectives*, July, 1995.

GANGS AND VICTIMIZATION AT SCHOOL

U.S. DEPARTMENT OF EDUCATION
OFFICE OF EDUCATION RESEARCH

[1]Public concern over violent juvenile behavior has *intensified* in recent years, especially in regard to safety inside schools. Included among the National Education Goals is a strong commitment to providing children with learning environments that are free of violence. Yet there are very limited data about the causes of either juvenile street violence or school-related crime. Journalists frequently blame street violence on the influence of gangs. This issue brief looks at the relationship between gang presence in schools and students' reports of victimization and fear. Data collected in 1989 and 1993 reveal:

Minority students living in urban areas are not the only ones who attend school with gang members. Similar numbers of white students and minority students report gangs in their schools. Also, similar numbers of students living in suburban neighborhoods and students living in urban neighborhoods report gangs in their schools.

Gang presence in schools is strongly associated with increased student reports of victimization and fear.

When gang presence is taken into account, differences in victimization and fear levels decrease between students living in *rural*, *suburban*, and *urban* areas.

(CONTINUED)

GANGS AND VICTIMIZATION AT SCHOOL (CONTINUED)

Which Students Are Exposed to Gangs at School?

[2]In 1989, 15 percent of students (approximately 3,301,000) reported "street" gangs in their school.[1] By 1993, in a different survey, 35 percent of students said "fighting" gangs were present in their schools.[2] Although the data from these two surveys cannot be compared directly due to the different wording of the gangs question, these data may signal an increase in the number of students exposed to gangs.

[3]Many people assume that gangs are confined to urban areas and schools with large concentrations of minority students. The 1989 survey, which asked students whether there were street gangs at their school, found that while the proportion of students reporting gangs was higher in urban areas (27 percent) than in suburban (15 percent) or rural areas (8 percent), the *number* of students in both suburban areas and urban areas who reported attending schools with gangs was roughly equivalent at 1.4 million each.[3] (See Figure 1.) In short, gangs are not just an urban-school problem.

Figure 1   Students Reporting Gangs in School, by Students' Residence and Minority Status

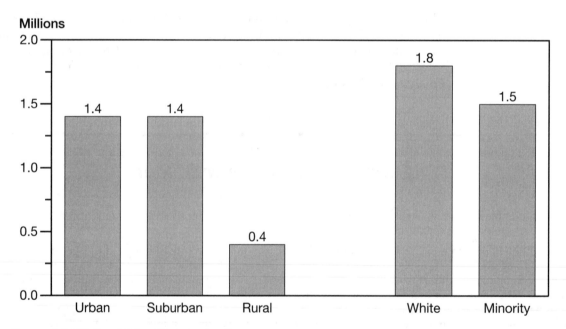

Source: 1989 National Crime Victimization Survey

[4]Exposure to gangs is also viewed primarily as a problem for minority youth, despite the fact that students from all backgrounds report gangs in their schools. In 1989, one in three Hispanic students reported members of street gangs were enrolled in their school (34 percent). Black students and white students were less likely to report gang members present in their school (21 percent and 12 percent respectively). Yet, because the school population of white students is much larger than that of other groups, more white students than minority students are estimated to report a gang presence in their school (in 1989, 1.8 million white students compared to 1.5 million minority students when all minority students are combined as shown in Figure 1).[4]

(CONTINUED)

GANGS AND VICTIMIZATION AT SCHOOL (CONTINUED)

[5]Analyses of 1993 data by race and ethnicity find similar patterns. In 1993, while the proportion of white students reporting the presence of fighting gangs in their school (31 percent) was less than that of black (42 percent) and Hispanic students (51 percent), the *number* of white students exposed to gangs at school (5.2 million) was nearly two million more than the number of minority students combined (3.2 million) exposed to gangs at school.[5]

Are Schools with Gangs Likely to Have Higher Rates of Victimization and Fear?[6]

[6]Overall, in 1989, 15 percent of students feared an attack on their way to or from school and an even greater percentage (22 percent) feared an attack while at school. A much smaller percentage (4 percent) said they had actually been *victimized* in the last six months.

[7]Reported rates of fear and victimization varied by whether gangs were present in the school. Students at schools with gangs consistently reported much higher victimization rates and levels of fear than students at schools without gangs (Table 1). Compared to students who did not report gangs in their schools, students who did were: nearly twice as likely to fear an attack at school; more than twice as likely to fear an attack while traveling to or from school; and more than twice as likely to have been victimized within the past six months. The overall proportion of students reporting they avoided certain areas within school (6 percent) or carried a weapon to school (2 percent) is roughly comparable to the proportion who reported being victimized in the past six months (4 percent), and again the pattern of gang-related victimization and fear is the same. Students attending schools with gangs were more than four times as likely to avoid certain areas within their school and more than three times as likely to report that they had brought something to school for protection in the last six months.

TABLE 1   STUDENT VICTIMIZATION AND FEAR AT SCHOOL,
BY GANG PRESENCE AND STUDENTS' RESIDENCE: 1989

| PRESENCE OF GANGS AT SCHOOL AND STUDENTS' RESIDENCE | VICTIMIZATION IN LAST 6 MONTHS* | EVER FEARING AN ATTACK | | AVOIDING PLACES INSIDE SCHOOL | BROUGHT SOMETHING TO SCHOOL FOR PROTECTION IN LAST 6 MONTHS |
		AT SCHOOL	TO OR FROM SCHOOL		
Total	3.5 percent	21.8 percent	14.7 percent	5.9 percent	2.0 percent
Gangs present	6.7	35.4	24.2	13.0	4.9
Urban	6.5	37.5	28.4	13.5	5.5
Suburban	6.8	32.4	19.6	13.0	5.1
Rural	6.9	38.0	25.3	13.0	1.9
No gangs	2.9	18.2	11.6	2.9	1.5
Urban	3.0	19.3	16.3	3.7	2.0
Suburban	3.0	18.1	11.0	2.6	1.4
Rural	2.6	17.5	8.9	2.9	1.1

*Victimization comprises the number of students who answered "yes" to either of two questions: "During the past six months, did anyone take money or things directly from you by force, weapons, or threats at school?" or "Did anyone physically attack you at school during the last six months?"

Source: 1989 National Crime Victimization Survey

(CONTINUED)

GANGS AND VICTIMIZATION AT SCHOOL (CONTINUED)

[8]These 1989 results are consistent with 1993 data, also based on measures of student-reported victimization and student reports of having "brought a weapon to school" (Table 2). As in 1989 data, the proportion of students affected is small, but the relationship of victimization and weapons-carrying to gang presence in the schools is clear. Students attending schools where fighting gangs were present reported much higher rates of victimization and weapons-carrying than other students. Students in schools with gangs were over three times more likely to report having something forcibly taken from them (over the course of the school year), more than three times as likely to report bringing a weapon to school, and more than twice as likely to report being physically attacked. Though the data indicate that gang presence is related to levels of student victimization and fear, these data do not tell us whether an already violent school climate *fosters* gang membership or whether gangs themselves are the *culprit*.

TABLE 2   STUDENT VICTIMIZATION AND FEAR AT SCHOOL,
BY GANG PRESENCE AND RACE/ETHNICITY: 1993

PRESENCE OF GANGS AT SCHOOL AND STUDENT RACE/ETHNICITY	PHYSICALLY ATTACKED DURING SCHOOL YEAR	SOMETHING TAKEN BY FORCE	BROUGHT WEAPON TO SCHOOL
Total*	3.7 percent	1.2 percent	3.4 percent
Gangs	5.9	2.3	6.2
White	5.5	2.3	4.6
Black	8.2	1.9	10.4
Hispanic	4.9	2.6	6.7
No gangs	2.5	0.7	1.9
White	2.5	0.5	1.5
Black	2.1	1.0	4.0
Hispanic	3.0	1.8	1.9

*Total includes racial/ethnic subgroups not shown separately.
Source: 1993 National Household Education Survey

Does gang presence outweigh where students live and student race/ethnicity in accounting for levels of student victimization and fear?

[9]All students, regardless of their race, ethnicity, or place of residence, tend to report higher rates of victimization and fear when there are gangs in school. For example, in 1989, whether they lived in an urban, suburban, or rural area, roughly 7 percent of students in schools with gangs reported they were victimized within the last six months (Table 1). Also, differences in students' reported rates of victimization varied little by urban status in schools without gangs—roughly 3 percent of the students reported victimization. Based on statistical tests of the 1989 data that simultaneously take into account where students lived and whether they attended a school with gangs, the likelihood of becoming a victim of violence at school was less related to place of residence than to whether the student attended a school where there were gangs. Similarly, based on statistical tests of the 1993 data that simultaneously take into account students' racial or ethnic background and whether they attended a school with gangs, the likelihood of becoming a victim of violence at school was less related to student background than to whether the student attended a school where there were gangs.

(CONTINUED)

GANGS AND VICTIMIZATION AT SCHOOL (CONTINUED)

Conclusion

[10]The problem of gangs in schools is limited to neither urban areas nor minority students—the actual number of students who encounter gangs in school is as great for suburban or white students as it is for urban or minority students. Gang presence, not a student's race or ethnicity nor whether the student lives in an urban area, accounts for most of the differences across students who report different levels of victimization and fear at school. When gang presence is factored in, urban and racial differences tend to become insignificant.

Notes

1. Based on the 1989 School Crime Supplement to the annual National Crime Victimization Survey (NCVS), sponsored by the Bureau of Justice Statistics (U.S. Department of Justice), NCVS surveyed 10,499 students, ages 12 to 19, and is a nationally representative sample of households in the United States. Students were asked, "Are there any street gangs at your school?"

2. Based on the School Safety and Discipline Survey conducted as part of the 1993 National Household Education Survey (NHES), administered by the National Center for Education Statistics. NHES surveyed 6,800 students in grades 6 through 12 and 13,300 parents and is a nationally representative sample of households in the United States. Students were asked "Do any of the students at your school belong to fighting gangs?"

3. NCVS, 1989. Residential areas are based on Metropolitan Statistical Area (MSA) classifications. Suburbs are inside an MSA but not in the central city of the MSA. Rural areas are all outside MSAs.

4. NCVS, 1989.

5. NHES, 1993.

6. See definition of victimization in Table 1.

CONTENT QUESTIONS—"GANGS AND VICTIMIZATION AT SCHOOL"

TRUE OR FALSE

If the statement is false, rewrite it to make it true.

1. Minority students living in cities are the only ones who have gangs in their schools.
2. The public is becoming increasingly concerned about violent juvenile behavior.
3. Students in schools with gangs are more fearful than students in schools without gangs.
4. The United States has a great deal of data about the causes of school-related crime.
5. The data may signal an increase in the number of students exposed to gangs in school.

COMPLETION

6. In general, which students are exposed to gangs at school?

7. What percentage of students reported "street" gangs in their schools in 1989? What percentage of students reported "fighting" gangs in their schools in 1993? What does this data probably indicate? What do you think the data would show today?

8. According to the 1993 data, what was most likely to make a student a victim—e.g., place of residence, race, ethnicity, attending a school with gangs? Why do you think that's true?

9. Why is the *proportion* of white students exposed to gangs at school less than the *proportion* of minority students, while the *number* of white students exposed to gangs at school is more than the *number* of minority students?

10. In 1989, how much more likely was it that a student in a school with gangs would "bring something for protection"? Do you think that likelihood is increasing or decreasing? Explain.

VOCABULARY—"GANGS AND VICTIMIZATION AT SCHOOL"

1. intensified (¶1)
2. rural, suburban, urban (¶1)
3. victimized (¶6)
4. fosters (¶8)
5. culprit (¶8)

CONTENT ANALYSIS QUESTIONS—"GANGS AND VICTIMIZATION AT SCHOOL"

1. What is the authors' purpose?
2. What is the authors' thesis?
3. How do the authors develop and support their thesis?
4. In paragraph 8, the authors say "...these data do not tell us whether an already violent school climate fosters gang membership or whether gangs themselves are the culprit." What do they mean?
5. One of our national education goals is a "strong commitment to providing children with learning environments that are free of violence." What are two ideas or steps you recommend to help meet that goal?

APPLICATION QUESTIONS—"GANGS AND VICTIMIZATION AT SCHOOL"

1. Assume that one of your night class instructors teaches full-time at a local high school. Yesterday morning she was shot and critically wounded trying to break up a fight in her classroom. You and several other students want to do something positive. What do you decide to do? Why?

2. As this brief indicated, there is limited information about the causes of either juvenile street violence or school-related crime. How could you design a small research project for a sociology class to gather information in one of these areas?

"GUNS AND DRUGS"

Susan S. Lang is the senior science writer for Cornell University and a freelance writer of more than 125 articles and 6 books including *Extremist Groups in America*. This selection—"Guns and Drugs"—is from *Teen Violence*, 2nd ed.

GUNS AND DRUGS

SUSAN S. LANG

How can America think of itself as a civilized society when day after day the bodies pile up amid the primitive crackle of gunfire across the land?

—*Time* Magazine, July 17, 1989

[1]There's no doubt about it, we are a heavily armed society. Our population is about 260 million—we have more than 201 million guns in the country.[1] Gun ownership is so widespread in our free and liberal land that there is one gun for every other household. Many youngsters can grab a gun as easily as a peanut butter and jelly sandwich. With a gun on hand at the critical moment, temporary problems too often turn into permanent tragedies.

[2]Consider these chilling statistics:

Since the beginning of the century, three-quarters of a million people have been shot dead in the U.S. with privately owned guns; that's 30 percent more than have been killed in all the wars in which America has been involved.[2] One-third of those people killed by guns, or one-quarter of a million Americans, died in the 1980s; that's four times more people than were killed in the Vietnam War.[3]

In 1990, 38,317 Americans were shot;[4] more people die of gunshot wounds every two years than have died so far from AIDS or in the entire Vietnam War.[5]

Six of every ten killings in the United States involve guns.[6]

One of every four deaths of teenagers is caused by a gunshot.[7]

Every day more than 100,000 kids tote guns to school.[8]

Every day, 14 children aged eighteen and younger are killed by guns.[9] Since 1986, gunshot wounds to children sixteen and younger have soared more than 300 percent in urban areas.[10]

In 1987, 3,392 children aged eighteen and younger were killed by guns;[11] in 1990, 4,200 were shot and killed;[12] in 1992, more than 5,100.[13]

Juveniles' use of guns in homicides increased from 64 percent to 78 percent between 1987 and 1991, during which time juvenile arrests for weapons violations increased by 62 percent.[14]

(CONTINUED)

GUNS AND DRUGS (CONTINUED)

Around the country, youngsters use guns. "City streets have become flooded with unregistered and untraceable handguns, available to anyone of any age with a bit of cash,"[15] reports *Newsweek*. In many cities, guns can even be rented on credit for the evening.

[3]In the inner cities, some 35 percent of teens report they carry guns, at least occasionally.[16] And the gun culture is not just in the inner cities. According to a 1993 Harris poll of 2,508 students in 96 schools across the country, 15 percent of the sixth to twelfth graders said they had brought a handgun to school in the past month; 11 percent said they had been shot at and 59 percent they could get a gun if they wanted one.[17]

[4]For many teens these days, using a gun is *the* way to settle an argument: "Why would you fight somebody when you can shoot 'em?" a bespectacled sixteen-year-old asked incredulously. "Instead of fighting, it's easier to shoot," the boy told the *Washington Post*. "If you fight, you could be there all day," said his friend. "You could just shoot 'em and get it over with."[18]

[5]Handguns, automatic and semiautomatic rifles and machine guns, teflon bullets that go through bulletproof vests, and plastic guns that can't be spotted by metal detectors are just a few of the weapons that are blanketing the American landscape and finding their way into the hands of children, hotheaded teenagers, hate groups, drug dealers, and gangs. Homicides, suicides, armed robberies, and gun accidents are so common that they often don't even make the local news.

[6]The United States of America is, in fact, the only modern industrialized nation in the world that widely and lawfully allows its citizens to freely own and even stockpile firearms. "The only such nation...so attached to the supposed 'right' to bear arms that its laws abet [help] assassins, professional criminals, berserk murderers, and political terrorists at the expense of the orderly population,"[19] says historian Richard Hofstadter.

[7]In 1992, for example, handguns killed 33 people in Britain, 60 in Japan, and 128 in Canada. In the United States, handguns were used to murder 13,220 people, according to the Handgun Control organization and the Center to Prevent Handgun Violence.[20]

[8]To many teenagers, especially those living in inner cities, guns have become an acceptable part of daily life, a ticket to more money, self-esteem, status, and power. "There is a cultural pattern in the community [in Detroit] that makes the carrying of guns an accepted and normal kind of behavior,"[21] reports Marvin Zalman of the Criminal Justice Department at Wayne State University in Detroit.

[9]Explains *Time* Magazine: "With a $25 investment, all the teasing from classmates stops cold. Suddenly, the shortest, ugliest, and weakest kid becomes a player."[22]

[10]At least 18 states already have laws that prohibit juveniles from having guns, and Congress is considering making the ban national. In 1994, the federal Brady law went into effect amid much controversy. The law now requires a five-day waiting period to buy a handgun, and during that time a background check on the person wishing to buy the gun is to be conducted. While supporters of the law believe that it will prevent persons with criminal records, drug addicts, and the mentally ill from getting handguns, opponents claim that the bill will do little to prevent violent crime and that the law is unconstitutional.

[11]Opponents of the Brady law also claim that it won't stop criminals who really want guns and can buy them on the street, and that the legislation focuses on guns rather than on criminals. Those opposed to the law say that tougher jail sentences, more prisons, and more police on the streets would be a far more effective way to fight crime than a law that tries to control guns.

[12]In the meantime, the Clinton administration in 1994 also declared semiautomatic shotguns to be "destructive weapons." Now owners of these firearms must register them and be fingerprinted and photographed by local police.

[13]In addition, a new bill, Brady II, has been introduced to Congress. This bill proposes a ban on the manufacture and sale of many semiautomatic assault weapons, requires licensing and fingerprinting, and a seven-day waiting period for all gun purchases as well, allowing only one weapon to be purchased a month per person. It would also raise annual fees for gun dealers from $66 to $1,000. All these efforts are intended to limit the number and kinds of weapons on the streets of America, but such legislation is expected to make only a dent.

(CONTINUED)

GUNS AND DRUGS (CONTINUED)

Drugs and Violence

[14]Compounding the problem of kids having easy access to guns is the soaring use of street drugs. The *New York Times* reports: "Experts attribute the increase in killings to a complex variety of factors.... Most often cited is drug use and its culture, including the tendency of newer drugs to cause aggression among addicts and the potential for huge profits by organized gangs of dealers."[23]

[15]Studies have found, for example, that people who use illegal drugs (heroin, cocaine, PCP, etc.) commit four to six times as many crimes as those who don't use drugs. Looking at it from the other side, half of those arrested for crimes are drug users.[24]

[16]When juvenile records in state detention centers were reviewed in 1988, authorities found that half of those arrested for violent crimes were under the influence of drugs or alcohol when they committed their crime.[25]

[17]Many kids start trying drugs as early as the fourth grade. As soon as they buy illegal drugs, they become part of a drug culture that is linked to violence at every turn, from addicts preying on the innocent for money to buy drugs to savage wars among drug kingpins.

[18]"Territorial disputes between rival drug dealers, robberies, violent retaliations, elimination of informers, punishment for selling adulterated, phony or otherwise 'bad' drugs, punishment for failing to pay one's debts, and general disputes over drugs or drug paraphernalia—all are common to the drug culture,"[26] says Gilda Berger, author of *Violence and Drugs*.

[19]From being a drug user, the step to becoming a drug loser is an easy one. Lured by the "easy" and big money involved, kids as young as nine and ten are recruited in the inner cities as lookouts. "For this, they can make up to $100 a day and be rewarded with a pair of fashionable sneakers, a bomber jacket, or a bicycle,"[27] says Berger.

[20]Harry Hamilton, as chief investigator at the Detroit morgue, says: "Kids can make $900 a week standing on a street corner whistling when a scout car goes by. There are plenty of fifteen- and sixteen-year-olds doing things like that, but they never get to be twenty-one."[28]

[21]Drug work not only promises ghetto children a fat wallet but it also provides status, risks and thrills, and the opportunity to work their way up into higher-paying drug positions.

[22]From lookouts, young teens can be promoted to "runners," making $300 a day by carrying cocaine and crack around the city. Then, if the youths aren't shot or locked up, they may score big by becoming dealers earning some $3,000 a day.

[23]If caught, juveniles—those under age sixteen—can easily slip through the cracks of the juvenile justice system and be back out on the streets within hours or days.

[24]The rising use of crack has made the problems much worse. Crack, a cheap, smokable form of cocaine, is thought to be one of the most powerful addictive drugs known. As Commissioner of the Nassau County (New York State) Department of Drug and Alcohol Addiction, Harold Adams says, "In all my years of experience, I've never seen a drug that's more frightening and more of a menace than crack because of the violent reaction and nature of those addicted to the substance."[29] And James Payne, chief of Family Court for New York City's Law Department, reports, "We've had almost a 50 percent increase in drug crime. Crack is the main reason. We are seeing kids as young as ten or eleven. They can make $800 a week. They only stay in school because that's where their constituency [customers] is."[30]

[25]In Los Angeles, crack is blamed for escalating violence to ten times what it used to be.[31] And PCP, or angel dust, is even worse than crack in triggering extremely violent behavior.

[26]The recent upsurge in crack has been getting even more youngsters involved in the drug trade, experts point out. "Crack has changed the role of young teenagers in East Harlem society, giving them more power and putting them under less community control than ever before...giving them new and enormous power over the older generation,"[32] said Dr. Ansley Hamid of the John Jay College of Criminal Justice in New York in the *New York Times*.

(CONTINUED)

GUNS AND DRUGS (CONTINUED)

[27]Recent studies have also highlighted that crack can stifle the parental instinct. In other words, when parents become addicted, their crack addiction becomes the most important thing to them, and parenting falls to a much lower priority. The result, experts fear, is that an entire underclass of children is being born not only impaired by drugs but also neglected by addicted parents. The cost to society is enormous, both financially and socially, as these children grow up on the streets with few resources and no one to care about them.

[28]The drug culture has also given rise to more and more street gangs, which pit themselves against each other in territory and status wars.

[29]Alcohol is also a big factor in crime and violence. It not only plays a major role in child abuse and family violence, but is involved in some 65 percent of all homicides every year in the United States.[33] Excessive drinking not only eases people's inhibitions but is thought to make them more likely to commit violent acts such as robbery, burglary, muggings, and rape. Furthermore, alcohol has been linked to delinquency and crimes of vengeance and passion in a number of studies.

[30]Experts agree that the mix of youth with guns and drugs, worsened by the desperation of poverty, is a lethal one, a blend so toxic that it is killing thousands of young men and women and thousands of innocent bystanders.

Notes

1.   Ted Gest, "Violence in America," *U.S. News & World Report*, January 17, 1994, p. 24.
2.   Jeffrey H. Goldstein, *Aggression and Crimes of Violence* (New York: Oxford University Press, 1986), p. 91.
3.   Sarah Brady, "...And the Case Against Them," *Time*, January 29, 1990, p. 23.
4.   Bob Herbert, "Deadly Data on Handguns," *New York Times*, March 2, 1994.
5.   "Seven Deadly Days," *Time*, July 17, 1989, p. 31.
6.   Andrew H. Malcolm, "More Americans Are Killing Each Other," *New York Times*, December 31, 1989, p. 20.
7.   John D. Hull, "A Boy and His Gun," *Time*, August 2, 1993, p. 22.
8.   Hull, p. 22.
9.   Bob Herbert, "Deadly Data on Handguns," *New York Times*, March 2, 1994.
10. "Handgun Violence: An American Epidemic" (Washington, D.C.: Center to Prevent Handgun Violence), 1989.
11. "Targeting the Children," *Time*, November 6, 1989, p. 36.
12. Hull, p. 22.
13. Herbert, ibid.
14. Barbara Allen-Hagen and Melissa Sickmund, Ph.D., "Juveniles and Violence: Juvenile Offending and Victimization," Office of Juvenile Justice and Delinquency Prevention, Fact Sheet, July 1993.
15. George Hackett, "Kids: Deadly Force," *Newsweek*, January 11, 1988, p. 18.
16. Hull, p. 22.
17. Ibid.
18. Patrice Gaines-Carter and Lynne Duke, "Guns Mean Status to Some D.C. Youths," *Washington Post*, January 1, 1988, p. 4A.
19. Richard Hofstadter, *American Violence: A Documentary History*, in Jack Zevin, *Violence in America: What Is the Alternative?* (Englewood Cliffs, N.J.: Prentice Hall, 1973), p. 77.
20. Herbert, ibid.

(CONTINUED)

GUNS AND DRUGS (CONTINUED)

21. "Kids Who Kill," *Time*, December 2, 1985, p. 66.
22. Hull, p. 23.
23. Andrew H. Malcolm, "More Americans Are Killing Each Other," *New York Times*, December 31, 1989, p. 20.
24. Peter Kerr, "Crime Study Finds Drug Use in Most Arrested," *New York Times*, January 22, 1988, pp. A1, B4, in Gilda Berger, *Violence and Drugs* (New York: Franklin Watts, 1989) p. 10.
25. Leah Eskin, "Punishment or Reform: The History of Juvenile Justice," *Scholastic Update*, November 4, 1988, p. 11.
26. Berger, *Violence and Drugs*, p. 16.
27. Ibid., p. 35.
28. "Kid Killers," *Time*, December 22, 1986.
29. Berger, *Violence and Drugs*, p. 26.
30. Peter Applebome, "Juvenile Crime: The Offenders Are Younger and the Offenses More Serious," *New York Times*, February 3, 1987, p. 8.
31. Seth Mydans, "On Guard Against Gangs at a Los Angeles School," *New York Times*, November 19, 1989, p. 1.
32. Gina Kolata, "Grim Seeds of Park Rampage Found in East Harlem Streets," *New York Times*, May 2, 1989, p. C1.
33. *Violence and Youth: Psychology's Response* (Washington, D.C.: Am. Psych. Assn., 1993), p. 28.

CONTENT QUESTIONS—"GUNS AND DRUGS"

TRUE OR FALSE

If the statement is false, rewrite it to make it true.

1. In America, there is one gun for every other household.
2. Since the beginning of this century, 30 percent more people have been shot dead in the United States with privately owned guns than have been killed in all the wars in which America has been involved.
3. Drugs and alcohol are not a big factor in crime and violence.
4. The increase in crack cocaine is responsible for getting more youngsters involved in the drug trade.
5. Crack cocaine can suppress people's instinct to take care of their children.

COMPLETION

6. List the number of people killed by handguns in Britain, Japan, Canada, and the United States in 1992. Why does Lang think there is such a difference in the numbers? Do you agree? Why or why not?
7. In 1994, the Brady Bill went into effect. What do supporters of the bill think it will/won't do? What do opponents of the bill think it will/won't do?

8. What, according to Lang, is "compounding the problem of kids having easy access to guns"? Why is this?

9. Why is crack cocaine such a multidimensional problem?

10. Why is alcohol a factor in crime and violence?

CONTENT ANALYSIS QUESTIONS—"GUNS AND DRUGS"

1. List three of the statistics Lang cites to support her opening statement, "…we are a heavily armed society." What kind of gun legislation do you think she would like to see enacted? Do you agree with her? Why or why not?

2. What are some of the reasons teens are resorting to guns these days? Which of these do you think would be the easiest to combat?

3. What are some of the reasons kids become involved in the drug trade? What do you think are some ways to combat the problem?

4. In paragraph 27, Lang states: "The cost to society [for children born impaired by drugs to addicted parents] is enormous, both financially and socially…." What are some of the costs she is referring to? Do you agree? Why or why not?

5. What actions do you think Lang would be in favor of to reduce the "toxic blend" that is resulting in the killing of thousands of young men, women, and innocent bystanders? What actions would you support?

APPLICATION QUESTIONS—"GUNS AND DRUGS"

1. Assume that a local elementary school principal has asked your college president if a group of students would present an assembly on "Staying Away from Drugs." You are part of the six-person team selected. What approach do you recommend—e.g., serious, funny, dramatic, scary? Why? What one idea or concept would you like all students to leave your presentation thinking about?

2. Assume that on your next city election ballot you will be asked to vote on a proposal to make it legal to carry concealed weapons. What factors would you consider? What would you read and who would you talk with to help you make your decision?

"THE BOOKMOBILE"

Arleen Knowles was a student at Mesa Community College in Mesa, Arizona, when she wrote "The Bookmobile," an award-winning remembrance of her childhood in a violent south Chicago ghetto. She is pursuing a bachelor's degree in business administration and plans to pursue a master's degree in social work.

THE BOOKMOBILE

ARLEEN R. KNOWLES

[1]Some say there is no God in the Ghetto. I would disagree. Yes, the violence, anger and poverty can be crippling, but what about the Bookmobile: an old *metal touring contraption* on six wheels, its walls filled with hope, knowledge, and freedom in each of its volumes. Like a *parable* spoken to the illustrious twelve, so the Bookmobile rambled down the streets of south Chicago. It is very visible, yet often unseen. The truth that is often sought is deemed out of reach, and many befriend despair. Yet there stands the Bookmobile; in it lies the answers to so many of my questions, to so many of my prayers. Another way of life is my dream, my quest; it is only attainable through the Bookmobile. I believe God had to have sent it.

[2]Walking down the familiar streets my steps are determined yet slow, and filled with foreboding. Looking around, it seems as if hopelessness has overrun our way of life. People are living in abandoned buildings. Through a broken window I can see men sleeping on torn, dirty blankets. A couple of guys are smoking dope in the doorway. I glance at them and look away quickly; I don't want to be able to recognize their faces. A group of men are laughing and talking loudly on the corner as they pass around an open bottle of Thunderbird. Just then, a car full of young men drives by, and I can hear them yelling comments to a mother pushing a baby in a stroller. "Eh, suga' you' lookin' good. Come 'ere and gimme a piece of that," the guy in the passenger seat says in an attempt to pick her up. She flirts with them for awhile and then continues her walk. I shake my head. As I get closer to her, I notice her face. She is young. In fact, she is just a couple of years older than I am. Didn't we go to elementary school together last year? I smile and make appropriate baby comments. As I reach the corner and cross over to the next street, "How sad," I say to myself. "She can't be more than thirteen," my thoughts continue. Her future is predictable, I remind myself. I am stunned by the sheer hopelessness of the choices she has made, realizing, of course, that I may be one of the only people who feels this way. They say that's the way it is in the Ghetto. But I want to scream, "It doesn't have to be!" What about the Bookmobile?

[3]The violence is everywhere. We can't escape it. I tried to for a long time. I used to be scared, but now, I don't feel anything at all. One of the most difficult things is trying to step over the people in the hallway of the building where we live. I have to check the banister and the walls when I walk down the stairs. It's hard to clean the blood out of our mittens or mend the snags we get in our coats from the *protruding* bullet holes when we lean against the walls. Someone is going to die tonight. They always do. Just like our neighbors, next door. First they used knives, and then they used guns. Why does violence always *escalate*? Then we heard them. The sound I had been dreading: the shots. We all had to dive for the floor because the bullets were flying everywhere. It looked like flashes of lightning. I opened the door when someone fell against it. I thought it was a knock. Our neighbor died that night. I watched him slide down the stairs held up only by the wall. The only thing left was the stain his blood made as he fell. We don't talk in the Ghetto; we always fight. Oh, sometimes we laugh, and love to dance, but we always die.

[4]When my family gets together for a barbecue at my grandma's house, I hear the adults talking. "It's the white man," my uncle says, "He tried to keep the black man down, always has, always will." These conversations confuse me, the "white man" doesn't hold the guns in our neighborhood. I just don't understand. Choices, there are so many choices. Why don't they ever go to the Bookmobile?

[5]They say we are poor, but my brother and I each have our own room. My dad works every day; he even likes his job. My favorite times of the year are Christmas and Easter. I get a new dress then. Other times we just wear the clothes my grandmother gives us from the white peoples' houses on the north side where she works. My grandmother's hands are always rough, callused, and tired. She's proud of what she does. "It's honest work," she says and "[I'm] giving [my] daughters a chance to go to college." My grandmother's hands are gentle, too. She is always baking cakes and cookies, always hugging us. My mother's hands are soft. She was supposed to be an artist, but she had to go away during the first semester of art school to have my older brother. Her hands are not gentle. They are full of anger. Twice, I almost didn't wake up from one of her bouts with anger. I think my mother is frustrated. Her lovely eyes are often sad. I have learned not to talk to her when she is unhappy. Quickly, she strikes out *like a predator seeking its prey*. I would like to help her, but I cannot. Sometimes I feel so helpless. If only she would dream again. If only she would go to the Bookmobile.

(CONTINUED)

THE BOOKMOBILE (CONTINUED)

⁶Smiling a brief greeting to a bum on the corner where the liquor store is, I notice the graystone apartment building that we call home. Just one more block, and I'll be there. My feet automatically slow their pace. Here it is, the best part of walking home: Mrs. Smith's house. The reds in her garden seem redder to me, the yellows brighter and the whites more *pristine*. Or does it just seem that way because of the empty beer bottles, discarded wrappers, and the other assorted trash that litter our block? Mrs. Smith has the best flower garden I have ever seen. There are flowers everywhere; all kinds of flowers like, roses, tulips, lilies and even Birds of Paradise. No one ever goes in Mrs. Smith's yard. It's a special place. We all stop and stare though. Just looking at those beautiful roses transports me to another world. The flowers often make me smile, even when I have no reason. Mrs. Smith is also very friendly. She always smiles and waves a greeting to us. Mrs. Smith likes to make things beautiful. I am certain that she has been to the Bookmobile.

⁷"Ghetto life is really not that bad," I think to myself, as I perch on the stoop. Once I take off my school clothes, we will pop popcorn and watch Dark Shadows on TV. My mom is always there. Maybe she will be happy today. I won't tell her about my A in class because she will be busy preparing dinner. Instead, I will go to my room and stack my library books in preparation for their return. Tomorrow is the best day of the week, the day that far away places, different and exciting people, and subjects that are not taught in my school come to the neighborhood. Tomorrow I will continue to learn how other people talk, react, and resolve conflict. When I grow up, I will not live in the Ghetto. God has something better planned for me. You see, I learned a long time ago, maybe when I was eight or nine, it is He who sends the Bookmobile to my block.

VOCABULARY—"THE BOOKMOBILE"

1. metal touring contraption (¶1)
2. parable (¶1)
3. protruding (¶3)
4. escalate (¶3)
5. like a predator seeking its prey (¶5)
6. pristine (¶6)

CONTENT ANALYSIS QUESTIONS—"THE BOOKMOBILE"

1. What is Knowles's purpose?
2. What is Knowles's thesis? How does she develop and support her thesis?
3. What does the Bookmobile represent to Knowles? Why?
4. As she was growing up, did Knowles consider her family poor? Why or why not?
5. Does it seem the time Knowles spent learning "subjects not taught in my school" and "how other people talk, react, and resolve conflict" was worthwhile for her? Why or why not?
6. What advice do you think Knowles would give a teenage girl living in an inner city ghetto? What advice would you give?

APPLICATION QUESTION—"THE BOOKMOBILE"

1. Assume that your city council is looking for ways to reduce street violence. You have an opportunity to suggest programs that would interest and educate young teens. What kinds of activities would you suggest? Explain.

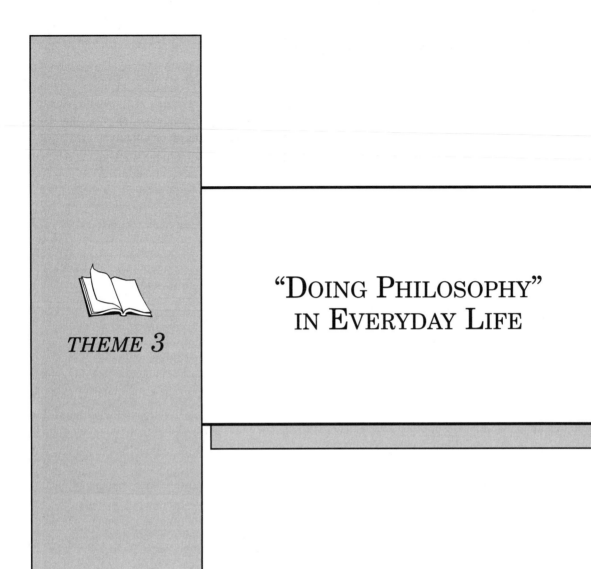

"DOING PHILOSOPHY" IN EVERYDAY LIFE

THEME 3

You're walking to your car in a shopping center parking lot. You see two people struggling and hear one of them calling for help. What do you do?

You're taking a biology course. A friend who has a later section of the class asks you for the answers to today's test. What do you do?

You're a food server in a restaurant. After closing tonight, you see one of the other food servers taking money out of the cash register. What do you do?

What you decide to do in each situation depends partially on your values. Values are your subjective reactions to the world around you. Your value system determines everything you do; how you relate to those around you, what you buy, how you vote, what television shows you watch, how you perform in school, what you do with your leisure time, how you perform your job, and who you believe is an authority.

This theme examines values with a focus on school experiences. "Beyond Materialism: Dark Hearts," a brief report on the "philosophical malaise of modern America" from research by psychologist Susan Krause Whitbourne, opens this theme. Then, "What Is Philosophy?" a textbook chapter by Dr. Thomas White, provides a framework for thinking about the basic issues of philosophy, life, and some less abstract issues.

Next, Pulitzer Prize winning author James Michener proposes that the nation's survival depends on our schools' teaching values. His article, "What Is the Secret of Teaching Values?" is followed by social studies teacher Helmut Manzl's "Feeding on Fast Food and False Values." This article describes the pressure on schools to counteract society's "undesirable values." Then Albert Yates, president of Colorado State University, proposes that "Universities Must Teach Both Facts and Values to Stave off Barbarism."

Next, in "Life Lessons," prominent travel writer Arthur Frommer shares what he's learned from forty years of traveling the globe. Then journalist Muriel Whetstone allows us a glimpse at one woman living her philosophy in "Beginning Anew."

And finally, in Guy de Maupassant's 1880s classic short story "The Diamond Necklace" we discover that "doing" philosophy has always been difficult.

Each of the readings is by a different author(s), of a different length, and requires different tasks.

STRATEGIES FOR SUCCESS

Develop a plan for each of the readings.

Determine who the author is and why he or she is writing.

Know the vocabulary the author uses.

Identify what the author is writing about.

Establish how the author develops and supports the thesis.

Recognize the author's stance.

Integrate graphic and text information.

Organize the information you need.

Decide what you can do with the author's information.

"BEYOND MATERIALISM"

BEYOND MATERIALISM: DARK HEARTS

PSYCHOLOGY TODAY STAFF

[1]A funny thing happened to psychologist Susan Krause Whitbourne. She thought she was researching how personality changes over the course of adulthood. But when she looked at the results of her *longitudinal study*, she was staring straight at the *philosophical malaise* of modern Americans.

[2]What she found was that since the mid-1960s, when she started her study, Americans have lost a sense of personal meaning. They're working more—but are far more full of despair.

(CONTINUED)

BEYOND MATERIALISM: DARK HEARTS (CONTINUED)

[3]In all three *cohorts of adults* she has added, tested, and retested over 22 years, every measure of psychosocial development improved with age. Except one. In her most recent round of testing, she was surprised to see a *"precipitous decline"* in ego integrity, a personality factor relating to wholeness, honesty, and meaning in life and to having a sense of connection with others.

[4]At first she thought it was restricted to the yuppie generation of her study—people with a "notoriously empty lifestyle focused on wealth and possessions," she reports in the *Journal of Personality and Social Psychology* (Vol. 63, No. 2). But when it turned up in all three groups at the same time, she could only conclude it reflects "a more general society-wide crisis of morality and purpose affecting adults of all ages."

[5]A professor of psychology at the University of Massachusetts, Whitbourne began testing personality variables at the University of Rochester in 1966. Students scored low on industry; they lacked "a focus on work and material success." Like others of their era, they were *disenchanted* with the work ethic.

[6]Over time, and with exposure to the real world, their personal industry began to climb. By 1988, when yet another cohort joined the study, the three groups were equally slaving away. But *ego integrity had plummeted*. All three groups were now questioning life's worth.

[7]What happened between 1977 and 1988? "People got caught up in chasing the materialistic dream. They got recognition for their achievements, yet don't feel that what they are doing matters in the larger scheme of things."

[8]The scores on life satisfaction were so low, Whitbourne says, they couldn't go any lower. She thinks people are now looking for ways to put more meaning in life. There are no data. "My belief," she confides, "is based on hope."

CONTENT QUESTIONS—"BEYOND MATERIALISM"

1. What was Whitbourne's primary finding in 1966? In 1988?
2. In general, what has happened to Americans since the mid-1960s?
3. What does Whitbourne hope is happening now?
4. Are you surprised by Whitbourne 's findings? Why or why not?
5. Identify one thing you think would help people to feel what they do matters.

VOCABULARY—"BEYOND MATERIALISM"

1. longitudinal study (¶1)
2. philosophical malaise (¶1)
3. cohorts of adults (¶3)
4. precipitous decline (¶3)
5. disenchanted (¶5)
6. ego integrity had plummeted (¶6)

"WHAT IS PHILOSOPHY?"

Thomas I. White is a professor at Rider College in New Jersey. This selection—"What Is Philosophy?"—is from *Discovering Philosophy*, Brief Edition.

C H A P T E R   1

WHAT IS PHILOSOPHY?

- What Is Philosophy About?
- The Basic Issues
- Why Studying Philosophy Is Valuable
- Previews of Coming Chapters

Most of us have either the wrong idea or no idea at all of what studying philosophy is all about. If you're feeling uncomfortable about the prospect of taking a philosophy course, perhaps the following will help ease your mind.

First off, you're probably feeling uncertain because you don't know what to expect from a philosophy course. You've already studied subjects like mathematics, history, English, foreign languages, biology, and chemistry. You may have also done a little anthropology, sociology, or political science. You have worked with computers. You know what art and music are, whether you studied them or not. Your previous experience, then, gives you some idea of what's coming in college courses on these subjects.

But philosophy? That's different. You haven't encountered anything like philosophy. So it's natural that you would be uneasy about a subject so new and different.

There is also something about philosophy and philosophers that's alien to the way average people see themselves. After you graduate, you probably expect to be a lawyer, computer programmer, sales manager, teacher, or corporate executive. You may even be able to imagine yourself as a rock-and-roll singer, or a movie star, or the president of the United States. But who wants to be a philosopher? You know the image most of us have—someone impractical, unrealistic, and absent-minded, some character with hair flying in every direction, lost in thought while pondering "great ideas."[1]

This image of the philosopher being "out of touch" is even suggested by the very word "philosophy." Literally, the word means "love of wisdom." (It

---

[1]One of the first caricatures we have of a philosopher is that of the Greek thinker Socrates. In the comedy entitled *The Clouds*, Aristophanes portrays the philosopher as someone absolutely useless and ridiculous. When we first meet Socrates in the play, he's sitting in a basket suspended in mid-air and staring at the sky.

1

2 • 1/WHAT IS PHILOSOPHY?

derives from two ancient Greek words: *philia,* "love," and *sophia,* "wisdom.") And who's going to go around saying that they "love wisdom" except somebody who's a little strange? Would anyone want to be like that?

Besides these concerns, you may also be feeling a little afraid. You don't know what to expect, and most people are afraid of the unknown. You don't know if you'll be able to do whatever it is when you've never done anything like it before, especially something so theoretical. You will find, however, that philosophy is a natural activity. In one way or another most people either already think like philosophers or can do so with just a little help. That's because when it comes down to it, as you're about to see, philosophy is a way of thinking that comes naturally. So you really have nothing to be anxious about.

WHAT IS PHILOSOPHY ABOUT?

What is **philosophy** about?[2] And how is philosophy such a natural thing to do that you're probably already doing it without knowing it?

More than anything else, philosophy is *thinking.* The main instrument that philosophers use in conducting their investigations is the human mind. They don't try to solve philosophical problems by conducting scientific, empirical research. They think. And so do you. You think just because you're human.

Of course, philosophers don't just think about whatever crosses their minds. They think about *life's most basic questions:*

- What is the purpose of life?
- Is there a God?
- How do we know the difference between right and wrong?
- Are our actions free or determined?

But who doesn't think about some very basic questions every now and then? You may not make a career out of it, but you have done it. You can't be human without doing it sometimes.

> **philosophy**   Philosophy is an active, intellectual enterprise dedicated to exploring the most fundamental questions of life.

---

[2]The first time a word listed in the glossary appears, it will be in boldface.

Philosophers also try to come up with answers to these questions, to explain them to other people, and to defend them against criticism and opposing answers. And you have surely also done some of that.

Philosophy even tries to get something positive out of uncertainty, confusion, and argument. If disagreeing philosophers can't prove which answer is right, they believe that discussion can still produce a greater understanding of the issues at stake. And you have probably had that experience as well.

"Doing" Philosophy in Real Life

Imagine, for example, that your friend Sam asks you to help him cheat on an assignment. You're torn between loyalty to a friend and uneasiness about doing something dishonest. You tell Sam you would rather not help him cheat. Sam tries to get you to change your mind, explaining that he doesn't see anything wrong with what he's asking. But you don't see it that way. The two of you get into a long discussion of cheating—why you think it is wrong, why he doesn't, why he thinks friendship is more important, and why you do not. It may surprise you to hear that this fairly typical event in the life of a college student contains all the basic elements of doing philosophy.

How you determine the difference between right and wrong is certainly a basic issue. We base all our actions on our sense of right and wrong. So the subject of your disagreement with Sam is philosophical. In your discussion with him you're forced to explain your decision, so you have to think seriously about your assumptions. In order to handle his objections, you have to think further about the issues and defend your position against his arguments. Let's say that ultimately neither one of you convinces the other. Has the discussion produced anything? Sure—a better understanding of the issue and of each other.

This is what philosophers do too. They think about basic questions and come up with answers, explain why they think that way, and defend their positions against people who disagree. Philosophers do this in the hope of either settling the matter or at least producing a greater understanding of the issues involved.

Now consider all the times you think about fundamental questions. You wonder whether God exists and if there is any way of proving it. Your best friend discovers she's pregnant and the two of you talk about whether she should have an abortion. You consider taking drugs, even though you know it's illegal. In all these cases, you're thinking about standard philosophical questions, coming to some personal answers, and growing in your understanding. The only difference between you and a professional philosopher is that he or she thinks about the same questions in a more technical, disciplined, and informed way.

So, you see, doing philosophy is one of the most common activities of life, something natural, normal, and, best of all, familiar.

4 • 1/WHAT IS PHILOSOPHY?

Philosophy—Activity, not Content

Note in particular that philosophy is an activity. Philosophy is active, not passive. It's a way of thinking, something you do, a skill you get better at as you practice, not a body of facts that you memorize. And there is a good and bad side to that.

The good news is that once you get the hang of it, philosophical thinking expands your ability to see things. It also encourages you to think independently. You can entertain all kinds of ideas or theories about an issue, then make up your own mind. No philosophy teacher will ever say to you, "I don't care what you think, just give me the correct answer to my question." How you think about the questions and about other philosophers' answers and how you explain and defend what you think is what it's all about.

Moreover, philosophers are not "authorities." They are only as good as their arguments. If their arguments are not convincing, forget it. The ancient Greek thinker Socrates may have been a great philosopher, but that doesn't mean that what he says is true. He still must convince you.

The bad news, however, is that since you probably haven't studied anything like this before, you're going to have to learn new ways of handling things. In a philosophy course, you can't fall back on memorizing the theories of great philosophers like Plato and Aristotle. You have to know what different thinkers say, but you also have to genuinely understand their ideas. And that's not all. After you think about it, you have to come up with your own reaction.

For example, do you agree or disagree with Immanuel Kant's ideas about what makes an action morally wrong? Totally? Partially? What are the strengths and weaknesses of his ideas? What would you change? Why? How would you convince Kant to change his mind? Suppose the person sitting next to you disagrees with you. How would you try to change her mind?

Philosophy is a dynamic process. That is one of the things that makes it so interesting—and hard to get used to. It isn't just learning the answers that earlier philosophers have come up with. It's also coming up with your own answers. So get used to the idea that you are about to embark on an active enterprise.

THE BASIC ISSUES

Since the subject of philosophy is the "basic issues" of life, it's not surprising that we encounter a wide range of issues when we study philosophy. Fortunately, philosophers are very logical, so philosophy has been divided into several branches, each devoted to different, but still basic, questions. What are these issues and what are the parts of philosophy?

The Most Fundamental Issues

Every philosophical question is basic. But some questions are more basic than others, and philosophy starts with those.

Reality

What's the most elementary thing you can say about yourself? That you're tall? Short? White? Black? No. That you are male, or female? Simpler than that. That you are human? Still simpler. Just that you are. What's the most fundamental characteristic of any object you can describe? Distinguishing characteristics? No. Simply that it is real. It exists. Now we've hit bedrock, because the nature of reality, or of existence, is the most basic issue we can talk about. The most fundamental philosophical question, then, is: What is the nature of *reality?*

What do we mean when we say something is "real"? What's the difference between "real" and "not real," or "imaginary"? Does something have to exist physically to be real? Or is it enough that it exists in our minds? Which are more real? Chairs and tables that present themselves to our eyes, but that will eventually wear out, break up, and be thrown out precisely because they're material objects? Or the circles and triangles that we see only with our mind's eye, which are "perfect" and haven't changed or decayed a bit since humans discovered the abstract world of mathematics thousands of years ago?

Personhood

Think again about yourself and the other things and people in your life. We've already seen that they have existence in common. They're alike in that they're real. But what makes each of these entities different from all the others? One way to account for these differences is through some distinguishing set of properties or characteristics. How are you different from this book in your hand, for example? For openers, you're alive and the book isn't. So now we're talking about the defining characteristics that make something be what it is. We're referring to what we call the "nature" or "essence" of a thing.

To narrow this down, let's focus just on human nature. What is a very basic characteristic of human beings? We're alive, but then so are all nonhuman animals, so we need something more specific. What in our life sets us apart from other living beings? Probably that each of us is a "person." This brings us to a point where we can frame another basic philosophical question: What is the essence of the special property, *personhood?*

What does it mean to be a "person"? To answer this question, use yourself as an example and contrast your kind of life with that of plants and animals. Notice that you have a particular kind of self-awareness and high intellectual abilities. You can communicate with other people. And you can control your own actions.

But are all humans "persons"? Fetuses don't have any of these characteristics, so some thinkers argue that they are not "persons" in their own right. But, then, infants cannot do most of these things either, and most of us recognize them as "persons." Furthermore, must a "person" be "human"? How about other animals? Some chimpanzees have learned sign language. Some people think that dolphins may be as intelligent as humans. And many individuals claim they've had encounters with intelligent beings from another planet. None of these entities is human, but they seem to have many characteristics and abilities that humans do. Should we think of them as "persons"?

Free Will

Consider another basic aspect of life. Think again about the most fundamental things you can say about yourself. You exist. You're alive. You're a person. Part of being a person means that you can control your actions, that is, your deeds are not merely automatic products of instinct. You have what philosophers call *free will*.

But now think about it. Sure, we all *feel* free. Yet aren't our choices influenced by our upbringing, the values we're taught, the norms provided by our culture? Perhaps some of our behavior is determined by our genetic makeup. What about the impact of our worst, irrational fears? What about the power of the unconscious mind? Perhaps you believe that God has people's lives all planned out; perhaps you believe in fate. And if the future is somehow already determined, what room is left for choice? These problems lead us to yet another basic philosophical question: How "free" are we?

Knowledge

Think back for a moment to our discussion of what makes a person. Surely one of the most important characteristics a person has is intelligence. A person can think and know things. Intellectual activity is such a basic part of human life that our species is named for this ability—*Homo sapiens* ("thinking man"). This brings us to another philosophical issue: What is involved in *knowing* something?

At first this might look like a simple question. We say we know something when we have acceptable reasons or proof for what we claim. I can say that I know that my computer is sitting in front of me because I can see it. I also know that the great English humanist Sir Thomas More died in 1535 because I've done research on More for years, and that is what the historical records show. I even know that the sum of the interior angles of every triangle that ever has or ever will exist is 180 degrees. Have I measured them all? Not very likely. How do I know it? Because this is, in fact, the definition of a triangle.

Each of these three examples involves knowledge, but each example is different. I claim to know something in each case, but the reasons I give keep changing. My first claim is based on direct sense experience. The second involves secondhand evidence, or hearsay, ultimately based on someone else's firsthand experience. And the third doesn't rely on sense experience at all. If they're all so different, do all these examples involve knowledge? The same kind of knowledge? As you see, questions about knowledge can be quite complicated.

So far our questions have focused mainly inward, on what it means to be a living person from the inside. When we turn our attention outward, however, we encounter different kinds of philosophical questions.

God, Life After Death, the Purpose of Life

What do we see when we look outside ourselves? We, and others of our kind, exist, but we're not alone. Plants and other animals also exist. So does the enormous universe that surrounds us. And if we reflect on its complexity and majesty, we've got to ask ourselves, "Where did it all come from?"

We didn't create our universe, so how did it get here? Is it the result of natural processes operating over billions or trillions of years? Or did someone create it? Are we alone in this universe, or is there a *God* as well? Not surprisingly, proofs for the existence of God have been debated by philosophers for thousands of years.

The question of God's existence raises other fundamental questions. For example, if there is a spiritual dimension to reality, does that mean that we have "souls" or "spirits" which continue to exist after our bodies wear out? Is there life after death? For that matter, have we lived other lives before this one? More people on this planet believe in reincarnation than reject the idea. Who is right?

And the idea of an afterlife, or of other lives, leads us to wonder, What is the *purpose of life*? Is it a test of some sort? If so, what counts as "passing"? Making a lot of money and becoming rich and famous? Doing some kind of important work? Devoting our lives to helping people less fortunate than ourselves? Growing personally or spiritually as much as possible? Questions of the ultimate purpose of life, then, are also common grist for the philosopher's mill.

So far we've identified the most basic questions of philosophy.

- What is the nature of "reality"?
- What is a "person"?
- How free are we?
- What can we "know" and how can we "know" it?
- Is there a God?
- What is the purpose of life?

8 • 1/WHAT IS PHILOSOPHY?

These, then, are the most fundamental, theoretical questions we ask in philosophy. But we also take up more practical issues.

Practical Issues

We've been looking at the issues raised by the simple fact that we exist (reality, personhood), that we do things (free will), and that we know (knowledge). What else is characteristic of human beings, but a little less abstract?

Standards of Conduct: Right and Wrong

When we choose what to do, we use certain standards or values to guide us. We also use these values to evaluate what other people do. Our society, like all societies, suggests some standards for our behavior, the most important of which are laws and customs. Organizations we belong to, schools we go to, churches we belong to, and companies we work for also have their rules, regulations, and policies.

But sometimes those are not enough, or they may conflict with each other. For example, even though it is illegal, many underage students use false IDs to buy liquor. Do you think they're doing something wrong? The traffic laws say you should stop at red lights and stop signs. But what should you do if you are rushing a sick friend to the hospital? Your religion tells you that sex before marriage is wrong, but you are deeply in love with someone and you don't feel that anything you do would be wrong. These ethical dilemmas lead us to yet another philosophical question: How do we separate *right* from *wrong*?

Questions about right and wrong can get as complicated as those about reality or knowledge. We need an ultimate standard of conduct. But where do we find something like that? How do you choose between two actions, both of which seem wrong to you? How would you explain the basis of your standard of right and wrong to someone who disagrees with you? Maybe your standard is influenced by your personal religious beliefs. Yet how could you convince an atheist that you were right? Even if you do have some standard for separating right from wrong, why should you act on it? Why should you do right and not do wrong? What if you can't afford to fix your car and you can steal a few hundred dollars from somebody who's rich? Is there any good reason not to steal, especially if you can get away with it?

So you see, many questions come up when we look at the everyday problem of evaluating human actions against some fundamental standard. And, it will come as no surprise, these are philosophical questions.

How Do We Organize Our Communities?

Questions of right and wrong come up because we live with other people and we need some standard for judging their conduct, as well as our own. But the fact that we live with other people in communities also creates some issues on a larger scale—and still more philosophical questions. How should decisions be made that affect the common good? Does everybody vote about every little thing? Or do you assign some of these decisions to others—that is, do you create a government? What kind of government do you want? Who gets to make the rules that everybody in the group must live by? What if the group's rules force some people to do things that they find wrong according to their personal standards? Are they entitled to disobey those rules? How do you decide if a law is "just" or not?

Other Concerns of Philosophy

We exist. We choose our actions. We know things. We evaluate what we do and what others do. We live among other people. Trying to understand and explain these most basic facts of life is what philosophy mainly does.

Yet philosophy also studies the conceptual foundations of some of the more complicated dimensions of human life—art, science, religion, law, education, artificial intelligence, genetic engineering, ethical issues in business and medicine and the other professions. In fact, the most abstract ideas of virtually every human endeavor are the domain of philosophy.

The Subject Matter of Philosophy

This quick survey of a few basic questions should give you a decent idea of what philosophy is all about. It is not some arcane study that has nothing to do with real life. It is an intellectual activity devoted to understanding the most basic dimensions of what it means to exist as a human being alone and in community with others. As such, it has everything to do with real life.

Philosophical Questions

The questions that philosophers ask are obviously varied. One thing they have in common is that all these questions arise from thinking about the fundamental aspects of life. But they also share something else that is distinctive of a philosophical question—their conceptual nature.

If I ask you if it's raining, how do you find out the answer? You look outside. And if I ask you how many students are in a particular classroom at noon on Monday? You go and count the people. In each case, you get the facts. Many questions are like this. They're answered by doing some empirical investigation. Scientific questions are empirical questions: they can be answered by "getting the facts." Questions that have factual answers are not philosophical questions.

Or what if you want to know if you can leave your car somewhere overnight without getting a ticket? You call the police. Or if you want to know what the Catholic church says about the morality of birth control? Ask a priest. In these cases, you're still getting facts, but they're facts of a different kind. There are specific answers that will settle your questions, but you must find the right person, book, or body of law that tells you what they are. You must seek the judgment of an authority. Questions like these are not philosophical questions either.

Instead, philosophical questions involve conceptual issues. Think about the account of the philosophical topics you just read. All those philosophical questions boil down to basic concepts, or principles. And that is the defining feature of a philosophical question. Reality, knowledge, right, wrong, justice, and the like are all concepts. The challenge of a philosophical investigation is exploring the principles and concepts at issue, and applying the results to situations that involve those ideas.

Philosophical "Answers"

Similarly, the "answers" to these questions share an important property that also characterizes philosophy. Because of the conceptual nature of the fundamental issues philosophy considers, philosophers can never give absolute proof that they are right.

Philosophical questions do not get "solved," as empirical questions do. The empirical question "How many pages are in this book?" has a single, correct answer; all others are wrong. But a philosophical question like "Is abortion wrong?" has more than one plausible answer. Depending on the positions taken on such debatable issues as "life," "personhood," and "rights," we can find even completely opposing arguments that are reasonable and believable. Similarly, we can make a plausible case for saying that we're free to choose anything we want whenever we want to. On the other hand, we can also make an intelligent case for saying that our sense of freedom is an illusion—that we fool ourselves into thinking we're free when our behavior is actually determined. It is simply a characteristic of philosophical issues that we fall short of absolute certainty. And this means that philosophical thinking deals more in probability and plausibility than absolute truth and falsehood.

The Parts of Philosophy

You now have an understanding of the subjects that philosophy discusses and something of the nature of philosophy. However, without realizing it, you also have acquired a sense of the primary branches of philosophy.

Very fundamental and abstract issues relating to existence in general (like the nature of reality and the existence of God) and human existence in particular (such as free will) are taken up in the part of philosophy called **metaphysics**. The ancient Greek philosopher Aristotle called this branch of philosophy "first philosophy," and that's a good way to think about it.

Metaphysics concentrates on the first or most fundamental questions we encounter when we begin studying the most basic issues of life.[3]

Another fundamental part of philosophy is theory of knowledge, or epistemology, which takes up the questions we saw above related to the nature of knowledge. "Epistemology" combines two Greek words, *epistéme* and *logos,* and literally means "the study of knowledge." *Epistéme* means "knowledge." *Logos* has many meanings, but in this context it means "the study of." The suffix "-logy" can be found at the end of many English words: "biology" (the study of life), "geology" (the study of the earth), and so on.

When we encounter the practical issues of philosophy, we move into **ethics,** or *moral philosophy,* and **political philosophy.** "Ethics" is the part of philosophy that discusses right and wrong, and the word is derived from the Greek word for "custom, habit, or character," *ethikos.* ("Moral" comes from the Latin word for "character," *mores.*) "Political philosophy" takes up the wider issues that arise from our living together, such as legitimate authority, justice, and speculation about the ideal society. Its root is *polis,* another Greek word, which means "city."

---

metaphysics   Metaphysics is the part of philosophy concerned with the most basic issues, for example, reality, existence, personhood, and freedom versus determinism. Metaphysics was originally referred to by Aristotle as "first philosophy."

epistemology   Epistemology, also called "theory of knowledge," is the part of philosophy concerned with "knowledge" and related concepts.

ethics   Ethics, also called "moral philosophy," is the part of philosophy concerned with right, wrong, and other issues related to evaluating human conduct.

political philosophy   Political philosophy is the part of philosophy that addresses the philosophical issues that arise from the fact that we live together in communities. These issues include the nature of political authority, justice, and the problem of harmonizing freedom and obligation.

---

[3] "Metaphysics" comes from two ancient Greek words, meta "after," and physika "physics." In light of contemporary usage, where "metaphysical" usually means "abstract" or "abstruse," you might think that "metaphysics" takes its name from the fact that it studies highly abstract issues "beyond the physical realm." While such questions are "metaphysical," the word is actually a historical accident. The Greek philosopher Aristotle gave a series of lectures dealing with the most basic questions in philosophy; as I mentioned, he called this "first philosophy." The treatise containing these lectures was never given a title, but after Aristotle's death his students traditionally filed it after Aristotle's lectures on nature, which the philosopher called "the physics." Thus, Metaphysics meant something more like "the scroll filed after The Physics" than "lectures on transcendental questions." That is why the best way to understand metaphysics is to remember that Aristotle called it "first philosophy," that is, think of it as the part of philosophy that asks the "first" or most basic questions.

12 • 1/WHAT IS PHILOSOPHY?

Metaphysics, epistemology, ethics, and political philosophy are the main divisions of philosophy. But given the wide range of topics that philosophers study, it should come as no surprise that there are also many important but more narrowly focused branches of philosophy, like philosophy of art, philosophy of science, and philosophy of language. Finally, in a class by itself, there is **logic,** the part of philosophy devoted to studying reason itself and the structure of arguments. Logic is the foundation on which any philosophical investigation is built, and modern philosophy of logic explores some highly technical philosophical questions.

WHY STUDYING PHILOSOPHY IS VALUABLE

So far you have seen that philosophy stems quite naturally from thinking about life's basic questions. And you have been introduced to some of those questions and to the different branches of philosophy. You should now be ready for what we're going to study in the chapters ahead.

Before we move on, however, we should address one more issue—why studying philosophy is worthwhile. Whatever you imagine you will get out of a philosophy course, let me assure you that if you work hard through this course, you will develop skills, abilities, and insights that will help you for the rest of your life.

Analytical Abilities

The skills you will pick up are easy to describe. You will develop better analytical abilities. You will handle abstract problems better. You will learn how to argue more effectively. And you will have a stronger imagination. Philosophy helps to shape in a positive way what we might call the "general cut of your mind." This is invaluable in whatever career you choose to follow. The most successful people use analysis and argument all the time. Successful people make their mark by solving difficult problems and convincing other people they're right.

In preparing this book, I asked several successful executives to tell me what they thought students should study if they wanted to succeed in business. They listed only a few technical subjects—accounting and finance, for example. (The technical end of business, they said, you learn mainly on the job.) Otherwise they suggested courses that help develop your ability to think

---

logic Logic is the part of philosophy devoted to studying reason itself and the structure of arguments.

about problems analytically and to communicate your analysis and recommendations to other people. Time and again, these executives identified philosophy as one of the most important areas you can study for learning how to think in a disciplined, analytical, and imaginative way.

Vision and Insight

The way that philosophy helps you see the world is no less real than its practical benefits to your career. Studying philosophy exposes you to a wide range of problems that you wouldn't meet otherwise. It simply lets you see more of the world. It stretches your imagination. It challenges you to come up with your own answers to tough issues that do not have ready-made solutions. If you take it seriously, philosophy teaches you different ways of looking at the world.

Studying philosophy helps you to develop insight into some of life's great puzzles and to fashion your own vision of what life is all about. As you go through life, you will be challenged all along the way to make decisions about who you are and what's important to you. What will you do with your life? What career will you pursue? Will you marry? And if so, what kind of person? Will you have children? How will you rear them? What will you tell them is important? What are you willing to do for money and success? How will you cope with the crises you will encounter in your own life or in the lives of those you love—illness, accidents, problems on the job or at home, death? Philosophy helps you develop a sense of what life is all about and where you're going.

In fact, Socrates, one of the first great philosophers, thought that philosophy is the single most important element in making our lives worthwhile. "The unexamined life," he said, "is not worth living." The habit of thinking philosophically lets us scrutinize our values, our goals, and the means we've chosen to achieve them, and it helps us keep our lives on course. In Socrates' mind, at least, philosophy makes it possible for us to control our own destiny. And that's no small matter.

As you now know, philosophy is simply thinking systematically about life's most basic issues. When it comes down to it, there is no way that thinking about these questions cannot make you better prepared for your life.

PREVIEWS OF COMING CHAPTERS

Now that you have a sense of what philosophy is, you're ready to plunge in yourself. What's coming up in the rest of this book? We cannot cover every important aspect of such a large subject in an introductory text. We will, however, talk about most of philosophy's basic topics and a few specialized ones.

We'll start preparing ourselves by "tuning the instrument," that is, the mind.

14   • 1/WHAT IS PHILOSOPHY?

Since we do philosophy by thinking, the best place to begin is by studying some of the "rules of reason" alluded to earlier. Chapter 2, "Philosophical Thinking," will introduce you to the ground rules regarding logic and critical thinking.

In the next section, "Exploring the Basics of Who We Are and Dealing with Others," we look at some of the most fundamental characteristics of our existence. We start with two chapters that consider opposing points of view about the issue of human freedom. In "The Case for Freedom" (Chapter 3), we look at the case for free will, and we explore the arguments in favor of determinism in Chapter 4 ("The Case for Determinism"). Then we examine basic issues related to our living with other people. We look at how philosophers talk about "right" and "wrong" in Chapter 5, "Right and Wrong." In Chapter 6, "Why Virtue?", we ask why we should bother doing what's right. And Chapter 7, "Democracy," inquires into the underpinnings of the political system we live under.

In the chapters that make up "The World of Theory," we explore basic philosophical issues of a more abstract nature. We start with absolute bedrock—the nature of reality—in Chapter 8. Chapter 9, "What Is Knowledge?", looks at the basic ways philosophers have looked at knowledge. In Chapter 10, "Does God Exist?", we examine the main "proofs" for the existence of God. In Chapter 11, "The Purpose of Life: Marx and Buddha," we tackle one of life's most perplexing questions as seen through the eyes of two very different philosophers. We conclude with three specialized topics in "Emerging Issues." Chapter 12, "Scientific Explanations of Reality," looks at philosophical issues raised by the ideas of theoretical physicists about the nature of the world. Then we consider some philosophical questions raised by some fascinating psychological theories that women and men have unique ways of thinking about knowledge and of engaging ethical problems (Chapter 13, "Psychology, Gender, and Thinking"). And in Chapter 14 ("Is a Dolphin a Person?"), we examine the philosophical implications of the remarkable discoveries that scientists have made about dolphins.

This book, then, will give you a basic but solid understanding of what philosophy is all about. It will serve as a road map for what many of us feel is one of life's most exciting, enriching, and engaging adventures—discovering philosophy. You will see new sights, explore new worlds, expand your horizons, and, most importantly, learn much about yourself. As with any journey, what you get out of it is mainly up to you. But if you give philosophy half a chance, it just might take you to a place you never want to leave.

MAIN POINTS OF CHAPTER 1

1. Philosophy is a conceptual discipline which focuses on life's most basic questions. It is the activity of thinking about these issues yourself, not simply understanding what philosophers from the past have said about these questions.

2. The most fundamental issues that philosophy investigates are highly abstract: the nature of reality, free will, knowledge, the existence of God, and the purpose of life. Philosophy also addresses more practical issues: right and wrong, and the organization of societies.

3. The main branches of philosophy include: logic, metaphysics, epistemology, ethics, and political philosophy.

4. Studying philosophy will strengthen your analytical abilities, your capacity for abstract thought, and your ability to argue.

DISCUSSION QUESTIONS

1. Have you already thought about any of the philosophical questions identified in this chapter? What spurred this? Another course? A debate about a controversial issue? An experience in your life? Your own proclivity to think about life?

2. Later chapters of this book will explore in depth the main philosophical issues identified above. But try your hand at taking a position and fashioning an argument on any of the following questions: How free are our actions? What makes an action morally wrong? Does God exist?

3. What do you expect to get out of studying philosophy? What will make it worth all the time and effort you will put in? Will just a good grade do it? If philosophy doesn't help you become more successful in your career, does that mean it has no value?

SUGGESTED READINGS

A superb source for detailed information about almost every philosopher and philosophical issue is *The Encyclopedia of Philosophy,* edited by Paul Edwards, 8 volumes (New York: Macmillan and the Free Press, 1967). For an excellent history of philosophy, see F. C. Copleston, *History of Philosophy,* 8 volumes (Garden City, NY: Doubleday, 1965). For a popular account of the development of philosophy, consult Will Durant, *The Story of Philosophy* (New York: Pocket Books, 1953).

"WHAT IS THE SECRET OF TEACHING VALUES?"

A Pulitzer Prize winner, best-selling author James Michener has also been awarded the U.S. Medal of Freedom. This selection—"What Is the Secret of Teaching Values?"—is from *Life* (April 1991).

WHAT IS THE SECRET OF TEACHING VALUES?

IN AN INCREASINGLY COMPLEX SOCIETY, OLD WAYS ARE NO LONGER GUARANTEED TO WORK

JAMES A. MICHENER

[1]Values are the emotional rules by which a nation governs itself. Values summarize the accumulated folk wisdom by which a society organizes itself. And values are the precious reminders that individuals obey to bring order and meaning into their personal lives. Without values, nations, societies and individuals can pitch straight to hell.

[2]I was a tough, undisciplined youngster, suspended three times from school, twice from college. I was a vagabond at 14, rode freight trains in my late teens. But because I had accumulated an iron-clad set of values, I was able to hack out a fairly acceptable life. In my day—and I am 84—young people acquired their system of values first in the home. I was raised in a terribly broken home, which never had enough money for normal living. But I had an adoptive mother who took in abandoned children, who worked around the clock, and who read to us at night. By the time I was five, I had the great rhythm of the English language echoing in my mind.

[3]I learned values in church, in school and on the street. I learned them through travel, military service and the movies. I acquired values through athletics, where a high-school coach took me, fatherless and *without a rudder*, and pointed me in the right direction. I learned values in the library and, in fact, it could be that my intellectual life was saved by the little library opened in our town of Doylestown, Pa. about the time I was seven. Records recently recovered showed that the first two cards taken out were issued to Margaret Mead and me. What a start for us; what a start for the library.

[4]Modern kids, regrettably, face extreme pressures that I simply didn't. This is a more complex world and the youngster of the 1990s absorbs a heavy hammering. There's an assault from all sides by news that's threatening; there's been a break-down of traditional safeguards like the family. Stanford University professor John Gardner, the founder of Common Cause, notes, however, that after many years of exploring "the limits of living without ethics, a lot of people are saying, 'It won't work.' I think there's a movement back toward commitment to shared goals." If so, it's mighty welcome.

[5]What should these goals be? Nationally, there must be a drive for public service, to see society protected and moved ahead. There must be encouragement to blow the whistle when something goes wrong.

[6]Individually, we must develop compassion, a willingness to work, loyalty to family and friends and organizations, the courage to face temporary defeat and not lose forward motion. I think we must learn fairness and honesty in economic matters. And we've got to keep reviewing our value decisions from decade to decade. You're never home free just because you went one way one time.

[7]Adults can keep updating their value systems from the best of what they read and see on television—and from the very fine adult study programs I've observed in places as diverse as Alaska, Maine and Florida. For young people, the home still ought to be the cradle of all values, but unfortunately a staggering proportion of them do not live in stable homes. It is thoughtless beyond imagination for older people to say rigidly, "The child must learn his or her values at home" when there is no home. Some substitute must be found.

(CONTINUED)

WHAT IS THE SECRET OF TEACHING VALUES? (CONTINUED)

[8]Religious training? It would be wonderful if every child had the warm, comforting experience I had in my Sunday school, with its songs, its stories, its bags of candy at the holiday, but many are denied that. And while religion is an admirable teacher for those connected to it, it is a silent voice for those who are not.

[9]The school is the only agency legally established by organized society and supported by taxation whose sole job it is to teach the child the knowledge, the skills and the values required for a successful adult life within the bounds of society. Its *task is formidable*, its achievement when things work well—that is, when teachers, children and parents unite in a common effort—can be magnificent. I know, for I attended such a school and taught in several. But it is obvious that today most schools fall far short of that ideal. They seem to *stultify intelligence*, not enhance it. Their *deficiencies are deplorable*, for the average student can spend twelve years in them and learn little, while gifted students are not challenged or helped to achieve at the maximum.

[10]I doubt that I could teach in a modern school, and for good reason. In my day parents and administrators both supported my efforts to be the best teacher possible; today it seems that teachers are not supported by anyone, and I doubt that I could fight undefended. Yet, even those of us who brood about the failure of schools must rely on them to help students build ethical codes and value systems. We must encourage the schools to demonstrate to a child that fair play pays off. That kindliness to peers pays off. That fairness in giving grades is taking place. The child has to see all this going on. We must show, as well as tell, what good values are all about.

[11]Young people these days are thrown into a hot-house of competition and social exchange that test their decision-making skills rather strenuously. The peer pressure I had to put up with was relatively simple. A boy would gain access to a jalopy and expect the rest of us to tag along on a joy ride. Today, there are drugs and gangs and unprecedented violence. There is the *incessant influence of TV*, heightening peer pressure to regard fashion and style, for example, as the highest values to which a *young person can aspire*.

[12]What television offers is so enticing. There was nothing in my youth to compare with its power. Statistics show that the eight or ten hours a week my generation of kids spent reading books are superseded by the 30 hours modern kids spend at the television set. The difference produces a radically different set of values. Beyond the *distorted consumerism*, there is an appalling amount of violence. Each week on TV I see endless shootings, stabbings and gruesome deaths. At Halloween I see sadism, abuse of women and slaughter for the fun of it. Young people cannot feed on such a diet without its having a *deleterious effect*, and studies that purport to prove otherwise are rubbish.

[13]I am disturbed by the *demeaning way* television depicts the American school. In too many shows, teachers are comic or pathetic and a student who works hard at his lessons is a wimp or a nerd. With so many people needing to rely on schools as the place to learn values, television could be of critical service to the future of our nation by rediscovering respect for the school. And schools, in turn, should direct youngsters to the best of television, to the portion of TV in which the disabled get support, racism is decried, minorities are depicted as heroes and heroines, and *patriotism is extolled* and rewarded. If young viewers select programs to ensure a mix of good with the violent and vicious, they can find material which illuminates the fight of the American people for justice and a decent society. Pressure can be—must be—mounted to promote the best, not the worst, of TV.

[14]As a young man I was taught to treat all races with justice, and I wrote numerous books testifying to that belief. I was taught that loyalty to one's nation was an obligation, and I have seen men who dabbled in treason come to mournful ends. I was taught the good citizen pays his taxes, supports schools, libraries and museums, and much of my adult life has centered on such activity. It was drummed into me that one looked after his own health and that of others, and I have tried to do so. At all levels of my education and upbringing I was advised to cling to good people and shun the bad, and I have tried. I realize there are considerations and pressures for young people today that did not exist for me—among them, drugs, AIDS and nuclear weapons. Yet, the values I learned must endure—and be taught—as the foundation for the America of tomorrow. They must be taught in the home, in religious training, in the Boy Scouts and Girl Scouts, in Little League, in the media. And most critically, as a guarantee that everyone will be exposed to them, they must be taught in school.

CONTENT QUESTIONS—"WHAT IS THE SECRET OF TEACHING VALUES?"

TRUE OR FALSE

If the statement is false, rewrite it to make it true.

1. People and society cannot function without shared values.
2. Today's young people spend approximately the same number of hours watching television as Michener's generation spent reading.
3. Nationally, there appears to be a movement back toward a commitment to shared goals.
4. Value systems should be reviewed and updated.
5. Michener has always been rich and successful.

COMPLETION

6. Where did Michener learn his values?
7. What does Michener think two of the nation's shared goals should be?
8. What does Michener think six individual goals should be?
9. What are three sources adults can draw on to help them update their values?
10. What are four of Michener's fundamental values?

VOCABULARY—"WHAT IS THE SECRET OF TEACHING VALUES?"

1. without a rudder (¶3)
2. task is formidable (¶9)
3. stultify intelligence (¶9)
4. deficiencies are deplorable (¶9)
5. incessant influence of TV (¶11)
6. young person can aspire (¶11)
7. distorted consumerism (¶12)
8. deleterious effect (¶12)
9. demeaning way (¶13)
10. patriotism is extolled (¶13)

CONTENT ANALYSIS QUESTIONS—"WHAT IS THE SECRET OF TEACHING VALUES?"

1. What is Michener's purpose?
2. What is Michener's thesis?
3. Explain what Michener means by "We must show, as well as tell, what good values are all about." Do you agree or disagree? Explain your answer.

4. Although Michener says "the home ought to be the cradle of all values," why does he think some substitute must be found? Do you agree or disagree? Explain your answer.

5. Why doesn't Michener think he could teach in a modern school? Do you agree or disagree with him? Do you think you could teach in a modern school? Explain.

APPLICATION QUESTIONS—"WHAT IS THE SECRET OF TEACHING VALUES?"

1. Assume that you have been asked by one of your professors to work with a committee preparing recommendations for parents on "what's good, and not so good, to watch on television." What type of programming would you recommend as "good" and "not so good"? Explain your rationale.

2. Assume that the local elementary school announces it is going to teach an "Ethics and Values in America" unit in all classes in all grades. How would you decide whether to be for or against the unit? Once you decided, what constructive steps would you take to convince school officials of your point of view?

"FEEDING ON FAST FOOD AND FALSE VALUES"

Helmut Manzl is a social science teacher at Oakville-Trafalgar High School, Oakville, Ontario, Canada. This selection—"Feeding on Fast Food and False Values"—was condensed from *Education Digest* 55 (January 1990).

FEEDING ON FAST FOOD AND FALSE VALUES

CAN STUDENTS OVERCOME INSTANT GRATIFICATION?

HELMUT MANZL

[1]Schools are under great pressure to counteract the hidden curriculum promoted by the social environment. Today, many students have unrealistic attitudes and expectations as a result of such sources of popular culture as the electronic media, advertising, and fast food. This has led to boredom, a *degeneration in work habits*, and a high dropout rate.

[2]The content of television programs places unrealistic expectations on schools and teachers. Programming is based on fast action, excitement, and glamour. Teachers are unable to compete. Students often have difficulty making the transition from the slick television world to the more routine, matter-of-fact daytime world of education.

(CONTINUED)

FEEDING ON FAST FOOD AND FALSE VALUES (CONTINUED)

[3]But it is also the process of interacting with a medium that shapes us. With the *advent* of cable systems, videotape, and remote channel changers, television offers a vast selection of programs, and this has considerable impact on how children approach learning. Their expectations for change and manipulation have been heightened by the media experience. Today's learner has a shorter attention span and a lower threshold of boredom than students from previous generations. Student boredom can often be *attributed to preconceived notions* about what should be going on in real life, based on television experience.

[4]Computers also affect how students learn, giving them a greater sense of control over the pace, content, and direction of learning. Schools do not follow that same *regimen*. Classrooms housing 30 or more students do not lend themselves to programming demands. Few teachers can give individual students the kind of undivided attention extended by the computer.

[5]The educational system cannot duplicate the electronic world outside. The increasingly obvious learning problems with which many students must cope do not stem from some inborn learning disability but from the incompatibility between the electronic environment and the classroom.

[6]But there are other equally powerful environmental messengers affecting the attitudes of young people. All around them, they receive messages that one's needs will be *instantly gratified*. From hamburgers to microwaves, from remote channel changers to computers, "fast" or "instant" have become important words in the student vocabulary.

[7]At McDonald's fast-food outlets, hamburgers are ready in 7.5 seconds, served with *perpetual smiles*. Television ads promise pizza delivery in 30 minutes or less and quick relief for a headache or other discomfort. Department stores promote total customer satisfaction. Dissatisfied patrons are told they can return products for a complete refund.

[8]This *subordination of trade* to the whims of the buyer falters beyond the marketplace. Students are well versed in their consumer rights and freedoms: They drop out of school and quit courses with the same frequency with which they would exchange an unacceptable garment or stereo.

[9]In schools, the instant gratification mentality translates into lack of application and hard work. Schools just seem to go too slowly. Many students believe they are entitled to fast, painless education. Trying harder to stay in school or working to meet the academic requirements of a course escapes many young minds *predisposed to consumerism*.

[10]Other equally powerful forces shape the attitudes of teenagers. Major credit card companies promise that everything is within the cardbearer's reach. No real effort is required to acquire even the most *coveted* consumer items.

[11]This message is not lost on young people. What they are often unaware of, however, is a lesson that many adults have learned the hard way: Instant gratification usually has to be paid off later, with interest. The motto of the credit card world is "Fun first, pay later." But the opposite is true in virtually all meaningful endeavors. The debt, in terms of work or energy expended, must be paid up front, and the gratification or payoff comes later, in the form of a job, a promotion, or a profit.

[12]What thus emerges is the attitude that one is entitled to goods and services whether one has the means to acquire them or not. The doctrine of entitlement runs contrary to the values of hard work, saving, and postponement of gratification. Success comes through struggle and hard work, and, in order to achieve, one must be prepared to compete in the social and economic arena.

[13]The Xerox machine may yet become an apt symbol for North American youth. Teachers are all too ready to fall into lockstep conformity while originality is sacrificed to the photocopy mentality engineered by the fashion industry and advertising.

[14]One of the principal reasons for the percentage of high school students who have part-time jobs is the need that young people feel to compete in our consumer-oriented society. They frequently hold down a part-time job because the youth culture places inordinate stress on money, and they want to fit in.

[15]The end result of this is a generation of followers. In a world where substance is subordinated to image, the designer-label generation equates status not with worthwhile achievement but with material gain.

(CONTINUED)

FEEDING ON FAST FOOD AND FALSE VALUES (CONTINUED)

[16]Teenagers and young adults may have an entirely unrealistic set of expectations. Inordinate numbers of young people think they will have a high-paying job and will soon be driving a luxury car, living in an expensive home, and spending large chunks of time on leisure activities.

[17]Our electronic and mechanized society tends to *supplant* qualitative judgment in favor of quantitative judgment. This is a most unfortunate attitude to take into the highly competitive career market where the doctrine of entitlement breaks down. Never before have so many young people competed for jobs and university and graduate school positions. Many universities have responded by raising their entrance standards. Likewise, job promotions are becoming more difficult to attain as competition intensifies.

[18]One of the most debilitating aspects of the hidden curriculum is that it requires little communication. Instant bank-tellers, fast-food outlets, drive-through services, television, and computers require a very limited amount of speech or no speech at all. But in the world of employment, communication skills will be even more important in the future.

[19]Parents, teachers, and educational administrators will be increasingly called upon to counteract the vocal isolation of the drive-through world in which children live. In the next 20 years, given the shift from an industrial to an information society, the majority of workers will be occupied with the creation, processing, and distribution of information.

[20]In the future, we will be compelled to challenge in some systematic way the pervasive environmentally generated values and attitudes to which children are daily exposed. If we fail to do so, no amount of curriculum shuffling will bring students closer to a sound education.

CONTENT QUESTIONS—"FEEDING ON FAST FOOD AND FALSE VALUES"

TRUE OR FALSE

If the statement is false, rewrite it to make it true.

1. Today's students have about the same attention span as students in previous generations.
2. The media may be giving teenagers and young adults a very unrealistic set of expectations about their world.
3. Instant gratification means getting what you want when you want it.
4. In the world of employment, communication skills will be even more important in the future.
5. Credit cards often encourage people to play first and pay later.

COMPLETION

6. What is the social environment's hidden message?
7. What are three "powerful forces" that shape the attitudes of teenagers?
8. What is the "lesson many adults have learned the hard way"?
9. Why does Manzl think so many high school students have jobs?
10. What is the "photocopy mentality"? Give an example of it.

VOCABULARY—"FEEDING ON FAST FOOD AND FALSE VALUES"

1. degeneration in work habits (¶1)
2. advent (¶3)
3. attributed to preconceived notions (¶3)
4. regimen (¶4)
5. instantly gratified (¶6)
6. perpetual smiles (¶7)
7. subordination of trade (¶8)
8. predisposed to consumerism (¶9)
9. coveted (¶10)
10. supplant (¶17)

CONTENT ANALYSIS QUESTIONS—"FEEDING ON FAST FOOD AND FALSE VALUES"

1. What is Manzl's purpose?
2. What is Manzl's thesis?
3. Does Manzl use primarily facts or opinions to support and develop his thesis? Give two examples to support your answer.
4. Explain what Manzl means by the "doctrine of entitlement." Do you agree or disagree that such a doctrine exists with Americans? Why?
5. Do you agree or disagree with Manzl that today's youth have "fast food values"? Explain your answer.

APPLICATION QUESTIONS—"FEEDING ON FAST FOOD AND FALSE VALUES"

1. Assume that a good friend of yours asks you to talk with her twelve-year-old son. She is concerned because his grades are dropping and he's cutting classes. He tells you that school is boring and doesn't have anything to do with "real" life. What do you say to him?
2. Assume that the professor in one of your required classes spends every minute of every class period lecturing in a monotone voice. You've been spending most of your time complaining to classmates or falling asleep. Now, however, you decide you want to take a positive approach to learn the information. What do you do?

"UNIVERSITIES MUST TEACH BOTH FACTS AND VALUES TO STAVE OFF BARBARISM"

Dr. Yates is president of Colorado State University, Fort Collins, Colorado, and chancellor of the CSU system. This selection—"Universities Must Teach Both Facts and Values to Stave off Barbarism"—is from *The Denver Post*.

UNIVERSITIES MUST TEACH BOTH FACTS AND VALUES TO STAVE OFF BARBARISM

ALBERT C. YATES

[1]Some forty years ago, as a boy of 10 or 11, I strayed some distance from my home. The unfamiliar surroundings seemed like an unknown, safe place where I could do as I pleased—and so I misbehaved. Unknown to me, I was watched. By the time I arrived home, my mother knew of my whereabouts and behavior—and I paid.

[2]During those times, our neighborhood *manifested and nurtured* the values we learned at home. There were accepted community standards of behavior which children were expected to uphold. We learned that if we crossed the line—if we strayed too far—there was a community of adults who had their eyes on us and were willing to step in and reinforce our parents' values.

[3]The world for most of us is quite a different place now, changed by a redefinition of family, an increasingly mobile society and the contracting boundaries of our neighborhoods. Community standards are more ambiguous, less easy to define.

[4]As a result of these dramatic cultural shifts, expectations of and demands on elementary and secondary schoolteachers have changed over the past two decades as well. A few decades ago, teachers accepted the reinforcement of parents' standards as part of their responsibility. Now, teachers often are expected to introduce children to the values and standards of behavior *requisite to membership* in a civil society.

[5]At the same time, changes of a different kind have occurred in our system of higher education. Once, under the philosophy of *in loco parentis*, universities acknowledged an obligation to monitor and discipline students as their parents might—a practice correctly abandoned during the social upheaval of the 1960s.

[6]Since that time, higher education has evolved effectively to meet the needs of a changing world in a host of important areas—technology transfer, educational access, research, economic development, extended studies and more—but with one notable exception. We have failed to address as well as we might questions critical to the shaping of our humanity. What, for example, is the academy's role in directing, or reacting to, the changing social fabric of our country? What level of responsibility should be assumed by our colleges and universities in *inculcating and refining values*? In preparing our graduates for citizenship? As higher education strives to regain the public trust, our institutions must become more certain of their responses to such questions. I don't pretend to have the answers, but some things are clear. We must resurrect the notion that universities play a critical role in developing human beings, and that our institutions themselves have an active part to play in determining the course of future societal events.

[7]In a 1981 essay, Colorado State Professor Willard Eddy warned of the danger of universities graduating students who are highly skilled in technical fields but lack an essential humanity. "Decency, civility, respect for others, are not stored in libraries or computers," he wrote. "Each generation comes into the world with more potential for becoming barbarians than for becoming saints. Consequently…a decent society is not easily sustained."

[8]No institution is better positioned to sustain such a society than a university. These are places which, by their very nature, are expected to model the highest values of civilization.

[9]For the public university, discussion and expression of values seem to occur in two contexts: The first is within the academic program itself; the second is within the example set by the university through the general conduct of its activities. These two settings are not unrelated and often at odds. But this tension between them—brought on by our quest for objectivity and dispassionate discourse on the one hand and our need to stand for something on the other—is a necessary part of the university's search for truth.

[10]Students come to college, in large measure, unshaped and uncertain. But they come with strong beliefs and assumptions, looking to the university for knowledge and guidance. Just as we expect a kindergarten teacher to educate young children in those simple rules that teach discipline and good behavior—say "please" and "thank you," don't cut in line, respect others' belongings—we should expect college professors to help students achieve understanding at a higher level of the finest attributes of a civilized society: the ability to act fairly, reason plainly, express oneself gracefully, behave honestly, define a position worth defending, and accept responsibility for actions taken.

(CONTINUED)

UNIVERSITIES MUST TEACH BOTH FACTS AND VALUES
TO STAVE OFF BARBARISM (CONTINUED)

[11]As well, our society expects university graduates to be intelligent people. J. Martin Klotsche, former chancellor of the University of Wisconsin-Milwaukee, once described an intelligent person as "one who has learned 'to choose between'. One who knows that good is better than evil, that confidence should supersede fear, that love is superior to hate, that gentleness is better than cruelty, forbearance (more noble) than intolerance, compassion (greater) than arrogance, and truth more virtuous than ignorance."

[12]A university's job is to help its students acquire the knowledge to choose wisely and to understand the consequences of their choices. In our classrooms and on our plazas, we must permit all manner of thought and debate, no matter how controversial or offensive. And within such forums we must be especially guarded in our advocacy of one position over another.

[13]But we still can do our very best to say, "Here are the results of choosing one set of actions over another. Here is what happened when someone embraced this course, and here is what happened to someone who chose a different path."

[14]In educating people to choose wisely, the *true mettle* of a college or university is *gleaned through* the *aspirations of its general education* program. Father Theodore Hesburgh, former president of Notre Dame University, captured the ideal in *characteristic eloquence* as he reviewed the possibilities of the curriculum:

[15]Language and mathematics stress clarity, precision, and style if well-taught; literature gives an insight into that vast human arena of good and evil, love and hate, peace and violence as real living human options. History gives a vital record of mankind's success and failure, hopes and fears, the heights and the depths of human endeavors pursued with either heroism or depravity but always depicting real virtue or the lack of it. Music and art purvey a sense of beauty seen or heard, a value to be preferred to ugliness or cacophony. The physical sciences are a symphony of world order, so often unsuccessfully sought by law, but already achieved by creation, a model challenging man's freedom and creativity. The social sciences show man at work, theoretically and practically, creating his world.

[16]Such values, expressed and debated throughout the academic program, offer the substance to permit an assessment of how the university itself chooses to conduct its business. Any university has a set of values it embraces and displays in decision-making, aesthetics, concerns about safety, about people and about funding—even in the programs and courses of study it offers.

[17]The emphasis universities place upon qualities such as service, community, integrity and decorum are *manifestations of* the things we treasure.

[18]Interpreted in this way, our universities model (or should) for their students—and others—principles and standards deserving of *preservation and emulation*. In the ideal, *faculty and staff elaborate the culture broadly articulated by the institution*. Through their behavior in the classroom and laboratory, as well as through personal contact with students, faculty can encourage students to embrace simple truths, like those which Klotsche named, which we know to be right and good.

[19]It is most important that the university be preserved as a forum for speech and debate that is unconstrained and unabashed. During their time on campus, students need to feel safe to venture into unknown territory, to push against the boundaries of what they know and draw conclusions based on their judgment and experience.

[20]But they should do so within the context of an environment which is itself secure and well-founded.

[21]The world is a different place from that in which many of us grew up. Those neighbors who watched me wander from home and get into mischief were part of a system of needed oversight and reinforcement of important things learned, but not yet owned.

[22]Much has now changed and new systems must be invented: Our colleges and universities surely must play a crucial role.

CONTENT QUESTIONS—"UNIVERSITIES MUST TEACH BOTH FACTS AND VALUES TO STAVE OFF BARBARISM"

TRUE OR FALSE

If the statement is false, rewrite it to make it true.

1. When Yates was growing up, neighbors felt a responsibility for neighbors.
2. Yates would like to see the university return to the philosophy of *in loco parentis*.
3. All colleges and universities have a set of values they believe and use.
4. Yates thinks some controversial topics should be off-limits on college and university campuses.
5. Yates thinks it is important that higher education be a forum for free speech and debate.

COMPLETION

6. What four changes does Yates say have made the world a different place today than when he grew up?
7. What does *in loco parentis* mean?
8. What six "attributes of a civilized society" does Yates think professors should help students achieve?
9. How does Yates think professors can help students achieve these "attributes of a civilized society"?
10. What is the importance of a college or university's general education program?

VOCABULARY—"UNIVERSITIES MUST TEACH BOTH FACTS AND VALUES TO STAVE OFF BARBARISM"

1. manifested and nurtured (¶2)
2. requisite to membership (¶4)
3. inculcating and refining values (¶6)
4. true mettle (¶14)
5. gleaned through (¶14)
6. aspirations of its general education (¶14)
7. characteristic eloquence (¶14)
8. manifestations of (¶17)
9. preservation and emulation (¶18)
10. faculty and staff elaborate the culture broadly articulated by the institution (¶18)

CONTENT ANALYSIS QUESTIONS—"UNIVERSITIES MUST TEACH BOTH FACTS AND VALUES TO STAVE OFF BARBARISM"

1. What is Yates's purpose?

2. What is Yates's thesis?

3. Explain what Eddy means by "Decency, civility, respect for others, are not stored in libraries or computers." What kind of advice do you think he would give professors?

4. In what ways do you agree or disagree with Klotsche's description of an intelligent person? Explain.

5. Yates writes, "A university's job is to help its students acquire the knowledge to choose wisely and to understand the consequences of their choices." In what ways do you agree or disagree? Explain.

APPLICATION QUESTIONS—"UNIVERSITIES MUST TEACH BOTH FACTS AND VALUES TO STAVE OFF BARBARISM"

1. Assume that your campus has an unofficial "soapbox corner" where students gather between classes to talk about events and issues. Recently there have been student complaints that the topics and language are offensive. You're now on a committee to decide what, if any, rules and regulations should be established. What is your personal point of view? How would you proceed?

2. Assume that as part of your English course you will to be required to participate in an computer-networked electronic forum each week. Your professor asks your class what, if any, rules and regulations it wants to govern the topics and responses. How do you respond? Would your stance change if some student responses consistently contained views or language you found objectionable?

"LIFE LESSONS"

Arthur Frommer is a prolific travel writer. His observations, comments, and evaluations of people and places are read throughout the world. This selection—"Life Lessons"—is from *Travel Holiday*.

LIFE LESSONS

WHAT I'VE LEARNED FROM 40 YEARS OF TRAVELING THE GLOBE

ARTHUR FROMMER

[1]To a hundred countries and over millions of miles, I've traveled for some 40 years, and now I am a changed person because of it. On every trip to everywhere, just being in unfamiliar surroundings, among new and different people, alters one's consciousness and creates new beliefs—like these:

We Are All Alike

[2]I am in the dark, dung hut of a Masai family in eastern Africa. Through an interpreter, the woman of the house tells me that she hopes to learn to read. And why? So that she can study a handbook on raising children. I am sitting cross-legged on a tatami mat in the apartment of a young Japanese couple. Their daughter, they tell me, is complaining about the harshness of her first-grade teacher. I am aboard a houseboat on the Nile. The owner is enthusing about a recent film.

[3]Travel has taught me that despite differences in dress and language and condition, all the world's people are essentially alike. We have the same urges and concerns; we yearn for the same things. And those who *patronize others* or regard them as funny or backward are foolish indeed; they have not yet learned the lessons of travel.

We All Think Ourselves Virtuous

[4]At the bar of an Amsterdam café I am talking with a Dutch friend. Last night, he tells me, a nationwide telethon raised the equivalent of some 80 million dollars for cancer research. "Only in Holland," he says, "would there be such an outpouring." We all consider ourselves the best; we all believe in the superiority of our own country and culture. How many times have you heard politicians proclaim this or that nation to be the finest on earth? Travel rids you of that *smug chauvinism*; it exposes you to the finest in every land and makes you distinctly uneasy when you later return home and hear people proclaiming their own nation to be better than others.

We Are Responsible for One Another

[5]It is the early 1980s. Dancing down a broad boulevard in Zagreb is a succession of laughing, gaily clad groups gathered there for a festival of Yugoslavia's national folk dances. From the curb, I watch Muslims and Christians, Bosnians, Croatians, and Serbs, celebrating in complete harmony. Now, years later, and because of travel, I remember them as distinct human presences, not as abstractions; I get almost physically ill when I read of the violence among them. I feel the same intimate bond with the Protestants and Catholics of Northern Ireland, whose cities I visited at the height of the troubles, and with the people of both Egypt and Israel, where I once led groups of tourists. Travel makes it impossible to ignore the sufferings of others simply because they are far away; it erases distance and transforms you into a more sensitive citizen of the world, the only kind of person who can contribute to peace.

(*CONTINUED*)

LIFE LESSONS (CONTINUED)

We Grow When We Confront Our Opposite

[6]I am at a residential yoga community in Lenox, Massachusetts, trying to open my mind to non-linear thinking. And though the guru's speech is at odds with my usual rationalism, I find myself enjoying it and savoring this clash of new ideas. I am visiting a Danish "folk high school" for adults. And though my middle-aged dignity is offended, I join in the breakfast song called "We Greet the Dawn" and find myself feeling less repressed, more open, than I've been in decades. I am at a personal-growth center on the West Coast, in a class of encounter therapy, where I am told that I must clasp hands with the elderly gentleman opposite me, look deeply into his eyes, wish him well, and give him a bear hug. While I am *initially loath to do so*, I then feel a surge of shame at being so emotionally controlled that I cannot offer *sympathy and succor* to a fellow human being. Travel exposes you to ideas, lifestyles, theologies, and philosophies that challenge your most cherished beliefs. It takes you out of a setting in which everyone thinks the same and sends you into the unknown, to your opposites, your *presumed adversaries*. You rethink your assumptions; your horizons expand; your life takes on new dimensions.

There Is No Single Solution for Human Problems

[7]I am walking the streets of Hong Kong, past signs for herbal medicines and acupuncturists, and all around are millions of people perfectly content with these approaches to personal health so different from our own. I am lying in a copper bathtub filled with naturally carbonated water in a bathing establishment in the Belgian city of Spa. And although my mind tells me that, scientifically speaking, water cures are rubbish, I feel something happening to my body and suspect that the 300 million Europeans who embrace such remedies may not be as wrongheaded as our own medical establishment would have us believe. I go to countries like Holland, where people by law may not be fired from their jobs, and to my astonishment meet wealthy conservatives who staunchly defend this prohibition. Travel reveals a whole range of unusual practices that may succeed in differing contexts; it suggests newer approaches for your own society and keeps you receptive to novel proposals and experiments in every field.

All People Should Be "Minorities"

[8]I walk the great cities of China and gradually realize that, in their midst, I am part of a minority in much the same way that others are of minorities in the city where I live. I stroll a great plaza in Nairobi, where I am in a minority. I experience the same illuminating impressions and insights over dozens of years and in hundreds of locations in Asia and Africa and India. Like many other travelers I feel the gradual weakening of whatever racist impulses still inhabit my subconscious. Travel teaches us that it is absurd to react to people according to their color. It makes everyone a member of a minority group on occasion. The experience changes all of us.

Travel Keeps Us Young

[9]I sit on that airplane, eating *execrable food*, breathing stale air, feeling jet-lagged and achy, and tell myself that travel is deeply fatiguing and unnatural. And yet when I emerge in an unfamiliar airport and city, I feel challenged and alive. There is still another language to attempt, a new history to absorb, another culture to encounter. And though some of it may dismay rather than enchant, it is never uninteresting; your mind is constantly awhirl with ideas and impressions. And even when you believe you have exhausted the store of new destinations and cultures, you discover that you can enjoy them on a deeper level. I'm currently studying Italian so that I can better enjoy a country I've visited a hundred times.

(CONTINUED)

LIFE LESSONS (CONTINUED)

Travel Teaches Us Humility, the Best Human Trait

[10]In the course of a long trip, I arrive at last at an English-speaking country say, Australia—and grab for a local newspaper. Wonder of wonders, there's not a single story in it about my own U.S. of A. Shocking and *impudent*, these "foreigners" dare to prefer their own concerns and matters closer to hand. We learn, through travel, that the world does not revolve around us alone, that we no longer rule the Earth, that not everyone worships our lifestyle or envies us. That kind of discovery makes us different from those puffed-up, closed-minded boosters and braggarts who sometimes dominate our public discourse. You become a quieter American and, in my opinion, a smarter and more productive one.

[11]Travel, for many, is merely a form of recreation. But travel is now becoming recognized as education. Certainly, it has a compelling effect, often greater than that of any other activity, even extensive reading. It has changed my life, and I believe that you, too, may want to reflect on how it has altered your own consciousness.

[12]Ours is the first generation in human history to travel to other continents as easily as we once took a trolley to the next town. Dare we hope that access to a larger world will result in more understanding, in human beings more tolerant and peaceful?

VOCABULARY—"LIFE LESSONS"

1. patronize others (¶3)
2. smug chauvinism (¶4)
3. initially loath to do so (¶6)
4. sympathy and succor (¶6)
5. presumed adversaries (¶6)
6. execrable food (¶9)
7. impudent (¶10)

CONTENT ANALYSIS QUESTIONS—"LIFE LESSONS"

1. What is Frommer's purpose?
2. What is Frommer's thesis? How does he develop and support his thesis?
3. In paragraph 5, Frommer writes because of his travel he remembers people "...as distinct human presences, not as abstractions." What does he mean? Why does he think that is important?
4. In paragraph 7, Frommer writes from his travel he has discovered "...a whole range of unusual practices that may succeed in differing contexts." What does he mean? What does he want us to understand?
5. Why do you think Frommer calls "humility" the best human trait? In what ways do you agree with him? In what ways do you disagree?

6. How would you answer Frommer when he asks in his last paragraph if we dare hope that travel will result in "more understanding, in human beings more tolerant and peaceful?" Explain your answer.

7. Of the eight "beliefs" Frommer lists, which two or three are most important to you? Why?

APPLICATION QUESTIONS—"LIFE LESSONS"

1. Since all students are not able to travel like Frommer does, what are two things you think the academic community should do to strengthen the attitudes, values, and human relations of students?

2. Assume that the company you work for has many branch locations. As part of your job training plan, you must work at a different branch for two months next summer. You can select an office across town, one in a major U.S. city about 1,000 miles away, or one in England. What factors would you consider as you make your decision'?

"BEGINNING ANEW"

Muriel Whetstone was a journalism student at Columbia College in Chicago when she wrote this article—"Beginning Anew"—for *Essence*. She graduated and is a full-time professional journalist in Chicago.

BEGINNING ANEW

MURIEL L. WHETSTONE

[1] I dreaded Sundays. I began living for the weekend at 8:30 Monday mornings. I resented my boss. The mere thought of answering other people's telephones, typing other people's work and watching other people take credit for my ideas and opinions would throw me into week-long bouts of depression. I hated my job. I hated my life. I hated myself for not having the guts to change either one.

[2] When most of my friends were planning college schedules and partying into the night, I was changing dirty diapers and walking the floor with a colicky baby. At 19 years old I was the mother of two, and a pitifully young wife. Everything I did for years, every decision I made, was done with my family in mind.

(CONTINUED)

BEGINNING ANEW (CONTINUED)

[3]And then I turned 29, and 30 was only a breath away. How long could I live like this? Certainly not until I retired. I began to feel that if I didn't do something soon, something quickly, I would die of unhappiness. I decided to follow my childhood dream: I was going to get my undergraduate degree and become a full-time journalist.

[4]I quit my job on one of my good days, a Friday. Almost at once I was *filled with trepidation*. What would I tell my husband and what would be his reaction? How would we pay our bills? *I must be crazy*, I thought. I was too old to begin again. I prayed, *Lord, what have I done?* I wondered if I was experiencing some sort of early mid-life crisis. Perhaps if I crawled back to my boss on my hands and knees and pleaded temporary insanity, he'd give me my job back. I spent that entire weekend in the eye of an emotional cyclone.

[5]But while I was feeling uneasy about the bridge I'd just crossed, I also began to feel a renewed sense of hopefulness about the possibilities on the other side. I had had a long love affair with the written word that was separate and apart from any of my roles. What we shared was personal: It belonged to me and would always be mine despite anything going on outside of me. I wasn't quite sure *what my journey would entail*, but I was positive who would be at the other end. *I steeled myself* to travel the road that would lead me to a better understanding of who I was and of what I wanted out of life. I shared my mixed feelings with my husband. He was as apprehensive as I was, but he was also warmly supportive. And so I stepped off the bridge and onto the path, nervous but determined. I soon discovered that I loved to learn and that my mind soaked up knowledge at every opportunity. My decision at those times felt right. But sometimes, after realizing what was expected of me, I would be *engulfed in self-doubt* and uncertainty.

[6]I was older than a few of my instructors and nearly all of my classmates. I was a social outcast practically that entire first semester. Finally I met a group of older female students who were, like me, beginning anew. We began to share our experiences of returning to school, dealing with husbands, lovers, children and bills that had to be paid. Over time we have become sisters, supporting ourselves by encouraging and supporting one another.

[7]I eventually had to seek employment to help with expenses. In fact, I've had more jobs in the last couple of years than I care to count. Many times I've had to stir a pot with one hand while holding a book with the other. More than a few times I've nearly broken under the pressure. I've shed tears on the bad days, but smiles abound on the good ones.

[8]However, I would not take back one tear or change one thing about the last couple of years. It hasn't been a snap: From the beginning I knew it would not be. And it's not so much the results of the action that have reshaped me (although that's important, too) as it is the realization that I have within myself what it takes to do what I set out to do. I feel more in control these days and less like a flag on a breezy day, blowing this way or that depending on the wind.

[9]I no longer dread Sundays, and Wednesdays are just as pleasant as Fridays. Now I get credit for my ideas, and my opinions are sought after. I love my new career. I love my life again. And I can clearly see a new woman waiting patiently just a little way down the road, waiting for me to reach her.

VOCABULARY—"BEGINNING ANEW"

1. filled with trepidation (¶4)
2. what my journey would entail (¶5)
3. I steeled myself (¶5)
4. engulfed in self-doubt (¶5)

CONTENT ANALYSIS QUESTIONS—"BEGINNING ANEW"

1. What is Whetstone's purpose?
2. What is Whetstone's thesis?
3. When Whetstone writes, "I wasn't quite sure what my journey would entail, but I was positive who would be at the other end," who does she know will be at the other end?
4. Explain what Whetstone means by "it's not so much the results of the action that have reshaped me...as it is the realization that I have within myself what it takes to do what I set out to do."
5. Describe the "new woman" Whetstone sees waiting patiently down the road. When do you think she'll meet her?

APPLICATION QUESTION—"BEGINNING ANEW"

1. Describe the "new person" waiting patiently down the road to meet you.

"THE DIAMOND NECKLACE"

Known for his simple, direct, realistic narrative style, Guy de Maupassant (1850–1893) is one of the world's classic short story writers. This story—"The Diamond Necklace"—is set in Paris.

THE DIAMOND NECKLACE

GUY DE MAUPASSANT

[1]She was one of those pretty, charming young ladies, born, as if through an error of destiny, into a family of clerks. She had no dowry, no hopes, no means of becoming known, appreciated, loved, and married by a man either rich or distinguished; and she allowed herself to marry a petty clerk in the office of the Board of Education.

[2]She was simple, not being able to adorn herself; but she was unhappy, as one out of her class; for *women belong to no caste*, no race; their grace, their beauty, and their charm serving them in the place of birth and family. Their *inborn finesse*, their instinctive elegance, their suppleness of wit are their only aristocracy, making some daughters of the people the equal of great ladies.

(CONTINUED)

THE DIAMOND NECKLACE (CONTINUED)

[3]She suffered incessantly, feeling herself born for all delicacies and luxuries. She suffered from the poverty of her apartment, the shabby walls, the worn chairs, and the faded stuffs. All these things, which another woman of her station would not have noticed, tortured and angered her. The sight of the little Breton, who made this humble home, awoke in her sad regrets and desperate dreams. She thought of quiet antechambers, with their Oriental hangings, lighted by high, bronze torches, and of the two great footmen in short trousers who sleep in the large armchairs, made sleepy by the heavy air from the heating apparatus. She thought of large drawing-rooms, hung in old silks, of graceful pieces of furniture carrying bric-à-brac of inestimable value, and of the little perfumed coquettish apartments, made for five o'clock chats with most intimate friends, men known and sought after, whose attention all women envied and desired.

[4]When she seated herself for dinner, before the round table where the tablecloth had been used three days, opposite her husband who uncovered the tureen with a delighted air, saying: "Oh! The good potpie! I know nothing better than that—" she would think of the elegant dinners, of the shining silver, of the tapestries peopling the walls with ancient personages and rare birds in the midst of fairy forests; she thought of the exquisite food served on marvelous dishes, of the whispered gallantries, listened to with the smile of the sphinx, while eating the rose-colored flesh of the trout or a chicken's wing.

[5]She had neither frocks nor jewels, nothing. And she loved only those things. She felt that she was made for them. She had such a desire to please, to be sought after, to be clever, and courted.

[6]She had a rich friend, a schoolmate at the convent, whom she did not like to visit, she suffered so much when she returned. And she *wept for whole days from chagrin*, from regret, from despair, and disappointment.

[7]One evening her husband returned elated, bearing in his hand a large envelope.

[8]"Here," said he, "here is something for you."

[9]She quickly tore open the wrapper and drew out a printed card on which were inscribed these words:

[10]"The Minister of Public Instruction and Madame George Ramponneau ask the honor of Mr. and Mrs. Loisel's company Monday evening, January 18, at the Minister's residence."

[11]Instead of being delighted, as her husband had hoped, she threw the invitation spitefully upon the table murmuring:

[12]"What do you suppose I want with that?"

[13]"But, my dearie, I thought it would make you happy. You never go out, and this is an occasion, and a fine one! I had a great deal of trouble to get it. Everybody wishes one, and it is very select; not many are given to employees. You will see the whole official world there."

[14]She looked at him with an irritated eye and declared impatiently:

[15]"What do you suppose I have to wear to such a thing as that?"

[16]He had not thought of that; he stammered:

[17]"Why, the dress you wear when we go to the theater. It seems very pretty to me—"

[18]He was silent, stupefied, in dismay, at the sight of his wife weeping. Two great tears fell slowly from the corners of his eyes toward the corners of his mouth; he stammered:

[19]"What is the matter? What is the matter?"

[20]By a violent effort, she had *controlled her vexation* and responded in a calm voice, wiping her moist cheeks:

[21]"Nothing. Only I have no dress and consequently I cannot go to this affair. Give your card to some colleague whose wife is better fitted out than I."

[22]He was grieved, but answered:

(CONTINUED)

THE DIAMOND NECKLACE (CONTINUED)

²³"Let us see, Matilda. How much would a suitable costume cost, something that would serve for other occasions, something very simple?"

²⁴She reflected for some seconds, making estimates and thinking of a sum that she could ask for without bringing with it an immediate refusal and a frightened exclamation from the economical clerk.

²⁵Finally she said, in a hesitating voice:

²⁶"I cannot tell exactly, but it seems to me that four hundred francs ought to cover it."

²⁷He turned a little pale, for he had saved just this sum to buy a gun that he might be able to join some hunting parties the next summer, on the plains at Nanterre, with some friends who went to shoot larks up there on Sunday. Nevertheless, he answered:

²⁸"Very well. I will give you four hundred francs. But try to have a pretty dress."

²⁹The day of the ball approached and Mme. Loisel seemed sad, disturbed, anxious. Nevertheless, her dress was nearly ready. Her husband said to her one evening:

³⁰"What is the matter with you? You have acted strangely for two or three days."

³¹And she responded: "I am vexed not to have a jewel, not one stone, nothing to adorn myself with. I shall have such a poverty-laden look. I would prefer not to go to this party."

³²He replied: "You can wear some natural flowers. At this season they look very *chic*. For ten francs you can have two or three magnificent roses."

³³She was not convinced. "No," she replied, "there is nothing more humiliating than to have a shabby air in the midst of rich women."

³⁴Then her husband cried out: "How stupid we are! Go and find your friend Mrs. Forestier and ask her to lend you her jewels. You are well enough acquainted with her to do this."

³⁵She uttered a cry of joy: "It is true!" she said. "I had not thought of that."

³⁶The next day she took herself to her friend's house and related her story of distress. Mrs. Forestier went to her closet with the glass doors, took out a large jewel-case, brought it, opened it, and said: "Choose, my dear."

³⁷She saw at first some bracelets, then a collar of pearls, then a Venetian cross of gold and jewels and of admirable workmanship. She tried the jewels before the glass, hesitated, but could neither decide to take them nor leave them. Then she asked:

³⁸"Have you nothing more?"

³⁹"Why, yes. Look for yourself. I do not know what will please you."

⁴⁰Suddenly she discovered, in a black satin box, a superb necklace of diamonds, and her heart beat fast with an immoderate desire. Her hands trembled as she took them up. She placed them about her throat against her dress, and remained in ecstasy before them. Then she asked, in a hesitating voice, full of anxiety:

⁴¹"Could you lend me this? Only this?"

⁴²"Why, yes, certainly."

⁴³She fell upon the neck of her friend, embraced her with passion, and then went away with her treasure.

⁴⁴The day of the ball arrived. Mme. Loisel was a great success. She was the prettiest of all, elegant, gracious, smiling, and full of joy. All the men noticed her, asked her name, and wanted to be presented. All the members of the Cabinet wished to waltz with her. The Minister of Education paid her some attention.

⁴⁵She danced with enthusiasm, with passion, intoxicated with pleasure, thinking of nothing, in the triumph of her beauty, in the glory of her success, in a kind of cloud of happiness that came of all this homage, and all this admiration, of all these awakened desires, and this victory so complete and sweet to the heart of woman.

(CONTINUED)

THE DIAMOND NECKLACE (CONTINUED)

[46]She went home toward four o'clock in the morning. Her husband had been half asleep in one of the little salons since midnight, with three other gentlemen whose wives were enjoying themselves very much.

[47]He threw around her shoulders the wraps they had carried for the coming home, modest garments of everyday wear, whose poverty clashed with the elegance of the ball costume. She felt this and wished to hurry away in order not to be noticed by the other women who were wrapping themselves in rich furs.

[48]Loisel retained her: "Wait," said he. "You will catch cold out there. I am going to call a cab."

[49]But she would not listen and descended the steps rapidly. When they were in the street, they found no carriage; and they began to seek one, hailing the coachmen whom they saw at a distance.

[50]They walked along toward the Seine, hopeless and shivering. Finally they found on the dock one of those old, nocturnal *coupés* that one sees in Paris after nightfall, as if they were ashamed of their misery by day.

[51]It took them as far as their door in Martyr street, and they went wearily up to their apartment. It was all over for her. And on his part, he remembered that he would have to be at the office by ten o'clock.

[52]She removed the wraps from her shoulders before the glass, for a final view of herself in her glory. Suddenly she uttered a cry. Her necklace was not around her neck.

[53]Her husband, already half undressed, asked: "What is the matter?"

[54]She turned toward him excitedly:

[55]"I have—I have—I no longer have Mrs. Forestier's necklace."

[56]He arose in dismay: "What! How is that? It is not possible."

[57]And they looked in the folds of the dress, in the folds of the mantle, in the pockets, everywhere. They could not find it.

[58]He asked: "You are sure you still had it when we left the house?"

[59]"Yes, I felt it in the vestibule as we came out."

[60]"But if you had lost it in the street, we should have heard it fall. It must be in the cab."

[61]"Yes. It is probable. Did you take the number?"

[62]"No. And you, did you notice what it was?"

[63]"No."

[64]They looked at each other utterly cast down. Finally, Loisel dressed himself again.

[65]"I am going," said he, "over the track where we went on foot, to see if I can find it."

[66]And he went. She remained in her evening gown, not having the force to go to bed, stretched upon a chair, without ambition or thoughts.

[67]Toward seven o'clock her husband returned. He had found nothing.

[68]He went to the police and to the cab offices, and put an advertisement in the newspapers, offering a reward; he did everything that afforded them a suspicion of hope.

[69]She waited all day in a state of bewilderment before this frightful disaster. Loisel returned at evening with his face harrowed and pale; he had discovered nothing.

[70]"It will be necessary," said he, "to write to your friend that you have broken the clasp of the necklace and that you will have it repaired. That will give us time to turn around."

[71]She wrote as he dictated.

[72]At the end of a week, they had lost all hope. And Loisel, older by five years, declared:

[73]"We must take measures to replace this jewel."

[74]The next day they took the box which had inclosed it, to the jeweler whose name was on the inside. He consulted his books:

[75]"It is not I, Madame," said he, "who sold this necklace; I only furnished the casket."

[76]They went from jeweler to jeweler seeking a necklace like the other one, consulting their memories, and ill, both of them, with chagrin and anxiety.

(CONTINUED)

THE DIAMOND NECKLACE (CONTINUED)

[77]In a shop of the Palais-Royal, they found a chaplet of diamonds which seemed to them exactly like the one they had lost. It was valued at forty thousand francs. They could get it for thirty-six thousand.

[78]They begged the jeweler not to sell it for three days. And they made an arrangement by which they might return it for thirty-four thousand francs if they found the other one before the end of February.

[79]Loisel possessed eighteen thousand francs which his father had left him. He borrowed the rest.

[80]He borrowed it, asking for a thousand francs of one, five hundred of another, five louis of this one, and three louis of that one. He gave notes, made ruinous promises, *took money of usurers* and the whole race of lenders. He compromised his whole existence, in fact, risked his signature, without even knowing whether he could make it good or not, and, harassed by anxiety for the future, by the black misery which surrounded him, and by the prospect of all *physical privations and moral torture*, he went to get the new necklace, depositing on the merchant's counter thirty-six thousand francs.

[81]When Mrs. Loisel took back the jewels to Mrs. Forestier, the latter said to her in a frigid tone:

[82]"You should have returned them to me sooner, for I might have needed them."

[83]She did open the jewel-box as her friend feared she would. If she should perceive the substitution, what would she think? What should she say? Would she take her for a robber?

[84]Mrs. Loisel now knew the horrible life of necessity. She did her part, however, completely, heroically. It was necessary to pay this frightful debt. She would pay it. They sent away the maid; they changed their lodgings; they rented some rooms under a mansard roof.

[85]She learned the heavy cares of a household, the *odious work* of a kitchen. She washed the dishes, using her rosy nails upon the greasy pots and the bottoms of the stewpans. She washed the soiled linen, the chemises and dishcloths, which she hung on the line to dry; she took down the refuse to the street each morning and brought up the water, stopping at each landing to breathe. And, clothed like a woman of the people, she went to the grocer's, the butcher's, and the fruiterer's, with her basket on her arm, shopping, haggling, defending to the last sou her miserable money.

[86]Every month it was necessary to renew some notes, thus obtaining time, and to pay others.

[87]The husband worked evenings, putting the books of some merchants in order, and nights he often did copying at five sous a page.

[88]And this life lasted for ten years.

[89]At the end of ten years, they had restored all, all, with interest of the usurer, and accumulated interest besides.

[90]Mrs. Loisel seemed old now. She had become a strong, hard woman, the crude woman of the poor household. Her hair badly dressed, her skirts awry, her hands red, she spoke in a loud tone, and washed the floors in large pails of water. But sometimes, when her husband was at the office, she would seat herself before the window and think of that evening party of former times, of that ball where she was so beautiful and so flattered.

[91]How would it have been if she had not lost that necklace? Who knows? Who knows? How singular is life, and how full of changes! How small a thing will ruin or save one!

[92]One Sunday, as she was taking a walk in the Champs-Elysées to rid herself of the cares of the week, she suddenly perceived a woman walking with a child. It was Mrs. Forestier, still young, still pretty, still attractive. Mrs. Loisel was affected. Should she speak to her? Yes, certainly. And now that she had paid, she would tell her all. Why not?

[93]She approached her. "Good morning, Jeanne."

[94]Her friend did not recognize her and was astonished to be so familiarly addressed by this common personage. She stammered:

(CONTINUED)

THE DIAMOND NECKLACE (CONTINUED)

⁹⁵"But, Madame—I do not know—You must be mistaken—"

⁹⁶"No, I am Matilda Loisel."

⁹⁷Her friend uttered a cry of astonishment: "Oh! My poor Matilda! How you have changed—"

⁹⁸"Yes, I have had some hard days since I saw you; and some miserable ones—and all because of you—"

⁹⁹"Because of me? How is that?"

¹⁰⁰"You recall the diamond necklace that you loaned me to wear to the Commissioner's ball?"

¹⁰¹"Yes, very well."

¹⁰²"Well, I lost it."

¹⁰³"How is that, since you returned it to me?"

¹⁰⁴"I returned another to you exactly like it. And it has taken us ten years to pay for it. You can understand that it was not easy for us who have nothing. But it is finished and I am decently content."

¹⁰⁵Madame Forestier stopped short. She said:

¹⁰⁶"You say that you bought a diamond necklace to replace mine?"

¹⁰⁷"Yes. You did not perceive it then? They were just alike."

¹⁰⁸And she smiled with a proud and simple joy. Madame Forestier was touched and took both her hands as she replied:

¹⁰⁹"Oh! my poor Matilda! Mine were false. They were not worth over five hundred francs!"

CONTENT QUESTIONS—"THE DIAMOND NECKLACE"

COMPLETION

1. When the story opens, why is Mme. Loisel so unhappy?
2. After the invitation to the ball, why is she unhappy?
3. What two actions does she take to solve her "poverty-laden look" problem?
4. What happened to Mme. Loisel after the ball?
5. In paragraph 73, Loisel says "We must take measures to replace this jewel." What measures did they take?
6. What is the ironic twist at the end of the story?

VOCABULARY—"THE DIAMOND NECKLACE"

1. women belong to no caste (¶2)
2. inborn finesse (¶2)
3. wept...from chagrin (¶6)
4. controlled her vexation (¶20)
5. took money of usurers (¶80)
6. physical privations and moral torture (¶80)
7. odious work (¶85)

CONTENT ANALYSIS QUESTIONS—"THE DIAMOND NECKLACE"

1. What do you think Maupassant wanted his reader to think about? Phrased another way, what do you think the moral of the story is?

2. This fictional story is set in Paris in the late 1800s. Do you think a similar story could be set in Los Angeles in the late 1900s? Why or why not?

3. Based on the words he used to describe her and the story's action, do you think Maupassant wanted his reader to like and be sympathetic toward Mme. Loisel? Use specific examples to support your answer.

4. After the loss of the necklace, in what ways do you think Mme. Loisel changed? In what ways do you think she remained the same? Use specific examples to support your answer.

5. In paragraph 91, Mme. Loisel muses, "How small a thing will ruin or save one!" What does she mean? In what ways do you agree? In what ways do you disagree?

APPLICATION QUESTION—"THE DIAMOND NECKLACE"

1. If this were real life rather than fiction, what do you think would happen next? What makes you think so?

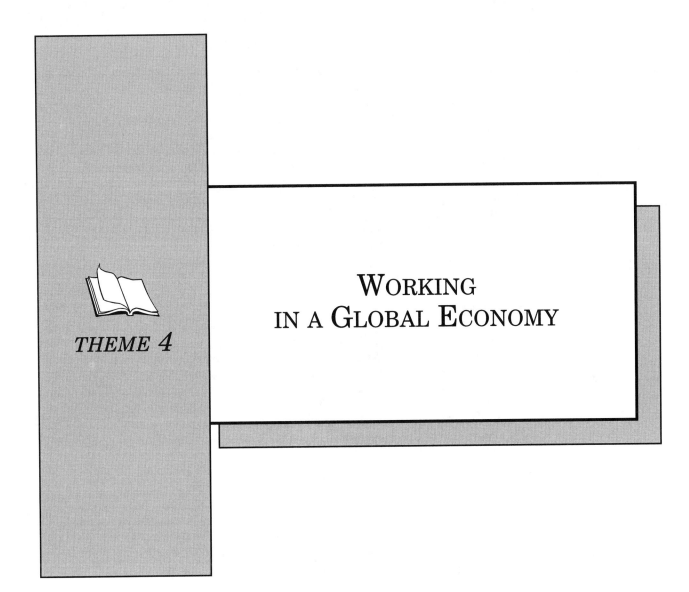

THEME 4

WORKING IN A GLOBAL ECONOMY

Selwyn Enzer, director of the University of Southern California's Project Overlook, warns, "Today's students and workers need to prepare themselves for a radically different job market by the year 2000." To prepare for the next century as we shift from the Industrial Age to the Information Age, Labor Secretary Robert Reich offers five career tips:

1. Whether you work in an office or manage a crew that cleans it, you must be computer literate.
2. Keep your skills sharp and continue your education.
3. Ditch the ladder; catch the web. Smart workers move along webs, earning more from expertise, not from seniority.
4. To hone your skills, "network" with others in your profession.
5. Tomorrow's workers will function as "teammates." Learn to play all positions and win as a team.

The readings in this theme consider predictions like these and encourage you to think about how changes in society, business, and school will affect you and your future work.

The textbook chapter "Recognizing Business Trends and Challenges" by Professors Griffin and Ebert provides the big picture—why the world you work in is so different from past decades. Among the trends and issues they examine are the impact of high technology, the transition from manufacturing to information services, the changing demographics of the workforce and the international trade dilemma. The articles in the theme focus on one or more of these.

First, in "Employment Challenges of the 1990s," Denver journalist Laura Anderson gives a glimpse of the workforce in the year 2000. Next, J. F. Coates, Inc., a firm specializing in futures research, provides an in-depth look at how changing demographics, modern technology, and new demands on workers is bringing sweeping changes to your workplace in "Future Work."

"Cutting through the Chaos," by Cassandra Hayes looks at not just the problems of the ever-changing workplace but at some ways to survive it. Then the staff of CQ Researcher gives us an overview of one specific issue: "Current Situation: Contingent Workforce."

In "Jobs 2000" Robert Lewis investigates the job prospects for midlife career changers in the twenty-first century. And finally, Harvey Mackay advises, "If you choose a job you love, you'll never have to 'work'."

Each of the readings is by a different author(s), of a different length, and requires different tasks.

STRATEGIES FOR SUCCESS

Develop a plan for each of the readings.

Determine who the author is and why he or she is writing.

Know the vocabulary the author uses.

Identify what the author is writing about.

Establish how the author develops and supports the thesis.

Recognize the author's stance.

Integrate graphic and text information.

Organize the information you need.

Decide what you can do with the author's information.

"RECOGNIZING BUSINESS TRENDS AND CHALLENGES"

Ricky W. Griffin teaches at Texas A & M University. Ronald J. Ebert teaches at the University of Missouri-Columbia. This selection—"Recognizing Business Trends and Challenges"—is from *Business*, 3rd ed.

CHAPTER

3
▼

RECOGNIZING BUSINESS TRENDS AND CHALLENGES

*L*EARNING
OBJECTIVES

After studying this chapter, you should be able to:

1   Describe five major trends that affect U.S. business today.
2   Explain why the U.S. government sometimes regulates businesses and how business seeks to influence the government.
3   Discuss changes in the U.S. labor pool and their effects on business.
4   Describe changes in demographics and consumer rights and their impact on U.S. business.
5   Identify and discuss four major challenges for U.S. business in the 1990s.

*C*HAPTER
OUTLINE

BUTTONING UP PROFITS

Once upon a time, in the year 1853, a German immigrant arrived in San Francisco and thought he saw an opportunity to sell tents to miners. As it turned out, miners weren't much interested in the tents he had to sell, but they were interested in buying rugged clothes. To salvage his investment, the merchant took his tent canvas and cut it into pants that proved sturdier than most. Encouraged by brisk sales, he took advantage of a good price on denim from a French firm (the word *denim* is from the French *serge de Nimes,* Nimes being the town that manufactured the cloth) and dyed the fabric a dirt-concealing dark indigo. In doing so, Levi Strauss built the foundations of an empire.

Not until the 1960s, though, did blue jeans truly take off. Adopted by the baby boomers—that fickle but huge generation beloved by businesses large and small—as a statement against "materialistic" culture, jeans became the uniform of the day and a symbol of the United States itself. Throughout the 1970s, sales of jeans continued to skyrocket. By the end of the decade, some companies had begun to market "designer" and "dress" jeans at prices that pronounced them a fashion item.

Unfortunately for jeans makers, however, jeans are most appealing to the young. As the baby boom generation grew older, its members—like generations before them—put on the weight that made jeans uncomfortable and unflattering. And like most other fashion statements, jeans eventually lost their cachet. At the same time, the new generation of teenagers—the so-called "baby bust"—was much smaller. In 1990, there were 16 percent fewer 14–24-year-olds—the age group that wears the most jeans—than there were in 1980. As a result, sales of jeans began to fall, sending Levi's profits downward.

Like many companies in the early 1980s, Levi's attempted to recoup its losses by diversifying. Selling suits and hats proved to be very different from selling jeans, however, and soon the company was in even deeper financial trouble. Convinced that drastic changes were needed if the company

was to survive, Robert D. Haas (great-great-grand-nephew of Levi Strauss) turned to that other business boom of the 1980s—the leveraged buyout. Buying out all the Levi's stock then held by members of the public wasn't cheap: the company took on $1.65 billion in debt in 1984 to finance the buyback.

Unlike many other leveraged buyouts of the 1980s, however, Haas's results at Levi Strauss have more than justified the buyout's cost. By the end of 1988, the firm had paid off more of its debt than anticipated—$950 million, to be exact. This success has continued into the 1990s. In 1990, Levi's sales rose to $3.6 billion and its profits increased to $272 million. In the first quarter of 1991, the company posted an 89 percent surge in net income over the previous year.

Levi's managers credit the company's improved financial picture to the leveraged buyout. They argue that the kinds of sweeping and often expensive changes they had to make to become highly profitable again could never have been made under public ownership. Publicly traded companies are often at the mercy of Wall Street brokers' projections of their short-term results. Levi Strauss's management has only to answer to the Haas family, which now owns 90 percent of the firm's stock. (The rest of the stock is held by Levi's employees.)

Moreover, Haas argues that being free from the pressure of outside investors has enabled the firm to commit itself not only to temporarily unprofitable activities but also to six long-term goals: communications, diversity, empowerment, ethical management, new behavior, and recognition. These items, Haas maintains, cannot be summarized in a line in an income statement, but they are vital to the continued prosperity of the firm. If such "aspirations," as Haas terms them, are unusual goals for a businessman, they are certainly understandable coming from a man who was once a part of another symbol of the 1960s—the Peace Corps.

Changing its product line to meet the needs of a new generation was just one of the challenges Levi Strauss met in the 1980s. But Levi's is not unique: today nearly every company must contend with shifts in its relationships with its competitors, the government, its workforce, and its customers.

In this chapter, we explore the nature of today's business world. We begin by discussing interactions among businesses within the United States. We then consider how businesses interact with other segments of the economy. For example, in discussing the production era in Chapter 2, we noted that business, government, and labor traditionally have acted as countervailing powers in the U.S. economy. In recent years, this balance has begun to change in subtle ways. Government and business remain strong, but labor's influence has eroded. At the same time, consumers have gained more power in their interactions with business. Thus business must contend not only with government and labor, but also with consumers. Only when you understand the complexities of these interactions can you appreciate the challenges facing business in the 1990s.

▼ BUSINESS TRENDS IN THE 1990S

Some of the changes and challenges confronting modern businesses involve the organizations themselves. Among the most important of these changes and challenges for U.S. businesses are the development of high technology, the shift toward a service-based economy, geographical shifts, and an increase in mergers and acquisitions.

THE IMPACT OF HIGH TECHNOLOGY

One trend that has affected virtually every aspect of the contemporary business world is the development and spread of high technology. The Bureau of Labor Standards defines a **high-technology (high-tech) firm** as one that spends twice as much on research and development and employs twice as many technical employees as the average U.S. manufacturing firm. The term *high-tech* often conjures up images of computers and robots. Firms that make these products are definitely high-tech, but so are firms in the aircraft, pharmaceuticals, biotechnology, and communications industries.

> **high-technology (high-tech) firm**
> A firm that spends twice as much on research and development and employs twice as many technical employees as the average U.S. manufacturing firm.

Several parts of the United States, including the Boston area, California's Silicon Valley, and Austin, Texas, have become centers for high-tech firms. The products offered by these high-tech ventures are affecting many other businesses. For example, high-tech robots produced by Fanuc Corporation, a Japanese firm, are used in virtually all automobile plants today.

High-tech has not delivered all that it originally promised. For example, it has not created the number of new jobs that many economists predicted. Some of the production jobs it has created have been in foreign factories. Many workers trained for industrial jobs have been unable or unwilling to make the transition to high-tech jobs. Finally, many entrepreneurs who rushed into the high-tech area did so with poorly conceived plans and were unsuccessful. While some high-tech companies like Sun Microsystems, Cypress Semiconductors, and Conner Peripherals have succeeded, many others have fallen by the wayside.[1] Still, high-tech is clearly here to stay and will play an increasingly important role in the U.S. economy.

> **M**any workers trained for industrial jobs have been unable or unwilling to make the transition to high-tech jobs.

THE SHIFT TO SERVICES

Developments in high technology have also contributed to another change in the business world. In recent years, the manufacturing sector—long the backbone of the U.S. economy—has declined in importance as an employer of workers, while the service sector has grown steadily. The **service sector** consists of jobs that involve providing a service rather than creating a tangible product. Banks, restaurants, retailers, transportation, and entertainment businesses are examples of service firms.

> **service sector**
> The sector of the economy consisting of jobs that involve providing a service rather than creating a tangible product.

The growth of the service sector since 1960 is illustrated in Figure 3.1. In 1900, only about 28 percent of U.S. jobs were service jobs. By 1950, the figure was 40 percent, and by 1991, it was almost 78 percent. No wonder, then, that many have begun referring to the U.S. economy as a "service economy."

Some service industries have grown less than others. While employment in traditional service industries has risen as a percentage of total employment, the growth of **informational services** in recent years is most notable. Informational services include those provided by lawyers, accountants, data processors, computer operators, financial analysts, office personnel, and insurance agents—all those who work on or with information.

> **informational services**
> Service industries that provide information for a fee. Examples are law, accounting, and data processing.

The demand for informational services has grown for many reasons. The increasing need to acquire and manage vast amounts of information in a highly competitive marketplace is one major reason. Another is the increasing govern-

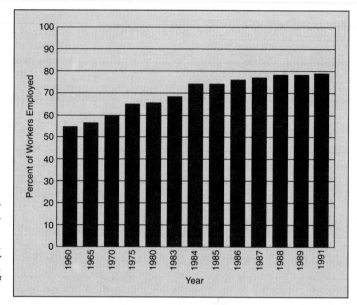

FIGURE 3.1 Service Sector Employment in the United States

The service sector of the U.S. economy has grown steadily over several decades. Today, it provides more than three-quarters of all jobs in the United States.

ment regulation of business. With more government regulations, companies have had to hire more people to study the regulations and to construct and implement appropriate policies to comply with them. Filling out government forms is another major task.

THE SHIFT SOUTH AND WEST

Another trend affecting business has been a gradual population shift to the so-called Sunbelt. The shift south and west picked up momentum at the start of the 1970s, when rapidly rising energy prices drove up the costs—and prices—of virtually everything. Consumers responded by buying less, causing many industries to lay off workers. But businesses in southern states like Florida and Texas and western states like Colorado and Arizona continued to hire. As people rushed to these areas, houses, retail stores, and restaurants could not be built fast enough to serve the growing population.

A favorable climate, a nonunionized workforce, and low taxes in the South and West have since resulted in a substantial relocation of the U.S. population. Some businesses have moved their headquarters from northern cities like New York to southern cities like Dallas and Houston. Other businesses have expanded to serve new population centers like Phoenix and the entire state of Florida. Such expansion, of course, carries with it more sophisticated communication networks, higher transportation expenses, and sometimes a loss of valuable employees who decide not to relocate.

The shift south and west continued through most of the 1980s. In the latter part of that decade, however, a glut in the world supply of petroleum hurt the economies of states like Texas and Louisiana. Major southern cities like Houston experienced dramatic economic downturns, and growth elsewhere in the Sunbelt stabilized a bit. But as the 1990s began, things started to pick up again and the shift continues. For example, J. C. Penney and Exxon both recently moved their corporate headquarters from New York to Dallas.[2]

MERGERS, ACQUISITIONS, AND STRATEGIC ALLIANCES

Another trend in modern business has been an increased emphasis on mergers, acquisitions, and alliances. In Chapter 2, we saw that businesses today buy and sell other companies like farmers used to buy and sell produce. An **acquisition**

acquisition
The purchase of one company by another.

occurs when one firm buys another. A **merger** is a consolidation of two firms. Under the terms of **a strategic alliance,** individual firms retain their independence but agree to work together in one or more areas.

In acquisitions, one firm (usually the larger) buys the other (the smaller). The transaction is similar to buying a car that becomes your property after the sale. In a merger, however, the firms are usually similar in size and the arrangement is more collaborative. A strategic alliance may involve the creation of a new enterprise jointly owned by the partners or may simply involve collaboration on new technology or marketing.

After a merger or acquisition, three things can happen. One possibility is that the acquired company will continue to operate as a separate entity. Even though K Mart bought Waldenbooks several years ago, the bookstore chain has continued to operate autonomously. Another possibility is that the acquired business will be absorbed by the other and simply disappear. For example, when Chevron bought Gulf, the latter company essentially ceased to exist—its service stations were either closed or converted to Chevron stations. Finally, the two companies may form a new company. For example, when Warner and Time merged, they formed a new company called Time Warner.

Types of Mergers. As Figure 3.2 shows, mergers can take several forms. A **horizontal merger** is a merger between two companies in the same industry.

merger
The union of two companies to form a single new business.

strategic alliance
A collaboration between two or more organizations.

horizontal merger
A merger between two companies in the same industry.

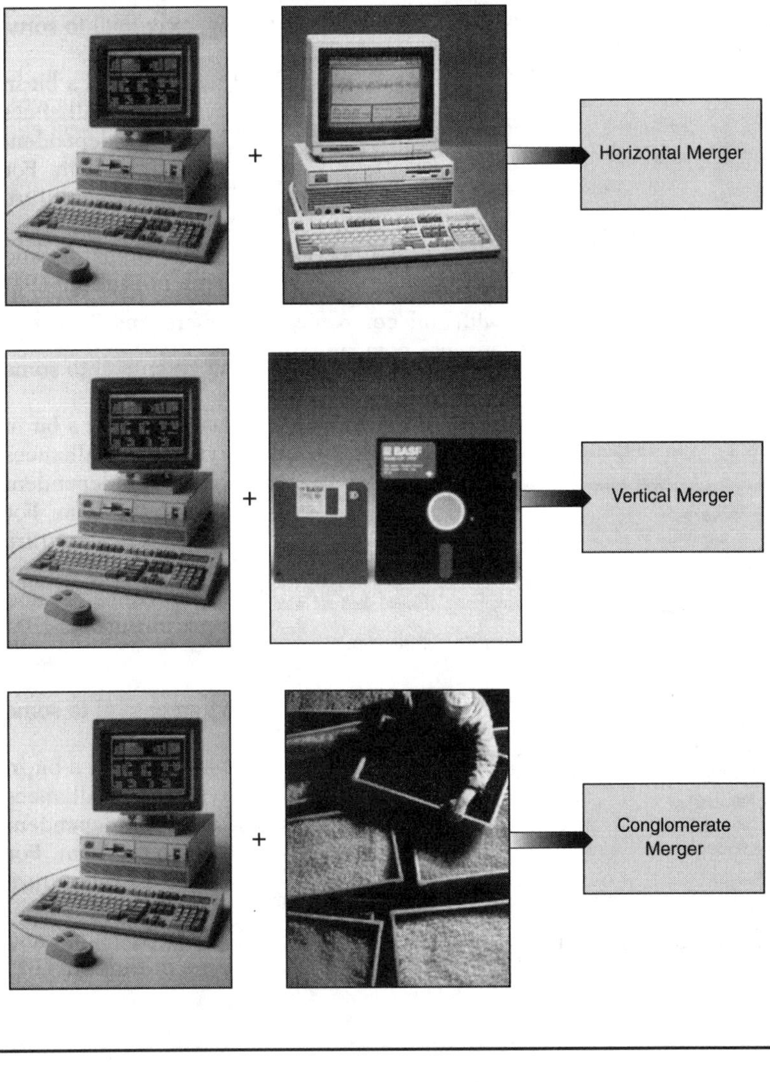

FIGURE 3.2 Types of Mergers
The three most common types of mergers are horizontal, vertical, and conglomerate.

Horizontal Merger

Vertical Merger

Conglomerate Merger

vertical merger
A merger in which one of the companies is a supplier to or customer of the other.

conglomerate merger
A merger of two firms in completely unrelated businesses.

friendly takeover
An acquisition in which the acquired company welcomes the merger.

hostile takeover
An acquisition in which the acquiring company buys enough of the other company's stock to take control, even though the other company opposes the takeover.

greenmail
A buyback of a company's stock at a large profit to one or more investors who are threatening a hostile takeover of the firm.

raiders
Investors who acquire a large block of a company's stock and initiate a hostile takeover.

Ford's purchase of Jaguar was a horizontal merger. **A vertical merger** takes place when one of the companies in the merger is a supplier or customer of the other. For example, Du Pont bought Conoco in part because it wanted a reliable source of petroleum for its chemical business. **A conglomerate merger** occurs when the companies are unrelated. Kodak's acquisition of Sterling Drugs falls into this category.

Takeovers and Greenmail. Mergers and acquisitions can take place in several different ways. Indeed, as summarized in Table 3.1, merger and acquisition activity has its own unique vocabulary. In a **friendly takeover,** the acquired company welcomes the merger, perhaps because it needs cash or sees other benefits from joining the acquiring firm. Chevron's purchase of Gulf was friendly. But in a **hostile takeover,** the acquiring company buys enough of the other company's stock to take control, even though the other company opposes the takeover. NCR initially fought AT&T's takeover bid and dropped its fight only after AT&T raised its offer price.

Closely related to the hostile takeover is the practice of paying **greenmail.** In this situation, investors (called **raiders**) acquire large blocks of a company's stock, threaten a hostile takeover, then let the target company buy back its stock at a price that gives the raiders a substantial profit. For example, Kroger recently had to pay a special dividend to all of its stockholders to fend off a takeover bid by a small group of investors. Such actions are costly, of course; often the firm has to borrow money to finance the stock purchase. Paying greenmail to some stockholders may also anger other stockholders.

Alliances offer the advantage of allowing each firm to remain independent while sharing the risk of a new venture with another firm.

While merger and acquisition activity has leveled off a bit in recent years, the number of alliances has skyrocketed. Alliances offer the advantage of allowing each firm to remain independent while sharing the risk of a new venture with another firm. For example, Nestlé and General Mills recently formed a new venture called Cereal Partners Worldwide (CPW). CPW will produce General Mills's cereals (such as Cheerios and Golden Grahams) and market them under the well-known Nestlé name in Europe. IBM and Apple have recently agreed to work together to create a new operating system that will be compatible with both companies' computers. And Boeing is working with three different Japanese companies to build a new long-range, wide-body jet.[3]

Table 3.1   The Language of Mergers and Acquisitions

Friendly Takeover
A merger or acquisition in which the acquired firm welcomes the takeover.

Hostile Takeover
A merger or acquisition in which the company being acquired does not want to be taken over.

Raiders (also called *Sharks*)
Investors who buy a large block of a business's stock and threaten a hostile takeover.

Greenmail
The buying back of stock from a raider for more than its market value.

Poison Pills
Actions taken by a business to make it less attractive to potential raiders (such as taking on additional debt or selling off valuable assets).

Golden Parachutes
Contracts with senior managers that guarantee them a large payment if the business is acquired and they lose their jobs.

White Knight
A company that takes over another company but allows the acquired firm to remain independent and to keep its existing management.

Because of the enormous complexities of large mergers, acquisitions, and alliances, and because of the potential for virtual monopolies to arise as a result of them, the government has become increasingly watchful of these activities. As you will see in the next section, this is just one of the areas in which business is affected by the government.

▼ BUSINESS AND GOVERNMENT

A few years ago, within the space of a few days, PepsiCo announced plans to acquire Seven-Up and the Coca-Cola Company declared that it would buy Dr. Pepper. The government intervened, however, and blocked both mergers, arguing that the mergers would place 81 percent of the soft-drink market in the hands of two companies.

At first glance, this type of governmental intervention might seem contrary to the nature of private enterprise and capitalism as we explained them in Chapter 1. Nonetheless, mergers are just one area of business that the U.S. government regulates and controls.

GOVERNMENT REGULATION OF BUSINESS

Regulation is the establishment of governmental rules that restrict business activity. Government regulates business for a variety of reasons, the two most important of which are to protect competition and to meet the nation's social goals.

regulation
The establishment of governmental rules that restrict business activity.

Protecting Competition. One of the reasons that government regulates business is to ensure competition. Regulation in this area protects both consumers and other businesses. As we saw in Chapter 1, competition is crucial to a market economy. If competition did not exist, monopolists would be able to charge high prices for low-quality goods. Laws prohibiting monopolies thus preserve competition and allow companies to offer goods that meet consumers' expectations at a reasonable price.

Similarly, without government restrictions, a large business with vast resources could cut its prices so low and advertise so much that smaller firms lacking equal resources would be forced to shut down. It was exactly this threat that prompted the Department of Justice (DOJ) to block the acquisition plans of PepsiCo and Coca-Cola. The DOJ feared that small companies like Royal Crown Cola (4.5 percent market share) and Cadbury Schwepps (3.7 percent market share) would go bankrupt if the larger companies were allowed to proceed. The DOJ's antitrust division and the Federal Trade Commission (FTC) are also empowered to enforce the laws relating to illegal competitive practices and deceptive advertising.

In some cases, monopoly may be desirable from society's point of view. In these instances, government regulation prevents companies from price gouging. For example, telephone, utility, and cable television rates are controlled by state agencies, city councils, or other governing agencies. Government regulation is also common in industries in which only limited competition exists. Fears that oligopolies such as the trucking, airline, and railroad industries will collude on prices have led the federal government to set rates in these industries at various times. Fears of the power of television and radio stations have been used to justify government rules and pressure on these organizations to run public service ads and to give equal time to opposing views.

Meeting Social Goals. Another reason that the government regulates business is to help meet social goals. Social goals promote the general well-being of society. In the United States, as in any market economy, consumers must have money to purchase goods and services. But our sense of fairness dictates that the ill should be treated, regardless of their ability to pay. Medicare (a federal insurance program for the elderly established during President Lyndon Johnson's administration) has not only made medical care available to many elderly citizens, but has also had a major impact on medical fees. For example, regulations now limit how much hospitals and doctors can charge Medicare patients for certain services. These limits have effectively created fixed rates.

Another social goal—a safe workplace—has also generated extensive government regulation of businesses. OSHA (the Occupational Safety and Health Administration) is the primary government agency charged with ensuring worker safety. In addition, state-mandated worker compensation programs require businesses to contribute to a fund that pays workers who have been injured on the job.

Through the EPA (the Environmental Protection Agency), the federal government has become the chief regulator of industrial pollution. But many states, counties, and cities have imposed additional restrictions on business activities that generate pollution. For example, New York and Florida forbid the sale of detergents that contain phosphates, which have been shown to affect water purity. In an effort to promote recycling, some states require bottle deposits. And California has placed strict limits on the level of emissions that cars sold and operated in that state may give off. OSHA and the EPA can affect a firm's profits by levying fines or even shutting down plants that violate government regulations.

Other federal, state, and local laws regulate countless aspects of business in order to "protect" the public. Federal laws regulate banks and stock sales. States license physicians, insurance agents, and barbers. Local ordinances establish where garbage can be dumped and who can serve liquor. Indeed, millions of laws, licensing rules, and legal actions regulate every aspect of business in the United States today, a pattern some small businesses find threatening, as the Small Business Report "David and Goliath: Small Business versus Federal Regulation" explains.

THE MOVE TOWARD DEREGULATION

Although government regulation has benefited the United States in some ways, it is not without drawbacks. Businesspeople complain—with some justification—that government regulations require too much paperwork. For example, to comply with just one OSHA regulation, Goodyear once generated 345,000 pages of computer reports weighing 3,200 pounds. It costs that company $35.5 million each year to comply with the regulations of six government agencies, and it takes 36 employee-years (the equivalent of one employee working full-time for 36 years) to fill out each year's required reports. In some cases, rate regulation has resulted in prices higher than those the market would have set without regulation. For these and other reasons, the federal government began deregulating certain industries in the 1970s, with mixed results. **Deregulation** is the elimination of governmental rules that restrict business activity.

> **T**o comply with just one OSHA regulation, Goodyear once generated 345,000 pages of computer reports weighing 3,200 pounds.

deregulation
The elimination of governmental rules that restrict business activity.

The Airline Industry.   For many years, the Civil Aeronautics Board set fares and assigned routes in the airline industry. Fares were so high that many airlines could cover the costs of a flight by selling only 15 seats on that flight! Because everything was regulated, the airlines had little incentive to control operating costs.

Since deregulation, however, the airlines have had to compete for customers by lowering their fares and costs. In recent years, many airlines that could not compete effectively have gone bankrupt, sold their assets to other airlines, or

Small Business Report

DAVID AND GOLIATH: SMALL BUSINESS VERSUS FEDERAL REGULATION

The statistics are frightening. Owners of small businesses spend as much as one-third of their time filling out forms to comply with government reporting requirements. These and other federal rules cost each of the United States's small businesses about $2,000 every year. Horror stories are common:

▶ A Virginia store owner ran afoul of Labor Department overtime rules when he let two of his employees have time off during the week in return for working for free on Saturdays and during lunch breaks. Getting the charge dismissed cost the Virginian $3,000.
▶ A Michigan gravel pit owner had to buy a first-aid stretcher for his facility—even though it's a one-man operation.
▶ A Wisconsin meatpacker with only eight employees had to spend $6,000 to sandblast a wall when a federal meat inspector was able to pry off a piece of paint—even though the wall was nowhere near the meatpacking area.

Worse yet, federal regulation of small businesses seems likely to increase. Under COBRA, the Consolidated Omnibus Budget Reconciliation Act, employers must continue benefits for ex-employees and their families at the employees' expense for 18 months. Adding to the paperwork burden, firms must give written notice of the benefits available to employees and to each of their family members.

Under amendments to the Resource Conservation Recovery Act, firms producing as little as 220 pounds of hazardous waste per month must obey complex disposal regulations and may be liable for damages if a disposal plan that is legal today is outlawed tomorrow.

Feeling buried under so much paperwork and regulation, small business has begun to fight back. Pressure on Congress and the White House has won some regulatory exemptions. For example, firms with fewer than 250 employees no longer have to have a written affirmative action plan. The Occupational Safety and Health Administration now performs routine safety checks only if a small firm has a higher-than-normal injury rate. Under the Equal Access to Justice Act, small businesses that can show arbitrariness on the part of regulators will be entitled to government payment of legal fees to defend themselves.

Then there are the small, private victories of small businessmen like George Poppas. Poppas owns a modest taxi operation. When the Federal Trade Commission threatened to send U.S. marshals to close down his business because he had failed to send in one form, Poppas let the FTC know that he would welcome the marshals. In fact, he promised to have a local television crew on hand to film their arrival. The FTC promptly lost interest in sending marshals and even in receiving Poppas's form.

---

reduced their operations substantially. For example, Continental declared bankruptcy twice, and Eastern and PanAm have shut down altogether.[4]

Ironically, the competition that has resulted since deregulation has not brought about any structural change in the airline industry. Some major firms did not survive the competition or grow as quickly as other airlines. But the overall structure of the industry—with international carriers, regional carriers, and local carriers—has not changed. What has changed is the cost of flying. It is now cheaper to fly than it was before deregulation. In addition, only those companies whose management was able to operate successfully in the new, deregulated environment have survived. For example, American, Delta, and United Airlines have thrived under deregulation.

The Banking Industry. Deregulation has also affected the banking industry. For years, savings and loan companies and banks were regulated by several different agencies. Since deregulation, some banks, like Nations Bank in North Carolina, have expanded rapidly and prospered. Many banks have also increased the range of services they offer. For example, some now offer a wide array of savings plans, discount brokerage services, and so forth.

Deregulation has forced the airline industry to cut costs and improve service to remain competitive. The result has been a wave of airline bankruptcies in the past five years. Northwest Airlines, for example, bought the planes of the now defunct Republic Airlines.

Deregulation of the banking industry has created some serious problems, however. To compete, some banks took greater risks in their loan making—a policy change that contributed to the large number of bank failures in recent years. Decreased regulation has contributed to hard times in the savings and loan (S&L) industry, too. A number of Sunbelt S&Ls, plagued by mismanagement of funds, bad debts, and outright fraud, have collapsed. Indeed, the federal government has had to pledge billions of dollars to avert a financial crisis in the industry. Several S&Ls have been taken over by other banks and many others have closed.

HOW BUSINESS INFLUENCES GOVERNMENT

As we have noted, not everyone agrees on the benefits of government regulation —or deregulation. Naturally, businesses want laws regarding regulation and taxation to do them the least harm and the most good. Toward this end, businesses attempt to influence the government through lobbyists, trade associations, advertising, and political action committees.

A **lobbyist** is a person hired by a company or an industry to represent its interests with government officials. Some business lobbyists have training in a particular industry, public relations experience, or a legal background. A few have served as legislators or government regulators. But all are required to register with the government as paid representatives of interest groups or particular businesses.

Employees and owners of small businesses that cannot afford lobbyists often join **trade associations,** which assist and promote the interests of their members. A trade association may act as an industry lobby to influence legislation. It may also conduct training programs relevant to its particular industry and arrange trade shows at which members display their products or services to potential customers. Most trade associations publish newsletters featuring articles on new products, new companies, changes in ownership, and modifications in laws affecting the industry.

Businesses can also influence legislation indirectly by influencing voters. For example, a company or an industry can launch an advertising campaign

lobbyist
A person hired by a company or industry to represent its interests with government officials.

trade association
An organization dedicated to assisting and promoting the interests of its members.

designed to get people to write their representatives demanding passage—or rejection—of a particular bill. (Figure 3.3 shows an ad used by Mobil to make a point about governmental actions.)

Finally, businesses may attempt to influence legislation by contributing to **political action committees (PACs),** which are special political fund-raising groups. The Federal Election Campaign Law limits corporate political contributions to individual candidates. But PACs can accept voluntary contributions from individual employees and distribute them to specific candidates. The enormous sums of money—millions of dollars each year—raised by PACs give them great power and influence in government.

Critics have argued that the growth of lobbying and the increased number of PACs in recent years have distorted the legislative process. They charge that legislators have become most sensitive to the best-funded arguments. For

political action committee (PAC)
A political fund-raising group that accepts contributions and distributes them to candidates for political office.

The wrong prescription

In an apparent response to the recent string of oils spills, the House of Representatives has expanded, by a wide margin, the existing moratoriums on the leasing of offshore tracts for oil and gas exploration. In addition, it voted for the first time to prohibit such leasing off the coast of Alaska. The measure makes as much sense as slapping a cast on the leg of a man with a broken arm.

The measure, attached to a bill for the fiscal 1990 funding of the Interior Department and other agencies, would prohibit, at least until October of 1990, all leasing and pre-leasing activities off California and a large area of the Atlantic stretching from Massachusetts to Maryland, including the Georges Bank, and including also the eastern Gulf of Mexico. Another affected area is Bristol Bay in Alaska, where some companies already have paid almost $100 million for leases, and where the government may have to buy them back.

Why is the House action the wrong prescription? For one thing, because it affects the wrong part of the oil business. The recent spills occurred as oil was being transported by large tanker. The industry has already recommended a detailed program to increase tanker safety, including the creation of a new spill-response organization, deeper involvement of the Coast Guard, improved maneuvering devices on vessels, and an onging research effort on how to clean up spills more effectively. To equate oil exploration and production with oil transportation is the archetypical—and erroneous—admixture of apples and oranges.

While a major oil spill at an exploration or production site offshore remains a possibility, that possibility is quite remote. The Minerals Management Service of the Interior Department recently reported that over the last 17 years, there has not been an oil spill resulting from a blowout at an exploratory well. Over the same period of time, only 840 barrels of oil were spilled during blowouts at production wells. Production in U.S. waters

during those years totaled five <u>billion</u> barrels.

Furthermore, the House action is wrong because it would be counterproductive. Most of the oil from wells in U.S. waters comes ashore by pipeline, not by tanker. At a time of dwindling U.S. production, any damper on the effort to find more domestic oil means an increase in imports to meet demand. Imported oil—currently 45 percent of consumption—does arrive by tanker, so more imports mean more tanker traffic in and around American ports.

There are also sound budgetary arguments against the banning of offshore exploration. The federal Treasury receives some $2.3 billion a year in royalties from offshore production. Cut the exploration rate and the production rate will eventually follow, and so will royalty income.

Other financial considerations are involved. We've already mentioned the $100 million or so that may have to be refunded because of the Bristol Bay moratorium. And another $184 million may have to be refunded for leases off the Florida coast. It hardly makes sense for Congress to frantically scramble for more revenues as it writes a tax bill with one hand, while the other hand busily adds to the budget deficit. Besides, as we have already noted, a slowdown in the domestic search for petroleum means an increase in imports—which translates into additional pressure on America's balance of payments.

In the decade of the 1970s, with its recurrent oil crises, the industry was often made the scapegoat during a frenzied search for easy answers and identifiable villains. The '90s is no time to replay past errors. Oil spills are tragic, but to compound the tragedy through hasty, ill-considered legislation benefits neither the nation nor its people.

We respectfully urge that common sense prevail when the Senate considers the House measure. Immobilizing a healthy leg won't heal a broken arm.

M⊚bil

© 1989 Mobil Corporation

This ad appeared in *The New York Times* on Thursday, August 3, 1989.

FIGURE 3.3 Advertising for Influence
Mobil attempts to influence legislators by advertising its position in the media. For example, this recent ad in The New York Times *criticizes governmental action regarding oil spills.*

*B*usiness Ethics

WHERE THERE'S SMOKE, THERE'S MONEY

"[P]olitical] power is an illusion . . . beautiful blue smoke rolling over the surface of highly polished mirrors," wrote Jimmy Breslin in *How the Good Guys Finally Won*. Thus it is perhaps fitting that until recently few in Washington have wielded more power over the Congress than the tobacco industry.

The industry's long-time influence depended on two factors: money and organization. Tobacco is a $35-billion-a-year industry in the United States, accounting for $4 billion in U.S. exports. Few members of Congress are prepared to write off the income the industry generates and the jobs it provides. Moreover, the tobacco industry is accustomed to "sharing" its profits with Congress. Long before political action committees became the fashion, the Tobacco Institute was funding political campaigns. In the 1988 election year alone, tobacco companies supplied $1 million just to congressional candidates.

But money and organization have not been able to protect the tobacco industry from increased governmental restrictions in recent years. As report after report from the U.S. Surgeon General has linked cigarette smoking and tobacco chewing to various forms of cancer and heart disease, the public has become more and more opposed to tobacco products. And reports that "second-hand smoke" (being in the presence of someone smoking) may also be a health threat have led to increased cries for limits on public smoking.

Today, antismoking forces are as well organized as the tobacco industry (if less affluent) and are successfully challenging the use of tobacco in many settings. Many of the restrictions on tobacco use thus far have been at the local level, but a few years ago Congress passed laws prohibiting smok-

The tobacco fields of Tennessee are just one small part of an industry that generates more than $35 billion a year.

ing on all domestic flights. In addition, many on the antismoking side are now calling for an end to cigarette vending machines. They point out that such machines make it impossible to prevent minors from buying cigarettes and that, of the 1 million new U.S. smokers each year, 80 percent are teenagers and 100,000 are aged 12 or under. (Indeed, the current U.S. smoker is most likely to be young, poor, and relatively uneducated.)

The tobacco industry is not giving up, though, and still wields considerable power in Washington. When the Environmental Protection Agency assembled a panel in 1990 to assess EPA studies on the effects of second-hand smoke, six of the eight panel members had ties to tobacco industry research groups. Only after word of the makeup of the panel was leaked to the press was one scientist who had previously expressed opposition to smoking named to the panel (over the objections of the tobacco industry, of course). It would appear that where there's smoke . . . there's still money.

example, they note that while public opinion polls show that most U.S. residents favor some form of gun control, the National Rifle Association's lobbying has kept such laws off the federal books. Similarly, farmers and ranchers have been given government subsidies not to grow or produce certain foodstuffs. And the same government that warns of tobacco's dangers allows the tobacco industry to make large contributions to political campaign funds, as the Business Ethics box "Where There's Smoke, There's Money" discusses.

For many lobbying efforts, however, there are opposing efforts. The American Cancer Society and the American Tobacco Institute have very different points of view on cigarette smoking and cigarette advertising, for example. So, in looking at business and its influence on government, it is important to keep in mind that competing interests can have vastly different effects on political processes. (We will discuss the legal and regulatory environment of business in more detail in Chapter 24.)

▼ BUSINESS AND LABOR

Because workers are an important resource to every company, relations with the labor force are another important dimension of the contemporary business world. As we noted earlier in this chapter, however, the influence of organized labor has been declining in recent years. This trend stems from several factors, including the changing demographics of the labor force and declining membership in many unions. At the same time, though, some organizations are giving their employees more power through increased participation.

THE CHANGING DEMOGRAPHICS OF THE U.S. LABOR FORCE

The statistical makeup—the *demographics*—of the U.S. labor force has changed gradually over the past several years. As Figure 3.4 shows, these changes have been in terms of age, the role of women, and the impact of immigrants.

The Graying Workforce. The age of the average U.S. worker has gradually increased over the past few decades. As you might expect, this increase is the result of more older workers and fewer younger workers. Americans are living longer than ever before, and some older individuals are taking advantage of changes in retirement laws and continuing to work beyond age 65. More important, however, is the so-called baby bust generation, those individuals born after the baby boom of the immediate post–World War II period. It was the baby boomers who embraced the jeans offered by Levi Strauss in the 1960s. The baby bust generation is relatively small, not only in comparison to the giant baby boom generation, but also in comparison to the individuals now in their 50s and 60s.

This trend has affected business in two ways. First, older workers tend to put greater demands on a company's health insurance, life insurance, and retirement benefit programs. Second, younger workers taking the places of retirees tend to want different things from employers—things like more opportunities for self-expression or more leisure time.

On another front, many businesses are now hiring retirees as part-time employees. Many retirees have a great deal of experience, are dependable, and require fewer benefits than do full-time employees.

Women in the Workforce. Another employment trend in the United States is the growing number of women in the workforce. In 1950, only 34 percent of the female population worked outside the home. By 1990, the figure exceeded 57 percent.[5]

There are many reasons for the increase in the number of women who work outside the home. Faced with rapid increases in the prices of goods and services during the 1970s, many couples found that they needed two incomes to maintain their standard of living. In addition, the women's movement and the greater number of women graduating from college have resulted in more career opportunities for women.

The large percentage of women in all types of careers has had and will continue to have a major impact on U.S. business. Millions of young children have mothers who work outside the home. Government leaders have described

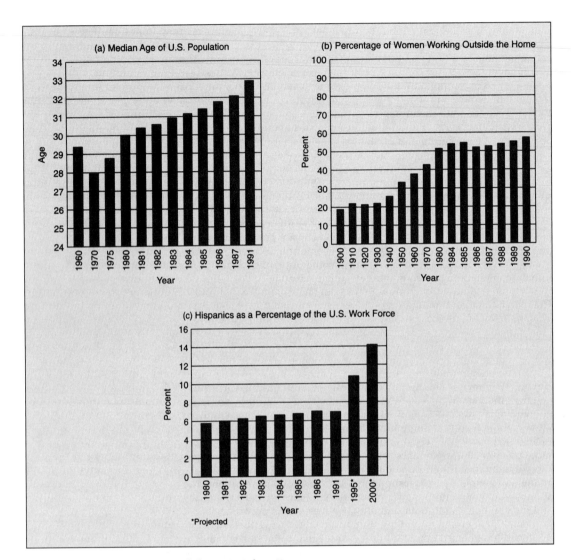

FIGURE 3.4   Demographics of the U.S. Labor Force
The demographics of the U.S. workforce are changing. The median age of the average U.S. worker is increasing, and women and Hispanic-Americans are a growing percentage of the workforce.

the problem of child care as one of today's most important business challenges. While everyone agrees that there is a problem, there is little agreement over how to solve it. Some people believe that the government should own and operate child-care centers. Others argue that companies should sponsor child-care centers for their employees. Indeed, many major companies have started offering such services in recent years.

Immigrants in the Workforce. Immigrants have long been said to make the United States a "melting pot." But immigrants have not merely melted into U.S. society; they have also changed it. For example, workers from some countries have religious holidays different from those celebrated in the United States. Some want more participation in decision making than is customary in the

Immigrants have not merely melted into U.S. society; they have also changed it.

Chapter 3 / Recognizing Business Trends and Challenges   63

Partially as a result of changes in retirement laws, older workers are staying in the workforce longer. Recent years have also seen an increase in the number of older Americans serving as volunteers for worthy causes after retirement. Volunteers are essential to many organizations, including this school in Donna, Texas, where Hispanic-American children receive special tutoring to learn reading skills.

United States; others want less. Some workers from hot climates are used to long lunch breaks, while others are accustomed to work weeks much longer than 40 hours. As a result of these various influences, some businesses have altered their policies regarding religious holidays, employer-employee relationships, and work-ethic expectations.

Tougher immigration laws have also increased labor costs for many companies in border towns. Accustomed to using the cheap labor of illegal aliens for temporary jobs like construction and agriculture, these firms now face stiff fines for such hiring practices. In addition, many companies have had to process additional paperwork (at additional costs) in order to document the citizenship of their workers.

THE DECLINING UNIONIZATION OF THE LABOR FORCE

Another important element affecting business's dealings with labor is the steady decline in union membership over the past several years. Several factors account for this trend. For one thing, the number of jobs in manufacturing, long a union stronghold, has declined. For another, younger workers entering the labor force in recent years have not been as interested in joining unions as their predecessors were. Furthermore, unions have been slow to enroll women and minorities.

Business, of course, reaps certain benefits from this trend. Labor costs don't increase as rapidly, strikes are not as likely, and there are fewer union-demanded "work rules" to worry about. (We will cover these and many related issues in more depth in Chapter 11.)

WORKER PARTICIPATION

Yet another trend in business-labor relations is the increase in worker participation. Traditionally, at least in the United States, managers made decisions and decided how things were going to be done. Workers carried out management's orders and had little voice in how they performed their jobs. In recent years, however, U.S. firms have learned that most successful Japanese firms give their

You might think this photo was snapped by an American on a visit to the Far East, but it was really taken in Los Angeles' Koreatown. Experts have projected that ethnic minorities will account for half of California's population by the year 2000. In Los Angeles, where they already do, shopping malls like Seoul (Na Sung) Plaza have sprung up to cater to the needs of various ethnic groups.

workers considerable responsibility. Impressed by the success of these firms, U.S. businesses have tried to become more participative as well. At Xerox, Federal Express, Westinghouse, and Apple (to name just a few), many managerial functions are being turned over to teams of workers. And those workers are not only accepting the responsibility for getting their own work done but are also doing a far better job than before.[6] (We will cover this trend in more detail in Chapter 8.)

▼ BUSINESS AND CONSUMERS

In addition to adjusting to the demands of government and labor, businesses have also had to adjust to a steady increase in the power of the consumer. Gone are the days of *caveat emptor,* "let the buyer beware." A business following that dictum today is apt to face boycotts, lawsuits, and government intervention. Consumer tastes and preferences are also more complex than in the past. There are several reasons for this trend, including demographic changes and the rise of the consumer rights movement.[7]

CONSUMER RIGHTS

consumer movement
Activism on the part of consumers seeking better value from businesses.

Activism on the part of consumers seeking better value from businesses—the **consumer movement**—has altered the conduct of many businesses. Although the consumer movement traces its roots back to the turn of the century, Ralph Nader's much-publicized attack on the unsafe cars being produced by General Motors in the 1960s (*Unsafe at Any Speed,* 1965) really gave consumerism its momentum.

consumer rights
The legally protected rights of consumers to purchase the products they desire, to safety from the products they purchase, to be informed about what they are buying, and to be heard in the event of problems.

Over the last decade, legislation has broadened **consumer rights** considerably. In particular, laws now guarantee consumers the right to purchase the products they desire, the right to safety from the products they purchase, the right to be informed about what they are buying, and the right to be heard in the event of problems. As a result, most products today come with extensive instructions regarding their use and, in the case of food products, a detailed list of their ingredients. Most products also have a guarantee or warranty, and many list telephone numbers or addresses to contact in the event of problems. We will consider consumer rights and related issues more fully in Chapter 16.

THE CHANGING DEMOGRAPHICS OF U.S. CONSUMERS

The same pattern of demographic changes that are affecting the U.S. labor force also reflect changes in consumer demands.

A Graying Population. Just as the average age of U.S. workers is increasing, so is the average age of the entire U.S. population. Because of this trend, companies are finding new market opportunities and challenges. Older adults are demanding recreational facilities, health care, housing, leisure-time products, and personal-care items designed specifically for them.

Working Women. Working women are also providing many new opportunities for business. For example, in recent years, there has been increased demand for convenience foods that require little preparation, such as microwaveable dinners and frozen pizzas. Products like telephone answering machines and home computers have increased in popularity, partly because of the increase in two-career families. Restaurants and home-cleaning services have benefited too. In addition, there has been more demand for professional "gear" for working women: business attire, briefcases, and the like. The fact that women are not staying at home to care for children has even created a whole new industry—the day-care industry.

Increased Cultural Diversity. The increased buying power of various ethnic and cultural groups has led businesses to respond with products requested or demanded by these consumers. Radio stations and even some television stations offer programming in several languages, along with special programs oriented to specific ethnic groups. Large grocery stores routinely offer Mexican and Chinese food products. Fiesta Markets in Houston has prospered by catering to Hispanic-American consumers. And the cosmetic industry now manufactures products designed for people with a wide range of skin tones.

> **T**he increased buying power of various ethnic and cultural groups has led businesses to respond with products requested or demanded by these consumers.

▼ BUSINESS CHALLENGES OF THE 1990S

Given the nature and complexities of today's business environment, it is not surprising that U.S. business faces a number of challenges in the 1990s. As Figure 3.5 shows, the four most important challenges relate to productivity, international trade, pollution, and technology.

IN SEARCH OF HIGHER PRODUCTIVITY

As we saw in Chapter 1, productivity is a measure of an economy's success. It is also a measure of a business's success, because it reflects the efficiency with

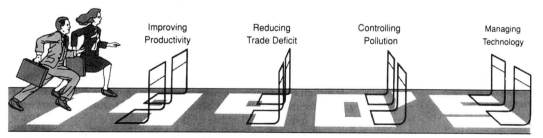

| Improving Productivity | Reducing Trade Deficit | Controlling Pollution | Managing Technology |

FIGURE 3.5 The Four Basic Challenges of the 1990s
U.S. business must confront four basic challenges in the 1990s: improving productivity, reducing the trade deficit, controlling pollution, and managing technology.

66   Part One / Introducing the Contemporary Business World

Carolyn Blakeslee, who singlehandedly produces every issue of ArtCalendar *(a monthly publication for visual artists that lists grants, juried shows accepting applications, and other forums to which artists can submit their work), is just one of many working mothers in the United States today.*

which a company uses resources. A company that uses fewer resources (whether materials, management, or labor) to make the same number of products as another firm is more efficient. While U.S. workers are the most productive in the world, for the last several years the growth of productivity in the United States has been slower than that in many other nations such as Japan and Germany. This has prompted U.S. managers to look actively for ways to improve productivity. The complex nature of the productivity problem and some proposed solutions are discussed in Chapter 26.

THE INTERNATIONAL TRADE DEFICIT

trade deficit
The situation in which a country imports more than it exports; sometimes called a negative trade balance.

trade surplus
The situation in which a country exports more than it imports.

Another significant challenge facing managers in the 1990s is the U.S. **trade deficit.** A trade deficit occurs when a nation is importing more products than it is exporting. For decades, the United States had a **trade surplus**—that is, it exported more than it imported. But the surplus turned to a deficit in the 1980s. The mid-1991 surplus was the first surplus in the United States in over 15 years, and it didn't last very long.

Why have so many foreign companies been more successful in the international market of late than their U.S. competitors? Some economists blame conflict among business, the government, and labor in the United States. Certainly, cooperation among these elements has helped Japan gain an advantage in the contemporary business world. If the United States is to compete more effectively in the international business arena, these economists argue, it must operate with more coordination and less antagonism. Perhaps the system that served us well domestically for so long must change to meet the challenges of today's global environment.

Some reasons for U.S. trade imbalances relate to the characteristics of other countries. For example, some countries pay their employees lower wages. This is one of the reasons that Levi Strauss recently made the decision to transfer some of its operations overseas. Lower safety standards and fewer pollution controls in many foreign countries translate into lower costs of producing goods. Fewer "paperwork" requirements mean that foreign companies do not have to employ as many accountants and lawyers—a substantial cost savings that is passed on to consumers in the form of lower prices. In addition, many countries have complex rules that restrict the import of U.S.-made goods. Some impose tariffs (taxes) on imports. Others have complicated inspection procedures that cost U.S. companies much time and money.

Finally, if unemployment threatens a particular industry, some foreign governments will subsidize that industry through grants, low-interest loans, or government purchases at inflated prices. Subsidies enable foreign companies to sell their products in the United States at prices lower than their actual production costs.

Because so many factors are involved in the international trade problem, any solution will have to be equally complex. We discuss the international business world throughout this book and devote a special chapter to the topic later on (Chapter 25).

THE CONTINUING CHALLENGE OF POLLUTION

By the end of the twentieth century, there will be no unused landfills in the United States. How will we dispose of solid waste then? Will we burn it? Will we recycle it? How will we meet the energy needs of the future? Will we use conventional power plants that damage the air and land? Or will we turn to nuclear-powered plants that raise the issue of safe nuclear waste disposal?

Unfortunately, this problem is not unique to the United States. Indeed, many areas of Eastern Europe are among the most polluted in the world. As the Executive Report "Turning Garbage into Gold" describes, pollution cleanup may be a new source of business profits. We explore environmental issues in more detail in the next chapter.

TECHNOLOGY: FRIEND OR FOE?

We have already introduced some of the opportunities and issues posed by technological innovation and advancement. Dealing with such technology and its role in modern society will continue to be a major business challenge of the 1990s. Is high technology friend or foe to U.S. workers and businesses? Critics fear the replacement of traditional middle-class jobs with automated machinery, predicting a depersonalized society in which people become nothing but numbers to a computer that receives telephone calls, handles banking transactions, maintains the temperatures in our homes, and even answers our doorbells. This fear of technology is not new. Charlie Chaplin movies in the 1920s satirized the industrial production line and George Orwell's *1984* (first published in 1949) painted a grim vision of a future government using technology to control society.

Is high technology friend or foe to U.S. workers and businesses?

Executive Report

DAVID L. SOKOL: TURNING GARBAGE INTO GOLD

It may be today's ideal industry. With so many disposable goods—disposable diapers, disposable lighters, and disposable razors, to name just a few—the United States is confronted with an ever-increasing garbage pile and an ever-decreasing number of places to dump that garbage. At the same time, everyone is worried about finding energy substitutes for expensive foreign oil. What could be more perfect than a company that burns garbage at high temperatures that generate steam, which, in turn, can be used to produce electricity? In the opinion of Ogden Projects' youthful president and CEO, David L. Sokol, nothing.

Sokol certainly seems justified in his optimism. Ogden Projects' first facility didn't open until 1986, yet by 1989, it had become the industry leader, beating out older firms such as Wheelabrator and Westinghouse. Of the 42 projects on which Sokol bid between 1984 and 1989, Ogden Projects won 22 contracts.

Much of the credit for Ogden Projects' success goes to Sokol's choice of market. Because Ogden Projects has confined itself to the municipal market, working with cities to build the necessary plants, it has faced less public opposition than its rivals.

Sokol's choice of technology has also helped Ogden's sales and profits. Because all of Ogden's facilities are exactly the same, the company has been able to construct them on time and at a relatively low cost. Because Ogden Projects has exclusive rights to the Martin incineration technology—which many say is the best available—Ogden has earned an attractive reputation for reliability.

Finally, under Sokol, Ogden's pricing policy has appealed to the cities with which it seeks to do business. Typically, Ogden Projects builds its plants for cost. It earns its money on 20- to 25-year guaranteed contracts with municipalities. Thus cities get low initial costs, while Ogden gets solid future profits that include a percentage of the energy revenues.

Occasionally, a hardworking entrepreneur finds himself riding the crest of a wave. The "Green Movement" of the 1990s, with its emphasis on environmentally sound trash disposal and recycling, has opened up a world of opportunity for David Sokol and Ogden Projects.

Ogden Projects' parent company, Ogden Corporation, couldn't be more delighted. Having pared its once far-flung holdings to focus on cleanup (everything from building maintenance to toxic waste disposal), Ogden Corporation is now reaping the benefits. And chief among these benefits is Sokol's Ogden Projects. In 1988, waste-to-energy provided Ogden Corporation with over $18 million, a third of the company's entire income.

And it seems that the best is yet to come. The firm's earnings have continued to increase substantially each year. Seven new plants were built in 1990 and 1991, and seven more are planned for 1995. With a recent ruling by the Environmental Protection Agency that incinerator projects must recycle 25 percent of their output by 1994, Ogden appears to have found a treasure trove in trash.

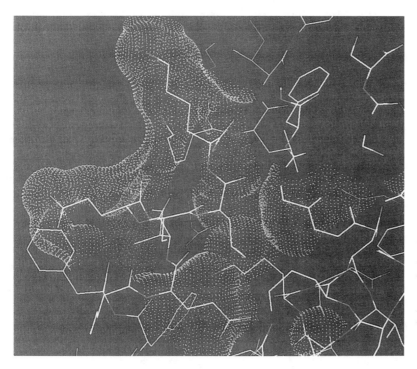

This is a small portion of the crystal structure of Actimmune gamma interferon, a virus-fighting agent produced by Genentech and pending approval by the U.S. Food and Drug Administration. Rapidly advancing genetic technology promises a safer world and a healthier population, but is not without its ethical problems. Should animals be used for experimental purposes? How extensively should a new drug or technology be tested before it is approved for use?

Defenders of technology point to its many benefits. New genetically engineered seeds that will increase agricultural production for a hungry world are now coming on the market. New vaccines that may help win the battle against cancer are in development. And new employment opportunities in safer work environments than the blistering hot and dangerous steel mills of the past are a reality for many workers today.

Some people argue that technology will provide solutions to the pollution problem and ways to increase productivity. Others raise complex questions about whether we will be able to control the technology we create. As future business and government leaders, you will be confronted with these and many other challenges in the decades ahead.

SUMMARY OF LEARNING OBJECTIVES

1 **Describe four major trends that affect U.S. business today.** Business, the government, labor, and consumers are four countervailing powers that influence and are influenced by one another. Over the last two decades, the influence of labor has declined, while that of consumers has been on the rise. The U.S. business world has also experienced a shift from manufacturing to services, a geographic shift toward the Sunbelt, the advent of high technology, and increased merger activity.

2 **Explain why the U.S. government sometimes regulates businesses and how business seeks to influence the government.** Government regulates business in order to promote competition and to help achieve social goals. Recent years have seen a trend toward deregulation, but businesses continue to use lobbying, trade associations, advertising, and political action committees (PACs) to influence government.

3 **Discuss changes in the U.S. labor pool and their effects on business.** Changing demographics in the labor force have influenced how business managers deal with labor. The most notable of these changes are an aging population, more working women, and increased ethnic and cultural diversity. In addition, the decline of labor unions has meant lower labor costs, fewer strikes, and fewer union-demanded "work rules." More organizations are giving their workers increased responsibility and allowing them greater participation.

4 **Describe changes in demographics and consumer rights and their impact on U.S. business.** The same pattern of demographic changes that has affected management-labor relations (see number 3 above) has also influenced business-customer relations, particularly in terms of the goods and services that customers are demanding. Consumer rights activism has forced businesses to become more sensitive to consumer desires and complaints.

5 **Identify and discuss four major challenges for U.S. business in the 1990s.** Businesses face a variety of challenges in the 1990s. Foremost among these are the need to increase productivity, the need to regain a competitive edge in international trade and reduce the U.S. trade deficit, the need to control pollution, and the need to harness technology.

OPENING CASE WRAP-UP

BUTTONING UP PROFITS

While Haas's commitment to creating a positive corporate culture has been a major factor in the success of Levi Strauss since 1985, of at least equal importance has been a host of internal changes to meet external challenges.

New Products. Much of Levi's increased sales come from several "new" products. The first of these new products is actually an old one—the revival of the company's trademark button-fly jeans, now hawked as "501 jeans." A switch to more stonewashed, acid-washed, and other "treated" denim has also helped to revitalize the firm's line of jeans.

More radical and possibly even more important is the introduction of the Dockers line. These casual nondenim pants, cut wide at the top and tapered toward the ankle, meet two baby boomer needs: comfortable fit and a more polished appearance than jeans. How successful is the Dockers' line? In just four years, it has become a $500-million-a-year line. Industry analysts describe Dockers as the fastest-growing product line in the history of the apparel industry. Little wonder that it has been expanded beyond Dockers pants for men to include coordinated tops and women's and children's wear.

New Promotion. Free of the short-term constraints of public ownership, the management of Levi Strauss has pumped millions of dollars into advertising. In 1991, the firm spent $15 million for the 1991 edition of its "Button Your Fly" campaign, directed by popular filmmaker Spike Lee, for its 501 jeans.

New Distribution. Levi's jeans have long been popular in Western Europe. By expanding sales and manufacturing operations into Eastern Europe and Asia, Levi's has been able to take advantage of relatively low production costs in these nations. Today over half of Levi's profits come from its overseas operations.

New Organization. Streamlining the firm's organization to eliminate layers of management has translated into substantial cost savings—and increased the speed with which other changes can be made. After maintaining a paternalistic attitude toward job security for employees for many years, Haas and other upper-level managers recently decided to shut 26 Levi's manufacturing plants in the United States. (Union officials admit that the severance plan for those let go was generous, however.)

New Technology. Thanks to the firm's LeviLink computer system, vendors can place orders and make payments electronically. The system also allows Levi's to order supplies and produce goods on a just-in-time basis to meet customers' needs (thus saving both Levi's and its suppliers the costs of high inventories). A sophisticated computer-aided design system takes initial designs, turns them into pattern pieces for a range of sizes, and designs a layout of the pieces to get the most out of the fabric.

What will the future hold? Will baby boomers abandon Dockers, as they have so many other products? Perhaps. But if so, count on Levi Strauss to find a way to get business "booming" again.

CASE QUESTIONS

1. Why do you think Levi Strauss's attempt to sell other forms of clothing in the 1980s failed?

2. What other savings might Levi Strauss realize by utilizing more high-technology equipment?

3. What changes in the labor force would you expect to see at Levi Strauss in the next decade? Why?

4. How do you think continued changes in U.S. demographics will affect Levi Strauss's products and sales in the next 10 years? The next 20 years?

5. In 1990, Levi Strauss agreed to sell stock in its Japanese operation to Japanese investors. The firm's management argues that such a sale is no threat to its management plans because Japanese investors are "in it for the long run." Do you agree or disagree with this decision? Why?

CONCLUDING CASE

ROLLING IN DOUGH

Though sometimes nicknamed "sinkers," doughnuts can float you to the top . . . just ask the folks at Dunkin' Donuts. While many firms in the United States spent much of the 1980s buying up unrelated firms and building conglomerates, only to dismantle them later (or see them fall apart), Dunkin' Donuts has stayed with what it knows.

Since its founding in 1950, Dunkin' Donuts has had a clear mission: "to make and sell the freshest, most delicious coffee and donuts." And quarter after quarter, year after year, that mission has translated into growth and profits. Today over 2,000 Dunkin' Donuts range from Massachusetts (the original store) to Europe and Asia, with more opening every year.

In the late 1980s, this very success made the firm a takeover target of Canadian oil and real estate magnate George Mann. But Bob Rosenberg, chairman of Dunkin' Donuts and son of the founder, fought back, deliberately taking on debt (a "poison pill" against a takeover). The firm also sold a large block of stock to its employees and additional stock to friendly General Electric Corporation. Left with only 15 percent of the firm's stock and the chance to buy only 20 percent more, Mann was stymied.

Unlike many firms that took on debt in the 1980s to prevent a takeover, however, Dunkin' Donuts may be in better shape than ever. For even as he took on debt, Rosenberg cut $7 million from operating expenses

Dunkin' Donuts' latest brainstorm is the "mini donut," a miniaturized version of its traditional donut. The minis were introduced in early 1992 at a price of five for 99 cents and were an immediate success.

by paring 14 percent of the staff—more than enough to service the debt. Remaining employees' morale remained reasonably high, thanks to the new stock ownership plan implemented by Rosenberg.

Rosenberg is also looking for new ideas to enable the company to continue to grow in ever more profitable ways. In the decade before Mann's takeover attempt, Dunkin' Donuts had expanded its kitchens to include ovens, its menu to include muffins, cookies, brownies, croissants, and soup, and its offerings to include lunch as well as breakfast. But such operations are expensive and space-consuming. Thus the company is now experimenting with kitchenless "satellite" shops in airports, train stations, shopping malls, and convenience stores. These shops sell products made and supplied by nearby full-service franchises. Not only are these satellite shops less expensive to build and operate, but they also provide an outlet for any excess production capacity at the supplying store.

All of which may make it a "hole" new ball game for Dunkin' Donuts.

CASE QUESTIONS

1. Do you think Rosenberg was wise to fend off Mann's attempted takeover? Why or why not?
2. What shifts in the marketplace do you think Dunkin' Donuts was trying to address with its addition of muffins? Of lunch?
3. What do you believe will be Dunkin' Donuts' greatest challenge in the next decade?
4. What demographic changes may force alterations at Dunkin' Donuts in the future?

KEY TERMS

high technology (high-tech) firm 51
service sector 51
informational services 51
acquisition 52
merger 53
strategic alliance 53
horizontal merger 53
vertical merger 54
conglomerate merger 54
friendly takeover 54
hostile takeover 54

greenmail 54
raiders 54
regulation 55
deregulation 56
lobbyist 58
trade association 58
political action committee (PAC) 59
consumer movement 64
consumer rights 64
trade deficit 66
trade surplus 66

STUDY QUESTIONS AND EXERCISES

Review Questions

1. Identify four significant forces of change that businesses must contend with.
2. In what ways do businesses attempt to influence government? What ethical implications can be drawn regarding these actions?
3. Why is union membership in the United States declining?
4. Why is productivity such an important issue today?
5. What four major hurdles face business in the 1990s?

Analysis Questions

6. Using periodicals such as *Fortune* and *Business Week*, identify six recent alliances. What do you think each organization expects to gain from its partnership in the alliance?
7. Locate three instances in which you believe business has been more responsive to consumer expectations recently than it was in the past.

8. Do you think that the continuing challenge of pollution will ever be solved? Why or why not?

Application Exercises

9. Interview a local bank manager. Identify ways in which deregulation of the banking industry has made banking more risky and more profitable.
10. Visit a local manufacturing company. Identify ways in which it has been affected by high technology.

"EMPLOYMENT CHALLENGES OF THE 1990s"

Laura Anderson is a marketing features writer for *The Denver Post*.

EMPLOYMENT CHALLENGES OF THE 1990S

LAURA ANDERSON

[1]Just 40 years ago, a man could expect to find a job relatively easily, work hard and stay with it, and retire at age 65 with a gold watch and a comfortable pension. His wife, in the meantime, stayed at home to give full attention to support of the family and management of the household. Needless to say, those days are gone.

[2]According to projections by the U.S. Department of Labor, by the year 2000, 80 percent of the United States work force will be made up of women, minorities and immigrants. Women will account for 47 percent of all workers and will be hired for 64 percent of all new jobs. By 2000, the largest age group of workers will be those 35 to 54 years old as the baby boomers reach their 50s. The disabled workers will find doors opened that have been otherwise closed, albeit illegally, as the shift in American industry puts more emphasis on intellect than muscle.

[3]Fifty percent of the new jobs created in the 1990s will require some education beyond the high school level and almost 33 percent will be open to college graduates only. According to recent surveys, 61 percent of the companies questioned are currently having difficulties finding qualified people to fill professional and technical positions; 66 percent surveyed indicate that applicants for entry-level positions now "lack basic skills such as reading, writing, mathematics, problem solving and communications."

[4]During the 1980s, the U.S. economy affecting the job market was replaced by the global economy. As imports and exports have broken down the geographic boundaries of business transactions and interests, the job market is being affected just as surely. As exports from the U.S. increase, jobs will increase. This presents a new challenge and great opportunity for businesses and the work force. Only the courageous will survive. Just as competition is stiff in today's American job market, tomorrow the competition will be just as stiff but will encompass the world....

CONTENT QUESTIONS—"EMPLOYMENT CHALLENGES OF THE 1990s"

TRUE OR FALSE

If the statement is false, rewrite it to make it true.

1. The makeup of the U.S. workforce is expected to remain the same into the year 2000.
2. By 2000, the largest age group of workers will be those 35–54.
3. Thirty-three percent of the jobs created in the 1990s will require education beyond high school.
4. The global economy is affecting the U.S. job market more than ever before.
5. With a global economy, the job market will be easier.

COMPLETION

6. Identify the three major components of the U.S. workforce in the year 2000.

7. What are the five "basic skills" many entry-level workers lack?

CONTENT ANALYSIS QUESTIONS—"EMPLOYMENT CHALLENGES OF THE 1990S"

1. What is Anderson's thesis?

2. How do these figures compare with Griffin and Ebert's data on the changing demographics of the labor force?

3. Why do you think a change in the amount of imports and exports has such an affect on the U.S. job market?

4. Explain what Anderson means by "as the shift in American industry puts more emphasis on intellect than muscle."

5. Explain what Anderson means by, "During the 1980s, the U.S. economy affecting the job market was replaced by the global economy."

APPLICATION QUESTION—"EMPLOYMENT CHALLENGES OF THE 1990S"

1. Would you rather have lived 40 years ago when a man could expect to find a job relatively easily, work hard at the same job all his life, and retire at 65 with a gold watch and comfortable pension while his wife stayed home with the family, or today? Discuss your reasons.

"FUTURE WORK"

Joseph Coates, Jennifer Jarratt, and John Mahaffie are the president, vice president, and research associate, respectively, of J. F. Coates, Inc., a firm specializing in futures research and policy analysis. This selection—"Future Work"—is excerpted from *The Futurist* 25 (May–June 1991).

FUTURE WORK

JOSEPH F. COATES, JENNIFER JARRATT, AND JOHN B. MAHAFFIE

[1]The North American work force faces wrenching changes in its structure and composition that will radically alter how employers recruit, hire, manage, and hold on to good people.

[2]Some of these changes are demographic. More women, minorities, and immigrants are entering the work force; the work force is aging, as is society in North America; and the number of younger, entry-level workers available is shrinking. Other changes are economic: for example, North American corporations confront growing competition at home and abroad from companies with lower labor costs and faster product-to-market rates. This means employers must contain labor costs and produce higher-quality goods and services with a smaller work force.

(CONTINUED)

FUTURE WORK (CONTINUED)

[3]What an individual worker can bring to the workplace—in terms of education, skills, self-reliance, and attitude—is becoming ever more important in reaching an organization's business goals. Businesses are recognizing that a worker is a resource and an asset, rather than merely a fixed cost.

[4]The North American work force has earned its reputation as one of the most vital and hard-working labor forces in the world. Other countries envy its education, mobility, and creativity, as they also admire the U.S. economy's capacity for generating new jobs. Maintaining this reputation and competing effectively in turbulent times will require flexibility and the ability to embrace and incorporate change. The ability of business planners and managers to anticipate changes and their effects on people in an organization thus becomes more critical, and competitive survival may depend on how well planners and managers can think about the future.

[5]More than ever before, people are the dominant factor in both service and production. People plan, invent, design, operate, manage, and service the large corporation. People are its suppliers and its customers.

[6]This increased attention being given to the demand for more-productive and more-effective workers is stimulating new ideas. When one thinks of innovation, one tends to think of science and high technology, such as robots and new ceramics. But now one also thinks of quality circles, innovative rewards, and new work arrangements.

[7]One of the most positive developments is the growing interest on the part of business organizations in identifying and analyzing trends shaping the future work force. This interest in the future is a first step toward planning for work-force needs over the next 10 to 15 years. Actions taken now that are based on an informed look toward the future can prepare a company for changes and shifts in its available work force over time.

[8]We have identified a number of trends that are likely to influence the North American work force in the next 15 years. The potential effect of these trends signals the need for action and response. Actions can range from merely continuing to monitor the trend to reviewing policies and creating major shifts in business strategy.

Increasing Diversity in the Work Force

The Continuing Aging of the Work Force Will Create Problems and Opportunities

[9]The aging of the baby-boom generation is raising the median age of the U.S. population. The median age, about 33 in 1990, will be 36 by the year 2000. By 2010, one quarter of the U.S. population will be at least 55, and one in seven Americans will be at least 65. The rapid growth of the U.S. labor force has been pushed by the baby boomers who have now matured into working-age adults. Between 1990 and 2000, the number of people between 35 and 44 will jump by 16 percent, and those between the ages of 45 and 54 will increase by 46 percent, compared with an overall expected population growth of 7.1 percent.

[10]In addition to the baby boomers (people born between 1946 and 1964), three age groups are influencing the shifting structure and composition of the work force: 1930s Depression babies (1929–1940); the baby-bust cohort (1965–1978); and the baby-boom echo (1979+).

Older Americans Will Increase in Number and Grow in Influence

[11]Older people are becoming a larger segment of the population, enjoying better health and longer life, and wielding economic and political power. More than 31 million Americans—12.4 percent of the nation's population—are estimated to be 65 or older. By 2020, when baby boomers reach 65, old people will be 20 percent of the U.S. population. At that time, there will be at least 7 million Americans over age 85.

(CONTINUED)

FUTURE WORK (CONTINUED)

The Middle-Aging of the Work Force

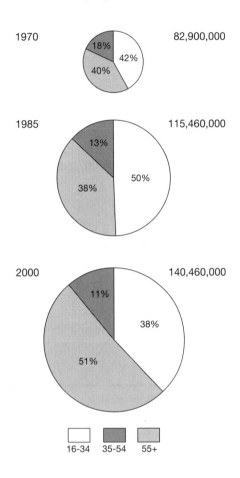

1970   82,900,000

18%
42%
40%

1985   115,460,000

13%
50%
38%

2000   140,460,000

11%
38%
51%

16-34   35-54   55+

[12]This aging of the U.S. society will have several significant effects. First, there will be changes in buying habits and consumer preferences. Second, there will be effects of the work force, such as aging workers and their productivity, health-care needs, retirement plans, rehired retirees as a part of the work force, and so on. Third, society will change with the rise of the four-generation family in which the older generation is active and economically independent.

Hispanics Will Be the Largest Fast-Growing Minority Population in the United States

[13]Hispanics are changing the face of America. The Bureau of the Census estimates that the Hispanic population grew from 14.6 million in 1980 to 21.9 million in 1990, about 50 percent in 10 years. Hispanic growth is five times that of non-Hispanics. By 2010, there will be 39.5 million U.S. Hispanics. Most U.S. Hispanics live in nine states. Mexican Americans are mostly in California, Arizona, New Mexico, Colorado, and Texas. Puerto Ricans are largely in New York, New Jersey, and Illinois. Cubans are mostly in Florida.

[14]Despite similarity of language, Hispanics are not a *homogeneous group*. Several different cultures, drawing on different national bases, make up the so-called Hispanic culture. But although there may be cultural differences, most Hispanics in the United States share North American values, including a desire for upward mobility.

(*CONTINUED*)

FUTURE WORK (CONTINUED)

PROJECTIONS OF THE U.S. LABOR FORCE—1988–2000 (ALL POPULATION NUMBERS IN THOUSANDS)

	U.S. LABOR FORCE			NET CHANGE		% CHANGE/YR.	
	1976	*1988*	*2000*	*'76–'88*	*'88–2000*	*'76–'88*	*'88–2000*
Total, Age							
16 and over	96,158	121,669	141,134	25,511	19,465	2.0%	1.2%
Men, Age							
16 and over	57,174	66,927	74,324	9,753	7,397	1.3%	0.9%
16–24	12,572	11,753	11,352	–999	–401	–0.7%	–0.3%
25	35,576	46,383	53,155	10,807	6,772	2.2%	1.1%
55+	8,846	8,791	9,817	–55	1,026	–0.1%	0.9%
Women, Age							
16 and over	38,984	54,742	66,810	15,758	12,068	2.9%	1.7%
16–24	10,588	10,782	11,104	194	322	0.2%	0.2%
24–54	22,925	37,659	48,112	14,734	10,453	4.2%	2.1%
55+	5,471	6,301	7,594	830	1,293	1.2%	1.6%
White	84,767	104,755	118,981	19,988	14,226	1.8%	1.1%
Black	9,565	13,205	16,465	3,640	3,260	2.7%	1.9%
Asian/Other	1,826	3,709	5,688	1,883	1,979	6.1%	3.6%
Hispanics*	4,289	8,982	14,321	2,693	5,339	6.4%	4.0%

*Persons of Hispanic origin may be of any race
Source: U.S. Department of Labor

Most Black Americans Will Advance—But Not All

[15]In 1987, blacks accounted for 10.8 percent of the U.S. work force and about 12.2 percent of the population. They will grow to a projected 11.7 percent of the labor force by the year 2000. About 70 percent of black Americans are advancing in nearly every aspect of American life. In their transition to the mainstream, they have already moved from the rural South to cities throughout the country and advanced in large numbers from unskilled and blue-collar work to white-collar work. They are moving up in corporations and government, making great educational advances, moving toward closer *income parity* with whites, and gaining political and economic power. In a generation or two, they have risen into the middle class and are moving to the suburbs. They are part of the mainstream.

[16]Nevertheless, 30 percent of blacks did not make these transitions after the great northward migration, which began in the 1920s and accelerated during and after World War II. They are stuck in a new American social situation—in urban ghettos, in multi-generational poverty, off the upward-mobility ladder—and locked into a goalless culture.

Women Will Move Gradually into the Executive Suite

[17]By sheer force of their growing numbers in management ranks, women will force open the door to the executive suite over the next two decades. They will be counted among the 15 to 25 people in each of the largest corporations who run the show.

(CONTINUED)

FUTURE WORK (CONTINUED)

High-Achieving Asians Are Out-Performing North American Whites in the Classroom and the Workplace

[18]For the most part, Asian Americans are affluent and well educated, but they are a diverse group differentiated by language, culture, and geography. Seven of the largest Asian groups in the United States are the Chinese, Filipinos, Japanese, Asian Indians, Koreans, Vietnamese, and Laotians. By the turn of the century, the number of Asian Americans will rise to more than 8 million.

[19]Asian Americans are outstandingly successful in education. Japanese males between 25 and 39 have a 96 percent high-school-completion rate. For Koreans and Indians, the completion rate is 94 percent; for Chinese, 90 percent; and for Filipinos, 89 percent. These rates compare with a white rate of 87 percent. Young Asian Americans graduating at the top of their class will be well *acculturated* and will have high expectations of the workplace and their prospects in it.

A Shrinking Labor Pool Will Create Opportunities for Traditionally Underemployed Workers

[20]A shortage of workers in the United States—especially entry-level workers and those with specialized talent—is making many *underutilized workers* more attractive. These workers fall into two categories: those of limited skill or ability and those who are only partially available for work. The first are underutilized because they lack particular abilities or skills; the second either are not available to work at preferred times and places or do not have the desired commitment. Both categories are a substantial part of the human resource pool. Labor shortages may make workers who are often considered unemployable or problematic—such as the disabled, emotionally impaired, or illiterate—more attractive.

The Scientific and Engineering Work Force Is Growing and Becoming More Diverse in National Origin, Gender, and Race

[21]Nearly 5 million scientists and engineers were employed in the United States in 1986, double the number employed in 1976, demonstrating the increasing importance of science and technology to U.S. society. At the same time, the scientific and engineering work force is becoming more diverse by gaining more foreign-born workers, women, and minorities. Women and black scientists and engineers are still a relatively small part of this work force, although their numbers are increasing. Universities and employers who need Ph.D. qualifications find themselves increasingly dependent on foreign-born workers.

SELECTED MARKET CHARACTERISTICS (WITH % AGES OF PARTICIPATION) OF SCIENTISTS AND ENGINEERS, 1986

	ALL SCIENTISTS AND ENGINEERS	*SCIENTISTS*	*ENGINEERS*
Labor-force participation rate	94.5	95.3	93.8
Unemployment rate	1.5	1.9	1.2
Employment rate	84.7	76.7	91.9
Underemployment rate	2.6	4.3	1.0
Average annual salary	$38,400	$35,700	$40,800

Source: National Science Foundation, *Science Resources Studies Highlights,* 1987

(CONTINUED)

FUTURE WORK (CONTINUED)

Home Life and Work Life

Corporations Will Adopt New Programs to Support Employees' Family Responsibilities

[22]Although it is currently focused on day care, the issue of workplace support for employees' family obligations is *indicative of a larger concern* for greater *integration of home and work life*. Employers, once able to assume that the demands of male workers' home lives were taken care of by wives and families, are now being pushed to pay attention to family issues such as day care, sick children, eldercare, and schooling. One reason why corporations may lag behind in this trend could be that their older senior managers have not experienced these pressures in their own lives.

[23]Drivers of this trend include more families in which both husband and wife work, the dramatic increase in the number of women in the work force who are mothers, and the growing need for long-term care of the aging.

Work and Education Will Influence Women's Childbearing Choices and Will Shape National Fertility Patterns

[24]Of the 50.3 million employed women in 1987, 59.2 percent were married and most were in their prime childbearing and working years. Women are returning to work after childbearing sooner than ever.

[25]For many women, especially those with more than average education and with career prospects, there is an economic and opportunity cost for bearing children that may be limiting their lifetime fertility, as well as encouraging them to postpone childbearing. Demographers now expect the average U.S. woman to bear fewer than two children, although she herself may anticipate having at least two. Many more women will be childless than had planned to be. While the consequences of these trends have yet to be fully estimated, one likely outcome is childbearing that is explicitly planned to coincide with career choices.

Work Will Move to Unconventional Sites and Arrangements

[26]Employers are becoming willing to consider almost any work arrangement that will get work done at less cost. Businesses are seeking to contain costs, are responding to the need for flexibility to meet sudden demands or slowdown in work, and are finding workers with critical skills either too scarce or too expensive to hire full time. Workers, on the other hand, find flexible schedules appealing, particularly in terms of childcare, and are more concerned about such factors as long commutes. Temporary workers, part-time contractors, and independent workers constitute the fastest-growing employment category. These workers accounted for half of the growth in the U.S. work force between 1980 and 1987.

[27]Companies are exploring options such as contingent workers and flexible scheduling. Contingent workers are paid only for working, may not qualify for benefits, and are less likely to join labor unions. At the same time, emerging computer and networking technologies are enabling work to be done anywhere, at any time, and at any distance from the office or factory.

The New Focus on Workers as an Asset Will Make Attitudes and Values More Central

[28]Pressed by demands for an adequate return on investment in the work force, managers are becoming increasingly concerned about factors shaping their employees' behavior. More is being invested in training. Expectations of the individual's productivity, skills, and capacity for responsibility are greater. Yet at the same time, the work force is increasingly diverse in its attitudes and lifestyles. It is better educated than ever before and more acquainted with psychology and sociology.

(CONTINUED)

FUTURE WORK (CONTINUED)

[29]As a result, researchers are prodding workers and their families about their values and attitudes toward work, their bosses, and the workplace. Surveying is becoming a tool for assessing employees' loyalty and productivity.

Mobility Continues to Be a Strength of the North American Work Force

[30]North Americans, more than others, are ready to pack up and go. The average American moves every six years—11 times in a lifetime. During 1986–1987, 18 percent of people living in the United States moved to a different home. Many of these movers moved more than once in a year. A steady stream of immigrants to North America adds mobility to the work force. Such mobility is a strength for the future work force. Workers can move to where the jobs are, acquiring experience and skills in the process. And a mobile work force means that employers can attract skilled workers to new sites, making it easier for business to relocate closer to markets and resources.

Countries Most Active in U.S. Mergers and Acquisitions, 1986

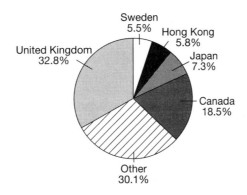

Source: U.S. General Accounting Office, *Foreign Investment*, 1987.

Globalization: Competing in a World Economy

Mergers and Acquisitions Will Continue—With More International Actors Involved

[31]Globalization encourages the flow of capital as barriers to the movement of capital fall. The increase in capital movement among countries results in mergers and acquisitions, with more foreign actors involved as nations look for more-productive investments. Over the long term, as a global economy emerges and structural and economic differences fade, there is the potential for large international shifts in corporate ownership and the development of new organizational structures for doing business internationally.

(CONTINUED)

FUTURE WORK (CONTINUED)

Work-Force and Market Demographics in Europe and Asia Will Present New Opportunities

[32]Birthrates are falling almost everywhere in the industrialized world. Between 2020 and 2025, the birthrates of Europe, Asia (including Japan, South Korea, Taiwan, Hong Kong, and Singapore), and North America are projected to have declined to about 12–14 births per 1,000 population. As the work forces of the industrially advanced nations of Europe and Asia grow in sophistication, those countries will grow economically and reap the benefits of world trade.

Sweeping Changes Will Alter Market Basics

[33]New stresses on time, the increasing diversity of lifestyles, the opening up of overseas markets, and the restructuring of many corporations will shift the basics of marketing. At the same time, workers at all levels will become integral to marketing, sales, and customer relations. Broad change will affect when products and services are marketed (time), and what is sold (quality, experience), how marketing and selling are done (technologies and new strategies), to whom products and services are marketed and sold (demographic change and segmentation) and by whom products are marketed and sold (worker as representative, customer as salesperson).

[34]Several factors are also pushing new approaches to marketing and sales. These include overseas competition and competition for foreign markets; changing social values in the United States and other advanced nations, including new demands for quality and service; and the opening up of new avenues and new markets through electronic technology, such as television, fax copying, videotex, home computers, and satellite transmission. One of the most important of these factors, especially in the United States, is greater demands on time.

Worldwide Technical and Scientific Competence Will Sharpen Competition

[35]Although the United States is the center of scientific and technical education, has the world's largest technically educated work force, and holds a sizable share of world trade in high technology, other countries are catching up. Their efforts are being driven by several factors: the greater significance of technical education as a route to economic success; transborder data flows and technical and scientific exchanges between nations; and new scientific and technical developments occurring world-wide, including the growth in research and development. Scientists and the technically educated are becoming the first truly international, mobile work force.

The Changing Nature of Work

New Critical Skills Are Emerging

[36]Skills critical to the future of the workplace are emerging, but some are or will be in short supply. Several factors are driving the shift toward new skills for work: greater use of information technologies, the move away from craft and assembly manufacture and toward computer-mediated processes, the larger amount of knowledge work in almost every occupation, new requirements for education and the ability to manage complexity, and the redesign of many jobs to include computer-based work. Frequently, several skills will be folded into one job, often with a new title and greater individual responsibility.

(CONTINUED)

FUTURE WORK (CONTINUED)

Training and Education Budgets Will Stay High as Corporations Stretch for New Results

[37]To boost competitiveness, many corporations are energetically training and retraining their work forces. At the same time, more managers and executives are exposed to new and sometimes eccentric methods and styles of training, aimed at shaping their behavior toward more effective leadership and greater productivity. In the name of leaner, meaner, and more-efficient management, corporate educators are forging ahead, with no evidence beyond the promise that these emerging techniques produce long-term results.

[38]There is, however, a solid base for all the technical training and retraining that needs to be done in factories and offices. In the next five years, four out of five people in the industrial world will be doing jobs differently from the way they have been done in the last 50 years. Most people will have to learn new skills. By the year 2000, 75 percent of all employees will need to be retrained in new jobs or taught fresh skills for their old ones. Corporate trainers, in the interest of saving time, will explore alternative and faster methods of delivering new skills and learning, including interactive video, audiotapes, take-home videodiscs, computer-based instruction, and expert systems.

The Corporation Will Reach Deeper into the Educational System to Influence the Quality of Its Supply of Workers

[39]At a time when the U.S. work force as a whole is becoming better educated than ever—one in four U.S. workers is a college graduate—corporations are troubled by deficiencies in basic skills among entry-level workers. As a result, more corporations are teaching reading, writing, and computing to new hires. More significant, perhaps, are corporations' efforts to influence the U.S. educational system and thus improve the skills of their future supply of new workers.

[40]To influence the future supply of workers, corporations are reaching into the educational system with a variety of incentives, new ideas, and cooperative agreements. In Minneapolis, for example, corporate contributions underwrote extensive participatory planning, which was used in the successful restructure of the city's school system, particularly its inner-city high schools. In Pekin, Illinois, IBM's "Writing to Read" program helped first graders, cutting the number who needed remedial teaching from 11 percent to 2 percent.

The Requirements of the Emerging Global Society Are Diverging from the Knowledge Base of the U.S. Population

[41]An emerging globally integrated society is demanding more knowledge and education. Sweeping technological change, the rise of worldwide communications, and competition in the global marketplace require specialized knowledge. The United States is failing to meet these requirements and struggles to sustain the literacy, math, and other abilities of previous decades.

Office Automation Will Thrive Despite Questionable Productivity Gains

[42]Spending on information-processing equipment is rising. Total fixed-capital investment rose an estimated 8.9 percent in 1988, to $490 billion; about 70 percent of this investment was on computers and telecommunications equipment. However, productivity in some industries is stagnant or slow to rise, despite increasing capital outlays.

(CONTINUED)

FUTURE WORK (CONTINUED)

Artificial Intelligence Replicating the Functions of the Human Brain

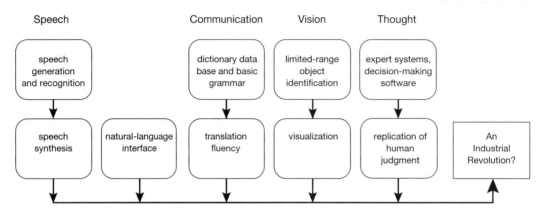

Artificial intelligence will allow computers to utilize many of the thought and decision-making processes of the human brain.

[43]Office automation is driven by the promises of increased productivity, efficiency, and effectiveness implicit in the technology. No one doubted that automation would streamline operations and increase worker's output. The promise, however, has not been fully realized. The service sector has posted virtually no productive gains despite huge spending on information-processing equipment. Several factors may be responsible: growth in productivity has not been high enough to offset large capital outlays for computers and related equipment, too little training is being put behind the hardware, and productivity in information industries is hard to measure.

Artificial Intelligence Is Jerkily Moving from the Laboratory to Practical Application

[44]Artificial intelligence (AI) promises a new industrial revolution by the turn of the century. That revolution may be bigger than the one created by microprocessing technology. Artificial intelligence mimics the human mind, and intelligent machines may eventually match humans in speech, vision, language, communication, and thought.

[45]Expert systems are available today that are the forerunners of AI applications. By the year 2000, AI will affect 60 percent–90 percent of all jobs in large organizations; it will augment, displace, downgrade, or even eliminate workers. AI's potential for teaching, training, and monitoring will also give us sophisticated new capabilities. The technology will make autonomous machines, free of a central control mechanism or wired networks, practical.

Employees and Health

The United States Is an Increasingly Sedentary Society

[46]As the United States changes into a post-industrial society, the characteristics of work will change. A feature of this shift is more indoor working and living. About 60 percent of American adults live sedentary lives. Americans are spending 90 percent of their time indoors, whether at home, in the office or factory, or in closed spaces during travel. Work is far more sedentary than in the past. Aside from sleeping, eating, and dressing, the big consumer of indoor time is watching television—six hours and 59 minutes daily in U.S. households in 1988—1989.

(CONTINUED)

FUTURE WORK (CONTINUED)

[47]The trend toward a sedentary society will lead to more exposure to the risks of an indoor environment, such as indoor air pollution; a sharp decline in muscular activity; new bad habits associated with a sedentary life, such as smoking, coffee and soda drinking, and candy nibbling; and even more social friction and interpersonal annoyances. Healthy workers lose less time and have fewer accidents. People in good physical shape live longer and healthier lives. Attention to health at the workplace also may be seen as an amenity and a factor in morale.

Strong Long-Term Forces Will Work against Cutting Health Costs

[48]The United States spends at least $500 billion a year on health care, more than 11 percent of its gross national product. As a percent of GNP, national health-care expenditures have almost tripled since 1940. Cost-containment attempts so far have only slightly slowed an inexorable rise. At the same time, there is no evidence that the quality of health care, of health maintenance, or of disease prevention is improving to match the increase in spending.

[49]At least four strong long-term forces are boosting the soaring cost of health care in the United States—and are likely to keep those costs high. The United States has huge institutionalized health-care obligations, created by factors such as the aging U.S. population. Insurance and liability costs in an increasingly litigious society are enormous. New medical technologies, such as those used for heart and other organ transplants, have been tremendously expensive. And the public's expectation of universal entitlement to health care and health protection continues to grow.

The Significance of the Worker's Contribution to Occupational Health and Safety Will Increase

[50]In the changing workplace, the worker increasingly is responsible for his or her personal health and safety, as well as that of fellow workers. The worker can contribute through awareness of and concern for health and safety or may aggravate workplace risks by inappropriate behavior or attitudes.

[51]New technologies and new workstyles have shifted occupational health and safety issues from the acute to the chronic and long term. There are also new issues (such as mental stress, eyestrain from computer use, and back fatigue) associated with the white-collar work force. In the blue-collar work force, averting injury is no longer strictly a matter of enforcing safety regulations. Greater use of automation requires more responsibility and cooperation from workers to ensure safety.

The AIDS Epidemic Is Killing People in the Prime of Their Working Lives

[52]What makes AIDS uniquely important to business is that those who are infected and die at present are mostly young men in the prime of their working years. At the same time, the long incubation period of AIDS will cause greater distress for individuals and higher medical costs for employers than any other acute epidemic.

[53]AIDS-related deaths are expected to rise to 68.63 per 100,000 U.S. population by the end of 1991. Evidence aside, most employers do not view AIDS as a problem. A Harris executive poll for *Business Week* showed little concern among the 1,000 companies surveyed; 89 percent of the executives reported that their companies did not have an AIDS policy.

(CONTINUED)

FUTURE WORK (CONTINUED)

Changing and Restructuring the Way Business Does Business

*Businesses Will Be Increasingly Committed
to Improving Performance through Innovation in Rewards*

[54]Small, medium, and large firms are exploring innovations in monetary, dollar-equivalent, and symbolic rewards—such as sabbaticals, mental-health benefits, and goodwill gestures such as special concert or other entertaining events for their workers. These innovations have high potential to stimulate and motivate workers without raising fixed costs. Both managers and employers, however, may need some help in thinking of and implementing any nontraditional rewards. Trade-offs between rewards and compensation, benefits, amenities, and perks will be common.

Organizational and Work-Force Restructuring Will Lead to Changes in Compensation

[55]New organizational goals for productivity, cost control, quality, and work-force restructuring are reshaping compensation patterns. Corporations are cutting the layers of managers that separate top executives from other workers. Between 1980 and 1987, 89 of the top 100 U.S. companies reduced their management layers; analysis of performance appears to show that companies with only seven layers perform better than those with 11. Compensation for those at the top, based on the old hierarchy, is rising to new heights, leading many to doubt that a system that is changing underneath can continue to support this pattern for long.

[56]Major new directions in compensation include the increasing popularity of incentive-pay plans in general (long-term plans in particular) and the use of other cash and non-cash methods of compensation—such as employee stock-ownership plans or savings plans—to substitute for wage increases.

Competition Will Promote Entrepreneurship and Worker Empowerment

[57]Encouraging innovation and entrepreneurship is the new goal of corporate management. Following the examples of many smaller companies, large organizations are also experimenting in empowering their workers. "Empowerment" is a voguish term for giving workers discretion, authority, and the power of self-management. To some, this is an old idea—a good business practice—with a new name. Driving the recycling of this idea are the greater use of worker participation as a tool for generating productivity, information technology that makes information available at all levels of an organization, and a better-educated work force, among other factors.

Downsizing Will Reshuffle the Work-Force Deck

[58]Begun in the restructuring of heavy industry, downsizing has continued into the white-collar work force and now affects the composition of all industries and companies, in all regions and of all sizes, and affects employees at all levels of skills and education. The resulting reshuffling of jobs will create a new business culture in which most people, as well as having more than one career, will have been laid off at least once, can expect to be laid off again, and are likely to behave as if their current jobs are fleeting.

(CONTINUED)

FUTURE WORK (CONTINUED)

Workplace Regulation by State
(Selected recent activity)

A   Parental leave legislation, 1987-1988

B   Family and medical leave

C   Raised minimum wage

D   Regulation of smoking in the workplace

E   Drug-testing bills or legislation

F   Ban on lie detectors in the private sector

G   "Whistleblower" protection for private-sector employees

H   VDT use/computer monitoring regulations considered and/or enacted

I   Health-benefits legislation

[59]Some believe that most U.S. corporations had hired too many employees and were suffering from payroll bloat. In any event, by some estimates at least 600,000 middle managers were laid off between 1984 and 1987. Factors driving downsizing include automation, mergers and acquisitions, the use of information technology that makes middle management and some clerical work obsolete, and new management concepts that call for fewer, cross-skilled workers.

Pent-Up Demand for Solutions to Workplace Issues Will Increase Regulation

[60]Societal problems that are important to the work force—family support, pay equity, drug abuse, job security, health care, and labor relations, among others—are not being fully addressed by U.S. employers or by the federal government. The relative neglect of these issues in the past decade has created a pent-up demand for new solutions. In response, state governments and the courts are reversing the United States' long-term tendency toward managing labor issues by federal regulation. In the process they are creating a crazy quilt of their own regulatory actions and decisions.

(CONTINUED)

FUTURE WORK (CONTINUED)

Corporations Will Be under Pressure to Explore and Redefine Their Ethics

[61]Business ethics is a growth enterprise. Frequently cited factors behind this uprush of interest in ethics include an increase in social concerns that began with Watergate; stock-market scandals; sexual-harassment issues; issues of privacy and testing; safety in products (as, for example, in cigarettes); the quality and integrity of advertising; and corporate fervor for belt-tightening mergers, acquisitions, divestitures, and downsizing.

CONTENT QUESTIONS—"FUTURE WORK"

TRUE OR FALSE

If the statement is false, rewrite it to make it true.

1. Managers planning for the future are giving most of their attention to the role of technology.
2. The median age of the U.S. population is decreasing.
3. The average American moves every six years.
4. Office automation has reached its peak and there will not be much change in the future.
5. In the next five years, four out of five people in the industrial world will be doing jobs differently from the way they have been done in the past 50 years.

COMPLETION

6. Identify three demographic changes in the workforce of the future.
7. What is the largest fast-growing minority population in the United States?
8. In the future, why will employers consider more unconventional work arrangements like contingent workers?
9. Name four societal changes that will cause changes in marketing products and services.
10. List three major health issues affecting business in the future.

VOCABULARY—"FUTURE WORK"

1. homogeneous group (¶14)
2. income parity (¶15)
3. acculturated (¶19)
4. underutilized workers (¶20)
5. indicative of a larger concern (¶22)
6. integration of home and work life. (¶22)
7. List and explain five additional phrases important to the understanding of the article.

CONTENT ANALYSIS QUESTIONS—"FUTURE WORK"

1. State the authors' thesis. Do you think they presented sufficient evidence to support their thesis? Why or why not?
2. Develop an informal outline of the article.
3. Why are businesses beginning to recognize employees as a resource or asset rather than just a fixed cost?
4. Compare and contrast the trends discussed by Coates, Jarratt, and Mahaffie with the trends and challenges discussed by Griffin and Ebert in their textbook chapter "Recognizing Business Trends and Challenges."
5. What do "The Middle-Aging of The Work Force" pie charts indicate? What does the text of the article say about this concept?

APPLICATION QUESTIONS—"FUTURE WORK"

1. According to the authors, the United States is failing the requirements of the emerging global society and is struggling to sustain the literacy, math skills, and other abilities of previous decades. What does this mean? Do you think this is true? If it is true, how might it affect you?
2. What is artificial intelligence (AI)? What kind of AI applications do you think we'll see in this century? What application do you think will have the most effect on you?

"CUTTING THROUGH THE CHAOS"

Cassandra Hayes, Mark Lowery, and Tonia Shakespeare are journalists. This selection—"Cutting through the Chaos"—is from *Black Enterprise*, February 1996.

CUTTING THROUGH THE CHAOS

HIGHLY SKILLED, MULTIPLE TASKMASTERS WILL DOMINATE THE EVER-CHANGING WORKPLACE

CASSANDRA HAYES, WITH ADDITIONAL REPORTING BY MARK LOWERY AND TONIA SHAKESPEARE

[1]You've heard it all before. Downsizing, reengineering, outsourcing and global competition—the change agents of today's workplace that will not let up. Unfortunately, economists, career counselors and futurists all agree that the epidemic of layoffs is still spreading.

[2]Kmart recently closed seven stores after 11 straight quarter losses, bringing their employee casualty rate to 25,000. Last November, AT&T mailed buyout packages to 78,000 of its managers. It's estimated that the merger of Chase Manhattan and Chemical Banks will result in 12,000 layoffs.

(CONTINUED)

CUTTING THROUGH THE CHAOS (CONTINUED)

[3]Downsizing is no longer just a response to a weak economy and dwindling profits. Early estimates predict that some 420,000 individuals were laid off last year, proving that even as corporate earnings rise and the economy improves, companies nationwide continue to slash payrolls. And the big boys are not the only ones cutting back.

[4]"Many more smaller and medium-sized businesses are taking advantage of the reengineering trend to rid themselves of less productive employees and superfluous functions," says John A. Challenger, executive vice president of Challenger, Gray & Christmas, an international *outplacement firm* in Chicago that tracks layoffs daily. Those threatened most by this phenomenon are the oldest and youngest members of the workforce, he adds. The reason: Companies feel that veterans are overpaid, while newcomers lack the experience and expertise necessary to compete.

[5]To combat the loss of talent through restructuring and to maintain flexibility, more companies are staffing strategically. They save money and become more efficient by changing the ratio of permanent and temporary workers during high and low workload cycles. The rise in contingent workers is a sign of things to come.

[6]In 1994, almost 25 percent of America's workforce were contingent workers—temps and independent contractors. From 1990 to 1995, temporary and full-time employment agencies were responsible for close to 900,000 of the 4.1 million new jobs created. As people continue to have difficulty finding work and lose lucrative middle-management positions, a new group has emerged, what Labor Secretary Robert Reich calls the "anxious class." Their anxiety is caused by the ongoing insecurity of the job market.

[7]Although President Bill Clinton touted an increase in jobs last year, it was low compared with the year before. The net gain of 2.1 million jobs from October 1994 to 1995 was substantially less than the almost 3.4 million jobs created during the same period the year before, according to the Bureau of Labor Statistics. What has not been said is that most of those jobs were in low-paying sectors and temporary employment.

Affirmative Action Backlash

[8]The recent furor over affirmative action will be the greatest threat to jobs for African Americans. "Affirmative action didn't make anyone hire anyone, but it planted a seed that told people they should think about particular groups and issues," says Frederick Miller, president and CEO of The Kaleel Jamison Consulting Group in Cincinnati. California's elimination of affirmative action programs in state universities and the ongoing political debate sends a message to employers that hiring minorities is no longer a priority. Companies say, "I'll just *raise the bar* on who I bring to the table, and as you raise the bar, a lot of people are left behind," adds Miller. Overwhelmingly, those are minorities.

[9]"If you hear that the unemployment rate is 5 percent for the general population, it's 10 percent for blacks; if it takes the average college grad two months to find a job, it takes four months for African Americans," says Washington-based economist Julianne Malveaux. "We (African Americans) are always caught between optimism and despair. We have to believe there is hope or else we'll give up."

[10]Both young and old have to be steadfast and realistic in their approach to careering. "Those students graduating from historically black colleges should not look to placement offices as the sole source of information because recruiters won't be coming," advises Malveaux. A further reality check: Fortune 500 companies are no longer the wellspring of employment. Individuals entering the workforce for the first time as well as those who are already there should look to smaller companies for employment or go out on their own, she advises.

[11]It's no secret that the road to success has always been rocky for African Americans. As opportunities decrease and competition increases, African Americans must maintain their drive and determination. There are plenty of career warriors who have maneuvered the vocational obstacle course and lived to tell about it—even thrived. What they say is that continuous education, upgrading of skills, developing contacts and keeping pace with the changing work environment will help you succeed. Stormy forecasts aside, there is still hope.

(CONTINUED)

CUTTING THROUGH THE CHAOS (CONTINUED)

The School-to-Work Track

[12]Despite present trends, a recent Gallup poll showed that today's college seniors are surprisingly optimistic about their futures. On average, most expect an annual salary of $98,000 by the year 2015. Nearly two-thirds expect their standard of living, 20 years from now, to be higher than their parents at the same age. No doubt this optimism is fed by their lack of conventional expectations—most have not seen their parents retire with a gold watch—as well as by *youthful bravado and naiveté.*

[13]The poll also shows, that most of the 1995 graduating class plans to work in business and nearly one in five seniors anticipate going to business school. With a 4 percent to 7 percent increase in salaries projected this year for MBAs, business school was the first choice for postgraduate study among college seniors. Yet, concerns about tuition expenses loom large.

[14]Gaining a competitive edge isn't the only reason students are pursuing graduate degrees. "More students are opting to go to graduate school because they can't find jobs," says Ada Green, placement counselor at Dillard University in New Orleans, who has seen a dramatic drop in the number of corporate recruiters on campus. She notes one bright spot, however. A nationwide teacher shortage has led to a buyer's market for education majors. "We have over 100 different school districts throughout the country begging our students to come to their states to teach." The demand has been so great, Green says, that last year Dillard placed every one of their education graduates.

[15]For those still in school, Green says, "Begin as early as possible to think seriously about a major that will get you a job. Do not major in psychology without knowing what you're going to do with it."

Gearing Up

[16]"Younger members of the workforce have the flexibility to work on temporary or contract basis, while older, more experienced individuals have a chance to play the entrepreneurial role in the job market by providing their work-tested expertise to companies," Challenger says. In fact, 88 percent of the companies surveyed by the Center for Creative Leadership in Greensboro, N.C., said that they were looking for employees with entrepreneurial leadership skills. The reason is simple: Organizations are reshaping themselves in an effort to get closer to the customer, and they want employees with the most customer contacts to make the decisions. Individuals who have run their own businesses are considered selfstarters, who require less management.

[17]The growth of self-directed work teams and "empowered" employees requires peripheral vision, the ability to see beyond the "box" of a job description. To drive this point home, companies are awarding bonuses and promotions in order to increase employees' entrepreneurial effectiveness. "There are senior executives with English and philosophy degrees, but that will not happen in the future," warns Miller. "Employers are going for a particular skill set versus hiring people who can come in and grow with the company—it's skills on arrival."

[18]Charting your career path will not be easy. The *popular adage* still holds true: be flexible. Do not set your career goals based on the growth of a particular industry. Stick to broad business functions such as sales, marketing, finance and data processing, Challenger says. Managers in these areas will always be in demand. People should look to *hone their skills* in one or two areas and plan on moving from industry to industry, if necessary.

[19]For the college educated, the fastest growing occupations are expected to be in human services, computer engineering and science, systems analysis, special education, paralegal work and physical therapy [see chart on page 392]. The projected increase in the amount of jobs within the health care industry will be driven by an aging U.S. population and the need to cut health care costs. Many of those jobs may not be in the hospital setting but in assisted care and long-term nursing facilities, says Alexis Waters, spokesperson for the American Physical Therapy Association in Alexandria, Va. With hospital stays decreasing, she adds, there will be a tremendous demand for home health aides and physical therapists and assistants.

(CONTINUED)

CUTTING THROUGH THE CHAOS (CONTINUED)

Some of the Fastest Growing Occupations (Numbers in Thousands)

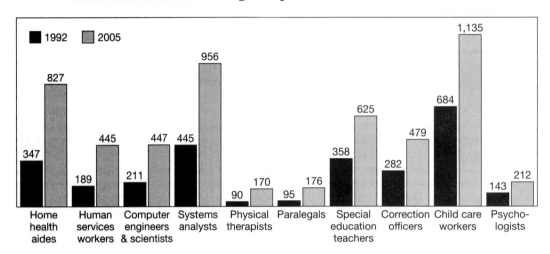

Source: Bureau of Labor Statistics, 1994.

[20]"Financial hiring is a *harbinger* of over-all hiring because companies add people in accounting and financing departments in anticipation of growth," says Marc Silbert, spokesperson for Robert Half International, a nationwide personnel firm. Silbert says there was a 6 percent net increase in financial hiring for the fourth quarter of 1995, with mid-sized firms showing 10 percent growth. Accounting has not suffered as much as other occupations, according to Beverly Everson-Jones, executive director of the National Association of Black Accountants. "Ten years ago people came out of school and went into public accounting or private industry. Now we're finding people who start out in nonprofit organizations and government. They're looking at industries other than the traditional large corporate environment," says Everson-Jones.

[21]According to the 1996 *Robert Half and Accountemps Salary Guide*, more companies are specifically seeking candidates with certified management accountant and CPA credentials because they reflect personal initiative and advanced accounting expertise. Those individuals with a combination of public accounting and private industry experience will also fare well. Knowledge of spreadsheets and accounting software is another important skill to have. In addition, accountants with international, tax and intellectual property experience will be in demand.

[22]The restructuring that has occurred in banking has slowed. Mutual funds, insurance, and other financial vehicles have changed the face of traditional banking. There will be ample opportunities for the highly skilled, particularly commercial and retail lenders, loan review and administration officers and auditors. The increase in electronic banking has resulted in the loss of tellers and branch managers. According to Sheila Crawford, president of the National Association of Urban Bankers in Silver Spring, Md., minorities held many of the staff positions in banks that were eliminated. Despite cutbacks, there will be a demand for more client services representatives and sales and marketing specialists, Crawford adds.

[23]Technology continues to drive the shift in employee demand. As businesses continue their migration to client server and network environments, there will be an inevitable demand for microcomputer programmers, programmer analysts and systems administrators. Those specializing in LAN or WAN environments can find great opportunities in regions of the country where there is a shortage of these experts. Industries increasing their information technology staff include health care, insurance, finance, entertainment, manufacturing, distribution and telecommunications.

(*CONTINUED*)

CUTTING THROUGH THE CHAOS (CONTINUED)

Changing Demographics

[24]The New England states have learned their lesson from the recession. Companies in Massachusetts, New Hampshire, Rhode Island and Connecticut are staffing cautiously. Major business hubs on the East and West Coasts continue to grow in specialized areas such as finance and high technology. Surprisingly, states such as Colorado, Utah, Minnesota, Tennessee and Florida have experienced unprecedented growth, particularly in manufacturing. Their low cost of living and affordable real estate have attracted a large number of companies and individuals.

[25]But few African Americans have benefited. More often than not, companies relocate to areas where African Americans don't live or want to live. African Americans may be less willing to relocate to an area that cannot offer a cultural and social landscape that they are comfortable with. As a result, the company's minority base diminishes, says Malveaux, and more jobs for minorities are eliminated.

[26]Understanding the job marketplace and possessing the skills necessary to compete will be the *definitive advantage*. Those who possess these skills and knowledge may find that the job search is actually shorter than five years ago, some experts say. "We are finding that if people are flexible as far as industry, salary, and position, and are willing to relocate, they can find jobs in a timely manner, depending on the salary. More money takes more time," says C. David Jones, vice president and general manager for career management services at Personnel Decisions Inc., Meredith-Lincolnshire in Minneapolis. Smaller firms are successfully hiring senior staff from the ranks of middle managers downsized from larger firms, he says. Because of their experience, the former managers work with less supervision and greater efficiency.

[27]You must be creative in your job search. "People have to prepare for periods of unemployment," says Challenger. In order to do that you have to develop a strategy and articulate it. Ask yourself how you can distinguish yourself from the competition. You must identify the areas that would be interested in you and determine how to penetrate that marketplace. You are really marketing a product, and once in the door, you add value by contributing more to the company. It will be tough, but your hard work will eventually pay off. Employment opportunities may be bleak, but people are still hiring. Malveaux advises: "Maintain your integrity preparing for the job you want, while realizing what kind of job you may have to take in the short run."

SNAPSHOT OF WORKPLACE 2000

Employees of the future will have to be quick-change artists to keep pace with the evolving workplace. These are some of the turnabouts to expect.

Short-Lived Assignments Will Be Common

Expect to work on a contract basis or spend time on several project teams, says Price Pritchett in his book, *New Work Habits for a Radically Changing World*. (Pritchett & Associates; $5.95) "You might end up working for more than one 'employer' at a time. You'll probably have a constantly new set of co-workers, more bosses, even new careers."

(CONTINUED)

CUTTING THROUGH THE CHAOS (CONTINUED)

SNAPSHOT OF WORKPLACE 2000 (CONTINUED)

Workers Will Have at Least Three Careers in Their Lifetime

Experts predict that people will turn over their skills, on average, three times. For example, a marketing manager may go into consulting and later go into academics and teach marketing. The career tracks of others may be more diverse as people continue to learn new skills and acquire different degrees.

Thirty-Hour Workweeks

Economist and author Jeremy Rifkin says that the age of technology is making us more productive. In his book, *The End of Work* (G. P. Putnam's Sons; $24.95), Rifkin says that companies will have to shorten the workweek to provide work for all those individuals out of work. In 1993, Germany's Volkswagen adopted a 30-hour workweek, and the French government has proposed a four-day workweek as well.

Nonprofits: The Next Career Frontier

Corporations and government are going to play an ever-reduced role in terms of jobs. "If the non-profit sector was an industry, it would be the seventh largest," says Rifkin. Over one million to date and growing, "It is the glue that keeps the country together." By building strong, self-sustaining local communities, jobs will be created for those displaced in the other sectors.

Flexible Schedules, Telecommuting and Virtual Offices

Today, managers are running departments from their home computers or holding meetings on the Internet or over a cellular phone. People are going online to apply for jobs and earn college degrees. Companies save money in reduced office space. Working at a desk from 9 to 5 will be history for some workers as offices become as close as a computer and modem.

CONTENT QUESTIONS—"CUTTING THROUGH THE CHAOS"

TRUE OR FALSE

If the statement is false, rewrite it to make it true.

1. The rise in contingent workers is a temporary phenomenon.
2. Most of the 1995 graduating class planned to work in education.
3. A majority of companies surveyed by the Center for Creative Leadership said they were looking for employees with entrepreneurial leadership skills.
4. Technology continues to drive the shift in employee demand.
5. When this article was written, college seniors were surprisingly pessimistic about their future.

COMPLETION

6. List six of the fastest growing occupations mentioned in the article and in the chart.
7. List six industries that are increasing their information technology staff.
8. What two skills/areas of knowledge will give the job-seeker the "definitive advantage"?
9. Why do companies like to hire middle managers who have been downsized from larger firms? What impact should that knowledge have for other job-seekers?
10. What was the anticipated outcome for African Americans from the "recent furor over affirmative action"?

VOCABULARY—"CUTTING THROUGH THE CHAOS"

1. outplacement firm (¶4)
2. raise the bar (¶8)
3. youthful bravado and naiveté (¶12)
4. popular adage (¶18)
5. hone their skills (¶18)
6. harbinger (¶20)
7. definitive advantage (¶26)

CONTENT ANALYSIS QUESTIONS—"CUTTING THROUGH THE CHAOS"

1. What is Hayes' thesis? How does she develop and support her thesis?
2. In paragraph 17, Hayes writes that employees need "...peripheral vision, the ability to see beyond the 'box' of a job description." What does that mean? Why do you think employers see that as important?
3. Hayes writes that career warriors advise African Americans that "...continuous education, upgrading of skills, developing contacts and

keeping pace with the changing work environment" are keys to being successful. Do you think the advice would be different for non-African Americans? Explain your answer.

4. Hayes writes that "charting your career path will not be easy." Do you agree or disagree with her prediction'? How does she suggest you survive? What other strategies would you suggest?

5. In the sidebar story "Snapshot of Workplace 2000," the author highlights five changes. Which one surprised you the most? Why? Which one already affects you? Explain.

APPLICATION QUESTIONS—"CUTTING THROUGH THE CHAOS"

1. Ask yourself how you can distinguish yourself from the competition. Make a list of the skills, knowledge and experience that you have to offer. Identify the businesses or work areas that would be interested in you and develop a strategy to penetrate that marketplace.

2. Assume that you are working with a group of students and faculty to set up a job fair on campus. What occupations would you definitely want to have represented? What local employers would you want represented? What resource or support people or services would you invite? How would you encourage students to attend?

"CURRENT SITUATION"

CURRENT SITUATION: CONTINGENT WORK FORCE

CQ RESEARCHER STAFF

[1]Despite the many jobs disappearing across the spectrum of American industry, the unemployment rate measures a surprisingly low 7.1 percent of the labor force. That's high compared with normal economic conditions but by no means as dramatic as the reports of permanent job losses would suggest. During the 1981–82 recession, for example, unemployment peaked at more than 11 percent.

[2]One reason for the relatively low jobless figure is that many unemployed people have simply stopped looking for work. The Labor Department estimates that these "discouraged workers," who are not included in the unemployment figures, number 1.1 million.

[3]Also left out of the statistics are 6.7 million people doing part-time work because they couldn't find acceptable full-time positions. "What we've got is large numbers of people cobbling together an income by doing less than a full week of work," says Audrey Freedman, a labor economist at The Conference Board, a business research organization in New York. She calls this approach to the job market "the contingent way of piecing together a living."

(CONTINUED)

CURRENT SITUATION:
CONTINGENT WORK FORCE (CONTINUED)

[4]The actual number of people who have joined the contingent work force is unknown. That's because the Labor Department has no measure for this group of workers. Some analysts, including Dan Lacey, editor of the newsletter *Workplace Trends*, and economist Richard Belous, who have studied the matter in some detail, estimate that contingent workers make up as much as a third of the total U.S. work force.

[5]But BLS economist Tom Nardone is skeptical, especially since the total may include not only poorly paid temporary and fastfood workers but also well-heeled consultants as well as doctors and lawyers who are self-employed. "It all comes down to a question of job security, and that is very hard to measure," he says. "The point is, how many lousy jobs are there? We don't have a measure for that."

[6]Whatever the number of workers involved, everyone agrees that there is a marked shift toward contingent workers, and that the change makes sense for business. For one thing, the shift can save employers a lot on fringe benefits, especially health insurance, whose costs are rising faster than any other employer-provided benefit. "If you look at who gets health insurance from their employers, it's much less frequent among part-time workers than among full-time workers," says Nardone, who adds that only 67 percent of full-timers have health coverage.

[7]Reducing the in-house payroll may also help companies become more competitive, says Freedman, enabling them to quickly change their products, their marketing techniques, even their factory or retail locations in response to new business conditions. "The rapidity with which they can adapt is very much affected by whether they have a long-term, stable kind of work force or whether they can pick and choose, in effect, by going to the supermarket and picking up a new crop of people to handle something that may not last more than three months," she says.

[8]According to Freedman, many companies turned to the contingent labor market in the 1980s. IBM is typical. As the company *pared* its permanent, full-time work force, it brought in outside firms to handle certain operations; it currently has contracts with 1,400 vendors and suppliers and employs about 33,000 contingent workers. "The trend is definitely to contract out to vendors the support-type services we need," says company spokeswoman Ryan. For example, Marriott Corp., the hotel and food service chain, operates some of IBM's cafeterias, while Manpower Inc., a temporary-help agency, provides clerical and secretarial services as well as more highly skilled workers.

[9]Sears also contracts out for many former in-house functions, including maintenance, type-setting, advertising and transportation. "To be competitive today," says spokesman Gordon Jones, "we have to have the cost structure that our competitors do, and one of the ways our competitors keep their costs down is by having outside companies do the work." While Sears offers health and other benefits to some of its permanent part-time workers, so-called "part-time regulars" who put in 30 hours a week, Jones acknowledges that many of the contingent workers do not receive benefits from the subcontractors.

[10]"If those outside companies provide minimal benefits, it's probably going to be one of the ways they hold their costs down when we go to them," he says. "In terms of the social impact on the country, I'm sure our senior executives are concerned, but at the same time there's the need to be competitive."

Core vs. Contingent Workers

[11]As more and more companies hire contingent workers, some experts say serious morale problems could arise between these lower-paid employees and the better-paid permanent, or "core," workers they often work with. Former United Auto Workers union President Douglas Fraser cites the problems that arose in the early 1908s, when airlines and other troubled industries tried to cut personnel costs by introducing the "two-tier" wage scale, which gave much lower pay to new hires—even when they had better skills than the older workers.

(CONTINUED)

CURRENT SITUATION:
CONTINGENT WORK FORCE (CONTINUED)

[12]"People lived with it for awhile," Fraser says, "but [the system caused] such friction that the companies that had two-tier just threw up their hands in despair. You rarely see it anymore."

[13]Two-tier wage scales may be on the *wane*, but some of the same problems afflict contingent work. "There's a big question about who's taking whose job away, and why somebody working side by side on the same job is earning half as much, with no security, no benefits and in most cases no union," says Thomas Kochan, a professor of management and human resources at MIT.

[14]For their part, Kochan adds, the permanent workers "feel that the company has an incentive to give all the work to these cheap folks and take their jobs away." He cites studies showing how resentment between core and contingent workers may even pose physical threats in certain industries, such as oil and chemical manufacturing, where safety risks already abound.

[15]Safety aside, Kochan says contingent work may do more long-term harm than good, even to the companies that promote it to improve productivity. "I don't think this employment relationship is good for the economy," he says. "You've got to have solid personal relationships to get along and solve problems in groups. You have to understand the culture and the setting because that's all part of what an organization is about."

[16]If contingent work becomes *entrenched* in the labor market, Kochan predicts, "quality and productivity will go down."

Contingent Work Spreads

[17]Once typified by the "Kelly Girl" and other low-level white-collar temporaries, contingent workers are no longer confined to low-wage occupations. "Contingent work is creeping up and becoming much more high-level white collar," Belous says, as corporations begin to subcontract for accountants and providers of other financial services.

[18]But contingent work has also moved much more into blue-collar occupations, particularly through "leasing" of employees for specific tasks. Leasing allows corporations to delegate a task to an agency that assumes all responsibility for the personnel who do the work. Although some leasing agencies provide benefits to their workers, Belous says they are usually less generous than benefits the corporation would normally provide full-time workers. He adds, "It's not unusual to read about some unscrupulous leasing operation that told its employees they had benefits but just pocketed the money."

[19]Contingent workers have fewer defenses against such abuses than full-time workers. "Unions have their collective backs to the wall," says well known economist Robert Reich, citing the fall in union membership to a mere 13 percent of the work force today. "In most industries, the unions are only a pale reflection of their former selves," he says. "It's very difficult for the unions to put contingent workers at the top of an agenda that's already crowded with the demands by unionized workers for protection from other corporate *incursions*."

[20]The move to contingent work is not bad for everyone, of course, especially among professional, managerial and technical workers. They can sell their special skills more easily to a number of clients than, say, a laborer or an assembler. "Contingent workers don't necessarily make less," says Dan Lacey. "Some who are consultants make a lot of money. So contingent working is not necessarily downward mobility, but it is certainly less predictable than the paycheck."

[21]Belous agrees that contingent work can prove beneficial for some workers. "Many workers view it as a way to gain increased freedom, and that's what they want. And let's face it, a lot of corporations would be out of business without contingent workers. It's *not an unmitigated evil*."

CONTENT QUESTIONS—"CURRENT SITUATION"

TRUE OR FALSE

If the statement is false, rewrite it to make it true.

1. Today's unemployment rate is higher than ever before.
2. It is estimated that as much as 1/3 of the U.S. workforce is made up of contingent workers.
3. The shift to more contingent workers makes good economic sense for most businesses.
4. Contingent workers are only found in low-level, blue-collar jobs.
5. Morale problems are likely to increase as more contingent workers are hired.

COMPLETION

6. Cite one reason for the relatively low unemployment figure.
7. Name three examples of contingent workers.
8. Identify three reasons companies are hiring more contingent workers.
9. List two reasons some workers like contingent work.
10. Name three reasons for potential friction between core and contingent workers.

VOCABULARY—"CURRENT SITUATION"

1. pared (¶8)
2. wane (¶13)
3. entrenched (¶16)
4. incursions (¶19)
5. not an unmitigated evil (¶21)

CONTENT ANALYSIS QUESTIONS—"CURRENT SITUATION"

1. What is a "contingent" worker? What is a "core" worker?
2. What are the major reasons companies are hiring more contingent workers and fewer core workers? Do you think this benefit outweighs the potential disadvantages?
3. What is Thomas Kochan's point of view on the increase of contingent workers and its effects? Give examples to support your answer.
4. In what ways do you think the increased hiring of contingent workers can help a business be more productive?
5. What does Belous mean by "It's not an unmitigated evil"? Do you agree or disagree? Explain.

APPLICATION QUESTIONS—"CURRENT SITUATION"

1. What companies in your local area make use of contingent workers, outside vendors, and/or leased employees? Does your college? What do you think their reasons are? Do you agree or disagree with their rationale?

2. What are two reasons a person might choose contingent work? Under what circumstances would you choose contingent work?

"JOBS 2000"

Robert Lewis is the editor of the *NRTA Bulletin*, a publication of the National Retired Teachers Association, which is a division of the American Association of Retired Persons (AARP). This selection—"Jobs 2000"—is from the January 1996 *NRTA Bulletin*.

JOBS 2000

MIDLIFE CAREER CHANGERS IN 21ST CENTURY WILL FIND A MIX OF GOOD NEWS AND BAD

ROBERT LEWIS

[1]Advice to midlife Americans who are thinking of job hunting in the next century: Get ready for a bumpy ride.

[2]A changing economy is going to put up roadblocks. "People in middle age will face a tough job climate," says AARP Work Force Programs Director Martin Sicker. "For good jobs that pay well, competition is going to get fierce."

[3]But the picture won't be entirely bleak for people in midlife seeking new jobs or changing careers.

[4]In fact, some growing job categories will be downright attractive, depending on your taste. Computer systems analysts, for example, will be in demand. So will teachers, registered nurses and certain types of retail salespersons.

[5]There also will be growth in some offbeat areas. For those with just the right background, there will be more openings for private detectives. And gardeners will be sought after.

[6]And if you look strictly at the government's just-released projections of job growth by the year 2005, the prospects for midlife job seekers appear almost favorable.

[7]According to the U.S. Bureau of Labor Statistics (BLS), the number of Americans age 55 and older holding jobs will climb 42 percent to 22.1 million between 1994 and 2005. That's double the 20 percent projected growth in the 55-plus population.

[8]Sounds great. Jobs for older persons will grow faster than their numbers. But there's a joker in the deck.

[9]The bulk of the new jobs, says the BLS, will be in low-skill, low-paying service occupations. There will be ample openings for salesclerks, cashiers, janitors, child-care aides, waiters and waitresses, for example.

[10]But more limited opportunities await applicants for high-skill positions, jobs such as chemical engineers, tool and die makers, geologists and purchasing agents.

(CONTINUED)

JOBS 2000 (CONTINUED)

[11]"We're seeing growth of low-paid service jobs," says economist Audrey Freedman, "and some growth in the high-paid, mostly technical fields. But there's not much growth at all of jobs in the middle range of pay."

[12]Be that as it may, there is one clear area of *burgeoning opportunity* for older workers: The aging of the population will, experts declare, generate explosive growth in some, but not all, health-care occupations.

[13]For example, openings for registered nurses, home-health aides and nursing aides, orderlies and attendants over the next 10 years will jump 36 percent to 4.9 million. (The overall work force itself will grow only 12 percent.)

[14]But certain other health-care occupations will grow only modestly as hospitals, doctors and other providers look for "alternative help" rather than higher-paid medical practitioners.

[15]"The general trend is to deliver health-care services [using] individuals who have the skills but cost the least," says BLS Associate Commissioner Ronald Kutscher.

[16]Consequently, the BLS projects a 72 percent increase in the ranks of occupational therapists and 80 percent growth in physical therapists, but only a 22 percent rise in physicians.

[17]While it may be impractical for a midlife worker to switch careers and become, say, a doctor or engineer, a paraprofessional occupation, typically requiring only a modest amount of preparation, may be within reach.

[18]All of which helps explain why there will be 58 percent more paralegals in 2005, but only 28 percent more lawyers.

[19]Another trend—the movement to independent living among the elderly—will fuel increased demand for home-health aides. Their ranks will more than double over the next decade, making the job they do the second fastest-growing among 512 occupations studied by the BLS.

[20](Personal and home-care aides, a related field, is the fastest growing occupation; its ranks will increase by 119 percent.)

[21]Welcome as this news would seem to be for those interested, there is, alas, *a caveat*. According to the National Association for Home Care, the average starting wage for home-health aides in 1992 was $6.31 an hour. The average maximum wage was $8.28.

[22]One reason the job outlook for midlife Americans in the next century isn't brighter is that the much-ballyhooed labor shortages—the staple of the business press during the 1970s and 1980s—aren't materializing.

[23]Everybody remembers the theory. The low number of births in the late 1960s and early 1970s would, experts believed, result in fewer new entrants into the labor force, diminishing competition for jobs. Employment prospects for older workers, the theory went, would improve.

[24]That isn't how things are working out. In the years since those predictions were made, "there have been fundamental changes in the economy," says analyst Christine Keen of the Domani Group, a Washington consulting firm. She cites increased automation as one example.

[25]"Technology is destroying jobs faster than it's creating them," adds AARP's Sicker.

[26]But while the computer revolution is *decimating the ranks of* bank tellers, meter readers, typists, switchboard operators and billing clerks, it is creating some high-paying computer jobs. The BLS projects a 92 percent increase for systems analysts and a 90 percent gain for computer engineers.

[27]These occupations could be fertile ground for older workers, who now hold only one in 20 of such jobs. And the pay is not bad. Median annual earnings in 1992 were $42,100.

[28]Another promising field for midlife workers considering a career shift is education. Many states are changing their teacher certification rules to make it easier for persons with professional or technical expertise to move into the classroom.

[29]For this and other reasons, over the next 10 years the number of elementary, secondary, preschool, kindergarten and special education teachers, and teacher aides, will record increases from 16 percent to 53 percent.

[30]Cashiers and retail salespersons—jobs considered well suited for older persons given their *reputation for diplomacy*—also will be expanding in the years ahead.

(CONTINUED)

JOBS 2000 (CONTINUED)

[31]There are other scraps of good news, at least for law enforcement officers. To be sure, retirement policies in law enforcement will continue to push many officers to retire early, typically at 55. But many retired cops, suggests the BLS, will find second careers as private detectives.

[32]Indeed, the field seems to attract men of a certain age. Right now, less than 3 percent of police officers and detectives are 55 or older. But 21 percent of private detectives are 55 or older. And their job outlook is good. The BLS forecasts 24,000 more private eyes by 2005, a growth of 44 percent.

[33]Still, the changing economy is darkening the prospects for many older workers. BLS analysts see slow growth for the real estate industry, the result of agency consolidations and home construction. The number of real estate agents, brokers, and appraisers will inch up only slightly by 2005.

[34]Forecasters aren't always correct, as their experience projecting the job future for travel agents amply demonstrates.

[35]Two years ago, BLS *prognosticators* confidently projected a 66 percent surge in the number of agents by 2005. Now they're seeing it differently. In a newly released forecast covering 1994–2005, BLS's 66 percent increase turned into a mere 23 percent rise.

[36]The lowered forecast reflects, in part the current expectation that more travelers will buy tickets through online services using personal computers, says BLS analyst Neal Rosenthal.

[37]Of course, any forecast of what the future holds is based on assumptions, and BLS analysts cranked more than 200 of them into their computers to produce their new assessment of job opportunities over the next decade.

[38]A key assumption deals with what the BLS calls the *"labor force participation rate,"* which is the proportion of adults who work. This tells the BLS whether people, as expected, will actually work longer before retiring.

[39]The rate for men, which had been declining since World War II as people retired earlier and earlier, leveled off in the late 1980s. Last year, 65.5 percent of men age 55–64 were in the labor force. The BLS sees no change in this percentage over the next 10 years.

[40]It's a different story for women. Last year, 48.9 percent of women 55–64 were in the labor force—a proportion projected to rise to 56.6 percent by 2005. Overall, the labor force participation rate for both sexes age 55 and over will rise from 29.7 percent this year to 35.2 percent in 2005.

[41]"The economics of retirement mean people need to work longer," says the BLS' Kutscher.

[42]Having the greatest stake in the job outlook, of course, will be midlife workers who lose their career positions to corporate downsizing, mergers, or plant closings.

[43]If the past is any guide, some 4.8 million workers 45 and older will be downsized out of their jobs between 1994–2005. That's the number of older workers who got pink slips between 1981–1992.

[44]But Kutscher says too much can be read into the unending flow of downsizing reports.

[45]"There still is a very large part of the work force that continues to work for the same employer for long periods of time," he says. "With all the publicity about job-moving and downsizing, our latest data shows that job tenure is going up, not down."

SECOND CAREER PROSPECTS FOR THE 21ST CENTURY

What are your prospects as you contemplate entering a second career in midlife? Below are five categories of employment that, based on Bureau of Labor Statistics projections, could hold the most promise for older workers in the next few years.

(CONTINUED)

JOBS 2000 (CONTINUED)

SECOND CAREER PROSPECTS FOR THE 21ST CENTURY (CONTINUED)

Some of these careers require a year or more of specialized education at a college or technical school. Others require so little training that workers can move into them immediately just to make ends meet and perhaps to get health insurance until their pensions kick in or while they train for new fields.

Retail sales—Salesclerks and cashiers will be in great demand in the coming decade. These jobs require only a little training, usually at the job site.

Computer careers—Openings for computer engineers and systems analysts are expected to grow. Such careers require substantial college preparation.

Health care—Increased demand for home-health care means growing demand for registered nurses, physical therapists and other kinds of therapists, and nursing aides, orderlies, and attendants. Training varies from just a few weeks to five years.

Education and child care—Preschool teachers and classroom aides are in great demand. Likewise, workers with experience and training in engineering and other technical fields are needed in high schools and colleges. Some schools are even relaxing certification requirements in order to recruit teachers with "real-world" experience for math and science courses.

Janitors and housekeepers—These jobs are often low-paying and tend to include no benefits, but there is a great demand for workers to fill them.

CONTENT QUESTIONS—"JOBS 2000"

TRUE OR FALSE

If the statement is false, rewrite it to make it true.

1. The number of Americans age 55 and older holding jobs will increase 42 percent between 1994 and 2005.
2. The bulk of the new jobs will be in high-paying, high-technology fields.
3. Now, less than 3 percent of police officers and detectives are 55 or older.
4. Over the next ten years the number of teachers and teacher aides needed at almost all levels will decrease.
5. BLS data indicates that job tenure is going up, not down.

COMPLETION

6. Why will most health-care occupations grow during the coming years?
7. Among the 512 occupations studied by the BLS, which is the fastest growing?
8. According to Lewis, what is one reason the job outlook for midlife Americans isn't more optimistic?
9. What are four of the most promising occupations for midlife workers?
10. In 1994 the BLS projected a 66 percent increase in the number of travel agents by 2005. In 1996, how and why did they revise their projection?

VOCABULARY—"JOBS 2000"

1. burgeoning opportunity (¶12)
2. a caveat (¶21)
3. decimating the ranks of (¶26)
4. reputation for diplomacy (¶30)
5. prognosticators (¶35)
6. labor force participation rate (¶38)

CONTENT ANALYSIS QUESTIONS—"JOBS 2000"

1. In paragraph 8, when Lewis says "there's a joker in the deck," what does he mean? What is the impact on workers?
2. The BLS projects an 80 percent increase in the number of physical therapists and a 58 percent increase in the number of paralegals, but only a 22 percent increase in the number of physicians and a 28 percent increase in the number of lawyers in 2005. What are some of the reasons for the increase in the paraprofessional occupations?
3. In paragraph 25, Sicker states "Technology is destroying jobs faster that it's creating them." In what ways do you agree? In what ways do you disagree? What can you do to lessen the negative impact of technology on your career?
4. Why does Kutscher think it's a mistake to read too much into all the reports on downsizing? Do you agree or disagree with him? (Have most of the people you know worked for the same employer for many years? How many people you know have been pink-slipped in the last six months?)
5. The BLS projects that the labor force participation rate for both sexes age 55 and older will increase into 2005 because of "the economics of retirement." What does that mean? How will that affect you?

APPLICATION QUESTIONS—"JOBS 2000"

1. What career planning advice would you give: an eighth-grader, a high school senior, your 35-year-old brother, your 50-year-old aunt? Please explain your reasoning.

2. Assume that a 54-year-old friend of yours was just notified that the plant where he has worked as a manager for the last 20 years is closing in three weeks and he will be out of a job. He asks your advice. What alternatives do you ask him to consider?

"IF YOU CHOOSE A JOB YOU LOVE, YOU'LL NEVER HAVE TO 'WORK'"

Harvey Mackay is a businessman, consultant, and writer. He is author of *Swim with the Sharks without Being Eaten Alive* and *Sharkproof*. This selection—"If You Choose a Job You Love, You'll Never Have to 'Work'"—is one of his *United Features Syndicate* columns.

IF YOU CHOOSE A JOB YOU LOVE, YOU'LL NEVER HAVE TO "WORK"

HARVEY MACKAY

[1]My favorite movie? *Father of the Bride, Part 1*. It's a movie for every father, wringing an alternating tear and a belly laugh. I think there also should be a "Father of the Groom" though, because all the emotions are different. Tender as the moments were at my daughters' weddings, a dad feels quite a different pride as his only son goes down the aisle.

[2]David Mackay had our blessing when he was about to say, "I do." Looking back at his wedding in Santa Barbara 18 months ago, I remember *silently appraising* the young men in the wedding party. Fluffed and buffed in their tuxedos, lined up in front of every cut flower that could be found in a 10-mile radius, they were still restless with *leftover adolescent exuberance*.

[3]David, the bridegroom/film maker in Hollywood (his *Breaking Free* was to be released soon); Jeff Kenline, president of an advertising specialty company; Tim Hall, Colorado ski instructor for the disabled; Dean Patterson, president of a courier service; Schaefer Price, consultant for biotech companies, and Tim Pogue, president of Ride Snowboards, one of the hottest stocks on the Nasdaq in 1995.

Purple-Haired Original

[4]Not so bad for the class of '81, Minnetonka High School. Of the group on that sunny California day, I mutter to myself, no one is more unique than Tim Pogue.

[5]Why? First of all, he has purple hair. Did I say purple? Yes, purple. Not to mention the tattoo on his fore-arm, thankfully covered by the tuxedo sleeve. Tim is an original.

[6]In 1988, when life was at the speed of light, and my first book, *Swim with the Sharks without Being Eaten Alive*, had found its way to the top of the *New York Times* best-seller list, Tim congratulated me and asked for a bit of time and advice, career advice I supposed.

[7]He had spent a long five years at the University of Minnesota, ending up a few credits short of a degree. He'd had several odd jobs but was *not exactly a guided missile on a career track* to corporate stardom.

[8]I liked him a lot, though. He wasn't, nor had he ever been, *intimidated by* adults. At ease in any situation, comfortable to be around, even a founder of a bike-repair shop in his garage in high school.

(*CONTINUED*)

IF YOU CHOOSE A JOB YOU LOVE,
YOU'LL NEVER HAVE TO "WORK" (CONTINUED)

⁹We finally got together as he took me to the airport.

¹⁰"What do you like to do?" I asked this fellow who would one day color his hair a verified 330 out of 365 days per year.

¹¹"Golf, music, sell things, snowboard."

¹²"Snow what?" I asked, with the look of a deer staring at headlights.

¹³"Snowboard," he said. "I think it's got real potential."

¹⁴As he explained this infant industry, I should have listened even more closely. Tim Pogue was just four years away from founding Ride Snowboards, today a Wall Street darling with $75 million in sales.

¹⁵He was seven years from a 500 percent per share gain in the '95 rally and a full-page, full-torso personal photo in Fortune.

¹⁶This was also a Perkins restaurant alum who had waited on me a few years earlier and was always scrambling for tips. He was tough, though, raised without his natural father on a very tight family budget in *an affluent ZIP code*.

"Follow Your Bliss"

¹⁷But I could tell that there weren't going to be many stiff white shirts and worn black wingtips in this kid's future.

¹⁸"Follow your bliss and find something you love to do, and you'll never have to work a day in your life," I said. I went on to say, "If you walk backward, you'll never stub your toe."

¹⁹He nodded like I was giving him my directions to a secret gold mine, and I was.

²⁰Did I have a strange passion to be an envelope manufacturer? No. But I always wanted to own a company that made something I could sell to people. Simple, but it rang my bell then, and it still does now.

²¹After our meeting, Tim went to work for Burton, the dominant board company in the world. He learned about manufacturing and marketing, and he built an incredible network in a few short years until he had a significant reputation in the industry.

²²In 1992, with two partners, he founded Ride Snowboards with $250,000 in borrowed funds and made money the first full year in business. Today, its stock has risen and split like baker's yeast, and he could buy 20 restaurants the likes of the ones he worked for in his busboy days.

²³And he did it all with purple hair.

Mackay's Moral

Follow your bliss.

VOCABULARY—"IF YOU CHOOSE A JOB YOU LOVE, YOU'LL NEVER HAVE TO 'WORK'"

1. silently appraising (¶2)
2. leftover adolescent exuberance (¶2)
3. not exactly a guided missile on a career track (¶7)
4. intimidated by (¶8)
5. an affluent ZIP code (¶16)

CONTENT ANALYSIS QUESTIONS—"IF YOU CHOOSE A JOB YOU LOVE, YOU'LL NEVER HAVE TO 'WORK'"

1. What is Mackay's thesis? How does he develop and support his thesis?

2. What does Mackay mean when he writes "I could tell there weren't going to be many stiff white shirts and worn black wingtips in this kid's future"?

3. List five adjectives you would use to describe Tim Pogue. Which of those characteristics do you think contributed to his business success? Could any of those characteristics be useful to you in your career search?

4. After he identified that he liked to "sell things and snowboard," what steps did Tim Pogue take to reach his success?

APPLICATION QUESTION—"IF YOU CHOOSE A JOB YOU LOVE, YOU'LL NEVER HAVE TO 'WORK'"

1. What do you like to do? Are you following your bliss? If not, what changes could you make in your future career path to work at what you love?

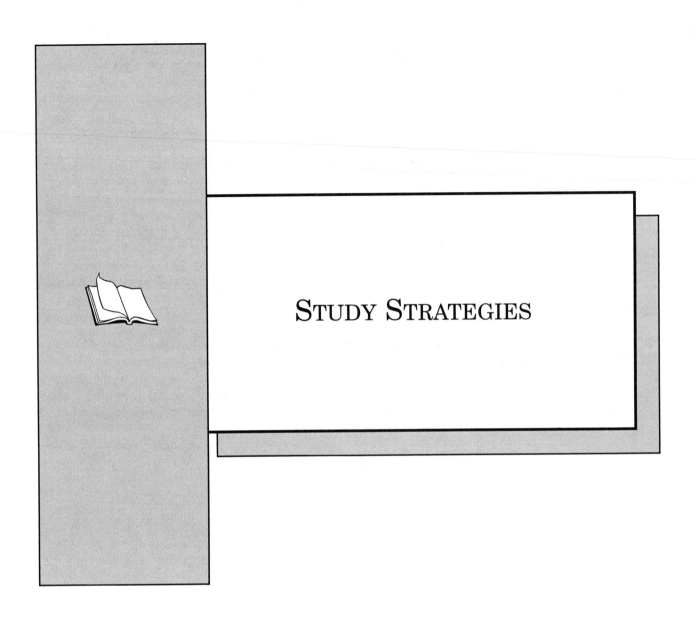

STUDY STRATEGIES

Effective study strategies are your keys to effective learning. Study strategies give you the opportunity to approach learning tasks systematically and independently. Building a large repertoire of effective study strategies for effective learning will help you be able to do the following:

Take more responsibility for your own learning
Spend your time effectively and stay on task
Select the best approach(es) for each assignment/task
Begin, follow through, and complete assignments
Access a variety of content and reference materials
Know when to ask for help

LEARNING TO LEARN

Learning is a very personal matter. There isn't one study/learning skill or strategy that works for every person in every situation. Therefore, learning to learn strategies are about learning what you know, learning what you don't know, and knowing what to do about it.

1. KNOW YOURSELF

Begin by honestly assessing your strengths and weaknesses in basic college skills—reading, writing, listening, and mathematics—and study/work habits such as organization, time management, concentration, listening, and note-taking.

Next, identify your learning style preferences. Many factors affect learning, but consider: Do you learn most effectively by reading, by watching, by listening, or by doing? You must also become familiar with your instructors' teaching styles to help you adapt your learning style to the best advantage.

In addition, consider when and where you are at your best for learning. For example, are you a morning person or a night owl? Do you concentrate best in a bright room with noise or in a cozy, quiet corner? If you're not sure about your strengths and style, check with your college's learning center or counseling office for help.

2. MANAGE YOUR TIME AND LIFE

The first step in learning to manage your time—controlling your own life—is to identify what your goals are and establish priorities to help you reach them.

Analyze how you are using your time. If you aren't spending time on your priorities, you must make the necessary adjustments or you won't reach your goals. If school, learning, and good grades are a priority, then you must make and follow a schedule that gives a significant amount of time to class and study. For more specific ideas, see the section titled "Managing Your Time Effectively."

3. IMPROVE YOUR CONCENTRATION

As a good student, you will not necessarily study more than a poor student, but you will definitely use your study time more effectively.

Learn to keep your attention focused on the task at hand: Concentrate. When you are in class or ready to study, give it your full attention.

And remember, how well you learn something, not how fast you learn it, is the critical factor in remembering. You must "get" something before you are able to "forget" it. For more specific ideas see the section titled "Concentrate⇨Comprehend⇨Remember: Improving Your Memory."

4. KNOW WHAT *STUDY* MEANS AND HOW TO DO IT

Learning takes more than just going to class and doing homework. It is a cycle built on the Plan⇨Do⇨Review reading/study strategy.

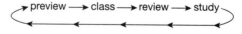

When you establish a learning-cycle routine, you will be able to learn more in less time with less stress.

5. DEVELOP A THINKER'S VOCABULARY

English is the richest language on earth. Each word is a symbol that represents an idea or object. Your ability to understand the meaning of the words others use and to select the right one(s) to communicate your ideas, information, and feelings is very important to effective learning.

To develop a thinker's vocabulary, you must become sensitive to words, and develop strategies for unlocking the meanings of new words and a process for remembering new words and their meanings. For more specific ideas, see the section titled "Improving Vocabulary."

6. BE AN ACTIVE READER

Did you ever fall asleep while playing tennis or watching your favorite television show? Probably not. How about when you're reading? Probably so. What makes the difference? If you are actively involved, physically and mentally, you stay interested and committed. When you become passive, you rapidly lose interest and drift away.

To learn from study/reading material, you must be an active, thinking participant in the process, not a passive bystander. Always preview the reading and make sure you have a specific purpose for each assignment. Read actively to fulfill your purpose and answer questions about the material. Keep involved by giving yourself frequent tests on what you've read. And always review. For more specific ideas, see the section titled "Plan⇨Do⇨Review."

7. BE AN ACTIVE WRITER

Writing that accurately expresses your ideas demands not only writing skill but also focused attention, critical thinking, and active involvement. You will be able to communicate your ideas clearly only if you become actively involved in the writing process.

Your writing must have a purpose, a controlling idea or thesis, organized development of your idea with major and minor supporting details, and a logical conclusion. For more specific ideas, work with a tutor or a member of your college's writing skills department.

8. BUILD LISTENING AND NOTETAKING SKILLS

Accurately listening to a lecture and deciding what is important are two skills that must be mastered before you worry about how to write the information in your notes. Again, being an active rather than a passive participant is the key to your success.

Taking good notes demands that you prepare for class, become an active listener, distinguish major from minor points, use a notetaking system, participate in class, and review often. For more specific ideas, see the section titled "Taking Good Notes in Lectures."

9. KNOW HOW TO STUDY FOR AND TAKE EXAMS

Exams are your way to show a professor how much you've learned. Preparing for exams will give you a better understanding of the material, lower your anxiety, and improve your scores.

Study and review the material over a period of time, using the night before as a final review—not a cram session. Pace yourself during the exam, and always go over your graded exam with your professor. For more specific ideas, see the section titled "Preparing for and Taking Exams."

10. SET YOUR OWN GOALS

Your professors can only set the stage for you to learn. You must create your own goals and achieve them through your own action. By assessing what you know and deciding what you want to achieve, you will expand your capabilities and improve your chances for success.

USING PLAN⇨DO⇨REVIEW

Everyone looks for ways to be more successful. American executives strive to compete with aggressive foreign competitors, teachers seek ways to enrich student learning, and students—like you—search for ways to improve academic performance.

So how can you, like a company president or a college professor, improve your chances for success? First, realize that whether your goal is to improve performance on a widget production line or on a sociology final exam, the basic blueprint can be the same: You plan what you need to do, you implement your plan, and you review how well you did. Then, since your goal, understanding more of what you read, can't always be met the first time you complete your plan, you view reading as a cycle instead of a one-shot activity.

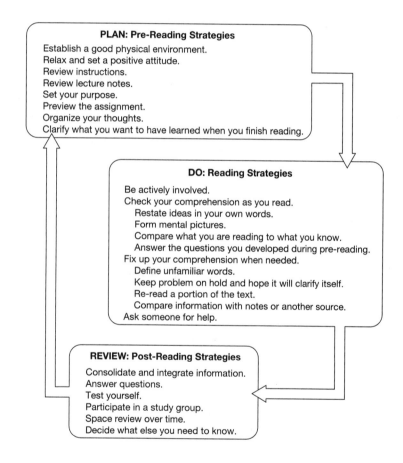

PLAN: Pre-Reading Strategies

Establish a good physical environment.
Relax and set a positive attitude.
Review instructions.
Review lecture notes.
Set your purpose.
Preview the assignment.
Organize your thoughts.
Clarify what you want to have learned when you finish reading.

DO: Reading Strategies

Be actively involved.
Check your comprehension as you read.
 Restate ideas in your own words.
 Form mental pictures.
 Compare what you are reading to what you know.
 Answer the questions you developed during pre-reading.
Fix up your comprehension when needed.
 Define unfamiliar words.
 Keep problem on hold and hope it will clarify itself.
 Re-read a portion of the text.
 Compare information with notes or another source.
Ask someone for help.

REVIEW: Post-Reading Strategies

Consolidate and integrate information.
Answer questions.
Test yourself.
Participate in a study group.
Space review over time.
Decide what else you need to know.

PLAN

Use the following strategies to help "prime your brain":

Establish a Good Environment Place yourself in surroundings that help you to concentrate, and that encourage good posture and a ready-to-work attitude.

Relax and Set a Positive Mental Attitude Set yourself up to be successful. Do your study-reading when you are at your mental best. Have confidence in yourself; know that you can read successfully and accomplish the goals you set.

Review Instructions   Check any comprehension guidelines you have been given such as "read this in preparation for tomorrow's lecture," or "read to see how this author differs from what I've said today," or "review all of the material we covered in preparation for the exam."

Review Lecture Notes   Reread any notes you have on this topic looking for topics, or ideas you need to clarify, words you need to define, or names and dates you need to fill in.

Set Your Purpose   Match the way you read to your purpose. For instance, reading for enjoyment does not require the full understanding that reading to prepare for a psychology lecture requires, and those demands are different from reading for a chemistry exam. Clarify your purpose before you begin to read, and you're more likely to be successful and less likely to waste time.

Preview the Assignment   To preview the assignment, do the following:

Read the chapter objectives.

Read headings/subheadings.

Read introductory and concluding paragraphs.

Read boldface and italic words and phrases.

Highlight/clarify unfamiliar vocabulary.

Examine graphics.

Review end-of-chapter summaries and questions.

Take advantage of anything that will help you understand the organization and core ideas.

Organize Your Thoughts   Based on the chapter objectives and headings/subheadings, jot down the major topics you are going to be reading about. Then write a few words about what you know on each of the topics.

Clarify What You Want to Know When You Finish Reading   If you don't read to find out something specific, you probably won't find out anything specific. One way to read for something specific is to phrase the chapter's objectives or headings/subheadings as questions, and then read to answer those questions.

DO

Use the following strategies to help you be active and think:

Restate Ideas in Your Own Words   At the end of a sentence or paragraph, rephrase the idea in your own words.

Form Mental Pictures   Stop and build a mental picture of what the author has written.

Compare What You Are Reading to What You Know   Ask yourself how new information fits with what you already know? Does it reinforce, contradict, or add new information?

Answer Questions   Connect what you are reading to questions you need to answer.

If you don't understand what you are reading, use one of these fix-up strategies to get back on track:

Define Unfamiliar Words   Understand the words the author uses. Check the context, glossary, lecture notes, or a dictionary, or ask someone.

Use Chapter Objectives and Headings/Subheadings   Reread objectives and headings/subheadings for ideas or concepts that help you to understand the unclear passage.

Review Related Graphics   Review corresponding graphics and their explanations to see if they clarify the text information.

Reread a Portion   Try reading the sentence or paragraph again with the specific goal of clarifying your question.

Keep the Problem on Hold and Hope It Will Clarify Itself   If the problem is just one sentence or paragraph, you can mark it and continue reading. It's possible the next sentence or paragraph will help you.

Compare Information with Notes or Another Source   Find and read about the topic or idea in another book to see if a different approach helps your understanding.

Ask Someone   After you've exhausted all other resources—clarified the vocabulary; reread the objectives, headings/subheadings, graphics, and unclear passages; and reviewed other information you have—and you still don't understand what you need to, ask someone for help.

REVIEW

Use the following strategies to help gain perspective and strengthen your memory:

Reread Thoughts You've Organized and Questions You've Answered during Reading   Make use of the work you did during your planning and reading.

Answer Questions   Write out or talk through the answers to the questions you set out in your plan.

Consolidate and Integrate Information   Combine your knowledge with what you've gained from reading and your lecture notes to form one coherent picture.

Participate in a Study Group   Join a group of classmates to talk about what you have read. Try reviewing concepts, sharing notes, and taking practice tests.

Test Yourself   Make up a test on the material or have a classmate make one up and test yourself. Make a set of question and answer flash cards for a convenient carry-along review tool by writing the question on one side of a 3" x 5" card and the answer on the reverse side.

CONTINUE THE CYCLE

Occasionally, on small assignments or familiar material, you will achieve your reading comprehension goals at the end of one Plan⇨Do⇨Review cycle. On the other hand, when you're reviewing, don't be surprised to discover gaps in your knowledge. When you do, just develop a new plan that will help you fill in the gaps. Reread the portion of the assignment you need to get the information and then review, making sure to integrate the new information with what you already have.

USING TYPOGRAPHY AND DESIGN CLUES

Good typography and design in a textbook aren't just decorations to make it look pretty. They are devices authors use to make information more accessible to the reader. Typography and design elements visually organize information with a structure that clarifies the hierarchy of ideas and the relationships among those ideas. As a reader, you can use typographic and design cues to help you gather information accurately from the printed page.

TYPE SIZE, STYLE, AND PLACEMENT OF HEADINGS

Although every textbook has its own way of organizing information for the reader, the size, style, and placement of heads and subheads is always a primary clue. Typically, authors alert the reader to different levels of information with techniques such as: varying sizes of type—the more important or broad the idea, the larger the type; using different styles, such as color, bold, italic, and underlining; using all capital letters; and differing the amounts of indentation from the margin—similar to an outlining technique.

Analyze the following example from Chapter 1, and then discover the organization scheme for your other textbooks.

WHAT DO I DO ONCE I START TO READ?

Did you ever fall asleep while playing tennis or while you were watching your favorite television show? Probably not. How about while you were reading? Probably. What makes the difference? Your active involvement.

Active physical and mental involvement keeps you interested and committed. When you become passive, you rapidly lose interest and drift away. So, to read successfully you must be an active, thinking participant in the process.

HOW CAN I CHECK MY COMPREHENSION AS I READ?

As an active reader, you use comprehension monitoring, or checking, strategies to make certain that your understanding is satisfactory for your purpose. Comprehension monitoring strategies include the following:

Restating Ideas in Your Own Words   At the end of a sentence or paragraph, rephrase the idea in your own words.

Forming Mental Pictures   Build a mental picture of what the author is describing.

TYPE STYLES WITHIN PARAGRAPHS

Authors use different type styles within their text material to highlight important words and ideas. Bold and italic are the most common type styles used for emphasis within paragraphs, although you may also see words underlined.

You can be sure, however, that authors use their methods of emphasis consistently. So again, your job is to analyze each of your textbooks, discover their patterns, and use those clues to improve your understanding of the information you need.

WHITE SPACE

White space on a page isn't an accident. It always serves a purpose: Authors use white space to help direct the reader's eye and to provide rest stops. For example, authors keep a consistent amount of space between lines and paragraphs on the same idea, but generally increase the amount between differing concepts.

Analyze how your text authors' use of white space can help you understand their ideas.

GRAPHIC ELEMENTS

Authors use a variety of graphic elements to cue you to different types of information. From simple single-line boxes around text, to bullets (•) in front of text, to a dingbat (◊) marking the end of a text section, all graphic elements are designed to alert you to a specific kind or level of information.

Often authors combine several design elements to more clearly communicate their message. In the following example from Chapter 2, notice how white space and the use of italics combine to highlight important information.

Inferring a writer's purpose is not just your opinion or a wild guess. An inference is your best reasoned conclusion based on the information you are given. Valid inferences follow logically from the information the author provides. As semanticist S. I. Hayakawa says in *Language in Thought and Action*, an inference is "a statement about the unknown made on the basis of the known."

Knowing an author's reason for writing will help you understand what the author writes. Four primary purposes for writing prose (writing other than poetry) are:

Exposition: The author wants to explain, set forth or make clear facts, events, and ideas.

Description: The author wants to paint a picture in words.

Narration: The author wants to tell a story.

Persuasion/Argumentation: The author wants to influence you—by engaging your emotions or by presenting logical arguments—to believe or feel a certain way or take a particular action.

But, just as in your own writing, authors often combine two or more purposes to clearly communicate their message. For example, an author may need to tell a story's sequence of events with vivid descriptions (but the primary purpose is still to tell you the story) or perhaps persuade you to take some action by giving you facts about the consequences of inaction (but the primary purpose is still to persuade you to act).

OTHER FACTORS IMPACTING COMPREHENSION

Line Length   Although you cannot physically change the length of the lines of type in the books you read, you can try to alleviate potential problems. Long lines of type are difficult to follow and may cause you to lose your place. To keep on track, try sliding an index card over the line you have just finished to keep your eyes moving ahead.

Capital Letters   The shape of words is a major clue in most reading. Text printed in all capital letters form uniform blockish shapes that are difficult to distinguish from one another. You will probably need to slow down when you have to read all capital letters. In fact, in the example from Chapter 1, notice how you must slow down to read the subhead that is in all small capital letters—"HOW CAN I CHECK MY COMPREHENSION AS I READ?"

MANAGING YOUR TIME EFFECTIVELY

Spending time, like spending money, is a very personal matter. Unlike money, however, you can't get a "time raise" or "save some hours" for a busy day. We all have to live on 168 hours each week. Successful students, like other successful people, must budget time according to their priorities to ensure that they spend it effectively.

IDENTIFY YOUR GOALS AND PRIORITIES

The first step in learning to manage your time—and controlling your life—is to identify what your goals and priorities are. You must decide what you want out of school and life and what you must do to get it.

Is learning—getting a good education—high on your priority list? How important is your current job? Your family? What is most important to you?

ANALYZE HOW YOU'RE SPENDING YOUR TIME NOW

Analyze exactly how you spend your time. For the next week, keep a detailed log of everything you do. Account for all activities: class attendance, study, work, eating, commuting, recreation, exercise, sleep, etc. Also note when (during what hours) you do these activities.

How much time each week do you spend...

in classes?	_____ hours
studying for classes?	_____ hours
working?	_____ hours
meeting the needs of others?	_____ hours
exercising?	_____ hours
relaxing?	_____ hours
sleeping?	_____ hours
_____?	_____ hours
_____?	_____ hours

MATCH HOW YOU'RE USING TIME WITH YOUR PRIORITIES

Now you can evaluate your use of time. No one—not even you—can judge your use of time as efficient or inefficient unless you do it in relation to your priorities.

In addition to looking at how much time you spend on each activity, consider if you are spending enough quality time on your priorities. For example, if learning is high on your priority list, do you study during your prime energy hours or only after everything else is done for the day?

DEVELOP A PLAN TO SPEND QUALITY TIME ON YOUR PRIORITIES

If you found some time blocks that are not in line with what you want to be doing to reach your goals, you can begin to systematically change your life by taking control of your time.

Start by building a realistic schedule, or time budget, that gives time to the activities that fit with your priorities and will help you reach your goals. If learning and getting good grades are high on your priority list, then you will have to budget time for attending classes regularly, for preparing, studying, and reviewing, plus additional time for papers, reports, and other special assignments.

Finally, you must stick to your time schedule. Some flexibility is necessary, of course, to take care of unexpected demands. But if you spend too much time on non-priority tasks, you will not meet your goals.

LIVE SMART: TIME MANAGEMENT TIPS

Maintain a "Things to Do" List and Keep the Items in Priority Order   Most people tend to do low-ranking, little things first and never get around to the important tasks.

Break Major Tasks down into Small Chunks   We often avoid big projects because we have limited time or we don't know where to begin. Break major projects into small pieces and tackle them one at a time.

Eliminate Tasks   Carefully evaluate each task and, when possible, don't do time-consuming routine tasks like washing the car weekly or dusting.

Delegate or Negotiate Tasks   Ask yourself "Who else can do this task?" (maybe not as well as you would do it, but acceptably). Ask "What tasks can I trade or share with someone?" Learn to ask for help.

Consolidate Tasks   Whenever possible, do more than one thing at a time—except thinking! If you're going to the library to prepare your biology report, also work on your research paper and look up that reference you need for literature.

Evaluate Your Habits   Why do you do routine tasks in a certain way? Are your routines the most efficient? Could you save time by changing your routine actions? Could getting up 15 minutes earlier be helpful?

Know and Wisely Use Your Prime Working Times   There really are "morning people" and "night owls"—find out when you're at your best and use those hours wisely.

Be Prepared to Lower Your Standards   Given the heavy demands on your time, it is doubtful that everything you do can be perfect. Based on your priorities, decide what you want to be "A" quality and what things can be "B" quality.

Learn to Say "No"   There is never enough time to do everything we want to do, so we must learn to do those things that move us toward our goals and say "no" to those that do not.

Be Flexible but Remain in Control   Expect interruptions, as they are bound to occur. If you are doing things in priority order—not leaving big things to the last—you and your schedule will easily survive.

STUDY SMART: TIME MANAGEMENT TIPS

Make a Study Schedule and Stick to It   The best way to ensure that you will have enough study time to meet your goals in each course is to plan for it. Daily, weekly, and monthly planners are available in most bookstores.

Understand Assignments and Write Them Down   Keep all assignments in one place to avoid forgetting something.

Develop an Understanding of Your Best Concentration Times   Arrange your schedule so that you have study time during your peak hours.

Remember That "Study" Includes Many Different Tasks   When instructors talk about the need to study, they mean you should: read/review material in preparation for class; complete all homework; and review class notes, text assignments, and supplementary material on a regular schedule.

Realize That Different Subjects Require Different Types of Preparation   Lecture classes require that you review your notes right after class and preview the new topic just before class; recitation classes, like languages and math, demand more specific study just prior to class.

Schedule Study/Learning Sessions to Fit Your Attention Span   Try studying for 45 minutes and then taking a ten-minute exercise break.

Begin Each Study Session with Goal Setting   Predict specifically what you want to accomplish and then work to meet your goals.

Study Difficult and/or Complex Material First   Leave routine and more mechanical tasks for last.

Vary Subjects and Type of Study for Maximum Efficiency   Within each study session, do some reading, writing, recitation, etc., to stay interested and alert.

Schedule Periodic Review Sessions   To remember material over a long period of time, you must review the information often.

Use All of Your Available Time   Even small bits of time, like waiting for the dentist, can be put to use—don't be caught without something to read or study.

CONCENTRATE⇨COMPREHEND⇨REMEMBER: IMPROVING YOUR MEMORY

You must "get" something before you can "forget" it! Often we say "I forgot" when what we mean to say is "I didn't pay attention and understand it." Good students do not necessarily study more than poor students; they use their study time more effectively. Top students use the strategies of effective learning—concentrating, comprehending, and remembering.

CONCENTRATE

By concentration I mean sustained attention, focused in one direction with no distractions. When you complain that you "can't concentrate," you usually mean that you can't keep your attention on your studies. You're probably concentrating, but on other things: what to eat, how to pay the rent, where to go tonight, and so on. To overcome distractions that interfere with study, identify the distraction and apply a technique to alleviate or overcome it.

Cope with Internal Distractions Internal distractions include daydreams and thoughts like "I have to remember to call the plumber" and "This is boring." Many people find themselves "reading" a paragraph and discovering they are really thinking about how hungry they are or the question they need to ask their professor next week. Some ways of coping with these internal distractions include the following:

Keep a notepad on your study table and jot down a brief reminder of the idea or problem; then let it go from your mind.

Turn the distraction, especially hunger or sleep, into a reward: Once you master the material idea, reward yourself with a snack or nap.

If you can't release your mind to concentrate, take a break and deal with the distraction.

To counteract boredom or lack of interest, try to identify the cause: lack of background knowledge, lack of purpose for the assignment, difficult reading material, or personal problems. If it is a textbook problem, try using the Plan⇨Do⇨Review approach or getting help from a tutor. If the problem is personal, consider talking with a counselor.

Eliminate External Distractions External distractions are related to the physical environment of your study area. They are easier to deal with once you've identified them:

The best way to combat most external distractions, whether it's the television, the telephone, family members demanding attention, or the smell of dinner cooking, is to get away from them.

Form the habit of studying in the same place at the same time every day. Make this place, whether at home or school, just for study. Pay your bills and read your magazines somewhere else—don't mix personal work, schoolwork, and leisure activities.

Select a study area with good lighting, adequate ventilation, and quiet surroundings.

When it is time to study, apply yourself totally with your full attention. If you feel you are not getting as much as you should from your study time and you cannot alleviate the distraction, take a short break and try again. The bottom line: You must learn to concentrate.

COMPREHEND

How well you learn something, not how fast you learn it, is the critical factor in remembering. Comprehending means you are able to translate information into meaningful ideas you understand. Five basic principles of good comprehension are as follows:

1. Something that doesn't make sense to you is hard to learn; the more meaningful you make it, the easier it is to learn.
2. The more you know about a subject, the easier it is to understand new information about it.
3. The more interested you are in a subject, the easier it is to comprehend.
4. Your ability to distinguish main points from details and to tell the difference between significant details and unimportant details is a very important skill.
5. Learning—understanding ideas—means you must fit each new piece of information into the subject's "big picture," not just memorize bits of details.

REMEMBER

Remembering is a skill. Improving your memory, like improving any other skill, is hard work. These tips and techniques will not necessarily make remembering easier; they will just make it more efficient:

"I have a poor memory" is just a convenient excuse to use when you haven't had the time to learn something. Being able to remember something usually depends on how thoroughly you learned it in the first place. Fortunately, you can improve your memory—it just takes time and work.

You remember only what you intend to remember. Do you forget your best friend's name or phone number? Do you forget how to drive?

Realize you can't (and don't need to) remember everything. Trying to remember every detail you read and hear is impossible. Therefore, your ability to identify important ideas and details in the study/learning process is critical to effective recall of information—remembering what you want/need to remember.

How you put information into your memory affects how easily you can access it. In many ways, your memory is like an office filing system:

Your sensory memory (momentary and very limited) is like a pink "while you were out" message slip that you deal with and forget.

Your short-term memory (30–45 seconds, with limited capacity) is like the "in-basket" where you sort out important from non-important information.

Your long-term memory (relatively permanent and unlimited in capacity) is like large file cabinets for storing important information.

Everything in long-term storage must first be identified through sensory and/or short-term memory as important, then organized by some system, and filed in the cabinet so it can be found easily. The same principles apply to your memory.

You must identify meaningful/important information, organize it, and then study it (file it) so you can retrieve it later from your memory.

Experiment with many memory techniques to see which ones work best for you. Once you have identified important information, there are several techniques that can help you organize and recall it. There is not, however, one best method for remembering everything.

Associate   Relate new information to something you already know. An isolated idea/fact is hard to remember; if you associate it with information that already makes sense to you, it will be more meaningful and thus easier to organize and remember.

Visualize   Organize information into a vivid, clear, mental picture. For example, to remember the elements of a novel, form a picture with all the important characters dressed in the style of the period, doing something representative of the character, etc.

Mnemonic Aids   For information that defies association or visualization, adapt a memory technique. Some mnemonic devices include:

Acronyms—form a word from the first letter of each word in a series, for example, "HOMES" for recalling the Great Lakes: Huron, Ontario, Michigan, Erie, Superior.

Acrostics—make a nonsense phrase so that the first letter of each word provides the information—for example, "Every Good Boy Does Fine" for the E, G, B, D, F lines of the treble music staff.

Word-Part Clues—for example, remember whether the denotative or connotative meaning of a word is the dictionary meaning by noting that *denotative* and *dictionary* both begin with "d."

Poems and Rhymes—make up short, catchy sayings that include the essential information—for example "In 1492, Columbus sailed the ocean blue."

Review and use information. Regular review and use of information will significantly improve retention and recall. So, rather than a single marathon study session, plan frequent short study sessions to learn new information, and always include a review of previously learned information (yes, even if you've already had that test).

IMPROVING VOCABULARY

English is the richest language on earth with the largest vocabulary—over 1,000,000 words. Yet the average adult has a vocabulary of only 40,000–50,000 words. Imagine what we're missing! Here are some strategies for unlocking the meanings of new words and a process for remembering new words and their meanings.

CONTEXT

You can often get at least part of a word's meaning from the way it's used in the sentence. So when you come to an unfamiliar word while reading, rather than first looking it up in the dictionary, try to figure out its meaning from the words around it. Often the author provides clues to help you unlock the general meaning.

> "Perihelion is the point in the earth's orbit when the distance between the earth and the sun is at its minimum, as opposed to **aphelion**."

GLOSSARY

If your book has a glossary, it will give you the specific definition for this field of study. A glossary, or mini-dictionary in the back of a text, contains only the definition that fits the use in this book.

> **aphelion**   The point in the earth's orbit when the distance between the earth and the sun is at its maximum.

DICTIONARY

To find out exactly what a word means and where it comes from, look it up in the dictionary. The dictionary is a reliable source for definitions, correct spellings, pronunciation, parts of speech, and derivations. To use this resource book effectively, however, you must understand the abbreviations it uses and the variety of information it includes. Since you may find a variety of definitions for a word, always fit the definition back into the original context to be certain it makes sense.

> **aph•elion**   (a-ˈfēl-yən) *n. pl* = **elia** [NL, fr. *apo* + Gk *hēlios* sun—more at SOLAR]: the point of a planet's or comet's orbit most distant from the sun— compare PERIHELION

STRUCTURE

Knowing the parts of words—prefixes, roots, suffixes—helps you understand and unlock the meanings of whole families of words. A prefix is the part that's sometimes attached to the front of a word; there are about 100 commons ones. The root is the basic part of a word; most of our root words come from Latin and Greek. A suffix is often attached to the end of a word.

> **apo**   prefix from Greek meaning *away from*
> **helios**   comes from Greek meaning *the sun*

Now, other words with **apo** or **helios** start to make sense, such as ***apo****lune* = the point in the path of a body orbiting the moon that is farthest from the center or ***helio****phyte* = a plant thriving in full sunlight.

READ, READ

In addition to using these strategies, it's important to read a variety of materials. The more you expose yourself to new words, the more words you will learn.

PRACTICE: REMEMBERING NEW WORDS

Unless you actively work at reviewing and remembering each of the new words you encounter, you will have to rediscover the meaning each time you see the word.

1.   Write each word to be learned on a 3" x 5" card.

aphelion

2. On the back of the card, write the definition (the one that most closely fits the way the word was used in your original sentence).

The point in the earth's orbit when the distance between the earth and the sun is at its maximum.

3. Below the definition, write an example sentence using the word.

The point in the earth's orbit when the distance between the earth and the sun is at its maximum.

On January 3, the earth is about 3 million miles closer to the sun than it is during **aphelion** *on July 4.*

4. Use these cards for study, review, and testing yourself.

Look at the word and try to recall the definition on the back.

As you go through the cards, sort them into two stacks: know and don't know. The next time you review, concentrate only on the don't know stack.

From time to time, review all the cards. Periodic review of information is critical to remembering.

TAKING GOOD NOTES IN LECTURES

Why take notes? There are three basic reasons: to learn, for reference, and to keep you thinking. But taking good lecture notes isn't easy. Good lecture notes must summarize the main points, include the important ideas in your own words, and list the specific details needed for your purpose in this class. To be successful, you must make what you hear part of your own thinking.

BE PREPARED TO TAKE GOOD NOTES

Understanding a lecture and taking good notes from it will be easier if you have prepared and know what topics will be covered before you go to class. You should read all assignments listed in the syllabus and given by your instructor. In addition, you should review your notes from the previous class session and any handouts. Finally, you should determine what your purpose is for this class session so you will be able to take the notes you need to fulfill your purpose.

KNOW YOUR INSTRUCTOR'S STYLE

Does your instructor: (1) simply review the text page by page, (2) use the text as a basis for lecture but add information from other sources, or (3) assign you to read the text—expecting you to read it on your own—and lecture from other sources? It's possible that your instructor will use a combination of these approaches during a semester, but your awareness of where lecture material is coming from is your first step in taking good notes.

Also consider the way an instructor organizes and delivers information. If you have an instructor start a class with, "Today we will discuss the three basic views of...," use that as a key to organize your notes as you take them. If, on the other hand, your instructor begins with an anecdote or some other illustrative material, you will have to write down ideas in the order the instructor delivers them and then spend time organizing them after class. Stay alert for cues your instructor gives you, such as the following:

Changing voice pitch, rate or tone
Writing information on the board
Using audio-visual material such as transparencies or computer presentations

UNDERSTAND WHAT YOU WRITE

Don't try to be a human tape recorder—trying to write a complete transcript of the class is not good notetaking. Your notes should capture the main points and only those details you need for your specific purpose.

Your notes should be simple and in your own words whenever possible. Aside from complex concepts or specific formulas that you must memorize and therefore need to write/copy, always translate ideas into your own words. Include supplemental and text references your instructor gives; the additional readings will help you clarify your notes and the concepts that are covered.

TAKE YOUR NOTES THE SAME WAY

Use standard 8 $1/2$" x 11" lined notebook paper. Title it with class, date, and whatever other information is needed to distinguish the notes you take in this class today from any other notes. Devise and use your own shorthand to make notetaking easier, and stick to it—remember that each note must be complete enough to be intelligible later. If you miss any information, leave a blank spot in your notes and ask after class. Don't crowd information together. Leave room for extra information and put only one idea or item on a line.

MAKE NOTES ON YOUR NOTES

Study from your notes; don't just look them over. Right after class, spend 5–10 minutes editing your notes. Fill in missing information, clarify abbreviations, and expand details. Annotate your notes by writing key words in the margins:

1. Leave a 2-inch margin at the left side of each page of notes. Do not write in this margin while you are taking notes.
2. After you have edited your notes, annotate in the left margin with words, phrases, or questions that briefly summarize major points. These key ideas should also trigger your memory to help you recall the complete information.
3. To study, cover the lecture notes and look only at your annotations. Read each annotation and try to recall all the information in your notes. Slide the cover over and check yourself.

A sample of annotated lecture notes is on page 427.

Standard Notes Heading

Melissa Student
College Study Skills
October 15
Page 1
See page 45 in textbook

Lecture Topic

Taking Notes from Lectures

Key Idea

Lecture Notes

My notes have to:

3 Things
Good Notes
Must Do

*1. Summarize main pts

2. List important ideas in my own words

3. Include significant details needed for this class

Prepare to
Take
Notes

• Read text assignment before going to class

• Read last class session notes and handouts

• Predict topics for this lecture

Instructor
Style

To organize my notes, I must know if the instructor:

• Reviews text pg by pg

• Uses text as base buts adds (info) from other sources

• Wants me to read text from other sources

Consistent Abbreviations

How a teacher can signal important (info)

4 Teacher
Cues

1. Changing voice pitch, rhythm, tone

2. Writing (info) on board

3. Using A-V materials-transparencies, etc.

4. Telling class directly that (info) is important

TAKING USEFUL NOTES FROM TEXTS

There are many techniques for taking notes from books. The one you select will vary with the type of book, the assignment, and the instructor's requirements. What won't change, however, is the necessity for you to take some type of notes. You must make reading and learning an active process and notetaking is a good way to ensure that you get involved with what you're reading.

BEING AN ACTIVE READER IS THE KEY TO GOOD NOTES

Ideas that are organized in a way that makes sense to you are easier to remember than isolated bits of information. Thus, your goal for notetaking is to identify information you need, and organize it to help you study efficiently and effectively.

Begin a reading/study session by previewing the entire assignment: Read the titles, subtitles, introduction, conclusion, and chapter questions to get an overview of the content. Set your purpose for the assignment.

Based on your preview, list the main topics in the reading assignment. Then, jot down information you already know about the topics, plus any questions you have, and any questions your instructor has given you. In other words, give yourself a reason to read: Identify some ideas and information you need to discover.

Now you are ready to read and take notes. As an active reader—one with a reason to read—you will be able to distinguish between information that is important to your purpose from interesting, but inconsequential, minor details. The following are two options for taking notes directly in the book:

TAKING NOTES IN THE TEXT

Annotate Write notes in the margins. This is a good strategy because it makes you an active, thinking participant.

1. Decide what level of information you need for this purpose.
2. After you read a section, do the following:

   Write words and phrases in the margins that summarize the information you need to know.

   Mark important information with abbreviations, such as *def* for definition, *ex* for example, * for key point.

   Jot down questions you have or challenges to the author's ideas.

3. After annotating a section, think about how what you've read and written relate to the questions you set out for yourself during your preview.

Underline or Highlight This is a questionable strategy because it is easy to become passive.

1. Decide what level of information you need.

2. Always read a section completely before you mark it. If you underline or highlight as you begin to read, you run the risk of marking information that is not important for your purpose.

3. Mark only those portions that meet your purpose according to the level of information you need—main ideas only; main ideas and major details; terminology only, etc.

4. If you underline or highlight almost everything on the page, it's no more helpful than if nothing is marked.

TAKING NOTES ON PAPER

Options for taking notes on paper include using graphic organizers, such as information maps and informal outlines, writing a summary, or devising a system of your own.

Like taking notes in the text, to take useful notes on paper, you must set your purpose and then read a section through at least once before you begin to take notes. Then, with your purpose in mind, you can write down in your notebook the ideas and information that fit your purpose. Restate information in your own words and organize it in a way that makes sense to you. One advantage of taking notes on paper is that you can combine your lecture notes with your text notes to enhance your overall comprehension of the subject.

A sample of combined textbook/lecture notes is on page 430.

When you have text and lecture notes on the same topic, coordinate and compare them. This will help you think about all the information, organize the ideas and details, and make future study more effective.

Sample Text Notes ↙

Sample Lecture Notes →

Text Topic

Melissa Student
College Study Skills
Efficient Study pp. 45–60
Page 1
Lecture: October 15

Steps to Good Lecture Notes

To be useful later my notes have to:

1. Include all main pts—organize around these!
2. Restate main ideas in own words
3. Put details in order of impt

Text Notes

✓ Key is to prepare before class:
• Read/take notes on txt assgmt before class
• Review last class session notes & syllabus
• ⟨Prepare notebook to take notes⟩

Different Info

Know what instructor style is:
• Lectures from text only
• Lectures from text and known reference bks
• Lectures from variety of sources

Instructors cue important info in many ways:
1. Voice cues—like raising voice
2. Key pts written: board, overhd, handouts
3. Repeating info
4. Giving reference info, extra readings

Standard Notes Heading

Melissa Student
College Study Skills
October 15
Page 1
See pages 45–60 in textbook

Lecture Topic

Taking Notes from Lectures

My notes have to:

* 1. Summarize main pts
2. List important ideas in my own words
3. Include significant details needed for this class

Lecture Notes

To prepare for class I must:
• Read text assgmt before going to class
• Read last class session notes and handouts
• ⟨Predict topics for this lecture⟩

To organize my notes, I must know if the instructor:
• Reviews text pg by pg
• Uses text as base buts adds ⟨info⟩ from other sources
• Wants me to read text from other sources

How a teacher can signal important ⟨info⟩:
1. Changing voice pitch, rhythm, tone
2. Writing ⟨info⟩ on board
3. Using A-V materials-transparencies, etc.
4. Telling class directly that ⟨info⟩ is important

Consistent Abbreviations

430

PREPARING FOR AND TAKING EXAMS

Exams show a professor how much you've learned. Find out as much as you can about the exam, study and review the material over a period of time (use the night before as a final review rather than a cram session), pace yourself during the exam, and always go over your graded exam with your professor. Preparing for exams will give you a better understanding of the material, lower your anxiety, and improve your scores.

PREPARING FOR ANY EXAM

Find out exactly what will be covered and what kinds of questions will be asked.

Begin your review preparation several days or weeks in advance.

Organize your review so that you will have time to study everything:

> Text chapters and lecture notes
>
> Previous exams, quizzes, and assignments
>
> Teacher handouts, summary outlines, lists of terms, sample problems, charts and graphs, or explanations of difficult concepts

Prepare and answer a sample test on your own or with a study group or tutor.

Reserve time the night before the exam for a last, once-through review.

PREPARING FOR AN OBJECTIVE EXAM (MULTIPLE CHOICE, TRUE/FALSE, ETC.)

Learn the overall structure of the content even though this exam may emphasize details. Knowing the thesis and main ideas provides a necessary framework.

Review text notes and lecture notes; turn headings and main points into questions.

Define all terms and any general vocabulary of the subject.

Work problems by actually doing them—don't just look over samples.

Know important proofs, diagrams, formulas, cycles, etc.

Review specific information with a study card system:

> Write a question on the front of a 3" x 5" card.
>
> Write the answer on the back of the card.
>
> Read the questions and try to answer them without looking at the back.
>
> Carry cards with you and review often—for example, while waiting for an appointment.
>
> Shuffle the cards often to change their order.

PREPARING FOR AN ESSAY EXAM

Remember that essay exams involve retrieving information from your memory, organizing it, and expressing it in your own words.

Look for trends and themes in your readings: Use text boldface headings, end-of-chapter discussion questions, lecture notes, and your text and notes annotations.

Concentrate on information that unifies, or brings together, all of the assigned material. This information will probably come from clues your instructor has been giving all semester—his or her approach, focus, and emphasis.

Spend most of your study time organizing and restating ideas in your own words rather than simply rereading information.

Form sample questions and write answers using your own words to clearly state the thesis, main points, and significant details.

Write a clearly stated paragraph on every topic. When appropriate, include your position on an issue and support it with logical evidence.

Give credit to reference and information sources.

Review complex or interrelated information with a study sheet system:

> Select information to be learned.
>
> Outline it using as few words as possible.
>
> Group together related points or ideas.
>
> Read it over several times.
>
> Write the first topic on a blank sheet of paper.
>
> Try to fill in specifics from memory.
>
> Repeat this process for each topic.

Remember and use information on your study sheet by doing the following:

> Choose a key word or phrase for each idea.
>
> Memorize each key word or phrase.
>
> Write the key words on the back of the exam before you begin your answer.
>
> Use the key words as an outline for the major points you want to include.

TAKING ANY EXAM

Bring all related materials—such as word book, dictionary, calculator, scratch paper—to the exam.

Get there on time—do not arrive too early or too late. If you do arrive early, don't let your classmates' nervous anxiety rub off on you.

Sit in the front of the room but do not begin until you have heard all the instructions. If you do not understand the oral or the printed instructions, ask!

Skim the whole exam to get an overview before you start answering questions.

Plan your time. Estimate how much time you should spend on each part of the exam. The number of points each section is worth should be your guide.

Pace yourself so you can complete all questions. Keep track of your time.

Read each question carefully.

Answer the easiest questions first.

Skip items you're not sure of and let other questions/answers spark your memory.

Stay calm and use logic and common sense to reason out answers.

Allow time at the end of the exam to read through your work, answer any questions you have left blank, and make grammatical corrections.

Concentrate and avoid distractions. Do not be concerned about other students finishing the exam before you.

Know the exam grading formula, including the number of points per right answer, and whether there is a "guess factor" penalty.

TAKING AN OBJECTIVE EXAM

Watch for absolute or categorical statements in true-false questions; they are usually false. Generalizations are usually only partially true.

Read the "stem" of multiple-choice questions and try to answer them for yourself before you look at the choices. Then pick the answer closest to yours.

Read all the possible answers in multiple-choice questions even if you think the first or second choice is correct.

Eliminate alternatives in multiple-choice and matching questions, thus narrowing your choice and increasing the probability of a correct answer.

Guess at an answer (unless there is a guess penalty) rather than leave a blank. Your guess might be right. If you have time, go back at the end and give it further thought.

Change an answer only if you can think of a concrete reason that makes your first answer wrong. When you "guess," your first answer is usually best.

TAKING AN ESSAY EXAM

Read the question and identify the topic(s) you are to write about, limiting words that restrict and direct your answer, and key words that tell you what type of information to include in your answer. For example:

Q: Compare the causes of the Vietnam War with the causes of Desert Storm.

Topics: *Vietnam War* and *Desert Storm*

Limiting word: *causes*

Key word: *compare*

Note key word(s) and do exactly what is asked. For example, don't *describe* if the question asks you to *evaluate*. Frequently used key words include the following:

Describe, analyze, develop, trace = descriptive and analysis questions

Explain, demonstrate, illustrate, justify = explanation and proof questions

Compare, contrast, relate = analogy and comparison questions

Criticize, evaluate, interpret, defend = personal judgment questions

Organize your answer and jot down a brief outline in the margin before you begin to write. This will help you write a clearer and more concise answer.

Write your answers in complete sentences and include only one major point in each paragraph. The rest of each paragraph should explain or support the major point.

Be direct; do not ramble or list random pieces of information.

Outline major ideas for an answer if you run out of time and cannot write a full answer.

Keep your paper legible. Instructors must easily read what you write.

Proof each answer, number all pages, and write your name and section on each sheet.

AVOIDING PLAGIARISM

Most students would never intentionally steal another person's belongings. All too often, however, they steal another writer's ideas and words: They plagiarize. To be fair and to avoid even the appearance of plagiarism, always use your own words and generously credit your sources.

Be careful when you use research that others have done. Only information that is widely available from a variety of sources—such as historic facts and geographic data—can be used without giving credit.

For example, if you were writing a research paper on earthquakes and you wanted to compare California earthquakes to others throughout history, you could find and use the dates and locations of other major earthquakes without referencing a specific source because similar information is available from any number of sources. If, however, you wanted to use a person's story about an earthquake, an analysis of the cause of an earthquake, or even a description of an earthquake, you would have to give credit to your source.

As an example, the following is an original paragraph from Joan Delfattore's book.

> In the Dick and Jane readers some of us remember from our childhoods, a family consisted of a married couple, two or three well-behaved children, and a dog and a cat. Father wore suits and went out to work; mother wore aprons and baked cupcakes. Little girls sat demurely watching little boys climb trees. Home meant a single-family house in a middle-class suburban neighborhood. Color the lawn green. Color the people white. Family life in the textbook world was idyllic; parents did not quarrel, children did not disobey, and babies did not throw up on the dog.
>
> —Joan Delfattore, *What Johnny Shouldn't Read:*
> *Textbook Censorship in America*

The following three paragraphs illustrate common ways Delfattore's paragraph is plagiarized:

Plagiarized: In the Dick and Jane readers some of us remember from our childhoods, a family consisted of a married couple, two or three well-behaved children, and a dog and a cat. Father wore suits and went out to work; mother wore aprons and baked cupcakes. Little girls sat demurely watching little boys climb trees.

Problem: This has been directly copied without quotation marks or credit to the author.

Plagiarized: According to Delfattore, the Dick and Jane readers of several years ago pictured an unrealistic family life. Stories always seemed to take place in middle-class suburban neighborhoods where life was idyllic; parents never quarreled and children always obeyed.

Problem: Although portions have been paraphrased and credit has been given to the author, quotation marks are still needed around the copied portion.

Plagiarized: In the past, elementary school reading books told stories of an unrealistic life style. Families always lived in suburbia where homes and life were picture-perfect....

Problem: Although this has been paraphrased, credit has not been given to the author.

Professional writers always credit their sources unless they are absolutely certain their information is available from a wide variety of references; you should too. Use the following general guidelines:

Use quotation marks and credit the source when you copy exact wording.

Use your own words—paraphrase instead of copying—when possible.

Give credit for words and ideas that aren't your own, even if you paraphrase.

—Donald Bower, ed., *The Professional Writer's Guide*, The National Writer's Club, 1990; and Ellen M. Kozak, "The ABCs of Avoiding Plagiarism," *Writer's Digest*, July 1993.

"The most important advice I can offer," says Myrick E. Land, "is this: Remember that you are a writer, not a compiler of previously published material. Although you will consult other writers, frequently for facts and background information, the value of your writing will depend on your own contribution" (*Writing for Magazines*, 2nd ed., Prentice Hall, 1993).

PRACTICE: AVOIDING PLAGIARISM

Rewrite these paragraphs. Quote when appropriate, paraphrase when possible, and credit when necessary. Check your rewrites with your instructor or tutor.

We as a society are caught in an information technology paradox: Information technology is thriving in a society that may not be ready for it.

Some of us want to wrap ourselves in information technology. Some of us want nothing to do with it. Most of us want it, but in moderation. This reluctant acceptance of information technology has resulted in many information technology-based opportunities being overlooked or ignored. For whatever reasons, business, government, and education have elected not to implement computer applications that are well within the state of the art computer technology. Literally thousands of cost-effective information technology-based systems are working in the laboratory and, on a small scale, in practice; however, society's pace of information technology acceptance has placed such applications on the back burner.

—Larry Long and Nancy Long, "The Information Technology Paradox," *Computers*, 4th ed. Upper Saddle River, NJ: Prentice Hall, 1996, p. ISS2.

The word violence has a generally negative connotation; it has been defined as "behavior designed to inflict injury to people or damage property" (Graham and Gurr, 1969, p. xiv). It may be considered legitimate or illegitimate, depending on who uses it and why and how it is used. Some special uses of violence, particularly in athletic activities like football and hockey are so socially accepted that they are usually perceived not as violence but as healthy and even character-building behaviors.

—William Kornblum and Joseph Julian, "Violence," *Social Problems*, 8th ed. Upper Saddle River, NJ: Prentice Hall, 1995, p.199.

The age of the average U.S. worker has gradually increased over the past few decades. As you might expect, this increase is the result of more older workers and fewer younger workers. Americans are living longer than ever before, and some older individuals are taking advantage of changes in retirement laws and continuing to work beyond age 65. More important, however, is the so-called baby bust generation, those individuals born after the baby boom of the immediate post-World War II period....

This trend has affected businesses in two ways. First, older workers tend to put greater demand on a company's health insurance, life insurance, and retirement benefit programs. And second, younger workers taking the places of retirees tend to want different things from employers—things like more opportunities for self-expression or more leisure time.

—Ricky W. Griffin and Ronald J. Ebert, "The Graying Workforce,"
Business, 3rd ed. Upper Saddle River, NJ: Prentice Hall, 1993, p. 61.

A compelling reason to preserve species is that each one plays an important role in an ecosystem—an intricate network of plant and animal communities and the associated environment. When a species becomes endangered, it indicates that something is wrong with the ecosystems we all depend on. Like the canaries used in the coal mines whose deaths warned miners of bad air, the increasing numbers of endangered species warns us that the health of our environment has declined. The measures we take to save endangered species will help ensure that the planet we leave for our children is as healthy as the planet our parents left for us.

—United States Fish and Wildlife Service,
U.S. Department of the Interior, *Endangered Species*,
Washington: Government Printing Office, 1994.

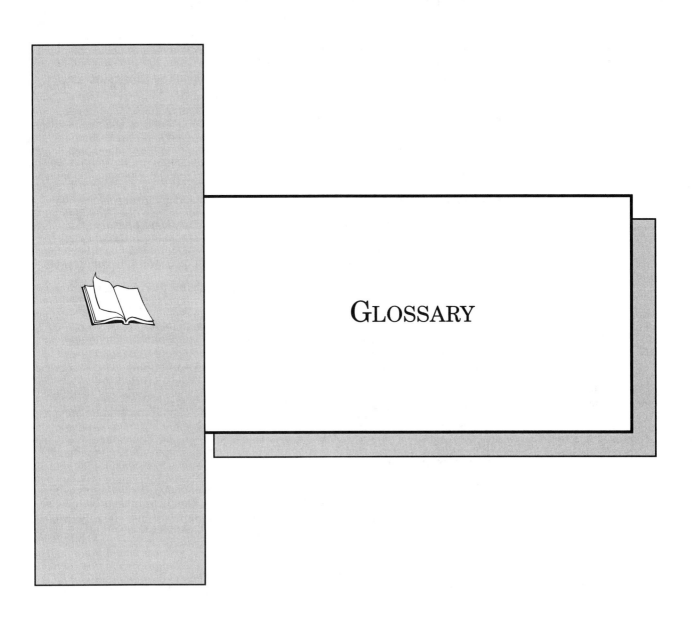

GLOSSARY

annotate   a way to highlight and organize main ideas and details by writing brief, useful information in the margins of a text

argument   the author's thesis that is intended to convince the reader, through logical evidence, to think, feel, or behave in a certain way

bias   an author's personal slant on a topic

caption   a brief description of the contents of a graphic

column   vertical lines of data in a table

comprehension monitoring strategies   tactics to make certain that the reader's understanding is satisfactory for his or her purpose

connotation; connotative   the implied meaning of a word triggered by the feelings and emotions it creates

context   the meaning of words taken from their surrounding words or phrases that can throw light on a term or concept—how they are used in conjunction with other words

context clue information an author provides within the sentence or paragraph to help the reader understand important words

controlling thought what the author wants the reader to know or understand about the topic

critical reader one who comprehends, questions, clarifies, and analyzes in order to reach objective, reasoned judgments

denotation; denotative a word's literal, dictionary meaning

description; descriptive text that paints a picture using words

diagram a general term that refers to any type of drawing an author uses to help the reader understand ideas, objects, plans, processes, or sequences

directly stated main idea the topic and controlling thought in a sentence; often called a topic sentence

Do the second phase of the Plan⇨Do⇨Review cycle; requires active physical and mental involvement

evidence the facts and opinions an author uses to support and develop a thesis or argument

exposition; expository text that explains, sets forth, or makes clear facts, events, and ideas

fact objective information that is true; a fact can change over time as new discoveries are made

figurative language words used in an imaginative way to help the reader comprehend the message more clearly by forming a mental image, or picture, of what an author is talking about; figurative expressions often compare something the author thinks the reader knows about to what he or she wants the reader to understand

flow chart a type of diagram that uses boxes, rectangles, diamonds, or circles, with connecting lines or arrows to show the step-by-step procedure of a complicated process

graph a type of graphic that uses bars or lines to show the relationships between or among quantities

graphic any visual an author uses to highlight, clarify, or illustrate (often through an example), summarize, or add to the text information

implied main idea the author doesn't directly state the main idea and leaves it up to the reader to piece together the information from all the sentences and infer, or put together, the main idea

infer; inference the best reasoned conclusion based on the information given

information map a type of graphic organizer for main ideas and details that uses different size boxes or circles and different size writing to create a picture of the relationships among the ideas

irony; ironic text that states the opposite of what the author means

key; legend a reference center on a graphic that defines codes being used

literal meaning dictionary definition

main idea the combination of the topic and the controlling thought

major supporting detail   a specific piece of information that directly supports and explains a main idea

map   a diagram that depicts all or part of the earth's three-dimensional surface on a two-dimensional flat surface

metaphor   a type of figurative language that uses an implied comparison

methods of development   how an author develops and supports the thesis or main ideas; the structure he or she gives the information. Six common methods of development are *example, comparison and/or contrast, division and classification, cause and effect, process, and definition.*

minor supporting detail   a very specific piece of information that supports and explains a major detail

multi-paragraph selection   a group of related paragraphs—each with a main idea—that support and explain one thesis, or over-all main idea—for example, an essay or text chapter

narration; narrative   text that tells a story

objectively analyze   impartial examination of the author's ideas and information separate from the reader's personal opinions and biases

opinion   subjective information that cannot be proved true or false; an opinion is not right or wrong or good or bad but, depending on the amount and type of evidence the author examined before forming the opinion, it can be deemed valid or invalid

outline   a type of graphic organizer for main ideas and details that uses differing amounts of indentation to create a picture of the relationships among the ideas

paragraph   a group of related sentences that support and explain one main idea

persuasion; persuasive   text that influences the reader by engaging his or her emotions or by presenting logical arguments to make the reader believe or feel a certain way or take a particular action

pie chart; circle graph   a type of graphic that illustrates the ratio of the values of a category to the total; the whole pie or circle represents 100 percent, and various segments, or pieces of the pie, show relative magnitude or frequencies

Plan   the first phase of a Plan⇨Do⇨Review cycle; developing a plan is based on a reading assignment's two critical factors: (1) the purpose for reading the assignment, and (2) how difficult the material is

Plan⇨Do⇨Review cycle   an approach that encourages the reader to become more successful at reading for learning; the reader *plans* before beginning, *does* the reading actively, *reviews* what has been read, and continues to *plan, do,* and *review* until comprehension goals are met

point of view   the author's position or opinion on the topic

pre-reading strategies   tactics that prime the reader's brain and give him or her a head start on good comprehension

prefix   a word part added to the beginning of a root word to change its meaning

preview   looking over material before beginning to read to get a general understanding of the organization and core ideas

prose   writing other than poetry

purpose   an author's reason for writing

reliable   a fair analysis of the topic without undue influence from others

Review   the third phase of the Plan⇨Do⇨Review cycle; information is put into perspective and the reader begins working to remember it; without good review, spaced over time, the reader will probably forget as much as 80 percent of what was read

root word   the basic part of a word

row   horizontal lines of data in a table

satire; sarcasm   an ironic tone that uses ridicule, mockery, exaggeration and understatement to poke fun at people and deride foolish or dishonest human behaviors

scale   a map element that shows the relationship between a length measured on a map and the corresponding distance on the ground

signal word   words or phrases to point the reader in a specific direction of thought or to alert the reader to particular types of information

simile   a type of figurative language that makes direct comparisons using the words "like" or "as"

stance   the author's position on a subject

strategy   an action a reader consciously selects to achieve a particular goal; strategies are means to an end

suffix   a word part added to the end of a root word to change its meaning or the way it can be used in a sentence

summary; summarize   a condensed version of the original; it begins with a restatement of the thesis or main idea and includes the main ideas and/or major supporting details in the same order and with the same emphasis as the original

table   a graphic that provides several pieces of specific data, often numbers or statistics, arranged systematically in rows and columns; the information often compares qualities or quantities or shows how things change over time

thesis   the primary idea of a multi-paragraph selection that combines the main ideas of all the paragraphs; the frame that holds the paragraphs of the essay or chapter together

tone   the emotional feeling or attitude created with words

topic   the *who* or *what* of the text

word analysis   defining a word by defining its root and any prefixes and/or suffixes

Suggested Answers for Practice Exercises

CHAPTER 2

PRACTICE: IDENTIFYING THE AUTHOR'S PURPOSE (PAGE 27)

1. exposition and perhaps persuasion
2. description
3. exposition and perhaps persuasion
4. exposition
5. narration and exposition

CHAPTER 3

PRACTICE: DEFINING WORDS USING CONTEXT CLUES (PAGE 41)

Always fit your definition back into the context to be certain it makes sense.

1. *slant*—their approach to the topic; I use punctuation as a clue
2. *Like terms* are terms that have the same variables with the same exponents; Angel gives a specific definition

3. *physical units* (i.e., quantity of production, number of errors), *time* (i.e., meeting deadlines, coming to work each day), or *money* (i.e., profits, sales costs); Robbins gives examples to define each term

4. *tempo*, or overall speed; Politoske provides a definition

5. Computerphobia, the fear of computers.... This relatively recent phenomenon, also known as *cyberphobia*; authors relate word to a word they have just defined

6. Although a person who is *chronically* drunk, as opposed to the occasional drinker; author gives clue by stating opposite

PRACTICE: DEFINING WORDS USING WORD PARTS (PAGE 43)

Always fit your definition back into the context to be certain it makes sense.

1. *biodiversity* (bio = living organisms; divers = different; ity = state): having a variety of living things; *irreplaceable* (ir = not; able = capable of): cannot be replaced

2. *illiterate* (il = not; literate = able to read and write): not able to read and write

3. *telecommunications* (tele = over a distance; communications = exchanging /transmitting information, signals, messages): exchanging/transmitting information, signals, messages over a distance

4. *empowerment* (em = within; ment = action): encouraging action from within the community

5. *intrapersonal* (intra = within): communication within yourself; *interpersonal* (inter = among, between): communication between/among people

6. *microbial* (micro = small; bios = living organisms; al = characterized by): populated by tiny organisms

PRACTICE: SELECTING THE BEST DICTIONARY DEFINITION (PAGE 45)

Always fit your definition back into the context to be certain it makes sense.

1. *harmony*: definition 1—a combination of parts into a pleasing or orderly whole

2. *acute*: definition 6—very serious; critical; crucial

3. *critically*: definition 2—characterized by careful analysis and judgment

4. *front*: definition 18—the boundary between two air masses of different density and temperature

5. *radical*: definition 1b—extreme

PRACTICE: DEFINING WORDS USING OUTSIDE RESOURCES (PAGE 46)

Always fit your definition back into the context to be certain it makes sense. In addition to the definition, name the resource you used to find your definition.

1. *megalopolis*: a large, heavily populated, continuously urban area; *notorious*: widely but unfavorably known

2. *Gutenberg revolution*: the invention of movable type by Gutenberg
3. *preemptory force*: commanding presence
4. *pervasive*: dominant; *apt metaphor*: appropriate comparisons
5. *raison d'être*: reason for being

PRACTICE: DEFINING WORDS USING CONTEXT CLUES, WORD PARTS, AND OTHER RESOURCES (PAGE 48)

Always fit your definition back into the context to be certain it makes sense.

1. *accelerating loss*: rapidly-increasing losses
2. *habitat destruction*: loss of native environments
3. *exploitation*: unethical uses
4. *predation*: killing by another animal

PRACTICE: CONSIDERING BOTH THE CONNOTATIVE AND DENOTATIVE MEANINGS (PAGE 50)

There is not just one correct answer. Discuss your answers with your classmates and instructor.

1. a. *jock*: athlete (negative)
   b. *athlete*: person trained in sports (positive)
2. a. *reserved*: self-restrained (positive)
   b. *inhibited*: unresponsive (negative)
3. a. *collect*: gather (positive)
   b. *hoard*: accumulate (negative)
4. a. *impertinent*: rude (negative)
   b. *bold*: confident (positive)

1. *unsuccessfully peddling his idea to every monarch of Western Europe*—message: negative; more neutral phrase: unsuccessfully presenting his idea
2. *crushing black leaders, ... inflating the images of Uncle Toms, ... able to channel and control the aspirations and goals of the black masses*—message: strong emotional negatives; more neutral phrases: by discrediting black leaders while encouraging ... were able to influence many black youths
3. *quintessential yuppie mother*—message: has many connotations—may tend to trivialize; more neutral phrase: outstanding working mother
4. *so-called God Squad*—message: negative; more neutral phrase: the commission

PRACTICE: UNDERSTANDING FIGURATIVE LANGUAGE (PAGE 52)

Always fit your definition back into the context to be certain it makes sense. There is not just one correct answer. Discuss your answers with your classmates and instructor.

1. *hew out of the mountain of despair a stone of hope*: comparing mining a single stone out of a mountain to mining hope out of despair—both take time and a great deal of work

transform the jangling discords of our nation into a beautiful symphony of brotherhood: comparing humanity to music—both can be clashing and noisy at times but can also sound together in harmony

2. *performance improvement efforts ... have as much impact on operational and financial results as a ceremonial rain dance has on the weather*: comparing performance improvement efforts and a ceremonial rain dance—both have little effect

3. *The year 2000 is operating like a powerful magnet on humanity*: comparing the year 2000 and a powerful magnet—the pull of both is great

4. *classrooms of the '90s are now more or less jam-packed with computer terminals*: comparing the rooms full of computers to a jar of jam—both stuffed full

   a spaghetti feast of electronic wiring: comparing how the wires look to a bowl of spaghetti—both contain an intertwined maze of cords

5. *The flowering of Etruscan civilization*: comparing the development of the Etruscan civilization to the development of a flower—both open slowly and produce beautiful results

6. *"Ted" Turner ... is crazy like a fox*: comparing Ted Turner to a fox—both are very crafty

Chapter 4

PRACTICE: IDENTIFYING DIRECTLY STATED MAIN IDEAS (PAGE 66)

Although there is not just one correct answer, you should include these ideas. Discuss your answers with your classmates and instructor.

1. To be successful in school, students must be able to understand and remember information presented in classroom lectures.

2. We created our twenty-four-hour society, in part, as a way to cut costs, a way to squeeze more output from our scarce resources.

3. The assessment of the economic status of the aged is far more complex than most popular articles and analyses suggest.

4. In spite of the good intentions of many writers, fictional characters are predominantly white and do not accurately portray reality.

5. Carbon monoxide is a by-product of combustion, present whenever fuel is burned.

PRACTICE: IDENTIFYING IMPLIED MAIN IDEAS (PAGE 68)

Although there is not just one correct answer, you should include these ideas. Discuss your answers with your classmates and instructor.

1. The families portrayed in many past textbooks were not representative of American life.

2. Be sensitive to the variety of human relations challenges you will encounter on the job; give and expect equal treatment.

3. Thomas More was an extraordinary man, a true Renaissance humanist.

4. The enchanting and familiar surroundings reminded me of what I would be leaving.
5. The Federal Clean Air mandates are causing a variety of U.S. businesses and agencies to consider telecommuting as a work alternative.

PRACTICE: IDENTIFYING MAIN IDEAS IN PARAGRAPHS (PAGE 69)

Although there is not just one correct answer, you should include these ideas. Discuss your answers with your classmates and instructor.

1. To keep pace with the rapidly changing workplace, business education has changed more in the last ten years than it did in the last century.
2. When your intended audience is a listener rather than a reader, you must write very differently.
3. It is generally accepted that adult behavior is acquired through a mix of genetic make-up and experience gained as the individual grows up.
4. Even if production of all ozone-destroying chemicals stopped today, those already in the atmosphere would go on destroying ozone well into the twenty-first century.
5. Although they are challenging to produce, 35mm slides usually make the best impression on an audience.

PRACTICE: IDENTIFYING THE THESIS OF A MULTI-PARAGRAPH SELECTION (PAGE 71)

Although there is not just one correct answer, you should include these ideas. Discuss your answers with your classmates and instructor.

1. exposition
2. a. *vigorous*: lively

    b. *caloric intake and expenditure*: amount of calories eaten and used

    c. *sedentary*: not active

    d. *hydrate*: saturate with water

    e. *when no thirst sensations exist*: when you're not thirsty

    f. *electrolytes*: water, sodium, potassium, and chloride

    g. *precipitates nausea*: causes nausea
3. [2]If you are neither losing nor gaining weight and have sufficient energy, you are probably taking in the correct number of calories daily.

    [3]It is necessary to hydrate approximately fifteen minutes before exercising.

    [4]Electrolytes should be replaced as rapidly as possible.

    [5]Iron is the only nutrient that adolescent female and male athletes need in greater quantity.
4. Athletes and active individuals have a few special nutritional needs to meet the demands of *vigorous* activity, to prevent heat exhaustion and heat stroke, and to maximize and store energy from food.

CHAPTER 5

PRACTICE: USING THE AUTHOR'S CLUES (PAGE 83)

1a. "the breakup of a family"

1b. A colon

2a. "many of the high mountains of the world contain glaciers"

2b. "In addition"

3a. They conduct research to identify early symptoms of brain disorders.

3b. "also"

4a. The common name for lipids is "fats."

4b. parenthesis

5a. The three primary conditions necessary for people to embezzle are: (1) have a financial problem that they do not want other people to know about, (2) have an opportunity to steal, and (3) be able to find a formula to rationalize the fact that they are committing a criminal act.

5b. "three basic conditions"

5c. "First," "Second," "Third"

PRACTICE A: DETERMINING HOW THE AUTHOR DEVELOPS IDEAS (PAGE 90)

Although there is not just one correct answer, you should include these ideas. Discuss your answers with your classmates and instructor.

1a. "The origin of the term 'Baroque' is uncertain."

1b. They provide an illustration or example; giving example of possible derivations.

1c. It continues the thought by providing another example of a possible derivation.

2a. "Couples seeking a divorce will not always find it easy to reach agreement on issues that affect their children, but they should attempt to do so before telling their children about the impending separation."

2b. It provides specific examples of how children need to be prepared for their parents' divorce.

2c. Sentence 3 contains major details because they directly explain and support the main idea.

3a. "Various behavioral theories have been studied as they relate to health." "These constructs influence how we view ourselves and also how we behave or seek to change behaviors."

3b. It provides examples of the behavioral theories that have been studied.

3c. They define each of the terms.

4a. Many North American Indian tribes made beautiful handicrafts while others lived very simply with few artifacts.

4b. It introduces a contrast.

4c. "however"

5a. Advertising plays an obvious role in the growth of the nation's economy.

5b. It summarizes.

6a. New machinery, technologies, and materials permitted companies to become more efficient and productive.

6b. They provide examples of industries that became more productive.

6c. It provides examples of industries that gained efficiency from new technologies.

6d. It provides examples of industries that benefited from larger and more efficient machine tools and a wider variety of semifinished materials.

PRACTICE B: DETERMINING HOW THE AUTHOR DEVELOPS IDEAS (PAGE 91)

Although there is not just one correct answer, you should include these ideas. Discuss your answers with your classmates and instructor.

1a. The increasing age of the average worker is affecting business in two ways.

1b. cause/effect—main idea is the cause; details are the effects

1c. "affected … in two ways," "First," "And second"

1d. (1) older workers put greater demand on a company's health insurance, life insurance, and retirement benefit programs; (2) younger workers want different things from employers

2a. "The most serious disciplinary problems facing managers undoubtedly involve attendance."

2b. examples

2c. probably the main idea

2d. probably more; you would need at least some detail

3a. "Being shy can cause many problems for adults."

3b. examples of the effects of being shy

3c. being shy; excluded from social relationships, less likely to be promoted, often taken advantage of by salespeople

3d. It continues the thought by giving another effect.

4a. To be convincing, presentation graphics must be fitted to the message and to the audience

4b. (1) develop a plan, (2) decide on one primary idea (theme), (3) state the idea in 12 words or less, (4) develop a complete outline, (5) decide on the time and the relative emphasis of each portion, (6) decide on the best way to illustrate, (7) draw small sketches of each visual

5a. Because public speaking differs from other forms of interaction in two important ways, communication difficulties often arise.

5b. division, examples

5c. (1) it includes two distinct and separate roles for speaker and audience; (2) the speaker carries primary responsibility

6a. We can influence people in our personal and professional lives in three basic ways.

6b. He divides or classifies ways to influence people.

6c. illustrations and/or examples for each of the three categories of influence

CHAPTER 6

PRACTICE: IDENTIFYING POINT OF VIEW (PAGE **108**)

Although there is not just one correct answer, consider these elements. Discuss your answers with your classmates and instructor.

1a.   Greenberg and Dintiman appear to be against smoking.

1b.   A representative of the tobacco industry would probably be in favor of smoking.

1c.   You need to read more than one source for a research paper to explore a variety of points of view. You could consult sources such as medical reports, current periodicals, tobacco company reports, books on addictive behaviors, and research compilations.

2a.   Trelease's point of view on the effects of watching television seems to be that critical viewing is fine; uncritical/unquestioning viewing is disastrous.

2b.   A television executive, an advertising person, and a politician are among the people who might have a different point of view about the effects of watching television.

2c.   Answers will vary.

3a.   They see a positive impact.

3b.   Because people have individual reasons for preferring types of foods, it's impossible (and unwise) to generalize about the attitudes of all people who prefer "health foods or natural foods." Some might view the impact of biotechnology negatively, others might view it as a positive step, while others might see both positive and negative aspects.

3c.   A pesticide company representative might have a negative point of view about biotechnology because of its potentially negative impact on the pesticide business.

PRACTICE: DISTINGUISHING BETWEEN FACT AND OPINION (PAGE **109**)

Discuss whether you think the sentences are facts, and whether the opinions are valid or invalid with your classmates and instructor.

Paragraph 1

1.   fact—whether more and more firms have adopted MBO can be verified

2.   fact—definition of MBO can be verified

3.   fact—whether this is a characteristic of MBO can be verified

4.   fact—whether such a meeting usually occurs annually with focus on next year can be verified

5.   fact—whether manager and subordinate are to agree on goals can be verified

6.   fact—whether MBO goals are to be stated in quantitative terms and written down can be verified

7.   fact—whether evaluation of MBO goals is typically done one year later can be verified

8.   fact—whether MBO has been shown to be effective can be verified

9.   fact—whether these companies have reported success with MBO can be verified

10. opinion—whether MBO involves quite a bit of paperwork and is used too rigidly might be difficult to verify; you would probably get different answers from different sources. If we think Griffin and Ebert are knowledgeable and reliable, we might tentatively accept their information.

Paragraph 2

1. fact—whether such a program was initiated in 1980 can be verified
2. fact—this information can be verified
3. opinion—whether the EPA's record was disgraceful would be difficult to verify; you would probably get different answers from different sources. If we think Nebel is knowledgeable and reliable, we might tentatively accept his information.

PRACTICE: IDENTIFYING TONE (PAGE 113)

Although there is not just one correct answer, consider these elements. Discuss your views with your classmates and instructor.

1a. Long's point of view toward the use and future outlook of computers appears to be positive.
1b. Long's tone seems to be optimistic and upbeat—any problem can be overcome.
2a. I think Barrett views Trump as a pretentious, publicity-seeking individual.
2b. Because of phrases like "smirked into a camera," "longest media dry spell," "laying claim ... with a lordly wave," and "willing to play posterboy," I'd describe Barrett's tone as sarcastic.
3a. I think White considers fear to be a most powerful force.
3b. Because of phrases such as "don't underrate the power," "what devastation ... can wreak," "damaging to our inner world," and "their dark energies," I would describe White's tone as serious.

CHAPTER 7

PRACTICE: READING AND INTEGRATING TEXT AND A GRAPH (PAGE 137)

1a. temperature curves for San Diego (maritime climate) and Dallas (continental climate)
1b. to give an example of the concept
1c. You probably wouldn't need any detail from the graph. The "why" is stated in the paragraph, not in the graph.
2a. sources of money available for starting a new business and buying an existing business.
2b. because it lists five specific resources
2c. personal resources
2d. lending institution

PRACTICE: READING AND INTEGRATING TEXT AND A TABLE (PAGE 139)

3a. attitudes of entering college students in 1968 and 1987

3b. Table 3-1 adds details not covered in the paragraph.

3c. Significant increases in the categories "improve reading and writing skills," "get a better job," and "make more money" (and perhaps even "prepare for graduate or professional school")

PRACTICE: READING AND INTEGRATING TEXT AND A PIE CHART (PAGE 141)

4a. how a typical item's price is increased from manufacturer to consumer

4b. Figure 19.2 gives an example of the concept of price markup.

4c. The manufacturer's cost for the item is $25.00. The consumer pays $60.38.

4d. Each member of the distribution chain marks up the item in order to make a profit. This information is in the paragraph.

PRACTICE: READING AND INTEGRATING TEXT AND A DIAGRAM (PAGE 145)

5a. Figure 20.3 illustrates what the paragraph says.

5b. The map illustrates the Federal Reserve System's check clearing process.

5c. probably not; it's just to illustrate the process

5d. The author probably wants you to remember that the Fed serves commercial banks by clearing checks, and that it is a somewhat complicated process.

PRACTICE: READING AND INTEGRATING TEXT AND A PHOTOGRAPH OR ILLUSTRATION (PAGE 146)

6a. The illustration provides a specific example of the author's thesis.

6b. "What you 'see,' then, is the meaning your mind imposes on the data, and your mind can reprocess that data so that they represent something different."

CHAPTER 8

PRACTICE: ANNOTATING TEXT (PAGE 163)

Although there is not just one way to annotate this excerpt, consider these elements. Discuss your annotations with your classmates and instructor.

Reading History

*T*An understanding of the fundamentals of historical writing will

make the student of history a more discerning and selective reader.

Although no two historical works are identical, most contain the

same basic elements and can be approached in a similar manner by

T: Understanding basics of hist writing can make me better rdr.
* Most have same elements & approach is same

the reader. When reading a historical monograph, concentrate on

the two basic issues discussed in the preceding section: facts ① and

② interpretation.

Imp: concentrate on ① facts
② interp

Interpretation   The first question the reader should ask is:

What is the author's argument? What is his theme, his interpreta-

Note:

tion, his thesis? A theme is not the same as a topic. An author may

select the Civil War as a topic, but he then must propose a particu-

lar theme or argument regarding some aspect of the war. (The most

common, not surprisingly, is why the war occurred.)

Ask: What is thesis/argument?

Discovering the author's theme is usually easy enough because most

writers state their arguments clearly in the preface to their book.

Students often make the crucial error of skimming over the preface—

if they read it at all—and then moving on to the "meat" of the book.

Since the preface indicates the manner in which the author has used

his data to develop his arguments, students who ignore it often find

themselves overwhelmed with details without understanding what the

author is attempting to say. This error should be avoided always.

thesis often in preface

The more history you read, the more you will appreciate the

diversity of opinions and approaches among historians. While each

author offers a unique perspective, historical works fall into gener-

al categories, or "schools," depending on their thesis and when they

DEF

were published. The study of the manner in which different histo-

hist works can be categorized by thesis & date

rians approach their subjects is referred to as *historiography*. Every historical subject has a historiography, sometimes limited, sometimes extensive. As in the other sciences, new schools of thought supplant existing ones, offering new insights and challenging accepted theories. Below are excerpts from two monographs dealing with the American Revolution. As you read them, note the contrast in the underlying arguments.

ex. of differing p.o.v.

1. "Despite its precedent-setting character, however, the American revolt is noteworthy because it made no serious interruption in the smooth flow of American development. Both in intention and in fact, the American Revolution conserved the past rather than repudiated it. And in preserving the colonial experience, the men of the first quarter century of the Republic's history set the scenery and wrote the script for the drama of American politics for years to come."*

Degler: Revolution conserved not changed colonies

2. "The stream of revolution, once started, could not be confined within narrow banks, but spread abroad upon the land. Many economic desires, many social aspirations were set free by the political struggle, many aspects of colonial society profoundly altered by the forces thus set loose. The relations of social classes to each other, the institution of slavery, the sys-

Jameson: Revolution major catalyst for change

*Carl N. Degler, *Out of Our Past*, rev. ed. (New York: Harper and Row, Harper Colophon Books, 1970), P. 73.

tem of landholding, of business, the forms and spirit of the intellectual and religious life, all felt the transforming hand of revolution, all emerged from under it in shapes advanced many degrees nearer to those we know."†

What you have just read is nothing less than two conflicting theories of the fundamental nature of the American Revolution. Professor Jameson portrays the Revolution as a catalyst for major social, economic, and political change, while Professor Degler views it primarily as a war for independence that conserved, rather than transformed, colonial institutions. The existence of such divergent opinions makes it [*] imperative that the reader be aware of the argument of every book and read a variety of books and articles to get different perspectives on a subject.

Imp: writers have differing views—
I must identify
Read widely for perspective

All historical works contain biases of some sort, but a historical bias is not in itself bad or negative As long as history books are composed by human beings, they will reflect the perspectives of their authors. This need not diminish the quality of historical writing if historians remain faithful to the facts. Some historians, however, have such strong biases that they distort the evidence to make it fit their preconceived notions. This type of history writing (which is the exception rather than the rule) is of limited value, but when

historical bias not bad if I recognize
it & if it doesn't distort

†J. Franklin Jameson, *The American Revolution Considered as a Social Movement* (Boston: Beacon Press, 1956), P. 9.

properly treated can contribute to the accumulation of knowledge by providing new insights and challenging the values—and creative abilities—of other historians.

Evidence: examine facts

Evidence   Once you are aware of the author's central argument, you can concentrate on his use of evidence—the "facts"—that buttress that argument. There are several types of questions that you should keep in mind as you progress through a book. What types of evidence does the author use? Is his evidence convincing? Which sources does he rely on, and what additional sources might he have consulted? One strategy you might adopt is to imagine that you are writing the monograph. Where would you go for information? What would you look at? Then ask yourself: Did the author consult these sources? Obviously no writer can examine everything. A good historical work, however, offers convincing data extracted from a comprehensive collection of materials.

Ask QS: type? convincing? sources? adequate?

*Imp: good wk uses convincing data from comp. services

As you begin to ask these questions, you will develop the skill of critical reading. Used in this sense the word critical does not mean reading to discern what is wrong with the narrative. Rather, it refers to analytic reading, assessing the strengths and weaknesses of the monograph, and determining whether the argument ultimately works. All historical works should be approached with a critical—but open—mind.

goal: be critical reader

① assess strengths & weaknesses
② be open-minded

③ *do not accept all or reject all*

One important point to remember is that you need not accept or ③ reject every aspect of a historical monograph. In fact, you most likely will accord a "mixed review" to most of the books you read. You may accept the author's argument but find his evidence inadequate, or you may be impressed by his data but draw different conclusions from it. You may find some chapters tightly argued, but others unconvincing. Even if you like a particular book, almost inevitably you will have some comments, criticisms, or suggestions.

PRACTICE: CREATING AN INFORMAL OUTLINE OR INFORMATION MAP (PAGE 169)

Although there is not just one correct answer, I think an informal outline would be more effective than an information map for this information. Consider this sample. You would include the same basic information in a map. Discuss your outline or map with your classmates and instructor.

Informal Outline

Understanding of the basics of historical writing will make me a better reader

      Most have the same basic elements

      Most can be approached in the same way

When I read history, concentrate on two basic issues: facts and interpretation

      Interpretation

            Ask "What is the author's argument/theme/ interpretation/thesis?"

                Often clearly stated in preface

            Historical works fall into general categories/"schools"

                According to their thesis and when they were published

                Historiography: study of the way historians approach their subjects

            Writers have a variety of opinions so I always have to identify the argument

            I should read several books/articles on the same subject to get different perspectives

            All historical works contain biases

                Historical bias is not in itself bad or negative; can be useful

                But watch for biases that distort the evidence

Evidence

> Once I identify the argument, l can examine the author's evidence
>> Evidence: the "facts" that support the argument
>> Questions to keep in mind as I read:
>>> What types of evidence does the author use?
>>> Is the evidence convincing?
>>> Which sources does the author rely on?
>>> What additional sources might the author have consulted?
>>> Where would I go for information?
>> A good work uses credible data from a broad collection of resources

I should become a critical/analytical reader

> Assess the strengths and weaknesses of the material
> Be open-minded
> I need not accept or reject everything an author says
> I can accept some things, reject some things and suspend judgment on others

PRACTICE: WRITING A SUMMARY (PAGE 170)

Although these are not the only words you could use to write a summary, consider this sample. Discuss your summary with your classmates and instructor.

> Because most historical works have the same elements and can be approached in the same way, understanding of the basics of historical writing will make me a better reader. I should concentrate on two basic issues: interpretation and facts.
>
> To discover the author's interpretation I should ask "What is the author's argument/theme/interpretation/thesis?" The answer, the author's argument, is often clearly stated in preface. Historical works fall into general categories or "schools" of thought according to their argument and when they were published. Because of these differences of opinions, I must always identify the author's argument. I should read several books and/or articles on the same subject to get different perspectives. All historical works contain biases, which is not bad unless those biases distort the evidence.
>
> Once I identify the argument, I can examine the author's evidence. Evidence refers to the "facts" the author uses to support the argument. Questions to keep in mind as I read include: What types of evidence does the author use? Is the evidence convincing? Which sources does the author rely on? What additional sources might he or she have consulted? and Where would I go for information? Did the author? A good work uses credible data from a broad collection of resources.
>
> My goal is to become a critical/analytical reader. This means I assess the strengths and weaknesses of the material with an open mind. I need not accept or reject everything an author says. After careful evaluation I can accept some things, reject some things and suspend judgment on others.

CHAPTER 9

PRACTICE: USING YOUR CRITICAL READING STRATEGIES (PAGE 184)

There is not just one correct answer. Discuss your views with your classmates and instructor.

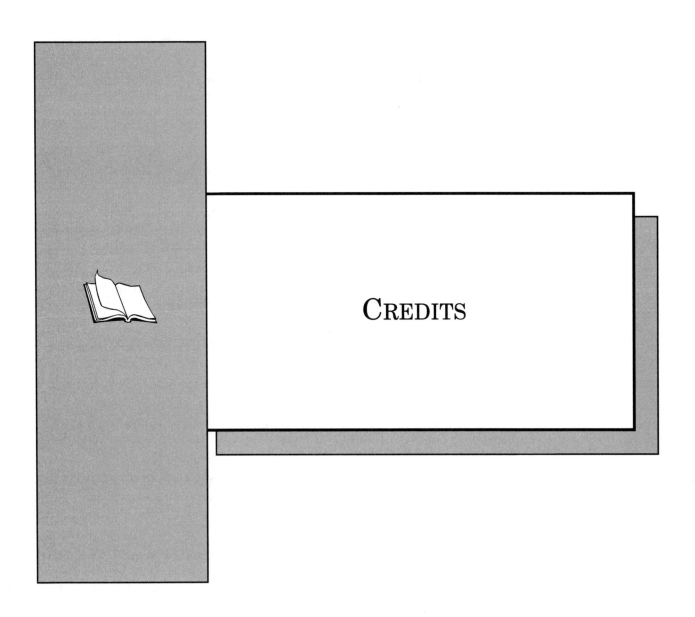

CREDITS

Pages 10–11: Amy Keating, M.S., R.D., "Nutrition for the '90s" from *Good Beginnings* (Winter 1993). Copyright © 1993 by General Foods Corporation. Copyright © 1993 by Retirement Living Corporation. Reprinted by permission.

Pages 13–14: Allen R. Angel, "Fractions" from *Elementary Algebra for College Students*, Third Edition, pp. 6–7. Copyright © 1992 by Prentice-Hall, Inc. Reprinted with the permission of the publishers.

Pages 15–16: Bernard J. Nebel, "Sources of Groundwater Pollution" from Bernard J. Nebel and Richard T. Wright, *Environmental Science*, Third Edition, pp. 274–275. Copyright © 1990 by Prentice-Hall, Inc. Reprinted with the permission of the publishers.

Pages 17–19: Larry Long and Nancy Long, "Computers: The Essentials" (text and figures) from *Computers*, Fourth Edition, pp. 12–13. Copyright © 1996 by Prentice-Hall, Inc. Reprinted with the permission of the publishers.

Pages 196–217: Rebecca J. Donatelle and Lorraine Davis, "Promoting Your Health" from *Access to Health*, Third Edition, pp. 1–21. Copyright © 1994 by Prentice-Hall, Inc. Reprinted with the permission of the publishers.

Page 212: Adapted from D. Girdano and D. Dusek, *Changing Health Behavior*. Copyright © 1988 by Gorsuch Scarisbrick Publishers. Reprinted with the permission of the publishers.

Pages 218–221: Mary-Lane Kamberg, "Fitness for Every Body" from *Current Health 2®* 17, no. 8 (April 1991). Copyright © 1991 by Weekly Reader Corporation. Reprinted with the permission of the publishers. All rights reserved.

Pages 223–226: Mayo Clinic Health Letter Editorial Staff, "Fruits and Vegetables" from *Mayo Clinic Health Letter* (July 1992). Copyright © 1992. Reprinted with the permission of Mayo Foundation for Medical Education and Research, Rochester, Minnesota 55905.

Pages 228–229: Deborah Jones, "Seven Keys to Good Health" from *Chatelaine* 67, no. 3 (March 1994). Copyright © 1994 by Deborah Jones. Reprinted with the permission of the author.

Pages 231–234: Carl Sherman, "The New Aging: The Research Is in: How We Grow Older Is Being Redefined" from *Working Woman* 17 (July 1992). Copyright © 1992 by Working Woman, Inc. Reprinted with the permission of Working Woman Magazine. For subscriptions call 1.800.234.9675.

Pages 236–237: Prevention Staff, "Good Friends Are Good Medicine" from *Prevention* 38 (April 1986). Copyright © 1986. Reprinted with the permission of the publishers.

Pages 237–239: Susan Goodman, "Jest for the Health of It" from *Current Health 2®* 15, no. 5 (January 1989). Copyright © 1989 by Weekly Reader Corporation. Reprinted with the permission of the publishers. All rights reserved.

Pages 241–242: Peggy Noonan, "Looking Forward: Are We Thinking Too Much about Prolonging Life, and Not Enough about How to Live It?" from *Good Housekeeping* (January 1996). Copyright © 1996 by Peggy Noonan. Reprinted with the permission of the William Morris Agency.

Pages 245–271: William Kornblum and Joseph Julian, "Violence" from *Social Problems*, Eighth Edition, pp. 197–223. Copyright © 1995 by Prentice-Hall, Inc. Reprinted with the permission of the publishers.

Page 248: Figure of Homicide Rates, Selected Countries, from Albert J. Reiss, Jr. and Jeffrey A. Roth, eds., *Understanding and Preventing Violence*. Copyright © 1993 by the National Academy of Sciences. Reprinted with the permission of National Academy Press, Washington, DC.

Pages 310: Table of Violence Against Children in Intact Families, from *The New York Times* (November 11, 1985). Copyright © 1985 by The New York Times Company. Reprinted with the permission of *The New York Times*.

Page 258: Figure of Homicide Arrests Nationwide per 100,000 People, by Age of Suspect, from E. Eckholm, "Teen-Age Gangs and Inflicting Lethal Violence

PHOTOGRAPHS

Page 212: Paul McCormick/The Image Bank

Page 245: Dunleavy/San Diego Express News/Sygma

Page 246: Charles Hlavenka/Sygma

Page 247: Scala/Art Resource

Page 251: UPI/Bettmann

Page 256: E. Elbaz/Sygma

Page 263: Paolini/Sygma

Page 266: Doug Mills/AP/Wide World

Page 267: Peter Byron/Monkmeyer Press

Page 353: Top, middle, and bottom left: IBM; Top right: Tandy Corporation; Middle right: BASF Corporation; Bottom right: George Haling/Photo Researchers, Inc.

Page 358: AP/Wide World Photos

Page 360: Karen Kasmauski/Woodfin Camp & Associates

Page 363: Bob Daemmrich/Stock Boston, Inc.

Page 364: Philip Saltonstall, Photographer

Page 366: Tom Wolff

Page 368: Andrea Brizzi Photography

Page 369: Genentech, Inc.

Page 371: Rona Tuccillo

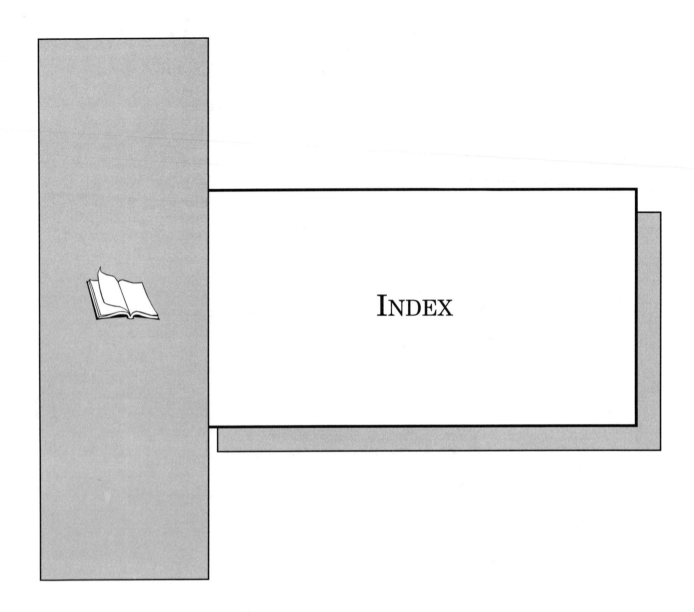

INDEX

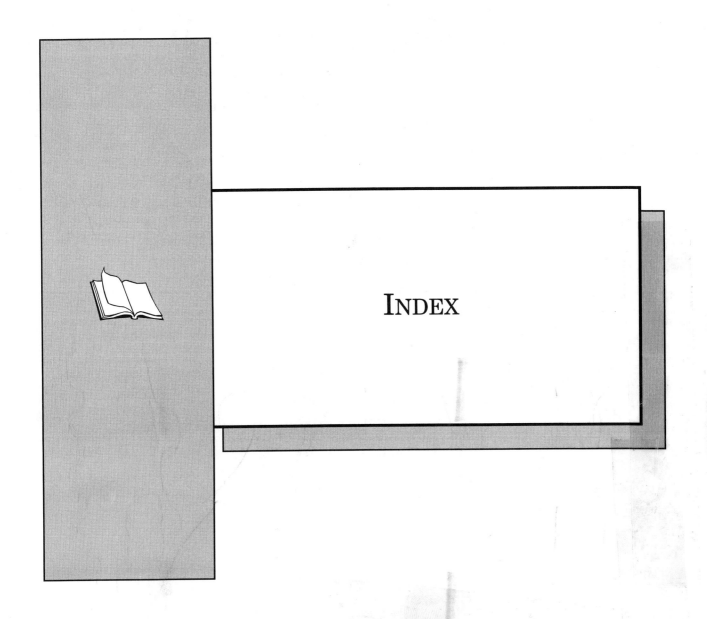

INDEX